D0194821

The Great American Magazine

The Great American Magazine

AN INSIDE HISTORY OF *LIFE*

BY

Loudon Wainwright

ALFRED A. KNOPF   NEW YORK 1986

THIS IS A BORZOI BOOK
PUBLISHED BY ALFRED A. KNOPF, INC.

Copyright © 1986 by Loudon Wainwright

All rights reserved under International and Pan-
American Copyright Conventions. Published in
the United States by Alfred A. Knopf, Inc., New
York, and simultaneously in Canada by Random
House of Canada Limited, Toronto. Distributed
by Random House, Inc., New York.

Grateful acknowledgment is made to the following for
permission to reprint previously published material:

Life Picture Service/Time Inc.: Selected excerpts
from *Life* magazine. Reprinted courtesy of
Life Picture Service. *Life* magazine copyright © 1936,
1941, 1942, 1943, 1944, 1945, 1956, 1959,
1967, 1969 Time Inc.

University of South Carolina: Selections
from the diary of John Shaw Billings,
South Caroliniana Library, University of South Carolina.

Library of Congress Cataloging-in-Publication Data

Wainwright, Loudon.
The great American magazine.

Includes index.
1. Life (Chicago, Ill.)   I. Title.
PN4900.L55W35   1986   051   86-45467
ISBN 0-394-45987-3

Manufactured in the United States of America

FIRST EDITION

For Martha Fay

Surely it is no more than fair that journalists, whose business is to record other people's fortunes and to chant other people's praises, should occasionally devote a paragraph or two to themselves and their profession. The meekest and most modest of men, (and such members of the guild proverbially are), have their moments of complacent meditation in which to review the past and look inquiringly into the future. And we really do not know what profession has a better right, in view of the great advances it has made of late years, to indulge in a little innocent boasting . . .

—WALT WHITMAN, 1858, IN AN EDITORIAL IN THE BROOKLYN *TIMES*

Contents

Acknowledgments

I COULD NOT HAVE WRITTEN THIS BOOK without the assistance of many people. One of those who helped me most was Lillian Owens, formerly the head archivist at Time Inc., who made repeated and substantial contributions to my work and to my understanding of it. Her assistant, Diana Franklin, was a big help in the early days of the project, and for their kindness more recently I am thankful to Elaine Felsher, the current supervisor of Time Inc.'s archives, and to her assistant archivist, Bill Hooper. The MacDowell Colony in Peterborough, New Hampshire, provided me with a wonderful place to work for several weeks, and I am very grateful.

I owe a large debt of thanks to the management of Time Inc., especially to Hedley Donovan, who was editor-in-chief when I began this book and who generously made it possible for me to have access to the company's archives. The present editor-in-chief, Henry Anatole Grunwald, approved continuation of that access, and I thank him as well. No book about *Life* could be written without repeated use of Time Inc.'s own record of its past: *Time Inc.: The Intimate History of a Publishing Enterprise*. These three well-researched and unblinking volumes were invaluable to me, and I feel an admiring gratitude for those who gathered the materials for them and for those who wrote them, Curtis Prendergast, Geoffrey Colvin and especially Robert T. Elson, a sensitive and perceptive observer who was also my boss at *Life* in the 1950s.

For the use of many entries from the diaries of John Shaw Billings, I wish to thank the South Caroliniana Library and its director, Allen Stokes. My good friend and colleague Ralph Graves not only often gave me his time in connection with this book, but he also generously made available his private diary for the winter of 1971. As well as offering his own recollections about various matters, Henry Luce III kindly gave me permission to use a letter his father had written to President Dwight D. Eisenhower in 1956. For their editorial assistance I am grateful for the care and highly professional skills of Barbara Baker Burrows, Jozefa Stuart and Josephine Reidy. The reporting done by Betty Ajemian in connection with the chapters on *Life* in the 1950s was truly invaluable to this project.

Over the years many others helped a lot, either with suggestions or recollections or both. Among them are: Philip Kunhardt, Robert Ajemian, Edward Kern, Edward K. Thompson, George Hunt, Joseph Kastner, Roy Rowan, David Maness, Tom Prideaux, Scot Leavitt, Thomas Griffith, Richard Stolley, Eleanor Graves, Don Moser, Allen Grover, Marshall Smith, Peggy Sargent, Muriel Hall, Marian MacPhail, Philip Wootton, Sally Kirkland, James Lebenthal, Timothy Foote, Dorothy Seiberling, George Silk, John Mulliken, Ray Mackland, Gordon Parks, Alfred Eisenstaedt, Charles Champlin, Charles Rubens II, John Neary, Nora Sheehan, Andrew Heiskell, Jay Gold, Don Weadon, Ann Morrell, Donald Wilson, Otto Fuerbringer, Richard Durrell, Jack Newcombe and Paula Glatzer, whose reading of the manuscript was a great benefit. Hugh Moffett and Bernard Quint, both of whom have died since I started the book, were particularly generous to me with their memories and their ideas about *Life*.

Most of those who helped me had worked on the weekly *Life* and were as deeply engaged there as I was. This was true also of my editor at Knopf, Chuck Elliott, who gave me excellent advice and powerful support from the beginning. Without his calm and sensible stubbornness about moving ahead, I might not have finished. His assistant, Sharon Zimmerman, cheerfully and intelligently guided me through many details. I wish that my agent, John Cushman, who helped get it started, had seen the book's completion.

I am also thankful to a number of people who have nothing to do with *Life* or its history. One friendly stranger, Perry Michael Whye, sent me from Iowa a copy of a master's thesis he had prepared on the astronauts and their relations with the press. Some others I know much better are Dan Rosenblatt, Ed Rosenfeld, Harold Rothwax, Peter Askin, Arthur Lockard, John Drimmer, Stuart Margulies and Robert Weber. The list very much includes Martha Wainwright and, of course, my children, Loudon, Teddy, Andrew, Sloanie and Anna, who must have all wondered when it would ever end. My dear mother, Eleanor Wainwright, loved the book without reservation, though she didn't live to read it.

Preface

THIS IS NEITHER AN OBJECTIVE NOR A definitive history of *Life*. And it certainly is not an authorized one, although I have received generous cooperation from Time Inc. and from many people there over the years of this book's preparation. To the best of my ability it is a reliable account of the magazine's career, modest in scope and unscholarly in its presentation. It is also biased, for I have no emotional distance from the subject and never will.

Obviously the book contains hundreds, even thousands of honest facts and largely accurate descriptions of events that took place and words that were spoken. I have surely gotten some things wrong, overlooked entire areas of interest, and to the likely relief of a few, including me, not told all I know. I have tried to be balanced in the presentation and selection of this material, sometimes in the teeth of my baser and possibly more reliable instincts.

But the book is the truth only in that it reflects my feelings and perceptions now. Many people who also know about these things may see them quite differently, and on those occasions where I was a witness or participant myself, I probably saw them differently then. Yet I can't remember for sure. Memory, as we all know, has a self-serving function. We rearrange the past to suit ourselves, and time itself helps muffle the truth—which we seldom want to hear anyway. Knowing the full truth is rarely useful, and in this case it helps that the subject matter is of relatively minor consequence—except for those hundreds of us whose lives were utterly tossed by it.

Life magazine had been in spectacularly successful existence for twelve years when I went to work there as an office-boy-with-expectations in January 1949. And twenty-four years later, on December 8, 1972, when its terminal shudders finally ceased and the pale and stricken bosses announced it was all over, I was among the final survivors. My career at *Life* was longer than most and shorter than some, including the careers of a very few who had been there almost from the beginning, in 1936.

All things considered, I had an awfully good time. Possibly I wouldn't choose to do it again with a second chance at life ("the one with the small 'l,'" we always called it), but it was an excellent fit for me. It offered the companionship and ready sympathy of a large circle of intelligent, energetic and generous friends with interests and enthusiasms roughly similar to mine. The weekly schedule brought quick rewards and recognition for good work—and mercifully fast forgettings of the bad, unless it was very bad.

Now and then the job threw up astounding moments. I remember sitting next to Marilyn Monroe on her couch in a Beverly Hills house— and forgetting the details of story arrangements I had come to discuss. There were others: interviewing the first American astronaut, Alan Shepard, and hearing his voice shake as he described his lift-off from Cape Canaveral a few days earlier; listening to the sound of my own laughter and leg slapping when President Johnson, in his White House office, told a barnyard-dirty story to just me and another reporter. And I recall riding in an open car through the Watts district of Los Angeles the day before Robert Kennedy was shot, hugging his legs tight along with his athlete bodyguards to keep him from being pulled out of the back seat by crowds of people clutching and hitting lovingly at him as we passed.

There were less high moments, and possibly higher ones, but through most of it, my self-esteem was amply supported—rather too well sometimes, a few might say, and I expect they're right. For most of my time at *Life*, I was among the specially favored, and I didn't always deserve it, particularly during those last bad years when I had soured on myself and on a magazine we all knew was dying.

But it was all right at *Life* in the high-flying years for people to act like children now and then. In fact, a capable man or woman who had passing seizures of mood or drink often made more money and was treated with more respect by the management than an equally talented person with a quiet, even disposition. So, in the final, head-chopping years, I was perhaps the beneficiary of an old tolerance for tantrums— and it didn't hurt that the editors who ran the place were my contemporaries and, indeed, my closest friends.

Old *Life* people tend to talk about the magazine as if there was nothing like it. And these include refugees from *Collier's, Look, The Saturday Evening Post* and even *Time*, where *Life* was often disdainfully regarded as a spendthrift and exhibitionist cousin. I never really worked anyplace but *Life* and have no trouble agreeing with those who claim its uniqueness. Much of this not altogether dry-eyed sentiment has to do with the collection of people who worked there and the kinds of camaraderie they shared. More of this later. But a lot of it had to do with what the magazine produced each week. By and large, the people who worked at *Life* believed they were turning out an honest product, and often they were very proud of it.

It would be a mistake to gather from that that *Life* people were especially naïve or uncritical about the magazine's contents. Hardly. In my experience, few harbored many illusions, and some devoted workers spent great segments of their careers in a lather of criticism and outrage at what they felt were mistaken or even malevolent editorial policies or offerings. It was clear to everybody that we were assembling each week a very mixed bag of goods. In *Life's* glossy pages, trivial and vulgar fragments about starlets and hairstyles nestled among splendid color portfolios about the glories of antiquity, titillating items about the weird habits of quirky socialites followed high-minded entreaties for American greatness, powerfully moving black-and-white picture essays illuminating the joys of childhood abutted shocking photographs of starvation victims and of people leaping to their deaths from burning buildings.

Of course, one might say, life is like that, the one with the small "l." But it was surely never the intention of the editors to reproduce, note for note, the real rhythm of banality, irony, suffering, comedy, exhilaration that is the human condition. Rather (and mercifully for the readers), they were, in the words of most editors who are up against deadlines and trying not to be intimidated by the persistent illusion that there is such a thing as a perfect combination of pages, "just trying to get out a magazine," and that always took a blending of hokum, crudity and fluff along with the better stuff.

But the fact that the magazine cranked out a lot of nonsense over the years (which many people might say was its most enduring natural function) did not keep the people who worked there from believing with some passion that *Life* was capable of being the best popular magazine in the world, and that it often was. This sense of big potential was very strongly held among the staff for most of the long run. Many of us felt, for example, that if an idea had real value, we would be able to get it in the magazine, and in front of the readers, even if the initial resistance to it was high.

Obviously there were limits. Henry Luce did not urge that the techniques of investigative journalism be applied to stories on Chiang Kai-shek. We did not deliberately set out to demonstrate that the products of our advertisers were shoddy or dangerous—which they sometimes were. But in its finest efforts (and in many hundreds of less well executed stories, too), *Life* did a sturdy, dignified and occasionally highly distinctive job of reflecting events as no other publication would or could, of presenting stories that now and then offered readers new possibilities for their own lives. Much of the staff's extraordinary loyalty and drive can be traced to the conviction that great things could happen in those pages, or grow out of them. In *Life*'s best years, there was always a sense of expectancy, as if huge surprises were lurking and plans could suddenly and marvelously change without notice—which they often did.

Not that *Life* was staffed by editorial missionaries or miracle seekers. We knew that most of what we did was perishable, like blueberries, and that a lot of our readers were just hurrying by, on the way to the barber chair or the end of the bus line. Still, we knew, too, that we would catch some of them, and we treasured our illusions besides. To survive the weekly grind, we needed them.

One recurring and contagious self-deception held that just by working at *Life* one was somehow participating in the events the magazine showed on its pages. We became identified with the contents of stories, often deeply, even though we didn't have the slightest thing to do with their happening or their outcome—or wouldn't in other circumstances have much interest in them at all. For instance, in a matter of hours one could become totally absorbed in Swiss avalanches—their causes, frequency, effects, incredible escapes from them—until, seated at a typewriter in New York, one felt as if he were burrowing in the snow with the rescuers.

Of course, this did not apply to people who worked in what we referred to solemnly as "the field." A reporter or photographer who covered a siege in Vietnam or a nasty campaign in the Congo, or who went along on a peace march broken up with horses, police dogs, fists, stones and tear gas, or who took a deep-sea dive with the mad inventor of a leaking submarine, very clearly exposed himself or herself to the uncertainties of the event. These people, who from time to time became casualties of stories they covered, emphatically were part of them, though they always had orders to stay out of the pictures.

On quite another level, many stories were hatched at *Life* and grew essentially from the imaginations of creative, loutish or even desperate people there. One very early example of this sort of staged story ap-

peared in 1937 and was called "How to Undress in Front of Your Husband." Written with mock-serious captions, it was a deadpan
demonstration of the right and wrong ways a wife could take off her
clothes; it was also a shameless exercise in editorial leering. Naturally
it attracted a lot of indignant attention, as did many of the hundreds of
journalistic concoctions produced over the years. And there were
other stories whose outcomes can fairly be said to have been arranged
or even bought by *Life*.

But in the normal run of stories, most of the people involved in
their production—the managing editor (always the top operational figure), his deputies and various attendants, the writers and researchers
in the New York office, where it was all assembled—were quite removed from the event. But it didn't seem that way at all in the heat of
putting a story to press. Then, under the pressure of time narrowing
against a deadline, of confining an event or an idea in pictures to a
limited space, a strange transformation sometimes took place. For those
who shaped it, *Life*'s treatment of an event somehow transcended the
event itself. In a long and curious jump of thinking (or of *feeling*),
whatever had happened to make the photographs possible took place
now and then, again and even better, in the pages of the magazine.
The production in light and shadow seemed bigger than the reality it
came from.

Of course, this wasn't always so. Some of our results were ordinary,
others were just awful, and disappointments were often strong. We
terribly wanted the magazine to be good, whatever that meant, and we
were outspokenly self-critical. When we weren't watchful enough of
ourselves, a kind of Olympian review often reminded us of our errors.

This had happened almost from the beginning. Virtually throughout *Life*'s history, the people at the very top were never really satisfied
with the magazine's performance or profits or even indeed certain that
they could define what sort of strange monster it was. And one sign of
their frustration was a high-level exercise in Monday-morning quarter-
backing. It was first carried out by Henry Luce and later by his successor, Hedley Donovan. In spite of his sense of humor and his
intellectual candlepower, Donovan especially was baffled by *Life*, and
his regular and most detailed comments on the specifics of various issues
sometimes read like a finicky teacher's notes in the margins of high
school essays and were received with glum dismay by his underlings
on the sinking picture magazine.

But in retrospect such nit-picking amounted to little when measured against the excitements of working for *Life*. For those of us with
relatively short attention spans, there was something new every week.

And the magazine's appetites and range of interests were broad enough so that photographers, editors, writers or reporters who liked to get buried in big, slow-moving projects could do that, too. The editorial staff was so big—250 or so in the fat years—that one could go for weeks or months without even seeing colleagues who were engaged in other *Life* enterprises. Much of the staff was often quite unaware of the plans for many substantial stories until they appeared in print.

For a lot of people at *Life*, no matter what their assignment, the job was a passport, a free ticket virtually anywhere, and the seat was in front of the front row. Photographers, reporters, writers moved from story to story in a continuous nibbling at the lives and experiences of others, and a man or woman thus involved mercifully had little time to reflect on how superficial his explorations commonly were. More often than not, "the *Life* people," the somewhat terrestrial tag usually given these journalist intruders, were received by the subjects of their attentions with the most touching sort of openness—even innocence. It was quite free of the understanding that these usually agreeable, presentable, sympathetic, solicitous people from New York or Chicago or Los Angeles or Atlanta could come and go in their gleaming Hertz cars, with free dinners for all involved at the best restaurants in town, and that in a few days or weeks a stack of shiny new magazines would appear at the corner store and abruptly change their lives. Not that the people from *Life* took advantage of them—at least no more than was necessary. But few subjects of these stories ever seemed really prepared for what was coming. Most were astonished at the images of themselves they saw in *Life*. Most, that is, except the rulers, politicians, moguls, stars, captains of industry and assorted celebrities and charlatans who were practiced at courting publicity and simply couldn't collect enough images of themselves.

For some, one crucial benefit of the job at *Life* was the opportunity to get lost in the work. Obviously such escape is available to people in other occupations as well, but it is particularly easy to come by in journalism, where big events can provide impressive cover for escapes from obligations of all kinds. *Life* was no exception, and its weekly deadlines could supply excuses for not taking part, for example, in one's own private life. Thus the job was often used to keep other realities—wives, husbands, children, the bills, planning for one's own future—at a tolerable distance.

The nature of the consuming routine at *Life* and the people there made this form of immersion easy if not irresistible. It could quickly become an addiction for those who needed the habit, and lives were much changed by it, some of them destroyed. The return to reality could be very hard, even when one had become lost in a single story for only a short period of time.

In the spring of 1968, for example, I was assigned to follow the presidential campaign of Robert Kennedy. His short and furious run overwhelmed me. I had started with great doubts about him but was completely won over by what I saw as his powerful convictions and great capacity for growth. Near the end I became a rooter and wanted him to win, which was rapidly becoming plausible.

With my objectivity thus impaired (but no more impaired than that of others in the group or than that of the Eugene McCarthy reporter-fans who were traveling with him or promoting his cause in the home offices), I let myself get tumbled along in the story. There were all the excitements of a furious national political campaign led by a driven man who suddenly damned well might win, unscheduled stops in an already jammed schedule, triumphs plucked from disaster, hilarity, despair and wild confusion along the trail, fascinating and outrageous fellow travelers, interminable motorcades, lost baggage, soggy arguments in a blurred succession of motel bars, rumors of every delicious and fearful variety, terrifying descents into rain-swept airports, all of it dominated by the candidate, his smile, his moods, his basic speech, his hair (is he letting it grow?), his silences, his jokes, his growing exhaustion—and the sense always there that something dreadful could happen to *him* at any moment. The rest of life, wherever one had parked it before joining the campaign, was virtually forgotten.

Then Kennedy was shot. The sense of grief and loss was overpowering; next to his family and close friends, we, who'd been with him that night in Los Angeles and rode the press bus to Arlington a few days later, felt ourselves to be the leading mourners. But mixed in with very real feelings of shock and sorrow was something quite different. For some of us there was the bitter realization of another kind of loss. A splendid joyride had ended, a magical tour was over. This story had come to its close. Now we would have to pack up and go home and pick up the less than glittering fragments of our own lives.

The best *Life* had to offer was its own people. As I look back, perhaps they are enlarged somewhat in the rearview mirror, but I doubt it. Often they were very bright (a few, more so), individualistic (now and then beautifully eccentric), imaginative, dogged, fierce, loving beings, and a lot of them would have been remarkable anywhere. Of course, we had our quota of jerks, sneaks and lackeys, too, and some of them thrived and rose to some prominence. But they were mostly lost in the crowd. Because of the nature of the group journalism we practiced, very few outside the magazine ever heard of most of them.

Goodness knows how enormous the list is, beginning with the little group around Luce and Longwell turning out the dummies before the start-up in 1936, stretching through to the 130 or so who were on the editorial staff when *Life* folded in December 1972. Several hundred, certainly, and possibly thousands were on the edit staff at one time or another over those thirty-six years, and when you consider all the other people who worked for *Life*, the whole publishing and business side, for example, the numbers get very big indeed.

For some of these, of course, their time at *Life* was not particularly important. For many more, though, working there was a big thing, and they invested much of their youth and energy in it. They recall their experiences at the magazine with passion and sentiment; they feel a powerful loyalty to it, a sense of kinship with all the others who experienced it, like ex-marines. In a way, both because it was a magazine where quite wonderful things really could happen and because they idealized it, the weekly *Life* became, in memory, more than just a good place to have worked. Somehow it became something that stood for the best in them.

Because this is a book about the place where I worked for twenty-four years (give or take a leave of absence, a resignation and a return), it is going to include me now and then, when it seems necessary or appropriate. In 1964, when a column of my comment began to run regularly in *Life*, I was given a brief introduction to the reader on the contents page in the front of the magazine. The intent of Wainwright's column, the introduction read in part (as approved by Hedley Donovan himself), "is to say how things feel, not to all of us but to one of us." I recall being a bit annoyed then at what I regarded as a somewhat hedged endorsement. But in retrospect the definition seems entirely appropriate, and on these pages, too, I speak only for myself.

The Great American Magazine

1

The Idea

THE FOUNDER HIMSELF, ADDRESSING HIS LAWYER in 1941 about a suit alleging that he, Henry R. Luce, and Time Inc. had stolen, actually *stolen*, the idea for *Life*, wrote in some impatience: "Don't you see—what you have to establish is that there is no such thing as an 'idea'—that there are only a thousand ideas, feelings, theories, practical considerations, experiments, hunches, etc. & etc.—and nothing valuable happens until all these thousand stream-of-consciousness rivulets get linked up in a living entity—a river in an established rivercourse?

"I didn't get 'the idea' sitting on a mountain. Nor did I steal it. There was nothing to steal. I had dozens of ideas—on mountains and elsewhere. . . . So did a lot of other people who worked here or who talked with us. . . . Eventually came the determination to do something—or to try to do it. We tried and we did."

In his characteristic staccato, Luce told an interviewer many years later: "Everybody who went to '21' and his brother, or to less expensive restaurants, in the journalistic or even any allied trade, or even not, said, 'Oh, well, there ought to be a picture magazine. . . . Anybody could make a million dollars or ten million dollars with a picture magazine.'"

From the available evidence, it does seem clear that various ideas about possible picture magazines were current among American publishers in those depression years of the early thirties. In fact, in May 1931, more than five years before Luce's *Life* got started, Clare Boothe Brokaw, a young editor at *Vanity Fair*, wrote her publisher, Condé Nast, about a notion she had for such a magazine. And she even had a name for it, a name that was then carried by a respected but floundering humor journal of the period. "There is a rumour that *Life* is now for sale," Mrs. Brokaw wrote Nast in this memo. "I do not know what the figure is, but I presume that it is fairly cheap, as *Life* has been slowly dying for some years.

"Of course, I know," continued Mrs. Brokaw modestly, "that this is probably a presumptuous suggestion on my part, and, in these depressed times, it is apt to seem an absurd one, but if the Condé Nast Publications were to consider buying *Life,* I can suggest a new editorial formula for it which I dare to believe would make the magazine a success.

"I should like to pattern an American magazine—and one bearing the title *Life* is admirably adapted to its contents—after the Parisian *Vu.* It would be a weekly, and would contain some of the editorial elements of *Time, Fortune,* and *Vanity Fair,* plus its own special angle, which would be reporting, not *all* the news nor, necessarily, the most important news, but the most interesting and exciting news, in photographs, and interpreting it editorially through accompanying articles by capable writers and journalists."

In 1934 Mrs. Brokaw told Henry Luce about her idea at a dinner party where they met for the first time. Possibly she said, as she had stated in her memo to Nast, that "the editorial point of view should be light but not frivolous, satirical but not bitter," and that such a magazine would have a broad appeal, attracting "Theodore Dreiser as much as the readers of the *Daily Mirror.*" Luce, who another woman recalled had the worst naturally bad manners of any man she'd ever met, was not uninterested. In fact, he must have found it fascinating; he'd already set up a special department to look into the possibilities of starting such a picture journal at Time Inc. And it is at least plausible that he found the young woman as striking for her beauty as for her imagination.

At their second meeting some months later, Luce drew her aside. "All right," he said, in typical fashion offering a problem instead of polite conversation, "so you have a magazine—a picture magazine. You're publishing in New York City. The Emperor of Japan dies, and you have to go to press within a week. What are you going to do about that?"

Mrs. Brokaw was not easily intimidated by rude men with vaulting eyebrows and rapid-fire patterns of speech. "Well, you know, Mr. Luce," she replied, "I should think anyone like yourself would have complete access to the best photographers in Japan. Make a contract with them, and buy first magazine rights from all the photographic syndicates."

"That solves the idea," he said dubiously, "if you can get the pictures from Japan on time."

"I don't know why that problem worries you," she said. "Because if *you* can't get it from Japan, Mr. Luce, I don't think anybody can."

At this point Luce suddenly pulled out his watch, "the turnip watch," she called it later, and announced: "Time to go. Good night." Then she *knew* that this annoying fellow was rude, although she recalled with affection years later that "he was always a master of the abrupt exit."

In any event, their talk about a picture magazine led to an intercontinental courtship, and as all devotees of American romance in high places know, Luce got divorced from his first wife to marry Clare Boothe Brokaw in 1935, about a year before his *Life* began. At the time of their wedding, the new Mrs. Luce was thirty-two, and her husband was thirty-seven, with a tremendous publishing success in hand and unabashed ambition for more.

Surely it was Luce's success with *Time* that made him the logical publisher of a magazine like *Life*. He clearly had a way with risks. With Yale classmate-friend-rival Briton Hadden (who many thought was the ranking genius of the two), he had started *Time* in 1923 on a shaky initial investment of $86,000. Back in its first years a lot of people considered *Time* a shallow gossip sheet whose rewritten gleanings from other sources just wouldn't catch on. But now with Hadden shockingly dead at thirty-one and Luce in unchallenged command, *Time* by the early thirties had become an established and profitable national weekly with a circulation of almost 500,000 readers. Luce himself was a man of growing power and influence.

The rising tycoon kept adding to his reputation as an innovator. Early in the depression, in 1930, after modestly predicting that his latest idea would become "a national institution," he started *Fortune*, a quality-paper, high-priced ($1.00) monthly for businessmen. In 1931 he launched *The March of Time*, a weekly dramatization of the news (which was actually created as promotion for *Time*), and in 1935 a monthly filmed version of *The March of Time*, its sound track echoing with the doom-filled voice of Westbrook Van Voorhis, began appearing in theaters around the country. But there had to be more. The ever-restless Luce, born and raised in China, where his father had been a Presbyterian missionary, a young man whose Hotchkiss schoolmates had called "Chink" until he stopped it with his fists, a man who'd once said he wished he'd had an American boyhood and come from Oskaloosa, Iowa, was always on the prowl for new projects in a communications field whose opportunities seemed literally endless.

To explore these possibilities he set up a small experimental department in 1933 that would, as Luce wrote in a memorandum announcing it, "sift through an accumulation of ideas about 'WHAT TO DO NEXT.'" Among the matters to be considered were an edition of *Time* produced for England, a children's magazine, a sports magazine, a women's magazine and a picture magazine.

Little came immediately of most of the ideas. Luce waited twenty years more to act on his interest in a sports weekly. As for the women's magazine, his reasons for *not* doing it are of some interest. Luce recalled later that "from the point of view of profits, a far stronger case could be made for it than for any case we had been able to work out for a picture magazine." And he also said with a candor that had only a modest trace of self-service: "Our criterion was not what was most likely to succeed. It was not then, I mean, and it never has been, because the first criterion in our minds as to publication is whether we could be genuinely interested in it ourselves and could really believe that it was a worthwhile thing to do. . . . In the end we decided that the plain fact was as a group of . . . general news journalists, we were not really very deeply interested in the matter of a woman's magazine. And so, however attractive the possibilities might be from a publishing standpoint, let's just forget it."

He had much more interest in a picture magazine. And there was a certain urgency about that project as well. In Europe many journals that made heavy use of photographs were being published—the *Berliner Illustrierte Zeitung*, *La Vie Parisienne*, *Vu*, the *Illustrated London News*, and there were similar magazines in America, too, *National Geographic*, *Town and Country*, *Vanity Fair*, though few had large circulations and the pictures were often used mainly to dress up the text.

Luce had already demonstrated his own fascination with photographs. Pictures and the flip captions under them had become a trademark of *Time*'s almost as noted as the backward-running sentences. "Captions to suit the human mug," Luce called them, and the writers tried to suit the circumstances, too. For example, the caption under two pictures of a Chicago socialite who failed to appear at a big tea read: "She reigns but she did not pour." "An artful codger" was the line under a picture of an aging prince who'd handed over his money to his son to escape inheritance taxes. In an exhortatory memo to the *Time* staff in 1932, Luce wrote: "Are your stories *terse*? Have you selected the *best* details? Did you miss an opportunity to suggest a surefire picture to the managing editor?" And photographs, of course, were absolutely essential to Luce's grand vision for *Fortune*. "It will be as beautiful a magazine as exists in the United States. If possible the un-disputed most beautiful."

To make it that beautiful, he had already acquired the services of Margaret Bourke-White, a driving, single-purposed genius who was well known as an industrial photographer though still in her twenties and who went on to become one of the most extraordinary photographers of the century. In a book she wrote years later, Bourke-White recalled her first meeting with Luce and the ideas he had about how pictures should be used in his new magazine. "The camera," she recalled him saying, "should explore every corner of industry, showing everything, Mr. Luce explained, from the steam shovel to the board of directors. The camera would act as interpreter, recording what modern industrial civilization is, how it looks, how it meshes . . ."

Luce's plans for the camera were not always that loftily stated. On another occasion he said: "Today I may not be in a mood nor feel the need to read the finest article about the Prime Minister. But I will stop to watch him take off his shoe." No matter how he expressed it, Luce was developing a growing preoccupation with what he called "picture-magic." Just exactly what he meant by that bit of deft imprecision can only be guessed, but it seems most likely he was talking about the simple eloquence of good pictures and how marvelously fast they tell us what they have to say. He recognized—and so had a lot of other people of the period—the potential for great journalistic power that photography held, and Luce was always hungry for that power.

Of course, much of the new interest in photography was a result of the then recent development of miniature cameras and so-called candid techniques. Much of this took place in Germany, where a Dr. Paul Wolff began experimenting with a Leica camera whose revolutionary fast lens (which let more light reach the film) made pictures possible that could not have been taken with the bulkier conventional cameras of the time, even when they supplemented the existing light with crude explosions of flash powder.

But the man who really put the small camera across as a journalistic tool was Dr. Erich Salomon, a former lawyer, banker and publisher who took up photography in middle life after hearing about Wolff's work. He covered a murder trial in Berlin after assuring the judge that his picture taking would cause no commotion, and his published results drew great attention. He began taking pictures of international political figures, and he was so cocky and assured in his approaches to them (as many *Life* photographers were in later years) that the French Foreign Minister called him *"Le Roi des indiscrets."*

Salomon and his family were driven out of Germany by the Nazis, and he did some work in the United States, taking pictures around William Randolph Hearst's palace at San Simeon, of the Supreme Court in session, and on assignment for *Fortune*. Luce used the word "Salomonesque" in conversation about photography, and Salomon's work caused some particularly enterprising photographers to start using miniature equipment. A man who knew Salomon well in Germany (and who eventually played a key minor role in the development of *Life*) was Kurt Korff, an editor from the German publishing house of Ullstein. "Dr. Salomon had several qualities that made his success," Korff recalled in an interview given more than fifty years ago. "He is distinguished-looking, he had high political connections, he speaks seven languages, he adores politics. His only failures occurred when he became so engrossed in the political discussions around him that he forgot to take pictures."

The experimental department had only three people assigned to it: a writer and a researcher from *Fortune* and an editor from *Time*. The researcher was a young woman named Natasha von Hoershelman, and the writer was Dwight Macdonald, a Yale graduate like many of the promising junior men on the premises in those days. Macdonald had worked briefly as a sales trainee for Macy's department store and would become renowned as an essayist and a critic after he broke away from Time Inc. The *Time* editor was John Stuart Martin, a figure of real importance and stature in the company. One of the original group who started *Time*, he was now its managing editor, a bright and testy man who'd lost his left arm when he was shot in a boyhood hunting accident. Martin was also a cousin of *Time*'s co-founder, Briton Hadden, and there is no question that this kinship made a difference to his colleagues at *Time*, very much including Henry Luce, who handled this talented and difficult relative of his dead partner with a gingerly solicitude he didn't often show others. And there were real problems with Martin. Like many journalists, he liked to drink and he drank too much. A man of quick humor and sensible judgment when he was sober, Martin was something of a show-off (he once shot a falcon from his office window) and a verbal bully when he was drunk, nasty to people who didn't dare drive his insults back at him. He was causing more and more difficulty with the *Time* staff, and it is likely that Luce put him in charge of the experimental department, among other reasons, to protect the morale of that staff. In Martin's place at *Time* during that period, Luce put John Shaw Billings, a far more reliable man—though he seethed with private angers—and a tough magazine journalist who three years later would be suddenly pulled away from *Time* and made the first managing editor of *Life*, only days before the publication of its first issue.

Still, Luce was serious about the experiments, especially those concerned with the picture magazine. Records of the time show that the group immediately began exploring sources for stories that might be told in pictures. In late 1933, Macdonald wrote to the director of the Field Museum in Chicago: "We are planning a new magazine, to consist mostly of photographs. News interest will predominate, but there will also be special departments and features. It has occurred to us that an excellent regular feature might be a survey of what is being done in the way of archaeological, anthropological and natural history exploration. We would try, by means of well-selected photographs and informative captions, to keep our readers informed as to current progress in those fields." The letter, touching subjects that would become regular preoccupations of *Life* during its whole run, went on to ask the museum's plans for the immediate future and how the experimental department could get pictures of the work. It ended with a more delicate request: "May I ask that you treat this new magazine project as more or less confidential?" The phrasing of the question was an acknowledgment that such secrets were hard to keep in the tight little communications world, and in fact people were quickly aware of Time Inc.'s special new interest. When a short-term option on the title *Parade* was quietly bought from a defunct Cleveland journal, one columnist speculated: "What they intend doing with it, of course, is another question, but my guess, and it's purely a guess, is an illustrated weekly, much in the manner of the British magazines that follow the smart people as they in their turn follow the seasons."

Of course, photographers were sought out, too, and Macdonald, who had submitted a dummy for a picture magazine to Luce in 1932, did much of the legwork. He wrote the already famous Henri Cartier-Bresson in Paris to tell him about "our new magazine . . . still in the formative stage." Macdonald, with a strong interest in photography and ambitions of becoming a movie director, wanted to assign Cartier-Bresson to do some work for one of the dummy issues they were preparing and suggested that he photograph "some such event as the Passion Play in Oberammergau." Cartier-Bresson did send in a set of pictures and was later requested to take more, this time of the Tour de France, a marathon bike race. But he couldn't do the job because of other work. In one letter to Cartier-Bresson, Macdonald indicated that publication of the new magazine might begin in the fall of 1934. Yet in July of that year he returned the French photographer's work "because we are not yet entirely sure that the new magazine will ever appear."

The experimental department cast a wide net, developing corre-spondence with various news and photographic agencies and with many individuals, too. As a result of a story someone had clipped from the New York *World-Telegram*, a letter went out to a man in Brooklyn expressing interest in "your camera with the human eye lens." Nothing came of it. Another letter to a possible source described the new proj-ect's requirements for "dramatic, interesting photography—not too tricky but not too conventional either."

Some years later Martin recalled the general setup of the experi-mental department and the way it worked. "We had a certain amount of talent in the office, talent for taking pictures, for editing pictures, selecting them, for layout, for caption writing, and that talent was combed over and certain individuals were assigned to me to make trial pages within various whole patterns of a magazine . . ."

They tried all sorts of formulas. "We might do a picture magazine this way," Martin continued, "and we might do a picture magazine that way, we might make it this size and we might stress pictures and we might stress text—so we were playing with a variety of ideas all having to do with picture reportage.

"That meant investigating sources of pictures, too. It meant ex-amining other pictorial publications [more than a dozen from all over Europe and the United States were subscribed to by Martin's depart-ment] and studying them for ideas or lack of ideas, finding out what was wrong with them . . . why they didn't have more appeal, how they could be improved. It involved hunting for pictorial representations other than the photograph, for map makers, people who do isometric drawings, cartoonists. I went on a rampage hunting for an all-American cartoonist, like Tom Nast, and trying to develop one."

Then Martin spoke of a matter that would be of continuing concern to most future *Life* photographers, editors and reporters: of looking for ways to win the confidence of the subjects of picture stories. ". . . we were planning," Martin went on, "to develop farther Dr. Salomon's idea of the candid camera and that meant you had to get into people's boudoirs and offices and take pictures of them in action, and to do that you had to learn how to approach people, how to handle them, how to kid them into being candid, candidly cameraed." *Candidly cameraed.* The way Martin put it, it sounded like a form of photographic seduction, and it often was. Such seduction is a commonplace of these times, especially by the more revealing and unblinking eye of the television camera. But in the thirties the mildest sort of photographic invasion of privacy seemed a considerable accomplishment.

As an example of this, Martin spoke of a set of pictures called

"Candid Weekend in Connecticut" that appeared in a pre-*Life* dummy. The photographs were taken at the home of the newspaperman Heywood Broun, and except for the fact that Broun and some of his companions were well known (actor Roland Young, *New Yorker* editor Harold Ross, writers Westbrook Pegler and Quentin Reynolds), it looks now like a quite ordinary affair, the kind of thing one sees through stifled yawns in an aunt's scrapbook. But Martin's comments about it accurately reflect the enthusiasm of that earlier moment.

"This illustrates," he said, "our experimenting in the technique of sending a camera man where no ordinary camera man would go, would be admitted." "There we were," Martin went on, "in the bosom of Broun's family and friends and they proceeded to cayort and carry on as they did normally and Russell Aikins made pictures all through the weekend and Lois Long recorded the events writing notes and taking captions." Wonder of wonders, here, quite possibly, was a photographic first, at the very least a rather lumbering forerunner of what became a regular feature, known as "*Life* Goes to a Party."

Martin's group ran several dry runs of the project and experimented with various styles of layout and typography. In February 1934, Martin wrote to a typographer in Boston to explain their operation. They were working, he wrote, "on a new magazine which can best be described as a BIG PICTURE MAGAZINE for 1,000,000 readers. Our work so far has consisted of evolving the editorial formula and assembling material which we then laid out roughly and captioned sketchily. The last issue that we worked on went to press theoretically night before last and we are going ahead this week and next with material to go to press Monday week theoretically . . ."

Dummies were made up in a wide variety of sizes, from *Time* size to the more spacious expanses of *Vogue*, *The Saturday Evening Post* and *Collier's*. The tone was generally lurid. One very early dummy featured a picture biography of Adolf Hitler, who had come to power in Germany just a year earlier, and the headline for the opening full-page picture of the dictator read:

HITLER
A News Camera
Biography
of
Europe's
MAD DOG?
SAINT?
BAD BOY?
SAVIOR?

Another story in the same dummy was called "Judge Lynch Rules Again" and consisted of a number of pictures of hangings, pegged on the fact that 1934 was turning out to be the worst year for lynchings since 1909.

Luce, who kept a close eye on the work of the experimental department, apparently thought of the picture magazine as something of a simpleminded alternative to *Time*. In what he called an apology "to be read before looking at Dummy No. 3," he wrote: "It would be partly for people who just find it too hard going to read *Time every week cover to cover*. And it also has a place because, though I'm continually against it, *Time* has developed an innate tendency to go more and more specialist; it is less and less willing to be simple and naive and to tackle these subjects in a broad perspective."

So, at that point, he thought the picture magazine should reflect a certain open ingenuousness, and another apology, to be read *after* looking at the dummy, offered some specifics. In his comments on a gossip section called "Private Lives," he mentioned three tabloid columnists of the time to make his point. "My notion here," he wrote, "is combination of very human and snob appeals. A sort of cross between Dorothy Dix (much concerned with consideration of life's problems) and Cholly Knickerbocker (very knowing about the snobs). (But hardly any Walter Winchell.) Captions to satisfy brief passing curiosity. But people would be expected to read the Dix-Knickerbocker article—at first laughing at it and razzing it, eventually admitting they *do* read it." Among Luce's other gifts, clearly, was a quite un-Presbyterian talent for titillation.

But in less than a year Luce suddenly broke off the work of the experimental department. "I felt that the thinking and creative imagination . . . had run into a dead end," he said later. "I was very dissatisfied with the whole procedure . . . thought that we had got off on the wrong track and . . . that the best thing that could be done would be just to forget the whole thing, at least for the time being." The project was abandoned, Martin went back to *Time*, the others to *Fortune*, and Luce, in the process of leaving his first wife so that he could marry Clare Boothe Brokaw (who had given up editing and was writing plays), took a trip to Europe. As far as new projects went, he ordered that work be speeded up on getting *The March of Time* on film. Over the next year, this exploration with *moving* pictures would contribute a lot to the eventual start-up of *Life*.

There were other reasons for temporarily dropping the magazine project. For one very important thing, there was the problem of quality reproduction of photographs at a plausible cost. Production techniques simply were not available then to turn out illustrated pages good enough and fast enough and in the great quantity Luce and his colleagues projected for the picture magazine. The kinds of coated paper and rotary presses necessary for the job had not been developed, and it took extraordinary effort and inventiveness to crash them into workable existence in the next two years.

Perhaps more importantly, the picture magazine needed a special guiding genius of its own to get started. Martin was not the man. And Luce himself was spread too thin, his mind racing from one problem to another, his ideas cataracting over his editors, his ambitions leaping far ahead of the moment.

The man for the job turned out to be Daniel Longwell, a fidgety, rather short, patrician-looking anxious fellow of thirty-five when he came to Time Inc. in 1934, a graduate of Columbia who worked many years at the publishing house of Doubleday, Doran, where his special interest was producing handsome illustrated books. Longwell, a Nebraskan always proud of his midwestern roots, was just what the situation needed, a bright, single-minded man who was fascinated with photographs, bursting with ideas for their journalistic uses and utterly obsessed with the idea that the time was at hand to publish a news weekly full of pictures.

When he came to work for Luce, Longwell buzzed around what was then a small company, serving in a number of jobs. Yet from the start he was thinking about a picture magazine, and had even brought a man along with him who he thought would be a good managing editor on such a project. He also told Luce, who had taken an interest in Longwell and his fanaticism about pictures since the twenties and had at least twice offered him jobs, that if he ever wanted to put out a picture weekly, "I was the one man in the United States to put it over." Longwell knew that would seem like boasting. But he meant it, and within limits he was right.

His first job was working on promotion for the projected *March of Time* movies. There he saw the great numbers of photographs submitted for consideration from the various agencies, and he wrote Luce: "Each week, news services give you enough pictures for a book. But— the trick is harder to accomplish than we think . . ." Luce knew perfectly well that the trick Longwell referred to was to arrange the photographs in a big weekly magazine. To get him more involved in regular production and certainly to increase the picture emphasis in his favorite magazine, *Time,* Luce put him there as a special assistant to John Shaw Billings, who with Martin was co–managing editor. A Harvard graduate,

Billings had come to *Time* in 1928 from the Brooklyn *Eagle* and a job as a correspondent in Washington, where he had been brought to Martin's and Luce's attention by cub reporter Henry Cabot Lodge. Billings had no special interest in pictures until he started running *Life*, and he had no pretensions about journalism, which he once described as "an honorable trade with a certain discipline, but . . . certainly not a profession." His solid stability, his energy and his self-discipline were a good match for the skittery genius of Longwell.

With Longwell at work, the number of pictures in *Time*, especially those arranged in what could be called picture stories, increased, and the style began to change, too. Longwell was greatly impressed by the candid camera techniques used by advertisers (he said later that *Life* "came right out of the advertising world of the United States"), and he started to look for photographers who used the miniature cameras.

One such man was Thomas D. McAvoy, a thirty-year-old news photographer working in Washington, and he sent *Time* some extraordinary pictures showing President Roosevelt at work in his office. Longwell was delighted with the photographs, and he wrote one of his contacts in Washington for more information about them, asking that the contact keep the matter confidential until *Time* ran the pictures. "Does Early [the President's press secretary, Stephen Early] allow Candid Cameras in the executive offices?" began Longwell's questioning. "What kind of a camera does McAvoy use? Did he have it out in the open or under cover? What was going on in the room? The President was signing the Brazilian Trade Pact, I believe. There is a pack of cigarettes on one corner of the desk. Are they Camels? They look as if they are ripped all the way down. Is that the way the President opens them? I want some dope on the whole scene for a little story to go with the pictures."

The reply to Longwell's query revealed that McAvoy, an admirer of the work of Dr. Salomon, had been shooting with a Leica camera equipped with a very fast lens. He had been the only one of the six photographers covering the President that day to be using miniature equipment. The President was in fact signing the Brazilian Trade Agreement, and as the pictures showed, he was also reading a letter, furrowing his brow, drinking a glass of water, getting whispered to by his secretary and smoking. The cigarette *was* a Camel. "He has NO special method of opening them," Longwell's correspondent reported, "although he most frequently splits the packs down the middle, and takes them out one by one for his long holder." McAvoy had made twenty exposures, thirteen of which came out just fine, in full view of the other photographers, who had shot only a few posed pictures of the session with their flash equipment and were skeptical about McAvoy's chances of success. "In that light and in that box, boy," one told him contemptuously, "you could not get anything."

What the photographers did not know was that McAvoy had prepared himself in advance by immersing his film in an ammonia solution that made it extra sensitive to the poor light. The pictures ran for what was then an extraordinary amount of space in *Time*—three pages—and were a sensation. McAvoy, described at the time as a man whose "ideal is to photograph things that you see but the camera can't," and as "diffident and devoid of the usual photographer's brashness," became instantly notorious among the Washington press, and his coup greatly boosted the growing interest in small cameras around the country.

There were less favorable reactions. President Roosevelt, who at first had been amused by the informal results of candid photography, quickly developed some serious reservations about it. A memo written by Longwell shortly after publication of McAvoy's pictures described the problem. "At the opening ball game the other day," Longwell wrote, "the President was eating peanuts. He saw a cameraman over at one side, so he tried to hide behind one arm while he popped a peanut in his mouth. The cameraman waited and got him with one going straight in his mouth. The White House was besieged with letters the next day saying it wasn't dignified for the President to eat peanuts. So last Sunday night Steve Early passed the word on to the cameramen, just before the fireside broadcast, that there weren't to be any more candid camera pictures of the President."

Longwell, of course, was enchanted with the kind of enterprise showed by McAvoy. It was a use of photography that promised new and revealing sources of drama, and Longwell, like a long succession of picture journalists after him, was particularly delighted by photographs that showed famous people doing ordinary or, better, ridiculous things. Another picture that pleased him at the time was taken by a young free-lance photographer from California named Peter Stackpole. This one showed ex-President Herbert Hoover obviously fast asleep on the outdoor speakers' platform during a speech by Labor Secretary Frances Perkins. Longwell began to use McAvoy and Stackpole regularly on picture assignments for *Time*.

In his work with pictures and picture layouts, Longwell soon had the help of a German journalist who would eventually play an extraordinary if minor role in the shaping of *Life*. This was Kurt Korff, an imaginative and knowing refugee from Germany who had been editor of the *Berliner Illustrierte Zeitung*. Hired as a special consultant at

$2,600 a year, with his presence quite literally kept secret from most of the staff, Korff helped Longwell to find picture sources and recommended photographers. One was Alfred Eisenstaedt, a tiny, stiff-backed, furiously energetic man who had been a private in the German Army during World War I but who then, in 1935, was a refugee from the Nazis. Eisenstaedt, of course, was already well known in Europe and had spent much time in Ethiopia, covering the Italian depredations there. Eisenstaedt, Bourke-White, McAvoy and Stackpole would be the original *Life* photographers.

But Korff's greatest value, according to Longwell, was as a teacher for the relatively inexperienced American editors. "What he largely taught me was what was a good picture and what wasn't," Longwell recalled some years later. "We would get a picture and look at it and say: 'Isn't that a wonderful picture? It shows Anthony Eden and so forth' . . . and Korff would look at it for a long while and say, 'But it's a poor picture.' And it taught us to look at pictures for a little something more than the content."

Longwell found ways to put his new understanding to work. With Korff and a solemn, handsome young man named Joseph Thorndike (who would eventually become *Life*'s third managing editor), he produced a little pamphlet called "The Pictures of *Time*," which attempted to describe for ambitious photographers the sort of picture qualities they were looking for. "*Time* is curt and frank," it said, "beats around no bushes . . . *Time*'s pictures must do likewise. A carefully posed photograph is likely to be about as revealing as a Congressman's carefully framed statement to the Press. As *Time* goes behind the statement, so *Time*'s cameraman must go behind the pose.

"Fifty percent of *Time*'s pictures are faces. If the subject has a hook nose, a double chin, a cauliflower ear, the picture should show it. But it should go beyond physical characteristics, reveal what manner of man the subject is. Some faces, like Hugh Johnson's [General Hugh Johnson was administrator of Roosevelt's National Recovery Act], almost always reveal something. Others, like Herbert Hoover's, rarely do. . . . Most people cannot look natural if they know they are being photographed. Hence the candid camera."

The pamphlet went on to describe and give photographic examples of the right and wrong techniques. Then it told of a pictorial supplement *Time* had been developing, a supplement that could run as long as eight pages in a given issue. "Its purpose," Longwell and his helpers wrote, "is not to illustrate but to tell a complete story in itself. Typically it includes close-ups, action pictures and group scenes. . . . Cameramen may well ponder," admonished the pamphlet in somewhat echoing tones, "the possibilities in this form of pictorial journalism."

One marvelous example of the sort of supplement Longwell was talking about appeared in an issue of *Time* in May 1934. It was about the famous bank robber John Dillinger, who had just escaped from hundreds of pursuing police in the course of a series of heists and gun battles across the Midwest. The four-page story featured a map of "Dillinger Land" and pictures of the room he'd most recently escaped from and of the dog whose warning bark had awakened him. The story also showed early photographs of Dillinger, including one of him as a boy. The caption under it read: "Great desperadoes from little urchins grow." Under a photograph of three women who had been left behind in Dillinger's wake was the caption: "To be plentifully loved and diligently hunted is the lot of desperadoes." The dead-serious developers of the new form of "pictorial journalism" were having themselves a certain amount of fun along the way. In that relatively beard-free period, for instance, John Billings was amused by beards and liked to run pictures of bearded men in *Time*. Longwell, on the other hand, was obsessed with flags and tried to slip pictures including them into the magazine. And whatever they showed, pictures in *Time* were coming to fill a more and more specific and blunt storytelling function. In November 1934, photographs of a caesarean operation were sent to *Time*'s plant in Chicago with the wrong instructions for their printing. Longwell wired a correction to the plant: "Instructions said touch out blood on six operation pictures in Press. Instead do not touch out blood."

However much Longwell was involved with increasing the number of photographs in *Time* and with changing their emphasis, his main concern was to get Luce going on a picture magazine. "I used to get a week's supply of news pictures," he recalled in 1956, "and edit them together in some kind of order and show them to Luce, saying, 'Look, we could make a magazine out of these.' He would agree, but we got no closer to a decision."

Longwell's sense of urgency increased in the summer of 1935 when he took a trip abroad to promote and launch *The March of Time* in England. He used the opportunity to visit people involved with picture journals both in England and in France. "I spent considerable time with *Paris-Soir* . . . ," he recalled, "and with Lord Beaverbrook and his colleagues, who were also doing a remarkable job of picture improvements in the *Daily Express*. Lord Southwood of Odham's Press had a picture magazine called *Weekly Illustrated* that with no effort at all was selling very well indeed. . . . I made tentative informal deals with several British publishers to secure their pictures when we got around to starting a picture magazine. I had no direct authority from Luce to do any of this."

He expressed his opinion very clearly at the time in a letter sent from England to Roy Larsen, a shrewd, attractive and ebullient businessman whom Luce had hired as his first treasurer in 1923. By 1935 Larsen was the driving force behind *The March of Time*, and he would become an enormously influential figure throughout most of *Life's* existence. "We've got to put out an illustrated paper," Longwell wrote Larsen. "Elias [Lord Southwood] has his weekly illustrated up to 300,000. . . . I saw the books—it's making money. Elias says as soon as he gets time he's going to push it to ¾ million. Dunbar, Elias' right hand, says we are saps not to do it."

When he got back home in September, Longwell redoubled his efforts to keep his employers from becoming saps. After a meeting with Luce, he ripped off one of his punchy memos. In part it read:

"Here is the gist of what I said yesterday morning.

"In our immediate program I suggest we include the picture magazine. The reasons are:

"A war, any sort of war, is going to be natural promotion for a picture magazine. The history of European illustrated magazines bears that out.

"Furthermore, a picture magazine is long overdue in this country, has been held back by big companies retrenching, but now, with things going up and the profit tax stimulating advertising, this magazine is going to happen—just as *Time, The New Yorker, Daily News*, etc., did in the 1920s. Crowell, for instance, having put in *intaglio* [a technique of printing], are snooping to launch a book like Elias' *Weekly Illustrated*. . . .

"I suggest #1 thing on our program is to get estimates, get a skeleton organization started, get ready. If the Italians march into Ethiopia, and if eight days later we can have a magazine on the stands, it ought to sell 100,000.

"I suggest the magazine be launched that way, as a surprise attack, that we don't promote it all over the place, simply say here's news that can be told in pictures, we make no commitments—we'll keep it up as long as we have pictorial news. . . .

"Isn't this worth a discussion and decision?"

The Italians *did* march into Ethiopia shortly afterwards, but Longwell's sense of urgency apparently didn't make much of a dent on Luce. He was too much involved with other matters. His divorce from his first wife became final that fall, and he was soon going to marry the beautiful Mrs. Brokaw. Pursuing her had taken a lot of his time, and she reported later that he had made her an interesting offer in the course of his suit. "I don't think Time Inc. wants any new babies," she recalled that he said. "But if you and I get married I will start the picture magazine and you can be co-editor."

They were married on November 23, 1935, and went to Cuba for an extended honeymoon. But not before a play of the bride's called *Abide with Me* had opened on Broadway to terrible reviews. Naturally this caused something of a problem at *Time*. The problem, managing editor John Shaw Billings noted in his diary, was to prepare a review that reflected "the proper degree of innocuousness." Such was finally accomplished when the bridal couple collaborated on a revision of the reviewer's copy that, in the fine, dry language of Time Inc. historian Robert T. Elson, "combined mild censure with faint praise." The new Mrs. Luce had been properly introduced to group journalism and its dainty power to fudge.

But before Luce had gone south, Longwell successfully urged him to set up a new experimental department, whose purpose was, according to a memo of Longwell's, to "learn all we can about photos . . . sign up important U.S. and foreign cameramen on options . . . explore picture sources." Longwell wanted to have an organization set up, with a budget and two staff photographers, by April 1936, so that "Time Inc. can move in any direction in the picture business." His anxiety about waiting much longer than that was clear. "What we do with pictures will not have noticeable effect in *Time*," he wrote. "Telephoto is developing, is destroying the old type of roto pictures—minds are getting restless."

Exactly whose minds Longwell meant—beyond his own—is not known for sure. But a lot was going on in the field. Longwell must have known, for example, that in the Midwest the Cowles brothers, John and Gardner, were thinking of expanding their newspaper-publishing interests into the picture magazine business. Luce and John Cowles were friends; Luce had once suggested that they get together and start a tabloid-size syndicated Sunday magazine for fifty newspapers. Soon the Cowles brothers would be asking their friend Harry Luce for advice (and money) for a periodical eventually named *Look*. Longwell wanted to get started ahead of the pack.

While he was waiting for Luce to return from his honeymoon, Longwell produced the dummy of a sixteen-page picture supplement, ostensibly to show the dramatic possibilities of the use of such a substantial picture section in *Time*. But this must have also been something of a cover for Longwell's bigger ideas. He arranged to have the dummy sent to Luce in Cuba, and it set Luce off about a picture magazine in a way that nothing else had. And it certainly helped Longwell that Luce's new wife was there, too, to push him along with her own enthusiasm.

Longwell sent a running narrative of the contents along with the dummy because there were no explanatory captions or text printed to go along with the pictures. "I simply took the pictures I had in one week," he began, "didn't take any special pictures, didn't research for any. . . . I got 600 pictures (the best I've seen) from Abyssinia. Taken by Eisenstaedt they were excellent. . . . I wanted to show what could have been done in four pages to tell people what Ethiopia is like. . . . On the first page I have Emperor Haile Selassie opening Parliament (the curtain is pulled down in front of his little stage and there he stands). On the second page I have the Parliament building and the meeting with the one lone delegate present. Below them the Cabinet stares down at him, ready to vote like a whip. . . . They are all known fellows. On page four, The People. Types at the top, then Mickey Mouse at the movies, to the right of that Children of the Liberated Slaves. Below that on the left a debtor. He's chained to a log and has to follow his creditor around and fetch and carry for him until he pays. Not a bad idea. . . . On page 5, a street scene at Harrar, just to give you the smell of the place."

Longwell's description of the dummy burbled along for several pages, and some of it touched on details that weren't shown but could be included in a bigger project. "Of course, if a bright fellow such as you were fixing this page up," he wrote to Ralph Ingersoll, the editor-executive who would show the dummy to Luce, "he would have re-searched the War Dept., got figures and instructions on bombing, then had Jimmy Williamson draw a strip cartoon showing how to sight a bomb, a perspective of its trajectory, etc., etc., all to run across the top of the page, with some remarks on the Italian's aim, etc., etc."

The dummy's contents also included pictures of ice-skating champion Sonja Henie and diagrams of the figures she executed, two pages on Mexican politics and similar space on the Czechoslovakian president, Eduard Beneš. There were photographs of the young actress Katharine Hepburn, "looking really red haired and freckle faced," and of royalty: "The Queen of England has gone nuts on giving movies publicity. Above, she . . . is photographed by infrared rays in a box seeing the opening of René Clair's and Korda's The Ghost Goes West."

The memo concluded with a typical burst of Longwell's enthusiasm. "With some help from me, much from Luce and you, Thorndike, Korff, a Friday and Saturday layout man, a roving staff cameraman

(Stackpole) and McAvoy (on his present arrangement in Washington) plus two good researchers could carry this thing out. You could always get 4, 8, or 16 pages. (Father [Divine] is crying to be done right now in 4 or 5 pages, then there's the Liberty League, the Democratic and Republican National Committees, the coming Republican, Democratic, Socialist and Communist conventions, T.V.A., etc. etc.—no end of stuff.) . . . Savvy?

"Of course Luce will say—now don't tell me we need cameramen (Luce 1934-5 ad infinitum)," Longwell continued, adding that *Newsweek* was getting a lot of attention because pictures were better displayed there than in *Time*. "I'm not criticizing," wrote Longwell, criticizing, "merely pointing out that *Time*'s editors, charming, affable and exceedingly intelligent, faced with a picture other than a face, become insufferable stuffed shirts, start talking about *Time*'s traditions. What the hell is *Time* doing with traditions?

"I grant, given the original definition of *Time*, picts have no great place," he concluded, "but journalism itself has gone pictorial since then. And I am not discussing *Time* as is, but this new thing that is abroad, pictures. Stay as we are and we have a comfortable old age ahead (the Century Club for tea and what our confreres on *Atlantic* and *Harper's* are doing, etc. etc.). But the quick nervousness of pictures is a new language as sure as Rudyard Kipling or Ernest Hemingway were. Or *Time* itself."

Luce's response to this memo has been lost, but its content was remembered with real clarity by Longwell. Luce was obviously excited by the dummy, and it seems certain that his wife shared that excitement. Surely she pushed him toward the big decision he finally made. He didn't want to do the *Time* supplement, he wrote. What Luce did feel strongly, according to Longwell, was that "we must go ahead and publish a picture magazine—big pictures, beautiful pictures, exciting pictures, pictures from all over the world, pictures of interesting people and lots of babies. It was the first definition of *Life*." In an entry written in February 1936, just nine months before *Life*'s first issue appeared, the compulsive diarist Billings commented on the boss's powerful enthusiasm. "The next day Luce came prancing into my office and cried, 'I'm pregnant!' That is, with ideas for his picture magazine."

2

Dime, See, Snap . . . Life

SOMETIME SHORTLY BEFORE HE WENT OFF on his honeymoon in Cuba, Henry Luce (his friends and close associates called him Harry, but now that he's dead the nickname trips easily off the tongues of many more) was visited by two important gentlemen from the printing business. They were Thomas Donnelley and H. P. Zimmermann of Chicago, top executives of R. R. Donnelley & Sons, the firm that printed *Time* and *The Saturday Evening Post*, among other large-circulation magazines. According to Zimmermann's recollection later, the printing men were just fishing for new business when they visited Luce.

"On our last day in New York," Zimmermann wrote, "we had some time, and I suggested we call on Harry Luce, whom neither of us had seen for some time. We had nothing specific to take up with him and in the course of our conversation I asked him what new publications he was planning, on the printing of which we might be of service to him. I remember his reply very distinctly: 'For God's sake, Zim, I can't be your salesman. What have you got to sell?'

"However, he then went on," Zimmermann continued, "and said substantially as follows: 'Now that you've opened up the subject, I would like you to figure out for me the best pictorial magazine package that we can lay down on the newsstand to sell for 5¢—or perhaps 10¢.' On our return to Chicago I sent for every form of picture magazine I could think of and we did some planning and figuring which, however, produced no definite results."

What the people at Donnelley needed, of course, was virtually a new technology. For the best reproduction of pictures, a heavy coated paper was required. This enameled paper was expensive, and it was then produced not in rolls but in sheets, an impractical form for use in a magazine that would have to be printed at speed and in great quantity (the early plans envisaged a print order of from 500,000 to 1 million copies per week). High-speed printing with coated paper also caused a dreadful smearing of the inks and a generally ruined result.

Thus, according to Charles Stillman, a glum and brilliant man who is widely credited at Time Inc. with vision approaching the supernatural and with making financial decisions over the years that brought great success to Luce and his company, two important advances were needed: "the ability of paper companies to make coated paper in rolls and the ability of the printers to print these on rotary presses with a folded delivery instead of a sheet delivery at substantially the same speed employed in the printing of mass magazines." Speed was the great consideration—the folded delivery of pages would make the binding process faster—and an economical process for machine-coating the paper would have to be worked out, too.

Perhaps the trickiest problems involved the inks. Somehow they would have to be dried almost instantly as the paper rolled through the presses. While some technicians pushed ahead on developing quick-drying inks, others worked on an ingenious system in which gas ovens would be attached to the presses. Under this plan, which was eventually used, the inks were "flash-dried" at high heat as the paper raced through the press, and the resultant horrible fumes were vented outside through connecting flues.

Luce was preoccupied with less technical matters. "I would say this about Harry," John Martin recalled with a certain bite. "He was always a very sainted person, a very consecrated person on anything you were talking about, but always just like chilled steel—cold as ice. Oh, a little smile here, and a little chitchat there, perhaps, and always this high titter." Martin clearly meant that Luce had little time for matters he considered extraneous, and now that he'd made up his mind, he was driving hard for the picture magazine. The first thing he did seemed almost like a diversion, but it really had a most important bearing on the eventual appearance of *Life*.

"I have in mind," he wrote in a memorandum dated February 18, 1936, "publishing within the next few weeks a handsome, fully illustrated book about *The March of Time*. . . . This book will be used for certain promotional purposes, but it will not be edited in any ballyhoo spirit and will not have any particular 'selling job' in mind." Luce would directly supervise the project himself, he announced, and he would be assisted in the project by Longwell and Laura Z. Hobson, a talented young promotion writer who later became a best-selling novelist (*Gentlemen's Agreement*).

Possibly Luce didn't have any special selling job in mind, but the slender, big-page hard-cover volume he and his associates produced was something less than low-key in its pitch for *The March of Time* and for Time Inc. Called *Four Hours a Year* (because *The March of Time*'s monthly twenty-minute films added up to four hours), it was a slickly produced hard sell that included maps of the United States and England showing the locations of theaters where the film could be seen and lavish testimonials from Lord Beaverbrook and H. G. Wells ("a brilliantly successful attempt to put real news into the news reel") and from such American filmmakers as Darryl Zanuck and David Selznick. One encomium from producer Irving Thalberg read: "*The March of Time* has justified the faith of motion pictures in its ability to give the American public thrillingly and informatively a vision of national and international events. It is this sort of vision and understanding which will do much to retain the American standards of liberty." Presumably by way of thanks for this stirring praise, a caption under Thalberg's picture referred to him as the man "who more than any other single person is responsible for the pre-eminence of Metro-Goldwyn-Mayer pictures for nearly a decade, with such achievements as *The Barretts of Wimpole Street, Mutiny on the Bounty, Grand Hotel, Smilin' Through*."

In somewhat more modest fashion, the opening text had intoned: "this book is published to tell how *The March of Time* is now established in the world, and how it began and grew in its first year. It is a chapter in the history of pictorial journalism—in the use of a new language, difficult, as yet unmastered, but incredibly powerful and strangely universal."

Thus rhetorically launched, the copy soared upward. "In summer 1934," it read, in words as pumped up as those often spoken by *The March of Time*'s commentator, Westbrook Van Voorhis, "Time Inc. despatched an expeditionary force into the fabulous land of Cinema, where many a wily Odysseus and many an earnest Jason before them had lost their all. Time's men were to establish themselves in that fantastic realm, not as entertainers, but as sober editor-publishers."

But if the book was a selling job for *The March of Time*, it also gave its producers another good opportunity to see for themselves how the picture magazine they wanted might work. Luce and his editors were, in fact, doing the biggest selling job on themselves. *Four Hours a Year* was filled with the sort of picture journalism that would turn up in the new weekly magazine. It was a model for the future; in later bursts of nostalgia and sentiment, Longwell referred to *Four Hours a Year* both as *Life*'s "Bible" and as its "Magna Carta."

There was wide variety in its seventy-two pages. Near the opening was a story, pegged naturally on a film *The March of Time* had shot, on the new and controversial Tennessee Valley Authority. The main focus here was on farm families uprooted from their land, which would soon be covered by a lake made by a TVA dam. There was a two-page spread copied from newsreel film of the 1934 assassination of King Alexander of Yugoslavia. There were pictures of babies, of operations, candids by Salomon (called "a first-class idea-fact journalist who hunted living history with the camera") of unwary statesmen, of Supreme Court justices and of Salomon himself getting out of bed at Hearst's San Simeon. A short picture story (or "act," as they came generally to be called) was entitled "Out of Time's Wastebasket" and consisted of publicity handouts of various beauty queens—the Orange Queen, Apple Queen, Sponge Queen, Nudist Queen, etc. The outright sexism of the pictures was amplified by the accompanying text, which began: "Fortunately perhaps for the race, all standards of news-value yield before the imperious desire to see, and see again, the female form divine . . ."

The book had a grab-bag quality that would become a characteristic—and a most important one—of the magazine to follow it in a few months. An item called "Cancel My Subscription" showed pictures of a lynching, an electrocution, a nude wedding with nude attendants, FDR and his wife kissing in the back seat of the presidential car, the soon-to-abdicate Edward VIII dressed in shorts. Another story showed what a witness called before a Senate committee (in this case banker J. P. Morgan) would see—hostile interrogators, an alert audience, scribbling reporters. Possibly the cleverest of these acts consisted simply of fifty mug shots on two facing pages. The headline was: "Time deplores the American face—and wishes it looked like these." On the left-hand page were the bland, unbearded photographs of members of the board of the New York Life Insurance Company, which included notables like former President Herbert Hoover, Alfred E. Smith and Columbia University president Nicholas Murray Butler. On the right-hand page were the much more interesting pictures of such non-Americans as Haile Selassie, Stalin and George Bernard Shaw—and better photographs of Hoover, Smith and Butler. The story was a perfect model for the lightweight trifle that became *Life*'s most successful and long-lasting feature, "Speaking of Pictures."

Thus *Four Hours a Year* was an easy-to-take mix of picture gossip, humor, sensation, viewing of the mighty at work and play. But putting it together also verified for its makers their feeling that photographic journalism—both in movies and in stills—offered a basic resource not often tapped by regular journalism, which relied more on big events and the big and little people caught up in them. In connection with one *March of Time* film, the text in *Four Hours a Year* read: "When the film was developed, Pa Perkins was real. Ma Perkins preparing supper, the Perkins kids, the simple men who worked for Pa Perkins in his battery shed—they were all real. From the Perkinses *The March of Time* discovered that real people can be photographed doing naturally that which it is their nature to do. . . . The result is a new gallery of American faces, as the reels unroll. Farmer faces, mining faces, faces of rugged individualists, Harlem faces, hopeful faces, tired old faces, smart night club faces—faces from Tennessee and Texas, faces from New England and the Pacific Coast—the faces of the U.S." Thus Luce and his fellow promoters played orotund tribute to the dramatic, touching, fascinating picture possibilities in ordinary folks doing their normal thing. In the magazine they planned, the faces of Americans of all kinds would stare back at millions of readers, who, here and there, would recognize themselves. And as *Life* climbed to its extraordinary popularity, this technique of holding up mirrors to its readers would quite transform the status of photojournalism, which, according to the writers of *Four Hours a Year,* was then "still regarded as a sort of mechanical sideline to the serious business of fact narration—a social inferior which, on certain regrettable and accidental occasions, may steal the show."

Work went ahead, of course, on more dummy issues, and Longwell and his secret German weapon, Korff, were deeply involved in this. Korff's talents came to be admired by more and more people in the office, including a perceptive young worker named Mary Fraser, who was one of the first women to become an important editorial executive on Luce's magazines and who eventually married Longwell. In a pre-*Life* memo to Longwell, Mary Fraser wrote of Korff: "He has been a god-send to me and whipped out a swell layout for the State Fair story in about 10 minutes—Billings came barging into your office, where I had hidden him, and met him but then forgot (I don't know how!) to ask me who he was, so he's still a secret. . . . I'm completely sold on Korff. . . . Our weekly conferences have been such swell fun for me—nice, calm philosophical cases in the complete nuthouse this summer turned out to be." And Longwell told Luce later—after Korff had left the project: "He was so game—worked any hours at the most menial tasks, and liked us. Besides he said such wise things. An expression of his somehow summed up everything you were going to learn in the next six months—you know the feeling."

Korff clearly enjoyed something of a guru's status in those early days. There were many mysteries in which to initiate his grateful new colleagues. He advised them about ways to set up picture files and the value of such resources. "A complete file is of excellent assistance, surely, but the thing to do is to use the file rightly," he admonished in in one memo. "The violin is not the miracle, but the man who plays it." About the use of staff photographers, he wrote that they should *not* be allowed to work for other magazines, that the photographers he had thus employed in Germany "were delighted to see their pictures in the best layout, in good representation. They liked it, and becoming famous is part of the fee." "The best star photographers," he concluded, "provide a magazine with the best pictures. They are like the best writers for a story magazine."

Perhaps the most fascinating trace of Kurt Korff remaining now, fifty years later, is a brief document he put together and headed: *ESSENTIAL OUTLINE FOR A NEW ILLUSTRATED MAGAZINE*. It began: "A good title is important—a short one." Some other items of wisdom:

> "Personally I don't like brown color for printing. I prefer black and white. Brown . . . doesn't cheer the mind."
>
> "You will never forget: Sometimes it is sufficient to have *one* very good, thrilling artistic picture . . . in one issue. Having seen only one picture in a magazine, a picture which he never forgets, the reader will open this illustrated magazine wherever he finds it."
>
> "Save no money on editorial material. Get the best you can. If you pay high prices for good material, the best photographers, illustrators and writers will get in touch with you. Rumors spread quickly that you pay best."
>
> "Never more than one similar theme in the same issue. One illustrated article about the life of an unknown tribe in Asia, about an expedition in Africa or somewhere—not two."
>
> "Try to have in every number pictures which depict lovely forms of animal life."
>
> "Articles and reports dealing with art, stage and literature in a popular form are profitable even for a cheap magazine. Actors and writers are propagandists for a paper; they usually speak about what they have seen or read . . ."
>
> "It doesn't matter whether a certain group of readers is offended.

To assail in an honest manner is always better than to bore. You get the attention of a large circle."

That uncluttered thinking, the sort of knowing and practical guidance Korff gave his American bosses, was followed by generations of editors who had, of course, barely heard of him except as an odd little gnome from picture journalism's prehistoric times.

As the months went by, the project became an open secret, although Luce kept denying in public that anything was up. Many in the publishing trade knew a picture magazine was in the works, and various columnists (Walter Winchell and Lucius Beebe among them) printed items on it. The management at Eastman Kodak, whose film and camera sales would certainly be stimulated by the appearance of a national picture magazine, got word of it, and when his inquiries were turned aside, one Kodak man wrote an acquaintance at Time Inc.: "All right, keep it a secret if you like, but I wish you would suggest to the people who are working on it that they come up and see us because we have a raft of material here which would be of value to them and even more experience—and of course we would do everything we possibly could to further such a venture." Longwell eventually got in touch with the anxious-to-please men in Rochester.

Luce, meanwhile, was spending some time trying to get together his thoughts for a prospectus he could present his board of directors about the new magazine. This compulsively energetic man turned out reports and memoranda with what must have been an intimidating frequency for his colleagues in those days. He was always analyzing matters that were interesting to him, then reanalyzing them almost before people got word of his initial conclusions. He sought weaknesses in arguments he had accepted earlier, and he worried problems the way a cat worries a wounded chipmunk. The picture magazine seemed to raise especially strong feelings of doubt in Luce, and he fussed about it, in fact, for the rest of his life, even in periods when its success, acceptance and influence were at their highest. He probably was never at peace with any of his projects, but he seemed most disturbed by *Life*, most uncertain of what it was and what it should be. Luce was a man who felt comfortable only with subjects he could define; a satisfactory definition of *Life* forever eluded him.

His notes for a prospectus in mid-1936, however, reflected little doubt about his current obsession. "Why not a picture magazine?" he asked, and proceeded to list a number of sensible reasons not to proceed—the fact that pictures were already seen in large numbers in the newspapers and magazines, that pictures were expensive to print in a way that showed them off best, that a picture magazine might not turn out to be a good medium for advertising. Then he went ahead and ticked off a number of reasons *for* such a journal—that people like photographs, that pictures, properly used, could turn out to be a good source of information for people. ("So," he wrote, "for the purpose of keeping well informed on subjects of general interest to intelligent people, we offer this combination: your daily newspaper, *Time,* and the Picture Magazine.") He also noted that pictures had a historical importance. ("A hundred years from now the historian should be able to rely largely on our Picture Magazine instead of having to fumble through dozens of newspapers and magazines. The contemporary reader must be given the assurance that he can count on the Picture Magazine for the pictorial record of his times.")

But the point Luce emphasized most in favor of a pictorial journal was one that publishers might be expected to avoid—or even deny. People just like to look through magazines, he said, and "there ought to be one magazine which is outstandingly the best magazine for look-through purposes. Unless it be *Esquire,* I know of no magazine which was ever designed to capture and occupy the position of No. 1 look-through magazine of America. . . . But *Esquire*—does *Esquire* boast about its tinted fornications? Certainly not—it is trying desperately to sell the works of Mr. Ernest Hemingway and other penmen. Now the Picture Magazine (in addition to all I have said about serious information) will, of course, immediately try to make itself and can, I think, announce itself as the damnedest best non-pornographic look-through magazine in the United States.

"If this comes anywhere near being true," Luce wrote, forecasting a sales pitch that would be *Life*'s for more than thirty years to come, "the Picture Magazine will have at least ten lookers-through per copy. And this gives us a clue to the advertising problem. . . . It may be the answer to a lot of what ails magazine advertising today. . . . It isn't a *good show.* Let the Picture Magazine advertisers put on a good show. Let them compete photographically with the editorial content. If we had 40 pages of striking photographic ads plus 40 pages of editorial photos, then there could be little doubt that the reader was getting a remarkable package of photographs for his dime."

Preoccupation with that sum of money led to the magazine's being named just that in the first prospectus. *Dime* it was called, and its center-ring subtitle was: *The Show-Book of the World.* The name immediately became a subject of company controversy. "*Dime* simply gives me the loud jitters," wrote a subscription executive. "One of the worst bugbears of subscription handling is the illegible writing of most people. We can now pick out the word *Time* without much difficulty, but when that is complicated by deciding whether it is *Time* or *Dime*, we will all be dizzy!" "I don't like *Dime*," said another, adding cogently: "After all, you may want to change the price sometime. . . . If people like to look why not call the magazine *Look*?" Of the top men at Time Inc., only Roy Larsen liked it. "It gives another meaning to a common word," he gave as one among his reasons. "But I am probably crazy. It just strikes me as crazy enough to make sense." In spite of Larsen's reputation as a promotion expert who knew when things could be profitably crazy, the name was dropped within weeks.

The language of this first prospectus was, by the standards of the genre, restrained and to the point. It listed specifications. ("Size: Approximately that of the *Illustrated London News*." "Quality: Shiny [coated] paper, much better than *Time*'s, not quite as good as that of the most expensive magazines." "Contents: A bigger and better collection of current news photographs than is available in all the current event magazines plus all the Sunday gravure supplements combined. Altogether about 200 photographs with full explanatory captions.") "The basic premise upon which *Dime* is published is that people like to look. They like to look at everything including themselves in the mirror. They also like to look at pictures, and especially in these swift-changing days they like to look at pictures which show them what is going on in America and in the world."

"*Dime* will *edit* as well as select pictures," the prospectus went on. "It will publish pictures in groups of 2 to 20 so that in all cases the whole will be more interesting and significant than the sum of its parts. . . . And it will supply captions written by alert and vigorously news-minded editors. Not only curt, clear captions to identify each picture, but in many cases, a highly concentrated 'significance' paragraph which will summarize the broad subject of which the group of pictures form a significant incident." The reader, in other words, would get the big picture, too.

"Nor is this all. As the only publication in America devoted solely to pictorial journalism, *Dime* will seek to advance the art and function of pictorial journalism. It will have its own staff of four or five outstandingly good camera men. It will also be a ready purchaser of the best products of the best free-lance camera men. And above all, it will have a constant stream of editorial ideas, which, through various agencies, it will seek to translate into significant pictorial achievements."

Barely pausing for breath, the prospectus hurtled along into a more detailed description of its specific content: "The Big News-Picture Story of the Week," "*Dime*'s Own Big Special Feature" (suggested subjects: Yale, Cancer, Greta Garbo, the Dust Bowl), "The Second, Third and Fourth Best News-Picture Story of the Week," "Great Photographs Which You Will Never Forget," "A Biography." "Each week," the reader of the prospectus was advised, "*Dime* will take some outstanding character, hero or villain, in politics, sports or art, and show him to you from childhood to now; show you his face in many moods, his figure clothed and if possible nude; show him with background of home, office, tools, friends—so that you shall have seen him without, *Dime* hopes, any possibility of ever forgetting." There would be sections on "Art," "Movies," others called "The President's Scrapbook," "Exposing Themselves" and "Private Lives," the last two pictorial equivalents of chatter and gossip columns. Occasionally, the prospectus declared, there would be maps and cartoons ("a little perhaps-necessary relief from photographs"). A last section was labeled "The Unpredictable." "Occasionally," went the explanation of that, "*Dime* . . . may publish a portfolio of a dozen super-magnificent industrial photographs. Or it may decide to devote two-thirds of an issue to The Queen Mary [the ocean liner], thereby making all other pictorial jobs on The Queen Mary look not like *Dime* but like nothing at all. Or on election eve, it may devote a whole bigger-than-average issue to a pictorial review of the campaign. So that while *Dime*'s viewers will usually know what to expect, they are never quite sure they won't get a whacking surprise."

Possibly the biggest surprise in this prospectus for readers who know how fast *Life* eventually took off is the modesty of the financial projections. And they were presented with a joking prediction that Luce and his colleagues might better have taken seriously. In fact, a substantial fortune was lost because they didn't believe it could happen. "It is easy to imagine how millions can be made out of *Dime*," the prospectus read, "since it is by far the biggest and best package of pictures for the money, and since 'everybody' likes to look at pictures, it will achieve millions of circulation and, having achieved five or ten million circulation, it will be the most potent advertising medium in the United States. Result: profits sufficient to pay off the national debt.

"But alas, short of this dream bonanza, it is difficult to find a logical profit formula. Truth is that *Dime* is not an investment—or even a speculation—which is likely to appeal to an unimaginative Scotsman." A budget was included for the board's study, and its unimpressive projection was that with a circulation of 500,000 and a turnover of $3 million, the magazine would just be breaking even. The problem, of course, was the ten-cent selling price for a product that was relatively expensive to produce. Normal publishing practice indicated the need for a higher price, but Luce wanted to keep it down within reach of the broad audience he felt sure was fascinated with pictures.

But apparently no one who mattered really expected that *Dime* would quickly find that broad audience. The modest publishing plan called for the magazine to start in the late fall of 1936 with a circulation base of 200,000 for 1937 and an advertising sales goal of 1,000 pages. "Investment in 1936," the prospectus closed, "will be between $250,000 and $400,000. If all goes well, *Dime* must drive on to bigger circulation, which will require an additional $300,000. If things do not go well, the $300,000 will be needed for repair and for retreat purposes. This comes to a total of $700,000 indicated outlay. Add to that another $300,000 for bad (or good) luck and it can be safely assumed that $1,000,000 will see *Dime* safely through to a break-even 500,000 circulation or to an honorable grave." With understandable apprehension that the latter might be the early result of their action, the directors gave their approval.

The prospectus underwent more changes before it was completed in the next few weeks. Most of them were made by Luce and involved refining the language of the original. The name *Dime* disappeared; *The Show-Book of the World* remained—with a footnote saying that the actual title of the magazine would appear on Vol. I, No. 1. But the changes in the flavor of the writing were notable, so much so that the authorship of the prospectus became a subject of real interest in the advertising and publishing trades. One admiring article in the journal *Advertising & Selling* read: ". . . If Mr. Luce didn't squander his time with publishing and editing, he could be a bang-up promotion man. In fact, one oldster has made the remark that Luce was born thirty years too late; that his real field would have been writing prospectuses for stock and bond issues as they were written around the turn of the century. He says that the fine promissory glow, conviction of success and siren seductiveness which Luce wraps in a prospectus is lost on a publication, but would make millions for an enterprising pre-SEC underwriting house."

Actually Luce had some helpers in the creation of that fine promissory glow, and one of them was the poet and playwright Archibald MacLeish, who had been a little ahead of Luce at Yale and was writing pieces for *Fortune*. He was a fast, versatile professional whose artistic pretensions did not interfere with his skill as a writer of popular journalism. Luce rightly placed great importance on the opening paragraph of his prospectus, and he wired his preamble to MacLeish, who was working at home in Massachusetts. His version began: "To see life; to see the world, the cockeyed world; to eyewitness the great events in the human comedy of errors . . ." MacLeish suggested some changes and wrote a few rolling sentences on "the revolution of the camera," which he thought might be placed ahead of Luce's beginning. "The great revolutions of journalism," he wired Luce collect, "are not revolutions in public opinion but revolutions in the way in which public opinion is formed." Luce did not buy that notion, but he drew several phrases here and there from MacLeish. The final result had both an eloquence and a simple aptness about the purpose of the new magazine that was never approached in the years of redefining and head scratching that followed. Even at the end, anyone who had worked at *Life* could read that lovely sell, that nice mix of pitch and promise, and see that, indeed, the magazine had done all those things Luce said it would. It read:

"To see life; to see the world; to eyewitness great events; to watch the faces of the poor and the gestures of the proud; to see strange things—machines, armies, multitudes, shadows in the jungle and on the moon; to see man's work—his paintings, towers and discoveries; to see things thousands of miles away, things hidden behind walls and within rooms, things dangerous to come to; the women that men love and many children; to see and to take pleasure in seeing; to see and be amazed; to see and be instructed;

"Thus to see, and to be shown, is now the will and new expectancy of half mankind.

"To see, and to show, is the mission now undertaken by a new kind of publication, *THE SHOW-BOOK OF THE WORLD*, hereinafter described."

Among the people Luce sent the prospectus was an old teacher of his at the Hotchkiss School. He wasn't much impressed with the plans. He wrote: ". . . the few people I've talked with about your new picture magazine are all 'agin it.' They feel you may sink your million and accomplish nothing but make your other publications less valuable to those who take them. . . . Overextension is a very common and easy mistake to fall into. So I say, *please don't*."

Reconsideration of his plans at that point would have seemed preposterous to Luce, but he answered the teacher courteously. "Your warning is, I assure you," he wrote, "taken much to heart. I do not like the idea of having too big an organization—not only for business headaches, but also for reasons of personal happiness. However, something just had to be done about pictures."

Naturally enough, one of the main preparations for the new magazine involved figuring out how to collect photographs. To ensure a supply of the best, Time Inc. made deals with the big foreign and domestic picture agencies, most notably the Associated Press, which would guarantee immediate access, usually on a first-look or an exclusive basis. The arrangement with the AP, for example, called for an exchange of pictures in which Time Inc. would "have all the American (Continental U.S.) rights, except newspaper rights, to all pictures originated and handled by the Associated Press for its members." For this, the AP would get access to Time Inc.'s pictures and $25,000 each year. Agreements like this enormously increased the volume of available photographs for the new magazine, and a special subsidiary corporation called Pictures Inc. was quietly set up to handle the flow. One of the functions of Pictures Inc. was to sell photographs that Time Inc. editors didn't want to other non-newspaper sources, but not long after the start of *Life*, the operation was dissolved. There didn't seem to be enough money in it, for one thing, and for another, some executives were haunted by the possibility that the picture group, in a natural effort to justify its existence, would sell pictures to the competition when they might have been useful to *Life* or *Time* later. But basically the AP agreement provided an important current resource to *Life* throughout its whole run, as did the connections with other agencies and independent groups of photographers like Black Star and Magnum.

While these preparations were being made, work went ahead on more dummies as the makers of the new magazine tried to sort out matters of style, pace and format. Longwell and a small staff, joined and led a bit later by John Stuart Martin, had gathered on the fifty-first floor of the Chrysler Building (where Time Inc. then maintained a relatively modest establishment on two floors) to collect and cut and paste and write. To keep down speculation about the activities of Longwell's group, Charles Douglas Jackson, a towering, articulate Princeton graduate then acting as Luce's special assistant, put out a cautionary and somewhat inaccurate memo to the staff. "The current moving activity on the 51st floor," wrote Jackson, who was always referred to as C.D. during the thirty years he spent in various high-level and occasionally indefinable jobs for Luce, "may give rise to the query 'What is up?' Something is up and until further notice should be considered an office secret. The Experimental Department is working on the idea of a Picture Supplement for *Time*. The least said about it the better."

An engaging sense of innocence dominated the experiments. And they produced some terrible stuff along with the better. They were making it all up as they went along, and they were not hampered much by precedents, by any choking sense of tradition, by feelings of heavy professional responsibility, by questions of taste. For the most part they had no burdensome intellectual pretensions and they had little shame. These inhibitions would all appear, and not always helpfully, later in the life of the magazine, but for the moment it was a free-floating adventure, exciting, hectic and offering new combinations of trial and error and reward every day. The giddiness of these men, in fact, was clear every time they tried to express themselves on the subject of photographs. It was as if Luce and Longwell and their equally wide-eyed helpers were the discoverers of photography, instead of simply its new journalistic salesmen. The foreword to one dummy produced in mid-1936 read: "Ahead of you lie 40 pages of pictures selected by us from 5,000-odd pictures that came into existence, or were for the first time available to U.S. magazines, during the week of May 18–23." One should not let the somewhat promotional tone of the writing shut out another truth—that these men were literally hipped on the subject of photographs. "These pictures," the foreword went on, "have been selected and arranged experimentally to demonstrate our conviction that, while the camera has achieved high efficiency as a reporter and recorder of our time, a journalistic job remains to be done in articulating a language of pictures." Self-serving perhaps, but they meant it, too. "Not to *see* our time is not to know it," the paragraph continued. "Thousands of cameras are seeing it, in fragments, all over the world every day. And more and more cameras can be sent to get even better visual fragments. Yet nowhere in the world, least of all in the U.S., is there a periodical devoted to piecing the world's picture story together intelligently as *Time* pieces together its factual story."

Describing the dummy, the foreword listed two general categories of contents. These were "Record" and "Revelation," and it isn't entirely clear how the distinctions between them were kept straight. Clumped among the "for the record" items were pictures of the French Socialist leader Léon Blum, England's Queen Mary with her grandchildren (including the future Queen Elizabeth II), Mussolini, Haile Selassie and the dirigible *Hindenburg*. A smiling murderer smoking his last cigar in the gas chamber qualified as "Revelation," and there was a picture biography of the tennis star Donald Budge. A story called "Nigger Hunt," which told of the police's tracking, trapping and eventual murder of a black man alleged to have shot a sheriff, was touted with the pitch that "you will see the ordinary news-camera given its due when it gets out and covers well a striking action story." Speaking of a section called "Private Lives," the foreword declared: "You will see us groping toward a page of what the U.S. public loves so deeply: Gossip. May ours be clean, harmless, and when possible amusing . . . But no popular magazine," the experimenters concluded coyly, "can be a Boy Scout all the time."

Much of the material in that dummy was well below any known Scout's honor. The captions that accompanied the dreadful police story were appallingly callous. Under one picture showing two policemen shaking hands after the black man had been killed was the caption: "*Well done*. Sergeant John G. Yeager, deputy sheriff of Orange County (Va.), and Superintendent Henry B. Nicholas shake hands on their grim night's work." The sly caption under the picture of Léon Blum, who Luce thought was a menace and whom *Time* had called "Jew Blum," read: "Communists raise clenched fists when the *Internationale* is sung. Socialist Blum does not. But he sings."

Some of the writers were having more vulgar fun with other material, and the crudity of the humor shows how tasteless the editors were ready to be if it would work. One picture showed a large, handsome young woman flexing her muscles. That caption read: "Six foot two in her stocking feet is Lois de Fee, 17, hired last week as Bouncer of Manhattan's Dizzy Club. Bouncer de Fee hails from Austin, Tex., weighs 184 lbs., likes to bulge her biceps and cry: 'I'm a good time girl.' Clothes, music, lights, dancing, liquor—what else is there when a girl is young?"

Another "act," several pages long, dealt with a family of nudists in a San Diego sideshow. "We sent a candid cameraman to report Zoro Gardens," the accompanying text read, "and the human story behind it. Is his report too strong for your taste? If such things openly exist in the U.S., should this visual magazine avert its eye?" The captions that went with the pictures frolicked heavily, and one next to a picture of a nude woman reading said: "Tanya, 22, gurgles: 'Our girl friends think we have orgies, but I have never had an orgy yet.'" Leered another: "Ruth, 21, irons a dress for a date. But the Cubitts seldom go out, explaining: 'Boys expect too much from us.'" Under a photograph of five nude women skipping rope, the caption read: "In Zoro Gardens the work is not just all posing and strip-teasing. There is also skipping, prancing, tag." Obviously the working staff thought that was pretty funny stuff. Archibald MacLeish, who was sent the dummy, took a more dour view of some of the material. "Mr. Budge is a magnificent tennis player," he wrote, "but he just doesn't swing the necessary weight to justify five pages of pictures from teething to the First Ten. Aside from the techniques pictures, those pages left me not even cold: just bored." Of the Zoro Gardens story he wrote: "One nude is nude: twenty nudes are just bare."

By midsummer, Luce and his experimenters were ready to go ahead with another dummy, this one actually printed—the others had all just been paste-up copies using photostats. Longwell personally carried the material to Chicago and "closed it" in the Donnelley plant. A print order of 30,000 copies was run off to "show advertisers and to establish a possible printed style." The size of *Dummy* (which was its printed title) was ten and one quarter inches wide by thirteen and one quarter inches high, near the size *Life* would be, but not as big as the next and final printed dummy, which accommodated Longwell's view that the magazine should "loom" over *The Saturday Evening Post* on the newsstands. *Dummy* would, however, take the plates of ads made for the *Post* and *Fortune*, which would be a plausible cost inducement to future advertisers already in those magazines. There were forty-eight editorial pages, including four in color, and twenty-eight pages of advertising, none of it paid for, of course. "This is a DUMMY," its editors wrote with a tone of apology seldom taken in Luce's publications, "which means that the editors did a lot of pretending and that the readers of this Dummy will please also pretend." The readers were asked to imagine that this was just one in a series that would appear every Thursday, and also coaxed "to simulate ordinary, and not too critical, reading conditions." This magazine, they were told with what Luce, Martin and Longwell must have hoped was an engaging modesty, "is not a special issue—indeed it is below par and suggests that the regular editorial staff had gone on vacation leaving this issue to be put to press by inexperienced juniors."

The dummy issue included picture stories by Eisenstaedt (on a steelworker) and Bourke-White (on a high jumper), stories about preparations in England for possible war, the movie *Mary of Scotland* starring Katharine Hepburn, the busy and stylish life of the beauty business's Elizabeth Arden, the tallest boy in the world (8 feet 5 inches) and the longest baby in the world (24.5 inches), color photographs of paintings depicting the life of Christ. It was not accorded universal acclaim among its readers. "It was a complete flop, as far as we were concerned," Longwell recalled. Only 3,000 copies were distributed. Still, advertisers were generally interested, though some commented that there was too much writing and that the tone (there were no pictures of nudes in this issue) was too "high-brow." Gardner Cowles agreed strongly with that, and thought the projected magazine promised to be so sedate that it would compete with *Time* and *Fortune* for readers and ad sales. Another reader was shocked by what he felt was *Dummy's* lurid content, and Luce wrote him that most people felt the other way, adding: "The point there is, of course, that we do not intend to appeal to the mob but we do hope that the magazine will appeal to a million or more people who are not all of them high-brow." His general manager, Ralph Ingersoll, who was known among his not always admiring Time Inc. colleagues as "the memo marathon," churned out a memo for Luce on the sum of the criticism. "Without equivocation," Ingersoll wrote, "laymen thought Dummy No. 1 swell, were to a man amazed by the 'package for a dime,' interested and excited by the pictures. With many equivocations, the professionals thought: a) the idea swell, b) the dummy confused, but c) confidence in the future of the magazine unshaken after seeing it." In a reply to another correspondent Luce was blunter: "The Dummy was a disappointment. Especially the people in Time Inc. were disappointed. Editors Luce, Martin, Longwell and others responsible for it got no praise from their associates. I hope it proves we can't do any worse. . . . We are now setting out to get the job done right."

Perhaps the biggest problem with the dummy, most people agreed, had to do with design, and one man who'd received a copy was a graphics expert named Paul Hollister, who was also a top advertising executive at Macy's. Hollister was appalled at the way the magazine looked, and possibly because he didn't realize at the time that a lot of other talented designers had been consulted about it, stepped right up and said so. ". . . It is inconceivable that even an avowed dress-rehearsal just for 'fun' should have turned out so far short. . . . Great God—that a magazine should make even a tentative peek looking like this. . . . The dangerous thing is you have good raw material; it must not be bootchered."

When he wanted to be, Luce could be most attentive in the presence of candor. He immediately telephoned Hollister, who was vacationing near Gloucester, Massachusetts. Hollister's account of the call follows:

LUCE: I got your note. It is very intriguing.

HOLLISTER: Oh.

LUCE: What do we do now?

HOLLISTER: What do you mean, what do *we* do now?

LUCE: I mean, what do you do next? I want your comments.

HOLLISTER: Better send me up twenty copies of the dummy, fast, and I'll go over to Gloucester and buy some tools, and see what I can do.

LUCE: How much money shall I send you?

HOLLISTER: No idea. What do *you* think?

LUCE: Would a thousand dollars be all right?

HOLLISTER: Sure I'll call you if I get something.

Their deal struck, Hollister bought himself a new drawing board, some rubber cement, a T square, lots of pencils and Artgum erasers and an excellent pair of scissors. When the dummies arrived from New York, Hollister started chopping them up and pasting them back together in ways he thought were better. "My task," he recalled, "was to make a better pattern of each page, conforming to a total 'basic format' character: to 'sell' each page for itself, each picture within that pattern; to suggest changes of pace; to clean up margins and gutters [where the magazine is folded at the center]; . . . to eliminate sloppy disturbances and tricks from the page."

For about ten days Hollister worked on his revision of the dummy, which he pasted together in an accordion pleat so that the whole thing could be opened up and studied all at once, without turning the pages. That way, he thought, "the whole 'feel' of the basic format could be grasped at a glance, and the change of pace seen quickly." Longwell came up on the overnight train to have a look. "I unveiled the accordion-pleated new dummy on the floor . . . and we walked up and down discussing it for a couple of hours," Hollister remembered. "Dan was delighted. He said it was fine-fine-fine-bully-fine. So we squeezed it back into shape, dined, and I put him back on the train to New York."

Then followed many days, even weeks of silence from Luce. First slightly troubled, then worried, then annoyed at not getting word, Hollister wrote Luce a one-question letter: "Was it that bad?" Next day, Luce phoned again—both men were in New York this time—and asked Hollister to lunch at the Chrysler Building's Cloud Club, in a private dining room where Luce often met with his colleagues. Hollister recalled that after an initial round of conversation about the possible contents of the picture magazine, Luce turned from his editors toward the visitor from Macy's. According to Hollister: "With the finality of a great man breaking up a momentous discussion, he said: 'Good! Now we have an editorial prospectus! Now we have a basic format—is that what you call it, that dummy? *Now* what do we do?' That is honestly what he said."

Hollister recounted his advice to Luce: "What you do is to get an art director and put him at a drawing board. Put tire tape over his mouth, because whatever he has to state should drain off through his fingers onto paper. Never let an art director talk.

"On a table at his left put your basic format dummy for reference.

Onto a table at his right feed him batches of photographs, with a note saying you want one, two, four, eight—any number of pictures you need, for each batch, and any suggestions you have for playing up any particular angles of the picture story.

"So he makes layouts from the pictures.

"If they are right, you pat him on the head. If they have strayed from the mood of the basic format, you take a small hammer, which you have chained to the wall for the purpose, rap him smartly over the skull, point severely to basic format dummy—cry 'No, no, no! Naughty!' He then repents and makes the layout right, or you get yourself a new art director."

Near the end of this advice, Hollister remembered, Luce was beginning to talk just like Longwell, saying over and over again: "Fine, fine, fine, fine." But he wanted one more small service from Hollister— the name of a suitable art director. Eventually Hollister suggested his own design man from Macy's, Howard Richmond, and he soon became *Life*'s first art director.

While the last dummies were being struggled over and reassembled, other work was going on in an area often referred to as "the business side," as if it were some gray zone where men and women without the fluttery nerve endings of editors and writers labored over grimy non-journalistic matters, like making money and keeping track of it. Generally speaking, men and women with editorial jobs on Time Inc. magazines have tended to regard people on the business side with a certain cool reserve, and in the case of advertising space salesmen, with some contempt, tinged here and there with jealousy. Editors sneer a bit at ad salesmen because, for example, they can be awfully hearty, raucous American Legionnaires in Brooks Brothers suits, because their dirty jokes tend to be tediously orificial, because their business is often conducted in places where other people play—at golf clubs and in fancy restaurants. And editors are jealous of the business side because they believe, with some justification, that many people there, including salesmen with their special commissions and bonuses, make more than editorial workers with similar or greater seniority.

Of course, the feelings run both ways. There can be no doubt that the business side is often put off and put out by editors, writers, photographers and reporters. These brooding, profligate, often unstable characters—as they are often perceived and sometimes are—are the glory boys of the operation. They inhabit the mastheads, get all the bylines and public recognition and, in the era of Luce's influence at least, were scrupulously protected against any undue influence for business considerations. The separation of spheres was kept as distinct as the separation between church and state, which is, in fact, the company language for the condition. People on the business side were often annoyed, dismayed, made frantic and now and then infuriated by what they considered the editors' smug aloofness from or even idiotic indifference to the facts of publishing life.

The advertising group set up originally to sell space in the new picture magazine went at its work with an engaging naïveté much like the editors'. No one really knew for sure just what the product was going to be. It didn't have a prospectus, rates or even a name when the first twelve-man sales staff began making the rounds. Nobody knew how big a market the picture magazine would reach or what was the precise nature of that market. Many advertisers, the new salesmen found, had a low regard for pictures: they were used to the content of rotogravure sections. Cheesecake pictures, they thought scornfully, snapshots of babies and dogs would never hold the readers' attention long enough to make it worth the advertisers' dollar. Both Robert Johnson, who was Time Inc.'s vice president in charge of advertising, and George Sadler, who had been moved over from *Time* to be the new magazine's advertising manager, thought there was a real problem with the November 1936 start-up schedule as planned, and some believed that the safest way to begin would be as a fortnightly, whose frequency could be changed when the going looked better.

In August, three months before *Life* appeared, the space rates were set. Advertisers could buy full pages at a rate of $1,500 a page, $800 per half page, $2,500 for a page of inside color. A net circulation of 250,000 was guaranteed. Advertisers with contracts made before the date of the first issue would be protected against increases for a year. This, of course, turned out to be a disastrously generous offering. When *Life*'s circulation immediately jumped far ahead of its guarantee and kept climbing, the first advertisers wound up with a quite unexpected bargain, and one that hurt Time Inc. badly.

In spite of the skepticism, there was a considerable amount of enthusiasm for the new magazine among many advertising professionals, and by late summer the small staff had sold over $1 million worth of space. Sadler sent Luce a list of advertisers who were committed to buy space—amounting to thirty-four pages—in the first issue. Some of the accounts were Zenith Radio, Seagram's Crown Whiskey, Maxwell House Coffee, United Air Lines, Four Roses Whiskey, General Motors. Luce replied that he thought the list was "fine except for perhaps a little too much liquor. I like Wrigley's and Maxwell," he said, "and would like to see a few more female advertisements." This last comment might well have been in response to pressure that Laura Hobson was putting on him to make a strong effort to reach the women's market.

Very often the salesmen used *Four Hours a Year* in their calls on clients. "Got a great new book," one salesman remembered telling prospective clients. "You'd better get in." Often they pasted up their own dummies with ads from other magazines to help them in their pitch, and one hot day Luce, chain-smoking and his sleeves rolled up, talked to the salesmen at length about his hopes for the magazine, went over the prospectus with them for possible uses of its rhetoric and gave them a bracing on the power of the camera. There it was again, that early sense of wonder about photography, that sense that pictures had an almost magical power to inform and touch a great audience. Of course, the audience would be influenced, too, by the advertisements that went along with those pictures.

By the time the magazine started, more than three hundred advertisers betting on that had signed up for space. And significantly, many advertising people saw in this new venture the opportunity to make enormous changes in their own approaches to selling. George Gallup, who was then research director of the Young and Rubicam agency, wrote his staff that the magazine "will doubtless create a new technique for pictures which an agency like Y and R should learn and be able to adapt for advertising." Another agency executive talked to Ingersoll, who naturally dashed off a memo: "His general enthusiasm for the whole idea was dizzying. As far as special advertising copy went, he said the minute we published the book he would put his whole department to work studying how to use this new medium effectively. . . . Said our ideas combined the best features of rotogravure and comic sections. He explained this last crack by pointing out that comic strips were comic no longer but made their appeal through visual story telling—and that was precisely the business we were going into. . . . He said anyone who paid a dime for a picture magazine would pay 15¢ for cigarettes and if we proved ourselves a good cigarette medium we could sell any kind of mass goods. Open to us: the whole field of mass accounts whose advertising cannot properly be adapted to the radio because they are best sold by showing the prospect the product." Another agency man who bought thirteen spreads of ads for Paramount Pictures said: "We're going to run you ragged—copy your technique so that you can't tell ads from editorial pages." Luce seemed delighted by the challenge, and the growing excitement near the deadline was beginning to make everyone feel, in the recollection of one of *Life*'s first space salesmen, Harry Dole, "that this was not going to be anything in between—it was either going to be goddam big or nothing."

"From now on," Luce wrote in a memorandum early in September 1936, "we must have an efficient, integrated editorial organization . . . with special responsibilities definitely assigned . . . but let the organization think of itself as a crew delegated by Time Inc. to seize an opportunity to do a big job. No one is indispensable; everyone who deserves to be on the crew at all is important.

"*The Managing Editor* of The Picture Magazine," Luce went on, "will be, for an unstated term of months or years, Henry R. Luce. *The Alternate Managing Editor* will be, for an unstated term, John S. Martin. When and if The Picture Magazine is successfully launched, it is probable that Luce will return to his sinecure as General Editor of Time Inc. publications, leaving Martin as Managing Editor of The Picture Magazine with a new Alternate Managing Editor to be discovered or developed. . . . A post of special authority on The Picture Magazine is that of *THE PICTURE EDITOR AND OFFICE MANAGER*, which will be filled by Daniel Longwell. He will be supremely responsible for the flow of pictures in and out of our offices, including the flow of pictures into the hands of the appropriate editors, through their hands into the magazine-dummy and out of their hands to the printer. Every picture deal, every nickel spent for pictures, must go through him. He will be the traffic officer for all assignments to photographers and also for the work of the layout men."

Thus, as the November publication date approached, Luce was serving notice that he was going to keep personal charge of the new project, that Martin would be his second-in-command and that Longwell would have special and important operational powers. How much Luce knew of any trouble is conjectural, but Martin was turning out to be a serious problem for the people under him on the small staff, especially for Longwell. "Martin couldn't stand Dan," a member of the pre-*Life* staff recalled. "Martin was quick and impatient and cruel when it suited him. Dan was prissy and sensitive and inarticulate and full of ideas and easily hurt. He would shrivel up under Martin's attack, like a caterpillar if you put a cigarette to it, and he would come out of Martin's office as if he were compressed. Martin was very pleased." He was also drinking enough to make him unreliable about afternoon appointments, and the group was uneasy about his moods. But Luce, at least at this point, seemed not to see the problem (and a strangely selective blindness and deafness frequently *did* afflict him), or quite possibly Martin's Hadden kinship made it particularly hard for Luce to act. But soon, in the clear interests of getting the new magazine out without a badly split leadership, he would have to.

"The pictures here gathered in rehearsal . . . are the harvest of a single week, the week ending September 21st. . . . Only when the new magazine is a weekly reality will the forces of inspiration and example work beneficently still further to improve the breed of the news photograph. . . . But it is from rehearsal that final stage directions characteristically emerge."

These words are drawn from the editor's message published in the second and final printed dummy, this one called *Rehearsal*. At 15,000 copies the print order was much smaller than for *Dummy*, perhaps because there was no doubt now that the picture magazine would be started and it would be pointless to keep making broad tests. Much of Hollister's basic format had been adopted, and the dummy looked tidier and more pleasing than its predecessors, though the headline type was one often used by advertisers—Luce ignored complaints that this would cause confusion between ads and adjacent editorial material and kept the Alternate Gothic type anyhow.

In *Rehearsal* were stories on a black family of cotton pickers in Mississippi (by Eisenstaedt), on the movie *Romeo and Juliet* with Norma Shearer and Leslie Howard, and a two-page drawing illustrating the problems of high-altitude flying. There were five pages about Helen Hayes and the play she was starring in at the time, *Victoria Regina*, an interesting little art story consisting of Russian-made paintings of Stalin ("as Communists *must* see him"), stories on the National Amateur Golf Championship and on women's tennis champion Alice Marble, a nature short on the life of the black widow spider. Also in the dummy were views of Hitler's Germany, including his Bavarian retreat at Berchtesgaden and the famous Nuremberg rally. Perhaps of special historical interest to fans of old movies, in the section called "Private Lives" there was a picture of a beautiful Austrian actress swimming nude in a film called *Ecstasy*. The swimmer was identified as Hedy Kiesler, wife of an "Austrian munitions magnate." Later, of course, she would travel to Hollywood and become Hedy Lamarr.

She was not the only nude in *Rehearsal*. In four pages showing the work in color of a photographer named Paul Outerbridge, there was a full-page nude called "Modesty," whose face was demurely turned from the camera, and a picture of a partially clothed dancer, who, the caption instructed, "might be a saucy Degas."

The nudes drew instant fire from the more shockable among Luce's readers. Thomas Donnelley, the man whose company did the printing, was very stiff in the expression of his proper views. His tone was a forecast of the occasional indignation of future generations of readers. "The magazine would be greatly improved," he wrote, "if Modesty's scarf was higher up and if the ballet dancer was left out entirely. This magazine is not only going to be popular with the adults of the family, but the younger children are going to look forward to it and pore over it with enthusiasm. . . . Such pictures as these are not necessary for the popularity of the publication . . . the second one is downright vulgar. You will lose no subscribers by leaving such pictures out." One man in circulation didn't even want his subscription agents to see the dummy because he thought the nudity "would rub our agents so wrong that it would prevent them from doing a good selling job for our new magazine." A man representing the company that would distribute copies of the future *Life* thought that while "Modesty" might stimulate some sales, "it would be better not to print a picture of this type in a magazine published by a publishing house that has the wonderfully fine standing of your company." Perhaps the most high-level expression of disapproval came from President Roosevelt's house in Hyde Park, New York, where a *March of Time* crew was making a film. The dummy and its poor "Modesty" came under the gaze of the President's terribly upright mother, Sara Delano Roosevelt, who pronounced that this was *not* the kind of magazine *her* family would have in the house.

Luce mostly agreed with the criticism on the nudes, and there is no record of what he thought about the comments on a story about Princess Juliana of Holland and her ancestors in the House of Orange. Apparently Luce had laid out the spread himself, so he must have been sensitive to the comments that it was "uninspired." Mrs. Luce didn't like it either, perhaps because the pictures were trimmed into odd shapes as if by a cookie cutter, and there weren't any more such layouts.

There were other non-compliments for the makers of the new magazine. The writer and political commentator Dorothy Thompson said that she and her novelist husband, Sinclair Lewis, thought it strangely "unmodern," "a combination of Bernarr Macfadden and the *Illustrated London News.*" She went on firmly: "In fact, Henry, the paper doesn't look like you. I should expect something handsome, dramatic, speedy, and creating, as your other papers do, an immediate recognition of first-class *organizing.* . . . It is not THE . . . MARCH . . . OF . . . TIME. It does not burst upon the eye with the sort of inevitableness which has always been your genius." The advertising manager reported that clients were agreed that *Rehearsal* "is a man's magazine; women are not expected to be interested in it as at present edited." Laura Hobson was upset; she deplored the fact that there was not in the dummy a

"lively, warm, human picture of the world. . . . The pages are intel-
lectualized, the captions are so cold, precise, full of *Time* and *Fortune*
locutions. My God, I want some feeling."

From the business side came an equally passionate assault. Pierre-
pont Isham Prentice, the top circulation executive, wrote Ingersoll:
"About half an hour after I sent you my memo yesterday telling you I
thought 370,000 circulation a not unreasonable expectation for 1937, I
saw the second dummy. If the magazine we turn out is going to be
anything like that, I do not believe we will hold more than 50% of our
prepublication subscribers, and I do not believe that our newsstand sale
will run more than 30,000 or 35,000 copies a week after the curiosity
buying settles down after the first issue. . . . You may gather from this
that I don't like the dummy. I don't. I think it is terrible."

From his sampling of people around the place, Longwell gave Luce
a much better report: "Encouraging is the attitude of Time Inc. people
who think in Time Inc.'s terms, people like Larsen, Billings, Eric Hodg-
ins, Noel Busch, Fraser. They criticize details, yet with publishing-
editorial imagination enough to see what we are aiming at and how we
are approaching what we shall be. Frankly they think we should go
right on the stands. It's in the bag, is their attitude." However much
Luce was able to accommodate criticism, however much he may have
wanted his new baby to be free of flaws, *that* was exactly the kind of
aggressive, charged-up, full-speed-ahead talk he wanted to hear.

One of the brightest young men on the pre-*Life* staff was Joseph Thorndike, a baby-faced but ambitious Harvard graduate who had been a
writer for *Time* until he got assigned to the experimental department.
Speaking much later of an interesting minor event from the dummy
days, Thorndike said: "I remember one day when Mike Cowles came
in with Harry and walked around the office—and the covers all over
the walls had *Look* on them."

Whether or not the Cowles brothers got the name for *their* magazine during that friendly visit, *Look* was only one on a list of about
two hundred possible titles being considered for the new picture journal. *Look* was C. D. Jackson's favorite choice, and Roy Larsen pushed
strong arguments for the title *March of Time*, largely because the radio
and film versions were so widely popular. "Here we are," he wrote,
"our minds made up to go out for a mass circulation for a magazine—
and as magazine publishers we have no mass following. But we have,
we have the biggest mass following of news-getting people in the U.S.,
people who like the way we give the news, people who are buying and
reading other magazines. I claim that if we put the name *March of Time*

on a magazine and put it on the stands and told these people it was there, they would buy it."

Other possibilities listed were, in no order of plausibility: *Album, Eye, Candid, Flash, Go, News Focus, Nuze-Vuze, Picture, Scan, Promenade, Quest, Snap, Vista, Witness, World, Spectator, See, Wide Awake!* One of the names on the list was, of course, *Life*. It is unclear whether any single person should be credited with picking it, although Clare Boothe Luce clearly thought of its aptness as a title for a picture magazine years ahead of her husband, who made the final decision. Longwell reported that he suggested the name, but he knew that others did, too. "I recommended it in a memorandum," wrote Ingersoll later, "and began negotiations unbeknownst to Mr. Luce six months before *Life* was born. Mr. Luce almost simultaneously arrived at the same idea independently in the course of writing his now-famous Prospectus." Ingersoll was referring, naturally, to Luce's use of the words "to see life," but whether Luce made that happy connection himself or someone pointed it out to him is unknown. James Linen, Jr., an old family friend of Luce's whose son, James Linen III, eventually became the president of Time Inc., wrote Luce after seeing the prospectus in midsummer of 1936: "I am disappointed in only one point and that was in reaction to the proposed name. . . . I do believe that in choosing the name *Show-Book of the World,* you are confining the initial appeal to a limited group. . . . *Life,* if it were preempted, would appear to me to best typify the proposed publication." Luce wrote back: "One of the reasons I did not answer sooner is due to the fact that we have been trying to get the use of the name *Life* and I had hoped to be able to write you before this that we had been successful in that effort. This is strictly confidential and to date there are only about five people in this organization who know that this is the name we would like to use. Among hundreds of names that have been suggested, I think you are the only one who has suggested that name, but as you can see, I agree with you fully that it is the perfect name." About the same time Luce sent a wire to Larsen in Nantucket, where he was vacationing. "Please," it read, "be careful not to mention proposed name for new magazine."

In early October, just a few weeks before the first issue was scheduled, Time Inc.'s executive committee met to approve Luce's proposal that the old *Life,* a weekly-turned-monthly humor magazine whose circulation had dwindled to 70,000, be purchased "largely for the purpose of acquiring the name *Life* to use on the new magazine. . . . It was the unanimous opinion of all present that the name was ideal." On October 7, the deal was completed. Time Inc. acquired the name, assets and goodwill of the old *Life,* which was in its fifty-fourth year of publication. The price was $92,000, and staff members got Time Inc. jobs. Alfred Eisenstaedt heard about the name when he was shooting pictures of beagles with John Martin, who gave him the news. "Well," recalled Eisenstaedt, "I thought, 'My God, let me see. *Life. Life. Life.*' And after five minutes I liked it. I had just photographed a dog covered with fleas—which was," he added, "a *Life* cover later." Allen Grover, a former Yale man who worked for Luce for forty years, became a Time Inc. vice president and was one of his closest confidants, remembered that on the day of the purchase Luce called him and *Fortune* managing editor Eric Hodgins into his office. "He was glowing," Grover said. "'Guess what?' he asked. 'We've got *Life.*' He was like a little boy with a new train."

3

A Vote of Confidence

WITH BARELY MORE THAN TWO WEEKS remaining before the first press deadlines, John Shaw Billings made this entry in his diary for October 23, 1936: "At five o'clock, Luce called me to his office, shut the doors, and proceeded to tell me that a great crisis had arisen on *Life*—a crisis due to Martin's behavior. Luce and Martin just don't pull together as a team and, as a result, *Life* is still badly disorganized and nowhere near ready to go into publication. Martin, said Luce, had contributed little or nothing to the experimental issues, had been off on his own and was just irresponsible. What precipitated the crisis was a Cloud Club lunch today at which Martin had appeared drunk and proceeded to criticize and abuse Luce before staff juniors. It must have been a bad scene. Now Luce wants to put Martin back on *Time* and make me managing editor of *Life*. He thinks he and I could work well together and so on.

"I was surprised and startled at this proposal," Billings wrote. "I know nothing of the philosophy of *Life* and am devoted to *Time*. I hate to think what Martin will do to the morale of my staff. Yet *Life* is a new job, with fresh excitement—and much harder work, I suppose. My answer to Luce was: I am ready to do whatever he thought best for the organization. If he wanted me with him, I would come and do my level best. If there was a change, it should come at once. Luce is leaving tonight for a weekend in his South Carolina place, where he will think over the decision."

At this eventful moment in his life Billings was characteristically honest with himself about his anxiety for the future. "Considerably upset and unsettled in my mind," he continued in his diary. "I am not picture-minded (Luce says Martin isn't either). Can I make a go of it? I told F. [his wife, Frederica] and Ma [his mother-in-law] about my talk with Luce. The only feature of it that really interested them was whether my new hours were longer or shorter. (I thought that was a narrow selfish view of a major change in my work.) I am sorry for Martin, who for three years has been a high-paid ($33,000) supernumerary, whose career is being wrecked by liquor—who may not get another chance. I am sorrier still for my staff, at whom he will bark and curse and mistreat and bully. But the decision is Luce's; to wreck *Time* to launch *Life*."

From that moment on, for eight years as the magazine's first managing editor and even after that when he became editorial director of all the Luce publications, John Shaw Billings held a position of commanding and unchallenged authority at *Life*. He imposed clarity and order upon a muddled beginning, and the discipline he applied to himself provided a solid example to the jittery and somewhat bewildered group around him. At thirty-eight, he was punctual, fastidious, tough-minded and physically strong, and bore himself with a certain aloofness that served both to scare away unwanted thieves of his time and to make people feel a filial devotion to him. He was a big man, heavy, with cold blue eyes, a rather jowly, impassive face, and he walked with a slightly duck-footed stride, his head down and his hands often clasped behind his back like a skater's. He could be cruel and icily indifferent when it suited him, and his small kindnesses were treasured by his underlings, who were moved to intense gratitude by his expressions of ordinary sympathy or by a simple invitation to lunch. He seemed a person of quite pervasive formality; he often wore his suit coat while he worked, and he commuted from his uptown Fifth Avenue apartment to the Time-Life offices—first in the Chrysler Building, then in Rockefeller Center—in a chauffeur-driven limousine, preferably a Packard. Only those who knew him very well and had the rank for it called him "John." To almost everyone he was "Mr. Billings," and many people made a point of not speaking to him at all unless he addressed them first or it was absolutely necessary. "He could have been interested in other people," recalled Edward K. Thompson, who came to work for Billings in 1937, was a protégé and great admirer of his, and in 1949 became managing editor himself, "but he did a superlative job of hiding it. I would think on an average that a new employee didn't get spoken to for about a year." Thompson remembered one new editorial employee who became almost unhinged by Billings's habit of silence, especially in the elevator, where, like Luce, he would not speak, one felt, even if the cable snapped. "This guy would say 'Good morning' to

Billings, and he wouldn't answer," said Thompson, a man who had his own unapproachable moments. "He became determined to make Billings answer. Billings was fairly predictable, and this guy would wait for him and get in the elevator with him and say 'Good morning, Mr. Billings.' Then when they got off he'd trot up the hall and say it again— 'Good morning, Mr. Billings.' He got fired shortly thereafter."

But Billings was not a man who put on any airs about his line of work or believed that it entitled him to any special status. "It always griped me to hear fatheads inflate the importance of journalism," he once wrote, "and attribute all sorts of high-falutin qualities to it I never thought it possessed." On another occasion someone had spoken to him of *"Time's* responsibility to the world in its hour of crisis." "Lord!" he wrote in disgust. "As managing editor, I make it a point never to consider public opinion or civic duty or any of that kind of twaddle invented to make journalism seem more important than it really is."

Billings did take pride in his ancestors, especially those on his mother's side of the family. They had been South Carolina aristocrats, and Billings's most prized possession was Redcliffe, the old family plantation near Aiken. It had been sold out of the family years earlier, and Billings had bought it back in 1935 when he was managing editor of *Time.* In a brief autobiographical sketch drawn for the corporate files, he wrote: "A large white house, Redcliffe was built in 1855 by Senator James Henry ('Cotton is king') Hammond, Billings' great-grandfather, half a dozen miles across the Savannah River from Augusta, Ga. A South Carolinian born and bred, Senator Hammond had nothing but contempt and scorn for Augusta and Georgia. Hence he put a cupola on Redcliffe's high roof from which, so he said, he could spit on the town across the river without straining. The Redcliffe plantation has now passed to the possession of Editor Billings who inherits his ancestor's feelings toward Augusta and, when the wind is right, uses the cupola to express them."

When he was fourteen, Billings began to keep a diary, and he kept it until shortly before he died at seventy-seven in 1975. He wrote in longhand in lined school notebooks about an inch thick. In the last years of his life he gave about seventy of these to the library at the University of South Carolina, along with family papers and big scrapbooks filled with his musings and ideas, with clippings, pictures, poems, sayings, songs—anything that had caught his interest, including his first wife's menus and grocery lists. They make an astonishing record. Billings was an obsessed collector of the shards of his own life: it was as if gathering and keeping these fragments, this running account of days full of anger and resentment, success and rejection, sorrow and bathos, elation and self-pity, was the only way to prove he'd lived at all. For all his curt, confident manner, Billings, as seen in his own journals, was a man who had much doubt and pain. "'Society,'" he wrote in his mid-twenties, "and its implied flattery and snub. I see Suydam and his fiancée made the objects of all kind of social attentions, dinners, parties, dances, teas. I suffer secret pangs of envy because I have been excluded from these affairs or because under similar circumstances I received no such attentions. In my heart I know such social activities would only be ashes in my mouth and that I would get no honest enjoyment out of them. . . . An upsurge of self-pity, a deep sense of being neglected and passed over. And yet I have a complete realization of why I receive no such invitations; I won't keep up my end by returning these social obligations; I won't make any effort on my part to win these flattering attentions. I lack money; I lack wit: so of course I am not asked out. Yet I try to comfort myself with thoughts of great future achievements which will put to shame all those who slight my company today. How I'll scorn them, how I'll reject their belated offers of attention! Such thoughts naturally breed a secret feeling of superiority. . . . Here, in my own case, is presented a complete set of facts from which a good fictional tangle could be developed."

In an entry made in 1924 Billings wrote: "I come into my office alone late one Sunday evening and write: Great winged ideas that rise in frightened flight from the soggy marshland of my mind when a piece of white paper is spread out and a pencil is poised to trap them—I sit in a pool of silence rimmed with city sounds. I am alone and the absence of other personalities gives my own room to expand. I could be brilliant if I could always be alone. But fear lurks in silence. The others—where are they, what are they doing? My sensation is one of missing something. I should hurry forth and find my comrades lest they lay schemes against me. If I were they, my very presence would forestall them— but I like loneliness. My ego can stand up and look about. I see the things of one day's work; the desks, the typewriters, the papers. How useless they seem in their silence. Six days a week they gear in with a devilish world—and then today they stand idle. How paltry are their products! They clatter nonsense, gigantic trivialities. . . . Scorn for the rest of the week and its poor labors fires up in me on Sunday."

Thus his scorn, his envy, his hurt, his tenderness were tucked away out of sight in the notebooks. A deep and growing disaffection with Luce, for example, is clear in the diaries, although Billings was regarded as "a good soldier," completely loyal to the boss and, for all most people knew, on excellent terms with him. But in an entry early in 1936, Billings wrote: "What does Luce really think of me? I don't think he likes me personally—and I know I don't like him. He doesn't want me around. He doesn't want me to talk personal matters to him—and he doesn't talk personal matters to me." Soon after that he wrote: "We [Billings and another *Time* editor] damned him for his strange kinks! I because he still carries Martin's name as a *Time* managing editor. I think Luce has changed greatly for the worse in the last year. His success has gone to his head, and he has grown hard and mean and coolly impersonal. I no longer feel I am working with a friend." An entry scribbled that summer in his curiously misshapen handwriting: "Luce asked me to lunch at the Waldorf (and as usual I had to pay the bill because he did not have money enough). We talked of the Landon-Roosevelt campaign first. (God, how he hates Roosevelt, as I do too.) Then he launched into his staff ideas. He wants to borrow some of my men for *The March of Time* [radio]—and the whole staff to help out with news for the new picture magazine. The project staggered me— and I wondered how I could get *Time* out. Luce is really a dog to work for—utterly cold and impersonal. Not once did he ask me about my vacation at Redcliffe or F.! Really I like him less and less and blame his second wife for his attitudes. She's just a yellow-haired bitch who is spending his money like water." On another occasion the entry was more moderate: "Regular work. Luce in. He told me that he had bought 7,000 acres near Charleston. Whew! I'm sorry—because I felt South Carolina belonged to me."

The "bad scene" between Martin and Luce mentioned by Billings apparently consisted of Martin shouting out "Buckeye!" at many of Luce's suggestions to a group of his editors. By that obscure epithet he meant that Luce's suggestions were corny, which certainly was the truth from time to time, though it was at least bad manners and judgment to say so publicly. For Luce clearly wanted no confrontation with Martin and was most reluctant to take any steps against him. He'd known for a long time that Martin created real problems with the staff, and he knew that among the worst of them was that Martin continually baited the sensitive Longwell.

On one occasion, a member of the first *Life* staff remembered, Martin came back to a story conference from a long lunch and immediately began harassing Longwell about the quality of his suggestions, which were usually offered in profusion. "Well, Dan, what crap have you got for us today?" was the sort of stone Martin is recalled as hurling at Longwell, whose excellent ideas were often buried among a lot of bad ones. At this meeting, Joseph Kastner, a young writer who'd been moved from *Fortune* to write the gossipy "Private Lives" section of the new magazine, offered a somewhat bizarre suggestion of his own. Reading from a news clipping, Kastner advised the group that doctors were becoming concerned about the violent way people were blowing their noses. If the noses were blown too hard over a long period of time, he read, there was the possibility that serious sinus problems would arise. Kastner's suggestion: a helpful picture story called "How to Blow Your Nose." The group, Kastner recalled, was silent for a moment. Longwell looked stunned. Suddenly Martin hit the conference table and roared: "A great idea, Joe! A great idea!" Then he turned to Longwell and said: "Goddamnit, Dan, why don't *you* have ideas like that?"

Even after it became plain to Luce that Martin would have to go, and even after he had told Billings that the change would be made, Luce stalled. Their long association, the fact that Martin was a cousin of the brilliant Briton Hadden, whose somewhat mocking ghost cast votes long after his death had ended the partnership, the fact that Martin had made substantial contributions to *Time*'s success, that he was, however difficult, a bright, charming, funny man, capable of kindness as well as cruelty, and a man who seemed unable to stop the downhill slide of a promising career—all these things contributed to Luce's reluctance to push him aside.

Others did not share his reluctance. "I went to lunch with Larsen at the Cloud Club to discuss the Martin matter," Billings wrote in his diary the day after Luce spoke of the change. "Larsen takes a hard-boiled, non-sentimental attitude toward Martin, who he considers impossible to work with. He says Martin must rule or ruin. Martin is evidently drinking as hard as ever. Larsen is for busting him completely out of *Time*. Larsen said his job and mine was to keep Luce's backbone stiff in dealing with Martin."

The backbone would need it. Two days later, Luce promised Billings he would deal with the problem that very day, but according to the diary he couldn't bring himself to do it. "Finally Luce came in at 7:00," Billings wrote, "and said everything was off until tomorrow. He had talked to Martin, who put up a great plea for a second chance on *Life*, promising to cooperate and so on. Luce had evidently got cold feet. He did not want to bring up Martin's drinking as one of the real reasons for the shift. Hence, he told Martin he'd let him know tomorrow, and he would then let me know. I felt let down and flat because Luce had failed to carry through."

The entry for the next day carried different news. Billings was at home. He wrote: "At 4:00 p.m., Luce telephoned: 'It's done. It was brief and painful. It made me sick.' That meant he had seen Martin, had ordered him back to *Time* as managing editor, had ordered me to *Life* as managing editor—a blow to Martin, who has boasted widely about the picture magazine he was putting out, and who will lose face with all his friends. It also means a great change and upheaval in my life." And he wrote later: "Luce shifted me so fast from *Time* to *Life* that I had no chance to tell the staff goodby or to cast a backward look over my three years running The Weekly Magazine."

The letter Luce wrote to Martin about the upheaval was oddly uncritical under the circumstances; in it, Luce was more critical of himself. "Dear John," he wrote. "It is surely unnecessary for me to say that you have contributed handsomely to the development of *Life* to date. Personally I have much to thank you for, and personally I have little to complain about. So, of what I have to say, I hope you will attribute as little as possible to any personal feeling or feelings of mine.

"What I have to say," he continued, "is that you and I have not been enough of a success to date as collaborators. This has been a disappointment to me—and one which I think can be partly attributed to bad luck or lack of luck such as the failure of an Art Director to arrive on the scene, etc. etc. And perhaps, without alibi, I should take most of the blame since it was my job to organize *Life* including the 'collaboration.' But I must express candidly the opinion, which is shared by the others, that you are a most able editor and an equally difficult collaborator."

His tender verbal spanking administered, Luce went on to say: "You can do a swell job on *Time*—and Billings is willing to suffer as 'Collaborator.' Your feelings on this subject may well be mixed. Perhaps best of all you would like to be managing-editor boss of *Life*. But I am sure you will like being managing-editor boss of *Time* better than the present set-up on *Life*." Thus it was finished, an absolutely necessary change made dangerously late, and one of the most astonishing things about it was that Luce's charitable and ambivalent attitude toward his old colleague permitted him to keep Martin in a position of considerable power in the company, at the operating top of *Time*, the magazine Luce surely was more attached to, cared more about personally than any of his others. But also perhaps it is a measure of Luce's confident regard for himself and his ability to deal with difficult problems in a situation he understood. Martin could be managed on *Time*, a thirteen-year-old success whose every page Luce ordered or approved. But *Life* was different. Nobody understood that. "We've been fussing around for six months with theory and philosophy," Luce told Billings. "From now on, to hell with theory and philosophy—you've got to get out a magazine."

There was one other high-level personnel problem in the days shortly before the new *Life* appeared, and it might even have been a more difficult one for Luce. Strictly speaking, it was not an office matter at all. This problem involved Luce's wife and the role she might reasonably play in this latest venture. Here even more than in the Martin affair, Luce acted in a curiously flaccid way, as if he couldn't bear to deal firmly with events over which he had, of course, absolute and final control.

Over and above the fact that she was the proprietor's wife, there were some good reasons why Clare Boothe Luce might have been considered a plausible candidate for a job at *Life*. She had been a magazine editor of real ability and imagination, and she liked to work hard. The new magazine would need experienced women editors. Clare Luce had a long-standing interest in picture magazines and many ideas about them. There is no reason to believe, in fact, that she wasn't at least as competent to work on *Life* as anyone there, including the bosses. And then, of course, she had surely been looking at the dummies right along and making her own comments and suggestions about them to Luce. Just exactly how much influence she had can only be guessed, but she must have had a lot. Clare Luce was an extremely bright, articulate, persuasive young woman, and she was well informed in areas—culture and the arts, for example—where Luce was a virtual booby, and he was very much dazzled by her, proud of her good looks and brains, very much in love with her.

She recalled that one night just a few weeks before *Life* started up Luce called home from the office. "He was giggly and sparkly on the phone," she told Robert Elson. Luce was calling with news about an invitation for them both. Longwell and Ingersoll had asked them out for dinner. According to Clare Luce's recollection: "Harry said, 'I think I know what's coming.' And I said, 'What?' He said, 'They want to offer you a place on the magazine.' So I said, 'Oh, that's wonderful!' I was very excited about it. We went to dinner at Voisin, the four of us, and the dinner hadn't been going on for more than twenty minutes before I knew that that wasn't what they wanted to say, and I began to get this very uneasy feeling. It was confirmed by Mac [Ingersoll] looking significantly at Dan and then at Harry and saying, 'Do you think we could go some place—to your apartment, because Dan and I have something to say to you and Clare.' Not 'something to *ask* you and Clare,' but 'something to *say* to you and Clare.'"

Back in the Luces' apartment on East Fifty-second Street, her account continued, "Mac Ingersoll got up and began to walk around the room, and told Harry what a great editor he'd been and how well he handled *Time* magazine. . . . Poor Dan sat there, not saying a thing, squirming and looking miserable. Then Mac said, 'Harry, you have got to make up your mind whether you are going to go on being a great editor, or whether you are going to be on a perpetual honeymoon. When you edited *Time* you stayed in the office until ten and eleven o'clock every night. Now you catch the five-ten back to the country; you clear out of that office at five o'clock every afternoon—' Now, mind you, we'd only been married less than a year! We'd only been married a very short while! And he said, 'Clare, if she really loves you, won't get in the way of the success of this magazine. And what I have to say to her is that you cannot publish a great magazine with one hand tied behind your back.'"

The message was as sloppy and insulting as a custard pie in the face. Not only weren't the editors offering her a job on *Life*, but Ingersoll, in a virtuoso display of effrontery, was chastising both Luces for an alleged crime of passion, the crime of letting their interest in each other come ahead of the needs of the new magazine.

Shocked and furious, Clare Luce waited for a moment to see if her husband had any response to Ingersoll's absurd candor. Nothing happened; the sharp-tongued editor-in-chief, the most powerful young man in American publishing, the cold and difficult boss, the ardent bridegroom was stunned to silence. His wife was not. "Mac," she said to Ingersoll, "I have something to tell you, and I hope you'll remember it and Harry will remember it. Harry Luce can publish a better magazine with one hand tied behind his back than you can publish with both of yours free—and both feet, too!"

Then, as she recalled it, "I got up and ran upstairs and had myself a little cry. It wasn't that I was really counting on editing the magazine—I was certainly wise enough to see the difficulties with a husband and wife in the same office. In fact, I was sort of hoping I'd be in the position of saying, 'I don't think it's the best thing.' But before I could say anything, here I was being accused of ruining the magazine, ruining Harry—all the rest of it." She added: "You know, this happened to me very often in the first two or three years."

Luce followed her upstairs shortly thereafter. Her account of their conversation: "I said, 'Well, what did you say to that?' And he said, 'Well, you know it would be an impossible situation considering the way they feel.' I said, 'Now, I'll tell you—as long as you and I are married, I will *never* put foot in your office or ever intervene in any way whatsoever with your magazines.' I think everyone would agree that that was a promise I kept—except insofar as I had some influence on Harry. . . . I was profoundly hurt, and I said to Harry about Ingersoll, 'There's something very wrong with a guy that would do that to a man who has just been married, and with no proof of any kind that I have been a drag on you.' And then I was a little cross at Harry that he didn't say something like 'After all, if Clare hadn't sort of prodded me on this, there'd have been no magazine.'" But Mrs. Luce was generous in her judgment of Luce's strangely passive response to Ingersoll's rebuke. "Maybe he felt," she speculated about her husband's behavior, "that an angry reply would further strengthen their position that it was all my conniving, because I wanted to edit the magazine, or something."

So Clare Luce did not carry the matter further, but said to him instead: "I've been hoping and thinking of how I could be the most help to you. But what is perfectly clear is that the way I can help you most is to set about my own business. And for some time now I've been thinking what I'd like to do is to write a play." She did just that, dashed off a play in a few months, and it was favorably reviewed with color photographs by the new *Life* only weeks after publication began. The play was called *The Women*, a clever and (for the times) venomous satire on the idle rich. With its all-female cast and its bitchy dialogue, it was a tremendous hit on Broadway and made a million dollars the first year. Then the play traveled all over the world, later became a successful movie and made a whole lot more. So much for the positive uses of anger.

Just what led Luce to react to Ingersoll's comments with such restraint can only be guessed. It is possible, of course, that Luce felt Ingersoll was right and decided on the spot that he had to drop such minor considerations as his wife's future as an editor and work much harder on the new magazine. It is possible, too, that he thought, as he told his wife, that her position on *Life* would be impossible if her colleagues didn't want her there. But there might have been other reasons, too. Perhaps Luce really didn't want his wife on the new magazine, didn't dare say so to her in those honeymoon days and was relieved and ready to use Ingersoll's opposition to his own ends. Or perhaps he *was* angry about it at the time and just didn't know what to do. His relationship with Ingersoll, who was a most considerable figure at Time Inc. in those days, certainly deteriorated over the next few years. Possibly Luce was just waiting for the right moment. Perhaps it came in 1938 when Luce decided that Ingersoll, who was quietly planning to bring out a newspaper called *PM*, was being disloyal to him. As a man who was present recalled, Luce called Ingersoll to his office and without preamble said with great calm and cold: "You're fired. I want you to get out of here as soon as possible." Ingersoll, the "memo marathon," went.

On the occasion of his family's purchase of the Minneapolis *Star*, little more than a year before the new *Life* came out, John Cowles appeared on the cover of *Time*. The story about this thirty-six-year-old friend of Luce's was most complimentary and read in part: "No corn-fed bumpkin, no dallying rich man's son, inquisitive John Cowles has stored behind his thick-lensed glasses and his moon face a wealth of essential fact. An excellence of perspective on top of a sound judgment makes him one of the most important young newspaper publishers in the land." About Cowles's brother Gardner, the story commented in just as friendly a way: "Mike Cowles is called executive editor. . . . He cooks up many a smart feature, directs the three radio stations. . . . Breezier, more imaginative than Brother John, Gardner Jr. is not so invariably right."

When the Cowles brothers began their preparations for the picture magazine that would become *Look*, there was much cordiality; strong efforts were made toward mutual cooperation and assistance. Early in 1936, Longwell had set up a meeting with a wire he sent to Gardner Cowles. It read: "If possible think it might be good idea for you or John Cowles to come here and see Luce, Ingersoll and me. Still a close secret but our picture plans are becoming fairly well developed and there are some things we might well do together." A few months later Mike Cowles had dinner with Roy Larsen, and among other matters they discussed Cowles's ideas for a picture magazine. In a few days Cowles wrote Larsen: "I am now attempting to give birth to a dummy along the line I outlined. I hope to have it off the press in about two weeks and at that time John and I will make a date with you and Harry and come to New York to give you an opportunity to tear the idea and dummy to pieces."

The meetings continued and included such subjects as cost estimates for *Look* and the possibility that Time Inc. would invest in it. Unlike *Life*, it would be produced with low-cost paper on rotogravure presses. There would be no advertising sold until a realistic circulation base had been established (a publishing strategy *Life* might better have followed), and circulation income would pay most expenses. "Please do not feel any obligation," Mike Cowles wrote Luce, "to buy this stock, however, if, after looking over the enclosed figures, the proposition looks less attractive to you than it did when John and I explained our plans to you in New York."

A presentation in favor of buying the stock in *Look* was made to Time Inc.'s board by Roy Larsen and Charles Stillman acting for Luce. In part it read:

"For $100,000 Time Inc. acquires 20% of a company which will have in it to start with $260,000 cash, plus two years of free management by Gardner and John Cowles, plus a very favorable contract with the Des Moines *Register and Tribune* for the availability of a substantial amount of editorial material at low cost.

"Examination of the dummy for *Look* makes it immediately apparent that *Look* will not compete very much with *Life*. It will come out after *Life*—will appear only once a month—will probably solicit no advertising until the latter part of 1937—will be cheaply printed with an editorial content geared towards the readers of the New York *Daily News* on a national scale. . . .

"The arguments advanced for this investment, which appealed to us, are as follows:

"1. There are no other publishers in the country with whom *Time* has more in common or for whom *Time* has more respect than the Cowles brothers.

"2. They have approached the problem of a national picture magazine for the American people at 10¢ a copy in a vastly different way than the plans which we have for *Life*. They may both succeed or they may both fail. If our plans for *Life* prove to be top-heavy with overhead and bigness, as they might, the modest scale of operations proposed by the Cowles brothers is so much the opposite extreme that they might well succeed where we might fail.

"3. Just as *Time* might do if it entered the newspaper field starting in a very modest way with a primary object of learning a new trade, so the Cowles have attacked the magazine business in an ultra-conservative way and are expressing in their modest budget their realization that they have a new trade to learn.

"4. Exchange of ideas and information should be of considerable value to both parties.

"5. A new field of publishing is being opened up by *Life*. There is already professed, if as not yet serious, competition in *Mid-Week Pictorial* [published by *The New York Times*]. It is better that we should protect our flanks with friendly cooperative enterprises which will tend to discourage less desirable competitors."

The executive committee of the Time Inc. board met to approve the investment on November 13, 1936, just ten days before the first issue date of the new *Life*. Luce was not present, and in his behalf Larsen brought up an interesting worry. According to the board minutes, Larsen "expressed the reservation in the mind of Mr. Luce on the unqualified endorsement of the Cowles brothers, namely, he was afraid their journalism would prove to be too 'yellow' for us to be in entire sympathy with it. However, it was reported by Mr. Larsen that the Cowles brothers feel that they will be able to become less 'yellow' as they go along." With confidence, then, that *Look* would be able to upgrade its color, the committee approved the purchase, and Time Inc. bought a sizable share (20 percent at first but shortly reduced to 17 percent) of *Look*.

Roy Larsen recalled one evening with the Cowles brothers with particular clarity. "Before our first issue came out—just before—in fact we had the dummy of the first issue with us—Harry Luce and I had dinner at the Savoy Plaza with John and Mike Cowles, and they had a dummy of their first issue of *Look*. So we compared notes on these magazines, and they thought at the time that they were going to be the mass circulation picture magazine and we were going to be the class. I volunteered the prediction that we would be the class *and* the mass, that their magazine was too sensational, too synthetic, that their appeal to the lower instincts would not take as a mass proposition. But, nevertheless, we thought it would be a success."

What happened, of course, is that after they got going, both magazines began to shift away from any extremes of propriety or sensation and to become more, in fact, like each other. Just before *Look*'s first issue and only a month after *Life* had started, John Cowles, in a letter he wrote hoping that *Look* would get a good editorial notice in *Time*, said to Larsen: "Although Harry is currently editing *Life* in a much more popular vein than Mike and I, judging from the *Rehearsal* dummies, had anticipated he would, I still believe as strongly as ever that there is a big potential field for *Look* wholly distinct from and non-competitive with *Life*'s circulation field." Not long after *Look* appeared, Mike Cowles expressed the view that he had "made a serious blunder in keying the first issue of *Look* too low." Some items in that first issue: scenes from Japanese houses of prostitution, a picture of a bull seeming to bite a bullfighter, a story about hermaphrodites called "When Is a Woman Actually a Woman?," newsreel clips showing an automobile skidding and killing a pedestrian, a doctored picture (a "composograph") showing the stripteaser Gypsy Rose Lee in apparent conversation with the best-dressed woman of that year, Mrs. Harrison Williams (their imagined conversation: Williams: "I never wear the same thing twice. And you?" Lee: "I never put off tomorrow what I can put off today"), and three pages of pictures on the various hats worn by Queen Mary of England. One of the photographs showed the Queen with her husband, George V, who had died more than a year earlier. A cartoon-strip dialogue balloon indicated that the King was saying: "Mary, I don't like that hat. I can't see your hair." Surely few people could have been upset by such harmless irreverence, but Mike Cowles made clear his intention to elevate the editorial tone so that *Look* would not be "in bad taste" in the opinion of "any substantial number of broadminded people."

The story in *Time* about *Look*'s first issue saluted it as "eye-popping photographic showmanship" but made no mention of Time Inc.'s holdings, although the magazine's financing was discussed. Actually the alliance would last only a few months longer. In July 1937, the Cowles brothers requested the opportunity to buy back Time Inc.'s shares in *Look*. Luce and his advisers, well aware by then that the two magazines were indeed competitive, happily complied—and turned a $67,500 profit in the bargain.

The arrangement came to an end with few bad feelings. Few, that is, except those that rankled in the breast of Dan Longwell. When *Look* came out, he sent a congratulatory wire to its founders. To copies of the wire he sent to Luce, Larsen and Ingersoll, Longwell attached the following note: "I am not sore at the Cowles boys. We were buddies in the exchange of pictures in the old days on *Time*—close buddies, like that. I was the first to invite them back here to see our experiments. Point was that they had represented themselves to me as wanting to syndicate *Life*'s pictures. What they got was a title for their magazine—and the impulse to start it. Same time they dropped me like hot cakes and have never been able to look me in the eye since. I am not sore. I've had fast ones pulled on me before. But I shall never trust the Cowles boys again in any way. Only the worst Jew in the publishing business ever pulled so smart a trick on me. He went broke. I don't think the Cowles boys will."

A letter, bearing Luce's signature, sent to *Time* subscribers in search of charter subscriptions to *Life* began: "It is at once dumbfounding and deeply gratifying to learn the response to our earlier letter inviting encouragement and support for the picture magazine we have been planning for so long—

26,151 answers in one day—
72,955 within a week—
162,450 to date, with still more pouring in—
And saying 'You can count on me as a Charter Subscriber.'

"This," the letter burbled on, "is such an overwhelming vote of confidence from America's most alert and newsminded audience—confidence in a magazine no subscriber has yet seen—that we are really at a loss for words to express our appreciation."

The response to the mailings truly was astonishing, even to the most optimistic *Life* boosters, and by the time the first issue was ready to go to press, there were more than 235,000 subscriptions on the books, at $3.50 a year. Almost 38 percent of *Time*'s subscribers signed up, and very special emphasis was placed on firing up their enthusiasm for the new magazine. "I think it is most important," wrote circulation executive Pierrepont Isham Prentice, "that we have our *Time* subscribers pretty damn excited about our new venture by the time they get their first issue, so that they will be in a mood:

1. to send in their checks;
2. to enter a lot of subscriptions for their friends;
3. to snap up all the copies that the newsstands offer for sale;
4. to rush around and tell all their friends about the new magazine and what a wow it is."

But Prentice, whose shortcut name was "Pierrie," did not seem terribly confident that the new project would last long—or that the magazine would build up much momentum of its own. "Of course, if the first issue is a lemon," he wrote his colleagues, "it won't do us much good to have our subscribers all hopped up to rush around as 500,000 unsalaried salesmen, but I honestly think we have got to assume that the editorial department will not let us down on the first issue (I am much more afraid they will let us down on the second issue, in case you're curious). It will be much easier to get our new subscribers hopped up about the new magazine this fall than it ever will be at any future time. I think everybody is interested in our new picture magazine right now. It is news and you have to know about it and talk about it if you are to appear well-informed. A year from now, the picture magazine will be just another magazine and we will have to fight for attention. . . . Instead of worrying too much about over-selling our subscribers, I think we should worry about making sure that the production lives up to our promises."

And Prentice did not like some of the promises being made about *Life* in its selling, especially the one made in Luce's almost euphoric letter to possible subscribers. "We can promise you," he wrote, "the biggest package of interesting and exciting pictures in the world—

10,000 pictures a year, intelligently edited and intelligently captioned." "I personally just plain do not believe," said Prentice, "that any large segment of the American public wants to see a lot more pictures. I am, personally, definitely bored by the suggestion of the biggest package of pictures in the world, and I am happy to report that a very large number of replies we have received from our trial mailing have indicated a similar feeling of 'Oh, my God, I see enough pictures already and here you are giving me more of the same thing.' The fact that after 22 years the New York *Times' Mid-Week Pictorial* still has only 10,000 newsstand sales is some confirmation of my belief that the American public's tongue is not hanging out for just any picture magazine. . . .

"Alas," Prentice went on with his lesson on how to market magazines, "it is my personal observation that 9 out of 10 successful magazine promotions are based on the proposition that the subscriber needs the magazine, rather than on the theory that the subscriber will enjoy the magazine. *Vogue* is sold on the idea that you can't buy your clothes wisely and economically without *Vogue's* advice. *Time* is sold on the proposition that you can't be well-informed unless you use this unique invention designed to get all the important news of the world into the head of an intelligent person—and make it stick. *Fortune* is sold on the proposition that you can't understand our amazing industrial civilization without taking advantage of *Fortune's* tremendous research. . . . *The New Yorker* is sold on the proposition that you can't hold up your end of civilized conversation in New York unless you have *The New Yorker's* help. . . .

"I am completely sour," he concluded, "on the idea that Americans, already struggling under such a tremendous load of pictures, will shout 'Hallelujah' when they hear the biggest load of all is approaching . . . and so I would be . . . satisfied with a campaign stressing the reader's inferiority complex, to sell our readers on the idea that they cannot be well-informed about our amazing world unless they have actually looked at it and seen it in the pages of the new magazine."

Prentice's was not the only voice edged slightly with doom. As Luce and his editors, salesmen, business managers, production men, circulation and promotion experts and various kibitzers of all sorts scrambled down to the deadline, there were many predictions of big and little trouble. Differences over budgeting techniques fired up David Brumbaugh, a young accounting genius who wanted Luce and his other bosses to think bigger. "Never in our history," he wrote, urging them to select a large page size for *Life*, "have we come out of any tight spot by a choice of conservatism or economy in the usual sense of those words, but always by expenditure of more money and more effort to gain greater income at greater expense. This will always be the right choice as long as the ideas and the vitality are flowing freely to keep pace with the increased outlays. This has produced profits which must be considered the result of the most effective and hence the most economical use of an enviable concentration of manpower, an element in success far scarcer than gold, no matter what price per ounce." Other urgings and worries were more pungently expressed. As the big day approached, a harassed circulation man in Chicago offered the view that plans were getting awfully sloppy, that it reminded him of the way that Baptists prepare for church picnics. They seldom take into account the possibility of rain, he said, and it is always sure to rain.

The ugly little feud between Time Inc. and *The New Yorker* dated back to *The New Yorker's* founding in 1925, when *Time* panned editor Harold Ross's first issue. Now, at the precise moment of *Life's* start-up, the row flared again, this time because of a wickedly funny profile on Luce by *New Yorker* writer Wolcott Gibbs, whose fame for verbal acid throwing was widespread. There had been other signs of increasing tension and trouble between the two young and cocky magazine companies. Two years earlier Ross had been angered when a *Fortune* story listed the salaries of *The New Yorker's* top people. With some justification, he was especially furious at Ralph Ingersoll, who had been his managing editor at *The New Yorker* before leaving to go to work for Luce at *Fortune*; Ingersoll obviously had inside information about salaries paid by his old employer. In retaliation, Ross ran a single sentence in *The New Yorker's* "Talk of the Town" section: "The editor of *Fortune* gets $30 a week and carfare." And Ross's editors had been taking public note of Luce's plans for *Life*. "This publication," one item noted, "promises to do away with the last vestigial traces of privacy in America."

But the Gibbs profile—which called *Life* Luce's "new whoop-sheet"—was clearly much bigger stuff, and when Ingersoll heard that it was in the works, he warned Luce and advised him not to cooperate. But feeling duty-bound as a journalist to sit still for the study of other journalists, Luce agreed to be interviewed. When the piece was completed, Ross submitted it for corrections of fact. There was an immediate response of fury and alarm from the executive offices in the Chrysler Building. Ingersoll was especially aroused and declared that Ross was guilty of "Hearst tactics." With the flushed reaction so well known to men and women given rough or insulting treatment in his own magazines, Luce was scandalized by what seemed to him to be clearly unfair treatment.

Possibly it was a bit unfair—making fun of somebody always is—

but it made hilarious reading and it must have delighted thousands of people, including some of his own friends and employees who wouldn't have dared to jest directly about Luce's quirky and arrogant ways. And Gibbs had written it in a parody of *Time's* punchy, word-coining style. "Backward ran sentences," Gibbs wrote, "until reeled the mind."

Other excerpts: "Behind this latest, most incomprehensible Timenterprise [*Life*] looms, as usual, ambitious, gimlet-eyed, Baby Tycoon Henry Robinson Luce, co-founder of *Time*, promulator of *Fortune*, potent in associated radio and cinema ventures. Headman Luce was born in Teng-chowfu, China, on April 3, 1898, the son of Henry Winters & Elizabeth Middleton Luce, Presbyterian missionaries. Very unlike the novels of Pearl Buck were his early days. Under brows too beetling for a baby, young Luce grew up inside the compound, played with his two sisters, lisped first Chinese, dreamed much of the Occident. At 14, weary of poverty, already respecting wealth and power, he sailed alone for England, entered school at St. Albans. Restless again, he came to the United States, enrolled at Hotchkiss, met up & coming young Brooklynite Briton Hadden. Both even then were troubled with an itch to harass the public. Intoned Luce years later: 'We reached the conclusion that most people were not well informed & that something should be done . . .'"

Along the way, Gibbs took another crack at the somewhat sainted Hadden: "Yet to suggest itself as a rational method of communication, of infuriating readers into buying the magazine, was strange inverted Timestyle. It was months before Hadden's impish contempt for his readers, his impatience with the English language, crystallized into gibberish. By the end of the first year, however, Timeditors were calling people able, potent, nimble . . . ; so fascinated Hadden with 'beady-eyed' that for months nobody was anything else. . . . 'Great word! Great word!' would crow Hadden coming upon 'snaggle-toothed,' 'pig-faced.'"

Gibbs made tough jokes about Time Inc. journalism, and if some were clearly too broad to be fair, the malice still was funny and not entirely undeserved. "Typical perhaps of Luce methods is *Fortune* system of getting material," wrote Gibbs. "Writers in first draft put down wild gossip, any figures that occur to them. This is sent to victim, who indignantly corrects the errors, inadvertently supplies facts he might otherwise have withheld."

What must have specially pleased Ross was the reference to his old employee, Ingersoll. "Looming behind [Larsen]," it went, "is burly able tumbledown Yaleman Ralph McAllister Ingersoll, former Fortuneditor, now general manager of all Timenterprises, descendant of 400-famed Ward McAllister. Littered his desk with pills, unguents,

Kleenex, Socialite Ingersoll is Time's No. 1 hypochondriac, introduced at palaces for study and emulation of employees, writes copious memoranda about filing systems, other trivia, seldom misses a Yale football game. His salary: $30,000; income from stock: $40,000."

Luce's own stock position was surveyed in a footnote: ". . . conservative estimate of Luce holding, 102,300 shares; paper value, $20,460,000; conservative estimate of Luce income from Time stock . . . $818,000; reported Luce income from other investments, $100,000; reported Luce bagatelle as editor of Time Inc., $45,000; reported total Lucemolument, $963,400. Boy!"

Another footnote stabbed Clare Luce, and in it Gibbs made use of part of a New York drama critic's review of her play. "One almost forgave 'Abide with Me' its faults," the review read, "when its lovely playwright, who must have been crouched in the wings for a sprinter's start as the final curtain mercifully descended, heard a cry of 'author,' which was not audible in my vicinity, and arrived onstage to accept the audience's applause just as the actors, who had a head-start on her, were properly lined up and smoothed out to receive their customary adulation."

But Gibbs had most fun with Luce himself and wrote: "At work today, Luce is efficient, humorless, revered by colleagues; arrives always at 9:15, leaves at 6, carrying armfuls of work; talks jerkily, carefully, avoiding visitor's eye; stutters in conversation, never in speechmaking. . . . Serious, ambitious Yale standards are still reflected in much of his conduct; in indiscriminate admiration for bustling success, in strong regard for conventional morality, in honest passion for accuracy; physically, in conservative, baggy clothes, white shirts with buttoned-down collars, solid-color ties. . . . Colder, more certain, more dignified than in the early days of the magazine, his prose style has grown less ebullient, resembles pontifical *Fortune* rather than chattering *Time*. . . . Certainly to be taken with seriousness is Luce at thirty-eight, his fellowman already informed up to his ears, the shadow of his enterprises long across the land, his future plans impossible to contemplate. Where it will all end, knows God!"

At a meeting set up between Ross and Luce to discuss the article in advance of publication, Ingersoll and St. Clair McKelway, Ross's managing editor, almost came to blows before their bosses separated them. The discussion was bitter and changed virtually nothing. Later Ross wrote Luce a letter in justification of his position: "After our talk the other night I asked at least ten people about *Time*, and, to my amazement, found them bitter, in varying degrees, in their attitude. You are generally regarded as being as mean as hell and frequently scurrilous. Two Jewish gentlemen were at dinner with me last night and, upon mention of *Time*, one of them charged that you are anti-Semitic, and asked the other if he didn't think so too. The other fellow said he'd read *Time* a lot and he didn't think you were anti-Semitic especially; you were just anti-everything, he said—anti-Semitic, anti-Italian, anti-Scandinavian, anti-black-widow-spider. 'It's just their pose,' he said. . . . I feel rather childish writing all this. It's all over now, anyhow. Sincerely yours, Harold Wallace Ross, Small man . . . furious . . . mad . . . no taste . . ."

"Dear Ross," Luce replied in part, ". . . it was not 'up to you' to make any explanations as far as I was concerned, but in any case I want to thank you for the personal trouble you took with the *Time*-Luce parody. . . . I only regret that Mr. Gibbs did not publish all he knows so that I might learn at once exactly how mean and poisonous a person I am."

Obviously his dignity was bruised by the piece, and he did not forget it. Years later he dropped in on a class in contemporary biography at a Florida college. To his astonishment and chagrin the students were discussing him and their text was the Gibbs profile. "That goddamn article," he said wrathfully to the man traveling with him. "Is this thing going to be engraved on my tombstone?" And Luce had some surprising support in his criticism of the article's bias. Much later James Thurber reflected: "As parody, the Luce profile was excellent, and often superb, but it seems to me that Luce and Ingersoll were justified in resenting the tone of the piece, here and there, and some of its statements." Fair enough, but it is doubtful that anything as interesting was ever written about Luce, and it surely increased his personal fame, from which he did not often flinch. Possibly it had exaggerated his ambitions (the piece mentioned a rumor "that Yaleman Luce already has a wistful eye on the White House"), but it also let a little air out of his ego. Perhaps it made him seem somewhat more life-sized to the men and women who worked with him and depended on his favor. Their reverence—or their fear—could always stand some cutting.

4

Birth of the Baby

THE FIRST EDITORIAL PICTURE PUBLISHED INSIDE Vol. I, No. 1 of the new *Life*, dated November 23, 1936, showed a surgical-masked doctor in a crowded delivery room. He was holding a newborn male child upside down in his gloved hands. It was a full-page photograph (originally considered a possible cover), and the bold headline under it read, naturally: "Life Begins." Next to that, the first *Life* caption hit the symbolism a little harder. "The camera," it read, "records the most vital moment in any life: Its beginning. A few hours ago, the child lay restless in its mother's womb. A second ago, its foetal life was rudely ended when the surgeon snipped its umbilical cord—through which the unborn child had drawn all existence from its mother. Then, for a second or two, the child hung lank and unbreathing between two lives. Its blood circulated and its heart beat only on the impetus given by its mother. Suddenly the baby's new and independent life begins. He jerks up his arms, bends his knees and, with his first short breath, gives out a red-faced cry."

There were moments in that last rush to publication when many of those involved must have felt lank and unbreathing, particularly the new managing editor, John Shaw Billings. Little more than two weeks before the final deadlines he wrote in his diary: "Because I am far behind on what *Life* is doing (and because *Life* itself is also far behind), I went to the office at 10 a.m.—and straight in to spend an hour with Luce. He made a speech to me on *Life*'s principles and purposes, explained the departments, etc. My job is to pick up his ideas as quickly as possible—and carry them out without too much criticism. (I think Luce is damned smart—and I have little or no criticism of his ideas.)—Longwell is ill with grippe—a sad circumstance because he is to initiate me into the *Life* personnel and machine. Back to my old office (I hate to swap it for Martin's smaller one), looking over layouts and captions, to get acquainted with material in the works . . ."

The next entry read: ". . . Tons of stuff dumped on me. Martin came in, friendly and nice. Later we ate a sandwich lunch together in my office while he went over stories and ideas he had been working on and is now transferring to me. —I had to see this or that thing, discuss the art schedule . . . go over the dummy and press schedule with Harry Luce and his brother Sheldon [Sheldon Luce, a younger brother, generally well liked at Time Inc., was briefly business manager of the new *Life* and left the company by his own choice in 1947]. . . . Everything was rush and confusion . . . and nothing was really accomplished. Longwell is still sick—which puts a crimp in everything. F. came down at 6 in the car. We dined at Schrafft's and went across to the Plaza to see Fredric March in *Anthony Adverse* (I've never read the book—so it was all new to me). Pretty good, though very long."

For October 30: "To the office. On *Time* I used to sit still and everything came to me at my order. On *Life* I must run around at a great rate to get anything I want. —Longwell is still ill—damn him! . . . Luce and I went to lunch at the Biltmore, where he talked of his *Life* ideas. He also told me a little about his South Carolina place. A figure: he had to spend $15,000 for lights and water plant."

Other entries as the pressure built: "My life on *Life* is now too full for more than notes here. . . . So many people in and out of my office that I could not settle down to real work. . . . Luce gave a Cloud Club lunch to talk about problems & jumped on Longwell for butting in with his ideas. Layouts & captions. I'll go crazy trying to do them." "Starting things but never getting time to finish them. I can't remember all I did, but I was steadily busy. Layouts and talks with Luce. He is being very nice and treats me well." "We lack a good opening story—a smash! And then Bourke-White's pictures of Whoopee at Fort Peck came in, as if in answer to our prayer. Now the first issue is all set! This story went to Ingersoll and MacLeish to work out. I had nothing to do with it."

The Margaret Bourke-White story (her famous photograph of the Fort Peck Dam was also *Life's* first cover) was one of the very few items Billings didn't have a lot to do with. Actually the already illustrious Bourke-White, who had joined the small staff a couple of months earlier, had been sent off to try to get some good material on WPA projects in the Northwest. Longwell, back at work from his grippe, wired her at Grand Coulee, Montana: "Have you got good Fort Peck night life pictures? . . . Up against it for party department first issue. Fort Peck might be swell. If necessary go back there and take more."

Bourke-White replied: "Think Peck night life will be very good. Have several bar scenes, crowd watching bowling, billiards, taxi dancers at work, two or three hard-won snaps of prostitutes, also exteriors their establishments, also famous Ruby Smith with her boy friends, also typical shanty-town orchestra, also assorted drunks. Films due Monday . . ." Luce warned Longwell in a memo that he would be waiting specially to see those pictures and wrote: ". . . pray God that your idea and Bourke-White's camera agree!" That they did, better than anyone had expected, was of course a bit of extra good fortune for those weary editors. But it was really more than that. The rawboned Bourke-White story about those Americans in a Montana construction town set a standard that would last as long as the magazine did. Whatever its preoccupations with royalty and politics and the high and low jinks of the famous, whatever its contributions in the understanding of art and science and the past, *Life*'s greatest resource for its best picture stories would always be the lives of ordinary people, their work, their pleasure, their follies, their anguish. Such stories touched virtually every reader.

The text and photographs for the first issue all had to be sent to Chicago for printing by November 13, ten days ahead of the issue date but only a week in advance of the magazine's newsstand appearance. Most of the work was completed on daily deadlines during the final week of closing; a mail pouch containing pictures and text with appropriate layouts was sent from New York to Chicago every night on the Twentieth Century Limited. The Billings diary indicated the extent of the rush. "This is the last week to get out the first issue," Billings wrote on November 9. ". . . Working on the French shooting party. Lunch at the Cloud Club with Luce and Longwell to discuss Vol. I, No. 2. Our big problem is to get future feature material banked up. At 3 I dashed to the Modern Museum to . . . pick out samples of surrealist paintings we are going to use in full color later. It was a breathless selection and I was back inside an hour. We began to make up the dummy on No. 1. To see Luce with it—and Larsen and others came in to look it over. Soon Luce was pulling it all apart."

The entry for November 10: "Office. Rush! Rush! The first forms of the first issue must go off today. All morning I wrote the copy to go with the French hunting story. Took it to Luce. O.K. Lunch alone. The first two forms got safely off on the 20th Century, *Life* on the American Newsfront and the President's Album with Thorndike. Pretty poor material. I complained to Longwell. Home at 7. F. in dumps. I knew something worried her but she wouldn't tell me at first. At 10 she cut loose and gave me hell for giving all my time and interest to *Life* and not to her. She felt very bad about it, talked wildly of divorce, etc., etc. But there was no quarrel because I just listened and agreed with her. She'll feel better now that this is out of her system." Thus Frederica Billings was apparently the first woman among hundreds to make it clear how cheated she felt by her husband's preoccupation with *Life*. More often than not, the complaints were just. The demands of putting out the magazine did not decrease over the years, and it took considerable discipline for one not to let himself or herself get completely taken over by the job. And sometimes, for some people, the work (and the intensity of the relationships developed around it) was much more stimulating and engrossing than the relationship they had parked uptown or at the other end of a commuter line.

The diary entry for November 11: ". . . Luce deep in thought on the introduction. . . . Lunch with him on Vol. I, No. 2. He gets all the ideas, makes all the decisions. I have contributed practically no original ideas to the magazine so far. . . . I made some layouts and Luce went into a brown study and remade them completely. I don't know how to satisfy him; it is pretty discouraging. Luce doping out the dummy— trying to get "unity and flow." Home at 6:30 and giving the whole evening to talk with F. She was in much better spirits."

The entry for November 12, right on the final deadlines: "F. went to the hairdressers and spent $38 on a wave, etc. Socko! But it has been driving her half crazy, her hair I mean. Office. President's album was no good the way Luce did it last night. We got Richmond [the art director] in to do it over—and he turned out a nice job in short order. A great rush of copy to make the train. Thorndike had much to write and I kept pressing him hard for copy. Even then he wasn't done in time. F. came down at 6:30. We dined at Schrafft's and went to the Plaza to see Gary Cooper in *The General Died at Dawn*—a Chinese warlord picture." Few of the top editors who followed Billings over the years would have things well enough in hand on closing nights to go out to a relatively early dinner and then to a movie. However much he complained in the diaries, he seemed a miracle of order and efficiency to those who worked with him.

November 13: "Not much to do. As Luce says, you can't make any forward passes in the last quarter on this magazine. [Late changes then were easier on *Time*, but last-minute forward passes became a big part of the game later on at *Life*, too.] I got the newsfront pages laid out and approved. . . . With Luce I went over ideas for Vol. I, No. 2. We are still shy on serious feature material. There is so much discussion with Luce, so much philosophizing, before anything is done." The entry for November 14, the last day of closing: "Office. All done but three news pages. These went through and Thorndike wrote the text. . . . I was through by 5. Vol. I, No. 1 is now behind us—and we get tomorrow off. Home at 7."

Four days later, early proof sheets were back in New York. "Luce in dumps when he saw mistakes in the proofs," wrote Billings. "Luce was in a bad humor—as if issue No. 1 had gone sour on the press." For a while at least, things didn't seem much better the next day. "To the office," wrote Billings. "Ingersoll told me that he and Luce had been up until 3 a.m. battling with Ross over a profile to run in *The New Yorker*. It was a malicious insulting piece and Luce had tried to get the facts straight. There was much drinking and bad temper. Luce didn't get in until about 11, looking red-eyed and bum. Realizing that he was useless he went home to sleep it off, returned about 4 in better shape." Then the tone of the entry changed. "The first complete issues of *Life* were in & they looked pretty good to me. Congratulations and cheers began to roll in and we all felt pretty good. But one issue doesn't make a magazine. I rewrote [for the second issue] the brain operation text running under 'Speaking of Pictures.'"*

The cover seemed to come out of a combination of ideas. Longwell and others promoted the notion put forth by artist Edward Wilson of a single black-and-white bleed photograph—i.e., one with no margins. According to Longwell, it would "just be the best damned picture we can find every week." The art director, Howard Richmond, remembered that during a discussion of covers he took a photostat of one picture, stuck it on a sheet of red paper so that the paper extended beneath the picture, put *Life* in simple block lettering, white on red, in the top left-hand corner, then showed the result to Luce, who said immediately: "That's it." The original idea allowed for the *Life* slug to move around each week according to the composition of the pictures and to vary in color as well. But Larsen, to whose selling instincts people generally deferred, wanted the slug kept in the upper left, and both he and Luce felt that the *Time* red was lucky. On one occasion in 1937, the *Life* slug was dropped entirely from a cover showing a huge white rooster, but the newsstand results were poor, so that variation was forgotten.

The Billings entry for that big day when the editors first saw the

---

*Time Inc. lore has it that the title for this famous *Life* department was arrived at in the following exchange that week: Billings: "Speaking of pictures, Harry, take a look at these [of the brain operation]." Luce: "Fine, wonderful. We will run them." Billings: "What department?" Luce: "Why not 'Speaking of Pictures'?" But it is interesting to note that a dummy made up two years earlier by a German adviser, Kurt Safranski, who worked with Kurt Korff, included a department by that name.

results of their work concludes on a typically domestic note: "Home at 6:30, with copies of *Life*. Ma and F. fairly devoured it after dinner. I did a little editing."

His apparent calm was not reflected by the rest of the people who had struggled to get out the issue. The editorial staff was exhausted. Everyone who knew about it was worried about the size of the print order, which was 466,000 copies, more than 200,000 of which were designated for the newsstands. No one was sure how the magazine would be received, and plans were laid to lessen the impact of a possible disaster. "As you will see," wrote the indefatigable Ingersoll in one memo in the blizzard of admonitions, advisories, situationers, recaps he churned out in those frantic days, including one seventy-four-page study on the philosophy of the new magazine that Luce simply didn't take time to read, "the distribution is arranged to provide against considerable deflation of our expectations. In other words, should the instant demand turn out to be only 50 percent of what we expect, we can still, by withholding copies, create an artificial sellout. . . . As noted, the program is to under-distribute from branch offices to actual newsstands, feeding out additional copies when, as, and if demanded."

The situation at Donnelley's in Chicago, where the printing was done, was close to wild. Other magazines were being printed at the same time, and the *Life* editors were sending instructions for copy changes well past their deadlines. One special problem involved collating the slick printed sheets as they came off the presses before they were stitched together and bound. Working by hand, crews of women were assigned to do the collating. Charles Stillman had been sent out from New York to lend an executive presence to the production closing, and he reported: "There were four rotary presses, supposedly all made ready and set to go, but it wasn't until 4:30 p.m. (on Monday, November 16th) that the first press, #41, started turning out acceptable work. The rest followed along, but it didn't make much difference how fast they turned over, as the bottleneck of the operation proved to be the collating of the twelve sections on the Christiansen stitchers.

"These endless chains were manned by girl workers and there were four gangs working. But the paper being slippery and the sheets larger and heavier and the line longer than they were used to, they made very heavy going. Furthermore, many of the girls were green, as Donnelley's had to recruit more girls to handle this job. Desperate efforts were made to speed up, including taking two crews off the *Farm Journal* and putting them on *Life*, making six crews in all. They averaged around 7,000 copies an hour and with all available girlpower on the job were just barely keeping their heads above water, running about 50,000 copies behind schedule. . . . Somebody slipped a cog when they didn't find out how difficult it was going to be to collate on the stitcher and give lessons by the hour—instead of using the first issue to teach them the routine. . . .

"The quality of the presswork improved as they went along, on the average, but generally speaking, it was very spotty, some excellent—some good—some poor. There is no doubt it will improve and ultimately be very satisfactory and consistently so."

Whatever its significance in the history of magazine journalism, Vol. I, No. 1 of *Life* was very much a grab bag—lots of stories, lots of pictures strung together without much discernible order. And although everyone had thought and struggled desperately hard to arrive at the decisions necessary to bring the magazine out, it looked in some places as if decisions *hadn't* been made. That first *Life* had the quality of an album jammed with snapshots the collector couldn't bear to throw away. Its look was earnest, amateurish and cluttered, its tone was variously wide-eyed, sentimental, smart-aleck, smug and foolish. Quite possibly, these were just the qualities that in some magical, quite indefinable mix (though Luce and his editors spent the next thirty-five years trying to isolate, define and capture the recipe) would guarantee *Life's* immediate and long-lasting success.

Of course, the first editors of *Life* tried, as all their descendants did, too, to make the issue appear as if it had been put together with some sort of purpose in mind. "Having been unable to prevent Bourke-White from running away with their first nine pages," they wrote in the introduction, "the Editors thereafter returned to the job of making the pictures behave with some degree of order and sense. So there follow, not far apart, two regular departments: *Life* On The American Newsfront and the President's Album. The first is a selection of the most newsworthy snaps made anywhere in the U.S. by the mighty picture-taking organization of the U.S. press. The President's Album is a kind of picture diary—a special focus on the personality-center of the nation's life. Luckily for *Life*, it can start its diary with a President who is a marvelous camera actor and is not above demonstrating his art.

"So strong is the President's hold on the attention of the people," went the galumphing essay, "that a hint from him is enough to bring even South America crashing into the headlines. South America is the continent Americans ought to be most interested in, and usually just plain won't be. But a month ago *Life* decided to do its duty and be interested—a duty which turned out to be surprisingly easy. This week, Brazil. Next week, The Argentine.

"On looking over what happened to the issue," the introduction waltzed clumsily on, "the Editors are particularly pleased that Art is represented not by some artfully promoted Frenchman but by an American, and the Theater is here in the person of an American lady who is being called the world's greatest actress. Hollywood's No. 1 Screen Lover is also here due to sheer coincidence of release dates. But that he is an American, is inevitable."

Thus in his first issue Luce struck the note of prideful chauvinism that would last at *Life* until the man and his magazine were dead. And in terms of attracting and holding the loyalty of a huge audience, he and the editors who followed his lead were surely right. A lot of people liked the magazine precisely because, in a national sense, it had the quality of a hometown journal, a journal that readers could open up each week and find, vicariously speaking, fascinating items about themselves.

The Americans Luce was referring to in that first introduction were John Steuart Curry, the Kansas artist perhaps best known for his painting of a farm family fleeing an onrushing tornado, the actress Helen Hayes and Robert Taylor, the newest male movie idol. The story on Curry was admiring and included four pages of his paintings in color; Luce had been determined from the beginning to use these big magazine pages for displays of art, and these became a staple of *Life*. The story on Robert Taylor, too, modeled thousands of movie stories to come. It included childhood pictures of Taylor and poked mild fun at his real name (Spangler Arlington Brugh). It also had pictures of him wearing a toga and headband in an early unsuccessful screen test after which Sam Goldwyn advised him to "go home and fatten up." By 1936 Taylor had made it as a star, and the story showed him working with Greta Garbo in the filming of *Camille*. But the captions tried not to be too admiring. "In his first love scene with Garbo," one read, "Taylor was so nervous that he allowed her to slip from his arms to the floor. But Garbo treated him much less like a schoolboy than she has some of her 16 previous leading men and by the time the scene above was shot, Taylor had acquired the confidence needed to carry her safely to a divan." This would be the mocking tone of countless captions about movies and movie people to come.

The piece on Helen Hayes, on the other hand, was an absolute gush headlined "Greatest Living Actress." The text was so respectful in its celebration of her starring as the lead in *Victoria Regina*, in fact, that it neglected to mention the author of the play (Laurence Housman), and the opening text block ended with words calculated to touch the coldest heart. "The story of her private life," it throbbed, "is as plain and happy as she is plain and great. She had a mother to fashion her childhood. She met her man. She had her child. Turn the next page and see all three." Thus *Life* began with an almost gaga devotion to the theater and its luminaries, who were, apparently, made of more substantial stuff than the pretty folks whose teeth gleamed from movie screens around the country. A bit of a cultural climber from the start, *Life* tended always to tug its forelock politely at the very mention of art.

The story on Brazil is, by contrast, both condescending and contemptuous. "Brazilians are charming people," the reader of this five-page article was advised, "but are incurably lazy. The original Portuguese conquistadors did not bring their wives, married Indian aborigines, and their descendants added the blood of Negro slaves to the strain. The mixture did not work." Such utterly racist comment was, of course, common in respectable American journals of the time. But it had a flip quality that was particularly characteristic of Time Inc. writing of the period, a sort of show-off stunting in which the writer rather wearily slapped his subject across the face with sentences like "Loafing through the 100° heat of the upper Amazon River Basin are the Indian women and children above, who sling their hammocks between trees to avoid crawling snakes and small animals and keep in the shade."

Much of the writing, though, was less smug than that, and some of it, notably by Archibald MacLeish to go with Bourke-White's Montana pictures, matched the plain tone of the good photographs and somehow enhanced them. "For $2 a month," wrote MacLeish about a new town near the Fort Peck Dam, "you can rent a fifty foot lot in Wheeler from Joe Frazier, the barber over in Glasgow, 20 miles away. Joe had the fool luck to homestead the worthless land on which shanty towns have sprouted. You then haul in a load of grocer's boxes, tin cans, crazy doors and building paper and knock your shack together. That will set you back $40 to $75 more. You then try to live in it in weather that can hit minus 50° one way and plus 110° the other."

"The pioneer mother," he wrote in closing the story, "can trek in broken-down Fords as well as in covered wagons. And she can crack her hands in the alkali water of 1936 as well as in the alkali water of 1849. When the Fort Peck project opened in 1933 the roads of Montana began to rattle with second-hand cars full of children, chairs, mattresses and tired women. Most of them kept right on rattling toward some other hopeless hope. Some of them parked in the shanty towns around Fort Peck. There, their women passengers got jobs like [washerwoman] Mrs. Nelson (right) who washes [the town of] New Deal without running water, or tried their feet at taxi-dancing like the girls on the preceding pages, or made money like [the madam] Ruby Smith on page 15, or gave birth to children in zero weather in a crowded 8 by 16-foot shack like many an unnamed woman of New Deal and Wheeler. . . . The group on the right, it will be noticed, resembles a statue recently erected to the Pioneer Mother of the old frontier. No statues are expected at New Deal." MacLeish's spare writing was much the best in the issue, and it set an unflorid style that many writers on *Life* would try anonymously to follow in the years ahead.

Much of the rest of the issue was a hodgepodge of almost random pictures of the famous or simply notorious—of Eugene O'Neill, James Farley, Winston Churchill, Benito Mussolini and his son-in-law Count Ciano, actresses Myrna Loy and Ina Claire, William Powell and Peggy Hopkins Joyce, a much-married woman of the time who was announcing her engagement, a fact noteworthy, the caption advised, "because it is the first time Miss Joyce has been engaged to an astrophysicist." Almost certainly because of Luce's fascination with most matters Chinese, there was a fluffy little story shot by Alfred Eisenstaedt about a Catholic school for Chinese children ("slant-eyed and shy") in San Francisco, a school where they were taught "to say *very* instead of *velly*, to distinguish *he* from *she*." There were miscellaneous items on shootings, awful deaths, high-altitude weather and a wonderfully gallant interview with a naval officer named Earl Winfield Spencer. He had once been married to Wallis Warfield Simpson, the lady from Baltimore whose love the King of England was finding better than a throne. Reflected Spencer: "She is one of the finest women I know. . . . She was the leader of social life here at Coronado but became lonely during the times I was at sea with the fleet." A half-page story showed a one-legged mountain climber, and among the advertisements was one for the Des Moines *Register and Tribune*, touting the paper's good news photographs. The picture in the ad showed the capture of two members of the infamous Barrow (Bonnie and Clyde) gang. Part of the hard-selling caption: "Note the animal snarl on the face of the captured girl. Her lover sits wounded at the right." And the text of the first *"Life* Goes to a Party" pointed out, as did so many that followed, in what fine company the lucky reader was traveling. "French hunting parties are hard to crash," one caption declared. "If the Comtesse Jacques de Rohan-Chabot (above) is a guest, you are at one of the most exclusive affairs in France."

But the story that *Life*'s first editors appeared to take special pleasure in was a two-page item simply called "Black Widow." A modest act about the arachnid of that name, it had appeared in the dummies and was the first nature story of thousands in which *Life*'s editors would get their anthropomorphic kicks—and give the readers theirs. Over the years the magazine's subscribers would again and again demonstrate that they were often more interested in animals than they were in people. Especially when the creatures were in trouble—or might be dangerous. "Hardly a week goes by," the opening caption intoned with glee, "that some newspaper doesn't carry the account of Man Killed by Black Widow Bite. Thriving in shelter afforded by cellars, garages and barns, the black widow spider has spread all over the United States, made its poisonous power more and more evident and made itself a growing menace. One out of every twenty people bitten die in wracking pain from the prick of the widow's tiny fangs."

Thus launched in delicious terror, the story included simple picture enlargements of the spider's life style and cycle. "The black widow," read one caption, "deadliest of all spiders, who can lick ten times her weight in tarantulas. Her venom is more potent than a rattlesnake's. Comes, too, a lover, a male black widow who is a quarter her size and knows that chances are the lady won't like him." The caption writer of the piece obviously got most fun out of the male spider's death by love: "It leaves him sucked dry and bloodless—a withered brittle corpse, solemnly enshrouded by his hungry wife who thus brings on herself her name: Black Widow." Few weeks of the next thirty-six years passed in which the editors did not directly appeal to the readers' insatiable appetite for news of *other* animals on this planet.

5

On a Winning Team

IN THE WORDS OF A PROMOTION BOOKLET written years later, *Life* was launched on a cool Friday in November. "The nation," it said, "was still in the midst of depression. Loyalists and rebels were fighting on the outskirts of Madrid, while many U.S. citizens were preparing to celebrate *two* Thanksgivings. The wars in Spain and China seemed remote and unreal to most Americans. The rising Adolf Hitler looked like a character out of comic opera. The U.S. Army numbered about 150,000. The CIO and the sitdown strike were novelties, and the United Auto Workers had only 80,000 members on its rolls. In the White House, President Roosevelt pressed a telegraph key to open the new San Francisco bridge. Alfred Lunt and Lynn Fontanne were at the Shubert, ambling through *Idiot's Delight,* and a few doors down the street, a pillow-padded Helen Hayes was appearing as Victoria Regina. . . ." And on that day, Luce and his colleagues were offering the public their newest product with something less than the optimism Kurt Korff had projected when he bade farewell to Luce a few months earlier and went to work helping William Randolph Hearst with some of *his* picture plans. "I am very sorry to leave you," Korff wrote Luce. "The spirit of your organization is my spirit too. It was easy for me—though I had to overcome the handicap of the foreign language—making friends and working in this milieu with my usual joy, having fun in everything."

"I have always been some sort of a mascot to publishers," he told Luce. "I predict a big success. You really are going to create the long-expected great American magazine."

When *Life* went to press Longwell sent the mascot Korff an advance copy of the first issue. "Naturally I am frightened at the results of the next few weeks," Longwell wrote. "I don't believe *Life* would ever have come into being if it hadn't been for you and Mr. Safranski coming to call on Mr. Luce that day. Certainly, credit for any of the virtues it has belongs to you and your wise experience and youthful enthusiasm which you taught us here. And all of its faults are our own. I wish you were here with us."

All 250,000 newsstand copies of Vol. I, No. 1 sold out the first day. The dealer in Cleveland, where 300 copies had been sent, telegraphed Time Inc.'s circulation office: "*Life* sold out first hour. Could sell 5000 more." "*Life* sold out by 12 noon," read the wire from Lansing, Michigan, where 325 copies had been placed. "Make order 1000 next week." From Los Angeles came the word: "First issue of *Life* caused heaviest demand in Hollywood and L.A. of any publication ever known. Clean sellout. We lost thousands of sales and still a heavy demand. Please, please increase numbers of copies for next issue." "Be a good fellow," was the message from Boston, "and see if you can't get up more copies."

The cry was the same everywhere—from Seattle, Denver, New Orleans, Buffalo came the urgent word that interest in the new magazine far outran the early guesses. Dealers all over the country wanted to increase their orders by as much as 500 percent. When they were told that this was impossible, many accused Luce's men of creating a controlled scarcity with *Life*, a scarcity they could use to force dealers to take more copies of *Time* in order to get enough of the new hot item. This was not the case; the capacity of the makeshift presses was simply not up to a huge immediate increase. But production efficiency improved very rapidly. Within three months, the Donnelley presses were turning out 1 million copies a week. By the end of the first year of publication, *Life*'s circulation had reached 1.5 million. That still wasn't big enough for the demand, but the scarcity *had* to be controlled, largely in an effort to manage the great losses (at least $5 million that first year) caused by the fact that advertisers were paying rates based on a much smaller readership.

Looking back years later on the near-catastrophic success of his venture, Luce said: "Of course, I didn't really *intend* to lose all that money, but then on the other hand I had to sort of *pretend* I had intended to. Otherwise all my friends would have thought I was a dope." Early efforts were made, however, to clear up the corporate ignorance about the demand, and they centered in Worcester, Massachusetts, then a town of 195,000, where 475 copies of the first issue had been snapped up from local newsstands. In what was later called "the Worcester Experiment," the circulation men decided to see how many copies of *Life* it would take to satisfy Worcester's appetite.

The experiment began with the magazine's third issue: 2,000 copies went to Worcester. They were all immediately sold. In the weeks that followed, the numbers of *Life* copies sent there were increased dramatically—3,000, 4,000, 6,000, 9,000—and the issues were all sellouts. In March, the joyous Worcester distributor wired: "Send 12,000 next week," and his request was filled. All the copies, of course, were sold, and on the basis of this remarkable record (and indications from other cities) projections were made showing that the demand for *Life* had a staggering potential: American readers apparently liked it so much that they would buy 5 or 6 million copies a week. The forecasts turned out to be surprisingly accurate in the long run, but the Worcester Experiment itself was marred by a certain imprecision. As Roy Larsen recalled with amusement almost forty years later, dealers from other communities all over the region were driving to Worcester, buying up as many copies of the new magazine as they could and then hustling them back home to sell to eager customers.

The readers' enthusiasm was apparent, too, in an outpouring of mail, though some of the encomiums surely were invited. "Best deck of pictures I've ever seen," wrote bridge expert Ely Culbertson, one of whose pupils was Luce. "*Life* is magnificent," burbled publisher Richard Simon. "I predict it will be the greatest publishing success of the decade." "*Life*," said Sam Goldwyn from Hollywood, ". . . is going to give life to millions of people in this country." "It is fascinating. It's all the newsreels on your knee," said artist James Montgomery Flagg, and historian Carl Van Doren was impressed enough to say: "*Life* looks like a natural to me." "It seems to me you have made an excellent start," wrote David Sarnoff of RCA, the communications mogul whose television empire would help make *Life* obsolete thirty-five years later.

Lesser-known correspondents were equally impressed. "It certainly made a hit with the entire family," wrote one father. "I can't imagine missing the next issue," said another. A housewife in Massachusetts was moved to verse: "You give life as it is / The sadness and the mirth / New *Life*, endowed by *Time* / Rejuvenates the earth." "Crackerjack," "swell," "snappy," "grand," "wow" were words that appeared frequently in the first batches of mail.

Naturally there were dissenters. Empire builder Robert Moses paused long enough in his labors with the landscape of New York to growl that he didn't think much of the new magazine. A man in Cambridge, Massachusetts, wrote: "It is with profound lack of enthusiasm that I look at your first issue. It falls far below expectations." Another in Rhode Island said: "If the frontispiece picture and text in the first issue of *Life* are indicative of your ideas of what is suitable and in good taste, we are in for some things that your subscribers will strongly disapprove of."

Imperfection of taste obviously was not much of a deterrent to the magazine's extraordinary reception. One memo from the circulation manager to Luce just two weeks after *Life*'s start advised: "Al Johns tells me over the telephone that we got 5,500 payment envelopes for subscriptions yesterday and that the percentage of checks in these envelopes is so high that we can come very near taking the envelope count as the payment count. . . . Johns also reports that they were completely swamped with new orders yesterday . . . and got so many that the cage was not able to count them and they do not yet have the count today." Another memo, this one to all employees of Time Inc. from the circulation boss, said: "I am afraid that you must be hearing a great many complaints from people who have tried unsuccessfully to get copies of *Life* at the newsstands. In order that you may be in a position to answer these complaints intelligently, I should like to get these points into the record: (1) The demand for *Life* is without precedent in publishing history. If we could supply the copies, the dollar volume of our newsstand sales this month [December] would be greater than the dollar volume of sales of any other magazine in the world. There was no way in which we could anticipate a bigger newsstand business than magazines like *Collier's* and *Satevepost* have built up in thirty years. (2) We are running the presses night and day clear through the week to squeeze out every possible copy. We do not take one issue off the press until we have to clear the press for the next issue. (3) The newsstand shortage is not a trick to force people to enter subscriptions. . . . We sincerely regret our inability to print copies fast enough to meet the demand. We realize we are losing valuable good will by our continued inability to print enough copies. We have ordered additional presses, and one of these fine days we hope to catch up with the demand."

The demand was naturally a selling point for the eager admen. In a report to Roy Larsen, one space salesman advised: "In a few cases where a laugh is important, we tell of the Boston barber who had a customer of 10 years' standing who never spent more than a fifty-cent piece and always got just a haircut. Recently upon entering the shop he grabbed *Life*, went to the chair and knowing others in the shop were waiting for the magazine, kept on and on reading until he'd had a shave, shampoo, massage, singe, shoe shine and manicure and his bill was $3.50."

While the business side struggled to manage *Life's* explosive growth, Billings and his editors kept plugging to satisfy the endless demand for stories. A few selections from his journal for the period immediately after the closing of the first issue indicate something of the pace and pressure on the new magazine.

> *Nov. 27:* Office. Noel Coward story with Luce. Also Japanese pearl-diving girls and Mrs. Roosevelt in Milwaukee. Took Luce to lunch at Schrafft's. We listed some features for a year ahead. . . . Another sellout today of issue No. 2. . . . Luce now thinks we may have hit on something.

> *Nov. 28:* Office. Got the Coward layout approved by Luce. . . . [Went over] Newsfront with Thorndike—and color text [for] two weeks in advance. Cloud Club lunch with Luce and Larsen. They were fairly bubbling with delight at *Life's* amazing success. Working all afternoon on late copy and future stuff. We are whipping the Simpson case [about the English King and his American beloved] into shape. A bale of pictures to work through.

> *Dec. 3:* Office. One cause of our press delays is that Luce must see every layout—and often revises them at the last minute. Also, in effect, the magazine is twice edited on text—once by me and once by Luce. . . . I felt that the issue is far behind—but Luce is not to be hurried. Issue No. 3 is a sellout again! We are on the crest of success. Still we have no lead piece—but Luce refuses to get excited. Home at 7, editing copy on the dressmaker's piece.

> *Dec. 7:* Starting work on issue No. 5. But a pretty slack day because Luce wouldn't buckle down. Instead he wanted to map out future material.

As Billings reflected some years later, the situation on the new magazine was quite different from any he'd experienced before. "Neither Luce nor I knew anything about type, with the result that the first few issues were a bastard conglomeration of different faces. We did not know how to open or close a story properly. The magazine was scheduled to go to press in sections, so every day was closing day with us.

Often we were working on three different issues at once." And, as the journal entries show, there were other problems.

Dec. 10: Rain. Luce really won't let go, let me edit, though he's immersed in business matters. Doesn't he trust me? We had no lead piece. I went to work on some biography spreads on Princess Elizabeth [the current Queen of England, then ten years old]. Also did Newsfront layouts. The Union Pacific story turned out a flop and was junked. Luce says we are now giving our readers too much good stuff and must hold down. I showed Luce the new Crystal Palace fire layout—and he got very mad because Richmond had cocked the pictures [placed them at angles]. It made me feel bad— as if I were to blame. And there was no time to change. F. came down at 6:20. We dined at Schrafft's and saw *Pigskin Parade* at the Plaza. Pretty funny—Amos, the Texas melon thrower, who beats Yale at football in a blizzard. Home. I spoke unpleasantly to F. when she interrupted my reading. It hurt her feelings. She sulked silently—then burst out in abuse to me, said I had "changed," that she had no life at all, etc., etc. I felt terribly, because I love her the most in the world. It took me two hours to pacify her—and get her to talk to me. . . . Edward VIII abdicated for Mrs. Simpson. I despise him!

Dec. 26: A day of devastating sickness at the office. . . . Luce telephoned he had fever of 101½°, which meant I would have to close out the issue. . . . Clare Luce's play *The Women* opened tonight, but Harry was too sick to go. Roy Larsen looked over the dummy, saw a hairy nude and got panicky about the postal authorities [who might judge the issue unfit to go through the mails]. A call to Nick Wallace in Chicago who assured us it would be all right. I finished up about 6:45 and home, feeling I had practically earned my bonus in one day.

Jan. 4, 1937: Luce in from his South Carolina plantation about 2 p.m. He was in a pleasant cheerful mood. I showed him what I had started in his absence. He seemed well satisfied with "Britain's Noble Beauties"—but wanted to do things with [a movie story on] *The Good Earth* (that's Chinese and he can't keep his hands off).

Jan. 5: Office. I laid out the Atlantic City Science spread. It had eye value, but made no great sense. Luce came in but was distracted and did not pitch in to the new issue. Instead he read the old one (done in his absence). He said it was "swell" in general (i.e. in pictures) but complained loudly of the captions, some of which he called "terrible" and "awful" (i.e. [the headline] "Fatal Fortnight" over the air crash spread). There was some merit to his criticism, I suppose, but I felt pretty bad about it. I had done my best—and he had small thanks for that. He fusses continuously about captions—but does not point the way to anything better. (I think he is pretty vain about his own creative ability and he thinks he can always do somebody else's job even better.) . . . I understand better now why Martin did not get on easily with him. Although I got a fat bonus at the year end, my base salary for 1937 is evidently not to be raised. That is disappointing.

Jan. 6: Paul Hollister of Macy's in Luce's office convulsed us with laughter with his criticisms of our layouts, etc. He said we let the nail holes show, that we seemed to be trying to sell white space— but the total effect of his criticism was pretty trivial. I laid out the auto strike lead, largely on Luce's ideas. I showed him what I had— and he didn't seem to like it very much. . . . If Redcliffe was not so big and so costly to keep up, I think I'd quit and go there to rusticate. (I often wonder what would happen if I told Luce I was leaving.)

Jan. 7: Office. I had lots of layouts to show Luce but he was too busy to see me. This slows up the whole machine and gets us all on edge. As a managing editor, I am in a tough position. If I put stuff through on my own authority without showing it to Luce, he is almost sure to dislike it and shuffle it all around. So I show it to him—and thus become hardly more than a messenger boy between him and the layout department. He won't do a full job of editing and he won't let go entirely. After lunch he read the Science captions and then tore up most of the layout just before train time. Hell! . . . F. came down at 6:30. We went to Schrafft's for dinner and then to the Plaza to see Edna Ferber's *Come and Get It*—a story of lumbering in Wisconsin. It was excellent—and we saw Frances Farmer for the first time. She is good—and pretty.

Jan. 15: Office. About 11 I showed Luce some layouts. He called for the paste-up dummy—and then blew up. "I'm very, very unhappy about this issue. It lacks balance. There's no charm in it." Then he went on a rampage about CHARM—how we must have it in every issue—and how we must get that first—and fill in later with news. . . . I spent a bad 30 minutes while he thrashed around in his dissatisfaction. He said he was "on a spot," that it was his fault (not mine) that the issue as a whole did not jell. . . . Luce finally blew himself out and quieted down to the point of accepting things about as they were. What really upset him were some fine Salomon pictures of Juliana's wedding [to Prince Bernhard in Holland]—and the limited space we had to play them in. Likewise, he yearned for some "pretty pictures," and "big smashes," which this issue lacked. His displeasures now were the direct result of his failure to take a firmer grip on editing earlier in the week—or to turn the whole job over to me. Home for a quiet evening.

Jan. 16: The paper came out with the *Time* salary lists—a New Deal release from Washington. Mine $25,480, Luce $43,000, Larsen $39,000, Ingersoll $20,000, Martin $33,640. When I told Luce they were out, he said they were really "modest." . . . He asked me to a business lunch of *Life* in the Cloud Club, with Stillman, Ingersoll, Sheldon Luce, [advertising manager George] Sadler and Larsen. The talk was new and interesting to me: *Life* lost $800,000 in 1936. It will lose $2,000,000 in 1937. In 1938 it will make $3,000,000, thus balancing the loss. Luce asked about paper prices—and Stillman launched into a long lecture on the subject of paper manufactures. . . . *Time*'s paper cost $88 a ton, ours nearly $250 (and we use much more). New methods may bring down this paper cost a little. 1937 budget: $9 million income, $11 million production cost. Circulation will go to 1,000,000 by April 1; to 1,300,000 by Jan. 1. Sadler thinks he will get plenty of advertising. He's got 1000 pages signed up for this year, 400 more promised. He needs 2000 in 1938 to show a profit. On the editorial side Larsen and Ingersoll made strong pleas that we follow *Time* and don't go too popular. They are all for spending money on digging up great Science features. . . . Back to editing at 3:30 and closing out copy on the last eight pages. Luce was in a mellow mood and raised these salaries: Thorndike $4000 to $7000, [foreign news editor David] Cort $6000 to $8000, Kastner $5000 to $7000. I did a little advance work—and home by 7.

Jan. 22: I got Ingersoll in to look over the Inaugural. He is snooty and I don't like to work with him. . . . Longwell complains of being sick—nerves, indigestion, fever. He phoned Luce and is taking next week off.

Jan. 25: Office. Luce came in at 12 and I had a great stack of advance layouts to show him. He seemed quite pleased: "Swell! Marvelous!" I need more office space—and a better office for myself. Luce promises to get it by putting Ingersoll and Jackson off the 51st floor.

Jan. 26: Where are all the good pictures that are supposed to flow through this office? We are always short on good pictures. . . . After dinner, F. and I drove down to see our second [Broadway] show of the season—Clare Luce's *The Women*, with an all-women cast. It dealt with the cocktail set—and I thought it was pretty unpleasant and not very funny. But it was a great hit and the [theater] was jammed. Harry, I suspect, is very proud that his wife has written a successful play. If I were in his place, I would be ashamed to have a wife who wrote so autobiographically. The play concerns a good wife whose husband is unfaithful. She is driven to Reno by her gossipy friends. Her husband marries the other woman—but the first wife *later* wins him back when the second wife starts misbehaving. Ugh!

The Billings entries flow on and on, packed with the beginning traumas and trivialities of those early days at *Life*. Observations about bickering on the staff, about frantic searches for pictures, on the sickness and death of a puppy that Billings's associates had given him for Christmas, on Luce's anxiety about losing his hair, on Billings's sense of gratification when he finally got the office that Luce himself had been sitting in for months—all these were part of his journal. And through all the mix of his reporting, through all the schedules and details about stories on disasters or on simple foolishness, through all his own admissions of anger and pain, one can always find his powerful obsession with Luce.

Luce's own preoccupations at the moment were centered on his extraordinary new project, and he soon became involved in the first of his many reexaminations of *Life*. It was as if he felt that the only way he could trap and preserve the mysterious elements that made the magazine work was to attempt a sort of dissection of the beast, as if rational dismemberment would produce a sensible, fail-safe formula for continuing success. In a fifteen-page confidential memorandum titled "Redefinition" and written in March 1937, he said: "Twelve issues of *Life* having come and gone, I have re-read the Original Prospectus." Then—which could not have much surprised the limited readership of his memo—he added: "It makes more sense to me today than when it was written. That, I think, is both surprising and hopeful."

He then proceeded to pick through the magazine, department by department, studying it in light of the definitions laid down in the prospectus. For example, he wrote of the magazine's main news story in pictures: "*The Lead:* I felt uncertain about this prior to Vol. I, No. 1, and I continued to be unhappy about it for eight or ten weeks. But now I feel it is okay, practical, manageable, definable. The Lead is what the Prospectus calls 'The Big News-Picture Story of the Week.' The Inauguration, the Sit-down Strike, the Sand-hog Murder, and above all the Flood proved that there is such a thing. But there isn't such a thing every week. Therefore I amend the Prospectus to say that the Lead is the Big News-Picture Story of the Week or, when there isn't such a thing, is a significant Picture Scoop by *Life*. That means we have to have a scoop always up our sleeve to play when the Big News-Picture Story of the Week fails us. Two scoops, very different, we have had. The Chinese Communists and Cancer. Both are important contributions to journalism. Both give the magazine kudos—even though most of our readers may not have been much interested in the Chinese Communists."

He seemed quite pleased and confident about the prospects for one other area of *Life*'s editorial output. And it was an area where, as the magazine developed over the years, its most penetrating and affecting pieces of picture journalism would appear. "The Feature," Luce wrote. "At the risk of being misunderstood, my comment on this is that it's a cinch—there's nothing to it—nothing except a crack photographer, which means nothing much for the Managing Editor as such to worry about. Here is where you get that 'pure pictorial journalism' that the picture-fanatics love. . . . What I mean is this: You can pick practically any damn human or sub-human institution or phenomenon under the sun, turn a crack photographer on it (after a little lecture by a journalist) and publish with pleasure in eight pages the resultant *photographic essay*. Fifty or twenty years ago, people used to write 'essays' for magazines. Essays for example on the bee. The essay is no longer a vital means of communication. But what is vital is *the photographic essay*. [The story on] Vassar, of course, is the best case in point. It is not a solid *Time* or *Fortune*-like account of that Institution. It leaves mountains to be written about education in general and Vassar in particular. It is not an account of Vassar. It is a delightful essay on Vassar. But it is vital. It does communicate. Both to those who know about girls' colleges and to those who do not, it tells something about Vassar and

America and Life in 1937. And it tells the kind of thing which only the most skillful (and now obsolete) literary essayists have hitherto managed to tell in words."

As for stories about art, Luce was satisfied with the magazine's performance, though he used the occasion to reaffirm the limits of his own immediate interest. "Especially this year," he said, "we want to concentrate on American artists, and especially on those who delight in painting the American scene with some degree of sympathy. Except when genuine news interest exists, we want to avoid artists who are too bizarre or who exhibit a tortured satire."

About Life's science coverage he wrote: "It is really amazing how little has come to us of a scientific nature which is really informative. But I have very little doubt that if we bend persistent and serious journalistic efforts to this task, we will develop a significant flow of scientific information—through pictures.

"We shall not insist that Science shall always be pictorially arresting. In fact, to Science we will give the privilege of not being pictorially arresting. We will be happy to have pictures which, if given a little time and study by the reader, will yield information which sticks. . . . The fact is that today most people—most educated people—walk through a world which has been amazingly analyzed by Science without having the least idea of what the world looks like to the eye of the Geologist, the Engineer, the Astronomer, the Biologist, the Chemist or the Bacteriologist. By learning only a little about how to see, Life can open many eyes.

"Here, as elsewhere, it is necessary in Life to achieve a reputation. Or perhaps what I mean is not so much that we must achieve a reputation as that we have first of all to put up our sign: 'Honest Science Sold Here.'

"Thus it is necessary to avoid printing inferior or foolish Science in order not to confuse the reader. . . . Foolishness there can be in Life. But let it be definitely in miscellaneous pages. Let us avoid foolishness or insignificance in Science and Art unless it is deliberately labelled as such."

In this, his first redefinition of Life, Luce was firm about some other things he wanted to avoid. "It already appears that, in Life as in our other magazines," he said, "what you do not print is almost as important as what you do." He had a list of Don'ts for his associates. "(a) Don't publish dull pictures—unless you have very precise justification for doing so. (b) Go easy on grue [gruesome pictures]. We always knew we would have to exert a conscious censorship against the camera's irrepressible tendency to produce grue. We have to exert an even stronger censorship than we supposed. (c) Sex? I still hope it will not be necessary to formulate an anti-sex don't. But perhaps we must admit the desirability of a temporary censorship on this aspect of *Life*—until people get used to seeing in pleasant pictures what for twenty years they have become accustomed to reading about in decidedly unpoetical words."

While he wanted his editors to be wary about sex and grue, he felt also that they should search diligently for two somewhat elusive qualities he called "Charm" and "Relaxation." "The first word to achieve a new technical meaning to the Editors of *Life*," he wrote, "was the word Charm." "Charm," he went on in words less than clear, "is the most important quality which *Life* needs which cannot be extracted from the ordinary processes of journalistic thought. We find that we must definitely plot and plan for Charm. Charm does not come naturally out of news. And the Charm which comes naturally out of the camera is mostly moonlit landscape stuff which we cannot use. Yet we intend that every issue of *Life* shall have the quality of Charm."

On the subject of that other quality, "Relaxation," he was a bit less murky. "An acute comment was made about *Look*," he wrote of the competition. "Someone said: 'The thing I like about *Look* is that you don't have to believe a word of it.' Something very different but something which is the equivalent for that quality lies in the true nature of *Life*. For lack of a better definition at the moment, I call it relaxation. There is nothing relaxing about either *Time* or *Fortune* or even *The March of Time*. They are exciting, amusing, and have definitely a 'life' quality. But they are all terribly important . . . you cannot get away from *Time*'s functionalism. It was, indeed, the first truly functional magazine. Well, *Life* is functional, too. *Life* is there to inform—indeed it exists to harness a whole new art of communication to the business of informing. But whatever the great picture magazine of 1950 may be, *Life* today does not come to its reader with any such burden of responsibility as does either *Time* or *Fortune*. . . . And so the reader can relax—and does.

"Now this may seem to contradict all that I said when I was speaking departmentally. I do not mean it so. . . . Nor must *Life* be irresponsible—it must be fundamentally respected. The departments as they increasingly define themselves and our canons of editing as they develop should ensure that we do a serious and worthwhile job. Taking that for granted, I think we may also recognize that *Life* can properly be a relaxing as well as a stimulating experience to the reader. The relaxation lies partly in this: that *Life*'s pattern of news and photographic comment is so different from all the other patterns of journalism. All

week long a man is harassed and his brow is beetled by the headlines
of the *Times* or the *Daily Mirror*—the dreadful (because newsworthy)
war in Europe or sex-murder in Hollywood—and he struggles with
Time or his favorite radio broadcasters to understand and grasp the
goings-on in this cockeyed world: and then along comes *Life* and its
whole angle on news and news value is so entirely different that he
takes a holiday from his almost continuous mental preoccupation with
the other news-patterns."

Then Luce indicated crisply what he thought was the big difference
between *Life* and other popular journals. "To *Life*," he said, "the sit-
down strike is not Labor Problems or Big Words between a dozen men
you really don't give a damn about. In *Life*, the hot news of the sit-
down strike is that people sit down! Or don't. So simple. So unlike the
New York *Times*. So relaxing. And yet so true."

But just the fact that his magazine was relaxing, he went on, did
not diminish its importance. "*Life* is so important," he wrote, offering
one of his suggestions that was never followed, "that I think a few copies
ought to be printed every week on paper which will last for at least 100
years."

Before concluding, he proceeded to touch on one relatively technical point, and once more he made clear the sense of continuing discovery he and his editors felt about the magic of photography and its
unexplored journalistic possibilities. "There is a new trick in the world
which pleases people," he wrote, "namely, the strip of photographs in
narrative sequence. One-two-three. One-two-three-four-five-six-seven-
eight. We ought to make more use of this than we do. Almost as we
say that every issue should have a few great photographs, so we should
say that every issue should have at least two strip sequences. I do not
think this trick is of any great importance in the development of civilization. . . . The strip act is only one way of telling stories. . . . But it
is a manner of speech which at the moment is most acceptable—and it
is a nice trick."

Luce concluded this memorandum on something of a homiletic
note, a note that surely showed signs of his missionary upbringing. This
was no ordinary urging by an entrepreneur whipping up enthusiasm
for the new product. He believed deeply what he had been saying—
and selling. For all his lack of sophistication about this picture form of
journalism, Luce sensed the enormous power his new magazine would
generate, and he wanted to make sure that he and his editors agreed
about what *Life* was and about what it stood for. Under a heading
labeled "Emotion," Luce wrote: "*Life* has a bias. *Life* is in favor of the
human race, and is hopeful. *Life* likes life. *Life* is quicker to point with

pride than to view with alarm. At some later time I will try to explain to myself why this is necessarily so. For the present, let it be acknowledged that this is inevitably *Life*'s bias so that it may not be thwarted or inhibited." To the end of his own life, Luce felt exactly that way about the proper bias for his picture magazine. In about 1960, speaking in some dismay about a story where *Life* had been both aggressive and wrong, Luce told Ralph Graves, who later became the magazine's last managing editor: "I always thought it was the business of *Time* to make enemies—and of *Life* to make friends."

Thus the magazine began—in conviction, confidence, naïveté, confusion, dread, furious energy, exhaustion, devotion, anger, determination and, as *Life*'s resounding acceptance became clear, feelings of exhilaration and wonder. "We never realized we were doing something totally elementary," recalled Andrew Heiskell, who began at *Life* as a twenty-one-year-old science writer in 1937 and was chairman of Time Inc.'s board of directors when he announced the magazine's finish more than thirty-five years later. He had been deeply shaken and near tears during that gloomy corporate ceremony, but in those earliest days, and in many thousands to follow, the men and women who worked on the magazine Luce said must be hopeful often had a joyful time doing so. Joe Kastner, the red-headed writer who'd suggested the story on nose blowing and who stayed on at *Life* until his retirement more than thirty years later, remembered the feelings of those beginning weeks and years. "We loved it," he said, "and we were proud of it. We were sick and tired of it and wished it would go fry in hell and—irritated, you know—go home and sort of swear we wouldn't come in the next day. And it was very exciting. And, of course, it was very successful. Here we were—we were on a winning team, you know—there wasn't anything that could stop us."

6

Billings in Charge

"IT HAS BEEN AN ENORMOUS SUCCESS. Evidently it is what the public wants more than it has ever wanted any product of ink and paper." So a cocky Henry Luce described his new baby, *Life*, to a meeting of the members of the American Association of Advertising Agencies in April 1937, barely five months after the first issue. But he wasn't there just to crow, though the astonishing performance of the big picture magazine (newsstand sellouts every week, circulation demand much greater than Time Inc. could satisfy for the moment) was in no small part attributable to his own peculiar mix of talent and drive. Luce had come to persuade this influential audience, whose enthusiasm for a journal would make the real difference between failure and a lasting success, to throw its heavy support toward his magazine.

"Should we publish *Life*?" he asked more or less rhetorically. "We have decided. . . . But it is also for you to decide. It is a question for each and every one of you to decide in your heart and in your mind because each of you is deciding it in the pocketbook of your client. . . . Here today I make application not for a few incidental pennies; I ask that you appropriate over the next ten critical years no less than one hundred million dollars for the publication of a magazine called *Life*."

That this grand figure would turn out to be relatively modest in terms of total advertising outlay (in *Life*'s first twenty years, for example, advertisers spent more than one billion dollars selling products in its pages) probably did not occur to anyone in Luce's audience. As much as they were impressed, most were still waiting for some more solid indication than they were already getting of the sort of magazine *Life* was really going to turn out to be in the long pull. Would it continue to rely, as *Saturday Review of Literature* editor Bernard De Voto suggested it had initially, on a "formula that called for equal parts of the decapitated Chinaman, the flogged Negro, the surgically explored peritoneum, and the rapidly slipping chemise"? Would it become something more than, in the words of young columnist McGeorge Bundy of the *Yale Daily News*, "a judicious combination of sensationalism, salacity and superb photography"? Such accusations stung Luce, an ex-editor of the Yale paper himself, who promptly sent Bundy copies of the five most recent issues and asked him to point out some examples of salacity (Bundy politely refused). But the big questions hung. Was *Life* going to develop some consistent, definable personality, some dominant trait of character that would make it, in fact, respectable? Or, more correctly, respectably *important*? Or would it, fueled by its own stunning notoriety, burn out and become just another in the lineup suddenly littering the newsstands?

The editors, of course, were trying in every way possible to make it clear to this potentially huge readership that *Life*, at the same time as it savored the fun in life and wondered at its twists and turns, really cared, too, about the important issues facing the American people and was ready to display a powerful public conscience. "Once again *Life* prints grim pictures of war," began the text of a picture story in the issue of January 24, 1938, about recent developments in China and Spain, "well knowing that once again they will dismay and outrage thousands and thousands of readers." The tone of the words was a sort of earnest but florid didacticism. "Obviously *Life* cannot ignore nor suppress these two great news events in pictures. The important thing that happens in war is that somebody or something gets destroyed," it went on. "Pictures of war are therefore pictures of something or somebody getting destroyed. . . . But even the best pictures cannot show war in all its horror and ugliness . . . they leave unrecorded the terrible will to kill, the even more terrible will to live, the long, lonely pain and the utter heartbreak of a whole people."

The impassioned voice of editors trying hard to rise above accusations of sensationalism is even more evident in the closing words of that brief introduction: "The love of peace has no meaning or no stamina unless it is based on a knowledge of war's terrors. Only then, by contrast, can the benefits and blessings of the absence of war be fully appreciated and maintained. Dead men have indeed died in vain if live men refuse to look at them."

Early in 1938 an opportunity arose that would profoundly increase *Life's* reputation as a magazine that cared. And the opportunity was fallen upon with a program of promotion that shrewdly engaged the sharp interest of hundreds of thousands of readers in advance—and inevitably aroused feelings ranging from honest curiosity to indignation to prurience. *The Birth of a Baby* was a film, a quasi-documentary about the pregnancy of one woman (an actress who actually became pregnant after she finished the movie) and the arrival of her baby. Made under the auspices of many organizations, including the American Association of Obstetricians, Gynecologists and Abdominal Surgeons, the American College of Surgeons and the Children's Bureau of the U.S. Department of Labor, it was an impeccably non-sensationalized, straightforward account beginning with the young mother-to-be confessing to her mother-in-law that she has missed her period. Mixed in with this and other dramatized scenes of such untitillating events as Mary telling her husband John that she believes he's going to be a father are drawings of the growing fetus in the uterus and footage, with a real infant and its real mother suitably draped, of the birth itself.

The need for such a film and its worthy propriety seemed beyond question, especially considering that both maternal and infant mortality rates in the United States were surprisingly high. The comments of advance viewers were extremely favorable; *The New York Times* found that the film was presented "with the simplicity, frankness and reverence that one of the supreme miracles of nature demands." But at that time public sensibilities on the subject were hardly as advanced as today's, and various censoring bodies, including one in New York, had imposed bans on the picture's showing. *Life*'s movie editor, Joe Thorndike, suggested that the magazine could do an important service by showing readers what the censors were holding up.

Roy Larsen, Luce's second-in-command at Time Inc. and a most important influence on *Life* matters in those early years, immediately saw the promotional possibilities of *The Birth of a Baby*. Here the magazine could look admirably responsible by publishing a vital health story at the same time as the readers were being stimulated to prepare themselves to see something too shocking for the censors. *Life*, if it played its cards right, could have it virtually all ways. Sensation, journalistic enterprise and the public interest were all elements of the juicy package.

Crucial to its selling was letting the readers know about it in advance, and here Thorndike had another good idea. He suggested that a letter be sent to all 650,000 subscribers a week ahead of time, announcing that the story would appear and giving reasons for its importance and endorsements of its merit. "To *Life* editors," the letter went solemnly, "this film posed new and serious problems. It is wholly and sincerely frank, dealing with the problems of motherhood, pre-natal care and actual childbirth. Before publishing it, *Life* consulted well its public responsibility and sought the opinions of many distinguished persons. The decision to publish it has been taken in the light of a striking unanimity of opinion that this is something which the public, and all the public, ought to see." In case any of *Life*'s readers thought their children should *not* see the pictures, the letter advised, the four pages containing them could be easily removed from the center of the issue. The kindly folks from *Life* had thought of everything.

As it actually appeared in the magazine, the story was a masterpiece of understatement. There were no big blowups, and no special emphasis was placed on the most exploitable pictures. The photographs, all small, were laid out in rows bordered in black, with dull pictures of people standing talking to each other given equal weight with others of the baby's actual arrival. The captions were utilitarian and undramatic. "As the actual birth takes place in Mary's home," read one, "the nurse has gone there to see that there is adequate lighting, plenty of bed linen, innumerable kettles to boil water for sterilization." That the magazine was trying terribly hard to stave off any possible accusations of sensation-mongering was evident, too, in the introductory text, which closed with the words: "Those who have seen the picture are impressed with the unfailing dignity and taste with which it is handled and its altogether wholesome spirit. In arranging its series of stills, *Life* has made every effort to preserve this spirit."

This commendable display of judicious propriety did not prevent *Life*'s managers, particularly Roy Larsen, from defending the story's appearance in a bold, even flamboyant way. He had some control of a situation that would make news and he was determined to make it. Sure enough, when the magazine came out on April 8, 1938, censors ordered it off the newsstands in the state of Pennsylvania and banned its sale in thirty-three cities, many of them in the Northeast. Customs officials grabbed it in Canada. In Bronx County, New York, after the district attorney confiscated magazines and threatened to bring charges against newsdealers, Larsen himself provided material for a test case. He went to the DA's office, sold a copy of *Life* to a detective waiting there and was promptly charged with selling an obscene publication. The Larsen case was an instant little sensation of its own, and interest in the issue went up everywhere. A lot of the bannings, it is fascinating to note, did not take effect until most of the copies had been sold at the stands. And Larsen, for the purpose of keeping demand very strong, had deliberately not increased the number of copies ordered from the printer.

By the time the Larsen matter came to trial in the Bronx later in the month, *Life*'s case had already been won. Many of the bans around the country had been rescinded and charges were being dropped everywhere. The U.S. Post Office had declared its confidence that the story was not dangerous to *Life*'s 650,000 subscribers and could be sent them via the mails. From editorial writers, broadcasters, pundits, medical experts, politicians and educators, from celebrities as important as Eleanor Roosevelt, came a constant stream of comment in support of the magazine's publication of the article. It was an absolutely ideal situation for *Life*; the magazine was courageously fighting the forces of censorship to bring its readers information that would only make their lives better.

Larsen's acquittal—by three judges who heard expert witnesses and decided that the subject had been handled with "delicacy"—was almost an anticlimax. "This means," said his lawyer, Morris Ernst, "that there will be no more of this nonsense in the country where petty police chiefs set themselves up as censors of the nation's reading." It also meant that *Life*, in the sense that it had most emphatically displayed its impressive and growing influence in a good cause, had really arrived as a conspicuous national force and would be there to stay.

The success of the baby story was evident in a number of ways. All available copies of the issue were sold, and the circulation manager reported an immediate substantial increase in subscription requests. *The New Yorker*, always on the alert for ways to prick Luce's balloons, did a cartoon-and-text spoof on the story called "The Birth of an Adult." The opening caption read: "From its title on, 'The Birth of an Adult' is presented with no particular regard for good taste. The editors feel that as adults are so rare, no question of taste is involved."

Of possibly greater significance, George Gallup's American Institute of Public Opinion, which found that the overwhelming majority of people who saw the pictures did not consider them indecent and approved of their publication, also estimated that upwards of 17 million adults saw the story. Given *Life*'s circulation, by then at 2 million, this suggested an extended, pass-along readership of more than eight adults per copy. To begin with, it was thought that such broadened power could be attributed to the presence of specific stories in the various issues. But gradually it became clear that the magazine had a much wider readership than the circulation figures alone suggested. Thus consideration of the pass-along readership provided a way of measuring impact, of measuring the real size of the *Life* audience. It would become one of the magazine's principal selling tools in the years ahead.

The fact that his magazine was doing remarkably well (although it was still losing money) did not keep Luce from brooding about it, and he was concerned enough in the summer of 1938 to produce a longish memorandum called "Redefinition of *Life*," at least the second of several such reevaluations he undertook over the next thirty years. "It is *not*," he admonished his readers, "intended as a piece of coherent literature—merely notes to focus practical discussion and practical *decisions* by the editors." The bill of particulars was rather long. The editor-in-chief felt the magazine wasn't beautiful enough ("Even when *Life* runs beautiful pictures, they don't always look beautiful"), funny enough ("*Life* lacks humor"), interested enough in people ("a non-fiction magazine which does not deal heavily in personalities has no chance of success"). He had complaints about the news coverage, the mix of news and features, the proper mingling of advertising with editorial material. He wondered about the ideal number of pages *Life* should publish, how it could be made more habit-forming, how the cover could better reflect the character of the magazine.

He burrowed into everything. In a supplementary memo on organization he worried over how his managing editor, John Shaw Billings, should divide his time on the job, how Longwell should dole out his energies in ways that would produce good stories and presumably keep tensions at a minimum, what the function of the art director should be. This last matter was very much on Luce's mind; he had just fired Howard Richmond, *Life*'s first art director. It was only the first of several sackings of art directors over the years; they seemed especially vulnerable to the need for a general cleanup by editors. Richmond's dismissal had not gone well. "Later Luce came down to talk about it," wrote Billings in his diary for July 29, 1938. "He said Richmond never fought back or gave him a chance to be forceful. It was, he said, 'like shooting a pet dog.' A horrid ordeal! A quiet evening, filled with thoughts of poor Richmond."

One subject that especially concerned Luce was the character of what was already being called "The Essay." By this he meant the long picture story that usually dominated the latter half of the magazine. The essay was not based on the week's news, though it was most often on a subject of topical interest. As he explained in his compulsively analytical way, Luce thought it was important that the magazine have two "rhythms," one the rhythm of "the nervous alert news-magazine," the other the rhythm of the essay, presumably more reflective. Ideally, they would work well together. "In learning this syncopation," he wrote, "we create a great new thing in weekly journalism. . . . We demand for it now a much harder-hitting dynamic journalistic quality. It has got to be an essay with a point . . . the mere charm of photographic revelation is not enough."

He went on to develop his point with current examples. "Contrast Texas High School with The Shriners," he wrote. "Shriners was okay—photographs in themselves sufficiently gee-wiz [sic] and there was good research adding up to a pretty significant 'Did you know this?' Texas High School pictures had great charm and were very revealing, but text and story did not point a strong enough moral or help you say 'gee-wiz.'"

The gee-whiz factor and a moral component were certainly present in the big essay called "Negroes: The U.S. Also Has a Minority Problem," which ran in October that year. An ambitious, fourteen-page production with pictures by Alfred Eisenstaedt and others, it provided a substantial journalistic look at a culture rarely seen outside the black press. It touched on the history, education, art, social stratification and progress of American blacks and ran a picture gallery of twenty of the most distinguished. The story was an earnest attempt to explore the big and difficult subject of blacks. "They are also the most glaring refutation of the American fetish," read the introductory text, "that all men are created free and equal. The Negro may be free but . . . he is a minority more sharply set off than any of the world's other minorities."

The essay drew widespread favorable comment from all segments of the audience. *Life* got praised for being courageous by the black press, one representative of which professed relief that the magazine had portrayed the Negro as something more than "a razor wielder, a crapshooter and a watermelon eater." Musician Duke Ellington wrote: "I believe this is one of the fairest and most comprehensive articles ever to appear in a national publication." Yet one has to wonder how Ellington and other blacks must have felt, for one thing, about the caption under a picture of a girl singing. "As she sings," it read, "with her eyes half closed, her ecstatic face becomes the face of the American Negro finding in music and religion his soul's two great consolations."

The article was littered with such avuncular racism. And worse. One small picture of two men loading cotton was captioned: "Tote dat barge. Lift dat bale." Another caption under a picture of men shooting dice read: "Baby needs new shoes." All in all, the *Life* essay was a great advance over the virulent nonsense often written about blacks back then. Even so, it was apparently impossible for white editors with the best of intentions in those palmy, segregationist days half a century ago to hear their own awful smugness in such words as: ". . . it must be remembered that the Negro is probably the most social and gregarious person in America. Nothing delights him more than a big lodge, with many a gold-braided official and many a high-sounding title." *Life* visits Amos 'n' Andy.

The magazine's acceptance by the advertisers had been complicated by fluctuation of the rates, which after being adjusted from their ridiculously low beginnings were then set too high. Advertisers balked at the idea of paying rates substantially greater than those of *The Saturday Evening Post* or *Collier's*, even if, as Luce kept saying and the salesmen were telling customers, *Life* did offer a uniquely powerful selling tool. It was only when improved production techniques—faster presses and a better bindery operation—were in place that costs began to come down enough to warrant a reduction in rates, which Larsen then persuaded Luce to accept as more truly competitive.

In a memorandum he wrote about *Life*'s position and future plans, Larsen speculated about continuing advertiser sluggishness. One of his lieutenants had reported that admen were saying two contradictory things about the magazine, either that "*Life* is a quickie. People don't spend enough time with it," or that "the editorial content is too fascinating to give our ads a chance." This only aroused Larsen's impatience. "These alibis are too silly to be the real answer," he wrote, "and to me it is clear that the real answer is simply what we have always known; that advertising men are like sheep, like most everybody else, and are waiting for somebody else to take the first dive." To help them take the dive, Larsen put Howard Black, one of the company's toughest and brightest executives, in charge of hammering the *Life* ad-sales staff into shape and of making it into the best-informed, most aggressive, resourceful and enthusiastic in the field, a standard it achieved and held for many years.

But Larsen's basic theme was that *Life* had to continue to be its own best salesman. He applauded the departmentalization that Luce and Billings had started, finding that it made the readers feel more at home in *Life* and thus susceptible to the profit-making habit of reading it regularly. And like Luce and many others, he thought that *Life* didn't have enough text in it, that the readers were flipping through too fast and could be best delayed by being offered more reading. "When *Life* publishes its first picture text biography," he wrote, "I think it will have taken over from the *[Saturday Evening] Post* enough of that dear old magazine's spirit to make our more traditional-minded and conservative followers, especially in the advertising and business field, justify their looking on *Life* as the complete replacement for the *Post* as the mirror and recorder of life in the U.S. today."

Luce was getting the same message from outside sources, too, including Condé Nast, the publisher of *Vogue* and a friend of many years. "Before you launched *Life*," he wrote in October 1938, "you were good enough to tell me of its proposed editorial formula. On that occasion, and from time to time since it was started in 1936, I have told you of an old conviction of mine that text, or at least an adequate amount of text, and not pictures, is what, in the publishing business, finally makes the mare go." Nast congratulated Luce on what he perceived as an increase in the amount of writing in recent issues, but urged still more. "I really think," he concluded, "that . . . compression or elimination of four or five of your picture pages, and the substitution of brilliantly written text, would bring you the advertising revenue to which *Life* is certainly entitled, even if some loss of circulation were to result from it. Please forgive this gratuitous interference with your private concerns."

"Believe me," Luce wrote back, "I am deeply touched by your great kindness in taking the trouble to write me as you did about the problem of *Life*." Then he made a strong defense of the necessity for keeping *Life* a picture magazine, the great value of which would soon be apparent to advertisers. "Finally, there has to come," he said, "a near-revolution in magazine advertising. The old mare ain't what she used to be. Answer: there must be new mare. . . . All right," he closed, relenting a bit, "what I have to worry about is what's wrong with me and us and not what's wrong with the advertiser. And, thanks mainly to you, I see that where we can do a lot better is in words. And so, duly agitated, again to work."

Of course, when he wasn't complaining about *Life*'s shortcomings, Luce was often engaged in praising it, both outside his company and within, where he showed signs of thinking of it as the benign, uplifting force in his array of publications. "It is the nature of *Life* to be *for* things," he wrote in a general memo, in which he had also noted with no discernible embarrassment that *Fortune* had been called "the most important magazine in America" and *Time* the most "powerful." "*Life* likes life. *Life*, if you like, is *for* the more abundant life—although *Life* is not likely ever to believe that the more abundant life can be poured out of a cracked pot or scooped from the end of a rainbow. And curiously this attitude of *Life*'s . . . arose from the nature of pictures, so far as we know about pictures. . . . You print a picture of a dog, and most of the time you simply cannot say simply 'This is a dog.' You have to say 'Isn't this a nice, cute doggy-woggy,' or 'I never saw such a damn mongrel son of a bitch.' So, if you're going to edit a picture magazine, you have to make up your mind whether you are going to print mostly pictures of nice doggies or mostly of mongrel bitches. Unless you are definitely morbid and sadistic, your decision will inevitably be to seek pictures of nice doggies. That is, you will desire and plan to sing out the good news and you will sing out the bad news only when you are compelled to do so by conscience or other journalistic necessity."

It doesn't really matter whether Luce was onto something about picture magazines or whether his words were the ravings of a powerful and ferociously determined fellow in search of a way to explain a process whose best practitioners were always much more motivated by intuition and taste than by formula. "This does not mean that *Life* is dedicated to a Pollyanna attitude," he wrote in the same memo. "[I]f human life is essentially tragic, *Life* aims at no cheap escape from that dilemma." But there can be no doubt that he preferred to think of *Life* as a nice, lovable, giving sort of publication, blunt maybe but not feisty or arrogant in its views. A sampling from one of several lists of story suggestions he gave Billings in 1938 is instructive: (1) Biography of Lincoln for Lincoln's Day; (2) Skiing; (3) The Kitchen ("And what about mama as a cook? Can she cook? What can she cook? Does she hate it? etc."); (4) The U.S. Post Office ("This could be a swell, big essay"); (5) Hawaii—Our Pacific Outpost Now ("We could do better than we did last time—with a little more emphasis on defense"); (6) The American Roadside ("It could now be a great *Life* crusade. Just about everything that is wrong with us Americans is symbolized by the dirty, messy dumps which are the American Roadside"); (7) Bourke-White Takes Beautiful Clouds.

One big and important essay published at the end of 1938 had none of the folksy quality of any of these, but it certainly reflected Luce's growing concern about America's reduced stature in a dangerous world. Called "Rearmament: U.S. is weak in arms and industry is unprepared," it was a fourteen-page assessment of the state of the U.S. Army, its weapons and the defense industry. The conclusion of the article: "Among the armies of the major powers, America's is not only the smallest but the worst equipped; most of its arms are outmoded World War [I] leftovers; some of its post-War weapons are already, in the military sense, obsolete; it has developed up-to-date weapons, but has far too few of them for modern war; if America should be attacked, it would be eight months before the nation's peacetime industry could be converted to production of the war supplies which the Army would need; whether there would be any Army left to supply at the end of those months is disputable." The impact of this story—researched largely and got ready for publication under the guidance of a young Harvard graduate, linguist and self-taught military affairs expert named

John Garrett Underhill, Jr.—was considerable, especially so since it followed by only two months Neville Chamberlain's alarmingly accommodating pact with Hitler at Munich. Underhill had been hired after he showed up for an interview with a number of loose-leaf notebooks full of comments about mistakes in *Life* stories. In years to come, many more seasoned experts, including such an authority as General of the Army and later Secretary of State George Catlett Marshall, said the *Life* story had had an important influence on beginning, however late, the upgrading of Army readiness.

Luce may have been the guiding genius, the driven, picky, furiously energetic gadfly who made himself felt in virtually every aspect of the *Life* operation. But the man who really made the magazine go week after week was John Shaw Billings, the managing editor. This big, intimidating, sometimes distant man (he could also be disarmingly informal and friendly) was thought of by his staff as a kind of god who had answers for just about everything tucked away somewhere in his formidable intelligence. But, of course, until he got thrown into the job at the last minute by Luce in 1936, he knew as little about pictures as the rest, maybe less than several. Joe Kastner remembered thanking Billings once for all he had learned under him. "The only reason you learned so much," Billings told him, "is because I was learning at the same time."

Whatever the case, Billings surely had extraordinary gifts as the editor of what in 1939 was already becoming a somewhat sprawling and hard-to-manage organization, a booming success on the verge of running away. Most who recall him refer to his astonishing memory (he could cite specific pictures *Time* had used ten years earlier or direct a researcher to a fact he remembered from an old clipping in *The New York Times*) or to his powers of order and selection (while photographers and other editors watched with a certain horror, he would go through a big stack of pictures very quickly, then pull out of the pile the dozen or so he would need for a layout). And he seemed—a blessing to subordinates who deplored indecision—to know just what it was he had in mind. If a writer, for example, couldn't come up with the language that Billings expected to end a text block, the managing editor himself would find the word or the phrase that would turn the whole piece in the direction he wanted it to go. And, under Billings, the magazine often spoke with an idiosyncratic boldness, a sauciness, a liberation that the *Life* of the 1950s and 1960s, much more conscious of the sensibilities of its many constituencies, never achieved. Billings, imperious, curt, often monosyllabic to a point chillingly past economy, ran the place with clear, demanding, consistent authority. All roads in those days led to him, and if he wasn't much of an idea man himself, he was the ultimate shaper of everyone else's.

He certainly wasn't a man of elegant tastes or lofty editorial purposes. His favorite actress was Shirley Temple, the dimpled and curly-haired child star, and he was so interested in railroads and everything about them that his obsession became something of a staff joke, as was his antipathy toward American Indians—or more correctly toward *pictures* of Indians, which he felt were usually so faked and old-hat that they should never appear in *Life*. He was unashamed of his other dislikes, including many sports. But his aristocratic background and his Harvard education did nothing to diminish his appetites for popular entertainment and culture. He loved the movies, which afforded him a frequent escape from pressure, and he eventually began to show them at home. Beneath his shyness and his sometimes haughty exterior lurked a strong, vital personality with a sure, quick news sense and a sound, unembarrassed feeling for sensation and scandal. He did not flinch at the sight of pretty girls without much on—but let's not have that nipple, please—and he had a real gift for concocting a lively mix of hard news, sex, travail, beauty, useful information, silliness and the other succulent elements that go into making a tasty picture magazine stew. The issues of *Life* that he edited, somewhat fewer than 500 in all, have a sort of raw look to them, as if they were thrown together less with care and artfulness than with a kind of scarcely contained excitement, a robust enthusiasm for the great stories being told and the thrilling ways that pictures made it possible to tell them.

For a man who exercised so much operational power on a daily basis on the magazine, whose every nod was the subject of close interpretation by his anxious underlings, Billings seemed oddly passive and excessively (if reluctantly) obedient when it came to dealing with the wishes of his boss, Harry Luce. This, of course, was always pretty much the case at Time Inc. (and in other corporations), but Billings's own accounts of it in his diaries make more clear the unsettling hierarchical phenomenon of excellent men putting their own professional judgments politely aside. One such entry was dated September 15, 1939, when Billings was in the final moments of closing a special issue devoted to the war just then engulfing Europe and threatening the neutrality of the United States. The Nazis had begun their invasion of Poland two weeks earlier.

"To an Editors' and Publishers' meeting in Luce's office," Billings wrote. "Speculative talk on war tactics and why the war wasn't moving forward faster. Luce and Larsen came down to my office and Luce went through the Special Issue dummy—with distressing results. He felt we didn't blame Hitler enough for starting the war, that we were too hard on Britain, that 'Hello, Sucker' [a headline later dropped] would delight Goebbels. Larsen chimed in with him—and I felt sunk! They want *Life* to go overboard for the Allies, because that is the way they feel personally. I have tried to keep [the] issue fair and objective—and now they say it is almost pro-German. Luckily I have no great conviction and serve as an umpire between strong-minded groups. To lunch with Luce at the Louis XIV—a dismal meal due to my anxiety about doctoring up the issue to satisfy Luce and Larsen. Luce talked high-falutin philosophy—Truth and Justice and Virtue and the need for Struggle (his Rollins College speech). Back to office—calling in Kay [Hubert Kay, one of the news editors] and telling him 'Hello, Sucker' was out and he must do history of Hitler and hate. 'When is Harry Luce going to declare war on Germany?' asked Kay with a groan. Larsen came in and a long discussion began. I kept out of it! I'm the umpire; let 'em all talk—and then I'll fix things up somehow. Here's where group journalism gets into trouble. Finally I get some ideas from the debate—fixed up the lead on Cort's British Empire [section], diddled other phrases here and there—and got the issue back on the track. A terrible ordeal—and to my staff, I suppose I appeared to be selling out to the Pro-British Management. It took all afternoon to calm everybody down to get back to work—a hell of an ordeal. . . . Home after seven, dead tired. Idle evening."

As the magazine evolved during those early years under Billings, two men played especially important roles on his staff. And considering the kind of manager he was, their skills were complementary to his and left him largely free for the complex job of putting the magazine together each week and actually getting it out. As is often the case with top lieutenants, their usefulness to the boss and their own competitiveness and zeal for the work sometimes put them squarely in each other's way.

One of these was Dan Longwell, whom Luce had hired with something big and vague about pictures in mind long before he even began experimenting with a dummy that became *Life*. Possibly more than anyone else, Longwell rates consideration as the father of *Life*—maybe not the founding father, which was Luce's role, but the stubborn guiding spirit whose unshakable conviction about photography as an immensely powerful journalistic force led Luce to take the big gamble. A nervous, somewhat jumpy man whose words tumbled over one another when he was excited, which was frequently, Longwell had showed himself not to be a gifted manager, though he would eventually, through a sort of familiar and regrettable corporate wishfulness, be made managing editor. In command, he turned out to be slow, cranky, muddled, indecisive and terribly anxious. But with somebody else taking the management heat Longwell gave abundant evidence of another, important gift—he was bursting with ideas, or scraps and swatches of ideas, for stories. Some of Longwell's ideas were awful—as is the case with most such talented people—others were half-baked. But a surprising number were just right for *Life*, or had within them the spark of a notion that could be worked into a picture story. In those innocent days when seeing a story told in pictures was new, Longwell had the gift of being unembarrassed when he suggested a story on wheat or college girls or garden clubs. He was afflicted with a sort of all-seeing naïveté, he took a daisy-fresh view of the obvious, and it paid off again and again for the young magazine.

Billings gave official recognition to these talents in an outline of staff organization he wrote late in 1938. "Longwell continues to be the great all-round Idea Man and planner of special projects," he wrote. "Working very closely with the department heads, he checks their ideas, helps them with angles and steers and slants, recalls 'that gee-whiz picture' which everybody else has forgotten and which alone will bring a subject to life. He keeps his eye peeled for covers and sees that Beauty gets into the magazine. He accepts or declines Parties. He sees to it that *Life* travels and goes Places. He alone on the staff is privileged to rove outside the contents formula bringing in all those stray things not covered by the present pattern." Billings went on to describe other duties he expected Longwell to carry out—working out essays and color features, making himself available each week to talk to virtually everybody else on the magazine. But Billings made it clear that he didn't want his gifted associate to become a loose cannon. "Longwell has no responsibility for any department," he wrote. "Nor is Longwell to stand between the department heads and the M.E. The success of his job is in being the M.E.'s *alter ego.*"

Oliver Jensen, a young editor on the staff during this period and a prolific idea man himself, described with admiration how Longwell often worked. "He traveled around the country," said Jensen. "He leafed through all the other magazines; he read all the publishers' lists; he had his nose in everything—the most agile nose I've ever seen. If Longwell took a trip out to Missouri, purely for vacation, the day he came back he *buzzed* around the corridors. He stuck his nose in every door and said to the youth in charge of radio, 'I heard the funniest radio program. You know, we ought to do some of this small-town radio stuff.' He'd stop in the fashion department and say that he'd never seen skirts so short or legs so pretty. He'd pull his head out of there and he'd walk down and he'd have an idea for the 'Speaking of Pictures' department, and he would also have discovered three basic trends for the domestic news department. I mean that he had a way of going around like a piece of blotting paper and picking things up and then squeezing them out, and the drops fall all over the place, and an awful lot of them are good ideas."

Maybe it was his relentless spraying out of ideas, maybe it was his often agitated air, but something made Longwell, unlike Billings and many of the hardy characters who followed him, the butt of laughter and occasional practical jokes at *Life*. One of the silliest of these took place late in 1940, when the magazine had put out an issue (October 28) almost entirely devoted to the U.S. Navy. Navy stories were spread throughout, and the first and biggest of these had to do with *Life's* coverage of an imaginary sea battle. "*Life* Goes into Action with the U.S. Fleet" it was called, and there were pages and pages of black-and-white pictures of officers and sailors and ships engaged in this mock action with headlines like "Fleet Strips for the Fight," "Enemy Attacks by Destroyers," "Enemy Planes Attack U.S. Line," "Fleet Takes Final Positions" and "Battleship Guns Prepare to Speak." That, in fact, was the headline just before the climactic spread, which showed the big guns of the battleship *Idaho* all firing at once in salvos that would settle the enemy's hash. The headline on that flame-belching spread was, in huge 120-point gray type, the word "BOOM!"

Longwell had been deeply involved with the story, engaged in most of the details, and had been especially taken with the "BOOM!" headline. On the Monday morning following the closing he was sitting in for the managing editor and asked to see an early copy, a "make-ready" of the issue that had just closed two nights before. Someone brought in a copy, laid it on Longwell's desk and tiptoed out. With the greatest anticipation Longwell began leafing through it, savoring the pleasure of looking at a fresh issue right after it's been produced and before the audience has seen it. He turned through the first big story, spread by spread. "Fleet Takes Final Positions." Fine. "Battleship Guns Prepare to Speak." The suspense was building. Then Longwell turned to the firing spread and suddenly howled in alarm. Holding his copy high, he dashed from his office. "What's the matter?" someone asked, stopping him. He held out the issue in horror. The headline for the spread, specially printed and artfully laid into just this one copy of the issue, was not "BOOM!" but "BOO!" Longwell simply couldn't believe it. "BOO!" And while the jokers in the layout room and others in the know rolled on the floor beside their desks, it took a considerable amount of time for the rest to persuade Longwell that it was all just a joke made up to give him a little jolt.

The other big man under Billings was Wilson Hicks, listed with Longwell on the masthead as executive editor. But of the two it was Hicks who eventually had the greater operational muscle because he was in charge of the photographic staff and supervised all the picture assignments. As such, he exercised important control over virtually everything *Life* did. He not only picked the photographers for the jobs but also discussed the work with them beforehand and then reviewed it when it was done. And perhaps most important of all, department editors wanting to get stories done had to persuade Hicks that their ideas were sound and that the photographers were going to have an excellent chance to bring off the assignments as requested. Thus dealing with Hicks was a central fact of daily life, and it was often not a pleasant one.

A Missouri newspaperman who came to *Life* in 1937 from the Associated Press, where he had been a top picture editor, Hicks dressed with care and kept every silvering dark hair in place. His cold look did not encourage conversation from juniors, and his whole demeanor suggested a somewhat disdainful skepticism. He did not receive requests for photographers with enthusiasm, and he was offended by anyone (except Billings, of course, or Luce) who had the temerity to suggest a specific person for a specific job. Sometimes he simply stared at supplicants and let them talk at him until they eventually drowned in his silence. According to Joe Kastner, some of the difficulty with Hicks was based on tension between him and Longwell and involved story ideas Longwell had already approved. "Hicks would turn down ideas that Dan was very strong on," Kastner recalled, "and we would find ourselves caught in the middle, shuttling back and forth between them. Hicks would say, 'Goddamnit, I won't cover this,' and Longwell would say, 'Tell him he can't intimidate me.' And occasionally Longwell would go down and close Hicks's door, and they'd have it out. It was exciting for everybody on the staff to see the big boys fight it out."

No matter how icy and difficult he was with editors (and several photographers found him a bully and a tyrant, too) and however much his own ambition may have increased the problems he had with his colleagues (like many of them, he wanted to be managing editor), Hicks made big contributions to *Life* in the thirteen years he was there. Many of the finest photographers—Leonard McCombe, George Silk, David Douglas Duncan—were hired by Hicks and nurtured by him, as others were, too. His toughness about assignments often made for sharper results in the magazine; his insistence on picture scripts, in which editors wrote out their expectations for stories and their suggestions for pictures, clarified objectives in advance. His choices of photographers for assignments were intelligent and occasionally inspired. Most of the great *Life* essays of the 1930s and 1940s—Gene Smith's "Country Doctor," Leonard McCombe's "Career Girl," Henri Cartier-Bresson's "A Last Look at Peiping"—were assigned by Hicks, who was always pushing to see that the photographers' best interests were taken care of.

That loyalty to the people who took the pictures reflected Hicks's position about a very big interior matter at *Life*. No matter how much Luce and Billings and many of the others raved about them and their vital importance to the magazine, the photographers, as a group, did not really enjoy the highest standing, even though their work made *Life*. Many, of course—Smith, Gjon Mili, Dmitri Kessel, Eliot Elisofon, among others—formed a sort of aristocracy of talent. But there were a lot of others who were less good—or less proficient at selling themselves. And these were considered by many to be slightly second-class, not as fancily educated or brought up as a lot of the editors, not as broad-gauge in their interests, technicians, really, clever with lights and electricity, often charming and brave, but—well, not really the kind of people you'd want to spend much time with.

Hicks hated that sort of snobbism and fought it however he could. In a speech he gave about *Life*'s operation to newspaper editors in 1940, he asked: "How many of *your* photographers are members of that exclusive club which centers in your and your city editor's and news editor's desks—are they a part of your editorial operation in the same way the reporters and rewrite men are? Here, gentlemen, in my humble opinion, is the most pressing problem about pictures today—the raising of photographers in general to the same level of prestige as writers. It is *Life*'s No. 1 problem and forgive me if I suggest it is yours, too."

This matter had been bothering Hicks for some time. The year before, he had persuaded Billings and Luce to take a public step addressing it: the classification of staff photographers was dropped from the masthead, and photographers were listed along with writers (and middle-ranking editors) as "Editorial Associates." In an advisory memo to the staff, Hicks wrote: "This revision takes recognition of a most significant point: that photographers are important in the Time Inc. editorial scheme of things *equally* with writers. The only difference is that one uses a camera, the other a typewriter to produce the essentials of our magazines."

The change lasted only a few years, and it didn't overturn old attitudes. Photographers were eventually listed by themselves again, this time higher than most people on the staff, higher than all but the most senior editors and—perhaps significantly—writers. The truth was that the editors always considered it *their* magazine. No matter how much Hicks or anyone else might have wanted it, photographers were usually kept out of general editorial operations and planning and only very rarely—as opposed to writers in the normal course of becoming editors—were given responsibility for any work other than their own.

Under Billings, Longwell and Hicks, there were several who played important roles at *Life* during those years before America went into World War II. Among them were:

Joseph J. Thorndike, Jr., still in his twenties, a handsome, bright, reserved, efficient fellow who acted as Billings's businesslike assistant managing editor, did some copy editing and handled special projects Billings turned over to him. Thorndike had come to *Time* in 1934 and then transferred to the picture magazine project. He liked to tell people that his only notable ancestor was hanged as a wizard at Salem in 1692. Ambitious, proud, marked from the start for bigger things, he would succeed Longwell as managing editor in 1946.

Edward K. Thompson, a graduate (at nineteen) of the University of North Dakota who came to *Life* in 1937 from the Milwaukee *Journal* and worked closely with Hicks making picture assignments, gradually extended his influence into other areas of the magazine, specifically its coverage of military and defense matters. Billings found Thompson, who produced a big story on the Southern Railroad with Eisenstaedt in 1938, "a joy," and wrote in his diary on March 3, 1940: "Thompson is a great help—and I like him personally a lot—much better than Hicks or Longwell." When he returned to *Life* after the war, Thompson became an assistant managing editor, then in 1949 replaced Thorndike as the top man.

Hubert Kay, who became national affairs editor in 1937 after first working on *Time*, was in his early thirties. As described by his colleague David Cort (in Cort's angry, disheveled, fascinating book *The Sin of Henry R. Luce*): "Kay was a man who plodded his way to the truth and presented it with crystalline honesty. He thought heavily but purely, though with an unnecessary anguish." In his diary (August 15, 1939) Billings was less complimentary. "Kay is getting very heavy and slow, hours of ponderous thinking and very little to show for it. . . . His sluggishness annoys me." By present-day standards, some of Kay's work seems quite lively. In a 1939 issue his summation of a furious 25,000-

word speech by Hitler was: "Poland, look out! England, take it easy! Roosevelt, shut up! Great going, Adolf!" Week after week, Kay wrote much of the front of the magazine and in 1941 left to return to *Time*.

David Cort, foreign news editor, also a transfer from *Time*, was brilliant, acerbic, erratic and, in Billings's judgment, at one time "a fabulous producer." He wrote of himself: "I had a sort of power merely by expressing the foreign policy of *Life* without contravention by my superiors." A cantankerous man, his unruly and outspoken behavior was sometimes a trial for the orderly Billings, who nevertheless valued his gifts highly. "Curiosity?" Billings wrote Luce in a memo. "Has the *Life* staff lost it? The classic example was David Cort, who would study a set of pictures for hours and send his researcher out to get answers to impossible questions. But when Cort wrote captions they had a relevance to the pictures that was startling." Of this technique Cort himself wrote: "I examined every picture for anything it had to reveal, no matter how trivial, if the reader could confirm it with his own eyes. My intuition would be that this procedure, faithfully pursued, would convince the reader that he could trust and benefit from the writer." Cort left *Life* in 1946, with a minimum of good feelings on both sides.

Noel Busch, a tall, elegant Princeton graduate who'd worked for *Time* as a movie and theater critic (and for the New York *Daily News*, *The New Yorker* and *Liberty* magazine) before coming to *Life*, was a prolific writer and story producer and eventually had charge of setting up all the long bylined pieces for the magazine. He looked and dressed the part of a dashing foreign correspondent (for a piece on the King of Arabia he grew a beard and wore a burnoose). His imperious style around the office may be somewhat explained by the fact that he was, after all, company royalty, being a first cousin to the deceased Briton Hadden, Time Inc.'s co-founder. His boldness was an asset. Shortly after the outbreak of war in 1939, Billings wanted an article about Stalin. To write it, Busch suggested Leon Trotsky, a colleague of Lenin's and a bitter rival of Stalin's then living in exile in Mexico City (where he was assassinated in 1940). Billings liked the idea but doubted it could be pulled together in time. Yet, according to Billings's diary (September 19, 1939), "Busch got Trotsky on long distance, told him what was want[ed]. 'How much?' asked Trotsky. '$1500.' 'I vill!' said Trotsky. And thus it was arranged—and Busch will fly to Mexico City tonight to keep Trotsky on the track." To Billings's delight ("a great coup," he called it), the article came out well, in spite of Busch's complaint from Mexico City that Russian was turning out to be a "very gnarled" language to translate.

Many others were deeply involved on a weekly basis, among them, of course, the original *Life* photographers, Margaret Bourke-White, Alfred Eisenstaedt, Peter Stackpole and Tom McAvoy. Other photographers had joined the staff, including John Phillips, a resourceful picture journalist who was one of the earliest to cover the European war, and Carl Mydans, a compact, bustling man, who married Shelley Smith, one of the most promising young reporters on the magazine. Mydans would rank among the finest of the combat photographers; he and his wife went to Europe as a working team in 1939 (where he covered the bitter Russo-Finnish War in 1940) and were captured by the Japanese in Manila in 1942.

Art director Worthen Paxton joined the magazine right after he'd helped Norman Bel Geddes design the huge General Motors "Futurama" exhibit for the 1939 New York World's Fair. Paxton didn't know the first thing about journalism, but he knew pictures and graphics and he made substantial contributions to the look of the magazine. He became an expert on the reproduction of color photography. His standing on the edit staff became high. To turn out the kind of detailed war illustrations and global diagrams that were his specialty, he assembled at *Life* one of the best map collections in the world, and he eventually helped gather a team of artists—among them Tom Lea and Fletcher Martin—who formed an important part of the magazine's war coverage.

Joe Kastner, the redhead who'd come to work as an office boy for *Time* in 1924 and would become one of *Life's* top bosses in the 1950s and 1960s, was writing picture stories on everything from sports to the beauties of the Hudson River valley. Lincoln Barnett, a blithe-spirited Princeton man (who got two additional degrees at Columbia, worked for five years as a reporter under the famed Stanley Woodward at the New York *Herald-Tribune* and was a skilled amateur tap dancer and ukulele player), was a roving writer being used wherever Billings needed him most. In the years ahead the graceful and versatile Barnett would become one of the country's best-known profiles writers and win awards as the author of "The Universe and Dr. Einstein" and a book that grew out of a long and very popular *Life* science series, "The World We Live In."

Oliver Jensen, a young Yale man who'd worked some in advertising and joined the *Life* staff in 1940, would play a considerable role at the magazine for the next ten years. Even while he was in the Navy during the war, his articles appeared frequently, and he later took on some management duties. He acquired a certain admiring notoriety on the staff because of the way he resolved a problem he had with Wilson Hicks, who was reluctant to assign a photographer to a story Jensen wanted done. Jensen then hired and paid his own photographer for the job and took his pictures directly to Billings. When Billings happily accepted them for "Speaking of Pictures," Jensen presented Hicks with a bill for the photography. Hicks paid it.

Without question the most idiosyncratic behavior on that prewar staff belonged to Alexander King, who stayed at *Life* only a few years. He'd been recommended by Mrs. Luce as a most talented man with a good eye for pictures and a sense of humor, and in the short time he was around, King (who became something of a talk-show TV star in the 1950s and 1960s and the author of a best-selling memoir called *Mine Enemy Grows Older*) contributed a number of offbeat and lively ideas. He'd written plays, and though he suggested stories in every area of the magazine, he was mainly the "Speaking of Pictures" editor. King is remembered for his unvarying wardrobe—green tweed suit, blue shirt, pink necktie. A brilliant talker, he regaled the staff with his colorful stories and outspoken opinions for hours on end. He once turned up at the office with a remarkable dwarf whose height of just twenty-two inches, King claimed triumphantly, made him short enough so that his picture could be printed, life size, across a spread of the magazine. On another occasion, he produced a series of pictures on the work of a plastic surgeon—who turned out, after the story ran, to be a well-known Manhattan abortionist. King's judgment began to make the management nervous (Billings thought he was lazy and that he counted on his connection with Mrs. Luce to keep his job), and in late 1940, this least orthodox and malleable of possibly all Time Inc. group journalists was fired.

By the spring of 1940, when *Life* was well into its fourth year, the success of the magazine was leading its advertising promotion writers to a near frenzy of number-inspired enthusiasm. In one document, called "Fantastic Facts of *Life*," it was reported that:

"1. The 2,800,000 copies of *Life* sold *each week*, if laid end to end, would make a footpath 618 miles long or from New York City to Detroit.

"2. The number of copies of *Life* sold *over a period of a year*, if laid end to end, would extend some 32,000 miles or 1 and ⅓ times around the world—or would make a street approximately 9 feet wide from New York City to San Francisco.

"3. *Life*'s weekly audience of 19,900,000 is equal to: (a) the combined population of Finland, Sweden, Denmark, Norway and what used to be Czechoslovakia, or (b) the combined population of San Francisco, Chicago, Boston, Detroit, New York City, Baltimore, Philadelphia, Providence, Cleveland, St. Louis, Pittsburgh, Atlanta, Portland, Seattle, Minneapolis and Galveston, with not quite enough left over for Ypsilanti.

"4. *Life's* total annual revenue from circulation, over $11,000,000, would be more than 110,000,000 dimes—or 1302 miles of dimes, more than the distance between New York and Kansas City.

"5. If a *Life* advertiser wanted to display consecutively all the page reproductions of his advertisement from any one issue of *Life*, he would have to rent a billboard over 445 miles long."

While it can be safely presumed that Henry Luce was pleased to know that *Life* was beginning to do well, he would have had little interest in such Ripleyesque applications of statistics. In fact, what was most preoccupying him at that time, and a lot of other worried Americans, was much more serious—the conflict exploding in Europe and the growing likelihood that the United States would become involved in it. And what seemed to be troubling him most about the situation, according to a confidential memorandum he sent to his company's top executives in July 1940, was "the persistence of an American phobia about War."

"Surely, in times like these," he wrote, "a great people should accept the risks of war just as cheerfully and confidently as they accept other major risks of life and death, of gain and loss, of pain and pleasure. Until the American people accept the risks of war as an inescapable element in the conduct of their affairs (so long as the World Crisis lasts)—until then everything else has only the value of a little preparatory time-saving."

The purpose of Luce's memo, headed "Subject: WAR," was to reach an agreement "in relatively exact terms, as to TIME INC.'s attitude and responsibilities in this critical hour of history." The founder asked his top echelon to consider an interesting—not to say mind-blowing—hypothesis. "If the Senior Group of TIME INC. were entrusted," he wrote, "with the management of the affairs of the United States of America, then its prime responsibility would be to *act*; we would then be guilty of criminal incompetence if we were incapable of making up our minds from day to day as to exactly what to do. But the Senior Group of TIME INC. is not responsible for the management of the affairs of the United States of America. That management is provided for, well or badly, in the Constitution of the United States."

But that did not mean, he explained, that there was no provision for Time Inc. in the document that shapes America. "As a matter of fact," he went on, "we are named in the Constitution. We do have responsibilities arising out of the Constitution. Our responsibilities are given to us under the clause of the Bill of Rights which guarantees Freedom of the Press. The responsibilities are not specifically named—they are left to the consciences of those who exercise the right of free-

dom of publication. Whatever other duties the Press may have, it has
no more vitally important duty than to tell the people what the situation
is. Therefore, if we have convictions as to what the situation *is*, and if
we do our damndest to convey these convictions to the people, we shall
have discharged our primary duty."

Luce had a very basic feeling about what the situation was. "Danger," he wrote. "The country is in danger. Danger. Danger. The country is in danger." As to the matter of Time Inc.'s journalistic duty in
the situation, Luce stated it in five parts:

"1. To continue to sound the Danger signal in all its aspects
—Danger to the Sovereign U.S.A., Danger to our Constitutional
Democracy.

"2. To cultivate the Martial Spirit—without which we shall by no
shadow of chance overcome the Danger.

"3. To show that America is worth fighting for—since, incredible
though it may seem, there appear to be those who doubt it.

"4. To be hawk-eyed in our observation of Preparedness and to be
savage and ferocious in our criticism of all delay and bungling.

"5. Among as many readers as possible, to develop a sense of
foreign policy."

Luce went on to outline a few details of what that foreign policy
might be. They included: "to take all reasonable risks to keep Germany
from subduing Great Britain" (including repeal of the Neutrality Act,
providing shelter in the United States for British children and selling
destroyers and other arms to Great Britain); to make sure that "Mexico,
the whole of Central America, and all countries bordering on the Caribbean . . . behave themselves in all important respects in a manner
agreeable to us"; in Asia, "to give maximum aid to China as long as
China is fighting . . . to foster good relations with all friendly elements
in Japan . . . to cooperate, on a cold diplomatic basis, with Russia in so
far as we find our interests parallel."

The response to Luce's memo from his senior people on *Life* was
prompt. Hubert Kay stressed the importance of explaining the nature
of the danger to the readers, "to bring home to Americans what fascism
in America would mean. . . . since time is short I believe that *Life*
should illustrate [Sinclair Lewis's novel] *It Can't Happen Here*." The
ever-vigilant David Cort reported that he found the memo excellent
but cautioned that "we might as well make up our minds (though perhaps this is not a thing to confide in our readers as yet) that when we
are armed to the teeth, we attack. This is so self-evident in a military
and economic and moral way that it is hardly subject to debate, yet
many people think we will sit on our 30-billions-worth of arms until

they are obsolete and play Post Office with Hitler. I also believe that we ought to tell our people the worst imaginable before it happens, on the psychological principle that they are then inoculated to the worst and do not fall apart when it comes. France was a sample of that latter."

Billings, too, was enthusiastic, but he wasn't quite sure how *Life* could best implement the boss's admonitions. "*Life* is swell for cheering," he wrote. "*Life* is a natural for raising the Danger Signal, cultivating the Martial Spirit, for showing that America and its way of life are worth fighting for. We're all for that and are already on the way. But technically, it is less easy for a picture magazine to promote, let us say, a strong foreign policy or to redefine the Monroe Doctrine 'in its pristine and simplest terms.' Likewise 'criticism of all delay and bungling' on preparedness. It is something we haven't found the answer to yet."

Actually *Life*'s coverage of military subjects, the widening conflict and general stimulation of the martial spirit was beginning to lead some readers to complain about the magazine on the grounds that it was pandering to rising fear and too deeply interested in the subject of war. *Life*'s frequent portrayal of the subject in all its aspects—including, as Kay had suggested, fantasized attacks against and lurid takeovers of the United States—prompted a hilarious spoof in *The New Yorker* just weeks before Pearl Harbor. A takeoff of a *Life* party story, it was called "*Life* Goes to the Collapse of Western Civilization: Pretty New York Models Get Thrilling Glimpses of Invasion and Insurrection." It purported to be the story—done in girlie-mag sexy drawings—of two models, "Meenie" Kronkheit and "Babs" Golcz, who are working in New York at the time the Nazis invade. "Both girls are good cooks," the caption writer explained, "hate to wash dishes. 'Babs' relaxes by walking in Central Park with 'Scotty,' her pet Scotty, 'Meenie' by reading Gibbon's 'Decline, Fall of Roman Empire.' In spite of numerous dates, both showed intelligent interest in invasion of U.S. by Axis and consequent civil disturbances. *Life*'s photographer spent day with them, raised skirts on still another news front of the world." The unidentified *New Yorker* writer's tongue fairly burst from his cheek in captions like those concocted for pictures showing the girls carrying a laundry basket full of greenbacks and consorting with Axis soldiers. "In this 'gag picture,'" read one, "'Meenie' and 'Babs' have dressed in scanty sports clothes for the task of lugging $3,450,000 in inflated United States currency to famed Elizabeth Arden's, to buy tube of vanishing cream. Corpse in foreground is real." The other read: "'Meenie' and 'Babs' pose in military brothel with two lads who can't believe their luck in meeting real, live actress, model. After this picture was snapped, girls declined drinks, went home on subway. Boy friends and careers don't mix, they say."

Stung to retaliation, Noel Busch sat down at his typewriter and composed a spoof on the detachment that *The New Yorker* might have brought to its own observations on the same event. It didn't really even the score, but it was a plucky try. "New York was noisy enough in 1929," it read in part, "when there was a new skyscraper going up on every block and a hundred riveting machines on every skyscraper. It is strange now to find that the same buildings make almost as much racket going down as they did when they were going up. Glancing out of our window a moment ago we saw the Empire State Building crumble and disappear, when a bomb hit the mooring mast. Things like this seem unnerving, when one stops to think about them. The Empire State didn't make too much noise, though. Too far away."

In those years just before Pearl Harbor, Luce's preoccupation with the state of the world and America's role in it was sometimes reflected directly in the pages of *Life*. Early in 1941 signs of work on what would be the best known of all his ruminations about the responsibilities of the United States cropped up in the entry in Billings's diary for January 31. "Office and work," he wrote. "Luce's two editorials, 'We Americans,' redrafted by [Russell] Davenport, came up for discussion. They are pretty good. Luce came down and Longwell came in. What to do? (Luce is like a man possessed—sick with his own abstract ideas. How to relieve him of them?) I was ready to run a series of seven. Longwell said they should all be in one big sock, to be presented as a special stunt next week. Luce immediately picked up the idea." Four days later Billings wrote: "Luce finished up his piece 'The American Century' (my title). It was pretty good—and is the only text I am using in this issue."

Signed by Luce, the essay ran for five dense, pictureless pages in the issue of February 17, 1941. Considering its forbidding look and the heavy subject matter, the piece drew a very large amount of mail, almost 5,000 letters, the great majority of them favorable. The most angrily vehement of the correspondents found the article "smug," "pretentious," "jingoistic" and "self-righteous"; one, Freda Kirchway of *The Nation*, wrote that Luce's program showed qualities that were "typical stigmata of the Anglo-Saxon in his role as imperialist." Most people who commented on "The American Century," however, seemed to feel that Luce had stated a timely and necessary call for clarification of American purpose and had offered a useful program for putting U.S. leadership into action. Looked at more than forty years later, Luce's proposals seem surprisingly close in general outline to what U.S. policy became and continued to be, starting in the years immediately after the war.

"In the field of national policy," Luce had written, "the fundamental trouble with Americans has been, and is, that whereas their nation became in the 20th century the most powerful and the most vital nation in the world, nevertheless Americans were unable to accommodate themselves spiritually and practically to that fact. Hence they have failed to play their part as a world power—a failure which has had disastrous consequences for themselves and for all mankind. And the cure is this: to accept wholeheartedly our duty and our opportunity as the most powerful and vital nation in the world and in consequence to exert upon the world the full impact of our influence, for such purposes as we see fit and by such means as we see fit. . . . As America enters dynamically upon the world scene, we need most of all to seek and to bring forth a vision of America as a world power which is authentically American and which can inspire us to live and work and fight with vigor and enthusiasm."

Luce, who earlier in the essay had written that America was really "in the war" however the nation may have deceived itself that such was not the case, found that such a vision could be realized in four areas. "First, the economic," he wrote. "It is for America and for America alone to determine whether a system of free economic enterprise—an economic order compatible with freedom and progress—shall or shall not prevail in this century. . . . For example, we have to decide whether or not we shall have for ourselves and our friends freedom of the seas—the right to go with our ships and our oceangoing planes where we wish, when we wish and as we wish. The vision of America as the principal guarantor of the freedom of the seas, the vision of America as the dynamic leader of the world, has within it the possibilities of such enormous human progress as to stagger the imagination. . . .

"Closely akin to the purely economic area . . . there is the picture of an America which will send out through the world its technical and artistic skills. Engineers, scientists, doctors, movie men, makers of entertainment, developers of airlines, builders of roads, teachers, educators . . .

"But there is a third thing which our vision must immediately be concerned with. We must undertake now to be the Good Samaritan of the entire world. It is the manifest duty of this country to undertake to feed all the people of the world who as a result of this worldwide collapse of civilization are hungry and destitute. . . . For every dollar we spend on armaments, we should spend at least a dime in a gigantic effort to feed the world—and all the world should know that we have dedicated ourselves to this task. . . .

"But all this is not enough. All this will fail and none of it will happen unless our vision of America as a world power includes a passionate devotion to great American ideals . . . a love of freedom, a feeling for the equality of opportunity, a tradition of self-reliance and independence and also of cooperation. In addition to ideals and notions which are especially American, we are the inheritors of all the great principles of Western civilization—above all Justice, the love of truth, the ideal of charity . . . It now becomes our time to be the powerhouse from which the ideals spread through the world and do their mysterious work of lifting the life of mankind from the level of the beasts to what the Psalmist called a little lower than the angels."

Thus this man, "sick with his own abstractions," fiercely proud of his country and determined to spread his grand vision of its highest duty, called for his fellow citizens "to create the first great American Century." At the far end of that year, ten months later, Billings spent much of Sunday, December 7, relaxing with his wife and dog. He had finished closing the issue of December 15 the day before. "F. and I napped comfortably from 3:30 to 5," he wrote in his diary. "I got up . . . and turned on the radio. 'The Japanese have bombed Pearl Harbor and Hickam Field—300 U.S. dead.' Well, here it is—War. I was shocked and surprised at its manner of coming and it took me minutes to collect my thoughts, as I ran around in a dippy dither in my underwear. A telephone call from Jackson brought me back to my senses—and I told him I would be down to the office in 20 mins. for an extensive remake in the issue. In great excitement I hustled into my clothes and kissed F. goodby. (You might have thought the Japs were right outside our door!) She was very woebegone at being left alone on such short notice—but I kept yapping 'This is war—this is war—' and dashed out and taxied to the office."

7

America at War

DEC. 15, 1941

WAR
JAPAN LAUNCHES RECKLESS ATTACK ON U.S.
IN DESPERATE GAMBLE ON VICTORY OR SUICIDE
IT STRIKES FIRST BLOW AT HAWAII

Out of the Pacific skies last week World War II came with a startling suddenness to America. It was 7:35 a.m. on a Sunday morning—the aggressors'
favorite day—when two Japanese planes, wearing on their wings the Rising
Sun of Japan, flew out of the western sky over the Hawaiian island of Oahu.

"A WAR, ANY SORT OF WAR, is going to be natural promotion," Longwell
had written Luce in 1935 as he urged Time Inc. to hurry up and bring
out its new picture magazine in time to take advantage of Italy's widely
predicted assault on Ethiopia. More than six years later, if there was
still any doubt that war—especially one passionately supported by the
overwhelming majority of readers but taking place thousands of miles
from home—was the ideal subject for *Life*, it was quickly dispelled by
the appearance of the first few issues after Pearl Harbor. Immediately
and with tremendous patriotic drive and ignited imaginations, the managers of the magazine rushed at this astounding global story (and one
from which Americans could no longer maintain the cool distance of
neutrality) and attacked it from every possible angle. "Though we did
not plan *Life* as a war magazine," Luce said much later, "it turned out
that way."

Of course, Luce and the editors of all his publications had been
busy for years focusing the attention of their readers on the growing

dangers of the world situation and especially on the responsibility of Americans to assert a leadership role. But now a real reckoning was at hand and the ordinary professional restraints of caution and reflection seemed almost beside the point. In the environment of war, Luce's tendency to think of Time Inc. and its magazines as an unofficial arm of government took on a heightened fervor. Ten days after the raid on Hawaii he wrote President Roosevelt: ". . . And in the days to come— far beyond strict compliance with whatever rules may be laid down for us by the necessities of war—we can think of no greater happiness than to be of service to any branch of our government and to its armed forces. For the dearest wish of all of us is to tell the story of absolute victory under your leadership."

The outpouring of journalistic loyalty in *Life* was amazing. From the outset until the war ended forty-four months (and more than 200 issues) later, the parade of war-connected picture stories was constant. In virtually every issue several stories dealt with battles, heroes, the home front, tactics, tips ("How to Tell the Japs from the Chinese"), trivia. The selections from the magazine accompanying this chapter are only a sampling, but they show how the writing that framed these pictures, the text blocks, headlines, editorials, bylined articles, captions, even the advertisements, reflected the many notes of U.S. patriotic opinion as the editors saw it and, in fact, experienced it—resolved, prepared to suffer, angry, cheerful, proud, bitterly contemptuous of the enemy, secure in the rightness of the cause.

It was as if—for this trying period only—the magazine became a sort of national house organ. Not that the editors abdicated their right to criticize the quality of the war effort and its leaders; *Life* exposed embarrassing shortcomings in war production, quarreled with military tactics and grand strategy and in 1944 came out strongly for the Republican Thomas Dewey in his failed effort to wreck Franklin Roosevelt's run for a fourth term. Still, the magazine was more often than not a great weekly cheering section in pictures and words, a voluble, reassuring, earnest, admonishing, indignant, aghast, tender, hugely admiring witness to a conflict whose victorious outcome for America it never doubted.

DEC. 22, 1941

These 30 young Americans (below) from Nebraska to Florida were on the first U.S. Army casualty list of this war. They were killed in action in Japan's surprise bombardment of Pearl Harbor, Dec. 7. They are only a few of the total casualties, now estimated at 3,000, and their names are among the last to appear in a public casualty list for the war's duration. Speaking for the Army and Navy, President Roosevelt declared last week that hereafter radios and newspapers

should refrain from announcing complete lists of dead or wounded, for such lists would give useful information to the enemy.

The magazine's determination to comply "with whatever rules may be laid down for us by the necessities of war" led immediately to an unpleasant and embarrassing little episode involving some of the magazine's foreign-born photographers. In the immediate aftermath of Pearl Harbor there was a presidential proclamation against the possession and use of cameras by enemy aliens, that is, citizens of powers at war with the United States. These people were forbidden to take pictures and ordered to turn their cameras over to "United States Citizens." Professional photographers who fell under the blanket of this edict were to be suspended from work by those who employed them.

To advise the government of *Life*'s compliance with this measure, Wilson Hicks, as he was required to do, wrote a letter to Francis Biddle, the Attorney General of the United States, giving him a list of the names and addresses of eight photographers, seven of them German-born. Among these men were some of the most outstanding magazine photographers in the world, including Alfred Eisenstaedt, one of *Life*'s original staff, and Hungarian-born Robert Capa, already a celebrated war photographer. "We have suspended these men from our active list . . . ," Hicks wrote. "They have surrendered their cameras to us or to other United States Citizens. Where the surrender of cameras was to others we are obtaining records showing with whom they are impounded."

Hicks clearly felt some obligation to speak well of the photographers. "We have assigned these men to picture stories for *Life* for periods ranging from three to five years," he told Biddle, "and have had confidence in their integrity. All have their first papers." But the editor also seemed to want the Attorney General to know that *Life* knew the value of homegrown loyalty. "Of course," he finished, "our main reliance is now and always has been on American-born photographers. If we can cooperate in any other way, please let us know."

The suspension of these photographers lasted only for a brief time, but feelings were naturally hurt in the process. Otto Hagel, one of the photographers involved, wrote a wry protest to Hicks. "I have looked under my bed," he said in part, "and in my scrap books, I've looked into a mirror and failed to find an enemy alien . . . But this is neither the age of reason nor of consent. The father of a mule goes by many names, and I'll answer to most of them, and take no offense. But to be labeled 'enemy alien' in a blanket indictment is hardly fair. However, this probably is beyond your jurisdiction, and at this juncture there is no need to quote Shakespeare."

JAN. 5, 1942

The army of Japan has one enormous advantage over the U.S. Army. It is an army of veterans, hardened and blooded by ten years of intermittent warfare in China. It knows the business of war, the small tricks of survival, the hard work, the cunning, the pleasure of victory. It is a cruel and ruthless army. Its men are absolutely convinced that they are right and their enemies are beneath contempt. They burn prisoners alive, rape and disembowel captive women, pillage and slaughter as though an atrocity were the most natural thing in the world. Their cruelties do not come singly, but in the indescribable hundreds of thousands. . . . The Japanese army has spread across Asia a tale of horror that will be told for a thousand years.

"In 1939," Carl Mydans wrote in his book *More Than Meets the Eye,* "Shelley and I were the first of the roving correspondents *Life* was to send afield—prototypes bearing little resemblance to the assured and well-instructed reporters who travel the boulevards and trails to-day. Then we were green. And so were our editors." By late December 1941, considerably less green by virtue of their experiences in China and in Europe (where Mydans had covered the war between Russia and Finland and later the fall of France and where his wife, Shelley, had reported from London, Scandinavia and Portugal), they were in Manila, where they were based while Mydans shot a big story on the preparations for Philippine defense against the Japanese. That they were in a very nasty predicament indeed is clear from a cable Luce sent them the day before Christmas, just two and a half weeks after Pearl Harbor. "For all that you are doing," he wired in anguished salute, "to transmit to us the spirit of valor we are all deeply grateful this Christmas." The Japanese, of course, were sweeping through the islands. The last message *Life* got from the plucky, dogged and energetic team (Mydans was thirty-four at the time, his wife was twenty-six) arrived two days after Luce's cable. It read: "Christmas morning was very quiet. Three raids kept us close to our base. We opened our presents under a tiny tree in our room while a Filipino serenader below sang 'God Bless America.' Manilans first choked on the words 'Merry Christmas,' but soon found the toast of the day: 'May this be the worst Christmas we ever spend.' Christmas night we can laugh because we are still free!"

The freedom of this articulate, tough little man from Boston and the bright and pretty Californian he married came to an end right after the New Year. "At dusk on January 2," the Mydanses wrote later, "the Jap vanguard moved warily up Dewey Boulevard, a column of tiny, single-cylinder motor bikes that coughed and sputtered. The little men on them with their tropical uniforms and their Rising Sun flags looked like dolls. We were amused and then ashamed. Slowly, these miniature soldiers embraced the city, then permeated it. With a minimum of direct contact and in good order, they separated us from the Filipinos interned with us, confiscated our property and businesses, then moved on toward Bataan, leaving Manila a breadless, inert city." This was the beginning of a captivity, first in a makeshift prison at the University of Santo Tomás for about eight months with 3,500 other Americans, that would last almost two years until Carl and Shelley Mydans became part of an exchange of prisoners and returned home late in 1943.

With the Mydanses when Manila fell was another young American couple, Melville Jacoby, who just recently had become the correspondent for *Time* and *Life* in the Philippines, and his wife of only a few weeks, Annalee Whitmore. Because Jacoby had reason to believe that the Japanese might deal with him with special severity if they captured him (he'd had considerable experience in Asia as a correspondent, radio broadcaster and photographer and had once been arrested by the Japanese for shooting pictures they confiscated), he and his wife (a writer herself who four years later collaborated with Theodore White on the book *Thunder Out of China*) and an Associated Press reporter named Clark Lee elected to try to escape. They fled by boat to the island fortress of Corregidor, where American forces under General Douglas MacArthur were holding out against constant Japanese bombardment, and from there to the Bataan Peninsula. The Jacobys worked there for a few weeks doing stories on American and Filipino troops under great pressure. Then, with the situation apparently hopeless, the Jacobys and Clark Lee decided to try to flee by boat to Australia, more than 2,000 miles to the south. This was arranged with the help of MacArthur. "He turned to Major General Sutherland, his chief of staff," Jacoby wrote, "and said: 'Dick, make arrangements immediately.' We had the General's signature on a letter, directing all military aid for us, his handshake and two sentences: 'I believe you will make it. Say goodbye to Annalee for me.'" Traveling at night to avoid being spotted by the Japanese, the Jacobys and Lee skipped by small boat down the long chain of islands. Seen from the air on a couple of occasions by Japanese patrols and stalked by enemy search boats, protected time and again by Filipino villagers along the way, they eventually made their way to an island where they were able to arrange to be taken by ship on the final long leg to Australia. They made it, but only a few weeks later Jacoby was killed in a freak accident at an airfield when an out-of-control fighter plane crashed into him and some others as they were about to board another plane. He was twenty-six, and General MacArthur remarked of him that "he could well have served as a model for war correspondents at the front."

APRIL 13, 1942

Life believes that a good deal of bunk has been written and printed recently about the morale of the American people. The morale of the American people, as a whole, is high and tough. It is in a mood for vigorous action. But there are always a certain number of yapping dissidents about the feet of a great nation marching to war. *Life*'s editors and correspondents, with the aid of trained investigators, have prepared this article, not to frighten Americans with bugaboos but to make them mad enough to see to it that their officials take the necessary action.

At home, the magazine's bosses were learning how to cope with the problems of getting stories done with the country on a war footing. "Coverage, of course, becomes far more difficult than it ever was," general manager Andrew Heiskell wrote the business staff in a memo. "When we were a neutral country, correspondents had certain privileges and warring nations tended to treat them with considerable respect. With the whole world and ourselves at war, a correspondent in the battle zone has an officer's status and is about as much a part of the army as any officer. This means that he cannot report his movements freely and, in turn, that we cannot get in touch. A wire to a photographer in the Far East may be delivered and again it may not. If it is, we sometimes will not get an answer for weeks. . . .

"Two years ago," Heiskell went on, "we used to be slightly vexed at the fact that it took a week for a set of pictures to reach us from the European battle front which was only 4000 miles away. Today the battle fronts in the east are 8000 miles off and methods of transportation are not only very slow but also totally unpredictable. All this means that *Life* must have more people on the fronts so that if one man doesn't come through with a story the other one does."

Of course, one of the biggest problems involved censorship, of both pictures and words. To help work out the difficulties of getting stories through the bureaucrats in the military, *Life* strengthened its Washington office and put a man in London to facilitate the clearance of valuable pictures there. Because the magazine had voluntarily sought official approval on some sensitive military stories even before Pearl Harbor, relations between *Life* and the censors were friendly. And Heiskell noted another reason for that: "Since *Life* first appeared the War and Navy departments have recognized it as a powerful instrument for public education and have gone out of their way to provide the editors with raw material such as no U.S. magazine has ever had at its disposal."

Still, just as *Life* could no longer send its photographers and correspondents anyplace the editors thought might provide lively action but instead had to wait not only for permission but to be told where the action was likely to be, it had to suffer the whims and built-in inefficiencies of the censorship system. Often persons other than the censor would have the right of approval over pictures or writing, and there were the inevitable conflicts. A story would be cleared by Navy authorities in Hawaii, and then be found problematic by some Navy bureau in Washington. Sometimes the censorship got down to sheer nit-picking. In one article, a picture caption spoke of exhausted Marines "snuggling" into makeshift tents. The Corps chauvinists charged with clearing the story fiercely contended that whatever Marines do, they don't "snuggle."

JUNE 22, 1942

Wedding bells are ringing more frequently than ever before in U.S. history. Estimates are that 1,600,000 couples will be married this year, an all-time high. Because so many of their bridegrooms are service men, most brides will marry in haste but with formal ceremony. Catering to this demand are bridal shops throughout the U.S. where a complete formal wedding can be arranged on a day's notice. Typical scenes in bridal shops are shown on these pages.

Love of frivolity continued to bloom among the editors of *Life*. Deeply engrossed in the serious problems of journalism in wartime, they remained fascinated with the lighter stories as well, stories, for example, about movie stars. One such star who clearly had a powerful grip on the imaginations of the top editors was Ginger Rogers, the show girl who became an actress and is now most famous perhaps for being Fred Astaire's lissome dance partner. A story done on Rogers in early 1942 put her on the cover for the third time, a distinction she shared with Franklin D. Roosevelt. The opening of this most recent story on her attempted to explain the attraction: "Ginger has become an American favorite—as American as apple pie—because Americans can identify with her. She could easily be the girl who lives across the street. She is not uncomfortably beautiful. She is just beautiful enough. She is not an affront to other women. She gives them hope that they can be like her. She can wisecrack from the side of her mouth, but she is clearly an idealist. She believes in God and love and a hard day's work. She is the living affirmation of the holiest American legend—the success story."

The adoring quality of the text indicates a rather high-level infatuation with Rogers, and indeed such was the case. Longwell and Hicks, both midwesterners like Rogers, had met her a year earlier. During a long session at the restaurant "21," Longwell had discussed with the star *Life*'s photographic depiction of *Kitty Foyle,* a popular novel about the problems of the modern working woman—who was played, naturally, by Rogers in the film. *Life*'s interest in this paradigm of beauty, humor and modesty grew, and in the summer of 1941 work was begun on a lengthy black-and-white picture essay about her, photographed by Robert Landry, a versatile fellow adept like her at wisecracking from the side of his mouth, whose most famous single picture remains one he took of Rita Hayworth kneeling playfully on a bed in her nightgown. According to an in-house newsletter, Landry and reporter Tom Prideaux had a delightful time with Rogers and her mother—who was always present—during the shooting, especially on trips when "to kill time the four sang (usually songs which Ginger or her mother had made up), played quiz games (which Ginger especially likes), and joked about Ginger's gum-chewing proclivities (Prideaux had the responsibility of keeping her supplied). Tom and Ginger played piano duets at night, 'Time on My Hands' ranking as their No. 1 rendition."

This happy spirit of camaraderie between the journalists and their subject culminated at the time of the closing, when Rogers came to New York and sat in on some of the work while the story was being put to press. This was an extremely unusual practice. Visits to the office by celebrated subjects usually consisted of brief walk-throughs and rather embarrassed handshakes from reporters and editors trying not to look too impressed. No one would dream of letting these people in on the final selection of pictures. But the adoration for Ginger was sufficient so that all the usual restraints (in many cases the photographers were not welcome at layout sessions) were off. "Billings, Hicks and Prideaux," according to the writer of the newsletter, "will testify that she behaved angelically and never said a word unless spoken to." Rogers apparently came in for several days, resisted the temptation to second-guess the choice of pictures and was on hand to give invaluable on-the-spot assistance with the writing of the captions. She revealed, for example, that one of her ancestors had introduced quinine to cure malaria in Missouri, "where church bells were rung every night to remind people to take their pills." Her biggest *Life* fan, Dan Longwell, was unfortunately away the week Ginger Rogers came to the office, but he telephoned, had her traced to a layout session with Billings and talked to her at some star-struck length while his colleagues fidgeted and waited.

JULY 6, 1942

In a friendly town like Harrodsburg, where neighbors call each other by first name and have watched each other's boys grow up and put on their first long

pants and graduate from school, the swallowing up of 66 of its young men in a single day is hard to bear. Even harder, in a way, is the lack of news about them—where they are, how they are doing, what they are getting to eat. It seems strange to read in the weekly Harrodsburg *Herald,* in the heart of blue-grass Kentucky, a list of instructions on "how to send . . . letters for prisoners of war in Japan or Japanese-controlled country."

Those first few months of the war brought many changes in the *Life* staff, and several of the men went into the service. One of the more prominent of these was Ed Thompson, who by mid-1942 and at the age of thirty-five had become a person of substantial influence on the magazine. Even at this time, he was probably better qualified to run the place than anyone but Billings, but the peculiarities of getting ahead in Henry Luce's company meant he would have to wait several years more—and a couple of managing editors—before he would get the chance. He acted as assistant to the two editors directly under Billings—Longwell and Hicks—and possibly exercised more operational control than either one of them. He ran the news section, he supervised the bureaus, he made many of the photographic assignments. Thus his departure left a real management gap. Billings acknowledged Thompson's special contributions to *Life* by abolishing his job and filling the parts of it with several people.

Naturally there was a sizable party to honor the popular Thompson on his departure to join the Army, in which he had a reserve commission and was assigned to the Tank Corps. (Because of his special professional expertise, he later was transferred, over his strong protests, to the Air Force, where he put together and edited an intelligence magazine called *Impact,* and eventually joined Eisenhower's staff in Europe.) The party, complete with huge photostatic blowups of Thompson's face and fake pictures of him with various luminaries including Adolf Hitler, was notable for its noisy quality and its affectionate songs. A verse of one, to be sung to the tune of a colossal hit of the era called "Deep in the Heart of Texas," went:

His mind is keen,
His ears are clean,
Clap hands for Captain Thompson!
His thyroid gland
Is simply grand,
Clap hands for Captain Thompson!

Another, to the tune of "My Bonnie Lies over the Ocean," reflected a little of Thompson's colleagues' real sense of loss at his going. The last verse:

Ed Thompson is joining the Army,
Who'll ever get out this poor mag?
Ed Thompson is joining the Army,
And Hicks is left holding the bag.

Billings, as usual, took note of the event in his diary. "Thompson was deeply moved by all this attention," he wrote, "and looked red and embarrassed. When I told him goodby at 7 he said 'Go quick now—or I'll cry.'"

JUNE 15, 1942

For the average Negro volunteer or draftee, Army life is no hardship. He is used to hard physical work, which is nine-tenths of a soldier's routine. He wants to learn about machinery and motors, and the Army gives him a chance. He likes the feel of a weapon in his hands, and thoroughly enjoys bayonet practice. The food is better than he generally gets at home. The base pay of an Army private ($21 a month, soon to be raised to $46 or more) does not look too meager. His living quarters, food, pay, furloughs, opportunities for recreation are equal to that received by white soldiers. There has been a decided increase in the number of Negroes attending officer-candidate schools. Except in the Air Corps, they are being trained in the same classes with whites.

The trivia that appeared in *Life* and the specifics of some of the home front coverage, even as the actual coverage of combat increased, inflamed some observers. One man, a *Life* public relations expert named Otis P. Swift, upset at what he thought was a government-inspired selling job on the "Hollywood War," fumed about the contents of one issue in a memo to one of the editors. "I would certainly use the June 29th issue as Exhibit A in an editorial on what is wrong with the U.S. attitude on the war," Swift wrote. "I have never seen a more trenchant exposition of U.S. mass imbecility." He complained about "an admiral who seems to have nothing better to do than pose and grimace for a photographer," 1,200 soldiers in "a traveling tent show in which men carrying Fourth of July sparklers join in a symbolic Wheel of Victory," other soldiers "snatching for cookies in a USO cookie jar, dancing the Lindy Hop with Dallas jitterbugs . . . competing in candle bowling, taffy pulling, tap dancing . . . lolling in a field in aviators' uniforms and putting flowers in girls' hair." "There is too damn much publicity in this war," he wrote, "and not enough war."

Swift also thought the ads in the issue reflected the insidious propaganda pitch that war is, among other things, "a delightful business." He cited one ad "proudly announcing that its wax is used in USO jitterbug centers," another proclaiming that the "U.S. War Effort [is] Speeded by Success over Athlete's Foot," a two-page picture of "a series of life rafts floating in the ocean containing bottles of Mr. Boston Sloe Gin."

Swift stressed that he was not "indicting" *Life*, and the editors seemed quite secure about the balance of coverage in any event. *Life*'s home front stories were not all froth. One in particular, which ran in August 1942, was a powerful attack on the progress of the war effort in Detroit and drew considerable praise and outrage around the country. Headlined "Detroit Is Dynamite," it told a story of failure at many levels in the production complex—failures of government, management and unions. "The result is a morale situation," the story read in part, "which is perhaps the worst in the U.S." And the writer concluded, not entirely hyperbolically, that it was "time for the rest of the country to sit up and take notice. For Detroit can either blow up Hitler or it can blow up the U.S." *Life*'s adman in Detroit, whose job it was to sell space to some of the very companies the article criticized, was leery enough about the backlash on sales to send all his clients a memo from general manager Heiskell explaining why *Life* did the story. "This country has been fed to the teeth with undocumented optimism," explained Heiskell in the course of a letter in which he forgivably if predictably pointed out *Life*'s history of taking courageous positions. "We published the story purely and simply because the people of the U.S. must know what is going on. . . . In times like these it is ever more important that we should be extremely realistic. Everybody in the country admits that things aren't going as they should be. *Life* simply states that belief—in concrete terms." More than a bit self-congratulatory, perhaps, but advertisers were generally mollified, and the story, possibly helped by the irate and independent action of some U.S. customs officers who ripped it out of copies of the magazine going into Canada, did well on the newsstands.

In Hollywood that first spring and summer of America's war, work on one of the magazine's most enduring interests, the photography of sexy women, went on apace. On the scene shooting a color portfolio of ten of the movie industry's most glamorous properties was a bright, brash, intensely competitive young man named Eliot Elisofon, who'd been born of immigrant parents on New York's Lower East Side and would give up free-lancing to join the *Life* staff late in 1942. His great energy often amazed his photographic subjects. "This lad reminds me," said Frank Lloyd Wright, "of a hungry orphan let loose in a bakeshop." Elisofon's interests were broad; he was a painter (he referred to himself as "a mild expressionist"), he'd been a social worker after graduating from college, later in life he became a fine cook and the author of cookbooks, he was an authority on African art.

But in Hollywood, where he came to be regarded as an authority on color by movie professionals, Elisofon was directing his formidable powers of concentration toward getting his pictures of the women. "I am going hog-wild on the color series," he wrote his boss Wilson Hicks. "Rosalind Russell tomorrow, and I will make her very ladylike, which I'm sure she is. On Sunday I'm doing Alexis Smith in a red bathing suit underwater [Smith eventually appeared in a light blue negligee stretched out on a couch that was a garish green]. And Monday Lana Turner against some sexy movie posters of herself, perhaps one of her and Gable. Turner will wear red [she wore blue in the magazine]. I have so far originated new color schemes for each girl and in keeping with her personality. . . . For Gene Tierney I have concocted a gray wall on which are placed at regular intervals white plaster casts of a hand. . . . We are going to try to get Garbo, too [they didn't succeed]. . . . The fun I am having doing the color series dates back to the days when I was a fashion photographer and never had enough props or pretty girls to work with. This is the town where you can go into a studio warehouse and point at anything you like. . . . Everyone in the studios [is] wild about the color already done. . . . Wait until you see Brenda Marshall seemingly floating (in Spirit) on a bed of fresh gardenias."

NOV. 20, 1942

General Patton rides his own tank, flying two white stars for his rank of major general, through the dusty, mountainous deserts of Southern California. From the desert heat and the dust, Patton learned many a lesson which will be valuable to him today in Africa. He says tank warfare is much like spaghetti. You can't push it from behind. A general has to be up front pulling it.

Within a few months Elisofon's concerns had changed greatly. "I was able to get excellent shots of the anti-aircraft fire," he wrote Hicks from North Africa after an air raid, "with several unusual shots of gunfire pouring into a well-lit spot. I saw the plane buckle under the fire and once again wished for the future film speeds and lenses which would have caught this scene."

A more aggrieved, competitive note crept into the communication. "Have heard from someone who came here from Algiers that Bourke-White expects to be back in America in a month," he said. "I still don't get the picture at all. I come here in the original operation. Have sense enough to get off and wait for a chance and then have her scoot in under my nose and she is lucky enough to be torpedoed on the way. I wonder if she'll get out a book on 'Torpedoed in the Med,' or afloat in a negligee. I am really dying of curiosity to know whether she had presence of mind to have someone in the lifeboat make a shot of her, chin outthrust, camera in hand. Oh, I've got the Bourke-White Blues."

MARCH 1, 1943

LIFE'S BOURKE-WHITE GOES BOMBING

First woman to accompany U.S. Air Force on combat mission photographs attack on Tunis.

Within a short time, such minor lacerations of ego seemed vastly unimportant. Elisofon was determined to be a great war photographer. "My ambition," he once said, referring to the Civil War photographer Mathew B. Brady, "is to be a small Brady." After photographing a battle in Tunisia, he wrote: "Sure enough an element of three [planes] decided to bomb our area. I was on my back ready to photo hits near us, but when I saw the bombs come out and start right for us, I must admit I turned over, put my entire body under my helmet and said 'Maybe this is it . . .' Of course I missed a great picture of bombs coming to the camera and a magic eye sequence or even three quick Contax pix would have been terrific but I am not ready yet for that. . . . I have tried desperately to avoid pretty pix. . . . I don't know what the censors will do with some of my pix of American casualties but they are enough to make any American fighting mad. . . . Plenty of blood, believe me. Too damn much."

MARCH 22, 1943 (Advertisement)

Under the flaring northern lights . . . a mess of Jap Zeros suddenly appears! But thanks to an amazing new Talon slide fastener, Arctic troops are out of their sleeping bags in a split second. This new fastener . . . developed after the war began . . . opens faster than any other slide fastener even known . . . saves precious time that can mean the difference between life and death.

The letters from photographers back to New York often began apologetically, oddly like letters home from camp. "I have been busy until now," wrote George Strock from New Guinea, where he had been covering a deadly jungle campaign against the Japanese. "Was covering the fight at the front lines every day until the fall of Buna village. Must admit that it's tough work as well as somewhat dangerous but I have the feeling that nothing will happen to me and so far I'm right. Our clothes were wet for a week," reported this nervy man who at one time had operated a portrait concession on an amusement pier in Venice,

California. "It rains almost every night. Shoes have been soaked and there is very little chance to take them off because of a possible night raid. We sleep in a helmet; this way we keep the body dry. Took one bath while there but the damn water smells like dead Japanese bodies. . . . Lt. Peabody and some soldiers with Tommy guns raided a Jap hospital supply dump one day and I took my Tommy and went along. Got swell pix of the whole thing. Ran out of film while in there but found some Jap film that fit the camera and used that. I saw Japs not more than 75 yards away. Sure would like to have shot some but that would have revealed our position. Was dangerous enough just getting through the Jap machine gun fire lanes. Gave a Rising Sun flag to the General that I got out of the raid. I have enough souvenirs anyhow." This cool, unassuming fellow, who exposed himself to the worst sort of danger again and again, was always going off on his own, and the New York office kept losing track of him. His photograph of three dead GIs lying on the beach at Buna was one of the first pictures showing American casualties that the censors allowed through. "You send a man into nowhere," Hicks reflected later, "and he gets the one picture that stirs the whole country."

The Pacific war was highlighting the work of other outstanding photographers as well. One was George Silk, a cocky, powerful New Zealander who'd served as an Army photographer with the Australians in the desert campaigns in Africa. Silk's picture of a New Guinea native leading a blinded soldier to an aid station was one of the most moving of the war, and Wilson Hicks hired him by cable on the strength of it. Another was Ralph Morse, a bouncy cheerful New Yorker who at twenty-four was the youngest man on the staff. The Navy cruiser he was on off Guadalcanal in the Solomon Islands was sunk one night along with three other ships, and Morse, his cameras lost, kept a young officer afloat for hours until they were picked up the next morning. When Morse got back to Guadalcanal with new cameras, he photographed a lot of heavy marine action on that bloody island where Americans won their first important victory in a Pacific campaign that would last three more years. On Guadalcanal at the same time as Morse was *Time* correspondent John Hersey, whose writing about the campaign appeared in *Life* (Hersey later moved over to the staff of the picture magazine) and then was made into a book, *Into the Valley*. A reviewer in *The New York Times* spoke of Hersey as "a new Hemingway, one whose single desire is to write 'truly,' basing every word on what the eyes have seen and the ears have heard," and said the book "should be pondered closely by everyone who has theories about the war and the world after the war."

MARCH 16, 1942

(by St. Clair McKelway)

He learned that his rifle must not be cleaned from the muzzle but that instead a patch soaked with hot water and coarse soap should be run back and forth through the barrel from the breech. He found out how to lay out his pack for inspection, how to clean spots from his clothes and how to mend them, how to roll his coats and set up his tent, how to administer first aid and how to carry the wounded and injured. He discovered, too, that every soldier should know how to make his will. Teed also learned not to think of commissioned officers as men like himself, but to expect them to be lofty, mysterious and inclined to look not at his eyes when they spoke to him but at his forehead.

As the war ground on, the magazine's efforts to get stories often caused conflicts with military authorities. "Relations between *Life* Magazine and the Pictorial Branch," wrote one frustrated Army headquarters public information officer, "are amiable. However, this branch feels that the management of *Life* Magazine has no regard for Army regulations or War Department policy and considers such restrictions, as we issue them, mere obstacles to be overcome rather than directives to be acted upon. . . . In attempting to explain our position in order to bring about a more satisfactory relationship, the writer got the impression that *Life* never had 'played ball' with the Army and didn't intend to do so; that it intended to continue in its efforts to break open every closed story possible and then seek BPR permission for release."

After including in his memo a list of more than a dozen instances of *Life* people's failure to follow military instructions about coverage, their continuing determination to get better treatment than the rest of the press and their generally duplicitous and high-handed behavior, the officer concluded—with little conviction—that things "would be much happier if *Life*'s present habit of refusing to take a Bureau negative as final could be curbed." His sense that the situation would not be easily cleared up was entirely called for. The notions of conforming to some bureaucrat's notion of what would make good pictures, of accepting setups that meant standing shoulder to shoulder with still photographers from newspapers and other magazines (especially other magazines), of giving up the pursuit of pictures that nobody else would even think of, were simply anathema to the best operatives from *Life*. From the management on down, they all shared the conviction that the magazine's requirements were special (if not unique) and that success depended on a certain exclusivity in virtually everything. Obviously there were other factors that had to be taken into consideration—national security, the legitimate needs of others, the pressure of time—but *Life* people looked at these most clearly only when reminded.

MARCH 22, 1943

Through a series of manuals, the Army is teaching its soldiers how to be expert killers. For one of these manuals Photographer Gjon Mili was asked to do a series of pictures illustrating the maxims "Be Alert," "Be Quick," "Be Quiet," and "Be a Killer." Mili came through with the pictures here, comparing the soldier attacking his enemy with a cat attacking a mouse. Like the cat, soldier must act stealthily and cruelly. On the next page are three methods for killing.

Possibly this constant pushing for a better vantage grew out of a sense of inferiority about the place of *Life*'s sort of journalism. However well tailored, well read, well heeled the best of *Life*'s operatives may have been, they were often regarded (and, in fact, sometimes regarded themselves) with a certain suspicion, as if they were a cut above burglars. In a memo to his boss, *Life* publisher Roy Larsen, Andrew Heiskell, an elegant type himself not easily looked down upon, wrote of this pervasive disregard. "Strangely enough," he said, "despite the fantastic success of *Life* and other picture magazines, news photography is not a respectable profession, and the photograph is not considered to be a complete and accurate medium for the reproduction of news and general information."

He ticked off a few examples of this: "1) We ourselves feel that to give weight, substance and solidity to *Life* we must run text articles. 2) The 'better minds' have a tendency to sneer at picture magazines and pictures. A magazine, because it is primarily composed of pictures, is not considered essential reading by those who want to know all about this world. I need not mention comments by various Time Inc. people about pictures. 3) News photographers are barred from many events open to reporters and placed in a lower and secondary category professionally. . . .

"It is probable that if we do nothing about this problem," he continued, "the natural course of evolution will bring respectability to photo-reporting in due course. I think it would be unwise for us to wait for this, particularly so since there is going to be an increasing belief that *Life* is a war baby, that photographs are good for covering war but that when peace comes they will not do the job."

Heiskell had some ambitious corrective steps in mind. "I therefore suggest," he wrote Larsen, "that we establish a broad program of action to emphasize the contributions of photography to this world, its value as a method of presenting news, its potential in terms of making complicated subjects simple, its great ability to make the normal as well as the abnormal newsworthy." To accomplish this laundering of the image of photography, Heiskell suggested a newspaper ad campaign, better promotion on the importance of the job done by photographers, the emphasis of photography's success as a selling tool to new subscribers, the establishment of scholarships at various universities for the study of news photography. "Use more photographers as speakers at advertising meetings," Heiskell offered as a way of stimulating *Life's* clients. "Everybody has a tendency to think of a photographer as a broken-down hack. They are always surprised when they meet *Life's* photographers."

Much of what Heiskell put forward, of course, made excellent sense and would be the basis, in fact, of promotion campaigns in the future. Even at the time he was writing, in early 1943, an ad printed in many newspapers all over the country stressed the unique contribution of *Life's* photographers. "No citizens," the ad copy declaimed, "far behind the fronts on which their fate was being decided, ever knew the sight and smell and flavor of battle as do today's Americans." This was because, the ad went on, of the amazing record made by "battle-wise photographers whose initiative and know-how are getting them to the newsworthy spot at the right moment. And that is but the beginning. For it also means the knowledge of how to make a picture story . . . how to get a series of pictures that will make *Life* readers feel they have actually eyewitnessed the great events taking place at the front." Twenty-five years later, the war that citizens eyewitnessed at home in their living rooms appeared not just in the pages of *Life* but in color pictures that moved as well.

OCT. 16, 1944

Midway through the first reel of *To Have and Have Not*, a new movie (see next page), the sulky-looking girl shown above and on the cover saunters with catlike grace into camera range and in an insolent, sultry voice says, "Anybody got a match?" That moment marks the impressive screen debut of 20-year-old Lauren (Betty) Bacall.

In Beverly Hills, Miss Bacall shares an apartment with her mother. Her favorite expression is "mad." She does "mad" scenes, smokes like "mad" and will go "mad" if the cigaret shortage doesn't soon let up.

Along with the photographers and reporters whose work was filling the pages each week, a small group of artists were providing dramatic oils and watercolors from fronts around the world. Some of these war artists had begun work for *Life* as early as 1941; the next year the Army took over the project. Then Congress, its members unconvinced of the value of this vivid documentation of the national war effort, refused to supply the funding, and *Life*, enthusiastically pushed by Dan Longwell, took over the contracts. The contribution of these painters—among them Tom Lea, Peter Hurd, Fletcher Martin, Paul Sample, Floyd

Davis, Edward Laning, Barse Miller, Aaron Bohrod, Reginald Marsh—gave an extra dimension to the magazine's coverage. Some were able to get places and to offer perspectives of the action or its background that no one else had shown. Tom Lea spent sixty-six days on the aircraft carrier *Hornet,* leaving the ship, in fact, just days before it was sunk by the Japanese. His paintings in a 1943 color essay gave a stark and detailed view of life aboard a carrier at war. And his account of a piece of the action, too, had great natural eloquence. One excerpt: "Around us the air is full of black popcorn, and we seem to be hearing a battle with our stomachs rather than with our ears. It pounds in on us and the smoke cuts at our eyes and covers our teeth with a kind of film. Men look up at the sky and read how close they are to death. A bomb hits off our stern—a near miss—throwing a towering, white, slow column of water high above the flight deck. The bomber that dropped it zooms up, as our anti-aircraft guns converge on him. He climbs into the cross fire and in the roar and confusion we see suddenly a burst of flame on his starboard wing and his climb slows, reaches the top and suddenly he is slipping back sideways. You find that your teeth are clinched so hard that you can hardly get the words out that you want to say—'Fall, you bastard, fall.'"

SEPT. 27, 1943

(by John Field)

LETTER FROM HOME

Dear Boys:
    Last week was a big week. The maples were red along the Warner River, there was a 40-lb. giant squash in Ralph Smith's garden in the village, and Muriel French exhibited a 2-lb. 6-oz. tomato which she had raised in her 4-H victory garden. The fishing and hunting were good. One man caught a 19½-in. black bass in Blaisdell Lake and on his way home from work Louie Bonette killed three hedgehogs (for which he got 50¢ bounty apiece). There was a sunflower growing 11 ft. 4 in. high near a house in town, and blue morning-glories twined about second-story windows on Tory Hill. The hay was almost in, the nights were cold, the summer was over.

With all the war coverage, the magazine kept churning out picture stories about the home front. The basic ingredient of these was immutable pluck; the guiding editorial vision was of an America that remained steadfast, calm, secure in its values, indomitable in crisis, facing the future with quiet humor and understated courage. It didn't matter whether the story was about a day in the life of Betty Grable's legs, the route of a rural mail carrier, a young girl in her first long dress, a visit to a small town in Iowa where twenty-three families awaited word of their men who were missing in action—there was a kind of overlay of unchanging resolve and determined cheeriness in almost everything.

One such story was called "American Sunday"; it was an attempt to link national purposefulness all across the country. In this somewhat grandiose and typically cornball effort, sixteen photographers from coast to coast took pictures on a single day that would emphasize our sturdy unanimity. For example, Fritz Goro went up to Eastport, Maine, to make a picture of the sun rising out of the easternmost point of America; Alfred Eisenstaedt traveled to Lincoln, Nebraska, to find a heartland family having a typical Sunday dinner; Peter Stackpole went to La Jolla, California, to photograph a soldier and his girl looking lovingly out at a Pacific sunset. What it all added up to was a forgivably dull exercise in patriotism by photography, a sort of Norman Rockwellism in pictures that was supposed to make its readers feel powerfully joined together in a common cause—which, in fact, they already did.

Far more likely to make Americans feel the reality of the struggle was a story done in the issue of July 5, 1943, the cover of which was a color portrait of the flag. In that issue the magazine ran the names of 12,987 men who had been killed in the first year and a half of the war. This astonishing compilation—each dead serviceman was listed by his state and hometown—took twenty-three pages, each bordered with stars, and was followed by an editorial that explored the ways Americans might find to justify the terrible loss of all these sons, fathers, brothers, sweethearts. It was a most powerful statement, and as well as being a rare and enterprising stroke of journalism, it also reflected *Life*'s deep sense of involvement with the cause.

JULY 5, 1943

Maybe you haven't got this message yet, maybe you haven't heard from the Adjutant General: well, you are just lucky—you can't know what it is to have your boy go over the Big Hill:

You can't know what it is to open the door of the garage and see the car he helped you buy—or to sit on the bed in his old room and see the picture of his girl there on the dresser, and his empty shoes in the closet—or to wander down into the cellar, as if looking for him, and see the holes he drilled in the cellar stairs when he was just a kid, and you bawled him out for it. You can't know any of this.

But maybe it would be a good idea to try to imagine it. For the people who get these telegrams ask a question: and this question is one that everybody in America must answer, and this question is, WHY?

What is it that called them over the Big Hill? What is the purpose?

The continuing war heightened everyone's feelings of mortality, not excluding those of Henry Luce, who invited John Billings to lunch one day in October 1943. The place was New York's stately and exclusive Racquet and Tennis Club. "Luce came in before I finished my cigarette and we went up to the dining room. He told me where he used to stay as a boy—with a Dr. Thomas on 52nd St. Then he said abruptly, 'What I wanted was that if anything should happen to me, if I should get run over by a truck, you'd take over my job as editor-in-chief of all the magazines.' I ohed & ahed with embarrassment and surprise. Did he think I could do it? He certainly did. Well, then, of course I would. That was fine! He hadn't spoken to anybody else about it—but he'd put it in a letter of intention or a corporate will. And that was that. And the rest of the lunch he spent telling me the principles of his personal foreign policy—Security, Prosperity, Freedom under law—all simple and easy. We went out. 'Well, let's shake on that other thing,' he said. So we shook hands & I left. What a vote of confidence from Luce! But it was secret & confidential and I couldn't discuss it with a soul (except F., of course). So I'm the heir apparent to Luce (but it isn't apparent, really)—which goes to prove you don't have to play around with him socially to get ahead. I taxied home by 2:30 and told F. She was depressed because it made the future look harder rather than easier."

Even in the midst of growing success and a circulation of 4 million, the sort of magazine *Life* had become and would be in the future was the subject of concern in the top echelons. "I have been greatly impressed," a troubled reader who was also a minister wrote Luce, "with some of the efforts which you have been making to lay the foundations for a better world and I appreciate what you have tried to do. Yet I wonder if you have ever thought that a better world is not made up totally of fair treaties and sound international relationships but that purity and decency are also important values in such a world. It seems a curious paradox to me that you would be working in one direction, on one hand, and in an opposite direction on another."

Luce neither bridled at this criticism nor ignored it as the unimportant complaint of a prude offended by some mildly titillating pictures from a theater story shot in Chicago. He wrote back: "You have, of course, put your finger on the major perplexity of any editor who is not merely interested in presenting the scandalous and alarming. That perplexity is what note to take of things which go on in the world that fall outside of what you describe as 'the beautiful and the kind and the good.'

"*Life* should mirror life. But how far? I should hate to think that anything which has ever appeared in *Life* should, because of this necessity, work against the high aims with which we are in such deep sympathy. . . . I am prepared neither to plead guilty to the indictment you imply nor to brush it aside as without any foundation whatever. But I shall take thought."

MAY 3, 1943

(by George Frazier)

Frank Sinatra, a gaunt, 25-year-old resident of Hasbrouck Heights, N.J., is what tired press agents refer to as the current singing sensation. His fans, who are tireless, have become so bold as to announce flatly that he is the new Bing Crosby. Inasmuch as there appears to be nothing wrong with the old Bing Crosby, this is a little perplexing. But Sinatra fans are a breed apart. The result of their purposeful worship is that in this, his first year as a solo attraction, Sinatra will earn approximately $250,000 from his work in night clubs, theaters, motion pictures and on the *Lucky Strike Hit Parade* radio program.

More specific, detailed questions about the magazine's future were being addressed by some of the top editors. The original prospectus, according to a memo produced by a small group under Longwell, "failed to forecast the future of *Life* accurately on two counts. It did not contemplate that a picture magazine could be edited for 4,000,000 purchasers at 10¢, and it did not give enough emphasis to the news picture." After the war was over, the memo went on, the magazine would be aiming for a circulation between 5 and 6 million. "If there is any one reason for our success," it continued, "it is the immense variety of editorial matter that appears in each week's issues. No other magazine can claim such a broad potential market as *Life*. . . . In addition to being a newsmagazine, *Life* is a combination of all general magazines, movie weeklies, the home publications, the scientific journals, *Harper's* and *The Atlantic*, fashion monthlies and the women's books. In general, we strive to outdo these publications in their own specialty. . . . As these publications perform a better service we, too, must improve our operation in each of these fields of interest."

There were several areas where these editors wanted substantial improvements. To increase foreign coverage, photographers and reporters would have to be based at permanent offices around the world and a bigger foreign news staff would have to be built up in New York. Because the magazine printed an average of only three color pages per issue and this on a very slow schedule, advances in the technology of color printing were necessary; the readers clearly liked color and the magazine should be offering them at least twenty pages an issue in five years. *Life*'s coverage of science and industry should be better, they said, as well as its treatment of the various areas of modern living, fashion, food, housing. The text department, where the major bylined articles were produced, needed strengthening. "Are we making full use

of books?" Longwell's group asked. "Do we publish enough poetry?
. . . Should we allow a small magazine like *The New Yorker* to go on
year after year publishing the best fiction in the country, or should we
try to deflect some of that talent for ourselves? . . . We must bear in
mind also that creative writing has been suppressed in Europe for a
great many years. After the last war there was a great upsurge of long-
dormant talent. That should happen again. And the editors who tap this
new talent will capture one of the great assets of the new world that is
coming."

Warming to the grandness of their vision for the blooming of the
picture magazine, already a powerful national force and only seven years
old, the editors went on with a certain orotund vagueness: "The American scene must have totally new expression after this war. If we win
the war on the terms we are now fighting, America enters into a new
era. It means American technicians and teachers throughout the world.
In spite of the ravages of war, the American should be a bigger person
with a broader outlook, and above all, with a thorough understanding
of his country and himself. Shouldn't we perhaps contemplate now
setting up a department to start studying America and the American?"
This would be a special "political, economic, sociological department"
that would take on large subjects, have prominent outside consultants
and "writers who are able to interpret the trend of living events. . . .
The department should grow so strong that if we wanted to, it could
produce a supplementary issue of *Life* on a single important subject
once a month." Positively simmering now with enthusiasm and optimism for the future, the memo writers envisioned "magazines that
might grow out of *Life*" and "supplements that would carry excess advertising and come out monthly or quarterly, or even form a mid-week
Life. If we want to publish supplements, our political-sociological department could even form the basis of a large pamphlet-of-the-month
club."

Among those who got a copy of this document was Roy Larsen,
Life's publisher, a hard-nosed reader of blue-sky memos. He took gentle
exception to the view that great variety had made *Life* successful. Larsen stressed the "importance of *Life* on the American scene" and went
on to write: "I think the thing—the one factor—responsible for *Life*'s
continued success is the outstanding nature of one or more of its articles,
whether picture or text, in almost every issue. Plus the accumulated
effect of an outstanding job on one particular subject covered over many
issues, to wit, our coverage and promotion of modern American art."

Larsen believed that for the future even more was needed. "What
I'm driving at is this," he wrote, "that true, we need a variety of ex-

cellence, but we need something beyond that to keep *Life* the outstanding American magazine and the most important, and that is a crusade, to describe it by an extreme word." He thought the instrument for such a crusade might be the special department Longwell's group mentioned. "In fact," Larsen finished, "as I read that section once more, I believe this is the 'soul' that I failed to find in your re-prospectus in my first two readings. . . . This, then, gives the opportunity for the importance which I feel is so essential to *Life* in the future, as it is today."

MAY 15, 1944

. . . The job will be the toughest American soldiers have ever taken on. It will be to breach the steel and concrete shore of Europe and annihilate the crafty and blooded armies of the Nazi Reich. The expectations are that they will do the job, but some will die doing it. Before they have died they will have confronted the Nazi with the qualities of the man America produces in the year 1944. Some of these men in England are shown on the following pages. Here at home those who pray may pray now for the immediate future of these American men. A responsible Army official has estimated that total casualties in the first month of the invasion, including wounded and prisoners, will come to 150,000.

D-Day (the D stands for Day) is Adolf Hitler's No. 1 concern today. The Germans have announced that D-Day will be preceded by a rolling Russian offensive and a concentrated air bombardment. The air bombardment has been on now for three weeks.

Early in May 1944 a big change for Time Inc. and for *Life* was set in motion. It began for managing editor John Shaw Billings on an otherwise slow Saturday. "I put copy through and got the issue closed without trouble," he wrote in his diary. "I didn't miss Hicks and Longwell much this week. All the speculation now is when is the Invasion coming? I hope not until I get South on the 15th. Lunch alone & the afternoon spent in advance planning and clearing accumulated trash off my desk. Luce came in, closed the door, pushed his hat on the back of his head and began a confidence: the company was too big for him to keep track of editorially. He needed somebody to ride herd on all three magazines—in fact, an editorial director and, not to beat around the bush, how would I like the job?"

"What's the matter with Gottfried or Grover?" the startled Billings asked, referring to Manfred Gottfried and Allen Grover, two of Luce's most senior and experienced men. Billings went on: "Luce had objections to both. Only I could fill the job, with my 'automatically perfect news sense.' I said I was an autocrat at *Life* and I wouldn't take his job unless I had the same autocratic power. He seemed to agree. But who to edit *Life*? Longwell? He says he wouldn't have it. . . . 'Well, think it over,' said Luce, exiting.

"I was flattered," Billings went on, beginning already to have appropriate doubts, "that Luce wanted me for top editorial boss of the company—but that's really his job and can it be divided up? Would I just be kicked upstairs and lose all identity with the magazines—another 33rd floor ghost? Would Managing Editors take my orders? After all, I have the seniority on them all now. A great question of my future usefulness which doesn't have to be decided now."

Even as he worried about the implications of this new position, Billings could not help chuckling to his diary about an old irony in his relationship with Luce. "It's a secret between Luce and me," he wrote. "But who says you've got to play up socially to your boss to get ahead? I treat Luce bad socially—and he still wants to promote me! Home with my head full of ideas on being 'editorial director' of whole company (how much I'd have to learn!) but F. said she didn't want me to take any job that meant more work and responsibility. After dinner I ran off [the movie] *White Cliffs of Dover* from 1940 poem. Not much good—trite story."

More than a month passed. The invasion of Normandy had begun. Billings had agreed to accept Luce's offer, with, as he wrote the editor-in-chief, only one outstanding reservation: "I don't want to lose my identity as a practicing journalist and editor in the Olympian mists of corporate responsibility." Now he was returning from vacation in South Carolina—but no one had yet told Dan Longwell that he was about to become the second managing editor of *Life*.

"Hicks and Longwell were on hand to greet me," wrote Billings about arriving at the office on June 19, "and tell me more details of their invasion make-over and coverage. Luce called me up, said he was glad I was back, that things were in a mess, a proof of the need for my new job. (An inky storm settled down on the city as we talked—a bad omen?) Luce was in his usual confusion and rush and had passed the details of installing me over to Larsen. Big question: Longwell as M.E. of *Life*? [Luce and Billings agreed it was the right solution.] I called Dan in, told him of my new job and offered him the job of *Life* M.E. 'Oh dear!' said Dan. 'This is a shock & a surprise,' and then his mind and words went whirling off on himself and his job. Yes, he would take it but only to work himself out of it quickly. (He was thinking too much of rest & holiday.) He babbled on about his plans of who would [do] this or that chore to relieve him."

Larsen took Billings to lunch in the Rainbow Room, a favorite spot at the top of the RCA Building for Time Inc. brass to talk over pressing business matters. Billings was annoyed at the thrust of the conversation. "All our talk," he wrote, "was of *Life* and Longwell and nothing about me or my editorial directorship. Nobody seems interested in that at the moment and I couldn't get Larsen down to the simple mechanics of announcement, office or masthead. I am still flapping around in the dark and am really left to appoint and install myself. Afterwards, Larsen and I had a session with Longwell, who gave a poor impression of himself by his constant chatter of how he hoped to get out of the M.E.-ship quickly, how he was getting old [he was forty-five at the time] & wasn't going to kill himself. The general idea was that we were going to seek a younger executive staff for *Life*—but what about Hicks? He needs special handling. A great flow of words from Longwell but no clear idea of an organization plan. Larsen sent him away to write one out."

Once more, Billings sounded a bit hurt about all the focusing on *Life*. "My job is eclipsed until Longwell and *Life* are settled. Back to editing *Life*—but not much heart for it. Home, pretty depressed about my new job, largely because its details are postponed. F. was in a whirl of home organization, too—and was also pretty tired and discouraged. After dinner I ran off *Arsenic and Old Lace*—but I was in no mood for a murder comedy and found Cary Grant's mugging anything but funny. More rain."

NOV. 22, 1943

This picture of Chili Williams, a New York model, appeared in the Pictures to the Editors department in *Life*, Sept. 27. Since then she has become the No. 1 pin-up girl of the U.S. armed forces. Even publicity-calloused Harry Conover, for whose model agency Miss Williams works, has never seen anything like the demand for her pictures. Three days after *Life* published a notice that he would supply them, his office received 1,035 requests. Letters since then have averaged about 500 a day until they have reached the total of more than 10,000.

Central to the whole business of making the erratic Longwell managing editor was that he have a reliable backup to support him and to fill in for him in his absence. "The key to the new set-up," wrote Billings in his diary, "is Joe Thorndike, who returned yesterday from the Middle East & Italy and who is to be Longwell's assistant managing editor and do most of the real work. Today Joe came to announce (confidentially) that he had decided to resign & go into the Army. Then I had to counter by telling him (again confidentially) about our plans for him. I left it with him to think over to give me a yes-or-no answer tomorrow. If he quit, he would seriously upset present arrangements. I didn't even tell Longwell about this possibility, just to spare him the extra worry. A [staff] lunch—big but dull as hell. I have little to worry about this issue:

a 12-page color essay on color [photography] & [John] Hersey's piece 'Joe Is Home Again,' both good enough to make any issue O.K."

The next day Thorndike reported he would stay, and Billings set about to advise the rest of the top members of the staff before Luce's memo on the changes appeared the following day. Hicks was the big worry; his rank was the same as Longwell's, and the two were natural rivals. "At first he was like a piece of frozen dough," the diarist wrote of Hicks's response when Billings, with Longwell present, told him. "But then he began to thaw out. Longwell began to talk about Hicks's increased authority & responsibility—the executive editor, etc. It was slow uphill work but finally I felt we were winning him over."

Soon afterward, as they were talking to people, Longwell suddenly left the office. "Then Longwell ran out on us," Billings wrote in clear annoyance, "to catch his train to Kent for a long weekend to rest up from the strain of editing during my absence. Dan is a weakling when it comes to responsibility!" But Billings charged ahead with advising the senior staff. "One by one," he reported, "I called them in and broke the news to them as an advance secret. Some liked it and some didn't— because they didn't like Longwell and his methods. Cort wanted to quit and become a 'swimming instructor.' [John] Field was all churned up about 'Longwell's confusion.' . . . This routine took up most of my afternoon—not counting a session with Luce, who tossed a variety of chores in my direction."

Luce's public announcement of the new job for Billings came the next day, June 23. "The simplest way to define this new post," Luce wrote, "is to say that the Editorial Director will henceforth be the only officer who is empowered to give orders or 'directives' to a Managing Editor or Producer of any of the company's publications. . . . Hereafter as heretofore, the Editor-in-chief will consult with Managing Editors and others. But all decisions directly affecting editorial operations will be made by the Editorial Director. The authority of the Editor-in-chief will be exercised by the Editorial Director. The authority of Managing Editors will be subject to the Editorial Director—and to no one else."

In an earlier memo sent only to his top editors and executives, Luce had been a little more succinct about the distinction between his own job and the one he was creating for Billings. He spoke of Time Inc.'s editorial activities as being in two rough categories: "1) those directly and inescapably related to getting out a current issue, 2) those . . . which have for their object the getting out of bigger and better issues months or years hence. . . . Billings will concentrate mostly on the first category. And one of the reasons for setting up this job now is to enable Luce to be more effective in trying to supervise the activities of the second category." So Billings, in short, as Luce's deputy, would be the operational supervisor of all the magazines, while Luce concentrated more on planning and policy. "[F]rom Billings," he wrote, "you may expect more action and less talk than from the Editor-in-chief." This last may well have been looked forward to as something of a blessing by managing editors who would welcome the sort of sensible, calm support that Billings would give—without the abundance of nervous cogitation Luce often threw in, too.

SEPT. 4, 1944

Within the first postwar decade television will be firmly planted as a billion-dollar U.S. industry. Its impact on U.S. civilization is beyond present prediction. Television is more than the addition of sight to the sound of radio. It has a power to annihilate time and space that will unite everyone here in the immediate experience of events in contemporary life and history.

Within a week, Billings's long and successful reign at *Life* was over. As he recorded virtually everything else that took place in his life, he reported the surprise party the staff gave him at the end. "Suddenly my door opened," he wrote, "and Larsen marched in leading the whole staff into my office for a farewell party. (I grit my teeth and was determined to take it nicely.) A hundred or so people flocked in, all the little Bobby-Sox girls, the Morgue girls, a swimming mass of unknown faces. Joe Kastner was Master of Ceremonies." They gave him two dozen red roses and a silver cigarette box. Then thirteen people lined up and each presented him with a volume of the Oxford Dictionary of the English Language. "Next the gags: a cover of myself as an Indian chief and a locomotive with me as engineer. I was pretty moved by this display and muttered a few words of thanks—then the tension was broken when [two of the layout crew] wheeled in a big keg of beer and the party really started. I circulated among the girls, giving each of the senior ones a red rose. I drank beer and cracked jokes and came close to enjoying this shindig in my office." It would be more than ten years before John Billings, at fifty-eight, finally retired in a mixture of bitterness and relief to live in South Carolina on the family plantation he so loved. In a letter to Luce, he'd characterized himself as "a silly old figurehead," and there can be no doubt that he never enjoyed his work again the way he'd relished it at *Life*. There he felt poised and powerful and needed. It happened pretty much as he feared in the years after he left. He was good at the new job Luce gave him, but "in the Olympian mists of corporate responsibility," working effectively and loyally as Luce's deputy, he somehow lost touch with the core of his pride, that he was "a practicing journalist and editor." Billings was more than that, really. He was one of the very best, and he was the perfect man—cranky, steady, nurturing, meticulous, energetic, honorable—to give the great American magazine a splendid start in life.

And his steadying presence was immediately missed. "I went down to see Longwell," Billings wrote in his diary a month later. "Things are still churning, copy was far behind and tempers were raw. Longwell seemed unaware of all the commotion. I dropped in to see [the head researcher] and she broke into tears at the pushing around Longwell had given the staff—and for no reason. I gave her a handkerchief and sat listening to her tale of woe. Three girls had collapsed in the copy room. 'Aw, to hell with it' was the reporters' attitude. The writers didn't know what Longwell wanted from them. The production dept. was about ready to brain him. [Worthen Paxton] was mad as hell. In fact, everything on *Life* was a mess—largely because Longwell and Thorndike lack executive ability. It's flattering to have people miss you and your system but the situation was dangerously bad. Psychologically the staff is suffering under illusions there is no end in sight—as when I return from vacation. I left Longwell a fine staff, with morale high, and now in a month he's on the verge of ruining it. *Life* is not the 'happy ship' which was my brag. I went to a quick lunch alone—and back to [the *Life* floor]. Longwell was racing about to catch the 3:40 to Kent; his week-ends always come first with him. I told him to go ahead and leave—but I also told him his ship was close to mutiny and he'd have to jack himself up. I hope he worries plenty at Kent. Anyway here's a new problem for me—or *Life* will become a hell-hole like *Time*. Luce was at my old desk racing through his editorial to catch the train to Greenwich. He finished & [John K.] Jessup and I put it in final shape to print. *Life* was a shambles when I left for home about 4."

APRIL 17, 1944

In the Army Effects Bureau, where the possessions soldiers leave behind are sent, the dead men's things are unpacked, sorted, packed again and sent to the soldiers' families. From this emptying of dead men's pockets come Bibles, prayer books, letters, snapshots, diaries. There are walrus tusks from men in the north, scarabs from men who died in Africa and souvenirs from all over— a stuffed alligator, a Japanese life raft, an almost-complete German machine gun, a pouch of unset diamonds. One boy carried a circular from a muscle-building company, still undecided as he went to his death whether he should buy the regulation "chest-pull-and-bar-bell combination" at $5.95 or the "super-strength set" at $6.95.

There was a lot of pious talk at *Life* over the years about the photographers—but as a group, the way people generalize about cops or baseball players—about how the magazine simply couldn't exist without them (which was true, of course), about how particularly sensitive and creative they were (which in some cases was true on either or both counts), about how they required especially deft and understanding management (which they by no means always got), like prima ballerinas or lions with painful splinters in their pads.

Now and then someone would haul off in one of these conversations and say that he really *liked* photographers, that they were, in fact, among his dearest friends. If the talk was in a polite stage, he might be given quizzical looks at this. Obviously what he said *could* have been true and actually was in a number of cases; there are many examples of lasting friendships, affairs, even marriages (and divorces, too) between photographers and people who did other things on the magazine. And when it was working well, the professional team relationship that quite often developed between *Life* photographers and reporters produced extraordinary journalistic successes.

But this sort of generous, sweeping evidence of esteem further obscured one immutable fact. It was that many staff members didn't really like the photographers at all, and the photographers didn't like them, either.

Editors, writers and reporters often looked down on photographers, thinking of them as marginally talented, babyish, unreliable, opportunistic, self-important, boring and even stupid. All these things were now and then so, and in amazing combinations, as they were so about many of the non-photographers at the place. For their part, photographers often considered the others snobbish, slow-witted, freeloading, blind, callous, treacherous, cowardly and incapable of knowing the difference between a really good picture and some hokey setup shot banged off by the clowns at the wire services. Some of the time, naturally, the photographers were right.

This great gap of understanding came about possibly because there was room for reasonable envy on both sides. *Life* was, after all, a picture magazine, and the photographers were the people who went out and actually got the exciting, touching, terrifying pictures that made the huge audience buy. Thus, when the stories were really notable, the photographers got most of the credit (after taking most of the risks); they were the famous ones whose names popped up in the columns, who hobnobbed with senators and novelists, whose bodies allegedly (not always) frolicked in the beds of grateful stars and starlets.

The editors, writers and correspondents, on the other hand, remained largely unknown to the readers. This was galling to some, who felt their own contributions deserved more notice, and a few reporters complained, too, that photographers used them as "donkeys" and "caddies," loading them up with heavy equipment, requiring them to make plane, hotel and restaurant reservations and treating them like lackeys.

On their own behalf, the photographers envied the others for the roles they played in the conception and execution of the stories. Most picture stories at *Life*, it is fair to say, were discovered or somehow dreamed up by non-photographers. And once the photographer had made his or her absolutely crucial (and often deeply personal) contribution to the job, the editors took over. Generally speaking, photographers did not select the pictures that were used in the stories (they usually played little or no part even in deciding which pictures the editors would see), and they had little or no say about the emphasis pictures were given or the space their stories got in the magazine. Likewise photographers were not consulted about the writing or the headlines in the stories, even those stories that had originated with them. This sort of exclusion was usually met with little more than grumbling—although at least two famous photographers, David Douglas Duncan and the anguished and brilliant W. Eugene Smith, broke with the magazine over their indignant (and rejected) insistence on maintaining substantial control over their own stories.

Yet it is at least reasonable to suggest the possibility that among the most considerable of *Life*'s gifts to twentieth-century American culture is the creation of the *Life* photographer as a recognizable stock character. The character appeared almost with the start of the magazine. He—and occasionally she—differed greatly from the public image of the ordinary newspaper operative who wore his press card in his hat, smoked cheap cigars, swarmed rudely all over his subjects, fired off flashbulbs in their eyes and hollered coarsely for the show of more bosom or leg.

The *Life* version was far more elegant. Miniature camera draped discreetly around his neck (it was only much later that the hanging of several cameras at once became fashionable), a Gitane—its ash just at the breaking point—sending a plume of smoke past a cool, unblinking eye, trench coat slung carelessly over one shoulder, he looked in his Italian shoes and his calming suit from Cork Street like the kind of fellow who would be presentable—even desirable—in any situation. Definitely a romantic type, he starred in movies and plays (*Rear Window, The Philadelphia Story*), doubled as a detective in mystery novels and was usually a wry, funny, sexy sort (brave, too, terribly brave, of course) who had been *everywhere* where he had done *everything*. There was little useful he didn't know, and he was a connoisseur of wines. The *Life* photographer never pushed his subjects around, he just

whipped out that little camera and took marvelous pictures before anyone knew what was happening. And when he left the scene, he usually
took the best-looking woman in the place with him.

JAN. 31, 1944

**A trench coat over him, an American's body lies where it fell. Wrote Capa:
"Most of the burial parties came under fire on this hillside and they too were
killed. With its trees scarred by shellfire, its mud and its dead strewn about,
the mountain slope looks like pictures of the last war."**

There's a photograph made in London in 1944 showing a sizable
group of *Time* and *Life* correspondents, artists and photographers just
before D-Day. They are dressed in uniform, and though the pose is
casual, there is a certain formality about the gathering. It is as if the
participants were posing for a class picture, something that mattered to
them, a picture of some importance that they could agree might be of
value later for the record.

But one of them, seated far on one side of the group, is behaving
quite unlike the others. He is offering an entirely impolite view of
himself to the camera. He seems utterly bored by the proceedings. He
is looking not at the lens but at what appears to be a paper airplane in
his hands. A cigarette hangs from his lips; his hat is pushed far back on
his head. This insouciant fellow (actually his bearing smacks a little of
playful contempt) was Robert Capa, and his artful separation from the
rest of the group was entirely typical. Capa, who was already the most
famous of modern war photographers, a man who embodied bravery
and professional skill and coolness under fire, was a supremely individualistic character who was never comfortable being just one of anybody's
group. He was, in fact, according to the phrase coined by his fellow
war correspondent and author John Hersey, "the man who invented
himself," and he seemed always, at least to dazzled and admiring observers, to be playing some facet of the glamorous role he had worked
out.

Born Endre Friedmann in Budapest in 1913, he literally concocted
Robert Capa in 1935 when, after a few years spent developing considerable photographic skills in Berlin and Paris, he decided that people
would be more likely to buy pictures from a mysterious American
named Capa (the name possibly lifted from movie director Frank Capra,
whom Friedmann admired) than from him. He was right, and within a
short time this intense, swarthy, black-haired young man with luxuriant
eyebrows had become renowned for his black-and-white pictures from
the battlefields of the Spanish Civil War. The best known of these, of

a white-shirted Loyalist soldier holding out his rifle and falling backwards at the instant he was mortally wounded, is one of the most famous combat pictures ever taken. In fact, it became so important as a symbol of man's pitiable vulnerability in war that it almost didn't matter that there were questions about how Capa got it and whether it was staged. Capa's own accounts of the making of the picture on the Cordova front vary somewhat, but recollections of shattering moments often vary, and virtually everything in Capa's record as a photographer in war action suggests that he should get the benefit of the doubt in his claim that the picture was made at the precise moment the soldier was hit by machine-gun fire.

In any case, his many pictures taken in action in Spain mark the beginning of a career forged under terrible risks in China, North Africa, Sicily, Italy, France and Germany and which came to its almost logical end when he stepped on a Vietminh land mine while photographing a mission French troops were carrying out not far from Hanoi. That was on May 25, 1954, Capa was forty, and he had without question become a legend in his own short time.

The legend was built of more than bravery and gut-wrenching pictures. It had to do with associations with famous friends (Ernest Hemingway, John Steinbeck), love affairs with beautiful women (Ingrid Bergman) and above all perhaps the constant projection of his own romantic image. The cigarette dangling from the lips, the taste for fine food and wine, the bedroom eyes, the richly rolled Hungarian accent— all were accouterments of the persona Capa so lovingly developed over the years. Even the things he said and wrote had a marvelous laconic quality, as if his pal Hemingway had written them for him. "I will be on my good behavior today," he told the men with him on the last day of his life. "I will not insult my colleagues, and will not once mention the excellence of my work." "War is like an actress who is getting old," he'd said more than ten years earlier. "Less and less photogenic and more and more dangerous." "The food was good and we played poker," he wrote for *Life* about his trip to Normandy on D-Day. "Once I filled an inside straight but I had four nines against me. Then just before six o'clock we were lowered in our LCVP and we started for the beach. It was rough and some of the boys were politely puking into bags. I always said this was a civilized invasion."

Capa's relationship with *Life* over the years he worked with the magazine somehow illuminates his determination to be independent, not one of the crowd. Many photographers—and editors, writers and reporters as well—pursued their association with *Life* hard and clung to it once they got it. For many of them, being part of the magazine's family enhanced their own identity. They didn't really amount to as much—or so they privately felt—without wrapping themselves in the logo. The benefits it brought—of access, money, camaraderie, convenience—were worth the losses of choice. A lot of people, in fact, did not miss the losses at all, though they may have complained about them from time to time. They preferred it that the managers made their decisions and shaped their liberties.

But Capa, though he was often identified with *Life* (and happily passed through whatever doors it opened for him) and was surely the prime public model of the cocky, debonair, woman-conquering *Life* photographer who was a familiar fiction in those midcentury years, remained basically quite aloof, even when he was attached. Though his pictures had been published in *Life* since 1936 and he had been quite ardently wooed by its editors ("I know your modesty will not lessen when I tell you that you are the No. 1 war photographer today," Wilson Hicks wrote him in 1938), Capa and the magazine never seemed comfortable together. The photographer, a very shrewd, even ingenious entrepreneur of his own skills, had various contractual arrangements with the magazine (and others, worldwide) and was actually on the staff for only about a year and a half at the end of the war. His last assignment in Vietnam was for *Life*, and it had come after a considerable hiatus.

FEB. 5, 1945

On the second day of the breakthrough the Germans added a detail to the frightful total of their guilt.

At a road junction near Malmédy, German tanks overpowered a little column of American trucks. The Germans herded some 159 Americans into a field by the road. A German officer spoke to a tankman, who shot at the prisoners with a pistol. Another German then set up a Schmeisser machine pistol in an armored car, massacred the Americans at point-blank range.

The men who were still alive lay among the dead for an hour. Some of them moaned and the Germans shot them in the head. Finally many of the Germans went away. Then the survivors, most of them wounded, got up and ran to a woods. Fifteen of them, weeping with rage, got back to tell what happened.

Even in the most productive period of his career, Capa chafed under the authority of the editors, became mistrustful of Hicks and was bored with many of the assignments he got in the United States in between his tours of duty on various war fronts. Many of the *Life* people were his good friends (and many less flamboyant and talented than he idolized him), and he obviously valued the times—relaxed, hilarious and desperately dangerous—he shared with them. But he simply did not intend to submit to the sort of control that working full-time for *Life* would involve. He wanted to be able to do as he pleased—with himself and with his pictures—and it was with this sort of independence in mind for himself and other highly regarded photographers like David Seymour and Henri Cartier-Bresson that he founded the Magnum agency.

The rich Capa legacy, which includes the refreshing fact that he occasionally had to break away from the pursuit of pictures of war just to chase good times, includes, too, a fatalism that was often expressed ironically. "I'm getting too popular," he told *Life's* Will Lang on the subject of how soldiers were always asking him to go along on their operations, "and someday this popularity will get me killed." For all his exaggerations and occasional distortions, he knew the value of understatement. "It was very unpleasant there," he said of his time on the beach of Normandy, where he made historic action photographs of Americans in the water, "and having nothing else to do, I started shooting pictures."

Proud, driven, fiercely competitive (he was very angry when another *Life* photographer, Ralph Morse, got sent to cover the German surrender at Reims), he took pictures of the war—of grim infantry actions at Salerno and Bastogne, of the liberation of Paris, of the exhaustion and horror and jubilation of soldiers and civilians throughout Europe—as if only *his* pictures, photographs by Robert Capa, would be left to tell the whole awful story. Sometimes covering it must have exhausted him—seldom more so, surely, than when he was working with the infantry as they took the city of Leipzig, Germany, in April 1945, days before the end. A soldier Capa was photographing as he set up a machine gun in a window overlooking the street was suddenly killed on the spot by a sniper. And the horrified photographer, the sickening futility of war once more in his viewfinder, crouched there and took pictures as the young man's blood pooled on the floor.

MARCH 12, 1945

Dead hands still thrusting his rifle forward, a marine lies where he fell a few yards up on Iwo's beach, a bullet hole drilled through his helmet. Jap marksmen killed many thus. But a shocking number of U.S. casualties resulted from mortar and artillery fire. Medical Corpsmen treating the grievously torn bodies talked wistfully of "nice, clean bullet wounds."

"In a few hours I shove off on something very tough, in an effort to get the twenty-four-hour period in a soldier's life that is worthy of these kids." This was the beginning of a short letter W. Eugene Smith wrote his friend Shelley Mydans in May 1945, just as he began work on his last assignment of the war. Within hours he would be seriously wounded by shrapnel; the injuries to his mouth, face and hand would trouble him for the rest of his life. The letter is not only a statement of the photographer's feelings about the importance of the job he was planning; it provides real insight into his feelings about himself and the integrity of his work.

"I know," he went on with obvious anguish, "that this is a completely impossible assignment to do with the power that I wish—but to God, and all, I must try. If it falls flat on its face and has no power, then I would rather die—and I know that I cannot say what must be said. This hurts so very deeply, and I am scared, I don't know whether this fright is from my own inadequacy, or from the physical danger involved. I think it is from the fright of failure, and I cannot bear to fail, and I live through this and on into the future—I cannot bear to fail. It would be much better to die tomorrow night than to live and fail these kids, and in the battle for peace. Oh damn, how I know that I cannot reach high enough, I haven't the power."

Gene Smith was going to try to shoot some of his pictures "by the light of flares," he told Mydans, "and they will be enemy, but I have to try for this terror in the darkness—people somehow must realize." In a postscript he added: "This would be so easy to ham and fake and gag to make a 'good layout.' But if this is what they expect I'll quit. Above all else it must be an honest story."

His fears of failure, that he wouldn't be able to do the job in the way it *had* to be done, that his editors would want him to distort his work or would try to distort it themselves, these ingredients of Gene Smith's torment appear in the letter and came up again and again in his life. Smith was a man whose fierce inner pain often came to the surface; even in 1945, when he was twenty-seven, he felt himself embattled. His sense of being misunderstood and betrayed, especially by his editors at *Life* (he did not actually join the staff until 1945), would only deepen over the years and would eventually lead to his resignation in 1954. "There was no way," writes Ben Maddow, the author of a perceptive illustrated biography of Smith entitled *Let Truth Be the Prejudice*, "to end the contradiction between the commercial ideas of *Life* and the social and aesthetic views of Gene Smith." Fair enough, but a lot of high hopes, great effort, need and even love went into the grinding quarrel, which was the despair of both sides.

Smith, who was born in Wichita, Kansas, in 1918 and died after having a stroke in Tucson, Arizona, almost sixty years later, was without question one of the photographic geniuses of his time. In the field of photojournalism, he stood out as an artist of extraordinary power and perception, and several of the black-and-white picture essays he did—

on a country doctor, a midwife, life in a Spanish village, mercury-poisoned sufferers in the Japanese city of Minamata—still haunt the memories of people who first saw them decades ago. Charming and boyishly friendly when he wanted to be, a good companion and an ardent lover of fine music, he was also—like many people of great talent—insecure, arrogant, jealous, inconsiderate of others, complaining, suspicious at times to the verge of paranoia and occasionally impossible to deal with. A man who suffered a lot of physical as well as psychic pain, he attacked his own health with drugs and alcohol. He was extremely competitive, endlessly hungry for acknowledgment of his worth (no matter how much praise was given to him) and furious about slights, real and imagined. He was also impressively hard on himself, full of dire expectations for his own failure, for his inability to get the job done according to his own unforgiving standards. With all that, when his great energies, technical skills and intuition were focused on the work, he performed superbly, time after time.

His pictures of the war first made him famous. But the young dropout from Notre Dame, whose mother had taught him how to use a camera, had moved to New York and was already known to magazine editors before the war. Wilson Hicks, among others, was interested in his work and gave him assignments. His willingness to take risks to make good pictures was evident as early as 1942, when he nearly blew himself up and damaged his eardrum in the course of shooting an utterly realistic explosion picture for the cover of *Parade* (it also won him a prize in a contest run by *Popular Photography*, and Smith, characteristically, thought it was "disgusting"). He chafed at not being in the war and felt demeaned by the sort of photography he had to do at home, pictures of pretty girls, of men being trained to fight. Finally, in mid-1943, he was overjoyed when the Ziff-Davis magazines got him accredited as a Navy correspondent in the Pacific.

Over the next two years Smith threw himself into combat coverage with the furious concentration Capa was showing on the other side of the world; he was on hand for thirteen invasions as Americans fought their way up the Pacific islands toward Japan. Often on assignment for *Life,* he landed on Tarawa (where he was outraged because he was let ashore too late), Saipan, Guam, Leyte, Iwo Jima and finally Okinawa. Before Tarawa he flew with Navy carrier forces on strikes, and late in the war he was the only photographer to go along on a raid over Tokyo itself. On this mission, according to his own later account, "I never really found out whether it was a serious order or not, but [Navy brass] said they would agree to my flying if I would give permission to my being shot in case of a crash landing in Japan." Smith, it seemed, had some advance information that no one wanted to fall into the hands of the Japanese. "I agreed to this provision after serious consideration," he wrote, "for the terms did not seem unjust when hundreds of lives might depend upon the keeping of the secret of the coming landings at Iwo Jima."

AUG. 28, 1944
(by Robert Sherrod)

What the Americans found at the battle's end staggered their imagination, strained their credulity. To understand, they had to throw away all their occidental concepts of the human thinking processes. There, on the northernmost point of Saipan, a large segment of the Japanese civilian population was calmly, deliberately committing suicide. Hundreds of human beings, perhaps thousands, had chosen to die as what the Japanese so fondly call "shields for the emperor." The sight which hit the Americans' eyes on the rocky tip of this far Pacific island is shown on the next pages.

Gene Smith's feelings of horror about the war and his compassion toward all those who were caught up in it are clear in his stark black-and-white photographs—of twisted Japanese dead at Tarawa, of exhausted and terribly hurt American men on Saipan, of terrified women and children being routed out of caves in Saipan. And his own accounts of the action are raw and moving. About Iwo Jima he wrote: "I walked up and down the beach amid the mortars, and the wreckage of man and machine, and soon we did not seek shelter, for you cannot dodge that which you could not see or hear. . . . During the night we estimated that from 1500 to 2000 mortar and artillery shells fell within 200 feet of us, and screams from the wounded begging for medics filled the silence between the whistle of shells and the crack of non-warning mortars. And in the gray morning a direct hit on an ammo-carrying 'duck' silenced the section of our artillery right behind us, and after the first violent explosions I leaped out of the hole, and ran over the bodies of our dead in the direction of the exploding duck, and the stuff whistled close, and after a few hurried closeups I tore once again to the comparative safety of the gun mount."

On Iwo Jima, on the day that wire service photographer Joe Rosenthal made his famous picture of the flag raising on Mount Suribachi (which Longwell refused to publish because it was a setup done specially for the picture), Smith got himself into a practically suicidal position between two deadly forces. "I was ahead of the front lines in a shellhole. I was in front of a [U.S.] tank and directly in line with a Jap field piece a good distance ahead. They were trying to knock each other out with point-blank fire. I, in between, would watch for the muzzle flash from the Jap gun, flatten out, then jerk to shooting position as the shell would land in the vicinity of the tank. This lasted for an hour, ended in a draw."

True to his perfectionist form, Smith berated himself after leaving this ghastly island battle. "I was very shamed and very depressed by the very poor pictures I had made on Iwo," he wrote. "My headaches and stomach were bothering me, so I went to a doctor on Guam to get some codeine tablets for my headaches. I have said that I was in the midst of heavy depression. This was no result of the war, for all of my photographic life I have suffered these periods of extreme depression after not being able to reach the photographic heights I had tried for." The doctor on Guam told Smith that he was indeed suffering from battle fatigue and should return to the States. But Smith ignored the caution and went on to Okinawa, where his wounds finally took him out of the action.

The war, and its intense demands on him, really brought Smith's genius into focus. And in the years after that, all through the 1950s and 1960s, it developed more. Observations he wrote for *Life*, for an article being prepared on photography, reflect his blunt directness about things that mattered to him. "The way we covered a war," he wrote, "or rather the way I covered a war, was to ask, each time I returned to the front, where I could expect to get into the most trouble for that day or series of days, for to get the picture that I needed, my subjects had to be in trouble, serious trouble, and the worse it was, the more possibilities there were for me to show the world what war was.

"Many people have shaken their heads in amazement at my 'iron nerve' and seemingly complete lack of fright. My only accomplishment in this direction was that my idealism and stubbornness gave me control over my nerves that let me isolate the turmoil to my stomach (thus ulcers) and left my mind clear and my nerves steady and capable of extremely slow exposures if necessary. Actually I am a very emotional guy, that explodes and splutters all over the place if there is no need to call forth the control necessary for coldly calculating work. . . .

"In closing," Smith wrote with his typical winning blend of idealism, naïveté, humility (of a certain self-important cast) and honesty, "I wish to sum up my photography in the war. I have made but a handful of pictures that have even been partially successful and are worth saving. And though I have no regrets with decisions I have made, I do regret the failure of my photography in this war, and the rest does not matter. It only matters that I have failed these men who fought this war, just as our leaders are now failing in the peace."

MAY 14, 1945

Elsewhere in Hitler's Reich, Germans stopped killing others and began killing themselves. In Weimar the mayor and his wife, after seeing Buchenwald atrocities, slashed their wrists. In Nürnberg the local Nazi leader shot the mayor and then himself. In Berlin, where the Russians reported mass suicides, Propaganda Minister Goebbels' chief assistant said that even Hitler and Goebbels had killed themselves. Hitler, reports went, had shot himself; Goebbels had taken poison.

The records of Capa and Smith do not diminish the accomplishments of the many other photographers who covered the war for *Life*, who put their own lives at risk again and again to bring home this painful light-and-shadow record of the great conflict. It was as if they all shared the sense—Mydans, Bourke-White, Silk, Morse, Frank Scherschel, John Florea, Dmitri Kessel, John Phillips, Elisofon, David Scherman, Peter Stackpole and at least a dozen others—that, more than anything else, their close-to-the-bone pictures gave meaning to the shocking life-and-death struggles being played out daily in front of their cameras. Nobody really wanted to say it (although promotion ads often burbled about the intrepidity of the photographers), but their photographs gave the magazine a kind of basic human dignity and even grandeur, a tone that spoke of suffering and pity and man's amazing ability to prevail, that only war could bring. The same thing would be seen again in Korea with the work, among others, of David Douglas Duncan, John Dominis and Hank Walker and in Vietnam with Larry Burrows, Co Rentmeester and John Olson. *Life* was never more powerful than when its photographers took their own awful chances and went out to cover the agony and chaos of war.

SEPT. 17, 1945

World War II formally ended at 9:08 on Sunday morning, Sept. 2, 1945, in a knot of varicolored uniforms on the slate-gray veranda deck of the USS *Missouri* in Tokyo Bay. When the last signature had been affixed to Japan's unconditional surrender, Douglas MacArthur declared with the accent of history, "These proceedings are closed."

8

A Strange and Wonderful Tension

WHATEVER HIS SHORTCOMINGS AS A MANAGING EDITOR of the magazine (he occasionally forgot that he had sent stories to press), Dan Longwell had a sparky, enthusiastic way of talking—and thinking—about *Life*. It was infectious, too. Even when his bosses (Luce, Larsen, Billings) had been complaining behind his back about what a mess he was at running things, they were somehow buoyed by the irrepressible affection he felt for their baby, now going on ten and still growing. "I can't sum up a philosophy for *Life* except this," Longwell wrote in a rambling memo to Luce about reorganization in 1946, "the title of the magazine is *Life*. Our first and primary duty as editors is to make the magazine reflect its title. It is a wonderful title. It is a wonderful magazine. *Life* can lash out, but *Life* does like people. It likes America, and is passionately for the democracy of the individual. It believes with great feeling in the dignity of man. *Life* will print the shocking and the horrid, but it loves the beautiful. And above all, *Life* has a sense of humor." Luce was so tickled with this section of the memo that he scrawled "Excellent! Swell" alongside the paragraph. Then, recovering his objectivity, he wrote another sentence: "But it is precisely *this* which hasn't recently come *through*." There it was again, the constant critical analysis that afflicted *Life* periodically from the beginning throughout its whole run, that recurrent need on the part of Luce and his top managers to figure out what it was that was keeping the magazine from becoming the mythological success they imagined was somehow possible. Another reappraisal was about to begin in the compulsive search for the magazine's "real" identity. And already, after only a decade, nostalgia was setting in—*Life* was beginning to look back fondly on its past as a way to find clues for solutions to new pressures. "One of *Life's* current problems," Longwell wrote in the same memo, "is that it is ten years old. That sounds trite, but it isn't. We've reached a high but dead level of competence. We're professionals. We've done everything. The first thing we must do, I think, is to forget all about that and go back and do everything all over again." Longwell wasn't talking about simply copying *Life's* approaches to the earliest stories; he wanted somehow to recover the spirit that drove the early magazine, the sense that anything was possible. "Then we must jack up our standards," he went on, "be more knowing and sophisticated in the arts. Perhaps in our enthusiasm to photograph the world we've been too foreign. Then we must turn our eyes to America. We must be more beautiful, have more charm, and be more human in spots." "Also more *meaningful*," Luce scribbled in the margin.

Among those then writing memos about the future was Joe Thorndike, Longwell's cool and sensible assistant managing editor and also his choice—to be put into place as quickly as possible—as successor. "*Life's* original editorial charter," Thorndike wrote, "was simply to show things: people, places, news events, social activities, everything. This had never been done before. Therefore every good big *Life* story—a college, a foreign country, a festival—was a revelation to the reader. *Life* was a huge success. . . . It would be foolish to expect that *Life* can ever recapture this first-look impact that it had before the war. . . . But it would be equally foolish to conclude that *showing* things as they are is not still a damned good editorial charter. . . . Looking ahead, there is one factor which, it seems to me, is of great importance to a mature magazine. It should aim to express in its pages the spirit of its time and place."

Included prominently among those composing memos about future plans was Ed Thompson, back from his years in the service and very much a commanding figure on the staff, which was pushing up close to 300 people. "Every once in a while," he wrote Longwell with an occasional trace of friendly irony, "I get the horrible feeling that we regard ourselves chiefly as purveyors of mass culture and charm. That we are rewarded for this charitable work with a tremendous circulation seems to us to be no more than we deserve. Sure, charm and culture are part of the package. We should improve our critical standards, although I'm perhaps not as penitent as I ought to be. . . . But let's not kid ourselves. The bulk of our circulation is attracted by the kind of sensational reporting that only *Life* produces. We're sensation mongers and have been, perhaps unconsciously, all the time. The underlying sensation was our founders' realization of how potent the photograph and other graphic devices could be. . . .

"Well, didn't other publications have the same material? Yes, but they didn't have the graphic approach which put our readers right at the ringside. The old Denver *Post* maxim about a dog fight in Denver being more important than a war in Europe was probably sound news doctrine but we brought the war into dog fight focus. Other publications didn't take the pains we did to explain the technique of conflict until the Army defined a military secret as 'something known only to the high command, the enemy and *Life* magazine.' . . .

"So, in planning our future let's make plenty of provision for book larnin' and gracious living but let's see that it's wrapped around some good solid sensations. Let's climb Mount Teddy White, let's shoot rapids with the most daring explorers like we jumped with the paratroopers, let's make our readers shudder with plagues and famines, exploit murders that have class with a capital K, let's capture the impact of a gusher, the speed of jet transportation. And we mustn't forget all kinds of conflict at home and abroad, including dog fights in Denver and even in Afghanistan if it looks like belligerency there will spread to Denver." In those last few sentences Thompson had provided his bosses with a capsule definition for just the sort of lively, aggressive, sensation-mongering magazine he would begin producing with great success within the next few years, right down to the emphasis on stories from heartland America.

Somewhat later in the year, Billings responded to a request for his thoughts on *Life* in a somewhat troubled tone. "*Life* seems to suffer from a jittery uncertainty, hard to define, from week to week. I miss a smooth, even flow of purpose—a sort of spiritual continuity from issue to issue. Why? Perhaps because too many top people are, directly or indirectly, pulling and hauling at the issue editor. [Longwell had started a practice of having one of his top assistants, Thorndike or Thompson, manage each issue more or less under his supervision.] Now advice and direction from above is a good thing, provided it flows from a unified source of intent and policy. I am impressed by the fact that there still seems to be a divergence of views of what *Life* is all about among its managers. This lack of philosophic unity at the top [he was referring to Luce, Larsen, Longwell, Heiskell and himself] is bound to affect the issue editor. Of course another explanation of this sense of uncertainty is the fact that Longwell is bringing up a junior staff and *Life* is in a wobbly transitional stage. If one man were editing straightaway for the next couple of years, there would be less feeling of fuzzy command."

Though he wasn't saying so in this memo, Billings clearly felt that Longwell, who did not hide his own feelings that he was a poor manager and wanted to get out of *Life*'s top operational job as soon as a successor was ready, was responsible for the problem of fuzzy command. Billings had been so good at the job himself; he seemed at times particularly irritated by the shortcomings of the man who followed him in it. "His uncertainties create uncertainty down through the staff," he wrote in his diary after a discussion about Longwell with Luce. "I said Longwell was afraid of Luce & me. Luce: 'He's afraid of everybody, down to the youngest checker.' I remarked on his stuttering & mumbling. Luce said he used that the way a deaf man does to avoid unpleasant topics. I praised Thompson—but Luce hardly knows him."

In his memo about *Life*'s direction and command, Billings's preference of a successor was quite clear. "Joe Thorndike as Managing Editor?" he asked. "The logic of the years says Yes, of course. But I'm beginning to have serious doubts. Technically, of course, he knows his way around admirably, but my doubts arise from deeper stuff—something to do with personality and the quality of leadership. Joe, I feel, somehow just misses inspiring his staff to greatness. He is smart and able—but there's still a quality of juvenile cynicism about him. He's in such deadly fear of being dull that he hesitates to tackle the stories of off-beat importance. What to do? I don't know. But if, in a moment of impulse, you should decide to make Thompson M.E., I think I'd feel a sense of good risky adventure, with the sky the limit. (I'm not recommending this: I'm giving you my reaction to it in advance.)"

In his comments about the content of the magazine, Billings expressed further displeasure. He didn't think *Life*'s trivia had enough fun in it. "Too often the trivia is just—trivia," he wrote. He worried about what he called "the decline of curiosity on *Life*" and the lack of "good honest 'pretty pictures.'" He thought the editors were concentrating too much on achieving variety within a given issue rather than over several issues. "When I was M.E.," he wrote with a pride that suggested he might really prefer to be doing the job still, "I always tried to think ahead: we'll use this as an essay next week, and that as a party the week after, etc., etc. One result was, I believe, that by juggling three or four issues in my mind at one time, I was able to get a 'change of pace' between issues as well as within issues. Another was that I came up to a new issue with a good deal of advance thinking and planning already done and didn't have to scrabble so hard to build from the ground up." Within the example of successful planning that Billings was offering, there also seemed a layer of nostalgia for the good old days gone by.

But he ended the memo with something of an attack on himself. "My views, on rereading them," he wrote, "all sound captious and destructive and I have no overall magic formula for solving the problems I've cited. I think what I'm trying to say is that I'd like to see the prestige value of *Life* raised by more serious intellectual sweat on the part of its huge and floppy staff. 'To work on *Life* [is] fun.' Well, maybe it ought to be a little less fun and more hard driving work."

Billings's concern was enough to trigger Luce into the composition of an utterly stupefying fourteen-page memorandum written in what he characterized as "an effort to reestablish a 'philosophical unity' for *Life*." Sent to the magazine's publisher, Andrew Heiskell, with copies to Billings, Larsen, Longwell and Allen Grover, the memo was in part a complaint about the current condition of *Life* and a sort of grand thrashing around in the search for ways to improve the magazine's content for the future. With all its headings (THE BASIC POINT, BASIC IN-GREDIENTS, SPECIFIC REMODELING, PRIORITY AA) and sub-headings (The Serious Offering) it suggests close organization, but it reads more like the somewhat annoyed ramblings of a worried and frustrated proprietor who wishes that his associates would just open themselves up to the obvious, for God's sake, and get on with the business of making *Life* the kind of resounding, something-terrific-for-every-reader success they all know it ought to be.

Among Luce's admonitions some were clearer than others. "*Life* has got to have the best pictures," he wrote. "*Life* has got to have a certain number of *great* pictures." "Too many of our supposedly 'serious' pieces are not really first class," he wrote under another heading. "We have room for only one or two serious efforts per week: they have got to be damned serious; by which, of course, I don't mean dull; they must avoid dullness by being astounding journalistic 'coups' or efforts." He was particularly determined to have stories somehow connected with Art (his capital) in almost every issue, to "be sure of having one Act which is dramatic, striking, thoughtful, beautiful, charming and inspiring." He was very clear about what he wanted for the major written article each week. "As for the Big Text Piece," he wrote, "hereafter it will never be a profile of anyone except a Very Important Figure unless it is an absolutely knock-out piece of writing. . . . And the Big Text Piece will not be a profile even of a Very Important Figure more than about 50% of the time. That is, the Big Text Piece will cover the whole range of possible prose subjects (and maybe poetry, too). . . . What we want for this Text Piece is terribly high standards of Importance and Literary Brilliance."

One of the matters that especially engaged Luce at this time was how *Life* should deal with stories in the general area of modern living, which he thought "should serve as a nexus between The Editorial and The Advertising [departments]." After launching into a minidisquisition on materialism and Christian morality, he got down to the duty of *Life*'s editors. "Concretely," he wrote, "it is the first job of Modern Living to show how the multiplicity of goods in an industrial age can be used with relatively better rather than relatively worse taste. . . . Being so deeply involved in the contemporary, *Life* can't, for example, refuse to have anything to do with clothes if it thinks that contemporary fashions, as a whole, stink. But it can, without becoming hopelessly eccentric, choose the less bad among the bad and, with a combination of subtlety and earnestness, try to point the way out of a period of bad taste (in anything) toward good taste. . . . There are problems of good and bad taste throughout the magazine. But in Modern Living the requirement is the positive one of promoting good taste in the use of the abundance of good things which our economy provides."

Among other things, Luce's schoolmasterish tone in this memo suggests the frustration he was obviously feeling about resolving the business of who would succeed Longwell, and when. Luce and Billings were having difficulties selling Longwell on stepping aside—even though he had suggested it from the start. Now, as it was on the verge of happening, Longwell kept throwing up roadblocks: he didn't want to appear to be leaving when Luce and Billings were dissatisfied with the magazine; he wasn't clear about what his new duties would be (Luce suggested that he act as a senior editorial adviser and troubleshooter in departmental problem areas, but cautioned that he could not interfere with the authority of the new managing editor); he wanted to time his departure with the date of *Life*'s tenth anniversary. Luce, as was often the case with him in dealing with people he wanted to remove from important jobs, was apparently unable to bring himself to insist on the immediate implementation of whatever result he wanted, and was on occasion troubled and hurt by Longwell's recalcitrance. After one unpleasant meeting, Billings took a hand. "Longwell came," he wrote in his diary, "all upset about Saturday's session—and I gave him a sharp critical talk about being too sensitive, with a chip on his shoulder. I told him he treated Luce badly, that we were trying to do what he wanted, etc. He said he'd been a fool, had been ungrateful to Luce for 'the honor intended'—and then blandly announced that Luce's plan [for the various top editorial posts] was really his own idea—and he just wanted to postpone it for the 'promotional value' of the tenth anniversary." No matter how much he talked about wanting to give up the job, it seemed, Longwell, like other men who would become managing editor, or like ball players and champion boxers and others in big positions with considerable perks and psychic benefits, was having a hard time actually getting down to leaving.

In late September 1946, Luce decided on the rough details of the change of guard. Thorndike would become managing editor, Thompson would be assistant managing editor and Hicks would continue as executive editor. Longwell, described in a later memo to the staff as "deputy Editor, working closely with me," wound up being listed on the masthead, where these changes were not reflected until the issue of January 13, 1947, as "Chairman" of an entity called the Board of Editors. It was all a bit unclear, and the whole thing was rendered a little fuzzier by the imposition of a divisional system under Thorndike. In place of a system with many competing departments, now there would be four divisions (news, culture, modern living and a ragtag mix of the departments not included in the others). The heads of these divisions would be responsible for producing stories from start to finish, until they were, in Thorndike's words, "ready to go in the magazine." Presumably this new organization would eliminate the confusion caused by the often conflicting demands of many different departments and reduce the pressure placed by them on the managing editor, who would find his supply of stories all neatly thought out, packaged and even written in advance.

But beneath this doubtless honest effort to simplify things at a magazine with an unwieldy staff and too many departments, there was also the evident determination of Luce—and Billings, too—to protect against the possibility of an ineffectual managing editor. In his day Billings had thrived on pressure and confusion and could handily play boss, father, uncle and occasional tyrant to any number of people as the situation required. Longwell had been far less good at that, and no one knew how Thorndike would turn out. This new plan was thus a hedge against the future, and it could not have been seen by Thorndike as a ringing vote of confidence in him. In fact, he seemed somewhat less than overjoyed about some of the circumstances surrounding his promotion. In his diary Billings reported he was having a problem getting Thorndike to make some suggested changes in the masthead. ". . . he quibbled about the junior listings. He says he doesn't want to make anybody mad with masthead demotions. Luce wanted only the assistant editors—and Thorndike wanted to throw all his writers into this category. Joe obviously doesn't want to do a real clean-up job, although we warned him he was just making future trouble for himself. But he's a mulish young Yankee and won't listen to his elders and betters. I sent him off to think it over and discuss it with his young colleagues."

And, of course, the selection of Thorndike didn't strike Thompson at all as the best idea in the world. "I spent an hour outlining to him the new *Life* organization," wrote Billings, so often the bearer of Luce's bad tidings. "I told him he was not to be M.E.—but to head up News department. I gave him all the angles and ideas. He sat silent mostly (hand stroking face) and didn't make it any easier for me by asking questions. I told him he didn't have to reply to any of this now—but I could tell he was greatly disappointed. 'I think you're making the wrong decision on M.E.,' he said. 'You know I'm 39 and can't wait forever.' I felt the results of my talk were highly uncertain." Thompson, of course, opted to wait longer for another chance at the job he so wanted, but it must have been especially difficult for Billings, who thought Thompson was the best of the rising managers and liked him personally, too, to try to persuade him to accept the proposition that Luce's decision was the right one for the moment.

The cover of the anniversary issue was a picture of a young model (presumably ten) holding a copy of *Life*'s first issue with Margaret Bourke-White's famous picture of the Fort Peck Dam on the cover. Bing Crosby appeared in two ads, one selling Philco products and the other something called Fleer's Candy Coated Chewing Gum. He cropped up again in a movie story charting the rise and fall of stars over the past ten years (Shirley Temple had been box office dynamite early on, then vanished from contention as she began to grow up). Also in the issue were stories on ten years of American Art, on "*Life*'s GIRLS," a confection of previously published pictures, including the one by Bob Landry of Rita Hayworth kneeling on a bed ("When they first saw it," read the caption, "*Life*'s editors thought it was the best girl picture ever taken. They have never changed their minds"), and on controversies stirred up over stories printed in the magazine. Among these were items on the problems occasioned by the "Birth of a Baby" story in 1938 and an especially fascinating one on the death of a fox in Ohio in 1944. The dustup here had been caused by a picture story showing how a bunch of men had cornered the animal and let a little boy beat it to death for their amusement. The piece had drawn more than 4,000 letters, 95 percent of them absolutely outraged by the brutality and more than a few by the magazine's depiction of it.

Basically, the issue (selling on the newsstands for fifteen cents with the paid circulation a little over 5 million) was a rather bland mix. It offered a friendly little package of looking back (via a gallery of memorable pictures from the past ten years), looking ahead (dream cars, dream houses, dream wardrobes), a picture-and-text survey of the state of the country and a pardonable collection of inevitably self-congratulatory stories about subjects remembered from *Life*'s short past, including items (about *Life*'s frequent mention in cartoons, for example) showing that the magazine now mattered. One of these—in a brief act called "Where Are They Now?"—showed a nice-looking young boy blowing out ten candles on a birthday cake. He turned out to be George Story, the seconds-old infant whose squalling, damp like-ness ran on the first page in the first issue. It was interesting to see that George had come along so well. He looked entirely presentable; one could believe he had a decent future ahead of him.

Much the same could be said of *Life* in 1946. It seemed tidy; there was no reason to believe that the future would not bring more of the success that had been piling up for ten years. But when one thought about the terrific, raw vitality of those first years and of the consistent (now and then excruciating) emotional impact of the magazine during the war, one could only wonder just what *Life* had come to. It seemed pretty tame, a little prissy almost, like a child uncertain of its power and a bit ashamed of its feelings. It clearly had some growing to do and it was not clear whether that growth would take it along a path toward well-mannered worthiness—or whether it would find new ways to ex-press some of the excitement, of the spontaneity, of the fun, of the brash muscularity that cropped up so often in the early years.

Thorndike's staff was a good one, packed both with solid senior people like Thompson and Hicks and with relative newcomers to the magazine like the ebullient Sidney James and Ernest Havemann, who brought extensive news experience on newspapers and magazines and considerable writing skills to their jobs. Such stars as Teddy White and John Hersey were gone, both after disagreements with Luce, but per-formers like Noel Busch, Winthrop Sargeant and Charles J. V. Murphy dashed off lively and opinionated articles. The end of the war saw a substantial beefing up of the staff in virtually all categories: John K. Jessup, in charge of editorials; Charles Tudor, the art director; assistant editors Maitland Edey, A. B. C. (Addison Beecher Colvin) Whipple and John Thorne; reporters Gene Farmer, Kenneth MacLeish, Earl Brown (*Life*'s first black editorial employee) and Robert Wallace; re-searchers Robert Campbell, Tom Carmichael, Mary Leatherbee and Dorothy Seiberling; bureau chief Robert Elson and correspondents Mil-ton Orshefsky and Irene Saint—only a handful of the men and women who would play important roles at the magazine over the next decade and more, some of them right to the end in 1972. The thirty-seven photographers on the masthead were an especially impressive crowd, including not only such already famous names as Alfred Eisenstaedt and Peter Stackpole, Dmitri Kessel and Gene Smith, but also many less celebrated but first-class photojournalists—Cornell Capa (Robert's younger brother), Mark Kauffman, Bernard Hoffman, Nina Leen, Fritz Goro, Wallace Kirkland, Walter Sanders. Virtually all of them were highly motivated, versatile, fast-moving professionals whose main preoccupation was getting as many good pictures as possible in *Life* magazine each week. They were unquestionably the best in the world in their line of work, and most of them were certain that *Life* was the best place in the world for them to appear.

Taken all together, the staff was a vital, talented, restless, even frolicsome group. Young geniuses from Harvard and Vassar mixed with returned infantry officers and bomber pilots, jazz piano players trained in politics and economics mingled with poetry-writing science writers, pipe-smoking experts on ancient Greek culture flirted with beautiful Egyptologists, hymn-singing newsmen from the farm belt shook bone-dry martinis for chic fashion consultants in the latest clothes from Chanel. The place brimmed with energy, enthusiasm, ambition and life. If a young man or woman wanted to be a journalist, wanted a job that offered opportunities to travel, to meet powerful, attractive people everywhere, to help produce stories that would be read (often next week) by more than 20 million Americans, among them the most influential people in almost every field, and all of this in the company of similarly driven, highly stimulating colleagues, what better place to work was there than this? Anything, obviously, could happen here, and much of it could be good. Thus the makings of a great postwar picture magazine were on the scene, waiting for Thorndike—or his successors—to give them the spark of leadership needed to turn their gifts and their pride into a renewed and resounding success.

Thorndike was thirty-three when he became managing editor. But as he pointed out, the publisher, Andrew Heiskell, was only thirty, and Thorndike had been working on the magazine since before the start-up in 1936. He had all the makings of a top Luce magazine editor of the period. He was bright, well-connected (a former editor of Harvard's daily *Crimson*), and he had a streak of toughness (Billings had called him "mulish") that suggested he might be able to withstand the fierce sort of pressures—fast-breaking events, the sudden collapse of big, important projects, bad errors in judgment on the part of staff members and himself, serious kibitzing by the editor-in-chief—that were inevitable in any managing editor's life. Indeed he did have a rather detached mien around the office—though friends found him warm and funny—and he didn't show signs of severe crankiness and agitation in adversity, the way Longwell did, or get stern and cold, like Billings.

He was, in fact, a thoughtful, seasoned and highly competent magazine journalist, and in his relatively short tenure in the top working job at *Life*, he made a big contribution, one that would influence the intellectual tone of the magazine for the next twenty years. Thorndike had a real interest in the role that *Life* could play as a teacher and popularizer of the culture and the history of civilization. He was the instigator of a number of substantial articles on contemporary American life (on art, atomic energy and the national character) and was responsible for the first major series *Life* ever ran, ten long, illustrated articles on the history of Western man. Written, among others, by *Time*'s foreign editor, Whittaker Chambers, and by Lincoln Barnett, it was a prestigious and widely read success for *Life* and later became a book, edited by Thorndike and Joe Kastner, that sold 500,000 copies. This project was the forerunner of many major *Life* undertakings (including series on the origins of the earth, on man, on Greece and Rome) that greatly enriched *Life*'s reputation as a contributor to popular education. Joe Thorndike's style was cool, not like his contemporaries', but more like that of Ralph Graves, who became managing editor twenty years later, and under much less promising circumstances. "Joe had a remarkable equilibrium," remembered Tom Prideaux, one of Thorndike's colleagues. "He was never promoting himself. He never seemed motivated by the desire to show off or disport himself conspicuously. He didn't have an arrogant bone in his body. Yet there was nothing at all self-effacing about him."

Quite possibly his style—a bit removed, not driven to maintain control over every detail—had something to do with the brevity of his stay at *Life*'s top job. Perhaps the imposition of the new division system shut him off from too much control of the editorial process; by the time stories got up through his underbosses to him, there wasn't much to do but decide whether or not to run them. In any event, he let his subordinates, especially Thompson, run their operations with very little interference. Nor did Thorndike have the sort of interest in news that the curious and aggressive Thompson had, and in the time he was in the job, he gradually let Thompson edit the final news closings of *Life* on Saturdays, the last day stories went to the plant, and finished off his own workweek on Fridays. Such laissez-faire editing would surely have struck a world-class backseat driver like Luce as quite odd, if not downright disturbing.

A period of two weeks or so in late October and early November 1948 must have been especially trying for Thorndike in his relations with the editor-in-chief. First, a *"Life* Goes to a Party" story about a ball held by a group of artists and architects in Honolulu struck Luce as being terribly vulgar and triggered a twelve-page memo, much of it about bad taste and when it may or may not be justified in *Life.* "Let our rule be this," he wrote. "'There shall be nothing in *Life* which is in bad taste unless there is some positive good reason for same.'"

Luce's judgment of the story was reasonable; it was basically a rather unattractive collection of pictures of people in various sloppy stages of undress, preliminary lovemaking and drunkenness. It was the kind of unzipped party that *Life* was invited to cover hundreds of times, and the wonder is that more of these mini-bacchanals didn't fall into the magazine over the years. When people, especially people who are somewhat respectable and passably dignified, behave like idiots in front of the camera, it requires a certain discipline to recognize that the pictures aren't worth more than a passing smirk among editors. But Luce, who got so worked up on this question of taste that he made it a substantial segment of a discussion he was already having with his editors on plans and procedures for *Life* for 1949, laid about him with some scolding of a rather heavy-handed nature. "Just remember," he wrote, "that nearly everything in *Life* is conspicuous; therefore when *Life* is vulgar, it is conspicuously vulgar." In his lecture, Luce posed an example of when it might be acceptable to run something that was in bad taste. "Suppose there is an aspect of bad taste which we wish to reveal, to expose, in order to denounce and to correct. There is no problem here." Then he shifted back to his scolding mode. "There's a rule of good editing," he wrote, "which says it's just as important what you *don't* print as what you do." He had a chilling solution for preventing future errors of judgment: "The Managing Editor should never settle a dubious question of taste without concurrence of at least one senior colleague."

Luce's memo, particularly this double-check procedure, provoked Thorndike into taking a surprising position. "Your latest memorandum on 1949 raises, I think, a serious question whether I should continue as managing editor of *Life,*" he wrote, adding that he believed that the views of a Time Inc. managing editor should be generally compatible with those of his boss, the editor-in-chief. "When I took this job," he went on, "I assumed that I was responsible for *Life's* editorial operation." His authority, Thorndike felt, was subject only to orders from above by Billings and Luce and would be diminished by the sort of consultation Luce was proposing on questions of taste. "I cannot admit," he continued, "that I *must* have the concurrence of any editors except those to whom I'm responsible." Thorndike then proposed that he and Luce discuss their differences. If the problems Luce saw in *Life* were attributable to differences between the two men, Thorndike would resign. "If a change is to be made," he wrote, "this is a good time to make it. The magazine, operationally at least, is in good shape. . . . A change in managing editors offers a good opportunity to shake up the whole staff. As for me I will leave Time Inc. with the best of feelings and much gratitude for the fine treatment and opportunities you have given me."

Luce immediately came back with a gracious and quite mollifying response. "I write this not to 'take back' anything in my memo," he told Thorndike, "though in what was labelled a hastily-written document, there might be much that I would be willing to take back." "May I say, from my point of view," he closed after he agreed it was important that the two men talk further, "that I never enjoyed happier relations with a Managing Editor and even the thought of parting company is most distressing. I shall certainly do my best to make the case against it—with full respect for your views and candor as to mine."

The very next week Luce had another reason to be concerned about the judgment on *Life*, though this time the error was very likely caused in part by a too ardent enthusiasm for the editor-in-chief's political position. In this case the issue closed a few days before the Truman-Dewey election, in which Dewey was heavily favored and which the incumbent Truman, of course, won. *Life* ran a full-page photograph of Tom Dewey and his wife taking a boat ride and with a certain defiant exuberance captioned it: "The next president travels by ferry boat over the broad waters of San Francisco Bay." By the time this message got to the readers, it was all wrong, and this, as well as other indications of reckless cheerleading for the Republican Dewey in Time Inc. publications, led naturally to an agonized reappraisal of political coverage. Thorndike was so shaken up by *Life*'s nationally laughed-at goof (and by the raw partisanship of the other magazines, too) that he wrote to Luce suggesting the need for "a very sober rededication to the principles of honest journalism." At the same time as one sympathizes with Thorndike and his own honesty, one has to wonder what principles of journalism would have been invoked if Dewey had won.

For all the politeness of their exchange, the working relationship between Thorndike and Luce continued to deteriorate. By this time the incompatibility was basic. Luce was clearly worried about the magazine, its editorial organization, the stories produced, the overall tone *Life* conveyed to its readers. In a memo he wrote a month after the exchange with Thorndike, he discussed what he called "the problem of combining serious and responsible journalism with 'enjoyment' of the magazine." He was even more determined than usual, it seemed, to find a solid working justification—and one with high purpose—for his sprawling, hard-to-manage creation. "Life as it is lived in America today," he wrote, "is a strange and wonderful tension between the particular problems of little people (all of us and our families) and the surge of great 'historic forces.' It's enough to drive anybody crazy—and apparently does. All the more then, *Life* is required to be good-tempered and sane. If we can bring together in one magazine a feeling for all the little 'human' problems and all the little episodes of human life together with an awareness and intelligent disclosure of the 'great historic' forces— that surely will be a very great achievement. And one which will surely contribute to a happier and less tragic outcome of the present 'human situation.'"

His reflections and his wishes for the magazine seem perfectly understandable and his right to voice them is clear, but within the context of his constant vigilance and his endless worrying of the problems, they would have been difficult for any managing editor. And Thorndike, proud, sensitive, a man who insisted on his own form of clarity, found the strains of working with his restless boss harder and harder to take. What upset him most was the fact that Luce discussed the shortcomings of Thorndike's operation in such an open way. "I have never objected to any amount of comment or criticism," he wrote in a letter of resignation he submitted in December 1948. "Indeed I would have welcomed more. But I believe that such criticism, made by a boss to a subordinate in an important executive position, should be made in reasonable privacy. I do not believe it is right for the boss to indicate his dissatisfaction publicly or to hold round table discussions of what is wrong with the way the subordinate does his job. To do so undermines the authority requisite to the job. . . . During the last few weeks it has seemed to me that your disposition has been to cut down the authority of the managing editor, to hedge it and qualify it and cut off segments for parceling out elsewhere." In spite of the firm tone of this communication from Thorndike—he did add to his request that the resignation become "effective today" the possibly hopeful words "unless you have any reasons to the contrary"—Luce asked him to stay on, though neither man could have had much confidence the association would last long.

The face *Life* put to the world in 1949 did not reflect this bothersome dissension at the top. Stories or photographs in the magazine chronicled the romances of seventeen-year-old Elizabeth Taylor (with former Army football star Glenn Davis), James Stewart (who got married at forty-one to Gloria McLean), Ingrid Bergman (who left her husband for Italian director Roberto Rossellini). Photographer Frank Lerner began work on a twenty-two-page color essay for the Christmas 1949 issue on Michelangelo's frescoes in the Sistine Chapel. Luce's delicate feelings on the subject of taste were certainly jostled by a story on the new-style Bikini bathing suits, whose caption writer, Robert Wallace, declared about their difficulties: "Top falls down at slightest provocation, such as exhaling. . . . Bottoms ride up, making already revolting condition even worse. . . . Abdominal scars are revealed. This has caused many women, whose surgeons have left their stomachs looking like old golf balls, to shun the sun." There were theater stories on the great Broadway hits *Kiss Me Kate, South Pacific* and *Death of a Salesman,* and there was a *Life* Round Table on the movies whose panelists included James Agee, Robert Sherwood, Alistair Cooke, Dore Schary, Hal Wallis, Claire Trevor and John Huston. *Life* ran pictures on U.S. politicians, world statesmen and each of the fifty-five victims of what was then the worst air crash in history, which occurred when a Bolivian fighter plane collided with an Eastern Airlines flight near Washington, D.C. In a long article about Ernest Hemingway by the critic Malcolm Cowley, Hemingway offered some advice to writers: "We play in a league with no favors asked or given. No writer worth a damn is a national writer or a New England writer or a writer of the frontier or a writer of the Renaissance or a Brazilian writer. Any writer worth a damn is just a writer. This is the hard league to play in. The ball is standard, the ballparks vary somewhat, but they are all good. There are no bad bounces. Alibis don't count. Go out and do your stuff. You can't do it? Then don't take refuge in the fact that you are a local boy or a rummy, or pant to crawl back into somebody's womb."

In a promotion ad that ran early in 1949 publisher Heiskell, listing some of the big numbers about *Life's* success, crowed that 5.2 million copies were sold each week and the magazine reached 36 percent of all U.S. families. With the pass-along readership, the audience was huge—12 million men, 10 million women. And you could buy this whole astonishing package (the editors looked at 500,000 pictures each year to pick the 10,000 they printed, 2,500 of them in color) for as little as $3.75 a year—that is, if you bought a three-year subscription and were willing to pay $6.00 for the first year and $4.75 for the second. "Advertisers," said Heiskell, "continue to invest more dollars in *Life* than in any other magazine." Their annual investment, he concluded with an optimism and an accuracy that wouldn't be appropriate too much longer in the booming age of television, is also greater than it is for network time over any of the broadcasting chains. We're hot, was the message, come warm yourselves with us.

Before his troubles with Luce came to a final head, Thorndike—responding to suggestions that had originated with Billings—made some changes in the division system. Thompson would become involved more deeply in overall editing, thus freeing Thorndike for more work on special projects. Thompson's old news division would be broken into two parts, domestic and foreign, headed by Sidney James and John Osborne (who later became one of the main editorial writers). Maitland Edey, who had been Thorndike's assistant, got promoted to division editor. All of this was calculated to improve things for Thorndike, who, as Billings wrote later, had become an unfortunate victim of a bad and decentralized system. "Thorndike was too far from the source of ideas and pictures. He did not get to see enough pictures in the raw. . . . Sometimes the issues were notably rough and jerky as he tried to carpenter together the miscellaneous and uneven lumber he was offered by his divisional editors. . . . If Thorndike had not been a competent manager himself, the whole system might well have collapsed in disaster. Loyalties among the staff became split as writers teamed up under their divisional editors rather than under the M.E. who seemed remote and inaccessible to the ordinary Lifer." But whether anybody really believed the largely cosmetic changes would work is doubtful. The truth probably is that Luce wanted a new man at *Life* and Thorndike was ready, even anxious, to leave.

When it finally happened, it happened fast. On August 5, 1949, Luce sent a memo to his top staffers announcing still another improvement he had in mind for the management of *Life*. "I believe it will go far," he wrote, "to fill a gap which we have always realized existed somewhere in both the theory and practice of *Life*'s editorial organization." He was proposing an entity he called the "Editor-in-chief's Committee." To be made up of Luce, Billings, Longwell, Thorndike, Thompson and Osborne, it would meet once a week. "The regular formal action of this Committee would be to give," Luce said, "the red, yellow or green light to all 'future' projects." Luce was seeking to get "a constant and continuous *evaluation* of the development of the magazine; specifically of how and where the vast editorial resources of the magazine are being used." The committee, in fact, some of whose members were junior to Thorndike, would have a power of approval or disapproval over virtually every major project *Life* undertook, and Thorndike simply could not accept it. Luce's implacable and insensitive persistence had completely worn him down.

"I took this job," Thorndike wrote on the same day, "on the under-standing that I would have full authority and responsibility under your direction to run the magazine. My authority has been appreciably di-minished over the last eight months, and the set-up you propose would, in my judgment, destroy it completely. . . . Last winter I submitted a tentative resignation, for the purpose of finding out where I stood. Lest there be any misunderstanding, this one is final and not subject to further discussion." The man Billings had called "a stubborn little New England cuss" packed up his briefcase and cleared out the same day. That was a Friday, and on the following Monday, Luce made the an-nouncement that Ed Thompson had been appointed *Life*'s managing editor. The news surprised no one at Time Inc., for this driving, Stetson-hatted, tough, make-believe rube from North Dakota was clearly ready and long, long overdue for the job.

9

EKT

EDWARD KRAMER THOMPSON, THE BRILLIANT and tough operating boss of *Life* during its period of greatest national influence and considered by many to be its finest managing editor, did not make a stunning first impression. In fact, after meeting him for the first time people routinely (and privately) expressed their surprise that a fellow who looked like that and expressed himself with such difficulty had risen to become the top man at one of the most powerful journals in the world. There was a doughy quality about Thompson. He appeared slightly underdone, unfirm, a poor soufflé in the act of falling. He seemed utterly sedentary, unadventurous. You wouldn't guess him to be terribly quick, vigorous, fierce, combative. Yet he was all those things—and more.

His preferences as an editor ran to journalism's red meat: catastrophe, heroism, crime, politics, conspiracy, heartbreak, the loves, lusts and downfalls (or pratfalls) of the rich and famous. Of course, he encouraged the ardent pursuit of much of the more trivial (and very popular) content of *Life*—the pretty-girl stories, stories about fads and fashions, stories about parlor games and pet elephants. But he was most preoccupied with the headline news, or the bigger news behind it, and he loved the often wild chase for it.

The chase brought out Thompson's ferocious competitive urges. He was delighted with situations, for example, in which *Life* and other big magazines came into confrontation over the same story. His eyes watered brightly and he pulled on his big cigars with a special gloating fervor when he heard that his photographers had got into secret smoke-filled rooms while the men from *Look* were still banging on the doors, when he found that his correspondents had outbid *Collier's* for the only existing rolls of film on a mid-Pacific plane ditching, when he decided to take advantage of *Life*'s faster production capability to beat out *The Saturday Evening Post* with a story about Princess Grace that was better than the one the *Post* had already scheduled and closed. Thompson dearly loved winning, and for the better part of the 1950s he ran *Life*'s most winning team.

Luce himself had allowed for the fact that magazines, like other human institutions, had a natural life span and couldn't be expected to go on forever. "Sometimes [a journal] can be born again. But certainly it must die," he said, and he would have agreed, too, that magazines have a period of peak vitality, a time when, in retrospect at least, they seem at their particular best. Such a judgment, of course, is based on a number of factors, not all of them measurable. One important factor, naturally, is circulation; acceptance by the readers is the first criterion. Without it, nothing else matters much. But it's a tricky area for measurement of success in a mass magazine, because—though many claim to—nobody really knows how much circulation is enough, or when enough, judged perhaps by the greedy or the overambitious to be bringing too modest a return, suddenly is transformed into too much by excessive promotion and giveaway subscriptions. Still, a strong circulation—and a high rate of renewals (say 70 percent) on subscriptions—is good news for any publication and is the first indicator most experts look at.

Another factor, with the virtue that it can be measured, is ad sales, an area where success or failure is constantly being calibrated in terms of actual pages and the dollars that advertisers are willing to put up to buy them. Space sales are a cruelly sound index of the mood of public acceptance surrounding a magazine. The makers of automobiles, cigarettes, whiskey, deodorants—and the advertising agencies whose whole reason for being is to see that the client's money goes where it will best sell his products—are constantly vigilant as to the changing capacity of a given journal—or radio or television program—to deliver an audience, the *right* audience. Agencies are always on the prowl for "a hot book," which simply means a publication that is catching the strong attention of a growing audience with money to spend. And because advertising budgets are limited, the decision to move a client into a new book often means the business is lost somewhere else. In pinched times, most publications lose advertising and the choices don't seem so pointed. But generally speaking, if ad sales are up, the managers of a magazine are gratified not only by the dollars (which are, of course, the lifeblood) but also by the enormously rewarding sense that the hard-eyed crowd on

Madison Avenue (which prefers to think of itself in more mellow, even artistic terms) recognizes the energy and conviction they are trying so hard to make jump off those editorial pages.

Certainly in terms of those two big business-side factors, circulation and ad sales, the decade of the 1950s was the weekly *Life*'s best time. The magazine had generated great power in the 1940s; during the war its patriotic fervor, its consistent currency with stirring photographs of U.S. troops in action, as well as its coverage of the home front, made *Life* a sort of journalistic cheering section. It developed an almost communal authority; people trusted the magazine with the big red logotype. That trust was reflected in the growing number of readers and the willingness of advertisers to buy space in 1940 at upwards of $6,000 a page. Guaranteed circulation went from 2.3 million in 1940 to 5.2 million in 1949. Ad pages sold in 1940 were 2,503; in 1949, 3,500.

But in the 1950s, specifically the first six or seven years of it, that public and commercial acceptance was expressed to an even greater degree. Circulation rose to 5.8 million in 1956; space salesmen in that year sold more than $137 million worth of advertising. For a surprisingly long time—even as television began to make its real strength felt—*Life* was clearly a hot book among major U.S. magazines.

What made it that? Why was *Life* such a success in this decade of rising prosperity and burgeoning aspirations? Obviously the answer is connected to some public sense of identification with the magazine. *Life* seemed to see things the way its audience saw them. It seemed to echo the hope, the curiosity, the impatience, the anger, the innocence of its readers. And if, occasionally, it also challenged them, the challenge was delivered in ways that were tolerable, even welcome.

A rare confidence was generated between the magazine and the great majority of its readers. Not that they found the magazine was always right, always reliable, always balanced. Few in the huge audience would have welcomed such insufferable virtues. Much more likely, the confidence had to do with reflections of themselves that the magazine offered its readers. Somehow, in a time of increasing affluence and great change from wartime austerity (and an accompanying need for reaffirmation of traditional stabilizing values), *Life* was playing back to these readers images of their country and of themselves that seemed both authentic and reassuring. One could, figuratively speaking, find himself or herself in the magazine's pages, or recognize one's hopes, or stoke one's indignation, or appease one's need for self-improvement or the need to identify with the great long line of humanity reaching back to the caves. The magazine of the 1950s was a place where millions of people could discover modern American life, be stimulated by it and feel part of it. Later, in the 1960s, as Americans saw the fragmentation of their society and were devastated by its implications, that mirror link between the magazine and its readers would weaken greatly. In many ways, *Life* in the 1960s looked better and offered its audience a more beautiful, thoughtful, balanced, imaginative mix of stories. But it did not, apparently, show the readers what they wanted to see of themselves, and it never had the power and drive of the earlier magazine.

The leadership of *Life* in the 1950s obviously played a big part in the magazine's success, and Ed Thompson's natural accession to power was probably the best thing that could have happened to assure it. A Phi Beta Kappa graduate of the University of North Dakota, of all places, Thompson represented a big change from the Ivy League types (with the exception of Longwell) who'd been running the magazine since its start-up in 1936. Luce and Billings were geniuses, to be sure, but they were also essentially elitist, aloof men who did not at all identify *themselves* with their mass audience. Thompson, as bright as they were and with a surprisingly broad and deep understanding of history and modern culture (not easy to spot because he hid it under his rube's hat), was much more a middle American, much more than the others was truly familiar with the huge general audience his magazine would have to attract to continue to be a success.

In the twelve years he ran *Life*, Ed Thompson edited some 600 issues of the magazine, roughly one-third the total churned out during its entire existence as a picture weekly. Because he was the kind of compulsively engaged editor he was—and the kind of inexhaustible and controlling man—almost every issue reflected his convictions, his tastes, his quirks, the way he saw America and Americans in the world. And because the medium was photography and because Thompson worked under the authority of one of the most imperious and idiosyncratic press lords of the time, he had to accomplish this in relatively subtle ways.

The choices of stories, the pictures used in them, the mix of stories (how one would work with another), the pace of the issues (deciding when to keep an issue moving fast, when to slow it down), the quality and tone of the writing, all these were areas where he could exercise control—and did. He also exercised it, of course, through his shaping and management of the staff. Virtually nobody got a raise or a promotion, or even an assignment, on the edit staff that Thompson hadn't approved personally.

The people who worked under Thompson at *Life* thought of it as *his* magazine. Though his despotism was generally benign, he could be capricious and hard to read, and there were inevitably people working for him who directed their energies not so much to figuring out what *they* should do as to guessing what Thompson would want. Even Luce did not attract such preoccupation from the staff. He was "the proprietor," a man who could make his power felt uncomfortably if he chose, but more typically a remote presence. On the other hand, EKT—those initials, scrawled on copy he'd approved and on all his memos, were the symbolic brand of his era—was at the heart of everything that mattered.

Thompson wasn't especially given to making general analyses of the magazine; he preferred dealing with particulars. But for Luce, who was constantly in the process of defining and redefining his products, Thompson revealed, only weeks after he became managing editor, that he saw *Life* as a quite specific character. "You have been very considerate," he wrote Luce on August 24, 1949, "to let me stagger through my first couple of issues before asking me sternly about my intentions. Now, though, I figure I had better expose you to some thinking out loud.

"I once thought," Thompson went on, with a beguiling blend of humility, flattery and good sense, "that it would be impossible to improve the promise of the prospectus, 'to watch the faces of the poor and the gestures of the proud; to see strange things . . .' Now, though, I will stop saying 'me too' long enough to state my strong belief that we mustn't be that detached. We must make the reader feel that his 20 cents gives him something more than a seat in the bleachers, he should feel a sense of participation in what the editors see and think.

"*Life*, to me, is a friendly neighbor, almost one of the family. He is kind of gabby, asks a lot of questions, always wants to get into a discussion, so there are bound to be some anti-social folks who don't like him too much. But where he is welcome he sidles up to the picket fence and says:

"'Let me tell you about that big fire I saw on my way through the county seat tonight. . . .

"'I've been studying up about this fellow Tito and I have a Jugo-Slav brother-in-law, who tells me . . .

"'Say, have you heard of a wonderful man named Schweitzer over in Africa? Well, he's doing fine things for those natives but he's an expert on Goethe, too, and here's what he thinks. . . .'

"And he ends up by saying: 'What do you think of that?'

"*Life* can get away with talking about philosophy, the atom, morality and what the missus ought to be wearing even though he has to get to know how to talk her language better. That's because this is what a lot of people say about him:

"'Yessir, that's about the smartest young fellow around here. He sure keeps up on things. But he isn't a smart-aleck, mind you, and there isn't a mean bone in his body. Even when he's talking about some of that deep stuff you can see he's been studying it real hard to try to understand it himself and make it interesting. Sometimes we don't figure we'll go for some of that but a lot of times we listen and get interested in spite of ourselves.

"'We figure he can speak right up to anyone but he doesn't try to talk down to us. He's good-natured and sometimes he gives us a real belly-laugh but he sure can get mad when people have it coming.'

"In short it seems to me," Thompson wrote in his own voice, "that *Life* must be curious, alert, erudite and moral, but it must achieve this without being holier-than-thou, a cynic, a know-it-all or a Peeping Tom. *Life* must always feel *privileged* to be the bearer of information or thoughts. When we do this largely as a matter of duty through the medium of a bored staff, we're through."

Thompson then offered Luce something considerably more personal, reflections on how he would like his own leadership to be viewed. "Maybe knowing the kind of managing editor I'd like to be would help, too," he wrote. "I'm proud of and sentimental about being a journalist. It comes natural to me to regard the managing editor (in this case myself) as 'the old man,' a newspaper term applied to m.e.'s from 21 to 71. 'The old man' to me is a guy who brings a strong personal flavor to editing. He has some crotchets which are the subject of wry office jokes, but all in all he is considered fairly Jovian. He rides his subordinates hard but is inclined to say nice things behind their backs. They feel he will not pass the buck to them when he gets into trouble with the owner or other higher authority. Being 'the old man' doesn't mean that one is a fatuous do-gooder. While a certain amount of rough-diamond kindliness is involved, it means that 'the old man' drives with a pretty tight rein, that he blows his top promptly when some stupidity is perpetrated, that he plunges zestfully into editorial projects that interest him (which should be almost all of them). . . .

"I'm certainly going to have positive and occasionally unpopular views, but I'm starting the job with humility and at least some knowledge of my own limitations. At the same time I feel reasonably confident because I think I can use my colleagues for the kind of thing I can't do."

Thompson followed that burst of candor with a characteristically wry, honest and somewhat difficult-to-read compliment. "Most of all, though," he finished, "I am approaching the job with a vast amount of goodwill. Please don't be embarrassed when I repeat that since the war

I've developed a sincere affection and feeling of loyalty to you personally. This isn't connected particularly with your conduct as a boss, but it ain't necessarily bad for boss-employee relationships." And it certainly wasn't bad for boss-employee relationships for him to say so.

Thompson's performance and his attitudes toward the job were, of course, subject to the most intense kind of scrutiny by many people. Most knowledgeable and influential of these was perhaps John Shaw Billings, Time Inc.'s editorial director and Thompson's longtime mentor. ". . . the temperament and personality of Thompson are chiefly responsible for *Life*'s present set-up," Billings wrote Luce in 1952, three years after Thompson took over. "He obviously derives deep satisfactions from the exercise of his power on the magazine. On occasion he may ironically refer to himself as a poor manager and bemoan his failure to delegate more of it to his juniors, but it is doubtful if he really means it. He is ambitious. He is indefatigably hard-driving. He likes the spotlight and applause. He is quite aware of his own capacities and the shortcomings of those around him. The *Life* set-up exactly mirrors his ego and whether you can radically change one and not the other is very doubtful."

In this memo, of course, Billings was deeply involved in that ever-popular Lucean game of reevaluating the performance of one of the magazines. Whether there was much need for it at this time was at least debatable, certainly in the eyes of Billings, who began his communication to Luce with the words: "*Life* is good. Its editorial staff is lively and competent. Its picture production is smoothly and efficiently organized. As the largest and most complex editorial operation in magazine history, the whole mechanism clicks along from week to week without crisis or breakdown. Why try to tinker with such a delicately-balanced organism at the risk of serious hurt to its functionalism? Everything seems to be going better than ever before, so why not sit back and enjoy this pretty marvelous spectacle of magazine production?"

But Billings was also too shrewd an editorial manager and had been too closely involved with the *Life* operation himself not to know that changes there could come suddenly. And he worried as well about his protégé and favorite, Thompson, and the exhausting way he ran his job. "His performance may be superb showmanship," Billings went on, "but it is not good long-range management. He is constantly so close to the buzz-saw that he never has time to back off and look at the lumber yard, much less the forest. If he could be persuaded to let up on some of the multitudinous details he now insists on handling, he'd undoubtedly prove to be a better and more useful top editor for *Life* for years to come." Then Billings undertook a piece of rare—and quite possibly accurate—analysis. "His behavior," wrote this man who knew a lot himself about such feelings, "sometimes suggests that he secretly feels very insecure in his job, for all his outward show of cocky self-confidence, and is compelled to these superhuman efforts because he is afraid somebody will snatch his job from him."

But after he had finished making numerous suggestions about reorganizing the editorial staff of *Life* in ways that would increase the responsibilities and rewards of the editors under Thompson (he was making about $75,000 in salary and bonus at this time, $35,000 more than the next man in the pay scale), Billings wryly proposed another alternative: "to do nothing but thank God you have such a gee-whiz M.E. as the present incumbent. Great newspapers and magazines have run for years on the operational stamina and virtuosity of one man— Ray Long, Lorimer, Van Anda, Swope. It may not be good theoretical management, but at least it gets sensational results for a time. This company has never favored such one-man performances, but we now seem to have one on *Life*. We could always recognize our blessings and not tinker with our good luck." There would be changes, but there wouldn't be much open tinkering with *Life*'s luck—or with Thompson— for many years.

Ed Thompson did not *look* at all like the sort of man who would inspire much confidence and loyalty in an overworked staff. He was forty-five the year that Billings wrote the memo above. His face was round and without particular emphasis, as if it had been sculptured carelessly from tallow. His eyes were blue and watery. His hair was a thinning brown that gave the impression it would come out easily if yanked. He was of average height, and he slouched. More often than not, he was somewhat overweight; he was scornful about exercise. He always worked with his suit jacket off and his sleeves rolled up just above the elbows. His forearms were pasty, and his trousers gathered oddly at the belly. Especially in the later years of his reign, he smoked cigars much of the time, and his beckoning or abruptly dismissing waves to his subjects rolled aside foul-smelling clouds.

He had distinct shortcomings as a communicator. A casual outsider watching Thompson in action at the peak of his power as operating head of the most widely read magazine in America might have wondered how he made himself understood. Insiders, in fact, frequently had a hard time figuring out what it was he was saying. Sentences began and died as Thompson suddenly looked around or lowered his head toward the floor. Distinct words were uttered and then sent floating away in gargle sounds. Strange new words bloomed and vanished. Coherent phrases leapt out toward the listener and then somehow fragmented and curled upward in the cigar smoke. Possible clues to comprehension, it was believed, lurked in every sound and movement. Hand gestures, for instance, were noted carefully by men and women seeking Thompson's meaning and so were shrugs.

Individual conversations with him were often baffling. A writer called to Thompson's office to get some editing directions on, for example, a political story would usually find him seated alone at the long wooden table where he worked with pictures and story layouts. The few white sheets of the writer's story would be in front of him, and off slightly to Thompson's left a large, open, leather-covered book. This was his dummy for the issue closing that week, and it was filled with photostatic copies of story layouts that would appear in the next *Life*. Thompson would look up and, seeing the writer standing diffidently in the doorway of the office, make a quick, almost embarrassed movement of the head signifying that the visitor should enter. "Gwaad-ark soonj block mass-ken whistlestop in the layout," the managing editor would mumble as the man stepped toward him. Naturally uncertain about what Thompson had said, the writer would respond with a weak "I beg your pardon, Ed?" Thompson would wave his cigar-filled hand with what might be interpreted as annoyance. "Look," he would say, "this is fine" (and the writer would be giddy not only with the news but with the fact he'd received it clearly) "but we need a little bafless tonse arsh here to Adlai in the caption. In politics you can't be too dwadletack or too oooom." For emphasis here, Thompson would perhaps bang his hand on the copy paper, dropping ashes on it, and then he would jab a thumb toward a photostatted picture of candidate Adlai Stevenson. "Parchur pondet useless unless we get mottle gravdend of this guy," he would say, a touch of impatience in his voice. "How else will the reader know where we're at?" He might then cock an eye up at his stunned listener and shrug, adding as he pushed the copy toward the writer, "You can fix it." Back in his own office, the man could be seen staring out the window over his silent typewriter. Occasionally he would make hunching motions with his shoulders or reach out with his open hands. In this strange pantomime, the writer would attempt a kind of replay of the conversation he'd just had with the managing editor, trying to dig his instructions out of the air by acting out Thompson's shrugs and hand movements and grunts. Surprisingly, it usually worked; a serviceable translation would be made and the revision accomplished.

A number of myths grew up around Ed Thompson, some of his own making. The one he seemed to take the most pleasure in was the fraud that he was a country boy. Possibly he looked the role, especially when the color was high in his pudgy cheeks, and he did, in fact, grow up in a small town in North Dakota. But as a few real country boys on the staff were quick to point out (though decidedly not to his face), Thompson had been a banker's son, had lived a sheltered life and, in the words of one observer, "couldn't tell a boar from a pig." Still, Thompson loved country music, hymns that required thigh and hand clapping, and he wore pale-colored, broad-brimmed Stetson hats. When he'd had a few drinks, he occasionally indulged in a breathtaking and even dangerous imitation of country dancing in which he would fling himself and his partner around the room with an abandon in extraordinary contrast to his normally dour behavior. Possibly there was something a little defiant, too, about Thompson's determined rube-ism. Surrounded by Ivy League types from Luce and Billings on down, Thompson may well have been determined to maintain an image clearly his own. His success in that, of course, was complete. And there just isn't any doubt that his lack of respect for many establishment values and his dogged lowbrow attitude (although he was extremely well read and well informed) gave the magazine a tilt away from New York and eastern provincialism that was very important to *Life*'s broad success in the 1950s.

But the real distinction between Ed Thompson and the other managing editors of *Life*, past and future, lay in his greed for crisis. Whereas the orderly Billings on the early magazine and Ralph Graves in the last years of *Life* took great pride in running tidy operations where things clicked right along according to plan, Thompson seemed to feel trapped with plans that committed him too firmly in advance. He sought opportunities to wipe them out. Perhaps it was his restless nature, perhaps it was his newspaper training, more likely it was his conviction that *Life* always had to have an urgent character about it: in any case, Thompson clearly preferred making big changes at the last minute to any other editor's prerogative.

In his sort of operation the breakage was considerable. Saturday was the magazine's final closing day for the issue that would appear the following week, and by that morning, or even a day or two earlier, the pages held for current use were in the process of being laid out and written or, in fact, had already closed. Thus, if a disaster—say, a plane crash or a mine cave-in—took place on a Friday or Saturday, other stories already in the works would have to be shortened or junked, on many occasions permanently. This kind of thing, of course, was a source of considerable pain for the reporters, editors and writers who had been involved with the killed stories, and it often devastated the photographers, many of whom took the whole business more personally anyhow, and because they were so exposed, with some good reason.

But Thompson loved it. Once he'd made up his mind to throw out six pages of pictures on, for example, a gathering of Republican governors, and to wait for a new lead (the opening news story near the front of each issue) on the ravages of a sudden violent blizzard in the western plains, the real joy he took in his job was apparent. His corner office on the thirty-first floor of the Time & Life Building echoed with scurry and command. If they weren't already on the scene, photographers and reporters were dispatched. Bulletins about the new plans were delivered—by personal summons, by telephone, by wire—to the printing and production people in Chicago, to the photo lab, to various subalterns who would check plane schedules, alert couriers, arrange escorts, provide, if necessary, infusions of cash to grease the passage of film to New York from wherever in the world it was being shot. The whole news staff lay in wait for the material, and on arrival it was processed with great haste and brought on the run to Thompson, who had been keeping semi-belligerent track of its progress every step of the way. Then in most cases the story hurtled to its closing, with the people involved—Thompson at the center—working right through the night. Naturally the costs for this kind of desperate operation were high—especially in overtime and energy—but those were rich years for *Life* and the staff was eager and strong.

There were variations on the late-closing crisis. Depending on the lateness of the story, the direction it was coming from and its news importance, Thompson might decide to take a team (usually consisting of himself, the art director, a copy editor, a couple of writers and production men and a few other assorted picture editors, reporters and copyreaders) to Chicago, where some time might be saved by closing the issue right at the R. R. Donnelley printing plant instead of sending the finished material from New York. These expeditions were called "crash closings," and they often did have a shattering effect on the participants, who usually worked around the clock and far into the next day to get the job done.

They seemed to be particularly exhilarating to Thompson, who for all his rather flabby appearance had extraordinary resources of energy and strength. He could drive himself to the point of stupefaction—and then disappear for an hour or two for a quick nap on an office couch before returning wide awake (and extremely testy) to the matter of finishing up. And the people who were chosen to go along with him on these exhausting trips were thrilled by them, too, however much they now and then complained. To be picked out by Thompson for a special job was simply the best thing that could happen for many of the young people at the magazine. It gave them a sense of status and of being at the very center of an exciting and important profession. It gave them powerful illusions of closeness both to the story, which may have taken place half a world away, and to those millions of readers they would never see. It gave young journalists the feeling that their work really mattered. But mostly it gave them the chance to work close to Thompson in a pressured stretch of time, a time when they could gather a new collection of his shrugs, winks, grunts, burbles, frowns ("Oh, God, what did I do wrong?"), now and then a quick look of approval. If things were going really well, if Thompson was pleased about the story, and the liquor and good fellowship were flowing, they might even join him in shouting a hymn, something rollicking and comradely like "When the Roll Is Called Up Yonder I'll Be There." In a way, these deeply tiring adventures presided over by Thompson were the central rituals at *Life* in the 1950s. To be invited to go along (and to be able to recall later shared moments of drunken hilarity or near-misses from disaster) was to be truly blooded at the magazine. To have been with Ed Thompson in Chicago was an admission to a very special club, a mark of acceptance that one couldn't get just by being good at the job.

Why did his staff so admire him? He was demanding, stubborn, often cranky and curt and occasionally unreasonable. He had his favorites, and he did not flinch at the adoration of sycophants. He had a cruel memory for past mistakes, especially if they had been made by people he didn't like. Though he repeatedly claimed innocence of it, he was practiced at playing his top assistants off against one another when it suited him (which Luce did, too) and at setting them up for conflicts he would then resolve later—to *his* credit. Billings was not the only one who suspected that real competition made Thompson uneasy. He was generally regarded as something of a wizard with pictures and picture-story layouts, but, in retrospect at least, his magazine sometimes appears choppy, predictable and ordinary in design, even dull when compared to issues turned out by his successor, George Hunt. Even when he wasn't working, he didn't bother much with efforts to be a good listener, a gracious talker, a delightful companion. His attention seemed always ready to take a walk. "Talking to Ed," one of his editors recalled, "was like falling into molasses. His whole technique was to keep you off balance."

But he had winning qualities as well. He was willing to work harder and longer than any of his people. He was extraordinarily persistent about getting the results he wanted, and he knew what those were even if he couldn't always define them. For example, Thompson placed great importance on story headlines, and he ordered them written over and over again until he was satisfied—or took over the writing of them himself and accomplished the miracle of condensation or resonance or punmanship he sought.

Thompson had more substantial attributes. During the years he ran *Life,* picture coverage of the news was still considered central to the magazine's function, and Thompson was a most intuitive, alert and aggressive journalist with a strong news sense. He was not intimidated by big daily newspapers like *The New York Times* and their capacity to get events into print almost immediately. In fact, he believed that *Life* could handle many of the mass stories better, and he insisted on trying to do just that virtually every week. He reveled, naturally, in exclusives, and it thrilled him to beat the other big magazines—including, of course, *Time.*

Thompson's slam-bang, beat-the-opposition approach to journalism was terrifically appealing to his staff, whose members regularly felt that they were on the winning side in a highly exciting game. It encouraged strong feelings of loyalty and esprit toward the magazine itself, some-times jocularly referred to as the Big Red Team, and, of course, toward its leader. And like any good leader, Thompson did more than rally his people and urge them on. In spite of his oddly unclear methods of verbal address, he managed to convey the unmistakable impression that he cared a lot about effort and quality of performance. This led quite naturally to a conviction held by many people at *Life,* a conviction that made it tolerable for some to work there for years under awful pressure. This shared feeling was that, given certain limits of taste and the polit-ical preferences of Henry Luce, pretty much of *anything* was possible, provided the idea was sound enough and the execution was good. A big idea always had a chance, and everybody believed it. Certainly Thomp-son was one of the chief beneficiaries of that optimism.

On a more personal level, Thompson was something of a slob, and he took a certain pride in it. For all his real toughness, he was easily touched by skillful appeals to his tender side. Once he had decided that he trusted someone, he was tremendously loyal, and it took evidence of the most extraordinary sort of venality or gross ineptitude to persuade him to change his mind. Just as he could be very harsh with someone he thought was covering up mistakes or otherwise trying to avoid re-sponsibility, he was disarmed by candor and confession. He responded generously to the individual troubles of his people, and though he had the reputation of being too talkative about professional confidences, he kept a lot of private secrets. He took a hand—with advice, backing and sometimes cash—in the lives of those who appealed to him. He put up his own money for therapy, abortion and bail. And several of his beneficiaries looked on him with more than the respect ordinarily directed toward a good boss. He was loved almost as a father by many who had lost or rejected their own.

So there he sat, a very bright, tough, driven, sentimental, tireless, decent man at the center of his own whirlwind. For a dozen years he managed the great American magazine, and he did it better than anyone else. The magazine was his life. Timothy Foote, a writer and editor who worked for Thompson in those years, remembered about *Life*: "A kind of extreme professional care that amounts to love was lavished on it night after night, year after year, by nearly everyone there." And a lot of the love was Ed Thompson's.

10

A Big Issue 1: Building a Magazine

EACH WEEK'S *LIFE* BEGAN AS A SINGLE SHEET of paper, a numbered list of
the pages for that issue. This sheet was called a mock-up, and it was
basically a simple diagram showing the location of all the advertisements
and the space available for stories, which the list makers labeled "edit
content." The mock-up also showed the order in which various sections,
or "forms," of the magazine were scheduled to go to press. Thus this
spare document was something of a timetable as well as a map, and a
managing editor skilled at reading it and alert to the several possibilities
of moving pages around within forms or even from one form to another
could tailor his issue as he went along.

As the magazine grew and took shape over the period of several
weeks it took to close any single issue, the mock-up would change
somewhat; a few ads would be moved around to open up better space
for stories, other ads might be dropped or new ones placed. And it
would gradually fill up, with inclusions to show where all the stories
would appear and what they were. In the last days of any issue's making,
only a few blank spaces were left in the mock-up. These indicated the
available pages remaining in the final closing forms. These were the
pages, as many as thirty in a large issue, that a managing editor kept
open for his most urgent or late-breaking stories. Much of this space
was up near the front of the magazine, and there were few or no ads
in the forms so that the stories there could run uninterrupted for greatest dramatic impact.

Life, Vol. XLI, No. 20, was the issue of November 12, 1956. Scheduled to hit city newsstands about a week earlier, it was a big one. In

fact, as one reading the mock-up could quickly see, it was a very big one, 212 pages long, not including the front and back covers and the pages on their reverse sides. The reason for its size, of course, was the amount of advertising in it; in their annual pre-Christmas splurge, advertisers had bought 134 pages of *Life,* much of it in color for about $50,000 a page, for a total price tag of close to $5 million. The ads hustled an enormously varied catalogue of goods for the American consumer: coffeepots, foreign cruises, clock radios, girdles, toothpaste, cheese, the Book of Knowledge, worm pills, shirts, cake mixes, mattresses, liniment, headache potions, Elvis Presley records, and for those who were thinking beyond Christmas, a burial vault ("Made of asphalt and concrete! Water Repellent! Guaranteed!"). And of course there were several pages of ads each for the dependables: life insurance ("How to paint a bright future for your child"), automobiles ("Announcing the trim, new 1957 Hudson Hornet V-8 . . . way up in power, way down in price!"), whiskey ("The decanter and gift wrapping are so distinctive they have received this year's Fashion Academy Award") and cigarettes ("New Filter SPUD freshens the smoke . . . *something wonderful!*"). The ads reflected the seasonal climax of a year so prosperous for *Life* that the eighty space salesmen around the country were able to sell 4,654 pages of the magazine (they could have sold more). It was the most successful year so far in *Life*'s history—and none of the years remaining would approach it.

But even in the euphoria surrounding this extraordinary success, there were surely some who noted the irony that among the magazine's finest customers were the makers of television sets, whose output had increased tenfold since 1950. In fact, page 1 of the issue of November 12, 1956, a choice location in any issue, had been preempted by the manufacturers of "Philco for '57 . . . Startling new mastery of Sight and Sound!" And from page 187 an earnest and terribly familiar face looked out over the headline: "To All *Life* readers from Ed Sullivan." "On Sunday night, November 11," this intimate memorandum began, "I will devote my entire CBS Television Show to a special celebration marking *Life*'s 20 years of publishing." Sullivan's heraldic burble was, naturally, a "house ad," one placed there by *Life*'s enterprising promotion department, whose writers possibly gave Sullivan a hand with his eloquence. "As a newspaperman," he went on helpfully, "I have always been especially impressed by the amazing journalistic job *Life* does each week in reporting the major news events of our time. How *Life* manages to round up so many wonderful photographs, weld them into forceful and informative picture stories and still print and distribute so many millions of copies so short a time after the news happens, is a never-ending wonder to me. And I have been used to frantic deadlines and pressure closings all my working life."

This salute from one professional to another, as it were, went on to describe how Sullivan's enthusiasm had led him to invite the editors to explain how they did it, specifically how *Life* had covered the sinking of the *Andrea Doria* late the past summer. "A highly dramatic 12-minute playlet," Sullivan announced, would take his 50 million viewers behind the thrilling scenes. "Seeing, on television," he continued, ". . . you'll get a better understanding of why *Life*, in two short decades, has become a national institution. Tune us in Sunday night at eight, won't you?" he suggested, winding it up: "I promise you some fine entertainment and a brand new insight into this magazine we all read each week." For the folks in the publisher's office at *Life*, that was the important part of this exercise in mutual back scratching, the admission of the magazine's enormous acceptance around the country. Never mind, for the moment at least, that all this cordiality among colossi wasn't going to last much longer, that the powerful embrace of television was soon going to start to hurt like hell.

A good managing editor for the weekly *Life*, along with his more prosaically laudable qualities, had to be an opportunist. That is, he had to be ready to pounce on events as they bloomed and use them to his advantage. He had to be prepared, at the sound of the bells of the most recent bulletin, to give up his established plan and firmly move to another, often giving the impression to those nearby that he welcomed or at least wasn't particularly surprised by this entirely unpredictable turn of events. At the same time, he had to be something of a con man, too, and somehow create the illusion for the readers that the mix of stories he was offering in a given issue had an integrity, a shape that he and his editors had deliberately imposed.

Almost inevitably the new material, especially if it was pictorially strong, would create problems. A big story—earthquake, assassination, uprising, plane crash—would come along late in the closing schedule, and any sensible use of its photographic power would tip the weight of the issue toward the new event. It would suddenly dominate the whole package; all else would seem pale and bland, even inappropriate, following it. And though any good editor was happy to be suddenly confronted with a story that brought unexpected vitality or raw emotion to the pages, he also wanted to maintain the sense that he was in control of the issue and was giving the readers as varied and balanced a blend as possible. Therefore the stories he picked for inclusion early, or at least a few of them, had to be substantial enough to work with almost anything that followed along later. And he had to make these decisions amid an incredible jumble of scheduling problems that demanded his prompt and careful choices. In the judgment of John Shaw Billings, *Life* in the 1950s "was the largest and most complex editorial operation in magazine history, and as such, Thompson had to juggle the contents of as many as six issues at one time: color forms closed six to eight weeks in advance, other forms from three weeks to forty-eight hours before press time; some form or other closed every day in the week except Sunday."

Back in late September and early October of 1956, when Thompson and his associates began putting together the issue of November 12, he obviously had no real idea of what its final contents would be. That is, he had no way of knowing which news stories would fill the pages he would save for them until the last possible moment. He did know, however, that in that issue he wouldn't be able to touch one of the biggest running news stories of the year, the election contest between President Dwight Eisenhower and Adlai Stevenson, the former governor of Illinois. Thompson would have to ignore it, though for reasons of timing, and not for any lack of interest in the second race between the two men. The November 12 issue was scheduled to close up tight three days before the election on November 6, and it would not appear on most newsstands or in subscribers' mailboxes until some days after the results were known.

Thus no story of current interest could be done, unless the editors decided, of course, to pick the winner in advance. And since the "Picture of the Week" debacle of 1948, the year that the incumbent Harry S Truman defied all the odds to beat Thomas E. Dewey, there had been absolutely no inclination by the editors of *Life*, or *Time*, to make rash predictions.

The greater caution exercised by Time Inc. editors after *Life* called Dewey "the next President" did not, of course, mean an end to partisanship: during the mid-1950s Luce and his magazines were solidly for Eisenhower and the Republicans. In the Ike era, in fact, Luce's political interests showed particularly strongly. A President of his choice and liking was in power, that same President had appointed Clare Boothe Luce as Ambassador to Italy (1953–56), and the presumptuous mind-set that Luce often showed—that his publications somehow spoke for the national interest and were, in fact, unofficial extensions of government—was in clear evidence during these years. A big and controversial story that ran in *Life* early in 1956 provided the basis for a rare illumination of how Luce would even undercut the work of his own reporters and editors to mitigate criticism being heaped on the policies of an administration he favored.

The story was about the operation of U.S. foreign policy, specifically the leadership of John Foster Dulles, Eisenhower's peripatetic Secretary of State. Billed on the cover as "Three Times at the Brink of War: How Dulles Gambled and Won," it told of the risk-filled occasions on which vital U.S. interests were preserved in Asia in spite of menacing Communist tactics. The author of the piece was James Shepley, the chief of the *Time-Life* bureau in Washington, who later became an assistant publisher of *Life* and eventually Time Inc.'s tough and somewhat feared president. Shepley, a journalist not reluctant to make clear his own position on matters of national policy, wrote the article with Dulles's cooperation. The Secretary, in fact, even was shown his own quotes before publication. The most provocative read: "You have to take chances for peace, just as you must take chances on war. Some say that we were brought to the verge of war. The ability to get to the verge without getting into the war is the necessary art. If you cannot master it, you inevitably get into war. If you try to run away from it, if you are scared to go to the brink, you are lost. We've had to look it square in the face—on the question of enlarging the Korean war, on the question of getting in the Indo-China war, on the question of Formosa. We walked to the brink and we looked it in the face."

Beyond its sensational revelations of what came to be called "brinkmanship," the article was a full-blown endorsement of Dulles's actions. "Today the world, free and slave," Shepley wrote with fervent enthusiasm, "knows not only where the U.S. stands on the question of Communism but what the U.S. intends to do about it. And they know because the U.S. Secretary of State has told them, in the greatest display of personal diplomacy since the great days of the Franklin-Adams-Jefferson triumvirate in the Europe of the 1780s."

And at the very end of the article Dulles spoke again in words that came very close to echoing exactly Luce's feelings on the subject of American responsibility in the world. "What we need to do," the Secretary told Shepley, "is recapture the kind of crusading spirit of the early days of the Republic when we were certain that we had something better than anyone else and we knew the rest of the world needed it and wanted it and that we were going to carry it around the world. The missionaries, the doctors, the educators and the merchants carried the knowledge of the great American experiment to all four corners of the globe."

When the article appeared, there was immediately a big flap, and the Democrats fell on Dulles with howls of partisan rage. His strategy was attacked in the Congress as a blow to the integrity of the United States in front of the rest of the world. Adlai Stevenson, among many others, accused the Secretary of playing "Russian roulette with the life of the nation." Columnists and editorial writers all over the country took indignant whacks at "brinkmanship" and charged Dulles with everything from poor judgment to dangerous arrogance. Dulles himself remained quite calm in the face of all the outcry; he did not protest the article or claim that *Life* had distorted his statements or his views.

Luce, on the other hand, seemed especially disturbed at all the commotion. Dulles, the editor-in-chief appeared to feel on second thought (he had approved publication of the piece), had been perilously exposed to his detractors by the article. The emphasis on war and going to the brink of it if necessary took important attention away from the fact that Dulles's essential aim was, of course, peace. Even though neither Dulles nor other administration figures were demanding relief from this embarrassment, Luce decided to come to the rescue anyway.

In a special signed statement in *Life*'s issue of January 30, Luce wrote that "the article as a whole was not an 'interview' and it was not cleared by the Secretary or any other official. . . . Responsibility [for its publication] belongs to the Editors of *Life* and to no others. . . . [O]ur use of [the words 'verge' and 'brink of war'] in the headlines was unfortunate in that they did not fully reflect the main emphasis of the lengthy conversation [between Dulles and Time Inc. reporters] which was on the Administration's vigorous pursuit of peace. . . . If anything in our account of the Secretary's position caused any misunderstanding among our readers or the public, we heartily regret it. At the same time, we are bound to say that any fault of ours was furiously compounded by those who, for the moment, put prejudice or personal advantage above the best interests of the United States."

In an editorial running on the same page as Luce's aggressive apology, the editor-in-chief (through the *Life* writer) reemphasized his confidence in Dulles, no matter how many brinks he'd come to. "In defending him against his critics last week," the editorial said, "President Eisenhower called Dulles 'the best Secretary of State I've ever known.' The Secretary fully deserves this praise. He has handled the fateful issues of war and peace with consummate personal skill. He has raised a standard of international morality and justice. His task, however, and that of Congress and the American people, is the greatest ever presented to American foreign policy: not only to avoid atomic war, but to disarm and surmount Communism on fronts that range from distant jungles and factories to the shallows and abysses of the human mind."

Luce's *mea culpa* and his spirited defense of Dulles (whose stewardship of U.S. foreign policy the editor-in-chief would find much more disappointing within a few months) naturally brought gleeful accusations from the Democrats. His magazines, they said, were little more than propaganda sheets churned out for the benefit of the Eisenhower team. Luce was undisturbed by such as that; he was confident of his own judgment in supporting Ike. Just days before the election—right at the time, in fact, that *Life*'s November 12 issue was closing—he wrote a letter to the President congratulating him on his handling of the Suez crisis, precipitated when the British and French joined the Israelis in an attack on Egypt a few months after Egypt had taken over operation of the canal. "This is just a fan-note," Luce wrote Eisenhower, "which you may come across in some calmer moment. The crisis of the last few days has been 'sickening.' (That's how many people describe their feelings about it.) Your conduct has been superb. Your T.V. statement on Wednesday night dealt effectively with the actual situation. And, in my opinion, it went far beyond that because you took this occasion to hold up the banner of Law as it has not been held up in a generation. More than ever, I look forward to living in the next four years. God bless you—and thanks." The President's reply was immediate and grateful. He wrote: "Yours is the kind of note that picks me up on those rare occasions when I allow fatigue to bring me a fleeting sense of frustration."

Luce's warm feelings about Eisenhower did not prevent *Life*'s vigorous and relatively evenhanded coverage of the 1956 campaign. An editorial endorsing the President ran in October, but before then there were several picture stories and other articles about the Democrats. The editorial page had actually been admiring of Stevenson from time to time, and there had been a fascinating article in the July 16 issue about Eisenhower's Vice President and the man the Republican convention would name to run with him for a second term. The story was called "A Debate, Pro and Con—The Subject: Richard M. Nixon," and its author was Robert Coughlan, a writer of experience, skill and elegant style. Coughlan, a fastidious, urbane and handsome man who had been on *Life* for many years and at one time had been the boss of the articles department, was one of the best of a small group of star senior writers who worked only on the long pieces, turning out between four and as many as ten of them a year.

Coughlan shaped his story in the conventional debate mode, with a chairman stating the proposition ("Resolved: that Richard Nixon would be a good President of the United States") followed by arguments and rebuttals on both sides. At the time the article appeared, Nixon had not yet been selected to be Eisenhower's running mate once more, and it is likely that it made interesting reading for the President's advisers (who probably gave Ike a much-shortened version of it) and the delegates to the convention. In his guise as chairman Coughlan reached no decision, leaving that to "the judges—the American people," but the negative side of the argument was put forth with rare vigor and candor. There had, indeed, been some internal debate about running the piece at all, but Luce eventually put his misgivings about it aside. Some of it was strong stuff to appear in a journal of Republican sympathies eighteen years before Nixon's final disgrace. "Nixon suffers from a fatal defect of character," it read. "Quite simply, he lacks principle." Later the point was made again—harder. "He is, apparently, permanently and incorrigibly irresponsible," Coughlan wrote, "a man who either does not know or does not care that partisanship carried to extremes is dangerous for the welfare of the country."

But there could be no such challenging a political piece in the November 12 issue. What Thompson and his editors really wanted as they made their early choices was something light and non-controversial. One such available item was a sprightly and affectionate bit of nostalgia about vaudeville by radio and television comedian Fred Allen, an important and widely admired figure in American entertainment who had died a few months earlier. Like many other articles that appeared in Life, Allen's was excerpted from a book then about to be published; it was perfect easy fall reading, full of vaudeville lore and stories about remarkable characters like Orville, who billed himself as "The Boy Hercules." According to Allen, Orville played the violin with an enormous English bulldog suspended from the crook of his bow arm and during his finale sang a song with a small upright piano resting on his stomach.

Another article slotted early for November 12 was by one of Life's frequent and most renowned contributors, Sir Winston Churchill, whose war memoirs had run in frequent installments over a period of five years in the late 1940s and early 1950s. Now the subject of Churchill's rolling periods was the history of the English-speaking peoples, which appeared in handsomely illustrated chunks of Life from 1956 to 1958. The title of the November 12 chapter, Installment #7, was "High Venture and Civil War," and the text, drawn by the editors from Sir Winston's book manuscript, touched briefly on early waves of English immigrants to America and in more detail on the growing troubles of the Stuart kings and the rise of Oliver Cromwell. It was a lively and informative account by a man who was unquestionably *Life*'s best rewarded author (more than $1 million for assorted memoirs, histories, speeches), and the come-on, teaser copy at the end of the piece urging readership for the following installment made it all sound positively delicious. "In Next Week's Issue," it barked, ". . . Cromwell's 'deed of frightfulness' in Ireland . . . the 'prying and spying' that characterized 10 years of dictatorship . . . the 'unceasing, flagrant and brazen scandal' of court life under Charles II." Next week, Nell Gwyn.

The editor who handled the Churchill closing in that issue was Ralph Graves, then thirty-two, a Harvard graduate who had been at *Life* since 1949. He had recently returned from Chicago, where he was in charge of the reporters and photographers in that busy bureau—and so popular that his staff had given him a green phone and a hat with "Chief" written on it. When he was first interviewed for a job at the magazine, Graves was asked what he would like to see changed about it. "There is too much news about things I already know," he replied, "and too little sports." This was really quite an artful answer, calling for a focusing of news coverage that no professional could find offensive, and indicating that he was interested in athletics, a blameless preoccupation. It suggested, too, that he was quite well informed. It was, in short, an answer that would appeal to most perceptive interviewers; it called for constructive change, and it was forthright, intelligent and earnest. These were the no-nonsense qualities that made him the choice, twenty years later, to become the weekly *Life*'s sixth managing editor—and its last.

At the time of the Churchill closing, Graves was an assistant to the top articles editor, Jay Gold, a sensitive and prickly man who had worked with Sir Winston on earlier projects with great success. Gold recognized Graves's abilities and gave him substantial responsibility. Graves made his selections for each installment from the full Churchill manuscripts, had them approved or modified by Gold and then sent the choices to Sir Winston's office in London, along with whatever connective writing was necessary to string the selections together. There were rarely hitches of any kind, and the job was easy for him. The methodical Graves never let his considerable ambition disrupt the orderly progress of his career. "I always saw myself getting the job of the guy who was immediately above me," he recalled. "Never five steps up, only one step." Yet he was not without humor, some of it even self-deprecating, a winning variety often useful for comers at Time Inc. "What I really hated about that period," he said, glancing back to his early days at *Life*, "was that there were a lot of young men and I looked like all of them. I never liked the name Ralph," he added. "It's always reserved for villains in bad books. And it's the Number Two villain who's Ralph, the guy who helps the Number One villain do his dirty work." Of course, Graves, a strongly built fellow with a crew cut then and a mouth that seemed small and alum-pursed until he laughed, didn't really look much like any of the others, and even though his gray eyes were cool—and possibly calculating—behind rimless glasses, few thought of him, at least in those early days, as a villain of any rank at all.

Ambition, it should be noted, was not thought of as a shameful condition at *Life*, although one caught practicing it too openly might be regarded as foolish or clumsy. It cannot be an exaggeration to say that a majority of the young men who came to work at the magazine in its years of greatest success thought of themselves at one time or another as potential candidates to become managing editor. Virtually all of Graves's contemporaries were guilty of that self-appraisal, some, myself included, more than others. The race looked exciting, the rewards were guessed to be high, the goal was obviously a worthy one—so people naturally wanted it. In the late 1940s Edward Kern, a brilliant young Harvard graduate who had just come to *Life*, shared an apartment with another of the magazine's newer employees, John Dille. Both were fledgling writers and soon after they moved in together, Kern noticed that Dille was bringing home photostats of pictures along with the big, *Life*-sized sheets used in making final layouts. He set up a table for himself and gathered a pastepot, gum erasers, soft-lead pencils, razors and large metal rule. He installed a strong light over the table. Kern, whose interest in the magazine switched quickly over to other matters as soon as he'd cleared the Time & Life Building each night, was surprised at this evidence of full-time preoccupation on Dille's part. He became still more so when he noted that Dille, a small, intense man with a large head who was a serious and precisely programmed worker and had performed heroically with his tank-destroyer outfit in France in World War II, was laboriously constructing his own version of layouts that were already in progress back in the office or even completed. A polite sort who respected the next man's eccentricity, Kern was nonetheless moved to ask Dille why he was doing this. "To get practice," Dille replied with some impatience. "I need the practice." Why? Kern wanted to know. Writers weren't required to make layouts. But *managing editors* had to know what they wanted, Dille answered crisply. "That's why I need the practice," he added, "so I'll be qualified for *that*." Furthermore, he added, he didn't really think a man should come to work for the magazine if he didn't aspire to be managing editor. Too astonished, perhaps, to speak, Kern shrugged—and stayed on at *Life* until the end, keeping his shocking lack of ambition to himself.

One slower-closing story that Thompson could easily count on for likely inclusion in the November 12 issue would involve one of *Life's* most predictable and productive staples over the years—the adventures of royalty. *Life* had an insatiable passion for crowned heads, their relatives, their loves and hates and hangers-on. This time the royal person was Britain's Princess Margaret Rose, the Queen's sister, and she would be traveling to East Africa for five weeks of feeding giraffes, applauding native dancers and reviewing endless lines of spear-bearing tribesmen in Kenya and Tanganyika. Such visits, attended on this occasion by *Life* photographer Mark Kauffman and covered in color, were perfect fodder for the magazine, offering a great mix of exotic scenery and funny costumes, all parading before the camera on a precise schedule. Already 1956 had been rich in the royal vein, with articles about people who were reigning, deposed or about to be crowned. In July there had been a long color essay on the Duke of Windsor's garden in France, enlivened with matter-of-fact captions ("The dog I am holding is Disraeli") by the abdicated monarch himself. And in the first months of the year there had been several stories on America's own stunning Princess Apparent, the movie star Grace Kelly, and her fairy-tale, sort of, courtship with the stocky Rainier of Monaco. No matter that Rainier's principality was less than half the size of Central Park and that its basic industry was roulette. If the Grimaldis of Monte Carlo were good enough for the fabulously popular Grace and the Kellys of Philadelphia, they were just fine for *Life's* readers, who were gleefully told virtually everything about the wedding festivities (among the presents were bonbon dishes from Princess Serge Wolkonsky and a bone-and-gold hatchet from the Speleological Club of Monaco) and then taken, photographically speaking, to the royal ceremony itself inside Monaco's St. Nicholas Cathedral.

While he was making early plans for November 12, Thompson was also beginning to think seriously about the year-end issue, a special edition on women that would come out about Christmastime and be on the newsstands for two weeks. This "two for one" issue, which cost thirty-five cents instead of the usual twenty, was becoming an annual custom at *Life*; with it the magazine could produce a substantial, single-topic product and attract enough advertising, which always fell off precipitously at Christmas, to make a respectable showing. Graves, too, as well as several of the other top editors, was working on the special, which was to be called, with typically grand-sounding all-inclusiveness,

"The American Woman: Her Achievements and Troubles." Graves's job was to assign writers to various articles, and he had picked several big-name authors to give the package some useful authority. Among them were Cornelia Otis Skinner, who would write "Women are Misguided," Phyllis McGinley ("Women are Wonderful"), Emily Kimbrough ("She Needs Time to Consolidate Her Position") and Margaret Mead ("Her Strength is Based on a Pioneer Past"). The redoubtable Robert Coughlan, who no matter how choked with deadline stress he became kept his hair neatly combed and dressed with Savile Row impeccability, was given a difficult and important subject: "Changing Roles in Modern Marriage: Psychiatrists find in them a Clue to Alarming Divorce Rise."

For this special, Thompson, who did not ordinarily make assignments himself, was on the hunt for somewhat bigger game, specifically Clare Boothe Luce. At the time, she was nearing the end of a three-year tour as U.S. Ambassador to Italy, and she had written an article about some of her observations on the job. Thompson wanted it for the women's issue, but Mrs. Luce apparently had another publication in mind for her writing, of all places *The Saturday Evening Post*, whose editors were interested in the magazine rights for an autobiography she was considering. Her years as ambassador were a natural part of that.

The idea of losing this prominent woman, and a family member at that, to the *Post* horrified the intensely rivalrous Thompson. Warned by Luce of her plans and his feelings sounding a bit hurt, Thompson wrote Mrs. Luce to ask her for the piece about her job. He wrote the final week of the closing of the November 12 issue, probably as he was waiting for the astonishing pictures of the Hungarian Revolution he would soon see, and he sat, as he usually did when he took care of his correspondence, hunched over a typewriter alone in his big office with a cigar held firmly in his teeth.

"Dear Clare," he began, "I would like, very earnestly, to ask you to reconsider your decision not to allow your article to be published. Harry, incidentally, says rather resignedly that it is o.k. for me to make this pitch. I gather that he agrees with me but thinks maybe I am wasting my time and yours. . . .

"There is one consideration which probably didn't and wouldn't have much to do with your decision. It is that it seems to me almost impossible to have an issue on American Women without having you in it. You know what I mean—you win all those Most Prominent polls, etc. You may be right in deciding that it is more chic to have the *Post* publish your full-length autobiography. It seems to me, though, that to leave you out of this issue would seem, to those who don't know the inside of it, to be leaning over backward to an extent that is positively silly. There is a limit to how much one can ignore one's family and obviously a *House & Garden*-type visit to the Villa Taverna [the ambassador's residence in Italy] would be inadequate.

"Harry is a good reporter," Thompson went on, readying his main pitch. "What he told me was that from what you knew of the issue you felt your article would be out of place. I think you may be leaping at conclusions. For one thing, the issue is for all of our readers and we expect men to be fully as interested as women. For another, we are trying to encompass, within admittedly a limited amount of space, all of women's interests and activities. Survey figures show that 98% of all American women consider a career, most seriously up until the age of at least 25. We will be concerned with women's careers on low to medium levels elsewhere in the issue and men will be interested in this because they not only hire but work with them and for them—and marry them. What could fit into the issue better than an article on how a woman does a job, according to man's—no, not man's, universal— rules. And the job is one to which any citizen, whatever sex, would be proud to aspire. This article seems to me the logical counterpart of whatever else we do about women and careers.

"The notion that you think this issue might be too frivolous to absorb such an important article has occurred to me. I rejected this because I think you know how seriously we assemble these special issues. I would be glad to go over the projected table of contents with you, though. As a matter of fact, I would like to talk to you anyway. May I?"

None of Thompson's arguments was persuasive enough for the ambassador, who cabled him from Rome: "Thank you for your kind letter of October 31, but *Foreign Affairs* magazine is publishing article, so regret I cannot release it to *Life*. Frankly I do not wish to appear in Women Issue at all either pictorially or in text. *Time* has indeed bent over backwards for many years to keep me out of its pages, and I have on the whole understood. One more backward bend cannot hurt you, but this time it will really please me. Warm regards, Clare Luce." For all her wire's cordiality, it suggested another message as well. There seemed a small but clear note of triumph in it, the possibility that an old score had been settled. Her pieces had appeared in the picture magazine from time to time, notably and frequently during the war. But now, with the managing editor virtually pleading for her contribution, she sounded almost happy, after waiting twenty years for the chance, to reject *Life*.

Organizing the special women's issue for Thompson—while he concentrated more on the current closings—was one of his assistant managing editors, Philip Wootton, a tall, shambling, rather wispy-looking man with glasses who had come to work for *Life* in 1941 when he was in his early twenties. Wootton appeared vague, as he blinked and said little even to people he was dealing with. But any conclusion about his possible slowness was a mistake; he was bright, a deft administrator, extremely sensitive to office politics, and because he had an interest in working with numbers, he managed Thompson's editorial budget, then running about $10 million a year. He had a clear distaste for *Life's* extravagance in this free-spending period, and he remembered with affection the tough old days when most of the office furniture was rented, when he had to repair the cord on his own telephone, when a deskless reporter did her typing on the floor. "We would do anything for the magazine," he said, "stay up all night, go without lunch or dinner, drive miles in our uncertain cars and rarely think of charging mileage. Before throwing memos away, we went through them page by page, removed the clips and then used the backs as scratch paper."

Wootton was not a popular figure in the office. He did not have the city-room gruffness of someone like Thompson. He did not have the gung ho drive and romantic approach to journalism of a man like George Hunt, the burly and even beautiful former Marine hero who was his principal rival for Thompson's job. He had, in fact, no qualities of flamboyance at all, and his general coolness was widely (and inaccurately) interpreted as apathy. His working habits helped to establish this conviction. Wootton, who had been raised under Billings's orderly rule and who plainly enjoyed his home life in Connecticut, frequently left the office early, about five o'clock in the afternoon. This was a most unusual time of departure in the Thompson era, although late arrivals in the morning were commonplace. Various observers often saw Wootton leaving early, slouched and waiting for the elevator in his grimy raincoat and banged-up fedora, and each sighting was widely reported with amused contempt, as if he had been caught stealing someone's newspaper.

He was also generally considered to be a special protégé of Henry Luce's, and that did not improve his standing. Actually, Luce did admire Wootton's calm capabilities, and there is evidence to suggest that he at one time preferred Wootton to the fiery Hunt as a choice to succeed Thompson as managing editor. But office gossip made much

Henry Luce and his right-hand man, **Roy Larsen**, in the 1930s

John Shaw Billings, the first managing editor

Dan Longwell, who helped Luce start *Life* and was its second managing editor, in an American Gothic pose   (Mary Fraser Longwell)

Wilson Hicks, longtime czar of *Life*
photographers
(U.S. Navy Photo)

oseph Thorndike, *Life*'s managing
ditor from 1946 to 1949
William Sumits, *Life* magazine
Time Inc.)

Alfred Eisenstaedt, one of the original staff who took pictures until the very end
(Leonard McCombe, *Life* magazine © Time Inc.)

Joseph Kastner, for many years boss of *Life's* writers

otographer **George Silk**, a New Zealander who joined
fe during World War II
arl Mydans, *Life* magazine © Time Inc.)

Carl and **Shelley Mydans**, one
of the first and best of *Life*'s
photographer-correspondent
teams
(Carl Mydans, *Life* magazine
© Time Inc.)

Margaret Bourke-White photographs a German fighter plane downed in Russia
(Margaret Bourke-White, *Life* magazine © Time Inc.)

Robert Capa
(George Rodger)

Photographer **W. Eugene Smith**
early in World War II
(U.S. Navy Photo)

Entertainment editor **Tom Prideaux** interviewing movie actress **Virginia Mayo**
(Ed Clark, *Life* magazine © Time Inc.)

more of the association. Because Wootton, like Luce, came from a family of missionaries who had served in China, it was suggested that there was some special kinship between the two. One woman who saved a special wisecracking scorn for Wootton developed the broad joke that his name was really Philip Woo Ton, that he was Luce's illegitimate son by a long-forgotten Chinese mistress.

Since the special issue was, after all, concerned with women, two women were in operating charge of it—under Wootton's supervision, of course. One was Mary Hamman, a tough, shrewd, funny, hard-drinking editor with long experience on women's magazines whom Thompson had hired in 1950 because he wanted more knowing and professional coverage of subjects like food and housing. Blond and blunt-spoken, Hamman was not in the slightest intimidated by Thompson or by the other men in senior positions at Time Inc., all of whom she called "dearie" with cheerful indiscrimination. The only thing that frightened Mary Hamman was the self-service elevators, which she would not ride unless she had a companion she could clutch if the rising or falling got rough. Working under Hamman on the special issue was Eleanor Parish, a younger woman, smart and good-looking, who hid useful steel behind a shy and sexy smile. She had come to *Life* from Barnard College in the late 1940s, had been a reporter and writer in the science department and was now beginning to get administrative experience that would be useful to her later when she replaced Mary Hamman as modern living editor in the 1960s. She was also beginning to see a lot of Ralph Graves, and in 1958 they were married, each, in the columnists' phrase, for the second time. It was not the ordinary conclusion of an office romance at *Life*, and it turned out much better than most.

A job of particular delicacy on the women's issue, even in those unliberated days, had been given to John Thorne, then just past forty, a former bomber pilot who had started working for *Life* as an office boy right out of Harvard in 1939. It was Thorne's job to edit the copy coming from writers working on picture stories for the special issue, and it required skill and taste to make sure it all went together without disastrous omissions, repetitions, slips or double entendres. A few of the stories in the issue were sheer fluff, and two of these were long photographic essays on beautiful young women, the first a collection of pictures of Americans, the second a portfolio of women from everywhere else. After the first story closed, Thorne addressed a memo to me; for some reason beyond recall I had been assigned to both stories. "Dear Loudon," it read. "We must not relax our vigilance just because we have got safely past one of these frightening essays. Thus I have taken the liberty of making a list of the modifiers you used in describing various of the American beauties. Possibly it will be helpful to know what we *can't* say about the beauties from abroad." His list followed: "fresh-faced, statuesque, unaffected, flirtatious, cameolike, wholesome, direct, warmly attractive, plain-spoken, composed, luxuriant, elegant, satined, stylish . . . Thorne." The memo, however, did not close off all descriptive possibilities. By drawing liberally from the vivid recollections of photographer Philippe Halsman, I was able to endow the foreign beauties—to Thorne's amusement—with "frisky gaiety," "languid grace," "innate nobility," "classic harmony," "unabashed voluptuousness" and "a boldness that is completely Irish."

John Thorne was an amalgam of gentility, competence, humor and talent—and, as he grew older at the magazine and gathered his disappointments with himself, of wry bitterness as well. The most distinguishing thing about his appearance, because it somehow enhanced his natural good looks, was a scar that lay diagonally across his cheek for perhaps the length of a cigarette and indented his ruddy skin to the corner of his mouth. It came from an automobile accident of his childhood, but it looked more dashingly won than that. People noticed it immediately, and on the street women often looked at him with open interest as he approached.

Like many of the men who worked at *Life* then, Thorne dressed in the Ivy League fashion, and more so than most. His style was unvaryingly conservative, his shirts at work always buttoned down, his sport jackets always tweed, his suits very likely brown or a special, not exactly khaki-colored gabardine sold only by Brooks Brothers. When he wore seersucker in the summer, it *was* seersucker and not some slippery fake. He never let his straight brown hair get too long, he put his feet up on his desk and talked to visitors with his hands clasped behind his head and he often put drops in his eyes to soothe them just before going out to lunch. He smoked Camels, a lot of them, but he tried not to start until midday.

John Thorne was often engaged in similar little actions against his more destructive tendencies. He loved to drink, as great numbers of his colleagues did, including me, and when he enjoyed something, his enjoyment made him wonder if it was wrong. Sometimes he took steps to cut back his pleasure, like shifting from martinis to Dubonnet, but he gave up self-improvement with relief. He often referred to people by their last names, in the boarding school fashion, and he was good at adding a single line to another man's luncheon story and making it better.

He was excellent at evaluating situations on the magazine, both personal and professional. He was one of those people who make continuous use of the past, and he had precedents for everything. His long service at *Life*, in which he took great pride, left him unsurprised by any event and occasionally wearied by it in advance. He maintained—with some justice—that all stories could be written by established formulas, and he could be very funny as he pointed out various openings and endings that could be applied to appropriate types of stories and then, as if recalling from a manual of instruction, gave them numbers like Lead Sentence 47 and Snapper Ending 16.

He did in fact know a lot about writing for *Life*. His own was perceptive and clear and straightforward; he was embarrassed by hyperbole. His work often strengthened and supported picture stories in ways that few other writers achieved. Yet, though he was aware of his strengths, he always underplayed them and mocked himself. For example, he often said (with some wistfulness) that he felt sure he could write a novel if only Ed Thompson or George Hunt would tell him to do it and tell him what it was supposed to be about and how long it should be and when it had to be finished. His modesty and genial cynicism worked against him. His good manners and fastidiousness made him perfectly suited to be passed by, run over by hardier types who often had less ability than he. Unassertive and outwardly mild, he was too ready to swallow his fury in the face of outrage. Preferring almost to cling to the wrongheadedness of others, to grumble about things later, he hugged his grievances, and nobody noticed, of course. They liked better to think of him as a charming and knowing fellow who always came up with the right thing to say. Coles Phinizy, a man hired by *Life* in the late 1940s, remembered well the first time he saw John Thorne. It was Phinizy's first day at work; he, too, had gone to Harvard, where he had belonged to an exclusive eating club whose members wore neckties of two different designs, one on Sundays and the other the rest of the week. When the recruit got off the elevator at the proper floor, a man hurried along the hall toward him. He had a scar on his cheek, and he smiled as he looked the newcomer over and glanced at his tie. "It's not Sunday," he said pleasantly—and passed on.

During his wife's tenure as ambassador, Henry Luce spent considerable time in Rome, but he kept close watch over his magazines, very much including *Life*. A lot of his communication about business matters was directed to C. D. Jackson, a large and elegant man, one of Luce's most influential lieutenants for many years and his powerful liaison with the Eisenhower administration, in which Jackson had worked for a time while on leave from his job in the company. Late in the summer of 1956, Luce, as was often the case, was fussing about the structure of the big magazine. "I write you first," he told Jackson, who would become *Life*'s publisher in three years, "about what is first of all important—namely, the Editorial Organization of *Life* Magazine. . . . Two things triggered this problem in my mind. One was a brief talk with Heiskell just before he left—in which he expressed doubts as to the overall editorial qualities of the several editors next in rank to Thompson and Elson [Robert Elson, then Thompson's executive editor and chief deputy]. . . .

"The other was a remark made by I forget who . . . in our luncheon session on *Life*'s future plans. The remark was that *Life* photographers are currently 'spread thin' over the many excellent ideas and assignments on *Life*'s Future list. Besides being a factual statement of the situation, this remark sharpened a feeling I had that *Life* was proceeding without a sufficiently firm control of priorities. . . .

"The problem broadens out into what might be called an intellectual-journalistic grasp of various subjects and stories. . . . We need under Thompson and Elson five or six first-class editors. Not all of them would have to be potential M.E.'s but at least three out of five or four out of six. The men we have to consider are: Wootton, Hunt, MacLeish [Kenneth MacLeish, Archibald's son and then a senior editor of *Life*], Farmer [Gene Farmer, then foreign news editor]—and who else? Wootton, MacLeish and Farmer may all be regarded as highly useful, but Hunt would seem to be the only potential M.E.—and he is not only eighteen months away but a couple of psychic jumps too.

"To get three or four potential M.E.'s is going to take a lot of looking—a studying of the entrails. Understand, when I speak of potential M.E.'s, I am *not* thinking of an actual replacement of Thompson—long may he live and shine—I simply mean that to handle *Life*'s $7,000,000 worth of editorial activity he needs, besides Elson, three or four people that should be worth at least $50,000 a year, and maybe $75,000—to put it in dollar terms. Who are they?"

Luce urged that Jackson and Heiskell look over the *Life* staff carefully. "And let's get their records, their dossiers in order," he wrote. Summing up, he declared: "So I would say that the No. 1 Objective of the Corporation for 1957 is to get a really high-class high-powered top management team for *Life*. . . .

"I would prefer that nothing be said to Ed about this until my return in mid-September because this is par excellence a subject I should like to handle myself—with informative assistance from you and [Heiskell]. . . . This is a subject of vital importance to us. But we must proceed with care. Capisci?"

For all Luce's insistence on caution, he was unable to wait until his return to the United States to talk to Thompson about *Life*'s top management. His sense of urgency about this was heightened because he was considering moving Elson, Thompson's top assistant, to another job in Time Inc. Luce began his letter with an almost apologetic reference to the fact that it made him "nervous to be way off here" when various problems came up. "Of course, there's only one real problem ever—and that's people," he wrote to Thompson. "Get the right people in the right place and there's nothing to it—either in war or peace. Simple. But how do you do just that? God knows. Like the fellow sings in *Fair Lady*, 'Wiv a little bit, wiv a little bit . . .'

"When the luck runs heavily your way, you don't want it to quit—you don't even want to think about it quitting. That's why it makes me nervous even to think about your thinking about doing anything except what naturally I think you were born to do. Sure, I know you can think of a lot of other things to do. So can I.

"But here we are. And here let us stay—until the Big Umpire unmistakably blows the whistle."

Then Luce mentioned the possibility of Elson's leaving *Life* and from that slid deftly into the personnel problem that most concerned him. "A few days before I left," he went on, "we had, as you know, a 'future' lunch and I was really overwhelmed by the amount and variety of *Life*'s future plans. This is splendid testimony to your staff as it is. Nevertheless what went through my mind was the question whether you had top editors who could direct and execute to best advantage all the variety of opportunity and the wealth of material indicated by the future list.

"I certainly don't have to remind you what an immense operation *Life* is. But it *is* truly immense. The figure of $7,000,000 (or whatever it is for the editorial budget) is only a symbol of its scope.

"To imagine all that enterprise being conducted to anything approaching perfection, one has to imagine, in addition to the Commanding Officer, at least five or six people of outstanding over-all ability. Each of the five or six people would, of course, have quite distinct personalities, would have more strength along some lines than in others—and yet each of them would have a fair share of qualities in common: e.g. something identifiable as flair for journalism, 'nose for news,' etc.; some depth of understanding; executive or leadership qualities, etc.

"Now and again, there appears a man with a touch of 'genius' in his field—and all the conventional tests of ability must make way for him. But short of such genius lucking into us, we have to make the best use we can of standards of judgment in selecting and bringing up men qualified to help run at the top the greatest magazine operation in history!

"All of this is mere prelude to talks I hope to have with you beginning in a few weeks and resuming throughout the autumn. What I've tried to indicate here is that I'd like to start with trying to define some general standards of ability, by which all top *Life* editors should be tested (in our estimates) and then see how each of the people you mention (and others) measure up.

"And I'm *not* thinking about who should be the next M.E. of *Life*. I'm just thinking that the fifth-ranking Editor of *Life* should be able to put out a better magazine than *Look* or *Paris-Match* (a *very* good magazine)—even if he had only $1,000,000 to spend!

"If none of this seems very pertinent—skip it. I may be too far away from where life is real and earnest! Yours, Harry."

For all Thompson's alleged inability or reluctance to bring along men who would someday be suitable replacements for him, he built a very solid working staff and kept reaching out for people who might improve it. He particularly wanted experienced professionals in certain fields; he didn't share the common Time Inc. confidence in the value of sheer journalistic exuberance, though he welcomed and rewarded both luck and high spirits. One field where Thompson especially wanted knowing coverage was sports—*Life*'s approach to that had been too amateurish in the past, he thought. And with some justice; one *Life* sports editor in the 1940s announced with some pride that he'd never seen a major-league baseball game until he got the job. And Thompson felt there should be a sports story of some kind, often two, in virtually every issue. In 1951 he hired away an expert from *Time*, a morose and rather handsome man named Marshall Smith, whom colleagues correctly regarded as a talented "bleeder" who had excellent story ideas and who also wrote well while giving off pitiful signs of distress. Smith was delighted at the chance to escape to *Life*. "Working at *Time*," he recalled much later, "was like walking in a tunnel with your shoulders touching the sides. Those were the worst years of my life. I still can't believe it."

Smith's agonies over his writing did not end when he came to *Life*, and he always suffered, whether the story going to press was just a page and a half of pictures and captions or a full-length article. "I never thought I was a good writer," he said. "I always figured I wasn't good enough. I had to write another piece to prove the last one wasn't a fluke. It's like committing another murder to make sure that the last one was okay." When he was in the early stages of writing an article,

Smith used to wander around the halls in pursuit of someone he could read a sentence to, or an opening paragraph. Friends learned to avoid him in this dangerous stage of his creativity—though he would ask for an opinion, Smith really didn't want one, unless it was spoken in praise—and they also tried to remember not to ask him how he was doing. This innocent query could get him started on perhaps a half-hour soliloquy on the difficulties of his current project and the likelihood that doom would prevent its completion.

When Smith was deep in his work, beyond his need for approval and companionship, he tuned the world out. He smoked heavily while he sat at the typewriter, and often flicked his butts away without looking up to see where they were flying—sometimes in the direction of the sports reporters seated at their own desks across the room. They usually just ducked and muttered. But on one occasion his staff of three decided to retaliate; at a signal they all fired their butts as close to him as possible, then reached into their ashtrays, reloaded and did it again. Totally unaware of the barrage, he went right on typing.

At *Life* the sports department was often the place where new young men on the magazine got their earliest reportorial experience, and the callowness of several of his reporters made Smith surly. "For Chrissakes," he would say to some cringing novice, "when are you going to snap out of your hop?" and his department became known as "the Detention Center" or as "Smith's Reform Academy." He liked to recall his own hard beginnings at the Providence *Journal*, where his boss told him: "Look, if you have to take a cab, bring back a receipt—or bring back the driver." He enjoyed shocking people mildly. When a young woman from *Time* came back to work after a maternity leave, she stopped off at Smith's office one afternoon with news. She'd had a baby boy, she told him proudly. "Oh," he replied with a grin, "so you got one with a bell on it?"

Smith's dour knowledgeability extended to virtually all the sports, but he was particularly expert on horse racing. His father had been a horse trainer from Baltimore, and Smith had grown up with him around the tracks of the Northeast. He had a powerful affection for his father, and his conversations about the older man were full of color and admiring wonder. "My father was an adult delinquent," Smith recalled on one occasion. "He shared everything with me. He treated me like another man. If I came home with a double dose of the clap, he'd say: 'Why, that's fine. I've had that, too. Let's go down to the doctor and see if we can get it fixed.'

"He probably put my mother in an early grave," he went on, "with all that gambling, drinking and women, but he was great to me. When we were broke, we'd sleep in the stall and eat out of the stewpot together. He'd put me in the best schools. But I'd only stay at each place one term, because he couldn't pay the bill. Then he'd send me to another. I went to fourteen schools.

"We never had real good horses," he explained. "We used to buy horses with problems like bowed tendons and fix 'em up. Then we'd race them. My father always said that ninety-nine percent of horses raced with something wrong with them. 'Now take the favorite,' he'd say to somebody. 'He looks all right, but he probably has four assholes.'"

But when he was involved with writing a story, Smith rarely let sentiment or anything else interfere with his glum absorption. In 1955 he was finishing up a ten-page picture story on the Brooklyn Dodgers. As usual, he was bleeding over every caption and had worked all the previous night long to turn out a clenched total of perhaps fifty words. He came back to the office after a hurried lunch and surprised one of his reporters, who had a visitor, a young woman who worked for another department. Years later, the reporter Jack McDermott recalled the moment well. "I'd proposed at lunch," he said, "and she accepted. And we'd had a drink or two, naturally, just a couple of shooters for me to get up the courage. There we were in the sports department kissing like two mad young fools and in walks the boss. He cleared his throat. Polly just vanished. Marshall took off his coat and sat down behind his machine. I said, 'Hey, Marsh, I think you ought to know what that's all about. I'd appreciate it if you'd keep it to yourself for a while, but Polly and I are getting married.' There was dead silence. Smith had this weird expression on his face. Then he lit a cigarette and put a piece of copy paper in his typewriter. He was pawing around through some research. He stared at the layout while I waited for congratulations. But all he could think about was his headline, and he said to me: 'For Chrissakes, Jack, what's a four-letter word for Roy Campanella?'"

Thompson's decision to bring Smith to *Life* had been a good one for the magazine. The wide-eyed amateurish view *Life* had offered for years, essentially a kind of gaga, superficial boxholder's view that told the readers little more than the obvious, was gone, and in its place the readers were provided more often than not with hardheaded illuminations and insights about the various games and the people who played them. Smith liked to tell readers, for example, how Sal Maglie's ferocious attitude made him a great pitcher, what was the secret behind Ben Hogan's powerful and perfectly grooved golf swing, how a marvelous football defense really worked. Smith's single-minded and demanding approach to stories in his own field rubbed off on the young men (there were no women sports reporters or writers at most places in those sexist days) who worked for him. But in one case in the summer of 1956, the ardent desire to produce a compelling sports story for Smith led, in fact, to a piece of journalistic excess that had its hilarious aspects but that also may even have damaged a most promising athletic career.

Ernie Shelton was a fine high jumper in Los Angeles, a man with good reason to think of himself as one of the world's best. He was almost sure of making the Olympic team that would travel to Melbourne, Australia, later that year. No one, up to that time, had jumped seven feet, and Shelton, who had come close many times and once cleared six feet eleven and a quarter inches, wanted terribly to be the first to make it. In fact, getting over seven feet was a subject that dominated his thought and effort. As *Life* reporter Philip Kunhardt and photographer Loomis Dean found out, Shelton was obsessed with the problem. He drew lines at seven feet on the walls where he lived so that his eye and mind would grow conditioned to the height. More dramatically, he put a set of high-jump standards at the end of his bed with the crossbar resting at seven feet so that his goal would be literally the first and last thing he saw each day. In every way he could think of, Shelton was trying to project himself over this unattainable height. "The Kid with the Seven Foot Psychosis" was the working title Kunhardt gave this fascinating little sports story. Nothing Shelton tried seemed to be working.

At this time there happened to be a flurry of national interest in the subject of hypnotism, thanks to the enormous popularity of a book called *The Search for Bridey Murphy*, which was about a housewife named Ruth Simmons who discovered through hypnotism that she apparently had had a previous incarnation 100 years before as a young woman in Ireland. People were commonly talking then about the various possible applications of hypnotism to dig into a person's past or to alter behavior, and Kunhardt, a powerful young fellow who later became one of *Life*'s top editors, suddenly had an idea. Maybe hypnotism, he thought, could propel Shelton over his seven-foot barrier. He and Dean, a talented, skittery and perceptive man who was utterly sympathetic to bizarre notions, talked it over and agreed that they might have a terrific story if they could get a hypnotist to work with Shelton, who would then go out and soar to a new world's record over seven feet, all the while being photographed for *Life*. It sounded wonderful to them and it also sounded great to me when they asked me about it in my capacity as chief correspondent in the Beverly Hills office, where we all worked. Shelton, anxious to find any avenue of success, agreed, and Kunhardt and Dean dug up a local hypnotist. This man began working with Shelton at no charge, thinking naturally that he would eventually make more money than he could carry if Shelton ever jumped seven feet.

This strange experiment in record seeking went on for some weeks, with Shelton repeatedly being put into hypnotic trances and told by his therapist that he was soon going to succeed in reaching his goal. The hypnotist even went to track meets with Shelton and worked with him right on the field while the jumper was ostensibly resting between tries at the bar. Dean, of course, was taking pictures of it all. Shelton was jumping well, still under seven feet but continuing to feel that his new training technique might work.

It all came to a climax at the final Olympic trial at the Coliseum in Los Angeles. This was to be Shelton's big moment. The results of this meet would determine the members of the Olympic team, and Shelton expected—and wanted terribly—to do well. The hypnotist, wearing a field pass that identified him as a press messenger, was on hand, as usual, to provide an extra boost.

But Shelton, under great stress, jumped badly in spite of all assurances that he could attain the magic height, and the odd experiment in record breaking came to a sad and inglorious end. He failed three times to clear six feet nine inches, finished fifth in the field and didn't make the Olympic team at all. After his final try, he lay in the high-jump pit for fully ten seconds, berating himself repeatedly, saying over and over: "I'm no athlete, I'm no athlete." Then, understandably angry and upset at the turn of events, he got up and literally ran away from photographer Dean, shouting back over his shoulder as he sprinted for the dressing room: "Get away from me! Get away from me!" To further add to Shelton's anguish, a relatively unknown nineteen-year-old named Charles Dumas won the event with a leap of six feet ten inches—and then went on, that same afternoon, to jump seven feet five-eighths of an inch, the first human on record to jump that impossible height.

In the issue of November 12, 1956, there were two sports stories, neither of them of lasting interest but each representative of a hardy and popular type of piece that appeared in *Life* again and again. The first, a fine example of what might be called the "My, What a Wonderful Family" picture story, celebrated in two and a quarter pages of black-and-white photographs the astonishing Majors family of Huntland, Tennessee. The most celebrated Majors at that time was Johnny, twenty-one, described in the story as "a thin-waisted, triple-threat tailback . . . the strongest All-America candidate the University of Ten-

nessee has had in years." There were four younger Majors brothers—
one a rising football star at Florida State, two others who were terror-
izing opponents of their hometown high school team and a fourth who
was already an accomplished passer at the age of seven. They had one
sister, a pretty girl of sixteen who was, of course, a Huntland cheer-
leader, "an avid fan" who "never misses an opportunity to . . . watch
Johnny play." The father of this group was the ranking football expert
in the family, being the coach of the Huntland High team, then un-
defeated in forty-six straight games. "The brothers were introduced to
family football as early as the age of 2," a caption explained, "and now
root hard for one another. Their biggest booster is Mrs. Majors, who
now accepts the game as part of the household. 'If I didn't like football,'
she admits, 'I'd be the most miserable woman in the world.'" If it was
demeaning to Mrs. Majors to dismiss her simply as her agile tribe's
number one rooter, the possibility certainly would not have occurred
to *Life*'s editors in those unliberated days—or by and large to its readers. They were entirely comfortable with the image of the self-effacing
and loyal mom she presented, just as they probably liked the idea that
her son Johnny—when he wasn't running over tacklers on the grid-
iron—"often speaks to children's groups in Knoxville on Sundays."

The second sports item fell into the genre of "Animals Are Smarter
Than You Think," a tried and utterly reliable variety of story the readers
always loved and responded to with admiration and ardor. Actually, this
one could be called a sports story only because its principal character
was a sporting dog, a Labrador retriever named King. It was the kind
of gentlemanly sporting story that Smith hated, and it had been produced by *Life*'s nature department, whose only member, Patricia Hunt,
was a well-groomed, rather distracted-appearing woman of intelligence
and powerful stubbornness who acted as a sort of ambassador for the
animal kingdom at *Life*; she was always speaking up for porpoises and
apes. Bats, snakes, marmosets and spiders, elephants and alligators all
came under her journalistic protection, and she had considerable scorn
for man's ignorance about his fellow animals and his cruelty to them.
She harbored her own cats and horses and thought of them as far more
substantial beings than pets—or humans, often.

Whenever possible, of course, it was important for animal stories
to be heartwarming, and this one was. It turned out that the handsome
retriever King was something of an animal lover himself. And instead
of training him to retrieve dead birds, his owner had taught him to pick
up only those that had been crippled by the gunfire of hunters. The
owner, a non-hunting feed salesman from Klamath Falls, Oregon, then
patched up the wounded birds and eventually released them or placed

the disabled ones in zoos. The dog had thus saved a thousand birds and was rewarded for these good works by being given (along with his master) a testimonial dinner and a medal. It was just the kind of chuckle-inducing trifle that Ed Thompson needed in great quantity to fill up the small islands of space created in these large, ad-filled issues, and he happily selected it for a page and two halves closing about three weeks in advance of the final pages of the issue.

Life's enthusiasm for lovable dog stories was not always reflected on the staff. Possibly the most famous dog in the magazine's history was a waif mutt named Lucky, who was found by photographer Leonard McCombe when he was on assignment in Texas in 1949. The pup's mother had been killed by a hit-and-run driver, and McCombe's pictures of the endearing survivor ran for four pages while a national audience cheered for Lucky's recovery. Then McCombe gave the dog to another photographer, Nina Leen, whose overpowering love for her new pet resulted in another story about Lucky. By this time the staff's delight in the saga was wearing thin, and upon hearing of the possibility that there would be still a third story, an anonymous memo began circulating on the editorial floors. "Notice to Life Staff," it was headed. "Nina Leen's dog, Lucky, will be graduating from school tonight. Naturally Life Magazine will cover the event. Al Fenn is the lucky photographer who has been selected for this assignment. It will be well if no one speaks to Al for a few days. When last seen, he was tearing the wallpaper off a saloon on lower Third Avenue. Lucky's graduation means that he's learned how to be a dog and is now fit to associate with dogs. Nina is very happy about it all. We are happy about the whole thing and expect to see some unusual pictures as a result of this assignment. Fenn did say something about using the biggest strobes in the house, plugging them into Lucky and making his shots by the lights in Lucky's eyes. . . . Eventually, we're sure, we'll be covering Lucky's demise. Let's face it. It's bound to happen, and this is no business for babies or squeamish people. Lucky is bound to pass away; it's only a matter of time. Only a matter of time. So Please—be patient."

Among the ways that Ed Thompson protected his popularity with his staff was to let selected lieutenants be unpopular instead. Supreme among these was Ray Mackland, Life's picture editor in the 1950s, a tall, slightly fleshy man who often dressed in dark blue suits and wore glasses he polished with a breath and his handkerchief while he listened to conversation around him. His sideburns were white. He walked with a kind of gliding languor, and he smiled frequently. In fact, he was called "the Smiling Assassin" by people who bothered to joke about him at all, and not many did. Mackland was the boss of all of the staff photographers, a job that might etch white at the temples of any man, and he supervised all picture assignments. Thus he exerted a degree of real control over virtually everything the magazine did, and many people resented it bitterly. Mackland was widely thought of as a boor and a bottleneck and he could be both. He was also honest, sensible and tougher than most of his adversaries.

Central to Mackland's exercise of power was the daily script conference, a noon meeting where new *Life* projects, large and small, were brought up for discussion and action. It was presided over by Mackland and attended by others who made local assignments and who supervised the magazine's domestic and foreign bureaus. Each person in turn reported on story suggestions or photographic requests received the previous day. It was thus a traffic meeting which served the useful function of keeping the traffic managers aware of what was going on all over the magazine. Since there would be scores, possibly hundreds of projects in various forms of development and readiness, this was one good way to prevent overlap, for example, on stories being prepared by two departments, to check duplication of effort or to head off conflicts. And since the people who attended these meetings had all been involved in the past with finding picture stories and working on them with photographers, they occasionally made sensible contributions as the new ideas came up.

But Mackland saw the function of the meetings as somewhat more than that, as a way to impose his own judgment on the operations of the various editorial departments and bureaus requesting the coverage. Sometimes he blocked suggestions, and if a department head or reporter was foolhardy enough to suggest that a specific photographer be given an assignment, Mackland and his associates would be at some pains to assign another photographer to the job. This naturally often infuriated the various department heads, who favored their own expert judgment in the field of fashion or sports or science or theater and were offended by what they considered sheer high-handedness.

Their anger, their occasional trembling outbursts did not bother Mackland much. Now and then he responded with an attack of his own, but his composure would return as soon as the other had left. "Somebody would argue and argue," he recalled, "and all the time there'd be people outside the office waiting to see me. If I couldn't get him out, I'd explode. Blow up. Just to get to the next person in line. Then I'd pass by my secretary and say: 'Well, how'd I do?' But it was fake." Mackland was a master of such office games. Years earlier, some considerable time after he'd been brought to *Life* from his job on the

Omaha *World-Herald*, he'd been working as assistant to Wilson Hicks, the slick-haired and lordly man who almost from the magazine's beginnings was czar of the photographers. Hicks decided at one point that he did not like Mackland's style and undertook a campaign calculated to persuade him to leave the magazine. He stopped communicating with Mackland and did not provide him with work; he even had Mackland's name removed from *Life*'s masthead, a rare and humiliating punishment. But Hicks withheld the final blow. He would not fire Mackland, possibly because that might trigger a confrontation with Thompson, a friend of Mackland's and Hicks's principal rival in those days. And Mackland, of course, would not take any number of hints. He simply ignored them and refused to be consigned to oblivion. He waited Hicks out. And when Hicks left the magazine after Thompson became managing editor, Mackland got his job.

Though the picture script became in its most ludicrous form a kind of sales document to convince Mackland and his colleagues of the worthiness of a project, it started as something more useful than that. Basically it was supposed to provide a brief description of the proposed story (who, what, when, where, why) and an educated guess as to how much space it would eventually occupy in the magazine.

For example, the script wired to a photographer in Detroit for one possible "*Life* Goes to a Party" story read: "November 12 will be Red Flannel Day at Cedar Springs, Michigan. The town of 1400 is high-geared for production of red flannel underwear and other garments, and once a year to commemorate the rebirth of Cedar Springs red flannel industry most people wear red flannel underwear and night-gowns. They spend the day walking, shopping and working in this state of dishabille. Party Department wants to cover Red Flannel Day with specific suggestions in mind for fast closing color [color that appeared only two weeks after closing instead of the much longer period usually required]. We would like best a picture in color of a whole family on street wearing spectacular red flannels while other citizens operate in background similarly dressed. Overalls of Main Street which promise to be crowded with people wearing red flannel, plus any other spontaneous pictures to suggest mass participation rather than individual eccentricity, should be shot in color as possible fast closer. Red Flannel Day also includes ceremonies—parade, float, queen—which we feel are best covered as black and white support. Any pictures of individuals trying to outdo each other in garb may also add up for a short black and white act to close story totally perhaps three pages and a couple of halves."

Another script, sent in from *Life*'s Beverly Hills office, listed the somewhat garish photographic possibilities for an upcoming film. "Suggest we add *The Prodigal* (MGM) to our plans," it began. "Movie has absolutely nothing of significance to say but for elegant decadence and grandiose depravity, it sounds hotter than Nero's fiddle. Movie is concerned with imaginary adventures in Damascus of the Prodigal (Edmund Purdom) and his love affair with a pagan priestess (Lana Turner).

"Three or four instances of prodigality stand out. (1) Gigantic wheel of fortune mounted horizontally like merry-go-round. Twelve girls occupy standing positions along outer rim which is propelled by four dwarfs. Recommend we shoot wheel in motion at slow shutter speed so girls go blurry as well as shooting at speed sufficient to stop the motion. (2) There is the love goddess Astarte's flaming sacrifice pit presided over by Lana Turner and huge black figure of the god Baal towering over one end. Into the pit will leap a character called the 'chosen martyr' which should compose nicely for a fiery vertical. (3) There is the 'Tinted Wall,' a row of niches in a bright and gaudy tile wall each occupied by an unemployed harlot. This is a sort of outdoor employment agency and virtues and prices of each girl are crudely advertised in writing under her niche.

"Also recommend gruesome scene in which Purdom is attacked by giant vultures and fights them off with carcass of another vulture. Studio will construct two mechanical vultures of twice normal size. For another scene in which birds appear on empty streets of Damascus, special set will be constructed and scaled down to half size so birds look twice as big. We can have some fun with the optical illusion of shooting scene both with and without human figure."

The perpetrator of this merry script was Jim Lebenthal, *Life's* movie correspondent of the period. A Princeton graduate then in his mid-twenties, Lebenthal, a bright-eyed, intense, very funny young man with so much energy that he seemed at times about to ignite and lift off, roamed his entertainment beat with wonder, huge enthusiasm—and his tongue often planted firmly in his cheek. "We sent you photograph other day," he wired one day in word-saving fashion to his colleagues in New York, "of chimpanzee Tamba tugging at blouse of pretty maid. More we think of it, feebler the humor seems. Nevertheless here's some dope should need arise. Girl is Columbia's brightest new gem of motion pictures, Kim Novak, about whom you'll be hearing more from us. Meantime, she was presenting Tamba with honorable mention scroll for acting excellence at American Humane Society's fourth annual P.A.T.S.Y. award presentation here last Sunday, March 28th. Humane Society is the outfit that supervises movie sets whenever animals are used for scene to safeguard against devices like the running wire used in bygone days to trip horses for spectacular falls in front of the camera. As starlet Novak handed Tamba scroll specifically for acting talents displayed in Columbia's *Valley of the Head Hunters,* a chain of anthropomorphic events happened in rapid succession. As Kim relates it, 'It was so funny. Tamba put an arm around me and began looking at my blouse wondering what was under there. Then he' (Tamba we learn is a female) 'opened the blouse and looked in. I pushed him away and he gave a puzzled look. It was so extremely human and yet the only reason he was able to get away with me letting it pass was because he was an ape.' This confirms what we've held all along: Apes have it pretty soft around here. Regards."

Lebenthal, who left *Life* to make films of his own and eventually wound up in his family's New York bond firm, for which he creates and stars in very successful and somewhat wacky television commercials, was always fascinated by the zany aspects of life in Hollywood. At one time in the mid-1950s he suggested a story on a woman who was the hostess of a horror show on a local television program. Her show name was Vampira, and Lebenthal's wired suggestion that the magazine do a story about her read: "Show opens with back-lit shot of the wasp-waisted woman preceded by her own shadow, walking towards camera down a long hallway spotted intermittently with candelabras and filled with the vapors of dry ice. She screams and titles fill the screen. Next she is seen in her attic playroom, languishing on a Victorian sofa from which the cherubic curlicues have been removed and replaced with death's heads. Between reels Vampira gives a spiel appropriate to the movie being presented or reads aloud from an oversize volume, *Embalming, Self-Taught,* or discusses such garden variety subjects as hands. 'I love hands,' she says in a sultry monotone. 'In fact my drawers at home are filled with hands.' Since Vampira sees herself as a bat and we find her slightly bats to boot, we'd like to have Dennis Stock, who brought her to our attention, shoot her hanging from a rafter upside down, her pet owl standing on the other side of the rafter. To cover ourselves we'll try it both upside down and right side up with her standing on the rafter and a stuffed owl attached by its feet to the underside." The story, like a great many Lebenthal suggested, got right in the magazine.

Another of those was an early-closing choice for the November 12 issue. It would be one of the big entertainment stories in the magazine that week, and Lebenthal's initial suggestion began: "As the swan song to 42 years of moviemaking, Cecil Blount De Mille, producer of *The Sign of the Cross* and *Samson and Delilah,* is preparing what promises to be his greatest Bible epic yet—*The Ten Commandments.* In no sense is the picture a remake of the silent he did 30 years ago under the same title. That picture dealt with Moses only as a prologue to a contemporary story. The current film purports not only to be De Mille's most ambitious and extravagant production yet, but as carefully a researched personal history of Moses, 30 years of whose life is omitted from the Bible, as has ever been compiled in one document. It will be a multi-million-dollar project, filmed in Egypt and Hollywood over the next two years on a scale so large that a $250,000 set of the Gates of Tanis will have to be constructed and shot in Egypt for elbow room and the necessary extras to fill its 325 by 107 foot vista." This promised all the ingredients of a big *Life* movie act.

As production of the film progressed, other scripts wired from Hollywood would urge specific picture possibilities. "Both De Mille and Paramount would be delighted if we elect to cover certain moments in this $13.5 million series of spectacles including the plagues God wrought, the fleeing Jews laboring over the desert, and the Bacchanalia before the golden calf. Or they will provide color stills themselves of such gripping items as Moses (played by Charlton Heston) leading the Jews into the desert or smashing the tablets when he comes down from Mt. Sinai. God's actual inscribing of the commandments in thunder and lightning will be filmed in the Paramount Studio in Hollywood and we definitely think our own man should be assigned to that for a possible full-page opener of the bearded and robed Heston holding the newly etched and smoking tablets of red granite. We have already seen stills of Egyptian charioteers drowning in the Red Sea as its waters close behind the retreating Jews, and they are terrific. We see this as a surefire six to eight pages of color with cover possibilities, too, perhaps of Heston in his flowing Moses outfit, perhaps of the woman he scorned, Princess Nefretiri, played beauteously by Anne Baxter. Obviously there are text possibilities here as well about De Mille, the driving and crusty titan standing at the Sinai of his production, the erudite and merciless giant, now 75, who made Hollywood's first feature-length picture, *The Squaw Man*, in 1913. Appreciate your reaction soonest. Regards."

On the receiving end of Lebenthal's communications from Hollywood was Mary Logan Leatherbee, *Life*'s movie editor and a person whose influence at the magazine far exceeded her specific responsibilities. A striking woman with prominent cheekbones in a very mobile, rather lined face, she had a strong husky voice that she used with great effectiveness in tones that carried little more than a suggestion of a Louisiana accent.

Leatherbee had a theatrical, declamatory way of expressing herself, and she did indeed have a background in the theater. She'd studied acting at the Royal Academy of Dramatic Art in London and then became a member of a theatrical group whose lights included Henry Fonda, James Stewart and Margaret Sullavan, as well as her brother, Josh Logan, who later became a famous stage and screen director. She came to work in the entertainment department at *Life* in 1945.

It was Leatherbee's quality of passionate involvement that made her stand out particularly. This colored her whole life. She recalled having a bit part in a play with Fonda and Sullavan and watching from the wings while she waited to go on. "I got so caught up with the play," she said, "that I started to cry and missed my cue entirely." Her sense of caring made her appear more of a key part of the place than power wielders like Mackland and Elson; people thought of her as having special qualities of dedication and devotion. She seemed almost a volunteer in the headlong fire of her enthusiasm, like an American Friends Committee ambulance driver on the North African front, and if there had been a club for team spirit at *Life*—which occasionally did resemble a school full of talented and balky adolescents—Mary Leatherbee would have been the obvious choice for captain.

Like the best of Thompson's editors, Leatherbee was a prolific producer of good stories. Her own fascination with entertainment made her seem to be caught up in the job all the time. She took several trips a year to the West Coast to meet industry people and dig out stories with Lebenthal and other movie reporters. She was always coming up with fanciful ideas (in one famous color essay by Richard Avedon, Marilyn Monroe was dressed up like famous sex queens of the past—Lillian Russell, Theda Bara, Jean Harlow; for other pictures she persuaded Cary Grant to play Chaplin, Frank Sinatra and Dean Martin to imitate George Raft and Jimmy Cagney) or cajoling the magazine's bosses into considering more space or special issues for entertainment subjects. Perhaps her impact had something to do with the fact that Mary Leatherbee seemed on the verge of celebrity herself; she somehow bridged the gap between *Life* and the glamorous characters who frolicked on its pages. Thus it wasn't surprising when the word got around that she was having dinner with Mike Todd or would be seeing the Goldwyns this weekend or the Hammersteins or that she actually owned a little piece of *South Pacific*. The operatic elements of her real life contributed to her office image as a dashing and colorful figure. Widowed after only two years of marriage, she became a pilot and during World War II ferried bombers from South America to Africa and towed targets for other fliers to shoot at in aircraft gunnery practice. On one occasion, the story went, she took over the controls of a twin-engine bomber whose pilot had passed out in a steep dive, and pulled out of the dive as she flew the plane *under* the San Francisco–Oakland Bay Bridge.

Not everyone found Mary Leatherbee a totally delightful woman. Her own sense of conviction and what would be the right thing for the magazine to do (in all areas that caught her attention, not just entertainment) usually melted the resistance of others. But continued opposition made her at first incredulous. Then fierce. Aroused, she was an utter partisan and campaigned furiously to get what she wanted. "She could put an arrow right in your liver," one editor remembered of her capacity to attack. "She was not devious," another recalled. "But she knew all the moves. She could be quite political. She would call in all her debts when she needed it." Her pride in the magazine, which had a proprietary quality and a touch of grandiosity, now and then led her to infuriate people whose intentions she got wrong.

More often she was easygoing and generous, supportive of the causes of others as she managed *Life's* show business coverage with her close friend Tom Prideaux, the magazine's theater critic and top entertainment editor. Prideaux, who had come to the magazine in 1938— after an interviewer reported he was "the leading literary man" of his Yale class of 1930, a big success "in spite of his poetic appearance and thoroughgoing individualism"—was a fellow with a bewildering array of interests and talent. A former English teacher, an expert on ancient Egypt, a student of the modern American theater, he had written books, plays, musical comedies, played the piano and was the composer and lyricist of more than two hundred songs, including one called "When We Were Two Little Comets in Love, and I Was Hot on Your Tail."

Like Leatherbee, he brought a quality of joy to his work, an ardent enthusiasm for his field, and was unshakable in his conviction that the magazine was capable of expressing his best wishes for it over and over again. He loved puns; his ordinary speech was packed with jokes, allusions, scholarly references, poetry. He looked rumpled and at times vaguely distressed, as if he had just missed a bus or a train, which indeed was always a possibility, and he was notoriously inept at managing his own money. Still, he had a sure, hardheaded sense of the news to be reported from his field. Confident of his own taste, he covered the theater and other areas of entertainment without a trace of condescension for such popular items as the Broadway version of *Mame* (which with Rosalind Russell in the title role of the wise but wacky aunt provided *Life's* color cover for the November 12 issue) or of special reverence for more highbrow material. In fact, Prideaux and Leatherbee together somehow provided *Life* with a continuing sense of zestful irreverence. They did not seem like journalists at all. Instead, they seemed—this rather frail, handsome man with bushy eyebrows (a fine-boned version of his first cousin Jason Robards) and this warm, good-looking, flamboyantly gesturing woman—a couple of bright, terribly curious amateurs who'd been put in charge of something amorphous and huge, like Making Discoveries.

The fashion editor, Sally Kirkland, like her friend Mary Leatherbee, was outspoken, energetic and totally wrapped up in her job. A tall woman with a kind of lanky grace and quite a penetrating voice, she moved around the office with a warning jangle of bracelets, often in the company of two or three women in her department, all of them dressed, in the view of unknowing colleagues who watched them pass, with intimidating stylishness. She often referred to the various male editors she had to deal with as "the boys," and when she and her cohorts were seeking one or another of the boys, they tended to look glitteringly menacing, like a war party. When Kirkland had an editor cornered, she often addressed him in a slightly aggressive, exasperated way, and her victims at such moments reported the feeling that anything they said would sound foolish.

Kirkland's demeanor was not really accidental. To some extent she clearly thought of herself and her fashion department as poor cousins engaged in a more or less running skirmish to get recognition and the right sort of space in the magazine, and she acted as if she thought confrontation, or the threat of it, was her most useful weapon. "The boys demand very little of a fashion story," she once told an audience of eight hundred fashion experts in a talk about her job at *Life*. "All they ask is that it appeal and be understandable to the male half of our 24 million readers as well as the female, that it contain pretty girls, general news, photographic interest, sum up the latest styles in one page and two halves, that it hold its own opposite a Campbell's Soup ad, not look too much like a Party or Movie story, and that it appear right at home tucked in between a sports story and a science piece.

"They are perfectly amenable to our word on what is a good or a bad fashion," Kirkland went on about the boys, "but they reserve the right to say whether it is also an interesting one. . . . And there's always the possibility that no matter how well behaved the men editors appear, once or twice a year they will rear up, accuse us of being too sincere and set forth their own opinions on what the dear little women are doing. As for the copy that goes with our pictures, any hint of fashion prose is anathema to them on the grounds that they can't understand it and not many other male readers can. Therefore a 'chignon' must be qualified as bun of hair at the nape of the neck. An 'ensemble' is simply an outfit. 'Versatile accessories' are thrown out of the text at sight. And 'smart' is a word to apply to a junior Phi Bete. You can't mention anything that isn't visible in that set of pictures. If we didn't know what we really thought about a fashion when we shot it, we certainly do by the time we have described it in six lines of black and white with no qualifying shade of gray."

The showy way that Kirkland conducted her business (she *did* have her sweeter, more restrained side) gave the whole *Life* working operation a kind of flash. The beautiful, tall models parading in and out of the office, the limousines dispatched to locations piled high with hatboxes and shimmering dresses, the noisy department parties with champagne celebrating the latest picture triumph on the work of Rudi Gernreich or Jimmy Galanos or just the fact that the fashion editor and her entourage were off for the openings in Paris or on a style safari to Beverly Hills—all these lent a panache nothing else offered. A lot of the big space that Kirkland filled several times a year—the showy color essays on Riviera beach wear, Spanish fashion and young British designers—were welcome islands of froth and beauty in issues packed with meatier stuff. But Kirkland, who came to *Life* from *Vogue* in 1947, had, as well as flair and intuition, a solid professional understanding of her complex field. And for all the occasional arm waving, she was utterly efficient. She provided short, newsy black-and-white stories for almost every issue. In 1950, as Kirkland once told colleagues in the fashion press, *Life* ran one hundred fashion pages in forty issues, including twenty-three color pages and eight covers. It was like that or better every year. But most of the stories were a page and two or three halves, confined to what Kirkland termed "a single fashion highlight." As the November 12 issue moved toward its final closings, Kirkland, as usual, was getting a number of items ready for the managing editor to choose from. Among them was the story he would eventually select, a brisk little act on the American response to the shocking fashion news of the fall, the big drop in hemlines initiated by the Paris designer Dior. For all her exotic and rather far-out interests in the world of clothes, the "rag trade" as she called it, Kirkland was very conscious of the fashion needs of American women, and sympathetic to them, except when they wore, as she often liked to complain, "little hats and little suits with little ruffles and little beads and little cuffs and a little bag."

11

A Big Issue 2: Hard News

WITH HIS NOVEMBER 12 ISSUE FILLING OUT with solid text and back-of-the-book pieces, Thompson had reason to feel some satisfaction. But *Life* was a news magazine, and if it had not been for some extraordinary photographs from Hungary, pictures that arrived in New York on the final days of closing, the issue would not have been remarkable for much more than its size. For Thompson, perhaps, more than for any other of *Life*'s managing editors, the fast-closing, hard news sections of the magazine were of key interest and importance.

The most shocking of the pictures from Budapest, taken by free-lance photographer John Sadovy, documented at point-blank range the killing of a group of Hungarian secret police who had been flushed out of hiding by furious rebels before Russian troops swept back into the city and crushed their brief revolution. Like most great news pictures, they were utterly explicit; the reader, thanks to Sadovy, was standing at the executioner's shoulder, watching as the victims, their hands up as if to ward off the gunfire, fell and died; one could almost feel the impact of the bullets as they ripped into the cowering prisoners.

The brutal quality of the pictures, in fact, was such that Thompson felt constrained to make a special point of it in the introductory blurb about the issue that usually ran next to the table of contents. Week after week, Thompson and the writer he had selected for the job took special pains with these introductions, and the copy for this one read in part: "*Life* has been reporting war and peace, depression and prosperity for almost 20 years. We have never shown horror for horror's sake, but as far back as 1938, in a story on the Spanish Civil War, we declared: 'Dead men have indeed died in vain if live men refuse to look at them.' This week, again, is a time for looking at dead men—heroes and villains." The special problem in this case, of course, was that, for the moment anyhow, the good guys were doing the killing in most of *Life*'s pictures. And to make sure that the readers did not let their natural feelings of horror lead them to the wrong conclusions about what they saw, the headline over the pictures of the multiple execution kept the political context straight. "Patriots Strike Ferocious Blows at a Tyranny" it read, and the caption under the final picture in that series stated: "Dead, the riddled enemies of freedom lie huddled in the street." Accompanying text further clarified matters: ". . . Communist henchmen reaped the frightful wrath they had sowed," it went a bit steamily. "These were cut down as ruthlessly as they had murdered countless anti-Communists."

To get this story *Life* sent two reporter-photographer teams to Budapest. Also on hand to help with the coverage was Erich Lessing, a free-lance photographer with the Magnum agency, and *Time*'s Vienna correspondent, Edgar Clark. One of the teams, reporter John Mulliken and photographer Michael Rougier, had been sent from the Bonn bureau; the other team, Timothy Foote and John Sadovy, had come in from Paris. There were, of course, staff photographers in the Paris office, but Foote had asked particularly for Sadovy on this assignment. "Many of the *Life* photographers," Foote recalled, "were monolingual and had no knowledge of European politics or history. They were very brave men, but they subconsciously expected people to make way for them." Foote felt that the Hungarian job would require special finesse. "Sadovy and I had been in Morocco," he explained. "We were stoned and shot at there. He's Czech, knew German and a little Russian. He was matchless on news, a mild man, also fearless and totally without pretensions. He had a Leica with a wide-angle lens. He would get up close to things and quietly pull it out of his pocket."

Foote and Mulliken, both in their early thirties at the time, were two of *Life*'s best young correspondents. Foote, very bright and somewhat acidulous with a didactic turn of mind, had come to the magazine in 1949. From very early on in his career, he expressed with a certain clarity—and often a persuasiveness—his feelings about what was wrong with and what needed doing about *Life*. The fact that he was right a considerable part of the time did not necessarily endear him to the recipients of his urgent messages, but he was respected for his skills and conscientiousness. Mulliken, a wry, funny and rather elegant Dartmouth man who had won a Silver Star while serving in the Netherlands with the U.S. 7th Armored Division in World War II, came to the magazine from an advertising agency and with a promising reputation as a writer. In New York he was first assigned to the military affairs department set up to handle the large number of stories turned out during the Korean war. After two years he was sent to London, and then, in 1955, to Bonn. He loved being a foreign correspondent. "We thought we owned the world," he remembered. "TV begged *us* for rides, then, not like now. I enjoyed being overseas. I went to Lebanon, the Congo. I never wanted to come home." In the early 1960s, both Foote and Mulliken, unhappy with their prospects at *Life*, took jobs on *Time*.

Mike Rougier, the photographer who arrived from Bonn with Mulliken, had been on the staff since 1947, when, at the age of twenty-two, he took some forbidden pictures of Eva Perón and smuggled them out of the country in spite of arrest, shakedowns and dire threats from the Argentine security police. Born in London, he'd been a combat photographer in Korea; his story about a twelve-year-old whose life had been smashed by that war, "The Little Boy Who Wouldn't Smile," won several awards. Boyish, handsome, inventive, he also had a reputation for coolness in tough situations. "He is crazy," said a *Paris-Match* photographer as he watched Rougier walk into a cross fire in a riot in Panama. "Tell him to take cover or get out of there."

The two teams met in Vienna, about twenty-five miles from the Hungarian border and one hundred fifty miles from Budapest, on Sunday, October 28. "Rougier and I drove to Vienna in the middle of the night," Mulliken recalled. "We'd been at a party at the American Club in Bad Godesberg. The weather was awful. We had the radio on all the way. The Russians were withdrawing to the outskirts of Budapest. [They would return in crushing force five days later.] All kinds of people were at the Hotel Bristol in Vienna trying to decide what to do. It was like a crowd going to a football game, a very moving event. There was only one way your sympathy could flow."

Even as the teams from *Life* tried to work out a plan of action to reach the story and cover it, there was some tension between them. "Foote and Sadovy came in as support, but there was a little competition here. This was our responsibility. They were invaders." What Mulliken was expressing was the territorialism common at *Life*. Every bureau operative was very protective of his area and sensitive to surprise invasions by people from other bureaus. Even in this case, where the magazine clearly needed several people on the scene, relations were a bit strained. After the four had dinner, Rougier and Mulliken drove out to the border and brought back word they didn't think it would be possible to cross until the next morning.

Later, in the room they were sharing, Foote and Sadovy decided they couldn't wait. "'This is the story,' we agreed," Foote said. "'We're fools to sit here!' We took a razor, a map, some brandy, a roll of toilet paper, my tweed coat, I remember, from Harvard, my L. L. Bean hunting boots, socks, soap, camera and film in a canvas sling bag. We didn't want to wake up Mulliken and Rougier, so we left them a note: 'We're going to try to go in on foot.'" Their secret departure from Vienna would be an infuriating surprise to the others when they woke the next morning.

"We got in one of those old Hispano-Suiza cabs," Foote went on. "It was raining. It looked like the last scene, the cemetery, in *The Third Man*. My passport wasn't even stamped for Hungary. 'Can we come in and talk?' we said to the guards at the border. This nineteen-year-old kid opened a door and showed us a bunch of nervous kids holding guns. We asked if we could get on a truck—supply trucks were going in—and we were told only a few Austrian doctors were getting through. We finally got a ride at five a.m. with a doctor in a Volkswagen. He had white on his sleeve and on the car. We left another note at the border for Mulliken and Rougier. We told them the situation and suggested they try for local stories in the area." When the other team got the note, this sort of advice did not go down well.

That morning the border opened, and the two *Life* teams met later in the day in Budapest's Hotel Duma. Soviet tanks ringed the city, which was crowded with armed and jubilant bands of Hungarians determined to make the most of this opportunity to wrench their city and nation from Communist control. The situation was alive with high excitement and danger, and violence was breaking out everywhere. Mulliken and Rougier were angry that the others had gone on ahead from Vienna, and the next morning refused them a ride around the city in the Bonn office Ford, which Mulliken had driven across from Vienna. Erich Lessing, the Magnum photographer, took Foote and Sadovy along in his car on a scouting trip for something that would make good pictures.

Both teams found plenty. "We had American flags on the car," said Mulliken. "Everybody cheered us. The first thing that happened was a half-track drove by. Young Russian boys were in it, about seventeen years old. They looked like marines. One of them was slowly aiming his gun. Somebody said: 'Don't move, that kid is scared.' Then we got in the middle of a cross fire by a bridge—between some rebels holding out in a barracks and some Russian tanks. The tankers were short guys dressed in black. One of them started walking toward us with a pistol. We left the car with all Rougier's equipment in the trunk and went two or three blocks away. They hauled the car away."

That night rebel students got in touch with them. By then the students had commandeered the car and led the *Life* men to it—and from there to more points of action. Next day, the Russians withdrew temporarily, and some journalists mistakenly predicted an end to the fighting. "The *Paris-Match* photographer," Mulliken recalled, "a terrifically good-looking, wealthy guy, said: 'Nothing ees happening. Zee story ees dead. Who wants to play cards?' Next day he was dead."

Foote and Sadovy came close to being killed in the street fighting that was breaking out everywhere. Told by rebels that there was some action a distance away, they approached the scene on foot. "We came to a square with a park in the center of it," wrote Sadovy in an account that appeared in the November 12 issue. "We heard shooting, and then we saw a tank facing a large modern building at the end of the square. It was held by the AVH [the hated Hungarian secret police, a Gestapo-like outfit loyal to the Communist government and the Soviets], who were firing from the windows.

"My first instinct," Sadovy continued, "was to get behind the tank. It would give us some shelter and I would be close enough to photograph the action. Halfway to the tank we found ourselves in the open park. Bullets began zinging past our ears. We fell flat on our faces. I tried to hide behind a young tree. I wished my tree was bigger and I tried to make myself smaller. It must have been in that rain of bullets that Tim got hit in the hand."

In this flurry of action, Sadovy got separated from Foote, who, as rebels soon assured the photographer, had been taken to a hospital where his hand would be attended to. In the park, the focus of the rebel attack was the police headquarters, and the return fire coming from it was extremely intense.

"People were dropping in the park like flies," Sadovy wrote. Then a number of additional tanks appeared, five of them flying Hungarian flags. It turned out they were manned by the rebels, and they began pumping more fire into the building. After a time, the tank attack let up, and rebels on foot began racing into the besieged headquarters, in front of which scores of freedom fighters lay dead. Then members of the secret police, attempting to surrender to the furious rebels, began to come out. Sadovy's most astonishing pictures showed the horrifying events that followed. "The first to emerge from the building," Sadovy wrote, "was an officer, alone. It was the fastest killing I ever saw. He came out laughing and the next thing I knew he was flat on the ground. . . . Then the rebels brought out a good-looking officer, his face white as chalk. He got five yards, retreated, argued. Then he folded up. It was over with him."

Sadovy's staccato account emphasized the raw brutality of the moment. "Two AVH men came out," he wrote next. "Rifle butts pounding. Punching and kicking. Suddenly a shot.

"Six young officers came out, one very good-looking. Their shoulder boards were torn off. Quick argument. We're not as bad as you think we are, give us a chance, they were saying. I was three feet from that group. Suddenly one began to fold. They must have been real close to his ribs when they fired. They all went down like corn that had been cut. Very gracefully. And when they were on the ground the rebels were still loading lead into them. . . . I could see the impact of the bullets on a man's clothes. You could see every bullet. There was not much noise. They were so close that a man's body acted as a silencer. This went on for 40 minutes. . . . Then my nerves went. Tears started to come down my cheeks. I had spent three years in the war, but nothing I saw could compare with the horror of this."

When the pictures by Sadovy and the others arrived in New York (in this case they had already been developed by the lab in the Paris office), their management was taken over by the foreign news department. This was considered by many to be the magazine's most glamorous section. Into its crowded corner of the old Time & Life Building's thirty-first floor streamed a parade of trench-coated foreign correspondents on home leave, peripatetic photographers like Dmitri Kessel, Brian Brake and Terry Spencer about to go off on assignment, mysterious, dapper-looking characters reported to be visiting diplomats from the French Foreign Office or undercover agents for the Free Poles. To journalists whose normal professional preoccupation was with such mundane happenings as flooding in the Midwest, changing trends in U.S. education or the pennant races, the exotic bustle around the foreign news department emitted a certain aura of intrigue and importance. Foreign news, known locally as FN, lent the place a touch of class it didn't otherwise have. Its presence amid the other *Life* departments was somehow like having an embassy mixed in with a row of dry cleaners, delis and hardware stores.

At this time foreign news was being run by Gene Farmer, who, like his adored boss Ed Thompson, did not look the part of an assured and accomplished journalist. In fact, he looked, with his round, little-boy face, his occasionally soup-stained shirts, his trousers slumping around his bulging middle and his cracked black shoes, more like a man one might find seated near a wood stove in some rural part of his native Arkansas. Here again appearances were deceptive. While he didn't have Thompson's ability to manage, intimidate and attract the unswerving loyalty of a large staff (there were only eight or ten people in foreign news; the section editor, however, had virtual control over several writers and the staffs of all the foreign bureaus), Farmer was quick, clever and aggressive in pursuit of his goals.

A Phi Beta Kappa from the University of Arkansas, where he'd also been state typing champion, Farmer had come to *Life* in the late 1940s with experience on midwestern newspapers. (There were fashions in hiring at *Life*. Sometimes all the new people were hotshot writer possibilities hired right out of college, usually the Ivy League. At other times only newspaper experience would open the door for candidates.) He worked for a while as the magazine's sports editor, and in that post he became known as a man with an impressive if relatively useless command of baseball statistics and the ability to produce and write stories with amazing speed (he typed so fast that reporters sharing his office were now and then reduced, at their own typewriters, to paralyzed embarrassment). He then became *Life's* chief correspondent in London and after that was named the foreign news editor. Still only thirty-seven in 1956, he was yet another on the long list of men and women who seemed more interested in the magazine than in anything else taking place in the rest of their lives, and he worked very hard to master his area of responsibility. He loved being foreign news editor of *Life* magazine and the implication it carried that he had access to the high councils of the world. He came back from London with a taste for derby hats and homburgs and he proudly wore the lapel ribbon of the Légion d'Honneur that the public-relations-minded De Gaulle government gave him after the publication of a story the French liked. He was fond of telling stories about influential people he had met on his frequent trips abroad—a failing he shared with hundreds of journalists from Henry Luce to Barbara Walters. In fact, he had just returned from a trip to Europe he had taken to try to improve his understanding of conditions in the satellite countries. His "appraisal" had run just the week before, and his interest in the pictures from Budapest had a special urgency.

The last week of the closing was a particularly busy one for Farmer and his section. Not only were the pictures from Hungary coming in, but world reaction to the crisis in Suez was powerfully indignant. There the Israelis, supported militarily by the French and the British, had attacked Egypt, driven Egyptian forces out of the Sinai Peninsula and threatened the Suez Canal. "The news-pot is boiling like it hasn't been for a long time," Luce wrote his top editors that week, and at *Life* most of the heat was on foreign news.

Farmer and the assignment editors had sent teams into the Middle

East wherever possible—to Israel, Lebanon, Cyprus and Jordan. The story was also being covered in London and Paris. In the United States teams were assigned to the United Nations and to John Foster Dulles, Eisenhower's Secretary of State, who was masterminding urgent efforts to bring about a cease-fire. In such a journalistic melee Farmer was, in the vernacular of some of the aggressively countrified types at *Life,* in "hog heaven." Lighting one cigarette after another, he bustled with nervous officiousness from one room to the next, keeping himself informed on the whereabouts of various photographers, reporters, film shipments en route (he had a mania for tracking packets, one colleague remembered), giving Thompson bulletins on exactly when pictures could be expected, when copy would be written. He made sure, even when the surveillance wasn't at all necessary, that researchers in his department were busy. The opinions they had of him varied widely. "Gene was very dynamic, very demanding," one of them recalled. "He kept his finger on every detail. By the time we got used to his mannerisms, we thought they were camp, but he didn't realize that." "He was rude, very tough to work for. He never once told me I had done anything well," said another. "He was a primitive, a terrific primitive." "I really loved Gene as a person," a third said. "He was warmhearted and soft under that 'grovelly' appearance."

It is not certain that the foreign news department had one, or perhaps two, of its traditional candlelight dinners the evenings that the horrifying story from Hungary was going to press. But it is likely; the dinners lent veracity to the department's well-cultivated image of special status. Besides, the staff, especially the chief foreign news researcher, the attractive and coolly elegant Lee Eitingon, liked them. The candles, napery and wine were a welcome respite from regular deadline routine, the long, tense layout sessions with Thompson and art director Charlie Tudor, the gathering of files and reference material for the writers, the checking of finished copy and the pursuit of additional information demanded by the editors, all the exhausting details that were part of every closing.

The ordinary routine for the staff's Saturday-night dinner was simple enough. People working late stood in line, chatting and holding their drinks, for the fancy catered meal served up on closing night by a red-jacketed squad of waiters from the Louis Quatorze restaurant next door. They usually then went back to their desks and ate while they worked; groups of two or three, more sociable or less in a hurry, sometimes sat together. But foreign news made much more of a production of the meal, clearing places for a group of ten or twelve to sit down together and turning off some of the overhead lights to make the candleshine more cozy. Frequently Farmer or Eitingon would invite a guest or two to join them—Thompson (who much preferred to eat outside the office) or a visiting foreign bureau chief. Now and then, on closing nights when the press of business was not too great, the conviviality stretched on and on, and researchers making last-minute checking queries sometimes had to take the phones into the wells under their desks in order to make themselves heard and to hear over the gay hubbub.

Things were pretty glum down the hall in newsfront on the closing nights when foreign news had the lead space in the magazine. Newsfront was the domestic news department, and its editor in the mid-1950s was a black-haired, deceptively boyish-looking man named Hugh Moffett, who had a flash of gold in his smile. Moffett felt keenly that his stories should almost always command the best space in the front of the magazine. He was too good a journalist—and too much engrossed with foreign news himself—not to have agreed that Hungary and the Suez crisis were stories that *Life* must feature that week. But still he was ferociously competitive, however much he may have believed in the *notions* of collegiality and everyone working together. When some other section carried off the best space, Moffett's usual jauntiness fled, and he looked a bit drawn, like a major-league baseball manager who sees his team's big lead blown in a ninth-inning fiasco.

More than any other editorial manager of that period, except for Thompson, Moffett had won the utter loyalty of his staff, who considered him fair, wise, funny and an absolute genius on stories. The dozen or so young men and women who worked for him in the New York office, like the mercurial Scot Leavitt, who'd gone on to become a top reporter out in the field, thought of him as a man of superior judgment and standards and a demanding and excellent teacher. It wasn't that Moffett had a lot of grand ideas or even particularly "important" ones. He liked to move hard on fast-breaking news stories, natural disasters like floods and earthquakes, man-made disasters like plane crashes. There was a large streak of the police gazette editor in him; he loved to do crime stories, stories on flashy and influential crooks. He was never happier than when he could somehow record the crimes and foibles of the rich and famous. When, in 1955, the socialite and racehorse owner William Woodward was shot coming home late one night (by his wife, who claimed she'd thought he was an intruder and used an elephant gun to defend herself), Moffett sent his reporters swarming over the story in high glee, setting up photographs of guns like the murder weapon being fired and collecting bad jokes like the one that said it would have been worse if Mrs. Woodward had shot Nashua, the horse. He enjoyed himself even more later in 1960 when an obscure heiress named Gamble Benedict decided to marry her grandmother's chauffeur, already married (and divorced) and fifteen years her senior. Moffett and his crew promoted the romance, then hid the happy couple from the rest of the press, provided cars and aircraft for an elopement and helped the pair have a quiet honeymoon (in a privacy they shared, naturally, with *Life*). The story ran as a nine-page lead and a cover. Following its appearance, there was a real outcry about the magazine's shameless marriage brokering, and Gamble Benedict's furious grandmother sued. Luce himself was reported to be very annoyed about what he considered *Life*'s overzealous performance on a tacky story. Yet word came back from one high-level lunch that he'd relented somewhat. "Maybe it would have been better," he is said to have reflected over coffee with true journalistic pragmatism, "if she'd been better-looking."

The year 1956 had been a tremendously good one for Moffett and newsfront. Election coverage alone produced many stories, and there were leads about plane crashes, the sinking of the liner *Andrea Doria,* an extraordinary rescue after an airliner had been ditched at sea, a uranium rush, an early missile launch, a story about a man who wrote his girl's name in huge letters in grass seed (they ran off and got married when it grew out). In a story about a bus boycott in Montgomery, Alabama, one small photograph of a hitherto unknown black man was captioned: "Boycott Director, Rev. Martin King, head of association which guides it, is mugged after arrest." In the same issue, March 5, Nobel Prize-winning author William Faulkner, a Mississippian himself, wrote a short piece called "A Letter to the North" in which he urged caution in forcing integration upon the white South. "Stop now for a moment," he wrote. "You have shown the Southerner what you can do and what you will do if necessary; give him a space in which to get his breath and assimilate that knowledge . . ."

In this same period the magazine produced a five-part series on segregation. Moffett was involved in the management of the series, especially of one story about a black family in Alabama named Causey. Mrs. Causey was a teacher in a black elementary school; her husband operated a little sawmill. In the published article, Mrs. Causey was mildly but firmly critical of differences in the quality of the treatment given black and white students in her district. She did not, in short, agree at all with the doctrine, then in effect throughout the South, of "separate but equal" facilities. Because of this rare outspokenness, her job was threatened, the family's credit in the area was cut off and her husband's business was boycotted and brought to a standstill. White disapproval was so great that the Causeys eventually had to leave their home and settle somewhere else, a change they made with substantial financial assistance from *Life*.

But before that happened, Moffett made a special trip from New York to the little Alabama town with Richard Stolley, the young correspondent who had worked on the story and had been Moffett's right-hand man in newsfront before being sent into the field. Moffett was upset about the revenge being carried out against the Causeys; he wanted to see if there was anything that could be done to reduce the community's anger at them. With Stolley he approached the head of the school board, one of the most indignant and influential of the local whites, stuck out his hand and said, for openers, one small-town man to another: "My name is Hugh Moffett. I'm from *Life* magazine and I understand we haven't got a friend in this town."

His blunt and engaging approach didn't help the Causeys, but it surely added to his good reputation with the people who worked for him. His laconic style delighted his friends, who were always quoting his jokes. He insisted on not taking anything too seriously, which some observers thought was his way of protecting himself from depression. In any case, his cracks sometimes took a macabre twist. "If you don't go to people's funerals," he said once at a friend's, "they won't go to yours." On vacation fishing trips he took each year with friends into the bush country of Canada, he always referred to the pilots as "Buck Duane," the name of the pilot who'd been flying *Life* reporter Terry Turner when they were killed in a crash in the Rockies in 1961.

Moffett liked to make fun of the little pomposities of his fellow workers. Holding a piece of copy in his hand, he'd drop in on a writer working on a newsfront story. "Now this word 'paradigm,'" he'd say, pointing to it in the writer's story. "You can just look at it and know you're up against a real word. But you know," he'd go on slyly, "I've been in a lot of towns where they don't use that word." The word would vanish from the copy. Moffett had considerable admiration for many photographers, but he was not the sort of man who would say that in public. What he did say once was that "photographers individually are just barely acceptable, and en masse they are preposterous." This comment was in reference to a meeting of all thirty-five of the staff photographers he'd arranged when he was in overall charge of them. As members of the group were preparing to sit down, Moffett had called out: "Will the good photographers please sit on the right and the bad photographers sit on the left?" His request was greeted with a certain amount of confusion. Possibly unable to believe their ears, the photographers largely ignored him. "They didn't pay any attention," Moffett said later with mock regret. "They were unable to sort themselves out."

This sort of irreverence only increased the affectionate veneration people felt for Moffett—which once prompted a large group of his friends to charter a bus in Chicago and drive nearly 200 miles to surprise him with cheers and banners at his old alma mater, Monmouth College, where he was getting an honorary doctorate of laws.

Moffett had little of the smooth, automatic courtesy so common among high-ranking Time Inc. editors. He made no real effort to make his bosses feel comfortable; he was not interested in learning to accommodate his thinking to theirs. Not that he couldn't cajole people when he thought it would be useful, or bend the truth if it would win an ally. He took his independence seriously, even if it sometimes endangered his career. When President Truman fired General Douglas MacArthur from his job as Supreme Commander in the Far East in 1951, Luce, a longtime MacArthur fan, was furious about it. Moffett, who was then Tokyo bureau chief and had spent a lot of time in Korea reporting the war at first hand, agreed strongly with Truman that MacArthur should go. Disregarding the obvious risks inherent in such candor, Moffett made no bones about his opinions either in his cables back home or, later, to Luce directly, when he told the editor-in-chief bluntly that MacArthur had been, among other things, just too old for the job. Whatever their disputes, Moffett respected Luce. "He had a great value in inspiring people," he recalled. "After I'd go to a lunch where he'd perform—brilliantly or erratically—I'd go back to my office thinking he's smarter than I am and I'd better work harder."

At *Life* Moffett worked hard for Thompson and later for his successor, George Hunt, but his zeal for the job was not overlaid with the kind of toady enthusiasm some showed the boss. He clearly took pleasure in being prickly and a maverick. Possibly his relative indifference to rank was also a reflection of a fatalistic attitude toward his own future. "I never was in contention to be the managing editor," he said after his retirement in 1967. "But I always said you gotta make out like you are around here, or they'll think you've had it." Then he added jokingly: "I was always terrified of the heights to which I'd inadvertently risen."

Moffett took great pride in his rural beginnings. Born in Kansas, the son of an osteopath, he spent much of his childhood on a farm in Illinois. He thought his country-boy credentials were better than those of anyone else on the staff. "Farmer was a phony rube," he said. "And Thompson didn't know anything about farming either. He pretended to, but he grew up in town.

"We had pigs, cows, corn, three hundred sheep," he went on proudly. "We drove cattle to town along the roads, like cowboys. We had a crisis a day. I've found it a tremendous advantage in this world to be a farm boy. There's nobody you can call up. No phones. You've got to fight your way out of whatever mess you're in. My father used to send me out to kill the kittens every spring."

Moffett recalled that Thompson had once kidded him for his ignorance about classic childhood stories, stories like Peter Pan or Pinocchio. "At about the time I should have been reading Peter Pan," Moffett said, "I was out plowing with a four-horse team. I remember once we drove over a bumblebee nest and the team ran away. The bees were stinging them and they were going wild. But I hung on and stayed with them. I got them back in the fucking furrow. I was probably eight years old."

But quite possibly it was his appreciation of the ridiculous that made Moffett more than just a hard-driving editor. When the young Queen Elizabeth II was making a visit to the United States in 1957, she was scheduled to attend a football game, her first. Wondering what she would possibly make of it, Moffett hired a lip-reader equipped with binoculars to work with the reporters and visually eavesdrop on the Queen's conversation. "My, it's exciting," said the Queen. On another occasion, at the Athens wedding in 1964 of King Constantine of Greece and Princess Anne-Marie of Denmark (for which Moffett had rented properly impeccable white-tie outfits in Paris for himself and the photographer), he persuaded the Greek stringer correspondent working for him to go to the royal stable and get the names of the six horses that pulled the wedding team. "Nobody else got the names of the horses," he recalled with pride in his absurd coup. Thus his stories, whether inconsequential or much bigger, often included a wink at the readers, as if Moffett wanted to let them in on the jokes inherent in almost everything in life. With Thompson, Leatherbee and Thorne, among others, he brought rare, idiosyncratic qualities to the *Life* of the fifties.

The writer on the Hungary story was Enno Hobbing, a very tall, handsome (he had almost cartoonish good looks, with prominent jaws like Christopher Reeve) Harvard graduate who'd been a reporter for *Time* in Europe after the war, then worked for the CIA before Thompson hired him. He was a friendly, obviously powerful man with a deep laugh. But he seemed a bit aloof from the rest of the staff. Perhaps his past government connections contributed to the sense that he stood somewhat apart from the others, especially the more raffish, fun-loving types who worked for Moffett and newsfront.

Two of the most audible of these were Charlie Champlin and Dave Snell, both excellent news writers who kept up their own spirits and those of others around them with an incessant barrage of patter and jokes. Snell and Champlin shared an office, and in off-hours it was something of a gag factory where writers and reporters—sometimes to the consternation of isolated or gloomy types who preferred a hospital quiet—gathered to share a mounting hilarity. They referred to their office as the Hotel Plunge (based on the typical tabloid headline: "Woman Dies in Hotel Plunge") and had special bath towels made to go with the joke. Snell, a former professional wrestler who had also been a cartoonist, occasionally splattered ink on paper or threw damp things against the wall or on the floor to see if he could achieve a pattern as interesting as something by the great abstract expressionist Jackson Pollock. In his wry, Louisiana accent, he launched scores of telling one-liners, including one about a nearby restaurant: "The food is not very good there, but they make up for it by serving small portions." Which is quite a lot like the self-deprecating comment served up in the same period by Robert Wallace, a deceptively mild-mannered Princeton graduate who for years was the magazine's best writer at just about any length and on any subject. "Well, it's short," Wallace once said of a piece he'd just finished, "but it stinks."

The man ultimately responsible for the work of Hobbing, Champlin and Snell—and the twenty-five or so writers turning out copy for picture stories in the magazine—was Joe Kastner, a Brooklyn-born Yale graduate, former *Time* copy boy and *Fortune* writer who had been at *Life* from the very beginning. Kastner, whose gentle outward appearance made only slightly unsettling his blunt determination to get the work done just as he wanted it done, was a man of considerable power at the magazine, absolutely central to the business of going to press each week. At one point in his career, he had been head of Time Inc.'s unit of the newspaper guild; now he was high in the management. He was called the copy editor, a title which fails to convey how much control he had over the substance as well as the style of the writing, and he was accountable only to Thompson.

Typically, a writer's first draft would come to Kastner, who would go over it quickly with a pencil. Seated at a desk jammed with a leather-covered dummy full of photostatic copies of the contents of the issue as well as the yellow flimsies he had of all the rest of the copy being funneled into the magazine, Kastner would then summon the writer to his side. If his editing points were minor, Kastner and the writer (whom the copy editor had usually tapped for the job) would work out the problems on the spot. Kastner would then "put the story through" with his initials in the top right-hand corner, and the piece would be moved along to Thompson for a final editing. Thompson often wanted more changes, but the major editing was usually Kastner's. Sometimes a little line of two or three writers would shape up outside the copy editor's office, and though one was not supposed to let on he was worried about seeing Joe, this was often a tense moment for those writers who felt shaky about their standing with Kastner.

Arriving at a version of the story that would satisfy him was often not easy. The writer would frequently be sent back to his typewriter for another try, or in extreme cases for several more tries. Kastner, whose curly red hair was getting quite grizzled above his high forehead by the mid-1950s, was particularly hard to please on a couple of basic matters. One involved the opening, or "lead," sentence in the initial text block for every story; these he considered crucial to getting readers "into the tent." He fussed just as much about the closing sentences, which jauntier insiders called "snappers."

The fact that Kastner was right about the emphasis he placed on these technical problems did not make it any easier for those writers who had a hard time getting the hang of it. And since text blocks were often very short, his displeasure over one or two sentences could take on dismaying proportions. There were no set rules about lead sentences, although if the opening photograph in a story was strong, it was deemed sensible to refer to it right away in a technique called "writing into the picture." For example, the text accompanying a 1956 photographic essay on the movie actress Kim Novak (March 5) began: "Kim Novak sits, beautiful and dreamy-eyed, only half listening as two agents discuss her prospects as if she were a commodities future, like oats or cotton." A story about a young classical pianist in the next issue led off more prosaically: "Glenn Gould, a 23-year-old from Toronto, has given only two piano recitals in the U.S. and made one record." But the closing sentences in that block provide an example of the sort of playful ending Kastner often liked. "Even pianos are against him," it goes. "One on which he records Bach he finds to be not suitable for his Beethoven, and neither a Bach nor a Beethoven piano is any good for his Brahms." A few weeks later, the snapper in a story about teenagers who were always on the telephone was purely utilitarian, written to let the reader know exactly where the story was going. "With a tape recorder and the family's permission," it read, "*Life* listened in on the Nyvalls' phone and on the next two pages gives a verbatim example of 14-year-old Ginny's conversation with 15-year-old Charlie Hoag."

Such were the weighty survival factors in a *Life* writer's existence, these and the problem of squeezing the facts of a story into a block whose length was dictated largely by the sizes, shapes and number of the photographs around it and was most typically anywhere from 200 to 500 words long. Kastner insisted on having lots of facts in the stories.

If there weren't enough in the initial versions (which the writers had usually prepared by reading reporters' files, the newspapers and material from the reference morgue), Kastner tipped them in himself at various places along the way. More precisely, he dropped in the word "koming," a Time Inc. copy designation meaning that a pertinent fact will be coming later, wherever he wanted this hitherto invisible information to appear.

Depending on the nature and number of his demands, writers, reporters and fact checkers hustled around trying to dig up information that would satisfy his requirements. Kastner was by no means the only one who fell back on the use of "koming"; some writers habitually drove their colleagues mad by using the device and making it seem that their stories could be brought to life with the addition of a few facts, like the addition of water to powdered eggs. The practice became a running joke on the staff, and science writer Ed Kern parodied it in a sample block that read: "For years scientists, exploring the koming of the koming, have had to be satisfied with the komingness of the komings available on ordinary komings. Now a new koming has been developed and perfected by Westinghouse for the armed services which produces komings koming times as koming as ever before (*above*). The device, known as a KOMING, is not only useful for komings, but can be applied to koming, koming and koming (*see next page*)."

If Kastner was tough with the *Life* writers, it was because he had been edited himself by a tough succession of professionals at *The New Yorker*, *Fortune* and then *Life*, where John Shaw Billings applied his own strict standards to the business of writing text blocks and captions. "Billings would butcher our copy," Kastner once recalled, "just in order to cram the facts in, and our fine phrases would go out. We soon found out that he had no room for fine phrases unless they moved the story along—which has been a rule *Life* has followed pretty much all the time under all the editors and which has broken the hearts of many writers and pounded sense into the heads of just as many." In the view of some of the writers, Kastner's editing amounted to a brutal oversimplification of the material, and several over the years who were subjected to the pressure of his dissatisfaction either left the magazine or went back to reporting or jobs that required other skills. It was odd but true at *Life* that even though the main emphasis was on pictures and the production of good photography, young men coming to work there very often wanted to become writers, first of the text blocks and captions that went with the bulk of the stories, then of the longer bylined pieces written by the people in the group designated on the masthead as "staff writers." The desire, of course, only increased Kastner's power, and he developed a reputation internally as a maker and breaker of young writers. "I suppose I made and broke writers," he said much later, "but I don't know how much of that was me and how much was the real demands of the magazine. We were very strict, and we were often rigid. If you got personality into it, you had to be very skillful. But a great variety of people became good writers.

"As I remember it," he went on, "I also had an unhappy habit of sticking with people who had a glimmer of promise. I hated to fire people, and I don't know how many really good writers got away." Kastner's moods and predilections were the subject, naturally, of much conversation and anxious thought by the writers. Most of them actually found him sensible, patient and even generous with his advice about the copy when he wasn't crushed by schedule pressures, and liked to sit around with him and gossip about office politics or affairs, which fascinated him endlessly. Though Kastner was kind and easily touched, his gruff refusal to settle for anything that failed to meet some undefined standard that lurked in his head ("How can he be so sure what he wants," I wrote somewhat boozily one night and left in my typewriter in showy frustration, "and not know what it is?") were the characteristics that intimidated most of the insecure people who worked for him. Dave Snell put a sign up on his cluttered wall that read, with a bow to the famed sportswriter Grantland Rice: "When the Great Scorer comes to write against your name, it matters not whether you won or lost, but how the Great Scorer's writing struck Joe Kastner."

The copy editor was one of a handful of people who worked closely with Thompson in those final hectic days each week when the pressure was greatest, when the last and often most important stories of the issue were going to press. Another was Peggy Sargent, a stout, cheerfully bossy woman who looked as if she'd been selected for the job from a foursome playing bridge in the New York suburbs. Sargent was the principal film editor, and it was her job to look over every frame of the thousands of pictures taken each week by the *Life* photographers and sent to the lab for processing. When they weren't out on other assignments, she worked with the photographers and often with someone from the department that had assigned the story.

Basically what Sargent did, working with a magnifying loupe on sheets of 35-millimeter contact prints or occasionally—if there was a special rush—on the not quite dry negatives themselves, was to select the photographs that would be blown up, as either 8-by-10 or 11-by-14 prints, as many as a hundred of them in each story, and shown to Thompson. Although the Hungary pictures for the November 12 issue had already been processed and printed in Europe, Sargent doubtless went over the film again herself in a hunt for photographs others might have missed.

By 1956 Peggy Sargent, who often scolded the young reporters as they begged for their prints, had already been working with pictures for twenty years. She had been Margaret Bourke-White's secretary–office manager when Luce hired the photographer. Bourke-White liked Sargent's judgment about pictures and brought her along to *Life*. Sargent then worked for a while in the early days as Thompson's secretary and became more and more involved with editing film. She had a superb natural eye for good journalistic pictures, and her years of experience with photography made it possible for her to tell which negatives would hold up and make the best enlargements. In the 1950s the great bulk of the photography at *Life* was in black and white, but Sargent and especially her associate Barbara Brewster began spending more and more time with the increasing volume of color pictures, most of them also the small-size 35 millimeter.

When Thompson was going over a set of prints ordered up by his film editor, he would occasionally flick on the interoffice squawk box on his desk and ask her to go back over a set of contact prints. He was often looking for a certain mood or expression or situation, and he counted on her more than anyone else to find it for him. Like Kastner, Peggy Sargent was an eager follower of office intrigue, and her pivotal job made her desk a hub for information, especially about the photographers, who were her pets and whose smiles, poses and other mugging gestures made up a huge photographic montage on one wall of her office. Having to look so closely at all the film gave Sargent a strong sense of participation in the magazine. Now and then it also gave her a special window on the lives of the photographers. Speaking of one woman-chasing fellow she was fond of, she said: "I could always tell after looking at about fifteen rolls who was his girlfriend on the story. She would always show up in the contacts. 'It must be this girl, eh?' I would say. And he would laugh and say 'Yes.'"

Many people who worked around Thompson gave the impression of being constantly alert to his wishes and thus to every nuance of his often indecipherable communications, ready at an instant's notice to do his bidding. Not quite toadies (many were brave enough to present their strongly held views when the opportunities came), they still conveyed a healthy sense of conviction in *his* rightness. This was not generally the case with Charlie Tudor, who as *Life*'s art director worked literally shoulder to shoulder with Thompson during the crucial phase of deciding how to use the pictures in the stories that were going to press. It wasn't that Tudor rebelled openly against Thompson or seemed even in mild disagreement with some of his ideas. It was more as if this handsome, barrel-chested man, whose main public show of any agitation was chain-smoking, was determined to maintain some pace of his own, some aloofness from the pressured events coming to a boil around him much of the time.

When summoned, he glided smoothly into the managing editor's office, weaving effortlessly through the human traffic that made these layout sessions a sort of levee with Thompson playing the Sun King. Making his way to the layout table and standing next to his cigar-smoking boss, Tudor would exchange an opening grunt or two with him. Then, while Thompson flipped through stacks of pictures, the two men engaged in an odd dialogue of guttural noises and body signals, shrugs, arm gestures and raised eyebrows. Some pictures would be thrown into one pile, others into another. At some point, this untranslatable conversation would come to an end. Thompson would offer Tudor rough sketches he'd made on little layout pads designed for the purpose. Tudor would accept these with a final, somewhat dubious arching of his eyebrows. Then he would grab up the smaller of the piles of pictures on the table and glide out the door to design the final layout and have it put together by one of his paste-up men. There, in the big room where his staff worked, away from the tense dance around Thompson, his temper sometimes flared briefly but fiercely.

Tudor, who'd worked as a newspaper artist after finishing art school in Cleveland in 1923, was a designer with the Rural Resettlement Administration's photographic group in the 1930s and then joined the staff of the early *Life*. He left in 1940 to join the staff of *PM*, Ralph Ingersoll's new paper, then returned in late 1941 and became art director in 1945 under Dan Longwell. Throughout a long career, he never gave up his desire to be a painter. He was extremely knowledgeable about the technological aspects of the graphic designer's craft; the new typeface he created, Tudor Gothic, was used extensively on *Life* in the 1950s and 1960s. He particularly enjoyed working on the design and production details of big color projects like the photography of the Sistine Chapel for the Christmas issue in 1949 or assigning and dealing with the artists and illustrators who produced the painting for hugely successful *Life* series like "The World We Live In" or "The World's Great Religions." His apparent poise did not save Charlie Tudor from the attrition of years spent under terrific pressure. Like many of his colleagues, he relied a lot on liquor as the years passed, and still gliding through the complex motions of his job, he retreated behind a glassy calm more and more into himself.

"You're getting a story *Life* was made for," Tim Foote had written the editors when he sent in the pictures from Budapest, explaining, in case there was any room for doubt, that the photographs were "what all popular revolutions are about: violence, bravery, hatred of oppressors." But certain difficulties were built into this great story. As stated earlier, the people being brave were sometimes doing so in a tremendously violent way. This made it necessary for the writing to emphasize, in that Cold War time, that the dead men in many of the pictures deserved to be dead and that the people mowing them down or spitting on the corpses were naturally expressing their rightful indignation.

Another problem had to do with the future safety of the people photographed in the streets during the uprising, which lasted only a few days. The men doing the shooting of the Hungarian secret police in Sadovy's astonishing photographs that Thompson selected as the story's opening spread were not visible in those pictures. Elsewhere in the story, many were clearly identifiable. One man with a peg leg and carrying a rifle was characterized as "a one-legged hero" who "joined the charge against police headquarters." Another, a baby-faced fifteen-year-old with a rifle slung across his back, was actually named in the caption, which said he was "one of the many brave teenagers who fought in the rebellion." The vulnerability of these people to the almost inevitable reprisals greatly worried a number of the reporters in the foreign news department; they felt also that the story was emphasizing the rebel violence without putting it in context with the long-term Soviet violence that had led to it.

"There was a kind of indecency, a pornography, about the way the magazine was selling death," one remembered of that specific issue. "I felt uneasy," recalled Patricia Blake, then the only person on the *Life* staff who spoke Russian and later a specialist in Soviet affairs for *Time*. "By this time [of the closing], we knew the outcome [that the Soviets had crushed the uprising]. There was no chance these people wouldn't be brutally punished. I felt it was irresponsible [to show them]. It was a terrible risk to human lives." To minimize this risk, Blake and others tried to persuade Thompson to substitute pictures or to obscure the ones used so that individuals would not be recognized. But he wouldn't make the changes, not wanting to lessen the impact of the story.

Blake and another reporter, Henriette Roosenburg, also complained about an early version of an editorial in the November 12 issue, which dealt with the British attack (along with the French and the Israelis) on Egypt. Headlined "Eden's Tragic Blunder," it was a review of the situation that had brought on the Suez crisis, in which the United States found itself at odds with its allies and feeling utterly let down by Britain's Prime Minister, Anthony Eden. Blake, who managed to combine striking good looks with an occasionally icy hauteur, and Roosenburg, a blunt and powerful woman whose writing had appeared in *The New Yorker* and who had been a ranking member of the Dutch underground during World War II, were formidable advocates. In this case they were upset because an early draft of the editorial made it seem that *Life* equated the British invasion of Egypt with the Soviet crushing of the rebellion in Hungary, in the opinion of Blake and Roosenburg an outrageous oversimplification.

Subsequent versions took into account this reasonable complaint, but Thompson still had his own problems with the current editorial, as well as the one that ran the previous week. He generally recognized without protest the right of "the proprietor," as Luce was sometimes called, to use this page of *Life* as a platform for his opinions, and in fact Thompson most often found himself in agreement with the editorials, which were approved by Luce but thought out and crafted by Jack Jessup, an erudite and graceful writer.

Earlier in the year, in fact, Thompson had pretty well defined the way he felt about editorial policy in his answer to a complaint from his art editor, Dorothy Seiberling—as blunt and outspoken as she was productive—about a Luce-directed editorial on art. "This," he wrote about the editorial page, "is the place in which to state the bias of the editor, in *Life*'s case HRL and/or his policy advisors. In the rest of the magazine we report as honestly and in as interesting a manner as we can on what seems to be worthwhile, newsworthy or whatever. . . . I disagree with some editorials. . . . [T]he editorial page is perfectly free to say [something] is outrageous. . . . As foreman of the editorial production department I sometimes question if the management is really saying what it means. I also frequently argue against an idea, but when the decision is made I say what the hell, it's their magazine. . . . There is room for a difference of opinion on Art."

At this time, though, Thompson thought the editorials were getting a bit wishful in tone. The comment in the November 5 issue, headlined "The U.S. and the Rebelling Satellites," found great opportunity for the United States in the explosive situation in Eastern Europe. "We face a whole new phase in the world struggle," it read. "A Tommy-gun empire is breaking up. Our task is not only to encourage the process but to design and build a world in which it can never be re-established."

In the November 12 issue, this rather rosy view of American possibilities in a precarious world persisted. One somewhat glowing sentence read: "We have even been presented with the chance to exert the moral leadership of the world, not only to make peace in the Mideast but to help create a new rule of law in the world which even Communists might have to respect."

This optimism seemed excessive to Thompson, and he wrote Luce a note about it. "I just talked to Jack [Jessup]," Thompson began, "and he told me about his talk with you and C. D. [Jackson] on the Near East editorial. Poisonously, I said: 'Do you intend to maintain stoutly your theme of "In Disaster, Opportunity"?' He said 'yes' but later weakened a bit to add, 'Well, for 24 hours, anyway.'

"I suppose it couldn't be helped but I have a feeling that our last two editorials seem, in retrospect, somewhat over-optimistic if not unsophisticated. Now I'm all for being constructive, for taking the situation as it develops and trying to build something good out of bad. I think we have to keep on doing this. This is merely a suggestion that, in this wicked world, we run a risk of sounding fatuous if we beat this optimism theme too strongly."

The last copy for the November 12 issue closed and was teletyped to the Donnelley plant in Chicago sometime in the early-morning hours of Sunday, November 4. The patient and knowing readers in the *Life* copy room had teased the final changes and fitting (all the captions and text blocks had to square off exactly, with no ragged lines) from reporters and writers growing progressively more stubborn or playful as the hours ground on and the flow of liquor increased. There do not appear to have been any special problems connected with the closing, as there were the night a couple of years earlier when one exuberant writer, intoxicated—among other things—by the fact that his first by-lined article was going to press, had badly scared all the copyreaders, including their stern and usually unflappable chief, Helen Deuell. Terror and confusion struck at once when the writer playfully hoisted one leg out of the copy-room window and was threatening slaphappily to follow it with the rest of himself until Joe Kastner, summoned by the unusual din, rushed to the scene and furiously ordered the writer to climb back in or face immediate firing. It was all part of an almost routine hurly-burly. "Every week," said Natalie Kosek, then *Life*'s chief of picture research, "we pretend we have never put out a magazine before."

The last of the Hungary pictures had been sent to Chicago by air on Friday and Saturday, with duplicate packets shipped overnight by train. Within a few hours the final forms were plated and running on the presses, with duplicate plates on the way to other plants in Philadelphia and Los Angeles. By the next day, when binderies at all three plants were in full operation, completed copies of the magazine were being turned out at a rate of 1,400 a minute. Within four days nearly 6 million copies, the whole run, enough to fill eighty boxcars holding thirty-five tons of magazines each, were in the hands of readers or on the way to readers all over the country.

The issue had a newsstand sale of 1,019,575 (at twenty cents a copy), which was about the size of the expected non-subscription sale. *Life*'s Hungary photographs and the reporters' files were put together quickly and in two weeks published again as a paperback book by a team including editors Bob Elson and Ken MacLeish and correspondent Foote. Called *Hungary's Fight for Freedom*, it sold 650,000 copies at a price of fifty cents, and Time Inc. donated the profits to the International Rescue Committee.

The issue drew fewer than 500 letters, respectable but nothing special. The story that prompted the most letters was not the Hungarian uprising, which had produced probably the most sensational pictures of the Cold War, but was instead a one-picture story on Sherman Wu, a college freshman who was forced to resign as a pledge from his fraternity at Northwestern when members expressed their conviction that Wu "would degrade their house because I am Chinese." The Hungary story did draw many spirited letters ("I can understand how Mr. Sadovy would find it necessary to sit down and cry." "What the rebels did against the Communists is only a reaction for crimes committed on themselves"), and so did the editorial on Eden. The rest of the issue pulled scattered comment on a few stories, including Churchill's history, a short on an inflatable globe and a brief picture essay on the Presbyterians' first woman minister, photographed by the redoubtable Alfred Eisenstaedt.

There were several minor offerings of note. A portrait by Philippe Halsman, who with Eisenstaedt led all other photographers in shooting more than 100 *Life* covers each, was included in the Fred Allen story. Carl Mydans, another of the first to work for *Life* and among its most outstanding war photographers, contributed an excellent black-and-white portrait of Anthony Nutting, the British Foreign Secretary, who quit in protest over Eden's move into Egypt. But the picture ran at something less than the size of a pack of cigarettes on a spread jammed with many others. Larry Burrows, who would years later die while on assignment for the magazine in Vietnam, produced color copies of a number of paintings in the Churchill story and then flew to Cyprus to be ready to take pictures there as part of the coverage of the Middle East. One of *Life*'s most famous combat photographers, David Douglas Duncan, was *not* among those whose work appeared in the issue. Duncan had resigned some months earlier in a dispute that grew out of a story he'd shot in Afghanistan. One part of the discussion included the assured, talented, determined and monumentally self-righteous Duncan's insistence that all copy on stories he'd photographed be checked with him before publication. Thompson refused, the resignation went through and, for the time being at least, an important connection was broken.

A young and hustling photographer from New York, Yale Joel, did his best in the issue with an extremely staid party that took place in an art gallery in Providence, Rhode Island. But he couldn't, in two pages, overcome its basic dullness, a distressingly frequent fault of the "*Life* Goes to a Party" stories of that era. As Thompson explained the general problem to publisher Heiskell later: "We've eschewed the screwball in favor of the graceful or couth party—perhaps some of the frolic has vanished." The magazine was pursuing these couth parties, of course, to create an appearance of new responsibility—and because *Life*'s operatives were being banned by mistrustful hosts and hostesses from events the editors really wanted to cover.

Still, the issue contained at least one flash of the magazine's insatiable fascination with the famous uncouth. A news picture from Memphis showed the young Elvis Presley, the fastest-rising star in show business, with an affectionate arm around a prettily smiling and even younger Natalie Wood, who was visiting from Hollywood. It wasn't a sexy picture, but it had—well—promise. "He's a pixie, and has a wonderful little-boy quality," the caption writer quoted Natalie as raving. And Elvis winked back to the readers: "I'd be crazy to get married now. I like to play the field."

So the issue passed into the indifference of history, silly and sad, crushing and trivial, quickly becoming just one of about a thousand that had been printed since the first in 1936. It would soon grow ragged on coffee tables from Fresno to Fayetteville, be chewed up by the dog, lent to the neighbors, thrown out—or now and then carried upstairs to join a growing and dusty pile in the attic, another leaf in one journal's rich and varied record of the life its cameras saw.

A couple of weeks later, in the November 26 issue, Thompson reflected—from the anonymity of the editor's note—on a big occasion and the passage of time. He wrote: "Now that *Life* is 20—the first issue was dated November 23, 1936—we of course feel proud that we've made it the way we have. We also reflect, perhaps a bit ruefully, that no one seems to be getting any younger either." There, right at the peak of his own and the magazine's greatest success, Thompson could feel the chill of inevitable aging and change. He couldn't know it, but the best years of the great American magazine were about over.

12

The Astronauts

Some fine early morning before another summer has come, one man chosen from the calmly intent seven above will embark on the greatest adventure man has ever dared to take. . . . These are the Astronauts, pioneers picked for America's first efforts at manned space flight. With this issue Life *begins an exclusive series that will chronicle their magnificent undertaking from start to stirring conclusion.*

LIFE, SEPTEMBER 14, 1959

PERHAPS IT HAS TO DO WITH A BASIC FEELING of insecurity in journalists, a sense many have of the precariousness of their own reputations and the fleeting value of most of their work, but there's little that makes a newspaper or magazine editor more comfortable than the knowledge that he has a good story all to himself. Under such optimum circumstances the crush of time pressure is diminished, the fear and paranoia aroused by the competition is all but gone and the editor is left with the luxurious sense that he can now develop the story in ways that would never have been possible if he'd been clawing for pieces of it right there in the pit with the rest of the press.

The best—that is to say, the most self-satisfying—story of this sort is the rare item that drops directly into one's net, ideally because the ground has been well prepared by a careful reporter and the sources well primed to deliver to that reporter ahead of everyone else. Such stories win praise, promotion and awards. Another, less highly regarded kind of exclusive is, of course, the kind that a journal gets—and keeps— because it is paying for it. Stories of this purchased nature are not often the object of high praise. They are more commonly regarded with skepticism by the general reader and a mixture of contempt and fury by the competition, whose indignation is typically fueled by an unstable blending of righteousness and covetousness. Hell has no fury like a journal outflanked for an exclusive—or outbid.

Life, in its high-flying prime as a weekly picture magazine, was always in the business of nailing down exclusives, when necessary with generous infusions of cash. Although in the ordinary course of events the overwhelming majority of stories were not purchased, Life reporters and editors were always ready—in the wake of a ship sinking, a fleeing bride or a presidential assassination—to offer money to those witnesses of history whose pictures or whose accounts would ensure that the magazine's stories were good, or at least better than anyone else's. That was the key—beating out the other publication. A story was never sweeter than if its appearance not only was trumpeted as news but also embarrassed the editors of Look, or The Saturday Evening Post, or The New York Times, or Time. More often than not, the routine acquisition of exclusive pictures and accounts went generally unnoticed and unchallenged. It took the buying of something really big, like the astronauts, to set off all the alarms.

Of course, the astronauts (more specifically, the pilots selected in 1959 for Project Mercury, the first U.S. program that would launch men into space) were precisely the sort of journalistic commodity that the editors of Life would feel they simply had to buy. This purchase had everything: history in the making, an incomparable adventure full of danger and the near certainty of heroics, the good possibility of accomplishments that would stir the national pride. And on top of all that, the makers of this history, the astronauts themselves, preselected by a committee of physicians, psychologists and other experts looking for the healthiest, sanest, most highly motivated and intelligent men they could find, were seven attractive and demonstrably intrepid Americans with bright, photographable wives and children. It was virtually too good to be true. Here, grandiosity was practically fact. Once Life had actually made the buy, an ad across two pages in the magazine (August 17, 1959) proclaimed this journalistic coup in a way that made the delight almost palpable. Crowed the gleeful headline: "The Astronauts' own stories will appear only in Life." "The lives that these seven men—and their wives—" the copy went on, "will lead between now and the day that one of them becomes the first American to orbit into outer space will in itself be one of the most absorbing, dramatic human stories of our time." Then the ad writer hammered the crucial truth home again: "Life—and Life alone—will bring you that story in the first-hand reports of the men and women concerned. And Life will illustrate that story in photographs as extraordinary to look at as the words are extraordinary to read. . . . *Life* is proud indeed to be chosen to bring you in these pages the continuing story of what will surely be man's greatest feat in the Twentieth Century—as viewed by the Astronauts themselves.

"We feel certain," the clarion copy finished, "that you will want to be with us for the beginning of the count-down three weeks from now—and to follow the almost-out-of-this-world adventures of the Astronauts until one of them (*which one?*) rockets out of this world in reality." The ad bore the signature of Andrew Heiskell, the *Life* publisher, who was himself rocketing upward in the Time Inc. world and would soon become chairman of the board.

Three weeks later, the first of a ten-year string of astronaut exclusives ran a whacking eighteen pages in the magazine's main news space and included individual 750-word pieces of self-introduction bylined by each of the pilots ("I've the normal desire to go a little bit higher": Gordon Cooper. "You just don't have time to get frightened": Gus Grissom. "I know it can be done, and I want to do it": Alan Shepard). It also included preview glimpses of the sort of training the astronauts would be undergoing in the months and years before the first flight.

But mainly the article's intent was to let the readers know what a sexy and attractive package *Life* had lined up for them. "They are the best of a very good lot," went part of the initial rave, "a bright, balanced, splendidly conditioned first team, willing—eager, in fact—to undertake an assignment most men would find unthinkable."

And lest the readers think the magazine might be a little overboard in admiration of its new partners-in-journalism, the story shifted into a mode suggesting a certain modesty. "In spite of their extraordinary qualifications," it confided, "the Astronauts [the reverent capital A was not dropped until 1961] have many of the preoccupations, and even the small weaknesses, of more ordinary men. Two of the four cigaret smokers in the group are trying—so far unsuccessfully—to stop. Two others are worried about their weight. They are concerned about the condition of the grass in their yards and proper schooling for their children. Even though they were picked from the same general mold, the Astronauts are seven individuals. For example, John Glenn is poised and articulate, Walter Schirra is lively and easygoing, Donald Slayton is frank and stubborn. But individual differences are subordinated to the main interest of all. In classes and in physical training they work in easy harmony. All are intensely proud of their exclusive fellowship—a pride reflected in a remark made by Scott Carpenter: "If I don't go first, I'll have had honor enough just being one of this group." The tone of admiration evident in this first article, a sort of wide-eyed, unquestioning, even proprietary pride in the men, somehow contributed to blurring both their outlines and the distinctions between them and would be typical of dozens of pieces that followed.

The acquisition of these modest paragons (for a package price of $500,000) had been the goal of intense planning for many months. Word of an exciting manned space project had been around for almost a year before *Life* announced its exclusive, and there had been close press interest in the process of selecting the pilots. The project was also the subject of concentration at a very high government level; following the U.S.S.R.'s triumph with Sputnik, the United States badly wanted a big space success. In early 1959, 110 military test pilots—service fliers with special expertise in developing new aircraft—were picked for an initial screening. After preliminary evaluation (which included all sorts of psychological and physical stress tests), the list was cut to 69, then to 32, then to 18, and then, in April, to the seven men chosen finally.

During the last months of this period, *Life*, under the enthusiastic direction of managing editor Ed Thompson, was preparing for the good possibility that the press would have an opportunity to bid for the stories of this historic covey of pioneers-picked-in-advance. "NASA and the White House are currently mulling over the question of whether to allow or forbid the Mercury astronauts to make private contracts for the exclusive story of the first man's first flight into space," *Life*'s Don Schanche in Washington wrote his bosses in New York in mid-February 1959. "Since we (and all other press) are to be completely frozen out of the Mercury program until the final . . . candidates are picked, there seems to be no way to do any advance paving for private deals if and when they are allowed. If they are allowed, everyone will have to jump the poor guys at once. Everyone, in this case, means all the networks, virtually all the magazines, the studios, and damn near every outfit that tells stories. About a dozen, including *Life*, have asked NASA to pass the word in to the guys that we are in the market. NASA has refused on grounds that the question [of permission] has not been decided yet and that when it is decided it will be up to us to make our own approaches. At any rate, we should be getting prepared to descend on the candidates when the doors burst open, and we should have in hand a really compelling offer. . . . I am hopeful of a break of at least a few hours, perhaps longer, on the names of the candidates."

Whether or not the government, in this case NASA, should have permitted anybody to buy a claim on the astronauts' stories became the subject of fierce dispute in the coming months—and years. Many editors, outraged at the eventual contract with *Life*, felt powerfully that the pilots never should have been allowed to sell their stories, that public interest in them was based solely on the fact that they were engaged in a national project being paid for by the taxpayers, and that therefore all publications and other media should have equal opportunities to get material from them.

Officials at NASA, on the other hand, saw certain advantages to such arrangements. With proceeds from their own deals, the astronauts, who were given flight pay according to their military ranks, could be reimbursed (and their beneficiaries given a form of life insurance) far beyond the government scale. And exclusive contracts could be a convenience for NASA in its public affairs management. Top officials in the agency sensibly feared that they would be drowning in requests for journalistic access if there were not some limits to coverage. Contracts would provide reasons for saying no—and the agency wouldn't get the blame.

Hoping for the best, *Life*'s editors began making preparations to buy, including drawing up sample contracts for possible use in nailing down deals with the astronauts. One such document stipulated: "If you are selected for the ballistic flight and for a flight in orbit, and are the first to complete such a flight, you hereby agree that TIME [the reference is to Time Inc. and means *Life*] shall have all rights of every kind throughout the world in and to the personal story or account of your flight. As soon as possible after your successful completion of the flight, you will relate your experiences on that flight to a writer selected by TIME for the purpose of committing your story to print. You will further cooperate with the editors of TIME for the purpose of completing the manuscript by making yourself available to them at reasonable times for consultation, checking facts, general editorial purposes and for the taking of pictures of you for publication in connection with your story."

For cooperating in these and other ways, the signers of such a trial contract would be promised $10,000 upon agreeing to the deal and the sum of $100,000 "in the event that you complete [the] first successful ballistic flight or [the] first successful flight in orbit." One particularly interesting clause declared: "If you are selected for either the first ballistic flight or the first flight in orbit, or a subsequent such flight after prior unsuccessful attempts, in the event that you die during or as a result of said flight, and before completion of the manuscript to your story, TIME shall pay to a person or persons designated by you in writing the sum of seventy-five thousand dollars ($75,000). TIME shall have the right to obtain insurance on you for the purpose of said flight if it so desires." Success, by that standard, was worth at least $25,000—and a life—more than failure.

By April 9, 1959, when the finally selected astronauts were presented to the U.S. public at a press conference (where John Glenn immediately showed his promotional alertness by saying with a soon to be famous grin that he had volunteered for space because it "probably would be the nearest to heaven I will ever get"), it was becoming clear that money offers would have to be made to the group as a whole and not to a single man. For one thing, choices for the initial flights would not be announced for many months, possibly years. For another, top officials at NASA, where the decision to let the astronauts sell their personal stories was near approval, realized the sort of problems they might have if, for example, Shepard sold his story to *The Saturday Evening Post*, Slayton to *The New York Times* and Cooper to *Life*. It would obviously be more tidy if one publication was the beneficiary of the whole package. Such an arrangement, where the men would share in the proceeds regardless of which one was selected for the big flights, would also promote a sense of unity and teamwork among them.

In anticipation of making just such a group deal, *Life*'s editors, on the day of the public announcement, drafted letters to the astronauts outlining the magazine's basic position. "This is a preliminary pitch by *Life*," it began forthrightly, "with the object of eventually obtaining exclusive rights to your reports on Project Mercury. We will of course get down to details later but . . . you all might want to think about an outline of the way *we* have been thinking.

"Basically we think it makes sense to specify an over-all sum which we would pay to the group of seven astronauts for story rights up to and including the first successful orbital flight. This could work like this:

"We would pay part of the total sum at once, part later on in the project and the rest upon completion of the first successful orbital flight.

"As you probably know, stories like those you will be able to tell have value beyond first magazine publication. They may become books, for instance, and bring in more money. Sometimes we contract for magazine rights alone, sometimes (as with President Truman's memoirs) we buy all rights in one package by paying a larger sum. One form or another of a package deal for all rights seems to make most sense for both sides. For instance, we will provide skilled writers to help you with the magazine material and they can go on to complete the full scale book or books as well.

"We can assess the price of the subsidiary rights in two ways. We can either include this in the total payment or we can handle the other rights on your behalf on a mutually agreeable arrangement."

Life's determination to make a better deal than anyone else then became apparent. "Money is of course the tangible thing we will be talking about and we don't intend to let that factor prevent us from making an agreement. But [let us also call your] attention to a couple of intangibles. *Life* is by far the most frequent popular publisher of serious science stories, so you know that your reports will be handled accurately. We will not allow the gee-whiz angle to overwhelm the great scientific contribution you are making. And our readers have been educated to understand what you will say.

"[We] hope this all works out. It will be an honor for *Life*, which specializes in great events, to include your experiences in the company of Winston Churchill and *The World We Live In*."

Beneath the friendly calm of that communication, *Life's* bosses were seething with competitive excitement. In a memo to publisher Heiskell, Thompson, on his way to Washington, where he hoped (prematurely, it turned out) to make a bid on the astronauts, wrote: "As we agreed, it seems unacceptable to let the *Post* outbid us. [One of Time Inc.'s lawyers] raised a question about board of directors approval on a project of this size. I assume this is your problem if indeed it is a problem. I just drop it in your lap."

Exactly what Thompson might have been prepared to bid under those circumstances is not clear, but something in the neighborhood of $1 million does not seem an implausible figure, given the magazine's earlier payments for other projects and its ardent desire to nail down this one. The strategies for making the winning bid had been worked out with great care. Thompson wanted to make very sure that everyone on his side understood the rules. From Florida, where he had briefly gone on business in April, the managing editor sent a telegram to Heiskell: "Be sure to get lawyers' formula on bidding and rebidding straight. As I understand it we get a 2nd bid if we are topped but if 2nd bid is under opposition's first bid we are out. If our 2nd bid tops enemy's first bid he gets another chance. If he does not come up to our 2nd he is dead but if he tops our 2nd we get another chance and so on. The minute bid from any bidder does not come up to a previous bid the bidder is out but check. See you in Puerto Rico. Best."

The propriety of a sale got top approval in May with the announcement of a policy directive from NASA. The document, which would soon cause a great outcry among the press, was drafted by NASA, checked out by the Defense Department and then okayed by Andrew

Goodpaster, a high-ranking official on the staff of President Dwight Eisenhower.

"The Mercury Astronauts have been detailed to NASA," it began, "by their respective military departments pursuant to an agreement approved by the President which makes them subject to the regulations and directives of NASA in performance of their duties.

"It is recognized that the experiences of the Mercury Astronauts through all phases of Project Mercury, from the commencement of training to accomplishment of orbital flight, will be of great interest to the public. NASA has therefore adopted the following policy on disclosure of information concerning the experiences of the Mercury Astronauts:

"1. All information reported by the Mercury Astronauts in the course of their official duties which is not classified to protect the national security will be promptly made available to the public by NASA.

"2. Public information media will be granted frequent accessibility to the Mercury Astronauts for the purpose of obtaining information from them concerning their activities in Project Mercury. The timing and conditions of interviews with the Mercury Astronauts for this purpose will be controlled by the NASA Director of Public Information so as not to interfere with their performance of official duties. During such interviews, the Mercury Astronauts will be directed to disclose all information acquired in the course of their activities in Project Mercury, except information classified to protect the national security.

"3. While detailed to NASA for duties in connection with Project Mercury, the Mercury Astronauts

    a. may not, without the prior approval of the NASA Director of Public Information, appear on television or radio programs or in motion pictures;

    b. may not, without the prior approval of the NASA Director of Public Information, publish or collaborate in the publication of writing of any kind;

    c. may not receive compensation in any form for radio, television, or motion picture appearances, or for the publication of writing of any kind, which involves reporting to the public their performance of official duties in any phase of Project Mercury; and

    d. may not endorse commercial products.

"4. The Mercury Astronauts are free, singly and collectively, to make any agreement they see fit for the sale of their personal stories, including the rights in literary work, motion pictures, radio and television productions, provided such agreements do not violate the foregoing restrictions."

Paragraph 4, of course, allowing the astronauts to put their stories up for sale, was the key section of the document, and the key word in it was "personal." The directive made clear that NASA officials somehow hoped to have it both ways. The project—and the men themselves—would be accessible to reporters and the world. Mercury, went the proud claim, was an open project: no impenetrable, Soviet-type secrecy for the U.S. manned space program. But only up to a point. Beyond that point, the astronauts, claiming, for example, that to answer certain questions would involve their opinions or feelings or material drawn from their pasts, could withdraw behind a veil of privacy.

Thus the men—and particularly their wives, who had no official standing within the program at all—were given a perfect out against pressure from the general press. "I'm sorry, but I'm under contract for my personal story." But more than that was involved. What would actually happen as well was pretty much what critics of the new policy feared. A deal with the astronauts for their personal stories made it easier for reporters working for the contract holder to dig out and develop additional material that was more clearly official. The fact that the astronauts were getting paid for full cooperation and confidences on one level would naturally make them inclined to be grateful—and friendly to questions about the mission and their duties. In fact, they developed relationships later with the team from *Life* that often gave the work a kind of social overlay, carried out over drinks or at dinner parties or picnics at the end of fishing or water-skiing outings. Though the astronauts sometimes complained about what they thought was an invasion of their privacy, they often found it useful to hide, quite literally, behind the convenient shield that the contract gave them.

Even before the contract was signed, before, in fact, any training had begun, the astronauts and their families were stunned at the onslaught by the press at the first word of their selection. "After that, it was a continual stream of writers, photographers and television crews," recalled Betty Grissom in a book, *Starfall*, she wrote with Henry Still after her husband, Gus, Edward White and Roger Chaffee were killed when their Apollo spacecraft burned up on the pad on January 27, 1966. "Where had they come from, this mob of reporters? What lines of communication had vectored them into position to strike so quickly with word and camera?" And the existence of the *Life* contract did not always deflect pursuit by others. After the program was well underway, in May 1962, at the time of Scott Carpenter's orbital flight, a team from *Life* (the author included) spirited Rene Carpenter and her four children into an oceanfront house secretly rented to hide them from the rest of the press. Encamped by the hundreds just a few miles up the Florida beach to monitor Carpenter's flight, they included many who wanted to know where the astronaut's wife and kids were, and some who had an excellent idea that *Life* had them stashed away in a special house. In fact, on a couple of occasions during the morning of the flight, Rene and the children (and naturally the *Life* reporter and photographer) had to dash back inside from the beach when helicopters rented by the television networks made low-altitude runs up and down the dunes in search of them. Later that morning, when Carpenter and his space capsule, Aurora 7, had been missing for almost an hour and appeared to be in serious trouble, those in the secret house listened with the rest of the world while commentator Walter Cronkite's voice grew gloomier and gloomier with each report. The *Life* team began making plans about where to take the family in the event the astronaut had really perished. Agents from NASA arrived at the house, too, to take charge of the family. But the discovery of Carpenter clinging happily to his bobbing capsule effectively ended any dispute. Rene Carpenter was driven to a motel, where she met the press and publicly stated her profound relief about her husband's recovery.

Shortly after issuing the policy memo about the astronauts' personal stories, NASA's public affairs chief, Walter Bonney, took a step calculated to see that the inevitable rush to buy (and sell) would be managed in a way that would work out best for the men—and for the agency. Bonney and his bosses had decided that the astronauts should be sold as a single package; to make sure this would happen, Bonney paid a call on C. Leo DeOrsey, a Washington lawyer whose practice included such big-time clients as Arthur Godfrey and Edward R. Murrow. DeOrsey agreed with Bonney that the men should stick together in their dealings. Outgoing and energetic, he was pleased to be asked to take some part in such an exciting national project. He told Bonney he would be happy to meet with the men and talk it all over.

The astronauts and DeOrsey hit it off immediately; some of the more sophisticated of the pilots, particularly John Glenn and Alan Shepard, already had a well-developed sense of how much a shrewd and seasoned agent like DeOrsey could help them. An agreement was concluded late in May; it gave DeOrsey broad power to act for them. "The Mercury Astronauts," read one part of the document, "transfer all of their personal rights, in and to their personal accounts of the ballistic flights [the brief, up-and-down missions that Shepard and Grissom later flew] and the orbital flights [the longer, earth-circling trips that made up all the rest of the Mercury missions] made by them in connection with Project Mercury, as well as personal rights in the literary work, motion picture, radio, or television productions, including personal appearances for compensation (other than those in line with their official duties) to C. Leo DeOrsey of Washington, District of Columbia, as their agent, with all rights to contract in their behalf as in his sole discretion he decides if for the best interest of the Mercury Astronauts." A concluding section of the agreement reflected DeOrsey's deep pleasure at being given this chance to help sweeten the financial futures of these seven preselected American heroes: "Said C. Leo DeOrsey agrees to serve the Mercury Astronauts without compensation and will also personally defray all expenses incurred by him in this project."

The actual sale of the astronaut stories turned out to be less of a suspenseful, wide-open auction than *Life's* editors thought it might be. DeOrsey, in his various contacts with journals he knew would be interested (*Life, The Saturday Evening Post, Look, Newsweek*), had put out word that $500,000 would be the minimum starting price for the personal stories. So it is possible that potential buyers were discouraged by the stakes. Although *Life* was often referred to later as the highest bidder, the amounts bid by any other organizations, if there were such bids, are not known. *Life*, in fact, appears to have won the big prize by simply agreeing to meet DeOrsey's price.

The contract that legitimized the winning bid was basically simple. It provided that Time Inc. (*Life*) was buying all rights of every kind worldwide for the personal stories of the men about "all ballistic and orbital flights made by the Astronauts during the course of and in connection with Project Mercury." The television and motion picture rights would be returned to DeOrsey and his clients *after Life* had published the stories in both magazine and book form. Also included in the agreement were rights to the personal stories of the wives "in connection with their experiences and life during the course of Project Mercury." A writer would be assigned to the job, and, the contract stated, "each personal account or story . . . will consist of biographical material of the individual Astronaut and his family and the experiences encountered by [them] during the course of their training and [the flights]." The contract outlined a schedule of payments over the life of the project. Included were clauses promising that *Life's* operatives would not interfere with training and forbidding astronaut wives to write or collaborate in articles outside Time Inc. without permission. One particularly interesting section put into legal language *Life's* worry that NASA might at some time down the road interpret its recent new policy in a way that would hurt the astronaut stories. In such a case, where "the value of the personal stories of the Astronauts and their wives is badly impaired or lost," *Life* could break the agreement with a minimum payment to DeOrsey. Whatever the caveats, the contract was generally a license for a rare kind of cooperation and easy access.

At the magazine, the news of the successful purchase was met with enormous pride, a pride reflected in the exuberant burst of ad copy proclaiming that *"Life,* and *Life* alone," would be bringing this incredible adventure to the American people. Even if it wasn't exactly true, the magazine had indeed bought something no one else had, and the enthusiasm was understandable. "It seems unacceptable to let the *Post* outbid us," Thompson had written earlier, and his words remained an example of *Life's* aggressive attitude on the matter. The astronaut story *belonged* to the magazine with the big red-and-white logo: in no other magazine would it seem quite so appropriately placed. And in 1959 this sort of arrogance still had the ring of reason.

For the astronauts, of course, this first contract with *Life* would provide them with at least a mini-bonanza. Before the sale, they were making an average of little more than $10,000 a year. This new arrangement would provide them with a total of more than $71,000 in cash over the four years before the Mercury program came to an end. It meant a new prosperity. For some the abrupt rise in their standard of living was reflected in an outbreak of sporty new cars. For all, the extra money provided a welcome cushion and a sense of expanding possibilities befitting their unique status of national heroes-to-be.

Life's acquisition predictably brought howls from the rest of the press. "The story of what the Mercury Astronauts do in Project Mercury," wrote managing editor Alfred Friendly of the Washington *Post,* "belongs to the public. It cannot be sold by anyone to anyone." The clamor was not diminished by *Life's* promotional department's insistent use of language that implied, again, and again, that the *only* place readers could be assured of getting the astronauts' *own* stories of this astounding modern epic would be *exclusively* in the pages of *Life.*

Naturally enough, NASA was embarrassed by the magazine's ebullient syntax and kept putting on a troubled bureaucratic face about it all, as if there'd been some unpleasant misunderstanding and the agency was being accused of giving away the store when all that had been really sold were a few odd socks and some nail parings. The fact, of course, is that confusion about the line separating information that was truly personal from what properly belonged to the public was inevitable. For all of the agency's troubled cluckings about the *Life* contract, NASA had made the arrangement possible. And the deal with *Life,* whatever its shortcomings, and however unfair it was to the rest of the press, was a marvelously reliable way to keep the burgeoning story of the U.S. man-in-space program reported and photographed in considerable depth, in front of a huge and influential magazine audience on a regular basis. As always, NASA needed public awareness and acceptance to keep its programs going—and viewed favorably by Congress. *Life* was a superb vehicle for that.

The wooing of the astronauts took on a new dimension after the contract was signed. With the suspense over, what remained was to develop good working relationships between the men and their families and the team of journalists charged with telling their stories. Much of this would work out naturally in the course of time, as the pilots and the *Life* men and women got used to each other.

But, in the beginning at least, the journalists came into the assignment with an extremely unusual set of mind. We had virtually abdicated skepticism. Possibly our attitudes had to do with the general innocence of the period or with a more ordinary need for heroes. Yet, from top to bottom, the *Life* group stood in some real awe of the Mercury pilots and were pretty wide-eyed about their mission. In a figurative sense, too, we had bought the story. A cold objectivity about national goals and the merits of this particular project were not at work here. We were not looking for trouble in the program. It was as if the team from *Life* had been charged with the protection of a valuable national asset. With a sort of sweet grandiosity, editors, reporters and photographers somehow took on a responsibility for telling the story in a positive way, one that would reflect credit on the men and on the space program. This was all quite subtle; no one gave any directions to that effect. We would have fought the idea, in those earliest days, that we were not really capable under the circumstances of reporting objectively on this story.

Still, the fact that the astronauts had become *Life*'s property, that we took pride in this and were determined to make the most of it over the long run (which would be a barrier to our resisting demands from NASA and the men along the way) and that our principal job would be the depiction—the enhancement, really—of a winning astronaut image, these inevitably combined to make us cheerleaders, too. Our pursuit and successful capture of the story—and the constant need to justify it—left us, in a very real way, imprisoned by it.

Yet in those earliest days the excitement of just having the story took over. Editor Thompson, in celebration, brought a big group from *Life* to Langley, Virginia, where the astronauts were training, and threw a party for the men and their wives. There were many exchanges of toasts and a number of glowing references to the successes that surely lay ahead. Over martinis and wine, editors met astronaut wives, reporters and pilots talked over possibilities for stories during the long training period ahead before the actual flights. As the evening wore on and the conversations grew more mellow, there was even a little modest hymn singing, though not on the raucous level often heard at parties on the magazine back in New York. It was all very friendly, almost family, and the people from *Life* were at considerable pains to leave the impression that what they most wanted was to be thought of as partner-confidants in this glorious effort who could be fully trusted in the necessary and honorable accounting. Communicating with his guests later, Thompson had emphasized his joy in the occasion, saying that "*Life* is highly honored," that he was "absolutely busting with pride over the privilege of reporting this challenging and purposeful scientific project."

The harmony of the event was not really diminished by the serious discussion taking place at one table. It was about whether or not *Life*'s money would exert a corrupting influence on the relationship between the journalists and the astronaut families—and on the whole enterprise. Didn't the fact that the stories were paid for in advance somehow change everything? asked Marjorie Slayton, whose husband, Deke, had been one of the Air Force's best engineering test pilots before being selected for Mercury. Didn't the money, someone else wondered, introduce an element that might subtly deflect the astronauts' loyalties? Didn't the fact that *Life* had gotten something everybody else wanted generate bad feeling that the astronauts might pay for later in the reporting of a frustrated and critical press? Good questions all, even if the group at the table could not agree on the answers. The astronaut wives seemed to have more doubts about the ethical problems of the arrangement than their husbands—and certainly more than were admitted to by the people from *Life*—although no one, in his or her party glow, was suggesting that the contract that had brought them together should be canceled.

The week immediately after the first big story on the astronauts the magazine produced another almost as big on the wives. As their husbands had been, the women were in a group picture on the cover, the billing of which read: "Astronauts' Wives, Their Inner Thoughts, Worries, Their Exclusive Stories." There it was, that pushy word again, and in the editor's note that ran each week with the table of contents, there was a cocky little definition of it—and of the story it labeled. "The word 'exclusive' is kicked around quite a bit," the note read. "It really means that a given journalist has what everyone else hasn't. One might say that the exclusive picture or story takes the reader to people and places where no other publication might take him. *Life* is in the business of doing this all the time.

"This week, for instance, we have a big exclusive which deals with one of the most keenly reported stories of the year: the Astronauts. It stars the seven attractive women above who tell, with intimacy and feeling, what it is like being married to a man who may soon be shot into space (pp. 142–163). We are proud of this article not just because it was hard to get but because it has produced individual statements of faith and courage which are variously romantic, religious or homely— and invariably warm and womanly. They will, we believe, endure as moving documents of the Early Space Age."

However the accounts survive through history, the picture that opens the wives' story should certainly endure as one of the most mem- orable—and odd—of all *Life*'s photographs of the space program. It shows the seven wives, in their nicest simple jewelry and brightly colored summer dresses, posing, like Rose Bowl princesses on a mys- tery float, around a full-scale model of the ten-foot-high capsule their husbands were planning to ride into space. It looks like a portrait of some eyeless, polymorphous household god, half vacuum cleaner, half ketchup bottle, surrounded by a cluster of his adoring suburbanite subjects.

For all the editors' enthusiasm about the women's stories, they showed, as the ghost-written accounts of the pilots showed a week earlier, that it was going to be difficult over the long pull to keep these pieces from having a deadly homogeneity. Possibly it was because we were asking them all the same questions (reporters Don Schanche and Patsy Parkin had interviewed the women, I had talked to the men) or because these were people who generally didn't speak much about their feelings, to whom it was important, in fact, to be able to be mostly laconic and jokey about serious matters like death and other unknowns. Whatever it was, the texture of their stories all had a vague sameness, as if they had agreed on what to say, or at least on a general way of saying it. Surely the culture they lived in as test pilots and the wives of test pilots dictated much of the similarity. And so did the magazine's need for easy impact and brevity. Here are small segments of these initial accounts by the women:

Louise Shepard: "I decided long ago during [Alan's] Navy career that it is not good to stand around and complicate things for him when he has a job to do."

Anna Glenn: "Religion plays an extremely important role in our lives. We try to live it every day, to be consistent in it and not, as John says, to use it as an ace-in-the-hole to pull us out only in the tight spots."

Betty Grissom: "It doesn't help to be afraid of something that has already happened any more than it helps to fear things you think might happen. [Gus] thinks flying is less dangerous than driving a car and I agree with him."

Josephine Schirra: "Wally never broods about anything. Neither do I. . . . I've found that the things I did worry about never happened at all."

Trudy Cooper: "I don't worry about Gordon's airplanes falling apart any more than I worry about our house collapsing."

Rene Carpenter: "For me there are no dark or foreboding feelings about having my husband prepare to rocket into space and there were none even when Scott first was asked to volunteer."

Marjorie Slayton: "I refuse to get dramatic about the dangers he faces. I'm disgusted with the Hollywood version of a test pilot's wife trying to keep her tears out of the dishwater."

The pattern of similarity in these comments is interesting—eerie, even—though *Life*'s editors could not have commented on that except in the most admiring way for fear the women would feel criticized by their publishers. Actually, as among the men, there were sharp personality differences among the women. Rene Carpenter, for instance, bright, articulate, ambitious, perceptive, very much wanted to maintain control over what she said and not have her meanings lost in the convenient elisions of some ghost writer or editor. In the article quoted above, she also wrote: "This is not to say I am never afraid. . . . If he was flying on a test project and did not come home by six o'clock, I just knew I was a widow." She had also included some selections from a log her husband had been keeping for her during his training. After the stories came out, she wrote Thompson a letter chiding him mildly for a number of things—there were no pictures of her sons, her face and Jo Schirra's were too white on the cover, there was too much advertising throughout the story—but particularly for a change the editors had made in her husband's log. The original had said: "If this comes to a fatal, screaming end for me, I will have three main regrets: I will have lost the chance to contribute to my children's preparation for life on *this* planet, I will miss the pleasure of making love with you when you are a grandmother, and I will never have learned to play the guitar well." In a sort of post-Victorian spasm of prudery—and with the somewhat lame claim of protecting the Carpenters from their own candor—the editors had changed part of the entry to read: "I will miss the pleasure of loving you when you are a grandmother." To Rene Carpenter's direct but good-natured query about it, Thompson admitted the editing was probably a mistake. "I can't believe any of our red-blooded

American men and women readers," he told her, "thinks intercourse doesn't go on."

The initial response to the astronaut stories was very positive. In *Life* and in journals around the globe (the magazine had recouped a substantial part of its investment by selling worldwide rights to the exclusive for $200,000) the articles were greeted with enthusiasm. "Stand up, America," wrote one subscriber in Evanston, Illinois, "and give hearty salute to the intrepid Astronauts, who have the stature of men and patriots." *Life* got saluted, too, by a man in Oneonta, New York. "Brave as these men most certainly are," he wrote, "it is you who are performing an equally laudable service in awakening the interest of the people in our national space program." The wives got a share of the praise. "I got the feeling," commented a woman from Michigan, "that whatever success the Astronauts achieve by their common assignment will be due chiefly to the bond of love, understanding and faith of their wives."

There were a few hoots. "After reading the article about the 'inner thoughts' of the Astronauts wives," wrote a woman from North Carolina, "I can understand perfectly why some of the Astronauts would be glad to be in outer space. All that 'togetherness' is enough to send anyone into the wild blue yonder." And a rather grumpy fellow from Huntington, New York, said: "I would suggest that before we publish sentimental articles about the Astronauts, we manufacture something for them to fly in. We are still likely to be admiring the Astronauts and their families long after the Russians have orbited several unsentimental Sputniks."

But the good general response showed an honest appetite for the astronauts and for stories about them. These energetic and engaging men were a welcome addition to the heroless American scene and a specific antidote for the national gloom and feelings of inferiority that had bloomed with the Russians' orbiting of Sputnik two years earlier. People *wanted* to believe that the projected Mercury flights, which many space experts thought were unnecessary stunts whose results could be topped easily by the unglamorous orbiting of instruments, would be successful, and they were, in fact, a wonderful way to ensure the return of achievement and pride. The first astronauts truly benefited from the climate of the times; there was a lot of goodwill and a rather broad conviction that the mission was appropriate. It is hard to believe that such a program, undertaken from scratch, say, ten years later, would have fared at all well in a period marked by attacks against "the establishment," the severe disaffection of youth and great malaise over the war in Vietnam. The first moon landing did, of course, take place in the summer of 1969 and was greeted with widespread enthusiasm. But Apollo 11 was a considerable technological success, with a payoff understandable and thrilling to just about anyone who had ever looked up at the moon. For pilots just getting into training and whose accomplishments were yet to come, a time of greater innocence was necessary.

To fill the gap of more than two years between the astronauts' selection and the first ballistic flight, *Life's* team produced—rather desperately as time wore on—a stream of training stories. Each of the men had a specific area of responsibility in the project (for example, Schirra kept track of developments in the pressure suit for the seven, Glenn the instrument panel, Shepard the tracking system), and some stories were possible in which the pilots talked about their specialties and the application of their training to the flight.

Much of the burden of coverage was carried by photographer Ralph Morse, an ebullient, cheerful, short, round, ferociously energetic New Yorker who for more than ten years simply turned over his life and his considerable imagination to the job of making the astronauts and their work (and family play) look fascinating, which wasn't always the case. Morse could do just about anything with a camera. Resourceful and quick, he'd been a good combat photographer. But he especially loved taking pictures that presented him with a technical challenge. His results with the astronauts were almost always good, now and then wonderful, occasionally amazing. In those first months, he did miraculously well taking pictures, often complex multiple exposures, of astronauts riding training devices like a giant accelerator called "the Wheel," which hurled them around under punishing G forces, or a real vertigo producer called MASTIF (Multiple Axis Space Test Inertia Facility), which spun the men every which way at horribly disorienting speeds until they were able to bring it under control.

Morse also covered the men learning to survive under varying conditions (in case their capsules got forced down in the jungle or desert or were somehow temporarily out of reach of the recovery forces), escaping from a sinking capsule (which Grissom actually had to do on his flight) or simply being with their families, relaxing at home or picnicking on the beach. The astronauts tolerated Morse's constant appearances in their lives with a mixture of admiration and amusement. Now and then, they got tired of having the restless and endlessly talking "Ralphie" around. But they respected his professionalism—and his results, which were contributing a lot as time passed to growing interest in the project and to their own increasing fame around the country.

Though all was not untroubled between *Life* and the astronauts as the training period ground on, the problems were mostly between NASA and the magazine, and they often had to do with interpretations of the contract. The team from *Life* naturally wanted to cover everything that might produce a story. But if *Life* began working on some phase of Mercury that the rest of the press hadn't heard about or paid much attention to, the word would inevitably get out that *Life* was onto something, and the project's public information people would begin taking a lot of heat. "What the hell's going on here?" reporters would ask. "Does *Life* think it owns the program or something?" If the stories involved Mercury "official business" (as opposed to the astronauts' personal stories), there was certain to be trouble.

Because the magazine was generally putting more manpower into Mercury than other press outfits and some of its sources were paid, this sort of thing came up all the time. And the NASA public information officer who had to deal with most of it in the early days was Air Force Lieutenant Colonel John A. Powers, known to all as "Shorty." A former pilot in the Berlin Airlift who switched to public information, Shorty Powers was a convivial fellow who enjoyed swapping stories with reporters and during the first flights became somewhat famous for his dramatic TV broadcast countdowns ("All systems are A-O.K. and the clock is started"). He took very seriously his work as a shaper of the astronaut image. Powers was also a scrappy and choleric man, and he hated the *Life* contract with a sour conviction. Directly charged with handling relations between the astronauts and the press, he obviously felt that the contract disrupted his management and reflected badly on the pilots.

He blocked *Life*'s efforts at every turn. On one typical occasion the magazine wanted to do a story with Scott Carpenter at Edwards Air Force Base, where Carpenter was working on some of the problems of weightless flight. Powers first stalled with necessary permissions, then held *Life*'s people off for a week until he could fly to Edwards himself and announce the flights (which offered no security or clearance problems) to the rest of the press. *Life* got its story, too, but the magazine's team felt it was actually being penalized for having more initiative than its rivals. Which may have been true, but such zeal was a constant embarrassment to Powers, whose noisy righteousness the *Life* group thought concealed a smoldering envy over the great financial deal the astronauts had cut for themselves.

But the astronauts, too, helped create the images of themselves that soon became current. "Bland," "boring," "Boy Scout"—all of these were applied frequently to describe the working portraits of the pilots that came out in *Life*. "They all run together" was a common complaint. "You can't tell one from another." The criticism was quite fair, and one reason for it was that the men, as well as the cold-eyed hero shapers from NASA, had approval rights over most of the copy that *Life* churned out on this big running story.

Typically, an article involving one of the astronauts would be sent to the pilot and to NASA headquarters, and changes of one kind or another could be expected from both places. If Wally Schirra, for example, didn't like the way he sounded in a quote, even if he'd said exactly that, he could insist on a change. He frequently did, and so did the others, with John Glenn and Alan Shepard, along with Schirra, seeming to be the most vigilant in the creation and protection of their images. They were very definite about *not* wanting ever to seem anxious, fearful, naïve, immodest, irreverent, unkind, angry, jealous or in any way uncertain that the whole enterprise was going to come out just fine. They didn't intend to own up to any "negative" feelings. They wanted to appear confident and positive and sensible. "Unemotional" was a word their *Life* ghosts often heard as being most desirable, as if the very thought of displaying emotions involved them in a possible loss of control and threat of breakdown. When Shepard, three days after becoming the first American in space in May 1961, told me about the moment of lift-off, his voice shook. Yet as we worked on the story of his flight, he would say very little about his feelings before the launch beyond the observation that his "stomach began to churn a bit" at one point and that he'd had "butterflies." He was the perfect Mr. Offhand. About walking out and looking up at the fueling rocket that would blast him and his capsule to an altitude of 100 miles at a speed of 4,500 miles an hour, he said: "I always enjoy the sight of a bird that's getting ready to go." After the orbital mission that made him globally famous in February 1962, John Glenn was determined to minimize his reporting of the content of a lengthy and emotional conversation he'd had with his wife by radio and phone hookup from his capsule a short while before the launch. She had had quite a lot to say about it in print just the week before, but Glenn, apparently not wanting people to know that he and Annie had virtually been saying goodbye to each other just in case, could manage little more than "I felt confident she was in good shape."

In the main, though, the changes the men requested were rarely big and did not distort the facts of the program or their parts in it; the astronauts wanted their pieces to be accurate. But the result of their changes was often a general flattening, and the distinctions between them tended to blur. The pieces lost bite and humor, which were real qualities of a number of the pilots, because seeing their complaints or jokes in print often made them uncomfortable.

But *Life*, too, was engaged in a kind of cover-up, an inflation and a smoothing out of the astronaut image. Headlines like the following for a John Glenn story—"An Unswerving and a Self Denying Man Engaged in a Stern, Dangerous Pursuit"—or sentences like this about Shepard—"Totally and somehow caressingly absorbed in [his jet airplane], he is very much its master"—have a certain hushed reverence, as if the reader is being warned that he is in the presence of supermen. "Decidedly ascetic" and "unswerving conviction" were among the typically euphemistic labels used to soften the truth about Glenn, which was that he was often rigid, driven and obsessive in his pursuit and that his repeated references to devotion to God and country didn't get in the way of conspicuous devotion to himself. What the reader didn't hear from *Life* about the "tough" and "poised" and "cool" Shepard was that he was also an arrogant and quite prickly fellow with a clearly visible mean streak. Like other men, the rest of the group were less than perfect, too, at various times small-minded, vengeful, crude, boring or even stupid. But their normal aberrations of character, or even the abnormal ones, were not grist for the *Life* stories. Such fastidious omittings are not uncommon in journalism generally; reporters often overlook the interesting human failings of subjects they deal with on a regular basis. Generosity like that, toward politicians, baseball managers and big businessmen, is a way of getting asked back. In the magazine's case, the contract was a further deterrent to full disclosure. In any case, the readers got a sanitized view of the men. *Life* here was in the business of promoting glory, and that contributed to the making of rather dull heroes.

It wasn't just that the articles lacked bluntness and gossip about the astronauts' off-duty exploits, though they certainly did that. There were always allegations of various kinds of frivolity floating around, including one unchecked item about a woman in the Cape Canaveral area who was determined to sleep her way through all seven. But what the *Life* people working on the story most regretted was not so much the lost gossip as not producing an overall tone of greater reality. It would have been impossible, for example, to tell from reading the stories that the Mercury astronauts were not really just one happy family. Actually, by the time of the first flights they had more or less split into factions. Glenn and Carpenter made up one; they thought a number of scientific experiments and observations should be carried out during the Mercury flights. Grissom, Schirra and Slayton believed differently;

they felt that the flights should be devoted purely to working out the worthiness of the "vehicle" and the system for future missions. Cooper joined forces with this group much of the time, and Shepard, the cool one, stood characteristically aloof from it all until it suited him.

There was a lot of rather pious talk about teamwork among the astronauts and throughout Mercury. Post-flight speeches by the pilots had an Academy Awards flavor; the grateful pilots invariably thanked the ground crews, the recovery forces, the makers of the capsule "and the thousands of hard-working people who made all this possible." As far as the *Life* people could tell (and our "in" with the astronauts caused most top managers of the project to shun us whenever possible), morale was generally high, a result to be expected on a project whose urgent success is suddenly given a top national priority.

But in spite of the spirit of teamwork and cooperation that prevailed, there was real rivalry among the Mercury seven for the first space flights. Obviously this was only to be expected with men who had been selected, among other things, for their high motivation and their need to excel. All were top-rated pilots of high-performance airplanes, and they were not accustomed to being ranked behind their associates. In their own rather narrow field, they were a bunch of All-Stars. For example, well before Mercury, Shepard was considered an admiral in the making, a man getting ready for the best that the Navy had to offer. Slayton, who performed amazing feats with the newest planes, was reputed to be among the very finest of military test pilots. Glenn, a combat flier, was clearly the best known to the public. He had already achieved a certain national notoriety for setting a new coast-to-coast jet speed record (3 hours 23 minutes) in his F84-1 fighter, and perhaps more importantly, for collecting $25,000 as a big winner on a TV quiz show (*Name That Tune*). The others all had variously comprehensible reasons for thinking themselves uniquely qualified to get selected over their fellows.

In a couple of cases, the rivalry was heightened by the fact that the men didn't like each other. Glenn, for instance, the earnest, boyishly grinning Marine hotshot from Ohio, thought that the off-duty behavior of a couple of the others was not becoming for men who'd been picked as symbols of American achievement in the new space age. They, in turn, thought he was a self-righteous prude. Whatever the merits of either position, the feelings generated were quite intense and grew greater as the time approached for the selection for the first flights.

Unbeknownst to us at *Life*—or to anyone else except the top people at NASA and the Defense Department and those underlings directly involved—the selection had been made on January 19, 1961, the day just before the inauguration of President John F. Kennedy. Mercury boss Robert Gilruth had called a meeting of the astronauts at their Langley, Virginia, headquarters and given them the word. The pilot of the first U.S. flight, a suborbital mission of about fifteen minutes' duration, would be Alan Shepard. Gus Grissom would fly the next, also suborbital, and John Glenn would be the backup pilot for both.

The next day, John Glenn and I traveled together by car from Langley to Washington, a distance of about two hundred miles. His usual friendliness and good spirits were completely missing. He seemed very tense and preoccupied, and as he drove—as the astronauts all did, with a skill somehow beyond ordinary drivers—his face was taut and unsmiling. I remember that he slammed the steering wheel hard with his bare hands a number of times. On that cold, clear and very windy day, as we tried to get Kennedy's inauguration speech on the car radio, the sound kept fading in and out. Was Glenn frustrated, I recall wondering, because we weren't getting better reception? Could he possibly have been moved from time to time by some staticky burst of Kennedy's eloquence?

Neither, it turned out, was the case. He was simply furious because Shepard, and not John Glenn, had been chosen as the first American to go into space. Glenn felt powerfully that he should have been the one. Weeks later, when the selection became public, Glenn admitted to a modest version of his disappointment and took a good-loser pose. But whatever he acknowledged, his rage had been severe. It reportedly led him not only to complain to project managers about losing out but even to suggest that those chosen over him were not really suitable to have been selected.

Even among highly motivated competitors, this seemed an extreme response to rejection. He was finally persuaded to stop protesting when it became clear that important people thought he was showing bad signs of not being able to handle the stress of a temporary setback. He was damaging his own chances for a selection for a later flight.

Even after he settled down, he stayed pretty glum for a while. When friends suggested that his designation as backup pilot surely increased the likelihood that he would be picked for the first orbital mission—and that *that* flight could bring the pilot much greater acclaim than Shepard would get for his 100-mile-high puddle jump—Glenn would not really be mollified. "First is first," he said. So much for his powers of prediction.

None of this, of course, appeared in *Life,* and the need to be silent about fascinating material increased the frustration of the reporting team. What at first had seemed like a great opportunity to work on one of the most interesting running stories of the age began to seem a bit tainted with public relations. NASA wanted its project to look good, the astronauts were busy taking care of themselves and *Life*—to protect its own interests—had to strain to keep the stories lively as well as make sure that everything worked out smoothly under the contract. It was not always an easy balance, and after several months of bickering with Shorty Powers, a kind of distance developed between the magazine and the astronauts, each side a bit disillusioned with the other.

But by no means entirely. The *Life* people remained basically smitten with the astronauts—in fact, gaga about them. This was not just a journalistic conviction about the importance of the space mission; *Life* was deeply proud to have this form of narrative custody of the astronaut story. As was often true over the years on Henry Luce's magazines, the interests of patriotism and successful publishing seemed somehow to meld together here in a warm, red-white-and-blue glow. The highest echelons of Time Inc. management regularly confused their journals with some nonexistent arm of government. For example, in June 1961, just a few months after Glenn's sorrow and only weeks after Shepard's flight, *Life*'s publisher, C. D. Jackson, ran an ad in the magazine and headlined it "The Aim of *Life*." The ad pointed out a few changes in appearance, some variations in typeface and layout here and there. The red band, Jackson advised readers, that had always been at the bottom of the cover was going to be dropped. Though the copy didn't say so, these design changes had been worked out by a team led by George Hunt, who would soon succeed Thompson as managing editor, and by Bernie Quint, who would be Hunt's art director.

But more importantly, the ad, emphasizing *Life*'s accomplishments at this time of its twenty-fifth birthday, also trumpeted its high patriotic intentions. "It is apparent to the editors of *Life*," Jackson's copy read, "that the national goals of our country can be stated in these two propositions: 1) Win the Cold War. 2) Create a better America. Can a magazine," Jackson asked solemnly, "presume to say that it will help win the Cold War, help create a better America?" Long one of Luce's trusted associates and a former speechwriter and adviser to President Eisenhower, Jackson had absolutely no problem with that at all. At the same time as he ringingly promised that the magazine would simply get better in every way over the next twenty-five years, he pledged: "*Life* dedicates itself to being a lively instrument of the National Purpose, to helping the people of America recognize their deepest aspirations and work unceasingly toward that fulfillment." The astronaut package, obviously, was part of that dedication.

Among those who worked on the stories, Glenn, friendly and ac-

cessible in spite of occasional outbreaks of self-interest and Boy Scout-
ism, was a favorite, and so was Scott Carpenter, a sweet and easygoing
Navy lieutenant. Glenn, a man of relatively wide competence and experience, always seemed, like Shepard and Slayton, to be highly qualified for the flights. In the advance betting he was the favorite, picked
as most likely to win the space sweeps. But Carpenter was really no
one's choice; his surprise selection for an early flight came only after
Slayton had been disqualified at almost the last moment because of a
heart problem. Carpenter brought less of a high-powered reputation with
him, and there was a modesty about him that was less visible, even
altogether missing, in many of the others. For one thing, he was quite
willing to express his doubts about things, including himself. He was a
romantic unafraid to confess his love for serious music, for example,
along with his feeling that he was really ignorant about it and ignorant,
too, in many other areas where he longed to know more—literature,
philosophy, history.

There was something truly touching about him; he projected none
of the cocky self-confidence of some of the others. He seemed genuinely
open, with an almost childlike enthusiasm for ideas that were new to
him. And compared to the typical astronaut determination to present
an image of strength, rectitude and good judgment, Carpenter's statements could be amazingly candid.

On at least one occasion, his candor about himself did not increase
the admiration of his fellows. This took place in the spring of 1962,
shortly before his own flight, which came only a few months after
Glenn's and was also a three-orbit mission. Before Glenn's astoundingly
well-received journey, *Life* had produced a sort of scrapbook of his life
up to that point, a ten-page album of pictures from his boyhood in New
Concord, Ohio, his high school and college triumphs, the beginnings
of his courtship with Anna Castor, the girl he would later marry, his
dashing career in the Marine Corps. Billed as the "Making of a Hero"
and headlined "A Man Marked to Do Great Things," it was an absolutely prototypical *Life* picture biography, complete with a close-up
cover of this splendid and freckled American in the helmet that he
would soon wear into space.

The story about Carpenter that preceded his flight was quite different. Though it offered many old pictures of his boyhood in Colo-
rado—including one marvelous photograph of him crouched on an
enormous rock—where the emphasis in the first story had been on
Glenn's All-American beginnings, Carpenter's was distinctly less adoring. The cover billed him as "The Loner Who Found Himself: New
Hero for Orbit." The headline on the article inside declared: "From a

Mountain Boyhood Filled with Roaming and Restlessness—Comes a Quiet Man to Ride Aurora 7." This story, the headline was saying, would offer a new wrinkle in astronaut coverage: the wrinkle of imperfection.

The revelations about Carpenter, even if they were unusual in the context, were not all that bad. As summed up near the beginning of the piece: "In his own words Carpenter was for many years a 'loser.' He was a hell-raising kid who stole the accessories for his car. He did miserably in college. He was profligate with his energies and reckless with his life. That he did not wind up dead in a mountain road ditch at 21, or carrying a hod, which he likes to do and for which he is remarkably qualified, he owes largely to luck. He feels fortunate, too, that he was ever chosen as an Astronaut, for at the time of the selection his naval career had seemingly reached a dead end."

The article itself did little more than amplify these and other facts of Carpenter's biography and develop such non-controversial matters as the astronaut's devotion to his wife and kids. But when the story appeared, the image protectors at NASA were upset. This was not what they'd come to expect. Here one of their charges had been depicted as something of a flaky character whose life had not been a succession of triumphs and whose career choices had sometimes been made out of impulse as much as from any disciplined drive toward a lofty or even discernible goal. In fact, some pointed out, from reading the piece a person might wonder just what it was Carpenter thought he was doing with his life. His views all seemed a little romantic and mushy. "Sometimes," he was quoted as saying, "I think I'd like to go back and live on a ranch. But more than that, I think I'd like to go back to some beautiful unspoiled island and get back to basics. I'd like to have a whole houseful of good books to read, an orchard full of banana trees and coconut palms and an ocean full of fish and a long sandy beach and a lot of surf to ride in. There I'd just take root and grow like another tree." Did *that*, aghast Mercury skeptics asked themselves, sound like the sort of man we ought to be sending into space for America? Let him ride waves or take root instead. We at *Life*, of course, were delighted with Carpenter—probably because he sounded more like one of us than one of them.

But there was nothing NASA could do to change things in this case. This was a story carrying my byline, not Carpenter's, and it had no reporting about the Mercury project in it. Thus it was beyond the censoring the agency did on more routine astronaut pieces. Carpenter had read it, of course, and gave it his okay, as the contract required. But that he could actually allow *Life* to print some of those things—

that he would even *tell* them in the first place—struck many on the project, including other astronauts, as showing awful judgment.

And when Carpenter, in his flight a couple of weeks later, made a basic and quite damaging error in the handling of his spacecraft, it simply provided evidence for the already harsh verdict held by some within Mercury that he really wasn't much of a test pilot. His uncool behavior under pressure—he'd gotten all excited by the views at 100 miles up over Australia and had improvidently burned most of his fuel to make more detailed observations—had contributed to the imprecision of his eventual landing in the Atlantic 250 miles downrange from the place he was supposed to be. He'd been missing for almost an hour, and people all over the world had been terribly worried about him. At NASA later, where near-perfection, after only four manned flights into space, was apparently to be expected, the open and ingenuous Carpenter was looked on as something of an embarrassment. As time passed, this lack of the confidence of others hurt him deeply and virtually ended his career within the project.

Working on the astronaut story, to be, in effect, a member of a tiny, private press corps, was a rare and occasionally unsettling experience. Closer inside than most reporters ever get on ordinary stories, yet without the freedom of reporting fully what we knew, we often felt anger and frustration toward the subjects, as if they were responsible for the discomforts of the compact between us. Still, there were real pleasures available for the reporter from *Life*. After Glenn's flight, he and his family came to New York with all the other astronauts to be the focus of the biggest ticker-tape parade in the city's history. The Glenns, with their kids and both sets of grandparents, were staying in the presidential suite in the Waldorf Towers. After the parade, I went back to the hotel with John to go over his first-person account of the flight, which we were trying to put to press that night.

The family sat down to eat—after Glenn had said a blessing—at a big table in the suite's formal dining room, and I recall feeling touched at the sight of these unfancy Ohioans, exhausted by the parade and all the events that had followed the flight, quietly making themselves at home amid all the gleaming glass and the rich napery. They were going to the theater afterwards, and one of the hotel barbers came upstairs to cut the hero's hair. I sat nearby, and to the accompanying sound of scissors we went over the story line by line.

When we finished, the barber undraped Glenn and dusted his shoulders with a cloth. Then John suggested that I could use a trim. So we traded seats and went right on with the editing. I remember being filled at the time with an enormous sense of gratitude and good fortune. Imagine—the free world's great new hero was buying me a haircut! Somehow, as my hair fell with his to the Waldorf rug, I became something more than his very tired ghost writer. His golden winning aura now included me. But reality nicked my grandiosity just in time. Shared haircut or not, Glenn stubbornly refused to give me any interesting details on the phone call he made to his wife from the capsule. That and the pressure of our deadline quickly put me back into a much less reverent frame of mind.

A few days earlier, during his flight, I'd felt almost the same disorienting sense of becoming part of the event. Along with photographer Michael Rougier, who was picked for this delicate assignment for his unobtrusiveness and sensitivity, I was ensconced in the Glenns' house in Arlington, Virginia. We'd arrived there late the evening before—so we could get inside without drawing the irate notice of the crowd of reporters, photographers and television technicians on the lawn. Annie Glenn, kind, cheerful and composed, made sure we were comfortable for the night. The next morning, just a few hours before the historic launch, she woke us for a very early breakfast.

The Glenns' two children, David, sixteen, and Lyn, fourteen, Annie Glenn's parents, a few friends and the family minister eventually gathered in the living room. Trying to be as invisible as possible, Rougier and I got ourselves ready to harvest the exclusive that would be billed on the cover the following week as "The Glenn Story Nobody Saw."

Things went along smoothly enough in those first hours. The crowd gathered outside. Scott Carpenter, Glenn's backup pilot, called from Cape Canaveral and put John on the line. I walked softly around the inside of the house looking at pictures and into open closets, making notes about the astronaut's loud bow ties and the pearl-handled Marine officer's sword that hung over the fireplace. I checked the spelling of the pet Siamese cat's name—C-h-i-n-k-a. My, this was exciting, I thought, to be in on something really big like this. Here Mike and I were, on the threshold of this huge event, right inside the family, practically part of it, in fact. Hundreds of other journalists would fight to be in our places. And nobody could get us out and crack our precious exclusive—because the Glenns wanted us there and we had the contract behind us.

Just three weeks earlier, when the flight had been postponed after a countdown had already begun, Lyndon Johnson, then the Vice President and overall czar of the space program, had tried to pay a call on Annie at the house. He would have brought the whole Washington press corps in with him. That would have brought terrific pressure on the Glenns to throw us out. But even Johnson had failed. Annie, un-intimidated by his power, turned him away ("You're so nice to call, Mr. Vice President, and you surely understand how it is. We'd just like to be together in the family at this time"), and now we felt quite beyond the reach of the competition. We were the men from *Life*, and we were going to do something wonderful.

Now, suddenly, we were into the last moments of the countdown. Glenn's towering Atlas rocket, with the Friendship 7 capsule sitting on top, filled the screens of all three television sets in the living room. No one there spoke. Annie, her white face composed and intent, began to rock ever so slightly back and forth. Lyn's fist was clenched at her cheek. Dave looked down into his lap.

When the belch of smoke and flame broke out at the base of the Atlas, Lyn put both hands to her face. "Lift-off!" the voice from mission control cried. When the tears began to run down her daughter's cheeks, Annie, without looking away from the triple view of the rising rocket, put one hand gently on her child's foot. The Atlas rose faster, the bright glare of its engines ringed by black on the television screens. "It is climbing nicely," the voice from Canaveral exulted. "Pilot John Glenn is reporting all systems go . . ." Finally then, as the television camera poked aimlessly through an empty sky, Annie put her head against her knees and sobbed.

And I, choking with my own feelings, didn't really know where to look. This was really much more than I thought it would be. Even protected by my job and by the knowledge that the Glenns had welcomed us there, I felt like a voyeur. This was a terribly personal moment, a moment of deep privacy beyond all contracts. A man's life was in the balance, in violent, unpredictable jeopardy right in the view of the people he loved most. I felt ashamed and unprofessional to think so, but there was something obscene about our being there to record it.

13

George Hunt Takes the Hill

FOR ANY IN SEARCH OF HARBINGERS, it is possible to say that the end of *Life* was really forecast at the close of its greatest year, 1956, when net income was at a peak ($17.4 million) and Thompson was in full stride as managing editor. It was then that another of America's mass magazines, *Collier's*, folded, the victim of constant punishing competition with *Life, Look, The Saturday Evening Post* and *Reader's Digest*, as well as the increasingly resourceful and persuasive salesmen from television. The unfulfilled subscriptions of *Collier's* (circulation: 4.18 million) were put up for sale, and Time Inc.'s bosses briefly considered buying the *Collier's* list to bolster *Life's* base circulation figure of 5.6 million and to put it far ahead of *Look* (4 million) and *The Saturday Evening Post* (4.85 million).

But various arguments—among them that *Life's* circulation was already strong at the current figures and that taking over the *Collier's* list would reduce *Life's* rosy (but still unsatisfactory by most hard-nosed standards) profits—were presented to make a final and convincing case against the purchase. *Look's* Gardner Cowles, on the other hand, saw the subscription offering as a potential bonanza for his magazine and quickly grabbed it. Almost immediately *Look's* ad rates were increased by 15 percent to reflect its new subscribers and within a year the magazine's revenues were sturdily up—by $9 million. In little more than a year, *Life's* gross ad revenues were off by more than 10 percent.

That Cowles had won that particular round of the furious and exhausting circulation wars seems beyond doubt. But the most devastating blow to *Life* may not really have been felt until more than ten years later. For all that time, while the trouble at *Life* was getting steadily worse, a pervasive corporate regret, a kind of Monday-morning guilt, was shared by Time Inc. managers who felt they should have bought the *Collier's* list when it was offered for sale—and were determined not to make the same mistake twice. Whether or not that would have made a difference to *Life's* long-run health is beyond guessing now, but what seems sure is that the failure to buy a list in 1956 assured *Life's* eager and ill-advised purchase of the *Saturday Evening Post* list in 1968 when that magazine began its final plunge beneath the waves. The subscribers bought from the *Post* led to an empty inflation of *Life's* circulation, an inflation from which there ultimately began an embarrassing, even ruinous public retreat.

In the frenzied competitive atmosphere of the late 1950s, the aim of all the big magazines was the capture of more and more circulation. The war for readers, such a combative fighter as Luce once reflected, "should be fought vigorously with every means. By all the editorial exertion and brains we can muster. And by Promotion. . . . Maybe we should cut back on newsstand price and subscription price. We would make things very expensive for *Post* and *Look*—and sacrifice our own profit position in the process."

Pretty much that sort of gasoline-war price-cutting would take place in later years, when the single-copy price of *Life* was reduced to an awkward nineteen cents in efforts to make it seem a shopping bargain. But for the moment, no reductions were made (*Life's* price in 1958 was 25 cents on the newsstand; $3.99 for an introductory 39-issue offer). Not long after this, Howard Black, one of Time Inc's shrewdest and most competitive executives, came up with a plan that was so utterly different from the conventional aggressive thinking of the moment that it didn't stand a chance of being accepted. Executive vice president Black, who had been a *Life* adman himself, put forth the fascinating if outlandish notion that the circulation wars were exhausting and self-defeating for *Life*. The magazine should stop pushing ahead for more and more readers, and concentrate instead on acquiring the best possible 4 million subscribers and selling the magazine to advertisers— at reduced rates—on the basis of the high quality of the audience. Black was right that the circulation wars would continue to be a big problem for *Life*, but those opposed to his idea felt that withdrawal from the battle would be widely interpreted as a signal of defeat and used by jubilant opponents to press their own cases. Big, it seemed then—very big—was the only thing that could be beautiful.

If trouble down the road for *Life* was more and more a consideration for the endlessly worried minds at the top of Time Inc.'s hierarchical pyramid, it wasn't reflected much in the day-to-day editorial operation. Journalistic matters were proceeding at full tilt, with big new projects being planned and the magazine appearing to move easily from one success to another. The staff, Thompson felt with some justification, was the best in the business, and if television was already beginning to lessen the impact of some of *Life's* newsier contributions, nobody seemed to notice much. At least on the surface, the magazine appeared to be bobbing securely along on a stream of high present accomplishment and expansive future hopes. *Life,* the people who worked there largely felt, was as solid as—well—General Motors, at least, or even the country. If there was something a little unreal about that sort of thinking, the euphoria certainly wasn't diminished by the atmosphere of the place, which was generally cheerful and often positively convivial.

Liquor wasn't everything at *Life,* but it was a lot. It did not make the machine go—or gum up the works too much—though the fumes were occasionally overpowering. But drinking there was widespread, often heavy and regarded by many with a certain reverence, as if it somehow enriched the work. It was distinctly a commonplace ingredient of the operation, widely thought of as a useful elevator of spirits, an easer of tension, a producer of merriment, a brightener of the imagination, an aid to teamwork, a suitable reward for a job well done—or, for that matter, almost done, halfway done, just begun, just dreamed up, or even abandoned. Drinking had the clear stamp of management approval, though the bosses were subtle enough about their enthusiasm not to draw unwelcome notice from such moderate drinkers as Luce or other corporate bluenoses who from time to time emitted worried cluckings about furniture or bones broken at office parties or about the launchings from windows high in the old Time & Life Building of such heavier-than-air objects as footballs. There was even one uncorroborated sighting of a falling typewriter.

The basic rule about drinking at *Life* was simple enough: drink what you want, have fun while you're at it, but don't let it interfere with your work. The last part of this was subject to wide interpretation. Few people were actually fired even when their drinking excesses had become painful and public. Many soggy workers, who were passably competent and inoffensive, were tolerated for years. Staff members whose talents were particularly appreciated were allowed a spree or two now and then, as a sort of unpaid bonus, even if the escapade turned out to be inconvenient for the magazine, or embarrassing.

It helped if a funny story went with the drinking. For example, shortly after I became head of the *Life* office in Beverly Hills in 1954, I was arrested for tossing firecrackers out of my car on a silent residential street at three o'clock in the morning. As if that wasn't amusing enough, I attacked the policemen who stopped me and insisted I get out of the car. After a couple of rough moments, I was wrestled to the ground, handcuffed and tossed in the back of the squad car for the ride to the station house, where I was held until court hours that morning. Even though this event was reported in the local papers ("Fourth of July Driver Booked"), there was no mention of my connection with *Life*, and the whole matter was regarded with kindly dismay by my superiors in New York. One even offered to help with my legal fees; in complete astonishment, I declined. As far as I knew, no one ever considered firing me over that or other damp capers. They were generally shrugged off and added with moderate amusement to the scores of similar drinking stories in the group memory.

Most of these stories actually began at the office, which became a drinking club one evening a week and often two when open bottles of scotch and bourbon were prominently placed out on a table in the layout room for the comfort of anyone who wanted them. This ritual took place on the final closing nights of each week's issue, and the liquor was displayed at a center of activity where virtually everyone came in the course of last-minute work on the stories going to press. The unofficial host on such occasions was the edit production boss, Bill Gallagher, a tender, funny and beloved man whose own fondness for liquor helped kill him. When the bottles were emptied, Gallagher put out fresh ones, and when the in-house supply was shut off, the thirsty took up collections and sent out for more to be delivered. It was not uncommon in the 1950s and 1960s that several people deeply involved in the closing operation—from the top to the bottom of the squirming editorial heap— were in various stages of inebriation late on the most pressured nights. On the liveliest occasions, the atmosphere was often as decorous as a beer bust; songs and loud laughter filled the air, various missiles were hurled playfully back and forth along the corridors. Amid the uproar, those who stayed sober did their best to get the work done efficiently. Now and then they had to scramble to keep the drinkers from making bad mistakes, from imposing their often loopy judgments about the way pictures might suddenly be moved around in layouts already pasted up or how captions and headlines should be rewritten to incorporate a gin-blown stroke of genius.

Of course, there was other drinking at the office, too, in the form of parties where little or no work got in the way. At the end of a slow day, a signal flag with a brimming martini painted on it might suddenly appear above the doorway leading to the foreign news department. The flag was an open invitation, usually marking the celebration of some less than significant event—a feast day in Nepal, a minor rallying of the pound sterling would be sufficient—and the happy guests would appear by the dozens. At *Life* in the lively 1950s there was almost always an excuse for a party. A correspondent's return—from Seoul or Fresno— a visit by someone's older sister, a successful request for the extension of an income tax deadline, all could set off the clink of ice and glasses. Another cocktail party would begin, and it might even be presented with hot hors d'oeuvres and icy shrimp if it was company-backed and celebrated something truly important, like an editor's new assignment to Paris or a visit by Marlene Dietrich on the occasion of her appearance on the cover.

From time to time, there were far more extravagant affairs. Back in the pre-1960s days before rising costs became such a dampening factor, there were Christmas parties each year in the ballrooms of big New York hotels where stars like Mary Martin would drop in to toss off a holiday song or two, now and then written for the event. These were lavish affairs, looked forward to for weeks by the staff. Many of the women bought new clothes to wear at the Christmas party, and some of the men, whose wives were not invited, booked rooms in neighboring hotels for the night in case office friendships took sudden turns for the better.

In the summertime, there were annual festivals called "*Life*-Outs" during which the staff would spend an entire day at a Connecticut or Long Island golf club playing tennis, golf and softball, getting sun-burned and variously better acquainted. Naturally the drinking at these outings was going on all day, and the affairs came to a splendid climax in the evening with dinner and a dance. Songs and skits all added to the general merriment and to the not altogether inaccurate impression that we were all great pals in this glorious enterprise together. It is miraculous that no one got seriously hurt either at or on the way home from these marathon parties, which were eventually stopped forever when people attached to *other* companies were maimed or killed on the way home from their outings.

As the magazine got older and some of its early settlers began to retire, there were truly lavish parties given to salute the departing. On the retirement of Joe Kastner, a notoriously light drinker, a party for five hundred people was thrown in the spacious company auditorium. An artist-decorator was commissioned to plan the festivities and to de-sign favor booths that lined the walls. Naturally there was music, and a group of women from the office sang "Hey, Joe," a song specially pirated from the Beatles for the happy moment. When Ed Thompson threw a retirement party of his own in celebration of his fortieth anniversary in the business of journalism, he was given a special present by a group of writers and editors. They made a film for him, an eighteen-minute comic salute, and they had worked on it for weeks for showing at this event. One of *Life's* best photographers, Leonard McCombe, had been sent to North Dakota to shoot scenes for it around Thompson's hometown. The movie had both a spoken sound track and music, and it was all put together by a professional film editor hired for the job. Its true cost in labor and materials surely amounted to many thousands and was buried artfully under assumed headings in the picture editor's budget. Some *Life* people, not altogether joking, said that their most creative work was done for the parties.

Such parties, and the oceans of alcohol on which they floated, were like Blue Cross, a virtual fringe benefit of working for *Life*, and people naturally got to depend on them. Possibly the most extraordinary was a series of celebrations that came late in the magazine's history, in the 1960s. These gatherings were called "Hunt Balls," after managing editor George Hunt, who in a characteristic display of hearty ebullience and grandiosity decided they would be good for staff morale—and not bad for his either.

These were massive, seated affairs, of course, given usually in New York's Plaza Hotel. They were attended by the whole staff of about two hundred and fifty, including bureau people flown in from all over the world, and, until he died in 1967, by Luce himself, who delivered speeches that were variously exhilarating, rambling, elegant, boring, hilarious, pompous, brilliant and incomprehensible. (One famous one dealt with his LSD trips.) After the dinner and the speeches—Hunt's own talks were a mix of exhortation, sentiment, somewhat clouded vision and hyperbole, as if a Marine captain or high school football coach had edited a speech of Winston Churchill's—there was dancing into the night and the bartenders were as busy as the musicians. Naturally a lot of the guests got loaded, but there is no record of anyone getting physically injured after a Hunt Ball. Some years earlier, before he became managing editor, Hunt himself had almost been killed after a long day's work and a visit to a particularly lively party given off the magazine premises by a *Life* reporter. Driving to his home on Long Island, Hunt had fallen asleep, and his car had run off the road and turned over. He was pinned unconscious and bleeding badly in the wreckage for a time, and his impressively regular features were severely cut and battered. The accident changed his face, and it pained him, too. In the years that followed he would often pause while he was standing looking at a pile of photographs—or, indeed, while he was having a martini (straight up, with an olive) at lunch—to rub his scarred and aching cheek.

Certainly the most disastrous outcome of drinking at *Life* came after the advertising sales convention held at Dorado Beach, Puerto Rico, in the spring of 1959. The purpose of these annual affairs, held over a period of several days in various attractive vacation surroundings far from New York, was to review ad goals and strategies for the coming seasons under circumstances that would keep staff morale high and enhance the sense that to work for *Life* was to work for a happy and unbeatable team.

Present at these conventions were the ad sales group headed by the publisher and the ad director, a large representation of many of the other business departments of the magazine and a good number of top corporate executives, often including such luminaries as Luce or Larsen or Stillman. A group of editors always came, too, and their principal role in the proceedings—beyond lending their presence to the extended socializing that took place—was usually to offer the admen (there were no women on that late-1950s sales staff) a discussion or program of some sort that would illuminate upcoming edit plans and projects and presumably make it easier for the salesmen to excite their customers about *Life*. Much golf and tennis, as well as such watery diversions as fishing and swimming, took place between the scheduled business events and speeches, and there was a lot of freestyle drinking, too, though it was rarely troublesome. In 1959, among the editors who went down to Dorado Beach were Ed Thompson, George Hunt, Charlie Tudor and the most recent addition to *Life*'s top staff, assistant managing editor Edward O. Cerf. A former *Time* senior editor, Cerf, forty-one, had by that time been at *Life* for little over a year. His presence on the staff was conspicuously unusual: only rarely—though Luce had shifted Billings from *Time* at the very start of *Life*—would an editor be brought in from another magazine and put in such a high position. And Cerf, it was widely known, had wanted to stay at *Time*, where he'd worked with impressive success since his graduation from Princeton in 1940, with time out for wartime service in the Marine Corps, during which he'd risen from private to major.

On *Time* Cerf, who had come from Oregon, had been a national affairs editor and then the top editor of several sections. At the time of his move, he'd had a special responsibility for the news magazine's illustrations and picture captions and had recently edited a company-produced book entitled *Three Hundred Years of American Painting*. Very bright, physically powerful, intense, the stocky and rather tousled Cerf was widely admired by those who knew him. "He lacked mendacity," wrote his friend and *Time* colleague Robert Manning. "He lacked pomposity. He lacked any tolerance for phoniness."

In the short time he'd been at *Life* before Dorado Beach, Cerf had won the affection and respect of many who'd initially regarded his coming with a kind of watchful dread, as if he was sure to be—in the hostile vernacular of inter-magazine rivalry—"another arrogant bastard from *Time*." That Ed Cerf drank a lot was noted by many, but few thought of it as any more dangerous than the drinking of several others on the staff.

Cerf had come to *Life* because Thompson thought he would be just the right man to oversee the work of the magazine's text department, which produced the long bylined articles that ran each week. The text department, Thompson and Luce agreed, was vital to the balance of the magazine, crucial to its substance and the sense of pacing, more important than the actual page volume of its weekly contributions. Few editors, in their judgment, had run it well enough; even the brilliant Emmet Hughes, a writer and editor of enormous ability, the man who wrote Eisenhower's famous "I shall go to Korea" speech in 1952 and had left *Life* and the text department to join the White House staff, found it difficult to produce a sufficiently rich and varied menu of articles and book excerpts week after week.

But Thompson had still more in mind for Cerf. Robert Elson, a solid and widely experienced journalist who had been serving as Thompson's firm if occasionally short-fused deputy, had recently departed to take a job on the business side of the magazine. That left Thompson with only Hunt and Wootton as his top staff, and he wanted to bring in Cerf as an assistant managing editor. "I would not consider," Thompson wrote Luce in proposing Cerf for the job, "that [he] should be confined to text as a specialist. I would consider him a key policy character, and available for other important duties, including a course for preparation to be a possible candidate for m.e.—if and when. This may be mighty ambitious talk, but it is motivated by my conviction that we have really got to be distinguished—and distinguished consistently—in text." Thus the proposal to Luce was that Cerf should be moved from *Time*, whose managing editor, Roy Alexander, could be persuaded to release him, Thompson thought, if "there was a real place in *Life*'s managing staff for him."

The trouble with the plan was that Cerf didn't want any part of it. Shortly before, he'd turned down the offer of a job as chief of correspondents for Time-Life International. "I think my present job on *Time* is more demanding," he wrote Luce, "more challenging and more satisfying than the TLI post. . . . I guess I don't have to re-emphasize—but I will—that I have really prayed over this."

The *Life* job, when outlined for him by Thompson after Roy Alexander had approved the offer, sounded no better to Cerf. "Naturally I am pleased and flattered at your invitation to join *Life*'s staff," he wrote Thompson. "I also realize that it is a Challenge and Opportunity—as well as such lower-case words as interesting and fun. But what it comes down to is . . . that what I most want to do is work for *Time*. I'm sure that you know of my admiration for *Life*, its personnel and its operations. But I guess in the end I think of myself as a *Time* man. I don't have to tell you that this decision was not lightly arrived at . . ."

Thompson had been prepared by Alexander for the possibility of Cerf's turndown. "Although I have a high regard for your powers of persuasion," Thompson then told Luce, "I really doubt if it is likely he will change his mind after talking to you. So I guess we have to go to work . . ." *Life*'s managing editor, who was usually most reluctant to push people when they were clearly unwilling, seemed to be saying here that it was time to work harder at persuading Cerf. In any event, Cerf was exposed to more persuasion, and he eventually agreed to come over to *Life*.

The clinching arguments may well have been presented by the boss he admired so greatly, Roy Alexander, and probably had more to do with his future at *Time* than the job at *Life*. Cerf rightly considered that he was an important man in the *Time* editorial hierarchy and believed his prospects for advancement were good. What he didn't know was that under *Time*'s *next* managing editor—who, Alexander already was sure, would be the cool and tough Otto Fuerbringer (he eventually took over in 1960)—Cerf would not be as favored as he was under Alexander. Fuerbringer seemed likely to appoint other people as his top deputies. Thus the move to *Life* was also a way to get Cerf out of a deteriorating situation on one magazine and put him on a more promising line of ascent. Still, when he finally accepted the new position, it was with both a sense of foreboding and the feeling he had been betrayed and rejected at a place he really loved.

Within a few months of his arrival, it was clear that Cerf had been accepted by the *Life* staff and had won the confidence of Thompson. His responsibilities were increased to include the special projects department (charged with suggesting and bringing together special issues and series), and he gradually began to fill in for Hunt, Wootton and even Thompson when they were away. His word carried weight at the magazine; he promoted the appointment of Ralph Graves as articles editor, and his suggestions for stories and for people to do them were listened to with care. People did notice that when he drank he got a little aggressive in his arguments and liked to needle people, including Hunt and Thompson. There was a story around that on an earlier overnight train ride with a group of *Time* editors he had punched Roy Alexander in the eye, and there was no doubt that Cerf, basically gentle and friendly, was—with his powerful upper body and bull neck—a little scary when he seemed to be getting belligerent. Some of his old colleagues on *Time* were concerned about what they thought was his heavier drinking since he'd moved over to *Life*. He asked one close friend if he thought he'd become a drunk, and Cerf didn't argue when the man said yes. But generally speaking, his new associates on *Life* didn't worry much about the matter or think of it as a problem.

When he got the word that he was expected to go with the selected edit group to the convention at Dorado Beach, Cerf did tell a number of people he didn't want to go. He didn't like, he complained, to be a performing bear for a bunch of advertising men. He didn't want to go to some awful goddamned resort hotel and spend several days trying to be friendly with people he had no real interest in. His time could be much more profitably spent on the job. This convention was just another Time Inc. boondoggle, a way for the usual gang of freeloaders to get a few rounds of golf and a good sunburn at company expense. More than anything else, he said, he hated to get up in front of a lot of strangers and explain himself and his work. Amid all his complaints, Cerf virtually buried the worst of his anxieties: he had been trying to cut way back on his drinking; at the convention he would be under— for him—almost unbearable pressure to throw over his restraint and drink with the rest of the boys. His requests *not* to go were shrugged off in the friendliest fashion. Oh, it won't be as bad as you think, he was told. These things can be pretty good fun. We'll all have a fine time.

The big company news on which the convention would focus was the fact that *Life* was going to push for a much-increased circulation— up to 7 million from the 6 million base currently held—and to bring down subscription prices from $7.75 a year to $5.95. There was a lot of speculation at the meeting, too, on the possible elevation of publisher Andrew Heiskell, who'd expressed a couple of years earlier to Thompson the worry that *Life* was becoming too much of an "institution," to an even bigger corporate post; within a month he would be elected to Time Inc.'s board of directors. And there was concern among the ad people about the sudden (and ultimately terminal) illness of Chuck Hansen, the popular deputy to advertising director Clay Buckout.

But the big gossip of the convention, brought back to New York along with the sunburns, the tales of miraculous putts, stirring wins in poker games and all-night carousing, was the disaster of the presentation by *Life*'s group of editors. It had been only a modest part of the program, just one of a number of events scheduled over the five-day run of the convention. Yet it was remembered with an appalled clarity and even embarrassment by most who saw it. *Life*'s top editors, four of them, were seated at a table on a raised platform, from which they were presumably going to hold a panel-like discussion on various aspects of editorial plans. But, as several in the audience of a hundred or so recalled, the program turned quickly into a shambles.

No one, with the exception of George Hunt, seemed adequately prepared to speak or answer questions. Thompson, marginally comprehensible in public in the best of circumstances, was very difficult to understand: his points often seemed buried in private jokes. Even more disconcerting was the fact that his face was severely discolored and swollen with what appeared to be a bad black eye. Charlie Tudor, for his part, mostly mumbled and shrugged, and Cerf, when it came his turn to speak, just glared at the audience in silence for a long time and finally blurted out: "Paul O'Neil is the best text writer." O'Neil, a former *Time* and *Sports Illustrated* writer, had just arrived at *Life*, and Cerf quite appropriately appreciated him. But his comment seemed strangely irrelevant at the time. People in the audience, many of them somewhat mellow themselves, had the distinct impression that members of the edit panel were quite drunk, an impression fortified by the fact that after the meeting ended and panel members had left the table, Cerf remained seated until ad director Buckout came up and helped him off.

The origin of Thompson's black eye was the subject of much discussion in Dorado Beach, and rumor had it that Cerf had delivered it with an angry punch. Later, back in the office in New York, Thompson and Hunt took special pains to deny this, and Hunt reported to a meeting of the staff that the managing editor had hurt himself by walking into a sliding glass door. Still, the punch version remained most popular, and there were other stories of the debacle—the terribly hung-over six-hour flight home: the ice ran out and at least one inert conventioneer had to be virtually carried from the plane. All in all, it seemed, even under those leisurely and protected circumstances, a disastrous performance, and one indignant high executive who saw it was said to have telephoned Ed Cerf at home and rebuked him for his part in it. In any case, two days after he returned from the convention, Cerf sent his ten-year-old son off to school and then, alone in his house on New York's Upper East Side, got out a .32 caliber revolver and shot himself to death. He left no note.

"All Ed Cerf's friends on *Time* and *Life* are suffering from a combination of shock and deep sorrow over this inexplicable event," said

Henry Luce in a statement for the papers. Indeed they were, and the event, considering what most people thought were Ed Cerf's great strength and his will to live, had its terribly confusing elements. Such things can never be fully explained. Cerf had been having difficulty at home, friends said, and his wife was in the hospital for a brief stay at the time he died. And it was also true that Cerf had been a most unwilling player (one might say the intended beneficiary) in a rather crude exercise of management power. That, combined with his drinking problem and his shame about Dorado Beach, could surely have produced a pressure on him that became unbearable. No one, of course, could be blamed for the tragedy. But what it did, as surely as the bullet that killed Cerf, was to set off a sharp sense of corporate regret—even guilt. It was suddenly clear that truly dreadful things could happen behind the happy atmosphere of success. In the years ahead, there would be more sad, self-destructive deaths by men and women caught up in the sometimes crushing whirl at *Life*; in fact, an ad salesman killed himself in the wake of that same Dorado Beach meeting. But with the death of the admired Ed Cerf, an age of jubilant, almost adolescent innocence was over and *Life* would never be the same.

Even though Luce had been thinking about it for months, even years, the removal of Ed Thompson as managing editor in July 1961 came suddenly. And it was concluded with a kind of cruel sloppiness that suggested fainthearted management—loss of nerve—at the very top. It was not that Thompson, after twelve years of putting out what was for much of that time the most powerful magazine in America, was dumped unceremoniously. But the final arrangements, so to speak, were concluded without his complete readiness, and he had to be told about them—by his successor—after the fact.

In his unending quest for the perfect *Life*, the *Life* he could understand, the magazine whose reasons for being and for being a great success could be easily explained by one sensible man or woman to another, Luce had decided to establish a dual management. There would be the managing editor, of course, and he would have a partner— a senior partner, it might appear to those interested in such mundane details as the order of appearance on the masthead—who would be named "editor." The managing editor would run the staff and direct and oversee the editorial production of the magazine. The editor, in Luce's words, would have "broad responsibility for the quality of *Life*," a job description so sweeping that it might have made any managing editor feel threatened by it.

Luce quite clearly expected that such an editor would be planning directions and shaping policy—under the watchful eye, naturally, of the editor-in-chief and his lieutenants. What he wanted to do was put Thompson in the new job and give the managing editorship to another, younger man. The leading candidate was George P. Hunt, a forceful and powerfully energetic former Marine of forty-two who'd worked for *Fortune* before the war and since then had had many jobs on *Life*, including supervising the magazine's Korean war coverage and tours as chief of the big Chicago and Washington bureaus. For the last six years he had been one of Thompson's assistant managing editors, in charge of such back-of-the-book departments as fashion, modern living, art, nature and science. Almost a year earlier he had written at Luce's suggestion a memo outlining some changes he thought might be useful to *Life*. Included in these seventeen pages of notes on "a new prospectus" were proposals that the magazine needed restructuring of its basic departments and a strong reaffirmation of the importance of the photograph and photography in the depiction of human events. Writing of the days ahead when *Life* would be continually challenged in a changing world (a world more and more dominated by television), Hunt said with characteristically ringing emphasis: "Every gain the competition makes seems like a step backward for us—which is not so. It is the levelling off after the great gold dust years. It is the time when leadership must suffer and when, in a place where the sensitivities and the individuality of the human being are held dear, it must take the step forward of stripping down for the fight."

For all Hunt's readiness and ambition, he did not have the successorship race to himself, even at the end. Ed Cerf, the reluctant and talented man Luce had placed on the scene three years earlier, was gone, of course, by his own hand, and Maitland Edey, a popular and imaginative editor, feeding milk to a recurrent ulcer that flamed up in his gut no matter how calm he appeared, had left in 1955 to write for a while before returning to the relative tranquillity of the Time Inc. Book Division. But Philip Wootton, the bright, rumpled, rather withdrawn assistant managing editor who was in charge of special projects (big series, issues dominated by a single subject) and the magazine's editorial budget, had been a strong contender for years and was, in the opinion of many, Luce's favorite right up to the point of decision. Maybe Luce thought Wootton was smarter than Hunt, an impression that in a tight grading situation might have proved accurate. And it is possible that Hunt's hearty flamboyance might have been unsettling to Luce when the moment actually came to decide on the operational leadership of his biggest (and shakiest) money producer. In any case, one story told by reliable sources at Time Inc. is that Luce was leaning toward Wootton—and was persuaded to go with Hunt instead by Hedley Donovan, Luce's deputy and successor-to-be, and by James Shepley, the tough and ready *Life* assistant publisher.

Whatever may have been Luce's intention, it is clear there was a misunderstanding at the last moment. His mind made up in favor of Hunt, Luce took him out to lunch at the St. Regis Hotel and told him he was going to be taking over as managing editor the next week. Thompson would be named editor. A memo to that effect, Hunt understood, would be coming out soon. Delighted that it was all settled, Hunt went back to his job and waited for Thompson to say something to him about the change. A couple of days passed and nothing happened. There was no memo. In their contacts with each other, Thompson acted toward Hunt as if nothing had changed. It suddenly occurred to Hunt that this man who had been his boss for twelve years had simply not been told about Luce's decision to replace him. It seemed quite likely that the memo, when it finally came, would catch Thompson by brutal surprise.

Hunt, it turned out, was right. Thompson thought he and Luce were still engaged in working out the last details of the editor's job. And however polite his conversations were with the editor-in-chief, Thompson must have faced the prospect of change with great misgivings and even dread. For he was—much more than his minions—an excellent power player and a realist, and he surely recognized that the move to editor, whatever the grand hopes anyone had for the job, signaled the real end of his grip on *Life*. Luce may have believed that Thompson as editor could play an important role (part of which might be keeping a close eye on the unpredictable Hunt), but previous trials with a similar hierarchical shifting at *Time* hadn't met with much success.

Whatever the euphemisms sweetening it up, the move smacked of being kicked upstairs. Tradition is strong at Time Inc.; managing editors run the magazines. They control the staffs, the schedules, the budgets. They're in daily contact with the people who feed the pages with their ideas and their energy. Virtually everything important that happens takes place because the managing editor demands it. In an operational sense, there can be no other top job, and Thompson knew it. He also knew he was going to have to go, but like most very successful men and women whose lives have their greatest meaning in seeking power and holding it, Thompson was terribly reluctant to lose it. And Luce was overcome with a kind of cowardice at the notion of telling him face to face that it was over.

Hunt did the telling, going into Thompson's office and saying with understandable discomfort: "Ed, I've been tapped."

"Tapped for what?" Thompson wanted to know.

"Tapped to take your place," Hunt replied, and he added that the only reason he'd taken it on himself to make this astonishing pronouncement was that he simply didn't want Thompson to read about the shift at the same time his staff did. Thompson later thanked Hunt warmly for giving him the news. But at that moment he was too shaken to do more than ask the next managing editor to take over the closing. Then Thompson, the apple-cheeked North Dakotan, the make-believe hick who had taken the great American magazine to its farthest limits of power and influence, the best all-around editor that *Life* ever had, left his office and went home.

Shortly after George Hunt was named managing editor, but before he actually stepped into the job, he took me out to lunch at a Chinese restaurant near the office called the Canton Village. It was popular with many people on the magazine and was referred to as "Pearl's," after the chicly dressed, cold-eyed woman in charge who froze out unknown drop-ins with silent contempt but took wonderful care of her favorite *Life* visitors by supervising the preparation of breathtakingly dry martinis and superb dishes like beef with lotus root and abalone with asparagus. A former dancer with a troupe of Chinese vaudevillians that traveled all over the United States, Pearl Wong had a sure and delicate feel for the precise location of power, and she hovered like a bee around Hunt that day.

Over drinks we talked about the great days that lay ahead. As far as I could tell, Hunt looked on his accession with a combination of joy and a calm satisfaction that his deserved segment of destiny was being carried out. For there can be no doubt that he had ached for the job for a long time and felt with some justification that he was the one most entitled to it. Years earlier, in 1952, on an overnight train trip to Chicago, where he was moving to take over the bureau and where I was going to work briefly on some story before returning to New York, he'd given me a hint of the size of his ambition—and the plausibility of it. As we rattled across upper New York State on the Twentieth Century Limited, I got warmed up enough on scotches in the club car to confess to George that I was getting terribly restless at *Life*. At twenty-seven or twenty-eight, I felt that my abundant gifts weren't being properly used. I'm not sure now just what it was that I thought should be happening to me, but I do recall telling this obviously rising star on the train that I was considering leaving unless something pretty special happened soon.

Hunt, at that point about thirty-four, a towering, rugged man who carried his convictions with utter confidence and was often surprised to the point of laughter when people disagreed with him, responded to my bitching in a way I found very stimulating and welcome. I should put aside my thoughts about leaving, he said in the urgent tones that later became so familiar to us all, and concentrate, for God's sake, on learning how to do my job—and whatever jobs might later be offered me—in the very best way I possibly could. It was clear to him, Hunt said with hearty ferocity as he stirred his drink, that I was a young man of great promise—anyone could see that—with a virtually unlimited future. I was one of a few people, he told me, who were particularly suited to great success at *Life* magazine, especially the magazine it would become. His intimation of knowing just what that might be was especially titillating, and I pressed for details. Well, Hunt confided, as I recall, nothing was ever certain, but he had reason to believe that he might play a substantial role in a future *Life*. We were alone then in the club car, and I waited for more. I must keep his confidence, he admonished me. Did he have my assurances? Of course, I replied. If I repeated our conversation, it could be very embarrassing. Don't worry about it, I said, awash with excitement and good-fellowship, I wouldn't say a word.

Well, Hunt said, he'd had a good long talk with Harry Luce* just the other day. The mention of the founder's name sharpened my attention still more, if that was possible. Hunt was not prepared to tell me, he warned, exactly what Luce had said. That wouldn't be right. Oh, I could understand that, I assured him. And it hadn't been anything really specific. But in general the things that Luce had said, Hunt went on, were very promising. Luce—the sort of man, Hunt reminded me, who took a keen interest in making the key appointments on his magazines and felt a special preoccupation with the health and well-being of *Life*—had told George he was very much counting on him for big things at the magazine in the years ahead. Exactly what that meant, Hunt did not say. But it seemed very plain that he believed Luce was saying that if all went well Hunt would one day get the top job. He would become the managing editor. And when that day came, Hunt said, he hoped he would be able to count on me as one of the important members of his team. I had the taste and talent for big things, he told me. Naturally enough, I found the prospect of my own success thrilling, and so we drank happily on into the night.

Now, perhaps eight years later at this slightly dingy Chinese restaurant (my choice—Hunt preferred grander places like the Forum of

---

*Hunt has since said that he was speaking of Thompson, not Luce, but my impression at the time was that the editor-in-chief was being invoked.

the XII Caesars), his dream had come true, and so in a way had mine. He had offered me the job of text editor, the title of the person in charge of producing the signed articles that ran each week in *Life* (as opposed to the anonymous blocks of text and captions that accompanied the picture stories). I would have preferred something a little bigger, like becoming one of his closest lieutenants, specifically an assistant managing editor, but this was really pretty good.

As text editor, I would be in charge of a big department that included two or three other editors, several reporters and some of the best articles writers in the country—among them, Robert Wallace, Robert Coughlan and Paul O'Neil. I would be able to assign pieces of varying sizes and importance either to *Life*'s own writers or to prominent free-lancers who might be interested in the jobs at our good prices (in 1961 writers were paid between $3,500 and $5,000 for a 5,000-word article). A substantial "text piece," as we called them, ran in the magazine every week, and there were often shorter articles, too, depending on the size of the issues. The text editor was in charge of managing book excerpts as well, shaping and cutting them to appear in the magazine, and they included everything from one-shot adventure stories about mountain rescues to the multi-part memoir extravaganzas of such towering figures as Churchill and MacArthur.

In short, Hunt was offering me an excellent job, even if my ambition wanted more. With it, of course, would come more money, status and a certain amount of autonomy. The text editor on *Life*, unlike many of the other department heads, was not confined to any single subject area for his assignments. Unless the ideas came into direct conflict with other plans, he could seek his stories wherever the ground looked promising.

Paradoxically, the fact that *Life* was a picture magazine gave the production of articles a particular importance. It was as if people believed that a good, solid written article would give the magazine a needed dose of respectability, a gloss of importance and semipermanence that would somehow make up for the flighty and trivial character of so much of the rest of the magazine. It somehow didn't matter really that many of the picture stories were instructive, dramatic and occasionally of real consequence—certainly more compelling than a lot of the articles. The old shamefaced embarrassment of journalists who aren't really convinced that pictures are quite in a class with words hung on, and some editors could only be reassured about the total value of the product by the weight or the impact of the weekly article. The text piece thus was a measure of *Life*'s seriousness.

This was very much on Hunt's mind during our lunch at the Canton

Village, and he was emphatic about the need—if the new team was going to be taken seriously—to make a good impression on Luce. Though the editor-in-chief was beginning to show some signs of relaxing his control over many details of the operations of his magazines, he continued to have a particular interest in the *Life* article. When my predecessor, Ralph Graves, had the job, Luce had kept regularly in touch with the work in progress, wanted to read all the manuscripts in plenty of time to make his positions on them clear and now and then offered suggestions of his own. His ideas often alarmed and even horrified the editors who received them, especially if they had to do with subject areas like the economy, or global strategy, or dealt with what we thought were formless abstractions like liberty or the national purpose.

We, his underlings, were more partial to stories that had an abundance of dramatic human content, stories about individuals who'd triumphed after great suffering or losses, about people who'd experienced amazing adventures that carried them right to the brink. We loved running pieces, for example, about a man of perfectly normal intelligence who'd been locked in a mental institution for his entire life, a singer winning out over her destructive alcoholism, an investigator trying to figure out why a certain kind of plane kept crashing, a commuter who had a heart attack on the train going home, a nuclear engineer having to climb to the top of a desert tower to disarm an atomic device whose timing mechanism was apparently stuck. These stories, which in many cases had very little significance beyond themselves, did not particularly appeal to Luce, who referred to them—in what must have been an attempt to demonstrate his easy way with current slang—as "gassers." It was clear to Hunt, and he wanted to be sure that I understood it, that we had damned well better keep our production of gassers to a reasonable minimum. We simply could not give Luce the idea that we were a bunch of utter lowbrows and adventure fans who had no real understanding of or interest in the major political and economic currents that shaped the modern world.

And how we looked to Luce—literally—was a matter that worried Hunt that day. He wanted his editors, no matter how turbulent their interiors, to seem comfortingly civilized to the boss. Appearances—grooming, neatness, shined shoes and the like—really mattered, he told me, casting a stern Marine company commander's eye over my somewhat casual ensemble. The members of his editorial team just had to look as if they meant business. We can't have anybody thinking we're a bunch of goddamn slobs, he said.

Therefore, he suggested with some ardor, it would be a good idea for me to get hold of a couple of nice suits, if I hadn't already done so, somewhat on the dark side. Then I could get in the habit of wearing them to the office (jackets and sometimes ties were removed during working hours) in case something came up, like a special meeting or luncheon called by Luce (always a threat), where it would be appropriate to look as unslobbish as possible. Warming up to the task of outlining a suitable dress and appearance code for the rising young editor, he glared at my head. We can't go around looking like members of the goddamn beat generation, he said. Putting out the best magazine in the world—and he just wasn't interested in anything less than that—was a job for serious people. And serious people, he concluded with a firm fist on the table, don't go around with their hair covering up their goddamn ears or growing all the way down their goddamn necks. He looked pointedly at my ears. They get regular haircuts, he said. We drank to that.

Life with George was like that a lot of the time. He was a great admonisher, urger, persuader; he was always stirring us up, driving us forward, reminding us of the grandeur of our task, telling us to reach deep for the resources he knew we had within. A lot of his exhortatory style, we felt sure, came out of his Marine Corps experience during World War II; he had been a company commander and won the Navy Cross and the Silver Star for his heroism in combat in the course of a number of ferocious Pacific campaigns. He looked on us as his trusted junior officers and noncoms; he looked on the difficulties of getting stories or getting the right people to do them or finding that the competition was beating us to the right stuff as military problems to be overcome with energetic military tactics.

We often joked about his style, saying behind his back that he was excessively gung ho, snickering at his references to "taking the hill" or "seizing the high ground." He spoke of the people in *Life*'s bureaus around the world as "the field forces." But he was utterly untroubled by our laughter—if, in fact, he was ever aware of it. Hunt's hearty techniques of leadership—he was as full of reminders about the pride we must take in ourselves and in our great mission as Henry V before Agincourt—never really varied much. Even his writing, in memos and a number of little editorial essays, reflected a kind of Teddy Roosevelt grandiloquence. When, eight years after he became managing editor, he turned the job over to his successor, Ralph Graves, he wrote in the magazine: "This is the last issue of *Life* that I shall edit. Next week the signature at the end of this column will be that of Ralph Graves, a bold signature, without unnecessary flourishes. . . . He was one of a team of editors who grew around me in the marvel of the excitement and thrust of our times." Describing the position he was leaving, he broke through to high, somewhat giddily high, rhetorical ground: "To reflect [on my tenure] is simply to say that this editorship is consuming to the hilt; that it is, in the purest sense, a quest for truth, that it insists on quality, that it demands a breadth encompassing points of view and fairness and bite in critique; that it sallies forth into crusades that ennoble society. It is—and must be—unrelentingly creative."

For all the traits in Hunt that were a bit broad and overblown, despite his physical power and his truly commanding presence—like Lyndon Johnson, he tended literally to lean into people he wanted to persuade—he had qualities of real delicacy and grace. He had studied painting during summers away from Amherst before the war and stayed interested and involved in it always. The problems of color, texture and design engrossed him, and he brought these artistic sensibilities to the problems of putting out a mass picture magazine. "Every issue was a tremendous challenge," he once said about running *Life*, "a potential work of art in the balancing of pages. Each issue had to be a painting, a tableau, a tapestry of the world involved in as many forms of life as we could get into those pages. You had to be brutal, to throw things out that would destroy the balance, the composition of the issue." His customary loftiness did not obscure his conviction about the value of the work. "This was a lot more than journalism," he went on. "Late at night after the last closings, I'd go through the dummies in my layout room, turning over the pages slowly, just feeling the issue, seeing where I'd done well, where things were not as good, where I'd goofed, where it just hadn't worked at all, as much as we'd tried. I had the feeling with every issue that a painting was going on exhibit in front of the world."

In his determination to get what he wanted, Hunt brought enormous energy to bear. When it was necessary, he could be an extraordinarily compelling salesman, winning over the opposition with the sheer power of his own conviction. On one occasion early in his editorship, he traveled to Moscow with his wife, Anita, and with his top news editor, Hugh Moffett, and his wife, Bette. Hunt was trying to get permission for *Life* to do a big color essay on the Hermitage Museum in Leningrad, and then possibly an entire special issue on the U.S.S.R. But at that moment in the Cold War the Russians were feeling deeply suspicious of the Western press and were most annoyed with *Time* for a blunt cover story done there recently on Leonid Brezhnev, the Communist Party First Secretary. When Hunt and Moffett went to call on Leonid Zamyatin, the Soviet press chief, he told them in excellent English that he foresaw great problems in getting any special permissions for *Life*, and he gave them a stiff little lecture on the place of journalism in the Soviet world. There was even a snide piece running in *Izvestia* that day about Hunt's visit, and the conversation between Zamyatin and the *Life* editors was not cordial. The meeting ended with Hunt trying to mollify Zamyatin by suggesting that they should stop the bickering and "find out what *Life* can do in this great country of yours." The press chief did not appear to be impressed.

The next day Hunt and Moffett were invited to a luncheon at the House of Journalists on Moscow's Zvenigorodskoye Causeway. This was the regular hangout for high- and middle-level Soviet journalists in the capital, and about two hundred of them had gathered to meet the Americans that day. The two *Life* men and the office interpreter sat at the end of a big table with Zamyatin. Their understanding was that this was to be just a relaxed and friendly social occasion, with no speeches or public comments called for from Hunt.

The lunch went along in an easy fashion, with amiable and informal talk between the Americans and neighboring Russians at the table. Suddenly, as Hunt recalled, Zamyatin began banging on his glass for silence. He rose and offered a friendly toast to Hunt and Moffett, to their health, to the success of their trip and to their deepening understanding of the Soviet Union. When he had finished and resumed his seat, there was a long silence, and as it stretched out, Hunt realized that the watching men at the table were waiting for him to speak. Horrified because he hadn't given this possibility a thought, he pushed back his chair and stood up.

"We'd been talking some about the war," he remembered, "and I decided I'd do better speaking to them not as a journalist but as a lieutenant colonel of Marines. With the interpreter standing next to me, I began talking about their tremendous sacrifices during the war, about the brave millions who'd died in the sieges before Volgograd [previously Stalingrad] and Leningrad. I talked about the great heroism of the Russians at Moscow in the face of the German hordes. I said it was they, the Soviets, who'd really won the war in Europe against Hitler. By that time, I could see that they were really listening to me with great care.

"I was talking to them as one fighting man to others. I told them a little about my own experiences in the Pacific against the Japanese, and then I came back and hammered some more on how brave the Russians were." As his interpreter gave the translation, trying to give the Russian version of Hunt's toast the proper seasoning of passion, the editor could see that a lot of his listeners had tears in their eyes. "They were openly crying," he recollected with some astonishment. "So I just

Henry and **Clare Boothe Luce**

Margaret Bourke-White with reporter **Lee Eitingon** in Pakistan
(Margaret Bourke-White, *Life* magazine © Time Inc.)

shion editor **Sally Kirkland**

anaging editor **Edward K. Thompson**
•sing a 1950s entertainment story with
porter **Laura Ecker** (left) and movie editor
ry Leatherbee
artin Iger)

The *Life* photographers pose with **Ed Thompson** at his retirement
(William Sumits, *Life* magazine © Time Inc.)

Henry Luce and his successor as editor-in-chief, **Hedley Donovan**
(AP Wide World)

News editor **Hugh Moffett**

John Thorne, one of the magazine's most versatile writers and editors
(Walter Daran)

A 1960s layout session: (from left) copy editor
Charles Elliott, managing editor **George Hunt**, photographer **David Duncan Douglas** and art director **Bernard Quint**
(Richard Meek)

Photographer **Ralph Morse** (top
center left) and picture editor **R●
Bailey** with a group of astronauts
including the first moon voyage●
(Ralph Morse, *Life* magazine
© Time Inc.)

y **Burrows**, who gave his life
et the pictures
rry Burrows, *Life* magazine
ime Inc.)

Ralph Graves, last managing editor of the
weekly *Life*
(Henry Groskinsky, *Life* magazine © Time Inc.)

Donovan and Chairman of the Board **Andrew Heiskell** at the press conference announcing the end of *Life*, December 8, 1972
(B. Little)

After *Life* folded, its editors threw themselves a last dinner. They are (from left) **Don Moser**, **Robert Ajemian**, **Richard Stolley**, **Loudon Wainwright**, **David Maness**, **Philip Kunhardt** and **Ralph Graves**
(Philip Kunhardt)

kept going. I didn't really know when to stop. But I did, finally, by toasting them, the heroes of the Soviet Union, and toasting Americans, too, as comrades and fighters together against the fascist scourge.

"When I was through, they all stood up in absolute silence and raised their glasses with mine. Then I sat down, and when they sat down, the applause came. It came hard, and it lasted a long time, and all of us in that hall were very moved by our kinship. And when we were leaving," Hunt finished, "Zamyatin turned to me and he said: 'George, I want you to know that you can go anywhere you want in the Soviet Union and I will help you.' Which was something of an exaggeration—there were lots of places they wouldn't let *anybody* go—but he always was a great help."

Getting together the right team was Hunt's first priority, and the people he chose to help him manage the magazine were already regarded as the pick of the place, talented, energetic and—unsurprisingly—ambitious fellows with a distinct sense of their own good possibilities for the future. The three he seemed to favor especially were Ralph Graves, Philip Kunhardt and Roy Rowan, all still relatively young (Graves and Kunhardt in their mid-thirties, Rowan about forty) and each with solid and varied experience of ten years or more on *Life*. Ralph Graves was bright and tough-minded, a good editor (and by then the author of two novels) who had sharpened up his skills running the articles department for Thompson, a steady manager not deflected by sentiment or nostalgia in his cool appraisals of the ebb and flow of the business taking place around him. He would be Hunt's right-hand man, supervising many of the big departments and always available for consultation and brainstorming with the boss in the next office. It seems entirely likely that Hunt chose Graves, in part at least, because of their enormous differences in style. Graves was not a dour man; he liked to enjoy himself. Yet at work he was brisk and largely serious; his enthusiasm never seemed overextended, the way Hunt's often did. Graves's emotions were much more under wraps, he was methodical and composed in the way he attacked his work, he disposed of details as they came up. His business conversations were to the point. The bottom of his in box was always visible.

Roy Rowan had more experience as a working journalist than any of the others Hunt was promoting. He'd worked as a correspondent in the Far East (in China in 1948) and run bureaus for *Life* in Germany and in Chicago (where Graves had been the magazine's chief, too). A popular and self-contained operator, Rowan kept his opinions and his emotions largely to himself. Though he had his playful moments, he gave the impression, as he moved efficiently and without much clatter and fanfare through his work, of making plans and solutions he would offer later, when he was good and ready. Collegiality was not his strong suit. He concentrated on his own interests—which were largely in the areas of news and politics—and appeared not to be much concerned about many of the other subjects—fashion, art, entertainment—that regularly filled great numbers of pages in *Life*. His seeming indifference to these non-news areas, in fact, probably worked against him years later, in the selection process for a successor to Hunt. For the present, Hunt made him, like Graves, an assistant managing editor, and put him at the head of "photographic operations," which meant that he had charge of the photographers and—much more—would have a strong say in the shaping of plans and any new directions the magazine took.

The third of these appointments went to Phil Kunhardt. Though Hunt wanted to make him an assistant managing editor like the others, Luce, who announced these major promotions on his magazines and had veto power over them, thought Kunhardt was still too untested for the burdens of such a grand title and insisted that he be named only a senior editor instead. This fine distinction didn't make much difference to the people on the staff, who recognized the real status of the big redhead blinking at them solemnly through thick glasses whose frames were too small for his face. A powerful man whose exuberance at parties tended to produce apocryphal stories about breakage, he was really sweet, quiet and rather modest, with a canny sense of his own abilities and the strengths of others. At this time, he had not yet held any big jobs at *Life*, but he'd shown real promise as a reporter working with photographers in Los Angeles in the 1950s and as a picture assignment editor in New York. He developed a kind of cult reputation as a creative young comer at *Life*, and he was clearly capable of inspiring zest and loyalty in the people who worked with him. Hunt put him in charge of the fashion, art, modern living and entertainment departments, all of them managed or largely influenced by women who were among the most highly motivated, creative and generally formidable members of Hunt's staff.

One holdover from the Thompson era was the assistant managing editor for news, Hugh Moffett, who was probably the most broadly experienced professional on *Life*. Moffett, in his early fifties when Hunt took over, had a tough and competitive side, too; he'd disagreed fiercely and publicly about stories with Ed Cerf when Cerf had been thrust into the *Life* hierarchy ahead of him, and it's likely he felt, as so many people at *Life* felt about themselves over the years, that he was as good a candidate to become managing editor as anybody else. Though he worked hard for Hunt—much of the time in Paris, in charge of European coverage—he kept his own counsel and his eyebrows wryly elevated at Hunt's bombastic approach to editing.

Another holdover was Phil Wootton, who was made executive editor by Luce when Hunt beat him out for the bigger job. In this new capacity he would still run budgets and special projects, but his real power was diminished. Hunt was now the main operational boss, and Wootton's clout was gone. Whatever contributions he tried to make at *Life* in the time he remained there, Wootton couldn't get anything substantial going without Hunt's approval. And it seemed plain to the rest of the staff, always watching for signals that would tell them who would next be floating belly up, that the two men had little use for each other. "He thought I was stupid," Hunt recalled later, "and I thought he was lazy." The two men came to their clearest and last understanding at a lunch in a hotel dining room where Hunt had taken Wootton for a privacy they couldn't find in the office. It was about two years after Hunt had taken over. In the course of the meal, Hunt told Wootton he was being fired. Such bluntness was not common at *Life*, and when Wootton looked utterly shocked, Hunt softened it a bit. "Well, then," he added, "you're being let go." Within days, his departure made somewhat easier by a new job in Time Inc.'s research and development section, Wootton was gone from *Life*.

And of course there was Ed Thompson, still very much on the scene, even if he had been removed from the operational chain of command and given a big new office down the hall from his old one. But the partnership he was supposed to forge with Hunt never really clicked. The two men were fond of each other, but the momentum now was all Hunt's, and Thompson, around whom everything had buzzed for twelve years, suddenly found himself trying to concentrate on a few big projects—he supervised *Life*'s working and contractual arrangements with the astronauts, and took charge of the acquisition of big-name memoirs (Richard Nixon; the letters of Svetlana Alliluyeva, Stalin's daughter)—overseeing the weekly production of *Life*'s editorial page and trying to make helpful suggestions about *Life* policy and planning. Such a kick upstairs is a kind of corporate euthanasia. People stop lining up outside the deposed man's office; the phone calls cut back to a trickle. All urgency is gone from his work. Nothing needs to be done this minute. Everyone knows something sad has happened, but even old colleagues are generally too polite to mention it. No one begs his decision. People drop in to see him, but they are like friendly mourners and have no real business to conduct. His calls and invitations to lunch or drinks, so highly valued when he was deciding on everyone's future, are received now with a kind of reluctance and even dread. Former toadies who spent hours plotting how to get his favor beg off his invitations. The days drag on, their tone of pressure and high excitement gone. In a palpable and tenderly brutal way, he doesn't matter.

For a man like Thompson, who had put his mark on everything *Life* did and managed a staff of almost three hundred men and women with a combination of direct persuasion, fatherly strokes and solicitude, arm twisting, the skillful use of fear, a high and stubborn intelligence and unbelievable energy, the shock of his loss must have been great. And in fact he showed it. Within weeks after the change took place, people began remarking on its obvious effects on him. He seemed to walk more slowly, his shoulders were rounder, his body bent forward. His color, too, was poor, and his face became less animated. His speech, difficult enough to understand when he was at his best, often seemed more slurred than usual, and friends noted that he had a tendency to ramble on in a boring way after a couple of drinks. He was only about fifty-five at the time Hunt took over, and he suddenly appeared, after years of miraculously quick recovery from the exhaustion of hard work and play, to be showing real signs of aging.

And contact with him over business in the office had lost its old tension and snap. One man who had worked quite closely with Thompson for many years was involved in a disagreement with him over the worthiness of a sizable project that Thompson, as the newly appointed editor, had developed a special interest in. The man felt strongly that *Life* should withdraw from the project, which he believed would never work out as its free-lance promoters were promising. Thompson insisted on going ahead. "But I thought it was going to turn out to be a real mess," the man recalled. "So I decided to fight for my position. It was the strangest feeling. I'd never really dug in against Thompson before. And now here I was, telling this man I'd respected over anybody else that he was doing the wrong thing, that we had to somehow change this deal he'd made or we were all going to look like a bunch of jerks. I remember being amazed at the sound of my own voice as *I* told *him* what we had to do. I kept waiting for him to give me one of those terrifying black frowns or to cut me off at the knees. But he just sat there looking at me sort of blandly through the cigar smoke. After I finished, he didn't say anything for a while. Then he kind of shrugged at me and in a very soft voice said something like 'Okay. Maybe you're right. We'll fix it. We'll try to work something out.' And that's all there was to it. It was over. I'd made my point and won. And I didn't feel good about it at all. I felt very sad, really, and guilty, like I'd pushed my father down the stairs."

It was inevitable that there would be tension of some sort between Thompson and Hunt after the changeover. Missing the excitement of his old job, a work junkie addicted to a camaraderie of stress and last-minute decisions, Thompson often hung around late on closing nights—when everyone else was very busy but there wasn't anything much for him to do. Usually he would just stand around and talk and drink with old friends in the layout room, where liquor was put out on closing nights and people gathered to relax in slack periods before they went back to fitting copy or making changes in captions or headlines. One story has it that during Thompson's worst period he wandered one night into a room adjoining Hunt's office. A last-minute layout was being sketched for the managing editor by one of his art directors while various other news editors and writers and reporters hung around ready to assist or make necessary points. It was a common scene during closings at the magazine, a lot of people milling around a big, picture-laden table in a big room, with all the attention being directed toward getting one man to tell them how he wanted this urgent problem solved. Hunt was the focus of things that night, just as Thompson had been on hundreds of similar occasions.

Thompson is reported to have begun to kibitz a little, to make suggestions when it would have been more prudent to keep quiet. But he persisted for a while, deflecting the attention of the people around the table, who were embarrassed at his being there. Hunt, it is said, tolerated this for a few minutes, but when it continued and the old boss began to get a bit more expansive, Hunt finally said with pointed exasperation: "Ed, I'm sorry. But I've got a magazine to close." In the silence Thompson left as quickly as he could.

The working relationship between the two men did not remain that strained in the more than five years that Thompson stayed on as editor. He worked closely and effectively with Luce and Donovan—as well as Hunt—on editorials and various other projects. But in a basic way, Luce's notion of a dual editorship really didn't have a chance to work with these two men. One had run the magazine for too long, and the other had been waiting too long to take it over. When Thompson left in 1967 to become the founding editor of *Smithsonian* magazine, his friends on *Life* were delighted to see him get a new job with the kind of operational control he craved and so clearly thrived on. That he made such a big success of it—and once more was the confident, competitive, sharp and canny manager they all remembered—came as a welcome relief and no real surprise.

Of all the appointments George Hunt made, the most important in some ways was his choice of Bernie Quint as art director. Very bright, intense, idealistic, affectionate, conscientious, demanding, irascible, unreasonable, Quint seethed with feelings, and he showed a lot of them. One of his proudest accomplishments was having been through psychoanalysis, and he didn't like to bottle himself up. Forty-seven at the time he took the job Hunt offered, he'd already worked for the magazine for twenty years. His standing there was very important to him. He told an especially illuminating story about his early days on the job. In the late 1940s and 1950s, the legendary John Shaw Billings passed him on countless occasions in the halls, offices and men's rooms—and never spoke. Quint would be walking along, and Billings would come by with his head down and his hands in his pockets and say not a word. Suddenly, as Quint told it with grateful laughter, after eight years of awful silence, the great man looked up as he was going by one day and said: "Hello, Bernie." He had arrived.

Like Mary Leatherbee and the handful of others who were totally immersed in the magazine, Quint invested his inner juice in *Life*. When it looked foolish or wrong, he was embarrassed, aghast, outraged. When it was tasteless, he cringed. Slightly bigger around the middle than anywhere else, with his white shirt sleeves rolled and his necktie on, he worked terribly hard and often with great patience to get things just right. He stayed late night after night, took work home and came in on the weekends and was at infinite pains with layouts he sketched in every detail on little white pads. When Hunt chose Quint, he was getting much more than his considerable graphic skills. Yet he was buying some problems, too, for Quint could be very difficult, rigid, ill-tempered with people who displeased him, hard on those who worked under him. Eight years later, in fact, Quint's badly controlled anger would cost him his job.

But for Hunt, what really mattered in 1961 as he began turning out his own issues each week was that Bernie Quint would be his partner in giving the magazine a bold and striking new look. Hunt, with his own strong artistic sensibilities, had long felt that *Life* was too cluttered, too chopped up with small pictures, too simpleminded in its straightforward sequential logic of presenting pictures. "First, you go through a door into the store," he once mockingly described a typical layout, "and then you go inside and then you see a salami. And then there's a close-up of the salami, and then there are pictures of everything else . . . one, two, three, four, five." Quint felt the same way and had suffered for years watching Thompson and his art director, Charlie Tudor, making what Quint thought were boring layouts that didn't take advantage of the pictures on hand. "Each picture has a design within itself," he once told a radio interviewer. "It has a pattern. It has shapes and forms and gray values and color values, and if no attention were paid to the particular relationship of these values to the values of the type, as well as the relationship of one picture to another in terms of the page on which these pictures exist—if you didn't pay any attention to it, you would end up with a hodgepodge." If his words were a bit pedantic, they reflected, too, his continuous need to define what he was doing. "We tried to make the magazine easier, simpler, more direct," he went on. "What we try to do is give it its own personality. . . . And at the same time we try to be not too obtrusive about the means with which we intrigue you."

That was the hallmark of the Hunt-Quint collaboration, an unobtrusive, spacious presentation, clean and without any graphic gimmicks, using fewer pictures at generally greater size. This new look was indisputably more stylish and beautiful than Thompson's—a lot of the old clutter was gone. Whether or not the big audience, more and more distracted by the nightly heat and tension of moving pictures on television, would like *Life*'s elegant, humane and reflective tone remained, of course, to be seen.

14

The Death of JFK

I had intended to speak to you a week ago about some of the extraor-
dinary signs and portents and wonders of our time. And that is still my
intention tonight. But back then, even before I had properly begun to
put my thoughts in order, an Event occurred, a real *event. By this I*
mean an event quite different from the cat's cradle of incidents and the
cacophony of episodes which ordinarily agitate our days and disturb
our nights. What is the effect of a real *event? Is it not, after the first*
thunderclap, to hush the world—or all the world within its range?
What does an Event say? . . . To some [it] says: "Be still—and know
that the Lord is God." To all it says: "Be still—and listen." Then grad-
ually the voices come.
—HENRY R. LUCE, IN A SPEECH TO TIME INC. EXECUTIVES
AT THE UNIVERSITY CLUB, NEW YORK, DECEMBER 2, 1963

DINING ROOM 1, AS IT WAS THEN CALLED, in the northeast corner of the
forty-seventh floor of the Time & Life Building, commands an excellent
if slightly antiseptic view of the city below, although the Equitable
Building just uptown chops Central Park from sight. Still, it has the
best vantage of any of the company dining rooms on that floor. It is a
big room, perhaps thirty feet long, and if one stands—as editors often
do in the rather tense drinking period that precedes lunch—at the big
windows that line the north wall of the room, he (and now and then
she) can see the gray shine of the Hudson to the left and far beyond
the graceful arc of the center span of the George Washington Bridge.
To the right on a clear day one can watch the planes rising out of La
Guardia Airport or sliding into it on flight paths that are precise linear

echoes of each other. From this comfortable perch the city—and the world—seem far away, the bitter reality of their textures muted by height and glass and napery.

At about 12:30 p.m. on Friday, November 22, 1963, approximately the time that 1,500 miles to the southwest the motorcade led by President and Mrs. John F. Kennedy was starting its swing through downtown Dallas, Henry Luce was arriving at Dining Room 1 to preside over one of his regular weekly luncheons with the managing editors of his magazines. Also present on those occasions were the various editors' senior associates and Luce's top lieutenant, editorial director Hedley Donovan. The managing editors' lunch, usually attended by from twelve to fifteen people, had become—since its origin somewhere deep in the mists of corporate time—a semi-formalized ritual of high-ranking editorial life at Time Inc., and remains so to this day. First Luce and then his successors tailored the affair to their own styles and made of it a tradition, which in that well-cushioned gustatory setting was nothing more or less than a celebration of power. The boss, not the subjects discussed, and certainly none of the other guests, and never the food, which was as unremarkable as the carpeting or the grass paper on the walls, was the center of attention. His every word, every movement, every look, every forkful was observed with care (if surreptitious) by most of the lesser members of the company. The studied air of casualness projected by some of Luce's guests, the fact that they bantered with him a bit and called him Harry, was little more than a show of informality, a polite fraud of company good manners. It was *his* lunch, and they were there on *his* business and no one forgot it. Which is not to say that Luce's editors, who after all cared deeply about their work as well as their security, were never impetuous or rude or too impassioned or argumentative. On rare occasions they were, and such outbursts, if they were bad enough, were greeted with embarrassed silence, as if someone had mistakenly flipped one of the big butterballs down the table.

This day, as on similar days, the lunch began with drinks being served from a big cart attended by a barman, with the assembled company standing near the windows and talking. Not all the guests arrived at the same time. Typically, they arrived by magazine, the dour and elegantly turned-out Andre Laguerre from *Sports Illustrated* with one of his colleagues, Duncan Norton-Taylor from *Fortune* with an editor or two, George Hunt from *Life* with an associate (on this day assistant managing editor Roy Rowan) and Otto Fuerbringer, the powerfully built and soft-voiced managing editor of *Time* (known to many as the Iron Chancellor), along with a couple of his top men. The *Time* editors, their weekly deadline coming up the next day, often came in a little later than the others. Luce and Donovan usually left the executive stillness of the thirty-fourth floor and arrived together.

After a few minutes of standing talk, Luce would often break away from one of the groups and, carrying his drink (seldom at lunch in those years more powerful than a Campari and soda, though many of his underlings preferred the midday lightning of a very dry martini or two), make his way to the long table, where he would then sit in one of the center chairs facing the north windows. At this point, according to the recollection of one of the regular participants, an odd sort of shuffle often took place. Like shy schoolboys at a dinner with their elders, many of these seasoned, well-paid and highly regarded professionals tried to get seats as far away from Luce as possible. Sitting right at the boss's elbow or within point-blank range of his cold blue eyes was not considered the best place to be, and the last chair to be filled was often one right next to the editor-in-chief. But this was the sort of social awkwardness that Luce simply wouldn't notice.

The scattered conversations begun at the bar cart would continue for a few moments until the waiters and waitresses had gone around the table and taken all the food orders and the reorders for drinks. Then Luce would wait for silence and advise the assembled company of the things he wanted to talk about that day. Usually he had two or three topics in mind, and occasionally he had them scribbled out on a piece of paper. Though it is not certain what the topics were for November 22, 1963, the subjects for similar luncheons in that period had been: Where does the Cold War go from here?; Negro Responsibility; Beauty in America; Bad Government—considering that we have a good system, but the budget is too big, the tax system bad, farm policy absurd; We could do more to discover New Intellectuals; Crusades or Causes in which *Life* and *Fortune* and *Time* could assert more leadership. The topics had a certain splendid size to them, like balloons in Macy's Thanksgiving Day parade. They were the sort of big, important sub-jects—one might reasonably say—that one of the world's most powerful editors *should* be thinking about, and challenging his help to think about. This flair for biting off huge chunks was characteristic of Luce. Neither of his successors, however informed, ambitious and intelligent they were, was blessed with even the slightest touch of his canny, sometimes inspired grandiosity.

One man present at the luncheon thinks that the state of the econ-omy was one topic that day. It certainly could have been; it was a favorite topic of Luce's, and so, of course, was politics. There wasn't much doing politically in that off-year season; *Time* was preparing to run a little story that week on President Kennedy's visit to Texas, where he'd gone to offer a show of support for Vice President Johnson's friend Governor John Connally. Although he had supported Richard Nixon in 1960, Luce had a special feeling for Kennedy. His father, Joseph Kennedy, was an old friend, and Luce had written a preface for *While England Slept,* the little volume Joe's second son, Jack, had written in 1940. While he was in office, the young President had occasionally invited Luce to lunch at the White House and chided him about the quality of *Time*'s coverage and about the anti-Kennedy bias of *Time*'s managing editor, Fuerbringer.

And it is possible that the group talked, as it now and then did, about major stories the magazines were publishing. On the previous Wednesday, just two days earlier, *Life* had closed the issue dated November 29, which would be appearing on urban newsstands the next Monday, November 25. On the cover was an action photograph in color of Roger Staubach, the All-American and star quarterback for the U.S. Naval Academy's football team. Even though Luce was extremely interested in the fortunes of *Sports Illustrated*, which he'd started up nine years earlier and which now was becoming a big success, it is unlikely that he would have cared much about any *Life* story billed on the cover as "The Houdini of the Backfield."

Still, there were articles in the upcoming *Life* that would have drawn his attention. One, billed on the cover as "Negro Demands: Are They Realistic?," was a long piece by Theodore H. White about increasing black power and militancy. Here the author as well as the subject was of interest to the editor-in-chief. Teddy White, who became a favorite of Luce's when White was reporting from China in the late 1930s, had fallen into serious disfavor in the 1940s for not agreeing with Luce about China or about his favorite world leader, Generalissimo Chiang Kai-shek. White and Luce had had a reconciliation of sorts in 1952, and White, following the enormous success of his book about the most recent national election, *The Making of the President*, had a contract to write occasional articles for *Life*.

Another piece in that issue that might have caught Luce's interest—or at least his amused notice—was the lead, the big picture story that opens the main section of the magazine and is usually devoted to news. That week, possibly because there was so little real news, and also because the editors always enjoyed making fun (but not so much fun that they wouldn't be allowed back the next time) of America's rich and prominent, the lead was on the current debutante scene. "Debsville Loses Some Dazzle," the story was headlined, and it consisted of several pages of words and pictures about the furor surrounding the decision of a Philadelphia debutante, Fernanda Wanamaker Wetherill, *not* to have a huge coming-out party, as planned. Accompanied by all manner of quotations from other Philadelphia girls about the difficulties of debuting ("You get tired of going to a party practically every night for three weeks in June and two weeks at Christmas. You don't meet that many boys"), the story also included a longish reflection on the serious problems that sometimes come with social notoriety. The writer was Brenda Frazier, the number one debutante of twenty-five years earlier: she had been celebrated then on *Life*'s cover and had become a victim of the pitiless glare of publicity even in those pre-television days.

"I was a fad—like miniature golf," wrote Frazier in this surprisingly moving piece about her unhappy life, and she reported on the chain of events that led to her total disillusionment and suicide attempt in 1961. All told, even in an off-week, the Wetherill-Frazier story had many succulent elements for the reader of *Life*—jealousy, fame, money, intrigue, ambition, sex, near-tragedy—that Luce knew well sold magazines and that, in fact, in 1974, with *Life* in its grave little more than a year, Luce's followers would exploit even more brazenly with the founding of *People*.

At some point well along into the meal—probably about 1:30 p.m., before the editors in Dining Room 1 had started their coffees or been offered their accustomed cigars—a telephone began to ring on a table in a corner. Someone picked it up—the call was for Otto Fuerbringer. None in the group thought much of it. Friday was a busy day for *Time*; obviously something needed the managing editor's attention. Fuerbringer walked over to the table and took the call. The others went on with their conversation, voices somewhat muted in consideration of the man on the phone.

But after a few seconds something Fuerbringer said or the tone of his voice as he stood there holding the phone silenced them. "What do you mean?" he asked his unseen caller sharply, "Where?"

"How is he?" was the next question.

To the men now listening to him openly, Fuerbringer's queries were suddenly alarming. "Is he dead?"

"Who shot him?" The men stared at each other in astonishment.

"Call back when you know more," he said, hanging up and turning to face the group.

The caller had been John Steele, Fuerbringer told them, the head of *Time*'s Washington bureau. Steele had received a wire report that President Kennedy had been shot in Dallas by an unknown assailant who'd fired on the presidential motorcade. There were no other details. It didn't look at all good. Steele was trying to find out more. Fuerbringer sat down again at the table.

The group simply sat still, shocked into absolute silence. Roy Rowan remembers that he and Louis Banks of *Fortune* exchanged stunned looks and that he then glanced directly across the long table at Luce, who was motionless and without expression. George Hunt remembers feeling a flash of admiration for Fuerbringer for being able to ask all those right questions at such a paralyzing time. For several moments the group, quite possibly the most assured, hardheaded, unsurprisable collection of working magazine editors in American journalism, just remained there waiting, suspended in time and space, waiting to hear that what they had just heard wasn't really so.

Suddenly the door that led from Dining Room 1 into the outside corridor burst open, and the maître d', a short, round-faced man who ordinarily revealed only the most poised sort of deference to guests in his charge, stuck his head inside. He looked stricken; he was in possession of some really dreadful news, and he felt he had to deliver it to these men who needed to know things like this. "The President is on his way out!" he virtually shouted. He'd heard it on the radio, he said. "The President is dying." At this, Fuerbringer recalls, Hunt jumped up in horror. Luce, Hunt remembers, put his elbows on the table, cupped his face in his hands and, looking pale and ill, stared straight ahead.

The lunch broke up almost immediately after that. Luce and Donovan went silently to their offices on the thirty-fourth floor, and the other editors hurried to their various magazines to start working out appropriate ways to deal with the President's murder. Even though *Time* had still not gone to press, Fuerbringer and his people would have to make over virtually the whole front end of the magazine, modify other sections as well and replace the cover of Thelonious Monk with one of the new President, Lyndon Johnson. No one, of course, had any idea of what the ramifications of this event might be. What would be the response to it around the world, from our allies, from the Communists? Was one man responsible? Were there several plotters? Would other killings or attempts follow? What would be our government's immediate course of action? *Time*'s extensive network of correspondents began looking for the answers.

In a production sense, *Life* had bigger problems. The issue of November 29, due out early the next week, was finished and running on the huge presses in Chicago, Los Angeles and Philadelphia. As it turned out, the cover on Roger Staubach and the bulk of the printing was already done; at least 200,000 copies of the issue (out of a total run of over 7 million) had been completed and bound and were on the way to distribution points around the country. If there were going to be big changes, the presses, which spit out 80,000 copies an hour, would have to be stopped right away to keep extra costs to a minimum. Without consulting any of the brass, Hunt had decided to do this. On the way downstairs from lunch he bumped into assistant publisher Jim Shepley. Hunt told Shepley what he planned to do. "I've already done it," Shepley said.

No one even seems to have considered the embarrassing and craven (but thrifty) possibility of doing nothing at all until the following week—which the biweekly *Look*, trapped with an issue completed beyond catching, had to do. But at one point in the flurry of those first hours, Hunt recalled, Luce phoned Arthur Murphy, who was *Life's* general manager (and thus the top operations man in production matters), and asked him what was going on. Murphy told Luce that the presses had been stopped and that the magazine was being remade. How expensive an undertaking was that? Luce wondered. It was going to cost a lot, Murphy told him, a million dollars, maybe more. Luce was startled at the sum. "Ridiculous," he snapped. Murphy said nothing. Was the boss going to step in, he wondered, and put a stop to the new plan? There was a long silence. Then Luce spoke in a milder tone. "Oh, okay," he said. "Go ahead." Weeks later, when all the costs were in and at $1.2 million turned out to be somewhat higher than the first estimate, Luce told Murphy and Hunt it was the best million he ever spent.

Back in his office, Hunt, fired up now to start remaking the magazine, was pleased to find members of his staff beginning to show up in numbers outside his door. Always buoyed by signs of loyalty and initiative among his people, he was moved at the turnout. Like Hunt, they'd heard the awful news at lunch, or in the street, or over someone else's radio, or by telephone calls from their wives, or in any of the myriad ways people become aware of such shattering events, and they were anxious now to get to work on what they were sure would be the magazine's strong response to this one.

Hunt and a few of his top editors—Hugh Moffett (when he heard the news, he'd been having drinks at "21" with former *Life* reporter Don Schanche, who'd made the date to offer Moffett a job on *The Saturday Evening Post*), Roy Rowan, Bernie Quint, Ralph Graves—began to figure out how to deploy the staff for coverage. Photographer Arthur Rickerby and reporter Tom Flaherty of *Life's* Washington bureau had been traveling with the President when he was shot and were at Parkland Hospital in Dallas. But it was already clear that more teams would be needed on the scene there, both to cover new developments and to recapitulate in pictures and text what had already happened.

Fragmentary details were coming in. The President's death was confirmed. As the afternoon wore on, there were reports that a police officer had been shot somewhere in Dallas and that the man thought to have killed both him and the President had been captured in a nearby movie theater. There was still no clear idea about the real shape of the assassination plot; no one really knew how many people were involved or if, indeed, there might be more killings planned.

But it was plain, too, that more *Life* people would have to be sent to Washington. The focus of the tragedy would eventually shift there. The new President, Lyndon Johnson, would soon be returning and probably bringing Kennedy's body home with him on the plane. Preparations for a huge state funeral were already underway. Among the scores of staff and free-lance people who urgently volunteered to help, Teddy White called in and went to the capital, where he eventually filed an elegiac report on the return of the fallen President on that sorrowful November weekend.

The critical factor, of course, was time. Once the decision had been made to rip the magazine apart to create slots for Kennedy stories, the new material had to be put in place with the greatest possible speed so the presses could get moving again with *Life's* enormous run. The number of copies of the November 29 issue originally budgeted for printing was some 7 million. To supply anywhere near the required number of copies, after making virtually a new magazine, and to get them out into the distribution channels, was going to require the greatest effort and ingenuity.

Hunt resorted to one time-saving plan managing editors had often used in the past; he sent a small edit team to Chicago, where all the magazine's plates were made and much of the printing was done. This team would be responsible for the final closing of much of the new material. In the team were Roy Rowan, writer John Dille, associate art director David Stech and layout artist John Geist. New pictures coming from Dallas and Washington after the first day would be sent directly to Chicago, where the film would be processed (with duplicate contact sheets flown back to New York). Rowan's team would make initial picture selections, produce layouts and write some of the captions. All this, of course, would be done in consultation (by phone, Teletype and Wirephoto) with Hunt and the main edit group in New York.

There, people were racing ahead with setting up the new space and getting the new stories started. The Staubach cover and story were dropped, and so was the lead on the debutantes (the article by Brenda Frazier was published a week later). Also thrown out were a little story about a Yale professor freed by the Soviets after they'd jailed him for sixteen days and a few pages of news pictures devoted to such disparate items as an underwater volcano and New York's Governor Nelson Rockefeller with his wife, Happy. *Life's* last routine picture of President Kennedy was dropped, too; it showed him standing in dark glasses with propulsion scientist Wernher von Braun as they looked over a Saturn I rocket being readied for flight at Cape Canaveral.

The original editorial, an item headlined "The Ice Cream Cone Congress," was junked, and chief editorial writer John Knox Jessup began work on an appraisal of the dead President. "He was beautifully equipped for the presidency," Jack Jessup wrote. "He had sought it hard, and he liked it fine. . . . One thing he left us beyond question: a high personal example of intelligence and grace." In the back half of the magazine nine pages were cleared out for a photo biography of Lyndon Johnson from his beginnings in Texas to the present. For the editor's note he wrote for the front of each issue, Hunt began wrestling with what he might write about his own last visit with Kennedy ("At the end of the sofas and facing the fireplace, with a wicker back and a seat with a cushion matching the sofas, stood the rocking chair"). For the very end of the magazine, Hunt decided to use some black-and-white pictures that photographer Mark Shaw had taken at the Kennedy compound at Hyannis Port a couple of years earlier. They showed the President, Mrs. Kennedy and their daughter Caroline playing in the dunes and on the beach together.

For the cover Hunt and Bernie Quint selected from hundreds of possibilities a formal color picture of Kennedy by the portraitist Yousuf Karsh of Ottawa. The close-up photograph, showing Kennedy holding his hand to his chin, was bordered in black. The familiar red in the *Life* logo was changed to black, too.

In making the choice of Kennedy, Hunt had gone against the traditional Time Inc. wisdom that you don't put a dead man on the cover. News magazines, somebody once said (possibly Luce, more likely someone thinking he spoke for him), must look ahead. To such cautionary advice from above, Hunt replied with customary bombast: "Kennedy belongs on this cover of *Life*. Let *Time* have Johnson." *Time*, indeed, did put Johnson on the cover—a fact that simply reinforced the feelings of everyone at *Life* that they worked for the magazine with the bigger and better heart.

By that first evening, pictures from the day's events were beginning to arrive in New York. Especially wrenching was a color photograph of a smiling President and Mrs. Kennedy taken when they arrived at the Dallas airport. In it, she was carrying a bouquet of red roses and wearing the pink wool suit that would later, as virtually everyone in the world would know, be stained with her husband's blood. Another picture was taken outside the hospital where Kennedy was driven after the shooting. It showed the empty interior of the convertible that Lyndon and Lady Bird Johnson had ridden in during that final motorcade; a similar bouquet of red roses had been discarded and was strewn across the back seat. Quint, using both pictures, designed a simple opening layout with a black *Life* logo and a headline reading: "The Assassination of President Kennedy." A short block of words was dummied into the space and would introduce the story. Writer Keith Wheeler, formerly a Chicago newspaperman and war correspondent who had been shot in the face in the Pacific, began to rough out his draft of that first block. It read: "Now in the sunny freshness of a Texas morning, with roses in her arms and a luminous smile on her lips, Jacqueline Kennedy still had one hour to share the buoyant surge of life with the man at her side."

That first evening as the magazine was reshaped there was little of the noisy bustle that sometimes developed on difficult closing nights. There had been more tension earlier in the afternoon as Hunt was working out his first emergency plans. At one point publisher C. D. Jackson, who had stopped in and was listening to a rundown of the work in progress as he sat in Hunt's chair, kept saying "Go! Go! Go!" in his enthusiastic approval. Now people were generally quiet as they went about the work. Little groups on the edit floor read wire service copy, listened to radio bulletins or watched the stream of television programming—old stills, old news footage, the latest film from Dallas, footage on Johnson, people grieving around the country—that would dominate broadcasting for the next four days. Nobody seemed to want to leave the office. It was as if only there would they be safe from their feelings of shock and loss. But the feelings were close to the surface. Hugh Moffett was the assistant managing editor who handled much of the Kennedy closing for Hunt. "When I left the building," Moffett wrote much later about finally going home that first night, "I found myself on Sixth Avenue bawling."

The magazine's response to the news from Dallas was no greater, really, than might have been expected. It would have been carried out, and indeed was, by any journal with the production capability to make the necessary changes and with a tradition of feeling obliged to respond immediately to events of big national importance. Good newspapers have always done it. Television reacts similarly today in times of sudden crisis—a taking of U.S. hostages, the Soviet downing of airliner K-007. And, of course, the networks made their own historic and profoundly significant contribution to a huge, grieving audience with its coverage during the four days immediately following the shooting of John F. Kennedy.

But the difference with *Life*'s assault on the subject was not so much that room had to be made in the magazine's pages for this tragedy. More, it was that *Life*'s operatives were simply determined to produce something unique, to somehow get hold of a piece of the event that would be quite unlike anything the rest of the journalistic pack would get. Considering the size and resources of the competition, such a notion was at least grandiose. But over the years that notion may have been motivated less by blind arrogance than by urgent need. In most cases, on very big stories the newspapers and the news magazines would beat *Life* out with the story and cover it more broadly and in greater depth. To counter that implacable truth, *Life*'s editors believed they had to offer readers a special premium, a prize that would be found nowhere else.

Often, naturally, the prize was *Life*'s own photographs, but these were not always possible to get. Under the sort of chaotic conditions that prevailed after the assassination, *Life*'s reporters were encouraged to try to get hold of some unmined aspect of the story—an eyewitness, a person who could speak with special authority on the event or the people in it, or pictures. The prime emphasis was always on the search for undiscovered pictures in the wake of big stories. The questions *Life* reporters always asked themselves as they arrived at the scene were: Who might have taken photographs that no one knows about? How can we go about finding them? Again and again during *Life*'s run, teams working in the field in these situations found wonderful pictures, often taken by amateurs at just the right moments, and made arrangements on the spot for their exclusive publication in the magazine. Under those circumstances, where the atmosphere was often ferociously competitive, *Life* sometimes paid considerable amounts of money to get the pictures—and to keep them from anyone else. If this was "checkbook journalism," nobody felt guilty about it. They were glad the checkbook was fat enough.

Two of *Life*'s most resourceful and competitive young story getters went to Dallas on the news that Kennedy had been shot. One was Richard Stolley, a tidy, boyish-looking man then in his mid-thirties, who was in charge of *Life*'s big West Coast office in Beverly Hills. The other was Thomas Thompson, a tall, rangy, baby-faced Texan about

thirty who was a reporter on Stolley's staff. With them came two photographers, Don Cravens and Allan Grant, and on the flight from Los
Angeles—packed, too, with other journalists, their equipment clutter-
ing the aisle—all four were trying to figure out what they could do
when they got to Dallas that would ultimately give *Life* the best story.

Had any amateurs, they wondered, been shooting pictures along
the parade route as Kennedy passed? What would such amateurs have
done with their film? How could they be reached? As the *Life* team
heard radio reports relayed over the plane's loudspeaker system, they
spoke, too, about the assassin. What sort of man was he? Where in the
Dallas area had he been living? Did he have any accomplices? Friends
who might be willing to talk about him? Relatives? Rudimentary questions, to be sure, of the sort that thousands of people, prominently
including cops and other reporters, must be asking themselves. By the
time they landed in Dallas, of course, Stolley and Thompson had no
answers. But they had set themselves in certain directions, and a combination of purposeful hustling and amazingly good luck, even as the
mournful White House entourage and the attention of most Americans
returned to Washington, soon produced two stunning scoops for the
magazine.

Well before his great success on the Kennedy story, Stolley was marked
as a real comer on *Life*, clearly one of the magazine's best young editorial managers. He wasn't one of the buttoned-down-collar crowd of
eastern, Ivy League hotshots who littered the premises in those days.
Rather, Stolley had grown up in a midwestern town, Pekin, Illinois
(where his father was a factory manager), he was a twin (just having a
twin brother, he claimed, gave him a special sense of support and self-
sufficiency) and he'd graduated first in his class at Northwestern's Medill
School of Journalism.

In little more than ten years at *Life*, this hardworking, earnest,
tightly controlled fellow, who kept his hair neatly combed and had a
kind of homespun handsomeness not much marred by traces of boyhood
acne, had shown himself to be fast-moving and enterprising on stories
on such disparate subjects as racial tensions, drug abuse and space
flight. He was also decisive and straightforward, bright if not strikingly
imaginative, and he always cultivated and won the strong loyalty of
people who worked under him. Detractors pointed out that there
was something remote about Stolley, that underneath the bland charm
he was both brittle and tense, that his life was more conflicted and
chaotic than it seemed to be, that he didn't delegate tasks well and that
he was clearly ambitious. But ambition, as long as it wasn't wielded

crudely, like a bludgeon, wasn't a handicap at *Life*. What counted in the ongoing editorial sweepstakes was guts, initiative, patience, pursuit and a canny understanding of magazine politics that would lead a good man to be ready to present himself for ripe opportunities when they arose. Dick Stolley had these.

By the time Stolley arrived late that afternoon, Lee Harvey Oswald was in the Dallas jail, and the town was swarming with reporters who'd flown in from all over the country. Like Stolley, many of them were on the prowl for something that would give them a winning edge. Thompson and Grant decided to look in on the scene at the jail, and Stolley went to the Adolphus Hotel to set up an interim office and to make a few phone calls to various local sources who might be helpful. He almost immediately got lucky. He got a call from a *Life* stringer correspondent, a woman named Patsy Swank. Calling from police headquarters, Swank said she'd heard from a local reporter that an amateur photographer had shot an eight-millimeter movie film of the assassination as the President drove by. His name began with a "Z," she said. She called back in minutes with the full name, Zapruder, Abraham Zapruder, a Dallas dress manufacturer. This, Stolley knew, might turn out to be nothing, but it was also the sort of lead that could give *Life* a tremendous exclusive. He found Zapruder's name in the phone book. Finally, after many attempts, he reached him about midnight.

Exercising all the tact and patience he could under the circumstances, Stolley learned from Zapruder that the film indeed existed, that it had already been developed at the local Eastman Kodak lab and that, along with authorities, he had seen it. Stolley was astonished to find that he was the first caller from the press. Three duplicate copies had been made, Zapruder reported. One of these had been sent to the FBI in Washington, another given to the Dallas police. Zapruder had the original movie film and the remaining copy in his possession. FBI agents, he said, had told him he could dispose of the pictures as he wanted. Subtly, he indicated that he knew the film was valuable and would like to talk about it.

It sounded to Stolley as if Zapruder was angling for a deal. Wanting to move as fast as possible so he could make an arrangement before the rest of the press began clamoring for it, he asked if he could come right over to Zapruder's house and see the film. But the dress manufacturer begged off. He said he was exhausted. He told Stolley to be at his office the next morning at nine.

While Stolley had been trying unsuccessfully to reach Zapruder earlier that evening, he'd also called Dick Pollard, *Life*'s director of photography in New York and a man with much experience in buying valuable pictures from amateurs. The two had agreed that the film might be just what they wanted. But it could be useless, too, or of little value, so they had not really discussed an offering price. When Stolley arrived at Zapruder's office the next morning, he was relieved to see that no other reporters were on hand. He was able to meet the bald, rather short and quite agitated businessman and talk for a few minutes before seeing the film for the first time, with Zapruder running the projector and a group of Secret Service men the only other observers.

Numb with dismay, they watched the shattering sequence, only seven seconds long, in which the motorcade carrying the smiling, gesturing President comes into view. Zapruder's panning of the camera is quite smooth and his focus good. Next to Kennedy is his beaming wife, and on the convertible's jump seats just ahead are Governor and Mrs. John Connally. Suddenly Kennedy's hands fly to his throat and Connally's mouth opens. Then there is the terrible bloody impact of a bullet smashing into the top of Kennedy's skull. In that famous pink wool suit, Mrs. Kennedy cradles his head; then she is somehow scrambling in horror across the trunk of the long car, and a Secret Service agent reaches out his hand and leaps to join her for the futile race to Parkland Hospital.

Shocked and sickened by the film, Stolley realized that this astounding bit of footage was very likely the only existing film record of the assassination and that its value as a piece of evidence as well as news was enormous. Absolutely nothing more telling was likely to come out of this dreadful event. And then, there in Zapruder's office, what Stolley had dreaded most began happening; other newsmen from the wire services and magazines began turning up, and Zapruder showed them the film, too. Stolley would have to make his pitch immediately.

Urgently, he asked Zapruder if he could speak to him alone. Fully aware that the man from *Life* would be trying to get the film, the other journalists started to protest with some heat. But Zapruder, because Stolley had been the first to contact him, said he would talk to *Life* first—privately.

With the others fuming outside—and in the case of the man from *The Saturday Evening Post*, sending in a business card to announce his interested presence—Zapruder and Stolley began to negotiate. Zapruder appeared to have a couple of points especially on his mind. He loved John F. Kennedy. He deeply wished, of course, that he'd never had the opportunity to become the maker of such an awful movie. But since the President's murder *did* occur, and since he, Zapruder, did take the pictures, it was clear that the film was potentially worth a lot—for him, and for his family in the future.

Zapruder also emphasized his fear that the pictures, in the wrong hands, could be given the worst sort of sensational play, even getting shown, he suggested more than once, to gawking audiences in tawdry Times Square movie houses.

With the friendly, surefooted poise of a first-class Mercedes salesman, Stolley began his reply. He felt instinctively that Zapruder would prefer to go with *Life* as long as the deal seemed sound. *Life* was the biggest and most powerful of the outfits interested. Surely, Zapruder might likely have thought, it would honor its commitments to him and, for its huge family audience, would certainly present his graphic, historic pictures in a way that would somehow dignify their garish content. Of course, he couldn't count on this, and neither, really, could Stolley, who would have little or no control of the film once he sent it off to his editors.

Still, he remained smooth as good meringue. He knew that they would try to deal with it responsibly, and without getting into specifics, he told Zapruder that the pictures would get "respectable display" in *Life*. As for how valuable the pictures were, he said, on a pure, fingers-crossed hunch, he felt sure his editors would go as high as $15,000. As he said it, he wondered if Zapruder, a man much more used to making business deals than he was, would find the figure ludicrously low. But Zapruder's smile welcomed the offer—without accepting it. While the rest of the press waited outside in mounting frustration, the negotiations went on.

The whole process would last only about forty-five minutes, and relations between the two men were entirely friendly and calm. Stolley felt he needed instructions from New York, and Zapruder politely stepped outside so that the *Life* man could telephone his superiors. In that call Stolley and Pollard agreed that the magazine should keep upping the offer, if necessary, with $50,000 being the limit for print publication rights. If that didn't work, Stolley should call New York again.

The talks went on, with the price edging upward as the furor outside the door increased. Stolley felt sure that if he ever let Zapruder go back into that outer room without a deal, all would be lost. He gave repeated assurances that the pictures would not be sensationalized in the magazine, and as the price moved up, made his top offer of $50,000 with utter conviction. This, Stolley said, was a great deal of money, and with it came all the support, resources and responsibility of the finest news organization in the world. The pictures, a great, historical document, he repeated, would get the extraordinary sort of showcasing and distribution that only *Life* could give them. This was the best thing to do under these terrible circumstances; Zapruder could be proud of such a deal with *Life*.

Suddenly, they had an agreement. Stolley sat down and typed out a makeshift contract for print rights for $50,000, and both men signed copies of it. At that point Stolley took both remaining sets of the film, the original and one duplicate, and left the office by a back door, leaving Zapruder to face the other, indignant newsmen, some of whom would surely have been willing to top *Life's* offer. But it was too late for that. Before it really began, the bidding was over.

Still, Zapruder would eventually get much more than $50,000 for his film. Stolley had sent the original to Chicago so that Rowan could select frames for printing in the magazine. The duplicate went to New York, where a number of *Life* people saw it, including publisher C. D. Jackson. Shocked as everyone else was by it, he proposed then that Time Inc. buy all the rights to it, including those for movies and TV. Jackson's intention does not seem just to have been to keep the film out of the hands of competitors; he appeared to be more concerned that the terrifyingly explicit footage of the shooting of the President should not be shown on television at a time when the country was still in anguish and sorrow over the loss.

In any event, Stolley and Zapruder two days later negotiated a total price of $150,000 for the whole package. On the afternoon that Kennedy was buried in Arlington, they completed the arrangements, with the artful Stolley leaving the session at various points to increase the pressure on Zapruder with fictitious calls for guidance to New York, while representatives of other organizations (including Dan Rather of CBS) clamored futilely outside the door. In part because of anti-Semitic feeling in Dallas and the fear that he would be seen as profiteering on a national tragedy, Zapruder directed that the first $25,000 installment of his payment be turned over to a fund for Officer J. D. Tippit, the cop Oswald killed before his own capture. *Life* made at least $100,000 around the world in syndication sales of still pictures taken from the film. Zapruder died in 1970, and Time Inc. gave the original and all rights to it back to his family in 1975. Zapruder's historic home movie, certainly one of the most horrifying bits of news photography ever taken, has never been shown for public viewing.

When Tommy Thompson and Allan Grant got to the Dallas jail that Friday night of Kennedy's murder, it was swarming with reporters and photographers waiting to grab pictures of Lee Harvey Oswald if the cops brought him out for a statement. A funny, natty, liquid-voiced fellow, Grant was one of those particularly versatile *Life* photographers who could take quality pictures of just about anything. He shot sexy pictures of movie starlets and poignant black-and-white essays on children with leukemia. He had a special talent for stories that required close-in, candid photography. He was also smart and very experienced, and he complained to Thompson almost immediately that the crowded scene was not good for making photographs that would be different from other people's. Thompson, relying heavily on his own Texas accent and a down-home demeanor that he hoped would separate him from this horde of out-of-town reporters, somehow got chatting with a deputy sheriff who seemed to know a lot about the case. Thompson persuaded the man to give him the address of the Dallas rooming house where Oswald had been staying. Then Thompson and Grant quickly conferred. This sounded really promising; it seemed quite possible that no one in this pack of journalists even knew about the rooming house. The reporter and photographer were off and running for the second big exclusive that *Life* got that weekend.

Of all the remarkable characters who turned up at the magazine over the years, Tommy Thompson, who was only forty-nine when he died of cancer of the liver in 1982, had a style that was unmistakably his own. There was nothing anonymous or self-effacing about him, and some disliked his style intensely, dismissing him as crude and pushy and shallow in his work. A brash, aggressive man, he often talked in a braying voice, filling the air and all ears around him with chatter. Barry Farrell, a marvelously elegant writer who'd transferred from *Time*, and I once cut Thompson's telephone line while he was out at lunch just to hear him rave when he got back and to put him out of action for an hour or two. Sitting in an office just down the hall, Farrell and I laughed until we cried at his rage. But part of our delight surely came from jealousy; Thompson's stories often got him more notice than ours did. We were cool and refined, sort of; he was hot and successful. That surface vulgarity covered up a real sensitivity and a canny ability to root out a story under difficult circumstances. He was an excellent reporter and a fluent, vivid writer, and he brought to his work important qualities of nerve and amazing energy. Some of his abrasiveness, good friends thought, came from his need to make sure that no one would ever take him for some rube from Texas. Much of the time, Tommy was as friendly and open as a huge puppy.

Even as he aged, Thompson was always something of a prodigy. He had completed a novel at eighteen. After graduating with a degree in journalism from the University of Texas, he became, at twenty-five, city editor of the *Houston Press*, youngest in the paper's history. He'd been at *Life* for only two years when Kennedy was shot, and his performance in Dallas was important to his rising career. He went on to become the magazine's entertainment editor and chief of the Paris bureau. But his main interests remained writing and reporting, and he was a top articles writer on the staff when *Life* folded in 1972. After that he turned to screenplays and books, among them the best-sellers *Blood and Money* (1976) and *Serpentine* (1979). He became quite famous and developed a powerful interest in the subject of fame and the people—like his friends Frank Sinatra and Natalie Wood—who achieved it. Just before his death he had finished a novel called *Celebrity*, in which one of the three main characters is a reporter who goes to Dallas in November 1963 and finds, just exactly as Tommy Thompson did, the family of the assassin.

Sure enough, when Thompson and Grant got to the address the talkative Dallas cop had given them, there was no sign of other reporters. The friendly landlady of the red brick house showed them the grimy little room she had rented to "O. H. Lee" for eight dollars a week. She obligingly remembered some things about the young man; he always washed the ring out of the tub after he bathed each morning. And he ate luncheon-meat sandwiches.

She also recalled, as Thompson explained in his novel later, that he often used a pay phone in the hall of the rooming house to call somebody in Irving, a little town between Dallas and Fort Worth. When he called, he spoke in a foreign language—the landlady thought it was German. She knew where the call was going because one day after O. H. Lee had phoned and left the house, the operator rang back and said he owed more money on his call to Irving. Thompson and Grant took off on the next leg of their search.

Once they got to Irving, of course, they had no idea where to look next—and they weren't really sure what, or who, they were looking for. By this time, it was past ten in the evening, and they drove around this quiet bedroom community about twelve miles from downtown Dallas until they spotted a small building with glass-block walls and a sheriff's car parked outside. Thompson and Grant went in and found a sheriff's dispatcher sitting at a radio console.

With cautious courtesy, or as Thompson put it, like a man who "sat down beside the campfire and warmed his hands, trying to appear like a needy stranger," he asked the dispatcher if anything had gone on in Irving that day "concerning the shooting of the President." Well, replied the man, as a matter of fact there were "feds" out earlier, "looking for some woman a few streets south." He gave them the name of the street he thought it was, but that was all—no specific address, no name for the woman. He didn't seem to want to talk more, and Thompson and Grant thanked him politely and left.

They found the street and drove up and down it, looking for some sign. The street was only a few blocks long; many of the houses were dark. Thompson had a hunch about one of the few where lights burned. He parked, and he and Grant walked to the front door and knocked. A tall, dark woman in her thirties opened it. When she saw Thompson and Grant, she did not ask who they were. Instead, and to their complete surprise, she said she'd been expecting the press and immediately asked them to come inside.

As Thompson wrote of the scene in *Celebrity*, there were several people in the living room watching television: "Air Force One had just landed in Washington. Its cargo a dead President, a bloodied First Lady, a new President." Thompson searched his mind for something to say to this unknown woman who had let them in. "Do you know Lee Harvey Oswald?" he blurted out. "Oh, yes," she replied. "Lee is my friend." And she added that they'd been studying Russian together.

The woman's name, it turned out, was Ruth Paine. She and her husband owned the house. When Thompson asked her if she thought that Oswald had killed the President, a distraught-looking elderly woman wearing a nurse's white uniform jumped up from a couch and shouted: "Don't you think *I* should answer that question? I'm Lee's mother."

Naturally, the *Life* men were astounded at this, and within moments they got another shock. A pretty, pale young woman carrying a baby came out of a side room on her way to the kitchen. That, said Mrs. Paine, was Marina, Lee Oswald's Russian wife. Their older daughter was asleep in the bedroom. This was almost more than Thompson and Grant could take in. With a winning combination of enterprise and dumb luck, the team from *Life* had stumbled onto the assassin's whole family. And, so far at least, there was no competition in sight.

While Grant began taking pictures as unobtrusively as he could, Thompson started to ask questions. How long had the Oswalds been living here? How much time did Lee spend at this house? When had they last seen him? His mother, Marguerite Oswald, sorrowful one moment and aggressive the next, announced that surely her answers should be worth something. Not entirely surprised at this, Thompson wondered what this woman would think her story was worth. Not wanting her to think that he could get her much, if anything, he first expressed some mild surprise at her inquiry. Then he asked her what sum she was thinking of. Something in the range of $2,000 to $2,500, Mrs. Oswald said.

Relieved that it wasn't a lot more, Thompson (whose reporter character in *Celebrity* wishes later that he'd paid the woman by personal check right there) said he'd have to get approval from his office in New York. Away from the rest, he called *Life* and spoke to managing editor George Hunt, who was busy remaking the issue. Hunt was as anxious as any of his operatives to get material no one else had, and he was very excited by Thompson's find. Nevertheless, he was horrified at the idea of paying anything at all to the family of the man who had killed President Kennedy. This would be completely improper, he told Thompson in his firmest Marine company commander's voice. Such a thing was wrong, and furthermore it would leave the magazine exposed to the most damaging sort of criticism. Who knows, he said, these women might actually have known something about Oswald's plans.

The answer about payment was no, absolutely no. But Hunt was sure, he said, expressing his typically blithe confidence, that his people could easily solve all difficult problems, that Thompson would figure out some way of getting the information he needed without paying for it.

Not at all sure he could do that, Thompson did not immediately give Mrs. Oswald the bad news that there would be no money. He'd have to talk to New York again, he said. In any case, he and Grant were extremely worried that a pack of reporters, photographers and TV people would be arriving at any moment at the door of the Paine house to snatch the story away from them. Then they had an idea. Both Oswald's mother and his wife apparently wanted very much to go see him at the Dallas jail. Wouldn't it be a good idea, Thompson suggested to them, if the women and two children came with him and Grant to the Adolphus Hotel downtown? They would have a very comfortable place to stay and could go practically next door in the morning to see Oswald. And although he didn't say so, Thompson thought, too, that the press wouldn't dream that the Oswald family was being hidden from them right in the hotel that many of the out-of-town journalists were using.

The older Mrs. Oswald seemed to like the idea of leaving the house. But Marina told her mother-in-law she didn't want to wake up the children. They'd have to wait until morning. With rising anxiety the *Life* team had to go along with the delay. They said their goodnights; they'd be back early next morning. They went to their car but didn't go far. "Throughout the night," as Thompson wrote of the experience in *Celebrity*, he "sat outside in a rented car parked on a nearby corner, eyes trained on the house that held the scoop of his career. He was prepared to halt, tackle, and if necessary tie up anyone who approached with a pad or a camera. He passed the cold night eating a stale peanut candy bar and drinking water from a neighbor's faucet and appreciating the absurdity of his life."

Next morning very early, their prize still undiscovered, Thompson and Grant took the Oswald women and children into Dallas, helping them first to load the car with diapers and wash fresh off the line in the backyard. At the hotel the men from *Life* took their guests upstairs via the freight elevator to a suite that had been booked for them the night before and where a Russian translator arranged by the magazine's stringer would come to relay questions and answers between Thompson and Marina Oswald.

But apparently someone had seen this odd little group coming into the hotel, and they had to change suites before Thompson could really settle down to his interviewing. The older Mrs. Oswald, whom Thompson later referred to as "Hurricane Mama," was alternately loving and abusive to her daughter-in-law, caressing her, then claiming from time to time that Marina was "a whore" who was responsible for the terrible trouble her son was in. Considering the unsettling circumstances, Thompson, who was able to flesh out his reporting with material from other sources later on that day, got an amazing amount of information from the women. In a short time, between baby feedings and quarrels and numerous interruptions, they told him a great deal about Oswald, his earlier life and the events leading up to the assassination.

He intended, of course, to question them for hours more, but about noon there was a loud and determined knocking on the door of the suite. It was the FBI, a voice announced. They knew Thompson was inside, they said, and they knew who was with him. Open up. For just a minute more, with the door still locked, Thompson tried to hold on to his scoop. There must be some mistake, he called back through the door. An official-looking identity card was slid into the room. Thompson sensibly surrendered, and while he and Grant looked on, FBI agents packed up the family and took them away. The *Life* men were disappointed, but there was consolation. Now, they realized, the government would be protecting their exclusive. Under increasing deadline pressure from his editors, Thompson sat down to produce the 2,000-word account he would file that night.

Earlier that day in Chicago, Rowan and his crew had looked at the Zapruder film after it arrived from Dallas. Using a hand-cranked Movie-ola projector, they ran the film through several times, fast and slow, jotting down the numbers of the frames they wanted to have converted into large black-and-white prints. Rowan was as impressed with the film as Stolley had been; these pictures were clearly a crucial part of the historic record of this appalling event. But they would have to run in the magazine in black and white; to print more color than the opening picture of the Kennedys at the Dallas airport was simply out of the question at this time. Rowan called Hunt in New York and told him how powerful the Zapruder pictures were; they decided to set aside four pages for the frames Rowan would ultimately select.

The magazine's photo lab in Chicago had made scores of eight-by-ten-inch prints from the Zapruder film, and Rowan and Stech laid them all out in sequence on the floor of an office in the R. R. Donnelley printing plant. Even though the film had been shot by an amateur in eight-millimeter color and didn't have the crispness and clarity one might expect from a professional using bigger film, the stills were horrifyingly clear. Rowan finally picked thirty-one pictures to make up a sequential layout that would show as much as possible: the President's motorcade approaching, his car starting to pass Zapruder's vantage point, the President's movements as the rifle fire hit him and Texas Governor John Connally and the signs of alarm from Mrs. Kennedy and the others in the car as her husband slumped forward and they realized what was happening. On the last two pages Rowan and Stech used what was certainly the most heartbreaking part of the sequence—Mrs. Kennedy's climbing out of the back seat where her dying husband lay, crawling across the nearly flat top of the convertible's trunk and reaching out frantically for help. At that point, as the pictures showed, Secret Service agent Clinton Hill threw himself onto the trunk of the slowly moving car and guided Mrs. Kennedy back toward the seat before the motorcade sped away to the hospital. Whatever else *Life* contributed to the coverage of this event and the mournful days that followed, this amateur's movie, viewed by 50 million readers, brought home the horror of President Kennedy's murder in a way that no other reportage would.

In Chicago, Dallas, Washington, New York, in various other places around the world where teams were reporting reactions to the assassination of the President, the big job of gathering and closing the story went on. It involved hundreds of people (including some who just came into the offices and hung around in case they might be useful) and a huge outpouring of energy. Rowan's crew worked straight through two nights with almost no sleep, and in New York the pages were being turned out and closed around the clock, too. In the midst of all this, plans had to be made and work started for the Kennedy coverage that would continue into the next issue: there would be another cover (this time, Mrs. Kennedy and her children), color photography of the state funeral, coverage of the beginnings of President Johnson's efforts to take charge of the office. And there was an intense, if quiet, urgency about getting all this done. Virtually everyone worked to the point of exhaustion—and past it—on that astounding weekend of violence, shock and sorrow.

By about noon on Sunday, not quite two days after the assassination, *Life's* story was all wrapped up in Chicago. The magazine, with its new cover and thirty-seven pages on the President's death, was running again on the high-speed presses. Rowan and his exhausted crew had already seated themselves and, in fact, had dozed off on a plane ready to leave for New York when Paul Welch, *Life's* Chicago bureau chief, dashed aboard. He had another piece of shocking news. Now Oswald had been shot to death, Welch told Rowan. Someone had taken a picture of it when it happened in the Dallas city jail; the picture was already moving on the wire to Chicago.

By this time, Rowan knew, it was already much too late to make any more big changes in *Life*. The best that could be done (and without leaving the plane he went over it with Welch, who worked out the details with New York) was to substitute the new picture of Oswald getting shot for a picture of him already in the layout—and to change the opening paragraph in Tommy Thompson's story to include the fact that Oswald had been killed by Jack Ruby, the owner of a Dallas nightclub. These last changes were made within a few hours and were included in 95 percent of the new issues. There was a revised headline, too, for the Oswald story. The old one had read: "Assassin: The Man Held for Kennedy's Murder." The new one read: "Assassin: The Man Held—and Killed—for Murder." It was just the sort of keeping current that suited *Life's* image of itself in those days when the editors still thought the magazine had a chance against television news. *Life* is up-to-the-minute, the headline said, you won't get it faster and better anywhere than you get it in *Life*. But in late 1963 the confidence already had a somewhat hollow ring.

Later that day Stolley called Hugh Moffett, who was at his home outside New York. Still another picture of Oswald getting shot had turned up. Stolley said it was "a better picture," Moffett recalled in a letter, "showing Oswald wincing as he was shot. The photographer wanted $5000. I said we got to stop somewhere and we are already late in Chicago. I goofed. The picture is 10 times as good as the one we ran. Aw, what the hell."

Such a minor goof, if it was that at all, made absolutely no difference to the readers of *Life*, who gobbled up the Kennedy issue within minutes of its appearance three days later on newsstands all over the country. Long lines formed in many locations to wait for trucks bringing new copies, and there were reports that the issue (which sold for a quarter in those days) was commonly bringing scalper prices of a dollar, and in some instances as much as ten dollars—or twenty dollars. Many subscribers had their copies stolen out of their mailboxes or lifted off their front steps. Thousands of inquiries came in from people who were upset because they couldn't get the issue. This sort of unprecedented demand continued for the issue of December 6, with a cover and another thirty-six pages on the somber aftermath of the assassination. Tommy Thompson wrote a piece for that issue, too, this time on the funerals of Officer J. D. Tippit, the Dallas policeman Oswald had shot just before his own capture, and of Oswald himself. Oswald, Thompson reported, was buried in a Fort Worth cemetery "in a dark-brown suit, white shirt, brown tie and brown socks." He also wrote that seven reporters who were on the scene volunteered to serve as pallbearers; from his novel it becomes clear that one of those helping out the pitiful family in this "furtive rite" was, of course, Thompson. The magazine story also includes an editorial parenthesis that indicates how sensitive *Life*'s managers were to charges of buying the accounts of Oswald's wife and mother. "Contrary to rumor," it read, "they received no sum, large or small, from *Life* magazine."

Another writer whose stories appeared in both issues was Teddy White. This time, he had been called by Mrs. Kennedy and asked to come to Hyannis Port so that she could give him her own account of the nightmare in Dallas and reflections about her husband. The magazine was held open far past its closing hours for the second week in a row as White conducted his interview and wrote his poignant piece. "She remembers how hot the sun was in Dallas and the crowds—greater and wilder than the crowds in Mexico or Vienna," White began in a Hemingwayesque burst. "The sun was blinding, streaming down; yet she could not put on sunglasses for she had to wave to the crowd." And while White listened, Jacqueline Kennedy looked back over some of her past life with the President. "At night, before we'd go to sleep," she told White, "Jack liked to play some records; and the song he loved most came at the very end of [one] record. The lines he loved to hear were: *Don't let it be forgot, that once there was a spot, for one brief, shining moment that was known as Camelot. . . .* There'll be great Presidents again," she went on, "—and the Johnsons are wonderful, they've been wonderful to me—but there'll never be another Camelot." Her grieving recollection to White had more emotional impact for millions of sorrowful readers than virtually anything else that was ever said about her husband or his time in office.

The outpouring of mail from the readers of these two issues was the greatest in *Life*'s history. Obviously the enormous popularity of the young President and the great national sorrow at his death were responsible for that. But the mail said something, too, about *Life*'s treatment of the tragedy. It suggested that the issues had somehow touched a deep need. People needed more than television's marvelous witness; they seemed to want a more or less permanent record of such an event.

Their response made the next publishing move entirely logical, and many people suggested it. *Life* made plans to combine the two issues in a special Kennedy memorial, and an eighty-four-page edition was turned out in just two days. It went on the newsstands December 9, right alongside the latest regular issue, which had a picture of Johnson in the Oval Office on the cover.

The memorial edition, which carried no advertising, was priced to sell for fifty cents. The original printing plan called for 1.5 million copies. There was one little flurry connected with the closing, and it had to do with the Zapruder film. In this special issue the film would run in color in bigger and fewer pictures. In one horrifying frame, not used earlier in black and white, it was possible to see a reddish shower of fragments arising from Kennedy's head at the exact instant a rifle bullet hit him. Many of the news people who'd handled the story originally wanted to use it now. That it was so dreadfully specific, in their view, only emphasized in a legitimate, journalistic way the enormity of the murder. Others, particularly art director Bernie Quint and associate editor Mary Leatherbee, vehemently protested the inclusion of the picture as being, under the circumstances, gratuitous, cruel to the Kennedy family and to grieving general readers as well and far beyond the bounds of acceptable taste.

At a high noise level, the dispute went back and forth for a brief time, and there were even rumors that Quint or Leatherbee or both had promised to resign if the offending frame was used, an offer which some wags on the staff suggested might be hard to resist. Hunt and Philip Wootton, the issue editor, decided in favor of good taste, a move most people welcomed, and particularly appropriate in view of the fact that the magazine had promised to give all profits arising out of the sale of the memorial special to a charity of Mrs. Kennedy's choice. All in all there were four printings of the edition, with a total of almost 3 million copies sold. The eventual profit came to $102,000, and this sum was donated to the Kennedy Memorial Library.

It was hard, naturally, for the managers of *Life* to refrain altogether from congratulating themselves about the excellent coverage on the assassination story and the extraordinary public response to it. It took some discipline not to exploit the approval washing over them or take a lot of extra bows for it. But most people tried to keep their ebullience in check, and made efforts not to crow about a great business success that grew out of a devastating national loss. The advertising director, for example, decreed that his space salesmen, each of whom had been sent a copy of the defunct issue with Roger Staubach on the cover, should delay a couple of weeks at least before showing it to clients. "It might be considered poor taste," he wrote, "if we sold too aggressively on the scrapping of the Staubach issue."

"It fell to *Life* to do what *Life* has always done best," wrote publisher C. D. Jackson, who died the next year of cancer at sixty-two, in a promotional memo bound into the December 6 issue. His language was surely noted by his friend and boss Harry Luce and had echoes, in fact, of Luce's original prospectus for the magazine. "To bring memorable events into sharp focus; to show with force and clarity the faces and hearts of people caught up in the news." In this tragic case, Jackson's little excess of self-congratulation was surely pardonable.

15

And Down the Hill Again

DURING THE LATE 1950S, AT JUST THE TIME when *Life* was showing disturbing signs of being in trouble, Henry Luce began the process that would gradually bring to an end the unceasing personal control he'd exercised over his magazines since he and Briton Hadden founded *Time* in 1923. His successor, selected by Luce himself and put in place far in advance of the actual turnover in 1964, was Hedley Donovan, a big, powerful Minnesotan and Rhodes scholar who'd come to Time Inc. in 1945 and risen to become managing editor of *Fortune*. Luce obviously saw in Donovan a lot of the characteristics he'd admired much earlier in John Shaw Billings, who had resigned as editorial director in 1954 and retired in somewhat embittered loneliness to his plantation in South Carolina (where he died in 1975). "A touchstone of good journalism and sound principle," Luce had said of Billings, and Donovan showed ample signs of those traits—along with common sense, self-control and stability. Deceptively slow-spoken—even, when it suited him, silent (a colleague called him "Old Flapjaw")—the extremely bright, honest, methodical, tough-minded, occasionally very funny Donovan was a superior choice, better qualified, really, than others of his rank at Time Inc.—Roy Alexander of *Time*, Ed Thompson—to be the next editor-in-chief. He had the intellectual size, one felt, the breadth of interests, the solidly based vision of a sound future, the essential *seriousness* it would take even to begin to fill Luce's shoes.

That, of course, would be impossible; the place was bound to be very different. Donovan could never be "the proprietor" in the way that Luce had been; he would never know the power of actual financial control, or savor the sense that it had all sprung from him. And, in fact, the extent of the new man's leadership would be different, too. In a changing company in a changing world, he would not possess Luce's autocratic imperatives to have his way in everything. Donovan's power would be largely confined to Time Inc.'s editorial enterprises; the business of a diversifying corporation would be run by the board chairman, Andrew Heiskell, and the president, James Linen III (succeeded in 1969 by James Shepley). Where Luce alone had always topped the pyramid, Donovan would be one of a management troika. The change was large indeed; for the people who worked at Time Inc., the change— at least subjectively—was comparable to the difference one might feel in a country after a demanding, charismatic leader has been replaced by a committee. The tension of a long-successful tyranny was gone forever.

Exactly what difference Luce's departure made to *Life* and what it contributed to its failure to survive cannot really be measured. An unfair joke common in the journalism community when *Life* folded went: "This never would have happened if Donovan had been alive." The likely truth was that the economic facts of magazine life in the early 1970s—increasing costs, high postal rates, the brutal competition of television—and not any failure of high-level leadership had brought the magazine down, as they had brought down all its big-page mass-circulation rivals. Donovan had no control over those factors, and Luce, for all his stubbornness and fantastic energy, wouldn't have had any either.

Still, the differences between the two men—or perhaps more correctly the differences in the ways they expressed themselves, their enthusiasms, their demands—were substantial, and *Life*'s editors certainly responded differently to Donovan than they would have to Luce. For all of Luce's continuing problems with the magazine, for all of his constant tinkering with it, for all that he was often out of sympathy with what he considered the errors and excesses of his editors, he was basically in sympathy with *Life* itself. After all, he'd started it; it was his baby. The big, sprawling, squalling, tender, shocking, sentimental, pompous, blunt, cheeky, silly, melodramatic, devastating, caring journal constantly surprised and stirred him with its beauty and power. And his feelings about it were clear.

Donovan's were less so. Though he admired *Life* and many of its people, he did not seem to have strong visceral connections with the magazine. *Life* often appeared to perplex him and to offend his senses of logic and propriety. It was untidy and lacking in order. Years after the magazine closed down, Donovan recalled that *Life*, back in the

1950s when he was managing editor of *Fortune*, had seemed "a huge and successful thing," almost beyond criticism. "But it also seemed," he said, "sufficiently different from what I was doing that I would have rather doubted my own judgment applied to anything about *Life*. The whole mystique in the company about *Life* photography and picture selection and layout and this being a kind of different world altogether from any other kind of journalism was pretty widespread. You know, I would imagine that Roy Alexander would have shared the feeling that this was a completely different art that was being practiced there." In the dozen or so years that Donovan, first as editorial director, then as editor-in-chief, had authority over *Life* and a lot to do with its running, much of that sense of strangeness surely wore off for him. But something aloof about his direction always remained. "Hedley Donovan," wrote Joan Simpson Burns in *The Awkward Embrace*, her book about executives in the business of culture, "is always watching from a distance, measuring things." And that is the way he seemed to many of the people who worked for him at *Life*, watching, measuring, focusing his cold blue eyes on the odd flailings going on in that "different world" of picture journalism. His encouragement and praise, when it came, was often buried amid little critiques on headlines and story presentation he didn't like. From a man of his obviously imposing stature and sense, many wished that his contributions might have been broader, more imaginative, possibly even inspiring, as disaster approached.

The outgoing personality of George Hunt, who was *Life*'s managing editor during the first part of Donovan's reign as editor-in-chief, was certainly in spectacular contrast to that of his boss and may have added something to Donovan's instinctive uneasiness with the picture magazine. There was an extravagant quality about Hunt, something a bit extreme and hyperbolic in his enthusiasms, something almost comically excessive about his passion for the magazine and its mission. Donovan, on the other hand, never seemed overboard about anything. Cool and analytical in his approach to professional matters, he appreciated the uses of logic and control. Exaggeration, exhortation and bombast, all occasionally employed by Hunt without a trace of embarrassment, were simply not Donovan's style.

One of Hunt's assistants recalled a small meeting in 1968 attended by Donovan where Hunt was giving vent to his great excitement about a special issue *Life* was planning to devote to the artist Pablo Picasso. This would be a tremendously important publishing event, Hunt said, banging a table with his hand as he got into his pitch. *Life* would be bringing its 50 million readers insightful, intimate, extraordinary, unique views of the life and person and work of the greatest artist of the age. The magazine had never done anything like it. No big magazine had ever done anything like it. Sensing perhaps a certain reluctance in his listeners or a skepticism that such a project was "right" for *Life* (actually this adventurous, handsome and well-produced issue did rather poorly on the newsstand), Hunt went into an even higher gear. He felt so powerfully about this Picasso project, he said, that he was ready to put his job on the line about it. If this special issue didn't turn out to be one of the greatest in *Life*'s history, he promised with ringing dramatic emphasis, he'd resign. There was a moment of heavy silence. Then Donovan, who was sitting near Hunt, reached out and patted him gently on the arm. "Oh, now, George," he said in his deep voice with the barest trace of a grin, "I don't think you have to go quite that far."

Hunt had been Donovan's candidate to become managing editor in 1961. But Luce, after he had decided on Hunt himself, apparently had some misgivings about the choice. He suddenly suggested that Hunt and Phil Wootton should be made co-managing editors, with Thompson being named editor. Donovan protested that this would create "an administrative nightmare" and persuaded Luce to go back to his original position, in effect saving the job for Hunt.

Later, Donovan was also supportive of many of the changes that Hunt brought to *Life*—the bolder look, the increase in the amount of text, the greater emphasis on more personal journalism through the addition of reviews and columns. (Among the items approved by Donovan: this author's page-long column of personal comment, "The View from Here," followed shortly by Shana Alexander's "The Feminine Eye," and then by Hugh Sidey's column from Washington. Frequent pieces of movie and television comment were contributed by Richard Schickel and John Leonard, writing pseudonymously as "Cyclops.") And the magazine rebounded from the alarming slump it had fallen into at the end of the 1950s. In 1966 *Life* rang up a net profit of more than $10 million—puny perhaps in view of its total revenues of more than $150 million, but still the second-best year in the magazine's history. The publisher at that time was Jerome Hardy, a smart and outgoing man who was almost as energetic as the managing editor himself. Jerry Hardy had come to *Life* from the book business, and he was so buoyed by the magazine's good performance that he gave Hunt and his top assistants big pewter mugs with dollar signs engraved on the sides. But the slide downward began again immediately the following year, the desperate purchase of the *Saturday Evening Post* subscriber list increased the ruinous pressure, and Hardy, disappointed at not getting a bigger job within the company when James Shepley became president, left *Life* and Time Inc. in 1969 for the position of president of the Dreyfus Corporation.

The years Hunt was in charge (1961–68) were among the most extraordinary in modern American history. "Oh, Jesus, what a time it was!" he recalled much later. "Three assassinations, one God-awful war, all kinds of other wars, riots, blacks marching, cities burning, dogs, fire hoses, colleges exploding, youth, hair." If Hunt sounded a little nostalgic, a man fondly remembering chaos, his position as a picture journalist makes it at least somewhat understandable. The items in his painful catalogue produced astounding images, and Hunt, however shocked and sorrowful he may have been about the events that caused them, was able to fill *Life*'s big pages week after week with photographs, more and more often in color, that reflected a national turmoil greater than it had been for a century.

Yet, for all that *Life* had never looked better or more conscientiously and imaginatively recorded its time than the magazine designed by Hunt and his art director, Bernie Quint, the great power of the *Life* of the 1940s and 1950s was gone. Why? The pages carried the big stories of the era and did them splendidly—the pageantry of the Churchill funeral in 1965 (when Hunt pulled off a cover and twenty-one pages by chartering a jet airliner, outfitting it as a photo lab and makeshift city room and flying a working crew of forty direct from London to the plant in Chicago even as the story was being developed, printed, laid out and written in the air), the painful struggles of the South as the civil rights movement went inexorably forward, the terrifying burning of cities like Newark and Detroit. When the three astronauts, Gus Grissom, Ed White and Roger Chaffee, died in the Apollo pad fire in 1967, *Life* again broke into an issue already finished and did a story on this first awful episode of the manned space age. In the astounding news year of 1968, when shattering events tumbled over one another, the magazine, as it should have, was responding to it all. A cover of Lyndon Johnson after he'd announced he wouldn't run again for the presidency was scrapped and replaced by one on the death of Martin Luther King, with seven pages of pictures inside. The next week there were fifteen more pages on King's death and an article by Gordon Parks, a *Life* photographer of amazing and varied gifts, written out of his own passion and growing anger as a black man. Two months later the pages echoed the special shock, grief and ceremony following the assassination of Robert Kennedy in a Los Angeles hotel kitchen.

Through it all, threads connecting these paralyzing big events of the time, were the stories on the rise of the counterculture, the student revolts, the disaffection of American youth. And, of course, there were the stories on the war in Vietnam, dozens of them, about individual heroism, about the battles, about the enemy, about the victims, about the tactics, about the hopes for U.S. victory. It was all there in *Life*, in its full horror and pain (with all the impact Dan Longwell said thirty-five years earlier that photographs brought to war). Yet somehow it was different, somehow the strong link that had formerly bound the magazine to its audience was gone, the sense no longer existed that *Life* was capable of reflecting things in America as they really were. For all its techniques, skills and good intentions, the magazine seemed somehow out of sync with the tumultuous times, showing its own middle age, truly aghast at hippies and dope and the counterculture, sensitive to attacks on the "establishment," shocked at the depth and violence of the protest against the root inequities of the system, fighting off the enveloping possibility that the truth about the war was that we weren't going to win it, that we were, in fact, going to have to get out of Vietnam. Suddenly, it seemed, America had too many faces, and *Life* was having trouble keeping track of its own.

The long terminal phase of the magazine's struggle to survive began in the years after the death of Henry Luce of a coronary occlusion in a hospital in Phoenix, Arizona, on February 28, 1967. He was sixty-eight. *Life* had marked his passing with thirteen pages of pictures and text, and Hunt would have run a cover portrait of the founder, too, if Donovan and the editors of *Time* had not decided (after some dispute) that it would be most fitting if Luce was on the cover of his first and favorite. The very least Luce would have done about *Life*'s troubles would have been to order up a fresh reexamination, still another study of what was wrong with the big picture magazine. Donovan was inclined to do that, too, and he gave Hunt repeated instructions to rethink the magazine. But Hunt believed, with some justice, that the action of week-after-week production spoke with greater eloquence than any analysis, and he deferred it. He couldn't do anything about the currents that were inevitably turning against him. As had happened with his gifted and high-riding predecessor, Ed Thompson, with Longwell and Thorndike, even to some extent with the imperious John Shaw Billings of hallowed memory, the pressure of the job, the inexorable corporate demands for improved performance were wearing the apparently inexhaustible George Hunt down. The focus was shifting to the next man, a man (as Hunt would observe in his final editor's note) "without unnecessary flourishes," who might—just might—provide a new and saving lift for the badly faltering magazine.

16

Stonehenge

THE MEETING PLACE WAS STONEHENGE, a reassuringly expensive country inn in Connecticut, about sixty miles from New York City. The four of us who met there for two days in the spring of 1969, who swam in the too cold water of the pool and picked lovely wines to drink with dinner, had just been chosen as the new editorial managers of *Life*, and we had come to this secluded place to begin planning for what threatened to be a very precarious future.

In fact, by the time we took over it was too late, though nothing in our comfortable pasts would have led us to believe it. Inheritors we were at last, the four of us at the top of the editorial heap when Ralph Graves became managing editor, and greedy for it, our own place in a line of succession that stretched back to those days when the giants Luce and Billings had made it all work by alternating strokes of genius with energy and luck. Now we had arrived, Graves and his three comrade-assistants, the mantle was ours, and somewhat overripe with seasoning, like promising athletes who slip past their peaks while waiting for star quarterbacks to retire, we were stepping up to take our turn at "running the magazine." Now we would be the guardians—or so we thought in our most hopeful moments—of the bold tradition we'd all grown up honoring, now we would give the orders that would turn on those immense and shuddering presses—and stop them suddenly, if we needed to—now we would be the ones to decide, in the stream of weeks and months ahead, on just the exact mix of sensation, sex, adventure, discovery, slapstick, patriotism, doom, folk wisdom to offer our huge and welcoming audience. In the fullness of our early middle age, we had reached the senior class.

All things considered, we were a worthy lot, and no one could seriously fault Hedley Donovan for believing that this team would provide *Life* with a stable and imaginative core of leadership. There was very little about the journalistic operations of the magazine we hadn't experienced at some depth firsthand. There were few mysteries remaining for us, few situations one could think of (short of the pervasive accelerating failure that awaited us) where we wouldn't have some practiced or remembered technique to fall back on in case of trouble. There was scarcely a story suggestion made, for example, that didn't set off in one or the other of us the clear recollection of ways of dealing with it that had worked or not worked at some point in the past twenty years.

Of course, and we all thought of it from time to time, there was something seriously limiting as well about our depth of experience with the magazine. A built-in smugness, even arrogance, came with it, and it all somehow implied that the ways that grew naturally out of our long experience would work fine in this new era of specialized magazines and the dominance of news coverage by television. And the world, even more so than usual, had changed utterly since we were young men growing up at *Life* in the late forties and early fifties.

Indeed, all four of us had grown up there; only one had had another job before coming to the magazine right out of college. Our solutions, learned by years, even decades, of listening to our elders over lunch tables and at story conferences, were often old solutions, our wisdom was conventional corporate wisdom, usually guaranteed to be sensible and safe. We tended to regard new approaches with suspicion and new people with wary condescension, as if we were waiting for them to say something ridiculous or to make a bad smell. In the boarding school term—which, incidentally, we all four recalled—we were very much "old boys," slightly superior beings who knew where everything was and when everything would happen. We did not suffer new boys easily.

To make matters somewhat worse, we were all close friends, forgiving and tolerant (at least in the open) of each other's mistakes, united against pressure from the outside, much more likely than not to reflect each other's views and to support them against challenge. We were a tight bunch, we spoke a common, comfortable shorthand and we shared a common professional history. We were quite satisfied now that we belonged in power, and quite certain, too, that it would work out all right, the way it always had.

At the center of the disaster that finally overtook *Life* three and a half years later was Ralph Graves, the best qualified of the four to become the magazine's sixth managing editor. However much anyone else suffered, he was the focal victim of the collapse, the one who more than any other had to bear each painful defeat that led to the end. It was Graves who somehow came to symbolize the futility of all efforts, many of them his own, to stave off ruin. Of course, the responsibility for *Life*'s sinking was not really his at all. There were several in Time Inc.'s management who had more control than Graves did over the fate of the magazine. But he was the captain in charge of operations and his was the manfully bailing form most visible at the end through the clouds of spray and the breaking waves.

Graves had wanted to be managing editor for a long time. Now forty-four, he carried himself with a certain authority, as if he was armed against all surprises. A solid and occasionally solemn-looking man with gray eyes behind strong glasses and an air of confident briskness, he was very bright, analytical, well organized, an excellent administrator who had the affection and respect of many who worked with him. He was a deft and perceptive text editor; he knew what he wanted from stories, and he presented writers in trouble with good working solutions to achieve it. Though he originated few stories himself, he responded well to the suggestions of others. He often referred to himself as a "counterpuncher," in fact, and he did have the valuable ability to translate another's energy or even half-formed thoughts into more substantial action.

He took considerable pride in his memory and suggested games where he could show it off. He liked to play bridge and to make election and sports bets for small stakes. He knew the words to old popular songs, and when he was feeling comfortable, he sang them in a strong baritone voice. He had a great capacity for hard work, and he was smooth enough to disguise some of his important shortcomings, including the fact that his judgments about pictures were ordinary and his ideas for their use were both predictable and unimaginative. He covered this up with a kind of technical expertise—he would comment, for example, on a photograph's suitability for reproduction or suggest odd croppings for dramatic effect—and he made his choices of pictures with crispness and speed. But his most apparent flaws grew out of his own need for order. He had to know where to find things quickly, including his own views on virtually everything, and this led him to tuck all sorts of items into handy compartments. For instance, he often gave completed articles a letter grade, A−, B, C+, in conversations with other editors, and he liked to compartmentalize people, too, in tightly composed terms of their strengths and weaknesses. The weakness of others brought out a bully in him, and he did not like to change his mind. And for a man of his experience, exposure and opportunities, he had an odd unknowingness about news and politics. He didn't, in fact, like to read the newspapers, an obsessional habit with most magazine editors on the prowl for stories.

By the time he was named managing editor, a quality of tight self-control was dominant in Graves. Capable of powerful feelings of both tenderness and anger, he kept them firmly in check except in the most rare circumstances. He was so chary of showing strong emotions that one could believe he feared their release might destroy him. Yet this buttoned-up, constipated quality, along with his real abilities, made him a more appropriate choice than any of the others, especially if the *Life* operation was going to have to be pinched hard to save it. That, it was already becoming clear, was the case. Graves had the right sort of coldness, of toughness, one might correctly assume, to do what he had to do in hard moments and at the same time to blink back any time-wasting tears.

Like Graves, Robert Ajemian had gone to Harvard, and he, too, had been at *Life* since his twenties. But unlike the rest of us, he'd worked on a newspaper—in Boston—where he'd first been a sports reporter and then a columnist. In that job, as Ajemian took light pride in telling, he'd had his name billed in big letters on the sides of the trucks that delivered papers to the city's newsstands.

He was a large man, slightly overweight, with very dark eyes and rounded shoulders. He slouched a bit when he walked and his hands were often in his pockets. He wore good, conservatively cut suits whose trousers were usually baggy, and some called him "Bear." The white shirts he always wore to work had buttoned-down collars, and he kept his thinning dark hair carefully trimmed. When Ajemian listened, he could look serious and absolutely deadpan, but he liked to tease, and his laugh began as a giggle and became a high parrot's cry. When he was enjoying himself, he touched his listener's elbow and leaned forward, eyes shining, utterly engaged and engaging. If he was angry, the eyes were cold, and he smiled stiffly, showing teeth.

His general reputation at *Life* was less resounding than either Graves's or the others'. His greatest strength was in the area of news and especially politics, which had fascinated him as a reporter in the 1950s and 1960s at *Life* and which he understood much better than his colleagues. He had certain failings as a manager, which he'd been in recent years. He tended to be compulsively thorough, slow and picky with daily problems and minor details that Graves, for instance, would have disposed of immediately. Ajemian explored—and then reexplored—the details of his projects to the point of his and other people's exhaustion. He could be too stubborn, and he was reluctant to forgive. But generally he was scrupulous and fair, supportive of the people below him, blunt and loyal with his bosses, candid and penetrating in opinions he gave in funny, unprofane and entirely explicit terms. In some ways he was the most solid of this group. Ajemian was regarded by the card-playing gamblers in Time Inc. as an extremely dangerous high-stakes poker player.

Philip Kunhardt had become a figure of quite special influence and power in his years at *Life*, a person who often aroused great loyalty, even devotion from those who worked with him. For many, he was a kind of guru and perhaps the most admired man on the staff. "What does Phil think about that?" would be a question many would ask in their uncertainty about matters. The statement "Phil *loves* that idea" dropped in the right moment would be enough to get a project moving, and he always assumed the chairmanship of little committees that would meet *after* bigger meetings to refine or revise decisions taken earlier. He had particular status as special champion and counselor for the powerful and talented women at the magazine, who heaped their ideas, their confidences, their frequent and considerable angers on his unprotesting head.

He had started at *Life* in 1950 as a big, enormously strong redhead just out of Princeton. He seemed shy then (and under some circumstances still was), and he was often silent, staring numbly at his questioners through thick glasses. As he became more important at the magazine, the silences tantalized many, made him seem full of secrets, and they often triggered the urgent desire to find out what he was holding back. Did he know something they didn't? Would he share some delicious mystery with them? Often, by his own winning admission, he was thinking of nothing in particular, or of something far removed from the situation—or was simply waiting to see what would happen next.

Kunhardt's heart attack in 1968, when he was forty, had somehow enhanced his standing at *Life*, although it did put him out of the running for the top job. A prudent management could hardly offer him a job that might kill him. Still, it enlisted the urgent sympathies of people who almost certainly would have been quite detached about the health of others. Friends, both men and women, would repeatedly remonstrate with him about his smoking—they would even snatch cigarettes out of his mouth as he lit them. "Don't *do* that, Phil!" they would scold him. He looked at these fighters for his life and smiled his mysterious sweet smiles. Kunhardt had big appetites. He liked to cook, and he threw ingredients into the pot with both hands. He poured glasses full, his and his friends', and sometimes he got rough, in ways he meant playfully, but which now and then hurt or broke things because of his great strength and surprising speed.

His gifts as an editor were considerable. He worked hard, he could handle big projects without a lot of attendant flame and smoke. He made people believe he cared about their problems—in fact he seemed to collect people with problems. He brought out their helplessness. He regularly had excellent story ideas and was good at pushing others to develop their own. He especially loved photography and photographs (his grandfather, Frederick Meserve, had been a renowned collector of Mathew Brady pictures), and his notions about their use in the magazine were consistently dramatic and original. Though he was an intensely knowing operator in office politics, he managed to appear at an almost saintly remove from them. What seemed to captivate his most devoted admirers particularly was that now and then he told them a secret, gave them some confidence, some glimmer of office intrigue, perhaps even a revelation of himself, that they felt very sure no one else would have.

I was the fourth man in the group, and while it lasted, I always felt a bit out of place, as if I were in some not quite convincing disguise. Of course, I wanted very much to be there, and Graves had wanted me as one of his top assistants. But I was aware of other feelings, too, mostly of the fact that I had been increasingly jealous of the success of these others, my closest friends at *Life,* and was determined to get a share of it. Now, for at least the second time in my career, this sort of envy was pulling me away from writing to the pursuit of a job as an editorial manager. That envy had been a big factor in my giving up a splendid job (and one I'd suggested and promoted for myself years earlier) of writing a page of personal comment that was printed every other week. I was getting stale and a little bored with it as well, and I thought—not altogether secretly—that I would really make a better managing editor than the others under, of course, certain ideal circumstances, circumstances where the efficiency of *my* assistants would provide a cover for my managerial ineptitude and free up my energy and ego for more soaring trips. I thought of myself as an idea man, as an intuitive person with a strong instinct for stories and a good sense of photographs, and with some ability to encourage and guide others in their work.

Those talents existed, and there were shortcomings, too. I got rattled and erratic under pressure and regularly drank too much to lessen my anxiety. I shuttled back and forth between ebullience and depression, and my attention to detail dropped off fast. I liked to make sure that I got proper credit for accomplishment and was not generous about the success of people I considered my competition. There were big blank areas in my understanding of the news; I knew little about international politics—and not much about domestic issues, either—and nothing about economics. But ignorance was by no means ruinous at *Life*, where flair, speed and the ability to improvise often counted for more than expertise. I felt I had enough of those qualities to be in the running.

Now we were all there together, and Graves was the boss. This was the time we'd all been waiting for since our beginnings at the magazine—or at least since we'd been around long enough for our youthful ambitions to seem reasonable. For years Graves, Kunhardt and I had talked and laughed and earnestly considered together over drinks and at private lunches how it would be that marvelous day when we were running *Life* together. It didn't make any difference, we three reassured each other staunchly over the second martini (or perhaps more flushed with friendship over a stinger on the rocks), which one of us got to be the boss. Each could work for the others, either of the others, in perfect harmony, we pledged repeatedly, and we would all have a terrific magazine and a wonderful time making it that way. We meant it, of course. We were the best of friends. We knew each other's secrets, strengths, weaknesses. We were like brothers, closer than brothers. But in the friendliest sort of way we were all lying. Because each of us thought, in the privacy of his heart, that there was really a difference between us. Each of us thought that *he* really was the best.

Even as we drank the wine at Stonehenge, we knew that our earlier hopes and plans for the future were out of reach. In fact, few of the editorial riches that we'd grown up to believe simply went along with a successful operation—the unlimited expense accounts and travel, the empire building that went on within the staff itself, the historic commonplace that we shot many more stories than we would ever use—and were common in the palmy days on *Life*, or even in the days immediately past under Hunt, would be available to us. Certain ugly realities were apparent to everyone who cared to look. Advertising revenues were off from the boom year of 1966, costs were rising fast and the circulation, force-fed by the acquisition of millions of names from the sunken *Saturday Evening Post*'s subscription list, was enormously inflated at 8.5 million. The magazine was showing signs of being in serious trouble; it was already certain that 1969 would be a losing year for *Life*. Just how big the losses might be, at least three of us at Stonehenge didn't know. That kind of bad news was kept close to the corporate vest. But it could be safely presumed to be an unpleasant amount, several millions.

And the huge success of the other medium emphasized our weakening position. Now television was winking its primacy and power day and night in 97 percent of homes around the country. The growing appetite of a national audience for news coverage and feature stories was being fed with a speed and breadth no magazine could match— and the color pictures *moved*. Ed Thompson's exuberant techniques of crash coverage and big spending would not work now the way they did little more than a dozen years earlier, in 1956, when *Life* had celebrated its twentieth birthday and its most successful business year. Another change, and a most important one: Henry Luce was dead. No one could guess what he might have done to revive a failing *Life*, and his own diminished ambition and energy might not have been enough for a big effort. But his absence was felt anyhow, if only in the fact that his inheritors in the highest reaches of corporate and editorial management, their individual gifts and competence all added up, were something less than he had been.

Graves had invited us to come to Stonehenge to begin dealing with some of these punishing realities. It was just two weeks before he was scheduled to move into the managing editor's office, and he wanted some concentrated and private time with his top editors away from the pressure of routine office business and the natural curiosity of the rest of the staff, which was utterly preoccupied with what was going to happen to them all under the new regime.

We arrived at the inn at midday on a hot Thursday in May; we planned to leave two days later on Saturday. That first day, before we got down to the heaviest business of the meeting, Graves had a little game for us, and the game itself was an indication of the sort of matter that would preoccupy us all in the coming months. It had to do with money, of course, and the saving of it, with which some of us were making a sudden and shocking acquaintance. The publisher's office had produced copies of *Life* covers made up in varying paper thicknesses and sizes. There was a cover, for example, made up in the rather heavy stock then being used, and there were covers printed on lighter, less expensive paper. There were also covers printed up in the current *Life* page size of 10½ by 13½ inches (it had shrunk half an inch in length since 1936), as well as smaller versions with half an inch or more trimmed off both the length and width. Obviously a lighter cover stock or a smaller page size could save us a lot of money in production costs.

Graves put the covers on the floor of the room where we were having drinks, first those of varying weights, then those of varying sizes.

He asked us if we could tell him whether we found any important differences between them. He didn't give any indication of what differences he might be talking about, and, just as he often did when he made bets or wrote reminders to himself at lunch meetings, he kept note of our responses on the flap of a book of matches.

Feeling slightly foolish and anxious to get the right answers, we hefted the pieces of paper, rattled them and held them to the light. The exact responses have gone with the matches, but we could find little to choose among the sample of, say, 50-, 44- and 36-pound paper. The covers all looked pretty good to us, although once we caught on to the game the more heavily coated papers may have had a slight edge. We were more picky about the size difference, though a couple did not spot the variations right away. Once we knew about it, the choice was clear. The size of the *Life* page has always been a source of pride (*Look's* page size had been trimmed in its declining years), and we all wanted to keep it big. Great pictures looked best on the *Life* page. Letting it be cut down was somehow too stark a symbol of our really shrinking power to accept. If we let the money boys do that, was the feeling over martinis, the first thing you know they'd have us shriveled down to some horrible little dimension, maybe even down to *Time* size. So, at least at this initial meeting, we agreed not to take the painful cosmetic step of trimming, and to investigate further the possibilities of using lighter stock, which didn't seem *that* bad on first consideration and might save us half a million or more each year.

But the Graves paper game was just an amiable deflection from the basic grimness of the Stonehenge gathering. Our purpose was to cut a lot of fat out of the editorial budget, which in this last year of Hunt's stewardship was running at about $14 million. Graves felt, with no serious disagreement from any of us, that important reductions could be made in that figure by cutting back on the staff, at that time consisting of about 250 people in all categories—editors, photographers, reporters, writers and others with such specialties as copyreading and layout design. We should somehow get rid of thirty to thirty-five people, Graves decided. The publishing side was committed to chop out a similar number drawn from the advertising, promotion, business and other non-editorial staffs. Thus Stonehenge was really a planning meeting for a mass firing.

Yet we brought to it a kind of cheerful purposefulness, as if such a drastic housecleaning was really going to make the difference at *Life*, as if our leanness would turn it all around and make the magazine successful again. This attitude implied, of course, that the trouble we were in didn't have much to do with what was in the magazine, with the face that we showed the world each week. And perhaps it didn't. But in retrospect, it's almost as if we saw tackling the organizational problems as plausible alternatives to the problem of trying to figure out what kind of magazine we were going to turn out in a changing and tormented country.

Although he would soon address, at least in a very broad way, the question of what he thought should be in *Life,* Graves had a special affinity for the organizational problems, a talent for dealing with them, and he took pride in it. His natural tendency to fix on the details came to the fore; he became consumed with questions of head count, of who was going to be in charge of departments, of what departments could be dropped or merged with others. This is the way out, he seemed to be saying. Let's tidy the place up and we'll be all right. The pressure on him from above was very great, and he remained stuck in the pursuit of workable solutions to an unfixable problem until the very end almost three and a half years later.

There was an air of unreality about it throughout. One usually thinks of firing as an isolated event involving a single individual and precipitated by some tangible piece or pattern of inept, unprofessional or otherwise unacceptable behavior. This was not the case now at all. Some of the staff members we would be saying must leave were marginally effective, but most were people who had been doing their jobs well enough not to draw bad notices under ordinary circumstances. Some had worked at *Life* for many years, for decades, and had made important contributions along the way. A few had been very successful.

But under these radically changed circumstances, they were the ones we decided were the weakest, the most difficult to work with or somehow the least desirable people for the smaller, tighter staff Graves wanted. Thus there was something particularly difficult about this cruel rite of choosing, even brutal, like shooting the slightly wounded. As much as we tried to rationalize our choices as logical and objective, much of the process was very subjective. And the fact that so many (we had no idea how very many more there would be) had to go made it seem even more of an execution. The numbers were so big, in fact, that we had all brought interoffice telephone lists and mastheads with us to make the job of selecting easier and to check out how the fired stacked up against those who would remain.

It must be said, too, that this was not the sort of reorganization that one would ever expect to take place at *Life.* At some other magazine maybe, but not at *Life.* A job at the magazine before this awful period carried with it an almost palpable sense of security. Firing was just not thought about except in the most extreme cases. Working there was like working for the United States government; nobody was going to get fired in the ordinary course of events. It was such a forgiving, *humane* place, too. If a person got in trouble, unless it was for stealing or something like that (or, as happened on one occasion, for taking a story without permission to another magazine), there was almost always some appeal possible. Tough decisions could usually be reversed; the ax was interrupted in its fall. But not this time. The indulgent employer wore a pitiless new face.

All this combined to make the meeting at Stonehenge very hard. A couple of us had been treated more than mercifully over the years ourselves. And it was made much harder by the fact that some of us were close to some of the people who had to go. They were close colleagues and more—good friends in some cases—and their leaving would be a substantial personal as well as professional loss.

There was little discussion about two of the most senior staff people leaving, and their departures would make a big difference. One was Roy Rowan, the capable, experienced, news-oriented man who had wanted the managing editor's job and decided not to stay once Graves got chosen over him. In a spirit of some magnanimity, Graves had offered the loser in this silent and polite conflict a job as head of the *Life* office in the Far East. But Rowan, most likely to Graves's relief, turned it down and planned to leave soon.

Much more difficult, especially for Graves but for the rest of us as well, was the fact that his wife, Eleanor, currently the magazine's modern living editor, would be going, too, and taking with her the energy and fierce enthusiasm she'd brought to *Life* for more than twenty years. Her leaving seemed to be a part of Hedley Donovan's decision to elevate Graves. Donovan apparently believed it would be risky management practice to have her in a high editorial position while her husband was boss. The potential for trouble was doubtless there; staff morale could suffer, at both higher and lower levels, if people thought Eleanor Graves exerted a disproportionate influence. She might well have. Open and even sweet at times, she could be headstrong and careless of others' feelings. And it would surely, many of us agreed, be hard for her, full of powerful opinions and ideas about the magazine and its running, *not* to throw her special weight around. Still, her going was a real loss; in some ways she was a better editorial executive than any of the men at Stonehenge. At the time Graves was stoic about the loss; some of the more cynical management watchers at Time Inc. guessed that he might really have been grateful to Donovan for getting rid of a nasty headache for him. But years later, Graves remembered emphatically how he'd felt. "I was very offended," he said. "I was deprived of a top editor I'd worked with for years."

For two days we pored over the lists, taking them with us to meals and working over the names long into the nights. Virtually no one on the staff was spared consideration as a candidate for firing; perhaps it made us feel that we could be most fair only by bringing up *all* the names. Not everyone picked, of course, would be fired outright. Wherever early retirement was possible with older staff members, it would be offered as a comfortable inducement to leaving without a fuss. Others would be offered contracts. A writer or a photographer, for example, would be given a guaranteed number of assignments at a reasonable fee. In some cases we guessed—without any advance regret—that the assignments would not work out and that the contracts, therefore, would not need renewing.

The analysis given each person was often not thorough; we spoke in a kind of blunt shorthand of complaint about several of the people we were willing to let go. In some cases it was sufficient to say of a person marked for the hit list that he or she was "boring about everything," "not aggressive enough," "too aggressive," "drunk for ten years," "a pain in the ass," "not really interested in the magazine," "over the hill," "not awfully bright," "too smart for his own good." The superficiality and banality of such judgments reflected the ugly nature of the job. In many cases we weren't getting rid of the people for cause; we were getting rid of them strictly for the sake of numbers, to keep the raft afloat.

So we moved through those nightmare days, writing out new lists, arguing over some of the more difficult cases, deciding who would do the actual firing (in most instances, especially among the higher-ranked people, the job fell to Graves), trying to take into account possible special approaches to soften the blow for staff members we feared would be hit particularly hard. At one point Phil Kunhardt told us he'd read a recent article on firing that suggested it was best for the victims to get the bad news early in the day, so that they had time to begin considering all its ramifications before going home.

One man whose response we were quite worried about had been at the magazine for many years. He was a brittle, pompous fellow whose status in the outside world, like that of many of us, was reinforced (at least in his own mind) by his rank at *Life*. We feared he might make a terrible fuss. As Graves found, that wasn't what happened at all. "He was absolutely gallant," the managing editor reported much later, leaning on *Macbeth*. "First-class. Nothing became his *Life* like the leaving of it."

Two of the firings had special reverberations for the little group at Stonehenge. There was no firm agreement among us about them; in both cases it was Graves who insisted that these people had to go—and the rest of us believed that he was entitled to his choice, especially about such key staff members. Still, there was a lot of pained discussion anyway. The cases threw into focus the essential, unanswerable question of how harmful to our future health these staff cuts might turn out to be.

The first involved Sally Kirkland, the smart, aggressive and difficult fashion editor who had come to *Life* in 1947. For more than twenty years she had produced variously elegant, raffish, stunning and often newsworthy fashion stories, and within the fashion field at large, Kirkland was a power who could jangle her heavy bracelets with the best.

But fashion stories, as Graves now felt with some real justification, in these lean and changing times at *Life* (and on these greatly reduced numbers of pages) no longer should play as spectacular or as regular a role as in the past. He wanted fewer and cheaper fashion stories and intended to give them less space. He intended, in fact, to abolish the fashion department—which at one time had included, besides Kirkland, two or three other full-time writer-editors, a couple of reporters, a secretary and two part-time scout-correspondents in Los Angeles and Paris—and to rely on one person working out of the modern living department to direct the fashion coverage on an occasional basis. Getting rid of Sally Kirkland, therefore, meant a big change.

Though the reasons for dropping her were mainly organizational, Kirkland presented some special staff problems, too. Her competitive zeal led her to run over other editors from time to time. She was charming and funny, but in her loud and rather nasal voice she could be formidably cranky and obtuse as well, resorting in her own behalf to heavy sarcasm when crossed and, at specially aggrieved moments, to a sort of controlled tantrum. Most of us were a little scared of her, and no one wanted at all to deal with her on the bad days, which seemed to be getting more frequent near the end of Hunt's editorship.

Still, she had contributed a great deal to the magazine, and Kunhardt and I wondered to the others if it might be a good idea to keep her on the staff in a changed capacity. She could still do the reduced amount of fashion coverage that Graves wanted, but we could also ask her to keep an eye out for trends, fads and interesting style movements of all kinds in the culture. She had a good eye for these things, wonderful contacts and a very sharp, wry sense of what made pictures. She also had powerful feelings about *Life* and, in spite of her sometimes justified complaints about the indifference and fatheadedness of her editors, an intense loyalty for it. We offered our solution to Graves, but he felt it really wouldn't work, that Kirkland had been playing her favorite role as herself for too long. More or less agreeing with him, but feeling—as her old friends—terribly guilty of ganging up on her and wondering how we'd ever replace that jittery creative energy, we went along.

The decision to get rid of Bernie Quint was even more painful for all of us—except for Graves, who was completely determined to see him gone. Quint had been *Life*'s art director since Hunt took over eight years earlier. Quint had many admirers; some of us believed he was really central to the operation, more so perhaps than any person other than the managing editor to the job of turning out a consistently good-looking, exciting, photographically provocative and thoughtful maga-zine. We were terribly worried about losing him for that reason—and worried, too, that he would be just devastated by getting fired. The magazine was very important to Bernie Quint.

That he had become *Life*'s art director at all was a source of huge pride. Largely self-educated, Quint preened himself on his knowledge of art, philosophy, psychology, history and politics, and he was not accommodating with people he regarded as ill informed or opportu-nistic. At times he seemed to think of himself as the Guardian of Truth, and this infuriated the pragmatists he worked with every day. He could be extremely difficult with the people who worked for him. He drove them hard, often rejecting their ideas and insisting that they follow his instructions in the smallest detail.

When he was happily engaged or feeling relaxed, Quint was ex-cellent company for the editors and reporters he liked (who had in-cluded—in the past, at least—all those at Stonehenge), explaining ideas with gentleness and clarity, and he was funny, too, a great storyteller, mostly of Jewish jokes he told with an impeccable accent and a lot of his own laughter. When he laughed, his eyes got moist behind horn-rimmed glasses, and when he was angry, his face was white and his mouth trembled. He was not as good at sitting on his anger as most of his Wasp colleagues.

It was uncontrolled anger that had completely finished him with Graves. On at least one occasion Quint's temper had landed on Eleanor Graves, who had apparently asked him an unwelcome question when he was preoccupied with something else. Immediately irritable, he said something insulting about her "dumb question," and she went right back at him, moving close and saying he couldn't talk to her that way.

The fierce confrontation then moved at high volume down the hall to Graves's office, where his work was interrupted by his wife's announcement that she wasn't going to take any more rudeness from Quint. Looking grim, Graves urged them both back to work. But he clearly felt that Quint's behavior was outrageous—and unacceptable in a civilized office.

Even in the face of Graves's implacable determination, we still tried to persuade the new managing editor to keep Quint. Scare hell out of him, we proposed. Tell him you will not accept any outbursts, that you insist he act in a responsible, courteous way with everyone. If he misbehaves, you'll can him on the spot. But he's so valuable, we insisted (with somewhat less courage than our convictions), so imaginative, conscientious, devoted and plain talented, we need him very badly. We'll never find another art director this good. He can make the difference between success and failure.

But Graves fended us off. He obviously didn't want to work with Quint. Surely he was offended by Quint's behavior. But there seemed to be more to his reluctance than that; some of us guessed that Bernie's talent and conviction could be extremely intimidating to an editor who was trying to discover his own style. At any rate, Graves just wasn't having any. Quint was out.

We knew how hard he was going to take the news. As he had already told two of us before Stonehenge, he had picked up Graves's complete coldness toward him. Something awful was coming, Quint feared, and he looked on his possible dismissal as totally uncalled for and shocking, like a mugging or a rape. The drama around his status was very depressing, and the regret and doubt all of us but Graves felt about firing Bernie dominated our feelings about the Stonehenge meeting. Those feelings contributed to sending us home from it deeply exhausted and with a sense of real anxiety about the value of the big surgery we'd just performed to save *Life*.

17

Vietnam: One Week's Dead

This is going to be a rather blunt speech. I am going to assume that for as long as I am managing editor, you would all prefer to hear the truth from me. I am not going to kid you, and I hope you will not spend too much of your time trying to kid me.

These are obviously hard times for general magazines and specifically hard times for Life. *That means hard times for me and hard times for you. We have television on one side of us and more and more specialized magazines on the other side of us. We also have an affluent, leisure-time society that has plenty of other things to do besides sit around and look at* Life. *Unless we make them look at us.*

It is not your job and my job to sell advertising or increase the circulation revenue or promote the magazine. That is Jerry Hardy's job, and good luck to him. Our job is to make readers care about this magazine. Not because it is an institution—let us never forget that The Saturday Evening Post *was an institution long before* Life *was even invented. Institutions have no built-in value unless they continue to be relevant. Readers will care about this magazine only if we talk to them about the right things.*

A SPEECH BY RALPH GRAVES TO THE EDITORIAL STAFF ON
JUNE 16, 1969, WHEN HE STEPPED INTO HIS NEW JOB

A NEW BOSS WANTS TO MAKE HIS MARK on the job as soon as possible, something distinctive, something emphatic to announce his arrival, to celebrate it and—most important—to set him apart from his predecessors. This was a particularly tough problem for Ralph Graves in 1969, arriving as he did at such a low point in the magazine's history, with fortunes in decline and compelling requirements for austerity and caution.

His situation wasn't helped by the somewhat overblown reputations of the men who came before him—Hunt, the powerful, impassioned, gung ho man of spirit, imagination and sensitivity; Thompson, the reigning genius of his time in picture journalism, the folksy but driving autocrat with a fine news sense and a peerless capacity for extracting loyalty and high energy from his people.

Graves had none of their flair. He did not create a stir with his appearance, he did not exhort his staff in Hunt's take-the-high-ground fashion or manipulate them into action with Thompson's artful blend of scowls, smirks, mumbles and shrugs. He was a much more prosaic type, on the surface at least, tidy and cool as a branch manager in a stuffy bank, rarely betraying with any flicker behind the glasses just how he felt about whatever was happening at the moment. Surprising broths simmered within, but he rarely let on.

That spring, before the announcement of his appointment, Graves became aware of the idea of doing a story on the Vietnam war dead. In the late sixties many of us on the staff used to talk a lot, naturally, about the futility of the war and our own dismay at the way the magazine covered it. For years Time Inc.'s editorial policy, as often expressed in *Life*, had bathed in a patriotic glow the American presence, buildup and execution of the war in Vietnam. Stories tended to glorify the American mission and fighting man; articles, including a couple by Time Inc. editor-in-chief Hedley Donovan—"Vietnam: The War Is Worth Winning" (1966) and "Vietnam: Slow, Tough But Coming Along" (1967)—were hopeful about a future our victory would bring. By 1969, editorial confidence about the outcome of the war had waned, yet a sort of journalistic numbness prevailed at *Life*. We kept getting great combat pictures and reporting out of Vietnam, but many on the staff felt that much more should be said, that *Life* should speak up for withdrawal. There were angry and frustrating meetings with Hunt and other editors where change was passionately demanded. Again and again we looked for ways to depict the war—we considered doing a story on the contents of a wallet taken from a dead North Vietnamese soldier—that would somehow give our readers an even stronger sense of its bitter cost on both sides. But no matter how great our clamor for a recommendation to get out, Hunt and the top brass were wary of any such reversal.

The Pentagon at that time was releasing weekly counts of the American dead and lists of their names—200, 300 young men each week. Like millions of others, we were horrified and outraged by the lists and the body counts. There was something about them that symbolized the terrible futility of the war, we told each other. It was just a step from that to the making of our own kind of list. During one conversation with Phil Kunhardt, it occurred to me that we could simply take one of these lists and run pictures of one week's dead, laying them out for page after page in a kind of unadorned album—a list of pictures—and let the readers look straight into every young face.

Kunhardt and I first tried the idea on George Hunt, who by that time knew he was leaving the magazine and was beginning to think about the transatlantic trip he would make on his sailboat when the congratulatory goodbyes were done. He recognized it as strong stuff and considered getting it ready for one of his last issues. Then, loath to make such a statement about the futility of a war he had strongly believed was just and necessary, he chose to let it pass. Graves, who had been in on the idea early, quickly decided to run the war dead in one of his early issues. Such a story, he saw, fulfilled definitions he'd set in his speech; it would make readers care about *Life* and believe in its relevance.

The critical problem, as we all knew, lay in getting the story past Hedley Donovan. Just bringing it up had all the potential for a big head-on showdown and one we would surely lose if Donovan decided to dig in against his editors. And that was a clear possibility. For one thing, Donovan had supported the conduct of the war for many years, had traveled to Vietnam himself on a number of occasions and was justifiably considered something of an expert on the subject. He was much better informed about it than any of his editors at *Life*. For another thing, the week's dead, we guessed, was just the sort of emotional, non-rational journalism that would make the editor-in-chief extremely uncomfortable. He might well kill the story before it was produced, we feared, because he thought it made the wrong sort of appeal to readers, to their feelings, to their sensibilities, and not to their good sense.

Yet, on the other hand, we were pretty sure that Donovan would be much inclined, especially in Graves's opening weeks on the job, to support the stories his new editor wanted to do. That would be a point in our favor, we thought, but we still wanted to be very cautious about it. We agreed it would be best *not* to ask for Donovan's approval of the idea in the abstract and instead to delay any confrontation with him until he could actually *see* what we were proposing to run. Thus Graves, at about the time he took over, told Donovan simply that we were planning a story on the war dead and that he'd be shown it when it was ready for publication. As we went ahead with our plans, none of us recalled—if, in fact, we'd ever known of it—the *Life* story that ran in

1943 with the names of almost 13,000 Americans who'd been killed up to that point in World War II.

Getting the story ready was a complex and ticklish job, and it had to be done in a big hurry, since we wanted it to come out as quickly as possible after the Pentagon released the list for the week chosen. Muriel Hall, one of the magazine's most poised and solid professionals, was put in charge of pulling the story together, and she attacked the problem with great seriousness and conscience. The daughter of an Episcopal bishop, a woman whose usually sweet and considerate behavior covered up tremendous strength and made surprising her occasional flashes of stubbornness and ferocity, Hall was in charge of the news reporters in New York and dealt closely with those in the field offices, too. She was a real Time Inc. veteran and had been a researcher at *Time* for many years before coming to *Life* in 1951.

When we decided to focus the story on those who had died in the war during the week of May 28 through June 3, it was Hall who took the list of 242 names and hometowns that Washington bureau chief Frank McCulloch had got from the Pentagon and broke the list down geographically so that correspondents and stringers could then make direct contact with all the families. Members of Hall's team approached the next of kin in every case—not just for pictures but also to make it clear to all the relatives exactly what the magazine was doing. There was some risk in that; some might decide they didn't like *Life*'s approach and didn't want their son's or husband's picture to appear. In cases like that—and there were a few—we decided not to make the usual effort to get pictures in other ways (from the Department of Defense, hometown papers, school or college yearbooks) but simply to run the names of the dead alone.

In magazine slang, such a quick, inclusive gathering of pictures and/or information from many different sources is called a roundup, and this, at the emotional level, was surely one of the most difficult and delicate roundups *Life* ever attempted. Talking to the relatives of the dead and asking them for information or photographs always involves an invasion of privacy that most reporters hate, and in this case we were doing it in hundreds of homes all over the country at the same time. In Detroit, Miami, Denver, Tucson, in cities all across the United States, in little southern or mountain towns, on prairie farms, reporters were sent out to make contact with stricken people, telling them what we wanted, hoping the requests would sound plausible, hoping they would be willing to look past their grief and decide that the story was something they should cooperate with and not just an exploitation of sorrow for sales and the promotion of a special political view.

The great majority of the families apparently felt they could co-operate. Some saw it as a way the sacrifices of their sons would be recognized. Others saw it as an anti-war statement and wanted it made. Others, with the kind of passivity and numb agreement that troubled people often give the press, just went along. A few, about twenty families, wanted nothing to do with the story or saw it as denigrating to the memory of their dead men, and the reporters did not push to get them to change their minds.

But how generously most of these mourning families treated the intruders from *Life*. They pulled out last letters from the dead: "Here's a picture of a 2-star general awarding me my Silver Star. I didn't do anything. They just had some extra ones." "Do you have tomatoes in the garden? 'A' Co. found [a North Vietnamese Army] farm two days ago with bananas, tomatoes and corn. This is real good land here. You can see why the North wants it." "I could be standing on the doorstep on the 8th [of June]. As you can see from my shakey printing, the strain of getting 'short' is getting to me, so I'll close now." "Everyone's dying, they're all ripped apart. Dad, there's no one left." "You may not be able to read this. I am writing it in a hurry. I can see death coming up the hill."

The families of these men were willing to share the most heart-breaking ironies. A PFC from the 101st Airborne was killed on his twenty-first birthday. A young woman waiting to get married had just bought her own wedding ring when she got the awful news. A mother received flowers ordered by her son and then learned he had died the day before they arrived. A lieutenant was killed serving in the battalion his father had commanded two years earlier. A Marine who wrote that the captured North Vietnamese mortars were lighter and more accurate than his own was killed by enemy mortar fire shortly thereafter.

They were not afraid, many of these relatives, to offer their most sorrowful recollections. When one young man had been home on leave some months earlier, a father recalled, he'd told the older man he was considering going AWOL. "I wish now I'd told him to jump," said the father to *Life*'s reporter. "I wish I had, but I couldn't." A woman spoke with great feeling of the nephew she had raised: "He was really and truly a conscientious objector. He told me it was a terrible thought going into the Army and winding up in Vietnam and shooting people who hadn't done anything to him. Such a waste. Such a shame."

The trust these people gave *Life* was reflected, too, by the pictures they offered. In many cases, they were the best or the most recent and the most treasured photographs in the family collections, and great care was taken by Muriel Hall and her staff to see that they didn't get lost in mailing or handling. That not one of these hundreds of photographs was damaged or destroyed in the course of this hurry-up operation was at least partly a sign of the way people felt about the story. More than any other the magazine had produced in years, this one on the war dead engaged everybody on a personal level. Special effort, special tact, special involvement, marked the job all the way.

The story came together more quickly than expected and was largely in hand about a week ahead of schedule. Graves planned then to make it the lead and the cover for the issue of June 27, and he wanted to have something to show to Donovan as soon as possible— even before we had the whole thing in closing shape. We would show the editor-in-chief four of the thirteen pages we wanted to use, went the plan, and eighty pictures, randomly selected, would go on the four pages. Graves asked me to have the opening block of writing ready to give Donovan at the same time; except for a few paragraphs at the end of the story reflecting the information the families had given our reporters about the dead, this would be all that *Life* would say. Under the pictures of each of the men would run his name, age, service, rank and hometown.

On the day of the crucial show-and-tell, the prepared pages and the introductory copy were set up in the layout room off Graves's office, and Donovan was invited down for a look. A big, imposing man in his suit, he seemed so much more serious and formal than his shirt-sleeved subordinates, and he looked very solemn when he grunted a greeting and walked up to the long, high table where the story waited. Graves and three or four more of us, not the usual crowd of kibitzers and tenuously connected onlookers who often crashed layout sessions on big stories, stood to one side and waited in silence.

Donovan put his hands up on the table and, hunching over slightly, stared at the faces. When the story was all done, Graves told him, it would run for thirteen pages, with about 220 pictures and possibly twenty-five additional names with no pictures. "Are they in any order?" Donovan asked. We did not plan to run them in any order, Graves replied, alphabetical or otherwise. Donovan kept looking at the pictures. "What kind of a headline have you got for the story?" he asked. "'One Week's Dead,'" Graves answered, "with 'Vietnam' in smaller type above it and the dates, May 28–June 3, 1969, below it." Donovan, we could see, was looking at virtually every face. Then he moved slightly and placed himself in front of the copy for the opening block. While he read it, he moved his hands only once—to turn a page—and it seemed to us that he read terribly slowly.

The faces shown on the next pages are the faces of American men killed—in the words of the official announcement of their deaths— "in connection with the conflict in Vietnam." The names, 242 of them, were released by the Pentagon during the week of May 28 through June 3, a span of no special significance except that it includes Memorial Day. The numbers of the dead are average for any seven-day period during this stage of the war.

It is not the intention of this article to speak for the dead. We cannot tell with any precision what they thought of the political currents which drew them across the world. From the letters of some, it is possible to tell they felt strongly that they should be in Vietnam, that they had great sympathy for the Vietnamese people and were appalled at their enormous suffering. Some had voluntarily extended their tours of combat duty; some were desperate to come home. Their families provided most of these photographs, and many expressed their own feelings that their sons and husbands died in a necessary cause. Yet in a time when the numbers of Americans killed in this war—36,000—though far less than the Vietnamese losses, have exceeded the dead in the Korean War, when the nation continues week after week to be numbed by a three-digit statistic which is translated to direct anguish in hundreds of homes all over the country, we must pause to look into the faces. More than we must know *how many*, we must know *who*. The faces of one week's dead, unknown but to families and friends, are suddenly recognized by all in this gallery of young American eyes.

When Donovan finished, he glanced at the pictures again quickly. His face was completely serious, unreadable. This had to be more than a story for him; it would be a statement of his company's new position. We waited through another heavy silence. "All right," Donovan said suddenly to Graves. "Thank you." And nodding to us all, he turned from the table and left the room. He'd said very little, but it was enough. In his own blunt way, Donovan had approved the war dead story—and much more. That was clear, but until he got safely out of earshot and off the *Life* edit floor, we kept our elation to big grins and noiseless hand clapping. Middle-aged schoolboys who'd turned the principal around, we were high with it, very high.

Donovan went along a little later, too, with our choice of a cover for the issue. It was an extreme blowup of a single face from the gallery, the face of twenty-year-old William C. Gearing from Greece, New

York, and surprinted on the cover photograph were the words: "The Faces of The American Dead in Vietnam—One Week's Toll." In retrospect, the cover was probably the only bad mistake we made with the story. Blown up as it was, the cover was grainy and hard to read and not at all as dramatic as we hoped it would be. Newsstand buyers, it turned out, were apparently quite puzzled or unmoved by it; the newsstand sales were rather poor, surprisingly so when one takes into account the fact that the story immediately generated a lot of good comment and people all over the country were quickly talking about it.

In hindsight, the cover would have been much better if we'd used an album page from the story inside. At the very least, that would have given our readers a clear idea of what we were up to with the whole story. Instead, we'd been reluctant to give away the punch we had inside and opted for a picture that was both indistinct and dull.

Still, by most standards the story was a huge success. While some newspaper editors hated it ("a destructive document"), it drew an extraordinary amount of favorable press and TV coverage. Mixed in with the comments were expressions of surprise at the obvious signs of changed attitudes at Time Inc. about the war. "An amazing turnaround," "profoundly important," "historic anti-war statement," were among the praise.

The readers hit us with a great volume of letters, more than 1,300 of them, some passionate in their fury at what one called our "ghoulish exploitation of the agony of America." There were several cancellations ("You have succeeded in turning the knives in the backs of grieving parents"). But there were many more letters reporting how deeply moved people were by the story. A small sampling of the mail:

> From a man in California:
> Your story . . . was the most eloquent and meaningful statement on the wastefulness and stupidity of war that I have ever read.

> From a woman in Missouri:
> All of us know someone who has lost his life there and we were grieved by it. There is enough dissension and unrest about this war and in my opinion your article will do far more damage than good.

> From the mother of one of the dead:
> Since my son was killed, we have had one more death in our town,

24 in all from this one small town. Five deaths in my son's 1966 graduating class.

From a woman in Canada:
One cannot escape the feeling that if America had been forced to look into her sons' eyes *every* week, the ghastly chronicle of May 28–June 3 could have been avoided.

From a man in Texas:
How unspeakably cruel to print pictures of 217 dead soldiers. How even more cruel to the parents of some not yet dead that this slaughter should continue.

From a woman in Michigan:
My husband is presently serving his year there and each face in that article is his face.

Looking back on the story more than ten years later, Ralph Graves somewhat ruefully expressed the view that it was perhaps ironical that, for his three and a half years at *Life,* he'd be remembered best for a story done in his first month and one that wasn't his own idea, to boot. In ways that were never really spoken of, the article about the war dead marked a great change in its own face that *Life* offered readers and the world. Here, for possibly the first time, the magazine dropped its life-long posture as the earnest, cheerful broker of the high-mindedness and the good intentions of the American establishment and declared itself on the side of the growing mass of dissidents, ready for a profound change. It took a lot of nerve for Donovan and Graves to come right out and do that. And in a very real way the story marked a turning point in public thinking about the war. It helped many Americans, growing desperate for a decent solution, to add their own voices to the call for an end to the exhausting conflict.

18

A Sense of Loss

"SOMEONE ONCE SUGGESTED," THE photographer Larry Burrows told a friend, "that maybe I had a death wish. But I certainly don't want to die, and I cannot afford the luxury of thinking about what *could* happen to me. When my lips go dry and my stomach turns over, I feel 'Should I be doing this?' But then I feel 'If I don't, what am I missing?' There is always this urge to go have a look and see what is happening, to my left, to my right, further forward. I can't resist it. The best thing that happens—and this is important to me—is when someone turns around and says: 'Well, you've taken your chances with the rest of us.'"

Larry Burrows's continuing and urgent need to move out and see what was happening led, of course, to his death in action in Laos in February 1971. His loss had a special crushing weight for his colleagues on *Life*, which itself was in the throes of a sickness that was beginning to feel ominously terminal to many of the men and women who worked there. For Burrows was virtually a *Life*-manufactured man; he had all but invented himself as a *Life* photographer from real versions he met and glorified while he was still an unformed English youth. He had always, in a career of almost twenty-five years, given the needs and purposes of the magazine the highest sort of priority. Like many others who worked there, he brought an amazing devotion to his job. For him—and them— the job was a calling, really, beyond ordinary loyalty, and it suggested, among other things, that in the work they found not only great satisfaction but also relief from the banality of the rest of their lives.

Even more, Burrows reflected the magazine at its most exciting and romantic. He was clearly in the glamorous tradition of the combat photographer, the bold, knowing operator who coolly exposed himself to terrible dangers to bring back pictures that showed what the experience of war was *really* like for the people who fought it and were devastated by it, the tradition exemplified by Robert Capa, David Douglas Duncan and many more. His death, therefore, in the line of duty and after so many years of calculated risk, had both a particular poignancy and an implacable logic. Like Capa's death in Indochina in 1954 and Paul Schutzer's in the Sinai in 1967, it somehow honored the whole profession. And it carried a profound sense of loss, symbolic as well as real.

As the year 1971 began, Ralph Graves decided he would keep a journal. He was too busy with sink-or-swim problems to sustain it for long, but the brief record it provides is a remarkably lucid and candid—if somewhat laconic—account by an embattled editor of painful months on a failing magazine. "Tomorrow, after a four-day weekend," he wrote on January 3, "we start back to work on what I am convinced will be the crucial year for *Life.*

"In 1969 we managed to lose a lot more money than was ever made public. During 1970 we made just about every business change you could think of: new publisher, new ad director, new general manager, new circulation director, as well as eliminating *Life International* altogether and cutting our own circulation from 8.5 to 7 million. Although the recession, capped by the General Motors strike in the fall, wrecked us for advertising pages, the biggest problem of the year was really circulation. Bill Conway, the previous circulation director, had made 1970 projections that turned out to be wildly untrue—untrue to the point of absurdity—and Jerry Hardy and the corporate business side accepted them, although with some misgivings. Renewals, new circulation and newsstand sales were all infinitely less successful and more costly than had been budgeted. The result, coupled with the ad collapse, was another ghastly year for *Life.*

"I have some real hopes for Bob Moore in circulation," Graves went on. "He is tough-minded, direct and properly appalled by the errors and predictions of Conway and Company. (Conway wasn't fired, of course. He was just given a new job. It is hard to say what it takes to get fired from the business side of Time Inc., once you reach a certain level.)

"I am less sanguine about Tony Mayer as ad director. I wish he weren't [retired Time Inc. president] Jim Linen's son-in-law, which would give me a little more confidence that he had earned the right to this job. However, that may be unfair. The question is whether or not he can sell ads, and it is too early to tell. At least the one gathering of ad sales managers was a blunt, straight-talking meeting in which both Tony Mayer and [new publisher] Garry Valk announced that the days of excuses, bonuses based on seniority and lovableness rather than performance are over. An improvement over the past. I think the first step, when you are in trouble, is to share that information with the people who work for you. At least they know then where they stand and what is expected of them. And if it is done right, they will respond to adversity.

"The big mystery on the publishing side is Garry Valk—a lot of joking coupled with a ruthless approach to facts. He works hard and cuts through nonsense better than Jerry Hardy ever did, but I don't detect any serious interest in or commitment to the magazine except as a business problem to be solved. He is shrewd and tough, which God knows is essential, but I wonder if he cares what we print except in so far as it costs a sale or helps make one. The commitment will have to come from the edit side."

Graves wound up this long first entry in his journal with a determinedly cheerful summary of how strong he felt recent issues of the magazine had been. "First we had four straight weeks of *Khrushchev Remembers* [the journals of the deposed Soviet ruler], and no editor could ask for a bigger property or more good publicity. Also, unlike *Look* at the time of the William Manchester book [on the assassination of John F. Kennedy], we surrounded the Khrushchev articles with excellent stories, so that people who were paying attention to *Life* because of Khrushchev could see what a good magazine went with it." Glad for the chance to crow, Graves then mentioned two other issues that pleased him, one Phil Kunhardt had managed that consisted of the best pictures from a *Life*-sponsored photography contest ("probably the best and most important issue of the year because it showed a great commitment to excellent pictures"), the other called "The Shapes of America" ("isn't as good as the photography contest, but it has a lot of meat, some fine pictures and stories, and makes a general and rather optimistic statement about *Life*'s most important and continuing subject, the U.S. today"). He closed by referring to a conversation he'd just had with Kunhardt. "We both feel that things are in good shape editorially. As Phil said, the right people in the right jobs [I had returned to writing by this time], and the system is working. It has taken longer than I thought it would, and of course it is never finished, never stable."

Roughly speaking, Larry Burrows had always wanted to be a *Life* photographer, and the fact that he became one, one of the very best, did not diminish the job's value for him. Henry Frank Leslie Burrows, a gawky London kid with bad eyesight and a stutter, came to the magazine as a sixteen-year-old in 1942. He'd been working earlier as an errand boy and picture messenger for the *Daily Express*. Then, in the blitz-and-blackout years, he'd got a job in *Life's* London photo lab, where, before he'd been around long enough to be trusted with printing and developing, he was sent out to fetch tea and cheese rolls for the great photographers of the era who were passing through town. Among the heroes Burrows served were such famous picture journalists as Robert Capa, Dmitri Kessel, Robert Landry, Margaret Bourke-White and Ralph Morse, who were in and out of England on their way to dangerous assignments at one of the war fronts. The shy, intense Burrows often saw their photographs before the film was dry. Naturally he idolized them and began to model himself after them, taking from each what he needed to form himself. He noted how they talked, joked, dressed, ate and drank and smoked cigarettes. He noted their tastes and their values, how they dealt with waiters or reporters and with other photographers. But mostly he noted their pictures, how they took them, what kinds of equipment they used to get them, what lengths they were prepared to go to in order to make the pictures they needed.

This kind of early schooling by observation served Burrows tremendously well in the future. Over the years he became a highly skilled and versatile professional, far better rounded and organized to do his work than many of his colleagues. And, of course, his exposure to the war photographers especially gave him the beginnings of a sense of mission about his journalism that would lead him, almost thirty years later and another war, to making the choice that would kill him.

The darkroom tea boy's work for *Life* during the war was interrupted by a call to service. His bad eyes kept him out of the military, and with a lot of other young Englishmen he was sent to work in the coal mines to dig out fuel desperately needed for Britain's war industry. He came back to the lab in London whenever he had enough time off, and eventually, when the mining seemed to be damaging his health, he was released from His Majesty's underground service. Burrows then came back to the darkroom, where, in the recollection of *Time* correspondent Honor Balfour, he became considerably more useful to the war effort printing pictures of the Normandy invasion and the Allied march to the Rhine. Soon, with used cameras he bought from other photographers, he began taking pictures, and by the late 1940s he was getting free-lance assignments from *Life's* London bureau. From the start, he was energetic and resourceful and determined to get better pictures than anyone else covering the same story. "We need a little elevation," was a common Burrows admonition, and to make sure he could count on it, he often took a lightweight ladder along on stories. If there was no ladder, he would occasionally resort to climbing on the shoulders of a sturdy working companion.

Larry Burrows practiced his profession with rare thoroughness. Getting the smallest details just right absorbed him; he wanted to leave as little as possible to chance. He spent hours analyzing parade routes in advance to pick the sites where the most dramatic action might unfold. He studied the movements of his human subjects, whether it was Winston Churchill or an infantryman in Vietnam, for just the glance or tic that would convey the heart of the moment. Anticipating the work an art director would do later, he often took pads and sketched page layouts showing just how he thought his pictures should be used in the magazine. Refreshing himself in hot baths at night, he soaked to the neck and brooded in soapy silence about the next day's shooting. He even designed his own camera cases and clothing with extra pockets for film (he also carried film in the tops of his socks). He shaped and outfitted himself, in fact, to the ultimate goal of being an effective photojournalist, readier, if he could do anything about it, than the rest.

Though Burrows got along well with people assigned to the job with him, he preferred to be alone, Milton Orshefsky, a veteran *Life* reporter and editor who often worked with him, remembers. "One man was less of a target," Orshefsky recalls of Burrows's thinking. "A helicopter might have only one spare seat. [And] he didn't relish the possibility of a correspondent's words eating into the space his pictures might get. Frankly, he didn't approve of words, especially if it meant sacrificing his pictures." Yet when Burrows, working alone, produced his own captions, they were detailed and precise, just what the editors needed for the pictures.

His determination to dig into all aspects of his work gave Burrows extraordinary versatility as a photographer, unlike many others who became known—and pigeonholed and limited—only for their ability to handle a particular type of assignment. A lot of Burrows's best-known pictures, of course, were candid and shot under natural conditions. But he was a superb technician as well and was adept at assignments that called for big cameras and extremely complicated lighting. He was truly an expert, for example, at the very delicate work of copying paintings for reproduction, a job many magazine photographers dismiss as inglorious drudgery. But for Burrows the business of duplicating on film the exact shadings and color values of the original artists was appealing, and he learned a lot, too, from their painterly uses of composition, texture and light.

One of the finest color essays Burrows ever produced was the story he shot in 1967 of the temples at Angkor Wat in Cambodia. Hal Wingo, the *Life* correspondent who worked with Burrows for five weeks on the story, recalled that the photographer spent the first week simply studying the way the light at various hours of the day struck the objects that interested him. Only when he had calculated the exact instants to shoot did he begin to take pictures. Some of Angkor's most important bas-reliefs were always in shade, and Burrows elected to photograph them at night, using floodlights operated by portable generators. An obsessed sculptor with a camera instead of an ancient chisel, he could thus create new shadows that would best show off the ancient stone carvings.

"I am very happy with the equipment I have," Burrows once wrote about his large supply of photographic paraphernalia. "All I need is time and patience to use it to the fullest degree, plus God on my side to help with the lighting problem—to move the sun, the moon and the stars to the positions of my choice."

"When we got back to closing our first regular issue [of the year]," Graves wrote in his journal on January 24, "after four Khrushchev followed by two special issues, everybody was out of practice. Disciplines, even self-disciplines, can't be relaxed for such a long time and then be automatically reimposed. There was nothing basically late (last-minute pictures or substitution of a story), and no complicated legal or checking problems, and the last copy went through me at 8:00 [p.m.]. Just the same, the copy room didn't close until 4:00 a.m. A lot of the trouble was a spread editorial on Nixon, sent down for typesetting around 6:00. Tom Griffith [Ed Thompson's replacement, in charge of the editorials] went out for dinner and after that it was greening and fitting and jiggling type all night. Howard Hughes text also took a long time. However, between the Hughes letters [to his staff], Tricia Nixon, dying swan pictures and [assistant managing editor] Don Moser's good piece on DDT and birds, we came out with a fine issue. Hedley's comment: 'one of the best regular issues of *Life* ever published,' and he is not what anybody would call extravagant in his praise. With the current issue and the two year-end issues, he gives us 'three out of three.'

"On Jan. 19 we had a meeting in Hedley's office with Heiskell, Moser, [Richard] Clurman and me to hear a proposal from Steve Somebody, a pleasant young man who used to work in ad agencies and now works on the 34th floor publishing side. His idea was that we should do three or four or six one-hour TV specials a year featuring one photographer and one subject. His list included the baby, fashion, travel, the portrait, animals. His pitch was that photography was the country's

#1 hobby, and that we were the #1 exponent of the still picture. He thought it would be a natural for Eastman Kodak to sponsor. Moser and I explained to everybody that we happened to have an awfully good pilot film already shot: the next Alcoa Hour on The Photographers. It's five different photographers and five different subjects, but it certainly shows how Steve's idea could be put into practice. We all agreed that Eastman Kodak was *not* a good idea ('There goes the Polaroid account again,' said Don), and in any case Alcoa should have the first crack, contractually and ethically. Alcoa might love it: wholesome, non-controversial, American, dealing with people. We agreed to see the Alcoa show and then meet again. I did not say at this meeting what I have said to Hedley and Heiskell and others before: anything that helps move *Life* and Time Inc. in the film field is desirable, because I am convinced that in the long run the physical cost of paper, printing and distribution make the old-fashioned magazine a bad bet. However, what we put *in* our magazines now could be put on film or tape and distributed electronically. The problem is to start translating while we have the time and system. Toward the end of the meeting when we got to talking about how eager ad agencies and newspapers are to knock *Life*, Hedley smiled and said, 'Maybe we should start a modest little magazine that they could knock instead of *Life*. They could call it *Madison Avenue*.'

"Personnel excitement for the first few weeks: Bill Lambert went through another endless cycle of talks about leaving *Life* for *The New York Times*. This time, unlike last spring when the [Supreme Court Justice] Fortas story was still fresh in people's minds and a Pulitzer still a possibility, I would not have struggled to hold him. Still, he went through all the soul-searching and talks all over again before finally deciding to stay. That's great if he will now settle down and do some work. He really is the best investigative reporter I know, but in the last year he has done one story, Senator Tydings, and that wasn't very good. . . . Barry Farrell, after struggling for something like three months, maybe four, over his Bucky Fuller article, finally delivered a piece which, after discussion and editing with [articles editor] Steve Gelman, was delivered to me at something like 8000 words. I sent back a critique, praising the portrait of Fuller but quarreling firmly with the structure and the lack of essential information. Prompt note from Barry: 'Ralph: Here is another piece of my writing that you can dismiss after one swift reading. So long. I've had it.' Considerable anger on my part, followed by answer: 'Barry: That was one slow, careful reading. I have waited patiently for many weeks for your piece. If you had so much difficulty writing it, I don't see why I should not be permitted to have difficulties reading it. In any case, I certainly did. You want to talk or not?' Issue unresolved at this writing because Barry had family disaster and went off to Vermont to deal with it. However, he left word he did, indeed, want to talk. As far as I'm concerned, he has resigned in that note. It may well be that he ought to leave or go on contract. He is a marvelous writer, one of two or three best on the magazine, but a wretched producer. The fights we had over his column a year ago took a lot out of him, and it may be that he simply cannot work as a staff member.

"On Thursday afternoon, Jan. 21, before he left for ten days' vacation, Hedley called Griffith, Ajemian, Moser and me to his office (Kunhardt was out). He reported that at the day's board meeting budgets for the year had been presented and that the board had asked a number of questions about the projections for *Life*. (He didn't say what the projections were, but the last I heard a couple of weeks ago was that we might lose $17 million. As far as I know, only [assistant managing editor] Dave Maness and I on edit know this horrendous figure.) Hedley and Heiskell and Shepley all spoke to the board about *Life*. According to Hedley, there are four things that can improve *Life*'s position: 1) strong improvement in the economy and therefore in advertising in general; 2) a deterioration in the TV advertising position, which has been predicted for years on the basis of the programming, but which shows signs of coming to pass at last (Hedley cited one study in Atlanta which showed the people didn't remember what the commercials were for, and in fact were just as likely to name a rival brand as they were to name the actual advertiser); 3) the collapse of *Look* (they are going for very cheap, short-term subscriptions, indicating that they are trying to lower their total subscription liability so that they can go out of business in 1972; they are also cutting ad rates); 4) improved desirability of *Life*. Since #4 is the only one we can do anything about, that's the one we editors must concentrate on. Now if all four of these things happen, or even two or three of them, without *Life* showing improvement, then, said Hedley, 'we would have to admit that this is a pretty sick property.' We went on to discuss some other matters, including the best news of the year so far, a sale last week of 110 ad pages, the best week we've had in a year. A continuation of that kind of activity would cheer everybody immensely. After the meeting Tom Griffith and I had a short 'interpreting Hedley' discussion: we agreed that the board must have been very tough on *Life*, and that Hedley, Heiskell and Shepley have probably agreed that if we didn't get improvement, something would have to 'be done.'

"I suppose it's proper for Hedley to tell us how important it is that we do well with the magazine editorially," Graves reflected somewhat ruefully near the end of this entry, "and yet I must say that all of us know that pretty well already. Furthermore, according to Hedley's tally, we've actually had not three but nine first-class issues in a row. I hope we closed number ten on Wednesday night, but in spite of a strong lead on the crippled Vietnam boy [by Larry Burrows], an excellent article by Joan Barthel on Bob Hope, and good shorts on hot pants, the mercury poisoning and a couple of others, there is a hole you could drive a truck through: an eight-page art essay on the Lehman Collection, full of madonnas. It might have been okay just before Christmas, or at least better before Christmas, but it sure isn't much now. It didn't really nag at me until too late."

Graves wrote his next entry on January 27, on a night when he was actually engaged in putting the magazine to press. It had been a day— and a week—of frustrating problems. "A closing night," he wrote, "recorded in some irritation while waiting for final copy on an essay about the oil spills in San Francisco and New Haven. First, we had Averell Harriman writing about his trip to Russia, and after he had talked a very good story about how the Russians were loosening up, he wrote a bland and quite confusing story. After much back-and-forth work by [articles editor] Steve Gelman, we finally got a piece that says something—but not all that loud and not all that clear. While Harriman was being worked into shape, we encountered the George Romney problem. Romney had talked to Jim Shepley last week about [a Romney answer to] *Life's* editorial summing up Nixon's first two years. A first-class editorial widely admired all the way from Hedley to the Nixon-haters on the staff. The [Romney] piece itself is no problem: a polemic in favor of Nixon and against *Life's* editorial, and it makes not the slightest difference really whether it runs or doesn't, as far as content is concerned. But it meant that we had to find a single page to make room for it. We couldn't throw out the [Hugh] Sidey column, 1) because Sidey hasn't appeared during the last month, 2) because Sidey is good, 3) because Sidey has news to report on how Nixon is cozying up to Congress. I would cheerfully have thrown out the editorial, which was the only other loose page, but Hedley is determined that the editorial page must run regularly, at least during this period when it is being reinstated. So we wound up wrecking a four-page Parting Shots, compressing it into three unattractive pages, and in the end Romney will complain because his riposte is running in the back of the magazine. After all this, Shepley had the bright idea of putting a slash on the cover, celebrating Romney, two days after the cover closed. When he was told that wasn't possible, much less desirable, he wondered if we

couldn't say something in the editor's note. Possible but equally un-
desirable. Romney is hardly a plus; he is simply a fact, one I feel perfectly relaxed about running. However, I would as soon think of billing
[his piece] as I would a Tampax ad.

"Ugly little ad crisis: two or three months ago I was brought a
layout for a new kind of ad; the edit space would be the top half of one
page and the top quarter of the facing page; the ad would have the
bottom half of the whole spread, plus the upper right-hand quarter. I
really hate these bastard-shaped ads, and during the entire period I
was growing up here, *Life* simply refused them, even though other
magazines accepted way-out shapes—as *Life* ad salesmen always
pointed out to the editors. Those are long-past days. Anyway, I accepted
the ad, specifying that it had to run in the review area. Several weeks
ago I was presented with the same ad from the same company (Mercury), only now the edit space was the bottom of the spread. I said no,
that wasn't what I agreed to. Who knows, I might even have agreed to
that if I had been asked (I don't really think so), but in any case, I had
been asked for something else. When I blew up, I was told that if we
refused the ad at this point, after it had been sold and plated, we would
certainly lose the business, since the agency understood it was already
accepted. Well, who hath honor?—he that died o' Wednesday. So I
said all right, God damn it, and fired off a strenuous memo to the
Detroit ad manager, Burns Cody, with copies to Mayer and Valk, saying
that I had been jobbed and that 'I cannot do business this way, and I'm
surprised that you can.' Heartfelt apologies ensued from Cody, Garry,
Tony Mayer. Then Louise Hunkins, who had to bear the initial brunt
of my intransigence, brought down this same misbegotten spread [from
ad production] and said that they now wanted to run an insert card over
this remnant of edit integrity. I had previously agreed that we would
indeed run insert cards over edit material, but I thought this was too
much to ask. I told Louise that I had been screwed all I was willing to
be screwed on this particular spread, and the answer was no. Bringing
us to today when [General Manager] Pat Lenahan came down and
explained to me that to run this insert card anywhere else in the magazine would either cost $10,000 extra or bitterly offend another adver-
tiser (General Foods), who had recently been bitterly offended by
having their turkey dinner ad run against the DDT story about 'birds
with cancer.' I said why don't we not run the circulation card this week.
Pat said we need it. It's the best way we have to get renewals and new
circulation at good prices. So: having said I would accept the ad only
on a top-of-the-spread basis, and been jobbed on that, and then having
said I would absolutely not be screwed further, I said okay.

"And then came the oil spill story, which I consider totally and peculiarly my business. For openers, it involved Humble Oil and Standard of California, whose advertising we do not have now and, after an 8-page story, wouldn't get even if we said the oil spills in San Francisco and New Haven were harmless and perhaps even beneficial. So in business terms the coast was clear. But in editorial terms the coast was absolutely clear anyway: the spills were a major event, and the pictures George Silk shot were marvelous. Nevertheless, I think it is a fair charge against *Life* and against the press in general that in our enthusiasm for a hot journalistic subject, the rape of the environment, we had not been balanced, fair or even-handed in our reporting. It is very easy, emotionally and journalistically, to be on the side of the birds and the seals, as indeed I am. More so for animals than birds, but that is an animal-lover's prejudice. However, it is not simple and clear-cut. It is easy to be indignantly righteous about wildlife without acknowledging that is a complex problem. I am still going to be on the side of wildlife, which happens to matter to me a lot personally, but it is very important—for reasons having nothing to do with the publishing side—to be accurate and fair. The conclusion may be the same, but it is lousy reporting to be simply a bleeding heart bird-lover. I think we have done far better in our recent stories to present both sides, to realize that it is a complex problem, and still to support the land against damage. So we expect some hours getting a rewrite of the story, and I am sure that the people who were working on it thought I was trying to be 'nice' to an advertiser—who isn't an advertiser anyway. Which must simply be lived with."

A key to the almost astonished regard in which many held Larry Burrows is the fact that he didn't look at all like the model of an intrepid war photographer, the way Duncan did, with those amazing good looks, or Capa, whose cigarette was always trailing out of his mouth in Bogartian coolness. Burrows looked quite a lot like Wally Cox, the actor who played Mr. Peepers in the comedy series of the 1960s. With his glasses and long face the photographer seemed more like a worried householder near the edge of some perplexing and possibly humiliating surprise than a man who would expose himself to hostile fire on jungle patrols or in the open doorways of helicopters.

In one recollection of Burrows written for the London *Observer,* a British war correspondent named Gavin Young said: "He had extraordinary modesty and courtesy. He was especially brave because, I think, he was frequently nervous. From the Congo to Vietnam, I have seen his lanky, nonchalant figure amble into a dozen hair-raising war situations in the last 10 years, and been comforted by the sight of it. Although he worked with the American magazine *Life*, he was an Englishman and remained ultra-British in manner and accent. He carried British understatement to the point of parody. In a Saigon restaurant one night, after we had returned from one of the bloodiest battles in Vietnam, a young American correspondent on his way there asked Larry what it had been like. 'Quite lively,' Larry drawled, with no conscious affectation. 'You want to be a little bit careful.'"

The gentle manner, the low-keyed analysis, even the nervousness, masked a steely determination to get the job done right. The occasional drollery was more an accurate reflection of what Burrows really thought than it was an expression of his sense of humor, which was unremarkable. One man who worked with him often said he couldn't conceive of Burrows falling into a depression or some other kind of funk about the things he saw happening all around him. "He reacted with his camera," the colleague recalled. "The feelings went right through him and came out on the film." And there was a kind of implacability about Burrows as he got on with his work; he wasn't going to be deflected by anything.

This single-minded absorption was largely confined to his photography. Although he was very attached to his wife and two children and often spoke happily and sentimentally of the times they were "all four under one roof" in their home on Hong Kong's South Bay, he was impatient with domestic chores and surprisingly was not, in his wife's recollection, at all a handy man around the house. "Do you think he ever opened a car engine and looked in it?" she asked rhetorically. "No. 'If it doesn't work,' he'd say, 'let the mechanic fix it.'" Yet he was a perfectionist at home and liked, for example, to have his dresser drawers arranged in an absolutely fixed and fastidious way.

Burrows was always ready to leave home on short notice. Like many of the best journalists, he always had an ear cocked for the phone call, the cable from New York or the news bulletin that would break into the fragile comfort of his domestic life and hurl him out into the world he loved best. Such interruptions were a kind of rescue, really, no matter how much discomfort or danger they brought. "He could pack ten or twelve cases for a major assignment," his son Russell recalled, "and be ready to leave for the airport within about half an hour."

His obsessive commitment to covering the war in Vietnam, of course, took precedence over everything else. In spite of the broadest variety of assignments during the nine years he'd been living in the Far East after moving from London, Vietnam remained his basic preoccupation. In response to a query about just that from editors who wanted to quote Burrows in a little biographical note about him in one 1966 issue of the magazine, he wrote: "You asked for my thoughts, so here goes. The Vietnam conflict is without doubt a puzzle to many, to me a challenge, and my only hope is that my photographs give people a closer understanding of the many facets of this miserable little war. If I were 20, then I could be accused of glory-seeking bravado, but at 40 I like to think that I have contributed a small service to people through my chosen medium." His somewhat stilted, touching words honestly reflected his enthusiasm and devotion. "Be it exotic meetings with Madame Nhu, sleeping on a stretcher with a Vietnamese patrol, being trussed like a turkey in a Phantom jet, or sharing a sack of rice with the Special Forces, this war, strange as it is, fascinated me, and my deepest wish is to be around to photograph both South and North Vietnam in peaceful times. Amen, Roger, and out."

The duty Burrows obviously felt about reporting on Vietnam worried his bosses a lot. They knew the risks for him were high—though his competence was so apparent that other journalists kept track of his movements on the job to minimize the danger for themselves—and knew that his survival this far, after literally scores of assignments under bad combat conditions, was little short of miraculous. They tried, in fact, to keep him busy with other work. (In a futile admonition, he'd been told he could keep living in Hong Kong, as he wanted, if he just would stay out of the war zone in Vietnam.) Burrows was on such a job in early February 1971 in Calcutta, actually quite a risky job having to do with corruption among officials there, when he heard a report over the portable radio he always carried with him that the South Vietnamese had moved into Laos. His sense of duty called. He packed up and left Calcutta the next morning.

Graves's next entry, for February 10, 1971, marks what was one of the saddest and most difficult of days for him and his colleagues. "Wednesday morning, closing day," Graves wrote. "At 8:30 in the morning I get a phone call at home from Murray Gart [Time Inc.'s chief of correspondents]: there is a cable in the wire room about Larry Burrows being shot down in a helicopter over Laos. I should call the cable room and have the text read to me. All of us have talked so many, many times about the danger that Larry goes through in Vietnam that it does not come as a particular shock. I call the cable room and get details: a wire from *Life* Correspondent John Saar beginning, 'I have to tell you the appalling news that . . .' Larry and four other photographers [were] flying across the border in a squadron of five helicopters . . . Four of the five helicopters got lost, wandered north and ran into heavy anti-aircraft fire. One helicopter exploded in mid-air. A second was hit, crashed and burned. Nobody knows which one Larry was in, but an aerial survey showed bodies and no sign of any survivors. 'Barring a miracle,' Saar says, 'he is almost certainly dead.'

"This isn't the first *Life* photographer or writer to be killed that I know. Terry Turner long ago on a plane crash in the Rockies. More recently Bob Capa in Indochina, and much more recently, Paul Schutzer in the Israeli Six-Day War. But I didn't know any of them well. Larry is a real friend, Eleanor and I knew him and Vicky Burrows well, and Larry Burrows is a *major Life* figure, one of the top four or five names on the staff, and revered by us all as an extraordinarily brave and wonderful man. I am to learn later in the day that he had spent nine years covering this war.

"I want right away to tell a few people that I think have to know, not so much because they can do anything but because they should know about Larry. Eleanor is taking a shower and I don't tell her— really because I don't yet want to face telling her until I have practiced telling someone else. I try to catch Phil Kunhardt at home, but he has just left for the train; I tell Katharine instead. Then I call George Hunt and get him and tell him. We don't say much: George has known even longer than I have that this might happen. I call Don Moser, who knew Larry well in Hong Kong, and Don has already heard from somebody else. The same compassionate, understood-in-advance lack of anything to say. I finally have to tell Eleanor, which is terrible to do.

"And then it is time to think, as one must, about what to do with the magazine, which is going to close tonight. Two days ago we had received an excellent piece by John Saar describing an incident that he and Larry had seen on the Laos border: they had been present during the accidental bombing of South Vietnamese and U.S. troops at Langvei by a U.S. plane. John told the story of that night, the shock of the attack, the scores of wounded and the handful of dying. He also described Larry's reaction: as soon as the bombs hit, Larry is moving toward the wounded, shooting pictures in impossible conditions. Larry gets John to help him bring in a wounded man, dying, who bleeds all over both of them. It is a harrowing night, one of those minor horrors of war seen close up by a good writer and a good photographer. However, Larry's film was delayed getting to us, and we still haven't seen it. We are due to get it first thing this morning, and because it is Wednesday, past our color deadline, we were planning to convert it to black and white.

"All right: step one—we have billed Alan Shepard and Apollo 14 on the cover [Shepard's crew had just returned from the moon], expecting to make that a lead. Now I have to find out if I can get the Shepard billing off the cover, because if Larry's pictures are in, we will go as far as we can with them, and Shepard has to come down in size and will not be the lead. The answer is yes: we can get the Shepard billing off the cover. Second question: can we bill Larry on the cover? Technically, the answer is yes, but I decide very quickly that, given the cover picture itself, a romantic Valentine picture of old movie stars, announcing a special half issue on nostalgia, any billing about Larry's death would be completely inappropriate. The thing to do is take Shepard off the cover, substitute nothing in his place, and do Larry inside: his story plus an editor's note. Question three: in this extraordinary situation, can we get color capacity on Wednesday, a day after deadline, and if so, how much can we get and how much will it cost? I'll find out all that at the office. I try to call Hedley to let him know about Larry, but his phone is busy three times, and I give up. (The rest of the day is so frantic that I don't try again. He and I don't talk about it until Thursday morning—a day too late.)

"One of the great things about *Life* is that when things are really in crisis, there is no horseshit. I'm in the office at 9:30, and only [news-bureau manager] Lucy Kelly and [picture editor] Ron Bailey are on hand. Our behavior to each other in those first minutes is what happens all over the staff all through that day: each of us knows—and takes for granted that the others know—that we have sustained a personal tragedy and a massive professional loss. We know that and proceed to do what we have to do without any wailing or keening or wringing of hands. It is the opposite of an absence of feeling; we all feel so deeply and know that everyone else does that it would be both a waste of time and an obscenity to go on about it. Everybody knows what everybody else feels.

"John Saar is still in Saigon, so a number of us troop down to the telex [room] to talk to him by typewriter. We agree by typewriter that Saar should reach Vicky and tell her, he being the last to see Larry and the only one to know any details first hand.

"Back upstairs we learn that we will see Larry's last rolls of film around noon. We also learn that we can handle up to four pages of color, provided we can get both transparencies and layouts to Chicago by 4:00 p.m., for a premium of $16,000. Money always counts: $16,000 is only the premium; we also have to pay $3000 a page for color, and this issue—because of the nostalgia package—is already way over budget. This is another of the easy decisions of the day: spend it. (In the end, this issue will be $64,000 over budget; one of the joys of staying under budget is that you can afford to shoot it when you need it. We were $60,000 under budget going into this issue.)

"A call comes in from John Saar in Saigon. He has talked to Vicky, but the transmission was so bad that they could not hear each other about any details. Vicky simply knows, in some garbled fashion, that Larry has been shot down and things look bad. I now get real details from John: the U.S. command had refused to take any press over Laos because it was technically a South Vietnamese operation. Larry and the other photographers had got onto a South Vietnamese helicopter tour of 'our' bases in Laos. The helicopter got lost in a way that, John says, U.S. helicopters never would have. He talked to a U.S. general in detail: there are no visible survivors, and it will take troops at least a week to get to the scene of the wreckage. John asked: is there any hope? General Sutherland said, there is always hope. John says, I'm afraid that's a joke. His best estimate is that there is absolutely no hope. This is my reading too.

"The next call is from Vicky. Vicky grew up in China; she is, like Larry, a British citizen. She is a strong-minded, outspoken, powerful woman. For nine years she has lived with Larry's exposure to constant danger. Beyond that, she is really the empress of the *Time-Life* Hong Kong bureau. Larry was always away and cared only about his work in any case. For the last three years she has had cancer of the throat. Reports have varied between Vicky is much better and there is no hope for Vicky. Cobalt treatments, surgery, etc. This is the woman who comes on the phone to hear details about her husband's presumed death.

"Vicky sounds very much herself, under control, wanting to know details. I tell Vicky what I know, withholding only one fact, that one of the two lost helicopters exploded in mid-air. Nobody knows whether that was Larry's helicopter; if it was, there is no hope whatsoever. I don't think there is any hope whatsoever anyway, but I simply tell her that two copters crashed and burned and that there are no signs of any survivors. Vicky takes it in, all the information. I then say that we want to send somebody out, and Vicky cuts in, very much herself: 'Larry always said that they should engrave on my tombstone, "She coped." I'm going to cope. It would be silly to send anybody out.' The only break in this incredible dike is that Vicky admits that if anybody, any-body at all, should come out to Hong Kong, it should be her son Russell, who has just graduated from college in California. For Vicky, this is a massive admission.

"Larry's pictures come in and they are marvelous. We race through selection: ten best transparencies go down for paper negs, and we know we have to work very fast to meet deadline. I find out we can expand from four pages of color to six. Meantime we have prepared a one-spread and a two-spread version of Shepard. L.A. has had an earthquake with some 50 dead, and we are holding open the possibility of a spread on that. Don Moser is writing an editor's note on Larry. Phil Kunhardt and Ron Bailey are working on a retrospective essay of Larry's best pictures for the following week's issue, which will have to close one day later.

"All this gets pulled together and closed at a reasonable time late Wednesday night. I go home around midnight with the magazine out of the way, and talk to Eleanor in bed about how I feel. How I feel is that I should go to Hong Kong, not really for Vicky, who really can cope, but because of how I feel about Larry."

The journal entry for the next day, February 11, was very short. "At the Thursday morning scheduling meeting I say that I am going to be in Hong Kong next week and that Don Moser will be editing in my place. In the course of the day I get visits from Phil, Loudon and Mary Leatherbee saying how glad they are that I am going. Mary says: 'I felt so good about it. It said *Life* cares.' At lunch that day Louis Banks said, with admiration, 'That's a typical *Life* beau geste.' I do not want to take any special credit for caring or for beau geste-ing, but I know that it is absolutely right. Larry Burrows gave everything he could to *Life*, and we should say thank you."

The terrible pressures of the war were more painful for Burrows than he usually let on. For one thing, he was acutely embarrassed by the raw invasions of privacy he had to commit when other men were dying. "It's not easy to take a shot of a man crying," he told Don Moser, who'd worked with him in Vietnam, "as though you have no thoughts, no feelings as to his sufferings." Such ultimate intimacy bothered him a lot and often. At another time he said about pictures he'd made of a dying marine after a helicopter mission: "I was torn between being a photographer and the normal human feelings. It's not easy to photograph a pilot dying in a friend's arms and later to photograph the breakdown of a friend. I fought with my conscience. Was I simply capitalizing on someone else's grief?" Of course, the ironic fact is that the most telling war photography (and the photography of other human disasters) depends on the unblinking exploitation of suffering. But Burrows's powerful sense of propriety sometimes overruled his virtually instinctual drive to get the best pictures. According to Moser, there were times when Burrows "would turn away from a scene of human grief out of his concern that his presence would aggravate the feelings of those involved."

This pervasive delicacy cropped up in other situations. In 1968 he'd photographed Tron, a ten-year-old girl who'd lost her leg in the war. Then two years later he did a story about another youngster, Lau, who'd just returned to his village after having been to the United States for treatment of his wound-caused paraplegia. In both cases Burrows took great care, as much as he liked these kids and wanted to shower attention on them, to keep a certain distance from these two pitiful victims of the war. He told friends that he was afraid that they would form strong attachments for him—and that then they'd lose this odd, foreign uncle with the cameras the way they'd lost just about everything else.

Very shortly before he took the South Vietnamese helicopter to his death (his compassion for the Vietnamese did not increase his confidence in their flying ability and he always tried to fly with U.S. pilots), Burrows and correspondent John Saar were helping to carry an ARVN soldier who'd been fatally wounded by a misdropped American bomb. As Saar recalled it, the dying man "let out a groan of terrible pain. The groan was echoed immediately and instinctively by Larry."

The last time the two men spoke was just hours later, when Saar was about to leave for Saigon so he could ship Burrows's most recent film to New York. These were Burrows's last pictures, and gaunt and exhausted, he was fretting about that most mundane of all photographic concerns—how the pictures would come out. "Don't forget to tell them," he called out to Saar, "that the light was absolutely marginal."

The next entry in Graves's diary is an inclusive one for the dates February 15–20. "Trip to Hong Kong," he wrote, "including 22 hours on the plane going out and 20 on the plane coming back, and not much sleep while I'm there. Still, I can't imagine a better-spent week. I know it helped Vicky to have someone there who admired and understood Larry professionally, because Larry cared passionately about his work and put the highest premiums on it. Vicky was tremendous, and Russell too. Memorial service for Larry at the cathedral; neither Vicky nor Larry could be called anything but an agnostic, so the service was really in honor of Larry for the sake of his Hong Kong friends. Vicky a bit nervous, hoping she wouldn't break up during the eulogy by Dick Hughes [an Australian journalist who was a friend of Vicky and Larry's], but she did fine, as anyone could have predicted. I had said, both in the note about Larry to the staff and in the editor's note in the magazine: 'I do not think it is demeaning to any other photographer in the world for me to say that Larry Burrows was the single bravest and most dedicated war photographer I have ever known.' This was quoted in Hughes's eulogy—except that the word 'war' was left out. I wonder if Vicky had edited it out. She had said several times that Larry was much more than a war photographer, which of course is true."

"I arrived back," Graves wrote on February 22, "to find that although [Lieutenant William] Calley was testifying this week in the Mylai massacre trial [American troops had slaughtered 102 Vietnamese villagers on March 16, 1968], no plan existed to close a story on him. We had to gear up a lead quite hastily. Fortunately, the artist had completed his paintings of Calley on the stand in the courtroom, of the jury, and of Calley himself, so we were able to close these along with two of the original Mylai massacre pictures and a couple of pictures of Calley offstage in Fort Benning. We also ran an extremely effective box showing what had happened to each of the 24 people who had been charged with either murder or covering up the event afterward. Name after name: 'charges dismissed.' At the time we went to press, 20 out of the 24 had either been acquitted (only two of these, I think) or had had charges dismissed. One wonders if it will finally be 24 out of 24."

"One of those superlatively unpleasant days," began the entry for February 23, "where not only do things go wrong, but they go wrong with unattractive overtones. One of the leftover stories from our January special issue on the New Shape of America was a round-up of individual efforts to clean up the environment. At the time that we decided to [delay] the story, I asked Dick Stolley to get a trailer of things that each citizen could do to improve the environment. Sounded harmless enough: I expected it to say things like use white toilet paper because colored toilet paper is non-biodegradable.

"The trailer text reached me Monday evening, and it was a very curious mixture indeed. They were all one-sentence items ranging from the sensible-and-serious (don't use pesticides, support and take part in ecology organizations) and the sensible-but-not-very-serious (use both sides of pieces of paper, never run the dishwasher half full) to the silly (save on paper towels by using shirt cardboards to drain bacon, put beer in a saucer in your garden to attract slugs to their death instead of pesticiding them). Anyway, I killed a number of items as silly or insignificant, cleared up some others. But there was one item that looked like real trouble: refuse to accept junk mail, return it to sender, lodge a protest with your postmaster. Time Inc. sends out millions and millions of pieces of mail each year; the Book Division operation is based

entirely on mail order, as well as a tremendous amount of magazine
subscriptions. Now I think of 'junk mail' in very specific terms: third
class flyers and unsealed envelopes addressed to 'Occupant.'

"I reached Pat Lenahan, the General Manager, warned him of the
problem and told the copy room to send him a copy of the edited text.
Half an hour later Pat was down in my office along with Garry Valk,
and I called in Dick Stolley. Pat was upset about the automobile section.
I found it innocuous and said so. Garry was very concerned about all
the paper items: don't use paper towels or napkins when you can avoid
it, etc. As Garry said, how are we going to reply to, say, the Scott Paper
Co. when they point out that Time Inc. must be the greatest paper
polluter in the country, shipping out some 15 million magazines a week?
Both Garry and Pat thought the junk mail item was impossible. I suggested we change it to: 'Refuse to accept mail addressed to "Occupant."'
We went through all the items in this fashion, and I sent Dick Stolley
off to do a crash rewrite, which I promised to send to Garry and Pat.
Then I put in a call to Hedley's secretary. It was beginning to sound
like something the editor-in-chief better know about.

"I saw Hedley an hour later and handed him the copy as revised
by Stolley. Hedley read it through and shook his head. He said it struck
him as a random, unimportant way to offend just about every conceiv-
able advertiser at a time when not only *Life* but Time Inc. as a whole
was fighting for magazine survival. Hedley asked why there wasn't some
kind of early warning system that could have prepared us for this. Was
there anything in the scheduling memo? Which made me sore: I said
yes there was something in the memo, but beyond that, I had told him
personally that we were going to do this trailer, many weeks ago.

"There wasn't much question in either of our minds that we ought
to drop it. Hedley said, 'When we are fighting to keep *Life* alive to do
really important things, this can't be justified.' With which I must agree.
However, there was no way to prevent [killing the trailer] from being
a terribly embarrassing event. This is the kind of thing that will be
passed around the staff, and it will come out—despite Dick's and my
concern and explanation—that the publishing side imposed a decision
on the editorial side. The fact that it is untrue may make no difference.

"Twice in the last year and a half I have thought that it might
become necessary for me to resign as managing editor over editorial
principle (once over Norman Mailer's article on the Astronauts, once
over Bill McWhirter's piece on the telephone company), but both
[questions] were resolved in my favor before the subject got all that
close. This time no such possibility arose in my mind, even though I
had been the one to suggest the ecology handbook. It was neither good

enough nor important enough to warrant such a stand. But it sure leaves a bad taste."

Graves's final item in the journal, written on March 1, found him worrying about the departure of staff members, a prospect he had often welcomed in these lean and increasingly desperate years. "Last week Paul Trachtman, an assistant articles editor," he wrote, "said he was leaving *Life* to live in Vermont and work on a novel that he had almost finished. An intelligent and attractive man but not a force on the magazine. Then Ron Bailey, perhaps the most crucial member of the next generation of editors, said that he had been asked to come to *Playboy*, which he didn't much want to do, but that he wasn't getting enough out of his job as Pollard's assistant, he wasn't making enough impact on the magazine, he wasn't making enough money, and he and his family didn't like New York. I told him he was down for a substantial raise, that he wouldn't like either *Playboy* or Chicago, and that he could have as much impact on the magazine as he was prepared to seize. This is an important holding action. The loss of Ron Bailey, the first top-notch picture editor in ten years, would be terrible both for the magazine and the staff.

"Today, John Neary came in to say that he was leaving. This is the only person to leave since I came in as m.e. that strikes me as a genuine loss. For all the others, I either wanted them to leave or didn't mind their leaving. John is a good all-purpose writer of picture stories, parting shots, leads, anything, and also a good writer of three or four articles a year. He says he likes *Life* and the people he works with, mostly [his editor] Chuck Elliott, and he feels fine about me, but he just doesn't like the life anymore and thinks he is old enough to do something more with himself. He hopes still to write pieces for us on contract and even come in to write picture stories in emergencies, but he wants to live somewhere else and do something more with his writing."

But these departures, or threats to depart, amounted to little next to the death of Larry Burrows. It wasn't just that the magazine lost a fine photographer, a superb craftsman who brought his high motivation and skill to every job. There were others who did that, though few if any could have been as brave. It was more that Burrows, though very much an Englishman, had somehow sprung from the fabric of the great American magazine. *Life*, in a way, had been the making of him, and he had returned the gift many times. Without him, the magazine was missing part of itself, and for Graves and his colleagues the loss was very heavy.

19

The Clifford Irving Caper

ONE OF THE NIGHTMARES OF JOURNALISM, like the threat of icebergs to ships at sea, is to get caught in a hoax. Such aberrant fortune focuses attention on the frailty of the hoaxed, on his gullibility, on his cupidity, on his fractured vanity. That comfortable sense of editorial poise, of well-being, of omnipotence nurtured over the years at clubby meetings and luncheons where editors gather to reinforce their mistaken sense of control over events, vanishes in a scalding fondue of dismay, anger and embarrassment. When it's all over, the victims of a good hoax feel both diminished and dumb—and rightly so.

As *Life* lurched to the end of 1971, what the magazine didn't need at all was to become the butt of a huge national joke. Even in the traditionally strong holiday season, the issues were painfully thin. The editorial staff had been cut back another 20 percent during the preceding twelve months, losses for the previous year had been over $10 million and Time Inc.'s management was choking over all manner of drastic options for money-saving change—reduced page size, lighter paper, fortnightly appearance. So the fraud brought off with such amazing success by the beguiling and fast-footed Clifford Irving carried a particularly heavy punch. Utterly seduced by Irving, *Life* bought a handsome share of his purported "autobiography" of the rich and reclusive Howard Hughes and thus got sucked into the most brazen journalistic hoax that anyone could remember. To make things worse, the editors and various other concerned magazine executives held on to their most hopeful convictions about the Hughes story for too long, even in the face of furious denials by the subject of the work itself.

From start to finish, in fact, the Irving caper was loaded with a laughable abundance of ingredients for a big, continuing national story about deception and ineptitude at the highest levels of the corporate world—code names, purloined manuscripts, handwriting experts, lie detector tests, weird coincidence, a big collection of witting and unwitting accomplices including a beautiful singing baroness with a memory for love that was much too good. And at the top of the whole thing—or more correctly the bottom—was the artful hoax master himself, a bold literary bandit whose sound sense of plot, steely nerve and outrageous luck led him to put one over, a huge one, on some of the coolest heads in American publishing. Except for his own ravening need for applause and recognition, Clifford Irving might even have escaped capture with a healthy piece of the boodle. Taken altogether, under less intimate circumstances the Irving affair would have made a wonderul story in *Life*.

Actually *Life* was just a co-dupe in the matter. First and best fooled was the big New York firm of McGraw-Hill, whose public relations office put out a release on December 7, 1971, announcing the publication a few months hence of the autobiography of Howard Robard Hughes, the multimillionaire aircraft designer, industrialist, hot pilot, movie mogul, all-purpose tycoon and mystery man who had been deep in an exile of his own ingenious making for more than ten years. For much more than that length of time, Hughes stories of one sort or another had held a deep attraction for many American journalists. His enormous wealth, his unmeasured power, his secrecy, his litigious combativeness, his paranoia and assorted eccentricities all conspired to make reporters want to track him down, see him, talk to him, find out all about him. Thus Howard Hughes became a mythical figure to a lot of the press, even though most Americans probably didn't care much about him, and the least important rumors and idly planted speculations about him carried a special resonance and significance.

The McGraw-Hill announcement, therefore, was big news. Now Hughes, for the first and only time, would be telling his whole fascinating story in the pages of a single 230,000-word volume. In emphatic words said to come from the great man's own preface to the book, the release offered: "I believe that more lies have been printed and told about me than about any living man—therefore it was my purpose to write a book which would set the record straight and restore the balance. . . . Call this autobiography. Call it my memoirs. Call it what you please. It is the story of my life in my own words." Assisting Hughes on the project was Clifford Irving, a man Hughes had selected for the job because of "outstanding qualities of sympathy, discernment, and, as I learned, his integrity as a human being." The real author of these touching words about himself presumably maintained a straight face through the shower of praise. Prior to book publication, the release announced, *Life* would publish three installments of 10,000 words each drawn from the work.

Staff members of *Life* got the good news that day from Ralph Graves, who called a meeting in the layout room next to his office. His delight was obvious. "We got it," he kept saying to various people in the overflow crowd, "we got it," and indeed there was in this meeting the sense that a real Hughes autobiography (in his alleged preface, Hughes had mentioned other "misleading and childish" biographies) was simply the finest buy that a red-blooded journal could make, and that *Life* was damned lucky to have it.

Graves was clearly relieved, too, to be able to end some of the secrecy that had surrounded the project. It had been called "Octavio," a name, according to Irving, that the endlessly conspiring Hughes (whose name, for code lovers, begins with the eighth letter of the alphabet) had given himself, and only a handful of Time Inc. people other than Graves had known anything about it. One of these was David Maness, who was Graves's administrator and a magazine journalist of competence and thirty years' experience. Early on, Maness, when asked for an appraisal of Irving's writing ability, had characterized him as "an untalented schmuck." But even the dour Maness had been impressed by the apparent authenticity of the reams of first-person material produced by the peripatetic Irving, who allegedly had captured it all on tape in the course of interviews with Hughes held in various cars and motels "throughout the Western Hemisphere."

Even the most boring parts of it were interesting, reported Graves. He obviously hoped, as did even the most skeptical of his listeners, that the Hughes installments would give the magazine new credibility and a fresh excitement, which in the proper large doses might just stimulate a real resurgence for *Life*. Before the meeting broke up, a wry joke was passed around about the possible aptness of the date, which was the thirtieth anniversary of the Japanese attack on Pearl Harbor. Whatever effect the Irving hoax really had on *Life*'s future, on December 8, 1972, exactly a year and a day later, the staff would meet again to hear that it was all over, that *Life* was done.

The magazine's interest in the Hughes book had begun much earlier, eight months before the public announcement, when a McGraw-Hill editor named Beverly Loo first broached the subject to Ralph Graves over lunch in a pretentious restaurant on New York's West Side. She and Graves had had business dealings in the past; they trusted each other. But this was bigger than anything they'd ever discussed before, Loo advised Graves, and she could tell him about it only if he promised to hold the information in the strictest secrecy. And if he was interested, only the barest few of his colleagues could be told. Graves agreed. He liked a good secret—it was one of the perks of his job.

Loo's story was interesting indeed. A McGraw-Hill author named Clifford Irving had won unique access to Howard Hughes. As Irving told it to his publishers, he first sent a copy of his most recent book (a story, entitled *Fake!*, about an art forger) to Hughes with a brief note saying they once met long ago, on the set of one of Hughes's pictures, where Irving's father had taken his screen-struck nine-year-old. Amazingly, Hughes sent back a cordial thanks, saying that he recalled Irving's father and was sorry to learn of his recent death. One little thing led to another, or so Loo had been conned into believing, until Hughes actually began to consider making Irving his biographer. "I am not entirely insensitive to what journalists have written about me," went a letter Irving had supposedly received from Hughes, "and for that reason I have the deepest respect for your treatment of de Hory [the art forger]. I do not question your integrity and I would not expect you to question mine.

"It would not suit me to die without having certain misconceptions cleared up and without having stated the truth about my life. The immortality you speak of does not interest me, not in this life. I believe in obligations. I regret many things in the past, but I have little feelings of shame about them.

"I would be grateful if you would let me know when and how you would wish to undertake the writing of the biography you propose. . . . Sincerely yours, H. R. Hughes."

The editors at McGraw-Hill were more enchanted by the whole scam than Irving could have dreamed, and by the time Graves had lunch with Loo, Irving and the publishing house had signed a $500,000 contract calling for "an untitled authorized biography of 'H' (Señor Octavio) with a preface by 'H.'" McGraw-Hill agreed there would be no publicity about the project until thirty days after the acceptance of a completed manuscript. This was especially important, Irving told his gaga marks. The skittish Hughes would cancel out if there were leaks. The delay also gave Irving a nice cushion of time to make off with the money.

Loo asked Graves if he had any interest in buying magazine rights for this meaty-sounding property. He did, of course, have terrific in-

·terest, though he made no offer at the time. But three months later, on July 21, 1971, *Life* agreed to pay McGraw-Hill a total of $250,000 for world first serial rights for a work that by this time had become thought of as a Hughes "autobiography." The payments wouldn't be completed until actual publication, and, in what turned out to be a vital reservation, McGraw-Hill would have to repay *Life* if Hughes did not authorize the book. But it was an extremely big deal for the magazine nonetheless, reminiscent, if not quite up to the giddy scale of the Churchill and Truman purchases of the past. It had an emphatic, confident thunk to it, as these two publishing giants put the legal finishing touches on an arrangement they felt sure would do well for them both. Not to mention Dell Publishing, which three months later agreed to buy the paperback rights for $400,000, or the Book-of-the-Month Club, which came aboard with an offer of $350,000. There was profit to be made here for all, it seemed, especially Clifford Irving, who would share nicely in everything.

Right after his meeting with Beverly Loo, the enthusiastic Graves, a man who always liked to keep current with the details of his job, wrote to Gedeon de Margitay, his Paris-based syndication chief, to try to get a line on how valuable the foreign serial rights for a Hughes biography might be. "The book will be very personal," Graves advised, "—why he lives the way he does, his personal phobias, etc.—but will also cover his big business deals. It will probably not deal with the women in his life, other than in the most gentlemanly and peripheral way." Obviously Irving was being fastidious in behalf of his client; the syndication man thought European journals would be most interested in the subject.

Graves also asked David Maness to see if he could find out anything about Clifford Irving in the Time Inc. morgue. "No vital stats at all," Maness wrote. "The possibility that he may have originally come from the Isle of Man. A clip referring to author Clifford Irving who became involved in protests about flogging students on the Isle. Could be another Clifford Irving, I suppose." Maness included in his report reviews of Irving's several books, one of them *Fake! The Story of Elmyr de Hory, the Greatest Art Forger of Our Time,* of which *Time* said: "An exuberant collage of skillful innuendo, succulent gossip, bitchery and elusive truths." No warning lights went on.

The object of the search was in fact born in New York in 1930, the only child of Dorothy and Jay Irving, a cartoonist whose most popular character was Pottsy, a cop. Young Clifford went to high school in Manhattan, and then—tall (six feet four), handsome and most successful with the girls—to Cornell University, where he began to consider the possibilities of writing. He got married in his senior year, at twenty, but two years later that marriage, his first of four, was over.

He traveled around the United States in various jobs—selling Fuller brushes in one—and writing in his spare time. Ernest Hemingway was one of his heroes. Early on, he completed a couple of novels—his first was called *On a Darkling Plain*—and discovered, in 1953, the delights of the Balearic islands, near Spain, especially the island of Ibiza. On that island he met his second wife, and the young Irvings began spending a lot of time in California, where Clifford, who had a short-lived interest in the beat movement, fluttered on the fringes of the Hollywood film community.

In the early 1960s, Irving, with his third wife and son, left Hollywood and went back to Ibiza, where he settled into the leisurely island life and the pleasures of being a member of its artistic community. There he began a long and ultimately ruinous affair with Nina van Pallandt, a pretty Danish folk singer who was married to a Dutch baron. There, too, among that tempting international smorgasbord of Ibiza, he met Edith Sommer, a twenty-eight-year-old Swiss painter with two young daughters and a divorce in the works. In 1967, after a courtship that included jeep rides through Israel in the wake of the Six-Day War, they were married. By the time Clifford had his big idea in late 1970, the Irvings had two new sons and were living more or less harmoniously in Edith's comfortable *finca* four miles outside the town of Ibiza.

By Irving's own account, he got the idea after reading an article about Hughes in *Newsweek* in December 1970. To a friend and fellow American named Richard Suskind, Irving first outlined a plan in which the publisher would be a party to the hoax. But he quickly discarded that as outlandish and worked out a scheme whose success depended on McGraw-Hill getting utterly sucked in. Suskind, a big, beefy man who lived on nearby Mallorca and was having trouble with a book he was writing about Richard the Lion-Hearted, got excited about the prospects; his experience as a researcher would be helpful in digging up material about their unwary subject. The success of the plan, according to Irving's extraordinarily dicey rationalization, would depend largely on Hughes's failure to respond to the news of his biography. That was possible, of course. He was notorious for his unpredictability. Deeply fearful about and involved in the litigation of more important matters, secluded and in hiding in the Bahamas (or, by some rumors, possibly even dead), Hughes, so Irving wrote, "would never be able to surface to deny it, or else he wouldn't bother."

As the fraud evolved, Irving then got in touch with Beverly Loo, who had been his editor on earlier books, and began to bait her with tales about writing to Hughes and starting to get the great man's interest in a biography. Early in 1971, when Irving returned to the States for his mother's funeral, he dropped in at the offices of McGraw-Hill, where the top editors were already so titillated about the moneymaking possibilities that they'd instructed Irving to drop the novel he was working on and concentrate on the mystery man holed up in the Bahamas. As the clincher, Irving brought to New York three letters he had supposedly received from Hughes, along with "copies" of the letters he claimed he'd mailed to the Bahamas. Irving's forgeries, handwritten on lined yellow legal paper, had been crafted from the sample and signature that had appeared in *Newsweek*. According to the letters, Hughes was very interested.

The folks at McGraw-Hill found them persuasive. Didn't everybody know, for example, that Hughes always used legal pads? But Irving got a terrible scare when someone mentioned a sample that had appeared recently in *Life*. When he left the meeting at McGraw-Hill, thoughtfully taking all his letters with him, Irving raced out and tracked down a copy of the *Life* issue he needed. Inside, much bigger than *Newsweek*'s and in color, was a far better Hughes handwriting specimen than the one Irving had worked from before. In fact, it was so good that the novice forger, armed with a fresh supply of legal pads and ink, immediately locked himself in his hotel room and carefully cranked out new copies of the Hughes letters that would be more suitable for close inspection. Next day nobody at McGraw-Hill knew the difference. When one McGraw-Hill man asked why Hughes had selected such a relative unknown as Irving to be his biographer, Beverly Loo, as Irving tells it, had the answer: "He certainly wouldn't pick someone very known—someone like Norman Mailer—would he? Then the book would be Mailer, not Hughes. Cliff's a perfect choice. He's a professional. He delivers. And he knows how to keep his ego in check."

The McGraw-Hill people could hardly wait for Irving to get to Hughes to offer him a contract that would eventually bring $500,000, a much bigger score than Irving had thought possible. With the publishers deeply hooked, he left New York, improvising along the way. His original plan called for fake contract meetings with Howard Hughes at Paradise Island in the Bahamas, where he was reportedly hiding. But Irving couldn't get flight reservations there at the last minute, so he flew instead to Oaxaca, in Mexico's southern mountains. Surely, he reasoned, the fictitious Hughes could travel anywhere. And with Irving on the trip to the tropics was the adventuresome Baroness Nina van Pallandt, whom Clifford promptly let in on the hoax.

When Irving returned to New York several gratifying days later, he brought a fresh batch of newly cooked-up Hughes stories for the hungry gang at McGraw-Hill. He told of a go-between named Pedro, who took him to his first meeting with Hughes ("a wreck, a thin and tired ruin") in an old Buick. He described a terrifying flight through mountains with Pedro at the controls and another meeting with Hughes where the two drank orange juice together in a hotel by the Pacific. Lulled by Irving's persuasive lyrics, nobody smelled a rat.

Then, suddenly, there was a hitch—and possibly a lethal one—in the plot. McGraw-Hill's lawyers decided that they needed Hughes's signature both witnessed and notarized on any contract. Alarmed, Irving told them emphatically that Hughes was just too independent and perverse to agree to something reasonable like that, but said that when Hughes next called him, he would ask. After a difficult delay, during which Irving, in Ibiza, considered the fraud so hopelessly snagged that he actually got back to work on his novel, Beverly Loo gave him incredible news by transatlantic phone. It seems that the lawyers had changed their minds. If Hughes just signed the documents in Irving's presence, she said, they'd be satisfied. Overjoyed, Irving allowed as how that might be arranged.

Just that sort of inadvertent connivance by his victims helped Irving almost pull the whole thing off. Some time later, after he had traveled to Puerto Rico to meet again with Hughes (who allegedly wore a black wig at this encounter) to work out details and get the contract signed, Irving met with Beverly Loo and Ralph Graves back in New York. Irving told Graves a story about buying a dozen bananas for Hughes ("He likes a man," Irving advised the Life editor, "who appreciates a good banana"), about Hughes's opinions on Mormons, women, old age and about his relationship with Ernest Hemingway. Then he showed Graves the letters he'd forged (by now for the third time), and watched with concern while the editor studied one with special care. A man with a remarkably good memory and an inclination to zero in on small details, Graves noted something he thought was familiar in the scratched-over way Hughes wrote the letter "I." He was sure he'd seen the same thing in other Hughes correspondence in the Time-Life files. "That's a habit of his," Graves said, as Irving recalled. "Very characteristic." This little aberration was very convincing to him—and it shouldn't have been. The scratched-over "I" was, in fact, the result of an accident in Irving's penmanship, and one he had decided not to correct because he liked its natural look.

The faked signature on the contract Irving brought back from the Bahamas was good enough to get him the first $100,000 installment in payment for the biography. Another $100,000 would be paid on acceptance of the "interviews" with Hughes (on the basis of which the book would be written), and the remaining $300,000 would be turned over on acceptance of the full manuscript and an introduction by Hughes. The deal between Irving and Hughes, according to the contract, called for $100,000 for the writer and the rest to Hughes, with any royalties in excess of the advance to go to Irving.

Irving got the first money in a check made out to him, and his slick plan for banking the funds got its crucial test. Edith Irving, dressed in a black wig and glasses and carrying an extra, altered passport to show at the bank, traveled to Switzerland, where she opened an account in Zurich in the name of Helga Renate Hughes. As her first big deposit, she turned over a bank check Irving had had drawn for $50,000 to H. R. Hughes, and Edith insisted that her own newly imprinted checks be initialed that way, too, without the Helga Renate, giving as her reason that she preferred to keep the fact that she was a woman as much as possible out of her business dealings. The account was opened without the slightest difficulty. Now it was available as a depository for checks made out to Hughes—and, of course, as a delicious money well for the conspirators to tap into.

The vital job of collecting the material on Hughes began. Irving and Suskind would need a lot of it, and it would have to seem awfully plausible—and even original in places—to reinforce the authority of Hughes's supposed participation. While Suskind went to Houston to check sources there, Irving traveled to Washington on a hunt for facts about HRH at the Pentagon and the Library of Congress, where he simply put one fat volume containing Hughes's testimony at a 1947 Senate hearing under his clothing and walked out.

In Nassau with Edith, he lounged around soaking up Bahamian atmosphere for fresh tales of meetings with Hughes, and after checking it out with a knowledgeable local man, he even sent Graves back word that a picture the *Life* editor had sent him for identification was not a picture of the famous recluse of Paradise Island.

Irving's great luck kept holding. In May 1971, a couple of months before *Life* had actually signed for the serial rights, he asked Graves for permission to look at the *Time-Life* morgue files on Hughes. These were certainly as good as and possibly better than the reference files of any other news organization on the subject; they would be packed with useful details covering most of Hughes's life. A lot of the basic material and raw triangulation necessary to a biography would be here, in tidy folders all carefully ordered and dated, a veritable mother lode of data for the conscientious hoaxer.

Ever winning and persuasive, Irving told Graves that access to the files would save "some dreary legwork" and said, too, by way of letting Graves in on a tidbit about the way things were going with the interviews, that "Octavio" got angry at his collaborator when he wasn't familiar enough with background material. Graves was understanding and he agreed to make the files available, although he advised Irving it wouldn't be possible for him to take anything out of the building or to make copies of anything he found especially helpful on the *Life* Xerox machines. According to Graves, those machines were only for the use of staffers. Irving expressed his gratitude for *Life*'s kindness and told Graves he'd be in the next morning—with his camera.

In a quiet office provided by the magazine, Irving worked alone and undistracted all the next day. He made no secret of his intention to use the camera and, in fact, recalled that in a conversation with Dave Maness, he discussed the difficulty of copying documents without having the camera mounted on a tripod. In any case, no one at *Life* betrayed the slightest uneasiness about his clear intention to copy portions of the files.

So he screwed a magnifying lens on the camera, and for seven hours put interesting pieces of paper about Hughes and his past on a well-lighted window ledge and shot twelve rolls of 35-millimeter film, about 400 exposures. When he finished pirating the files and left the office late that afternoon—after telling Maness that his search had been disappointing—he was really delighted. He had just lifted an absolute treasure in research. A month later, Irving fell into still more incredible good fortune. This stroke, even more than the *Time-Life* haul, would provide him with material suitable for transplanting into his book. In fact, the trove this time was a book about Howard Hughes, unpublished, and its aged author was Noah Dietrich, a man who had long been a top Hughes employee and one of a handful ever really trusted by the boss—at least until their predictable falling out. The book actually had been ghost-written from conversations with Dietrich by a reporter named James Phelan, and Dietrich, dissatisfied with the results, was looking for someone to rewrite it. Irving heard all about this on a trip to California, and managed to get a copy of the manuscript through an old Hollywood friend, Stanley Meyer.

Back in Ibiza with all the results of their various researches into the life and times of Howard Hughes, Irving and Suskind got down at last to the heart of what has to be one of the most extraordinary collaborations in the history of letters. In Irving's studio overlooking the Mediterranean, with first one of them and then the other playing the part of Hughes responding to an interviewer's questions, the two inspired con men spent most of the summer of 1971 spinning a detailed, dramatic, often hilarious life onto a tape recorder. It was an exhausting and exhilarating experience for them. The concoction they produced over those weeks was an artful blend of biographical fact, documented history, social comment, miscellaneous local color, gossip, myth and outright lies. As they acted out the real and fictional scenes in the life of a man they'd never seen, grabbing snatches from documents here and remnants from their own lives and memories there, they really invented a whole new person, and they were entirely captivated by their creation.

It was as if their excitement about the stunt they were pulling off somehow freed them from all caution and inhibition. Caught up in this artistic outburst, they tossed off almost everything that popped into their heads. In their building of Hughes's boyhood, for example, they constructed a phobia for his loving mother (by their account, she thought a person could get leprosy from eating cornbread). They dreamed up a homosexual experience for Hughes (in Mary Pickford's Hollywood house, where, after being accosted, he indignantly punched out the actor Ramon Novarro). On the basis of Dietrich material in which Hughes's fondness for cookies was mentioned, they fabricated a long, involved story about how his passion for Oreo cookies caused a man who was then president of Lockheed Aircraft to get collared for stealing Hughes a package of them from a supermarket. As a sort of private joke, they invented a Hughes affair with a diplomat's wife whose name was Helga, as in the Swiss bank, and reported lengthily and circumstantially on a purported friendship between Hughes and Ernest Hemingway (whom, as far as anybody knows, Hughes never met).

Whatever its flaws of legality, morality and taste, the product Irving and Suskind spun out was a marvel of imagination and hard work. Somehow the lies, in vivid combination with the overpowering preponderance of factual material they had lifted from other sources, gave the whole package a colorful and convincing verisimilitude. The opposites reinforced each other; the truths made the lies hard to find, and the lies made the truth seem fresh and authentic.

And the Hughes tone of voice, it turned out, was particularly persuasive, impressive even to those who had known Hughes quite well, like *Time* correspondent Frank McCulloch. There was a good reason for that: Irving and Suskind had based their imitation of Hughes's speech patterns on lengthy quotes they found in a secret memo McCulloch had written for *Time* years earlier (and which unaccountably turned up, not in the *Time-Life* files Irving had photographed, but in a verbatim copy in the Dietrich-Phelan manuscript).

However persuasive the conspirators' product, however incredible their luck, a kind of wild boldness worked in their favor, too. When things got threatening, when the flow of events started to turn against them and toward the cracking of the hoax, Irving didn't cower or cut and run, either of which would have ended it early. More typically, he took flagrant action, and that action, in turn, put the other side on the defensive.

Late that summer, for example, when he was finishing up the tapes in Ibiza, Irving got word from Beverly Loo that another book, horrifyingly like theirs, this one an authorized autobiography of Howard Hughes as told to a writer named Robert Eaton, was beginning to make the rounds of New York publishers. Frightened at this stunning news, Irving and Suskind first speculated about what this other book could possibly be. Was it the real thing? It all sounded pretty real. The perpetrator of this new version of Hughes apparently used lined yellow legal paper, too. Had the mystery man of Paradise Island really begun a collaboration with another writer? It could happen, of course. Or was this quite simply a second hoax being attempted by a man who'd just had the same brilliant idea they'd had?

Irving and Suskind decided (possibly because it was a more tolerable answer for them) that the Eaton book was indeed a hoax. Furthermore, they decided that the best defense against it lay in some convincing piece of cranky behavior on the part of *their* Howard Hughes. What they cooked up then was based on Hughes's well-documented animosity toward Time Inc. and *Life*. Hughes had often, in fact, been upset with one Luce magazine or another, and the McGraw-Hill people, worried about that, had instructed Irving to hold off telling Hughes that *Life* had bought the serial rights. The Irving emergency plan now called for Hughes to find out and to be furious about it. He was so furious, as Irving-Suskind spun out this latest dream, that he was suddenly demanding $1 million as the doubled price for his book and threatening, too, to call off the whole deal.

The plan fairly shimmered with special angles. Reporting back to McGraw-Hill on his imaginary communications with Hughes, Irving told the publishers that the enraged Octavio was screaming that the Eaton book was a fraud. Still, Irving claimed, he'd been able to cut the new price down to $850,000. And Hughes had agreed, too, that the book could now be called an autobiography. During all of this, the hoaxer made it very clear to McGraw-Hill, lest they think—horrors—that he was trying to make more money for himself on the deal, that his share of all this remained at the original, honorable $100,000. Basically, this was a dazzling mix of stonewalling, fancy dealing and cover-up, and it eventually worked much better than Irving—who thought that McGraw-Hill, however shaken up, would insist that Hughes stick to the original $500,000 contract price—could have expected.

Naturally, tempers got short in New York with these developments. The folks at McGraw-Hill were outraged, and Irving got word that the *Life* editors were getting suspicious and felt that he must be getting a kickback from Hughes. Irving rode it out. By this time he and Suskind had returned to Florida, where, on the pretext of getting more material from Octavio, they were really finishing up their 1,000-page *chef d'oeuvre*. These transcripts, they believed with some reason, would put an end to a lot of muttering about the project. In case of possible inquiries later, the tapes they'd made of each other being interviewed were burned, and so were the Dietrich-Phelan manuscripts and the bulk of the photographed items from the *Time-Life* morgue. They even abandoned a typewriter as potentially incriminating.

But before they went north, they hopped to the Bahamas, where Irving knocked off two more handcrafted Hughes forgeries on the stationery of a local hotel. They were addressed to Irving, and one simply verified the earlier promise that the book could be published as an autobiography. The other, dated September 11, 1971, was calculated to show Hughes's ruthless skill as a bargainer. "In the event," it read, "that no agreement is reached between you and McGraw-Hill [within ten days] concerning the publication of my autobiography, I authorize you to offer my autobiography for sale to another publisher on the terms to which you and I have agreed in our Letter of Agreement, and also to show them the manuscript in your possession." Just to make it all very clear that Hughes was willing to give McGraw-Hill back its money and go somewhere else with the project, Irving wrote a check drawn on the new Swiss bank for $100,000 (which by that time would have bounced over the nearest Alp), made it out to McGraw-Hill and signed it "H. R. Hughes." The big bluff was on.

It worked, of course, the way almost everything did during Clifford Irving's hot streak. The bigwigs at McGraw-Hill, and *Life*'s Graves and Maness, a natural worrier who was beginning to get very powerful feelings that something was wrong, all sat down and read the transcripts. Without exception they were utterly captivated. In Irving's recollection, Graves, who was aloof and distant when he began reading, coolly and carefully went over the whole package in two straight days. When he was through, he said it was "fantastic," "the most exciting and revelatory story that *Life* will ever have published, at least while I've been there." Readers from Dell, owners of the paperback rights to the book, were equally thrilled—which was especially gratifying since they had seen the Eaton manuscript, too, and thought Irving's was "the real McCoy."

Various segments of the story raised concerns about libel, but Irving's thoughtful selection of dead characters eased the problem considerably. However, one long story about a Hughes loan to Richard Nixon's brother Donald did cause something of a flap with McGraw-Hill's executives. The company did quite a lot of business with the U.S. government, and they didn't want to offend the President. But *Life* was interested in that section for their excerpts, and Irving claimed that Hughes himself insisted it be printed. Eventually, McGraw-Hill's big boss, Shelton Fisher, decided that nothing of Hughes's story should be cut for political purposes. "He may be crazy," said Fisher admiringly, "but he's a helluva man."

The high quality of the transcripts made Irving's renewed financial negotiations easy. Basically, he waved around the fake Hughes check for $100,000, threw in the bizarre possibility that the totally unpredictable Hughes might even attempt to *buy* McGraw-Hill to get his way and just generally bullied his frustrated suckers. But he didn't really expect that the publishers would up their ante. Thus he was astounded and delighted when he got a brief note from top editor Albert Leventhal of McGraw-Hill that ended: "We are more than eager to make certain that Mr. Hughes is happy with McGraw-Hill as his publisher. In that spirit, therefore, we are willing to amend our original contracts, increasing the advance from $500,000 to $750,000." The pressure Irving had applied to make the fraudulent package seem more convincing and desirable had just earned him an additional $250,000.

Now all that remained was to give everybody the impression that he had cleared the new offer with Hughes. This he did in typical traveling fashion by flying south for another imaginary meeting. And this time he carried with him two more McGraw-Hill checks, one drawn to Irving for $25,000, the other to Hughes for $275,000. According to Irving, that did it. He wired back to New York: "All well, check transferred, Octavio pleased." The final payments, totaling $350,000, would be made when the book was completed. But even as he brought off this precarious step in the hoax, Irving had daintily skirted disaster. The large check had originally been made out to "Howard R. Hughes." But that, of course, was not the name of the person who held the Swiss bank account. So Irving simply asked the McGraw-Hill treasurer if he would issue a substitute check, this one drawn to the order of "H. R. Hughes." It might seem like a small detail, Irving explained, but that's the way Hughes wanted it. He had his quirks. There was no use taking a chance he'd get upset over a little thing like that, now was there? The treasurer agreed, and the new check was promptly issued.

Irving's luck flashed in one more truly spectacular display before the Hughes book was announced and before the hoax, under the constant pressure of open exposure, began at last to unravel. A dreadful message from McGraw-Hill arrived in Ibiza. *The Ladies' Home Journal*, Beverly Loo reported, was intending to print excerpts of the Robert Eaton book, and would make an announcement to that effect in less than two weeks. It was absolutely imperative that McGraw-Hill and *Life* beat the competition to the gun by publicly saying first that *their* Octavio was the real Hughes. But the contract, which Irving had carefully structured to delay any dangerous publicity until all the money was in hand and the book was ready, specified that there could be no announcement until thirty days after final payment had been made. Now, Loo told him, Irving must persuade Hughes to permit an immediate announcement so that McGraw-Hill and *Life* would get proper advance credit for having the authentic Hughes autobiography.

Irving protested furiously that Hughes would never allow the change, that the Eaton book was a transparent hoax, that Hughes would sue the *Journal*. His points did not impress his publishers. Finally, Irving said he would pass the word along to Hughes—if he could. Here, of course, he was relying on another of his built-in safety devices to prevent discovery of the hoax. As Irving had much earlier explained it to his dupes, he could never call Hughes first; he had no number, no address, no way to reach a contact. In every case Octavio himself had to initiate the connection.

After the talk with Loo, Irving quickly decided that this was an occasion when Hughes had better call. On very short notice he worked out a clever plan. As usual, it depended for success on everyone's conviction that Hughes was difficult, stubborn and frighteningly unpredictable. In execution it went like this: first allowing a few days to pass, Irving would call Loo and tell her that he had indeed heard from Hughes, who after fussing a bit agreed to the early announcement. But the agreement was hedged by special conditions; these Hughes would outline in a letter he was sending from the Bahamas to Harold McGraw himself. Wearing gloves to prevent fingerprints, Irving had in fact already written the letter, a rambling, nine-page effort that included complaints about McGraw-Hill and *Life* and bitter, threatening denunciations of the Eaton book, and arranged to have it mailed from the Bahamas.

This weird document, ranking high among Irving's masterworks as a con artist, was simply the knockout punch for the admiring folks at McGraw-Hill. Its cranky, slightly paranoid style made them feel terribly certain that their Howard was the only Howard. Thus they were relieved and happy—yes, happy—to have it, and completely undaunted by the "special conditions" Irving had warned them that Hughes would require. These included a demand that the final payment to Irving— and from Irving to Hughes—be made simultaneously with the announcement. "I would also ask," the letter requested, "that you provide to me a copy of your public announcement, either before or after it is made, through Mr. Clifford Irving, as I do not read newspapers, and I respectfully request that your announcement lean more to the side of dignity than sensationalism."

Possibly this touching plea for dignity softened the urgent requirement for fast payment. In any event, no hackles rose at McGraw-Hill. But at *Life*, as it turned out, Graves was feeling some doubts about the newest development. He suggested an important test of Hughes's credibility. Why not send this most recent letter to a handwriting expert, the same man, in fact, who had studied the authentic Hughes sample *Life* used (and Irving copied) a year earlier? He could now compare the two samples. McGraw-Hill agreed and the letter was sent to Dr. Alfred Kanfer, who on December 2, 1971, provided what was surely the novice forger's most amazing (and useful) endorsement. "It can be stated," said Kanfer's report, "that the two handwriting samples were written by the same person." The report then enumerated the similarities between the original Hughes piece and the Irving forgery, similarities in word spacing, margins, height and width of letters, letter forms, "even the irregularities and fluctuations of size and pressure."

"The chances that another person could copy this handwriting," concluded Kanfer, "even in a similar way are less than 1 in a million." Understandably, that virtually unqualified statement of confidence in the Hughes letter made Graves feel easier, as did the word from McGraw-Hill that Howard Hughes had cashed the check drawn to him in September. Actually McGraw-Hill had it seriously wrong; what the bank in Switzerland had really advised the New York bank was that *H. R. Hughes* had cashed the check, and everybody just assumed that meant Howard.

The announcement came on Tuesday, December 7, 1971. That Hughes, the real Hughes, did not immediately make himself heard somehow to deny the validity of McGraw-Hill's project remains one of the whole matter's continuing mysteries. But locked in his problems and paranoia, not in good health, accustomed to subterfuge and to dealing with most matters only through intermediaries, he did not at first respond. His publicity men, unable to reach him themselves and caught by surprise at the announcement, registered no more than disbelief and confusion. Yet on that first day there came the stiff word from reputable sources close to the boss himself. "The Hughes Tool Company," was the tight-lipped reply to repeated inquiries, "denies the existence of a Hughes autobiography."

Nobody at *Life* or McGraw-Hill was much impressed with this odd, distant, undetailed statement. "We believe what we say is correct," replied one of the book's editors. Donald M. Wilson, a former *Life* correspondent, who'd risen to become Time Inc.'s vice president for corporate and public affairs, told one reporter: "Oh, we're absolutely positive. Look, we're dealing with people like McGraw-Hill and, you know, we're not exactly a movie magazine! This is Time Inc. and McGraw-Hill talking. We've checked this thing out. We have proof." With confidence that diminished very slowly, they would be clinging desperately to this proof in the rough weeks ahead.

Whatever fears they had, the publishers were more concerned for the moment with plans to get out the product. McGraw-Hill had its operations geared up for a crash schedule and a publication date in March. They intended a first printing of 500,000 copies, with other big printings to follow. *Life*'s three installments would be timed to appear consecutively just ahead of the book. Now that the secrecy was off, the magazine's syndication man was busily selling the package in Europe, and a small staff of editors and researchers was at work on the manuscript, carving out the installments and checking out the facts. In the course of their work over the next few weeks, surprisingly little would come up that would make this working team think the package was a fake.

Along with the hundreds of old Hughes pictures that *Life* was collecting from all possible sources, there was some fascinating new material, too, though not photographs, of course, which—as Irving kept claiming to a persistent Graves—Hughes always refused to allow. The new illustrations were specially commissioned oil paintings produced by David Walsh, a friend of Irving's from Ibiza who did the job by using old pictures as guidance and following Irving's "recollections" about expressions, postures and clothing—and was kept innocent of the truth.

Matters simmered along for a few days with McGraw-Hill and *Life* maintaining the authenticity of their big purchase. "We're very solid guys," came the word from a Time Inc. spokesman to one reporter, "and we wouldn't dream of coming into it unless we had so much documentary evidence that we couldn't be wrong. And we're not wrong."

On December 14, one week after the announcement, a big new development made all hearts tremble. Word came from the Hughes empire's top publicity men that the boss himself would like to speak. In characteristic fashion, he didn't intend to come out openly and make a flat statement. He wanted instead to talk privately on the phone with Frank McCulloch, a most senior *Time* correspondent who knew Hughes better than most reporters did, and in fact had had the last known face-to-face interview with Hughes in 1958 when McCulloch had been *Time*'s Los Angeles bureau chief. A gruff-voiced ex-newspaperman from Nevada, McCulloch had long been a notable figure at Time Inc. Vietnam bureau chief in the 1960s, he had something of a tough-guy reputation, kept his head shaved and often conveyed the impression that he considered many of the folks at Time Inc. a bunch of incompetents and sissies. He had also worked for *Life* as the head of the magazine's Washington bureau and was well regarded by Graves. If anyone could tell whether the man at the other end of the line was Hughes, it would be the smart and savvy Frank McCulloch.

The call was placed from the Time & Life Building (to the annoyance of the people at McGraw-Hill) by Chester Davis, Hughes's chief counsel in the tool company. He dialed the call himself, so nobody else would know where Hughes was. While various worried executives from both big publishers waited for word in nearby offices, a hastily briefed McCulloch talked for thirty minutes to the raspy-voiced man who said with angry emphasis that he was, by God, Howard Hughes. No, he said, he wouldn't allow McCulloch to record the call; he wanted it off the record. But in the course of a rambling tirade he was awfully clear about the book and about Irving. The man claiming to be Hughes said indignantly that he'd never met (or heard of) Irving and had absolutely not taken part in any project of his.

After the call, McCulloch felt sure he'd been talking to Hughes—and told Irving so when he called in a little later for a report. The anxious author of the work under such scrutiny had been waiting down the hall with the others at the start of the call, but understandably became so agitated during it that he made an excuse about having a previous engagement and fled in something nearing panic. His feelings weren't buoyed by his brief conversation with McCulloch—Irving had simply expressed his disbelief—or by the further word he got later, that the *Time* reporter was inclined to think that Clifford Irving was a phony.

In the next few weeks, McCulloch, then forty-eight, whose advice and investigative zeal might have made a big difference if applied four or five months earlier, would spend a lot of time trying to find holes in Irving's story. Skeptical as he was, when he read the manuscript he found it—as virtually everyone else did—very convincing. To a large extent it rang true, and in the course of several conversations with Irving, McCulloch found his accounts of the meetings with Hughes and his recall of the man himself persuasive. In his own book on the case Irving remembers that after one such talk McCulloch said: "By God, you've met the man. There's no doubt about it." Whatever he said, it seems clear that McCulloch was impressed with Irving's presentation of his own case. As late as January 18, 1972, McCulloch's confidence in the project was expressed in an affidavit he provided the court when Hughes's lawyers were attempting to stop publication of the installments. "I am convinced beyond reasonable doubt," McCulloch stated, "as to the authenticity of the Howard Hughes autobiography. This conviction is based upon my long-standing personal familiarity, my readings of the manuscript, and my interviews with Clifford Irving. My belief in that authenticity was not shaken by denials of that story, nor is my belief in the authenticity of the autobiography shaken by the denials which I have heard from a man I believe to be Howard Hughes. Such actions are perfectly consistent with the Hughes I know."

The incredible luck kept running. Ralph Graves, his own suspicion alarm set off again by the Hughes phone call, decided that he'd feel better if the documents were given another look by still more handwriting experts. Somewhat reluctantly, the people at McGraw-Hill agreed. The firm of Osborn Associates, holographic experts since 1905, was engaged, and eventually wound up comparing a set of *photographed* Hughes documents from Nevada with a set of *photographed* documents from McGraw-Hill. The fact that neither set examined was made up of originals may have contributed to the finding the Osborns then made. After a week's study, an informal report said, echoing the earlier validation in a faith-provoking way: "The evidence that all of the writing submitted was done by one individual is, in our opinion, irresistible, unanswerable, and overwhelming." Once more the editors at *Life* and McGraw-Hill were overjoyed, and a formal report, delivered by Osborn on January 10, 1972, was just as strong. "These basic factors," it read in part, "make it impossible as a practical matter, based on our years of experience in the field of questioned handwriting and signatures, that anyone other than the writer of the specimens could have written the questioned signatures and continuous writing." The ranks of the duped were growing every day.

Still another test of Irving's veracity took place as a result of his own suggestion. He was anxious to head off another phone call between McCulloch and Hughes, this one for the record, and in a letter written to Shelton Fisher of McGraw-Hill, he proposed instead that he and Hughes lawyer Chester Davis, in a sort of *mano-a-mano* by polygraph, each submit to a lie detector. If either man said he couldn't or wouldn't answer any one of ten questions asked by the other, wrote Irving, "the ball game would be over." The Davis part of the suggestion was overlooked entirely, but the idea of quizzing Irving by a machine that recorded his physical responses was picked up immediately. Within hours he was wired up and lying in answer to such questions as: "Have you taken any or all of the $650,000 meant to go to Howard Hughes?" and "Have you conspired with anyone else to defraud McGraw-Hill of any sums of money?" The polygraph technician, who'd been quickly briefed before the test by Frank McCulloch, saw evidence that his subject was very nervous, but he felt that the questioning was too minimal to provide the basis for a conclusive report. He hoped to continue the test on another day. Irving, who later conceded that the whole notion of the test was "pure bluff," was pressuring everyone now to let him catch his plane home to Ibiza for Christmas. And so they let him slip off the hook and fly away with his reputation as a truth-teller still awaiting the sort of confrontation that would blow the hoax wide open.

Then Hughes himself struck again. The first phone call had badly upset the various publishers. But their belief in the manuscript and the documentation provided by Irving led them to think that Hughes had gone along with the book project at first and then, persuaded by Davis and his other advisers that publication would hurt him financially by exposing him to the legal actions of his enemies, decided to deny the whole thing.

This time the telephonic voice from the Bahamas spoke to seven sweating reporters sitting in an expectant semicircle in a Los Angeles hotel room. The conversation lasted for three hours, and it was most emphatically on the record—parts of it were run on network television two days later. All the reporters but one had dealt with Hughes in the past and were qualified to make judgments about whether or not the man they spoke to was the man he said he was. In the course of the conversation, Hughes touched on many subjects—his health, the fact that he hoped to end his exile soon, various aircraft he'd designed, the relative shortness of his fingernails (falsely rumored to be six inches long), his enemies, the material used in some shoes incorrectly spoken of as canvas tennis shoes (he said they were made of imitation leather). He was clearly fascinated with little details, and there were some surprising gaps in his memory about people from his past.

But he was entirely clear about Clifford Irving. "I don't know him," said Hughes. "I have never even heard of him until a few days ago when this thing first came to my attention." Furthermore, he had not left the Bahamas since arriving there in November 1970, Hughes went on, and he had certainly never gone to any of the meeting places Irving had named. There must be some kind of plot behind the whole thing, he thought. "To assume that it's all an accident," he said with understandable suspicion, "takes a lot of assuming." He indicated that he was making every possible effort to find out all about those big checks McGraw-Hill and *Life* so wrongly thought he'd cashed. He was cranky, threatening, discursive, sharp, jumpy, impatient, condescending, all the qualities a person could expect to find in a fabulously rich eccentric calling in from his hiding place, and when the call was done, the reporters were unanimously agreed that the fellow at the far end of the line just had to be the elusive Howard Hughes.

In the face of this, the publishers maintained an equanimity that was nothing less than amazing. Obviously they felt that any public show of anxiety would be damaging not only to the book and magazine projects but to their corporate reputations as well. So they acted as if things were just fine, and the day after the broadcast they released a joint statement that began:

"McGraw-Hill and *Life* reaffirm that they possess the authentic autobiography of Howard Hughes and they plan to publish it as was originally announced on December 7, 1971.

"It is alleged that Howard Hughes made a telephone call Friday repudiating this material and the man who worked on it with him, Clifford Irving.

"We cannot accept this . . ."

The release went on to outline the evidence of the letters, the checks, the handwriting analyses, the contracts, and it ended with a ringing endorsement of their own fondest hopes.

"Finally, we have a completely convincing manuscript; no one who has read it can doubt its integrity, or, upon reading it, that of Clifford Irving."

At the press conference where he released this statement, Harold McGraw had underlined the rightness of his position by waving around a couple of photostatic copies of the checks endorsed by H. R. Hughes for deposit in the Swiss Credit Bank. At this moment, McGraw's picture was taken, and the name of the bank, which McGraw-Hill had refused to give to Chester Davis and the forces claiming to represent Hughes, showed up plainly on the back of the checks. Armed with this information, Davis began to try to get details from the bank about their

mysterious depositor. Swiss laws strictly forbid the release of such information, and Davis was rebuffed. But the pressure would be kept on
the bank by both the Hughes people and agents of the publishers, and
it was only a matter of days before everyone would know that whoever
H. R. Hughes was, it wasn't Howard. In the meantime, the bulk of the
money had been invested or transferred to another bank in Zurich
during the last of Edith Irving's flying visits to Switzerland, and when
she came home, she brought with her about $50,000, which was stashed
in various locations in and around the house in Ibiza.

By mid-January the press corps assigned to the Hughes story was
enormous (one paper had nine reporters covering it, another six), and
the pressure for new developments and information increased daily.
Juicy details about the book's contents and Irving's dealings with
Hughes were escaping with growing frequency via such leaking con-
duits as Martin Ackerman, Irving's lawyer, and Clifford Irving himself,
who made a television appearance with Mike Wallace (and self-servingly
recalled that Hughes had said about the secrecy connected with working
on the book that "none of my people know about this, and none of them
are going to know"). Worried that such blabbing and all the digging
around the story were going to undercut the value of *Life*'s installments,
Graves, who by this time was working on the Hughes matter full-time,
pushed up the schedule so that the articles would appear a month
earlier, in February.

Lawyers for the magazine were literally in court fighting a stop-
publication order that the Hughes people were trying to get when the
hoax really began to collapse in Switzerland. There, bank authorities
and police, bombarded with queries and information from investigators
representing Time Inc., McGraw-Hill and Hughes himself (a lawyer
working for Hughes had incidentally informed the IRS that his client
had no intention of paying income taxes on the $650,000 paid to some
other person named H. R. Hughes), became convinced that something
fairly criminal was probably taking place. They revealed that H. R.
Hughes, the big depositor everyone was asking about, was indeed not
the fellow holed up in the Bahamas. In fact, the depositor was not a
fellow at all, but an attractive woman named Helga R. Hughes. *Life*'s
lawyers told the court the magazine would voluntarily postpone publication until all this was cleared up.

Following these explosive developments, another crash meeting
took place between Graves, McCulloch and some of the McGraw-Hill
brass. Clifford Irving was there, too, and as usual his response to the
crisis was brazen. He invited the gathering to consider three alternative
possibilities: (1) he had been dealing with an imposter; (2) Hughes had

used a trusted agent to cash the checks and thus make it difficult to trace the transaction; (3) he, Clifford Irving, had pulled off a big hoax. "I discard the third possibility," he said with engaging sincerity to the glum group, "and I hope you do, too."

Irving then disposed of the theory that there had been a Hughes imposter; such a character would have had to be a tall, thin, consummate actor in his mid-sixties who knew all about Hughes—and was a great forger, too. This left only the trusted-agent theory, which Irving pushed with enthusiasm. Before the meeting ended he upset everybody present, including his lawyer, by announcing that he simply had to get back to Ibiza to see Edith, who needed him there. What he didn't say was that Edith was being questioned by Swiss cops who were leaning heavily to the notion that she was Helga.

Irving's insistence on going home again at this time just about blew away the last bits of trust remaining among his editors. They were furious, and so suspicious of him that they sent someone to the airport to make sure that he really got on the plane. Before he went, McCulloch and William Lambert, a seasoned investigative reporter and *Life* staff member, had a long, probing conversation with him. They concentrated particularly on details of his last meetings with Hughes in Miami and descriptions of a purported go-between, George Gordon Cooper. McCulloch and Lambert (who had won the Heywood Broun Award for his story in *Life* on the career-busting improprieties of Supreme Court Justice Abraham Fortas) persuaded Irving to sign two notes to be sent Cooper in care of General Delivery at the main Miami post office, the fake mail drop Irving had dreamed up for Hughes communications. Irving continued to impress with his convincing passion for lively (if outlandish) details. He told, for instance, of a pre-dawn session with Hughes in Palm Springs, which was interrupted by an introduction to Vice President Spiro Agnew (and *Life* was able to check out that Agnew had indeed been in Palm Springs that weekend). Lambert and Mc-Culloch reported to Graves that if Irving was a con man, he was certainly the best they'd ever seen.

But the game was almost over. Investigators in Europe and the United States were attacking the Hughes story from every angle. The Irvings faced the threat of serious criminal charges in Switzerland. Because of the possibility that the mails had been used as part of a fraud, the U.S. Postal Inspection Service had entered the case and one of their investigators working with Bill Lambert had begun turning up holes in Irving's artful narrative, one in particular showing a crucial inconsistency involving the records of a car-rental agency in Miami.

At just this moment, *Life* was putting to press its own story about the whole affair, a cover and eight pages headlined: "Howard Hughes as Clifford Irving Sees Him—The Writer and the Recluse." On the cover and several of the pages were paintings and drawings of Hughes in various situations by David Walsh, Irving's artist friend from Ibiza, who had based his work on Irving's detailed descriptions. According to the magazine's story, "Irving told *Life* that Hughes has seen the portraits and, with some minor criticisms, approved them."

The bulk of the text consisted of an account by Ralph Graves about his dealings with Irving and about Irving's description of meeting Hughes for the first time. Writing about his own feelings about the project early in the game, Graves said: "I was right to be excited and right to be skeptical—and wrong to be relaxed." The piece ended on a relatively upbeat note. "In view of the recent pyrotechnics," he concluded, "it is difficult for outsiders to believe that the manuscript makes even livelier reading than the mysteries that surround it. But it does, and we still hope to publish it."

But the upsetting news about the car-rental records in Miami cast the whole Hughes package in even greater doubt, and the editors (Louis Banks, then editorial director and Hedley Donovan's top lieutenant from the thirty-fourth floor, was managing *Life* while Graves wrestled with the Irving mess) set about to make crash changes in the article and cover, which was already printing at high speed. Simultaneously, Irving had returned from Ibiza with Edith and their children and almost within hours made a climactic confession. Under fierce pressure from various law-enforcement agencies and the press, and after first spilling it to Frank McCulloch and another reporter, Irving confessed that Helga was none other than Edith.

That ripped it with *Life*. The editors, after first considering changing the cover entirely from one of the Walsh paintings to a picture of Liza Minnelli, settled by replating the fabricated portrait of Hughes and having a banner slashed across it that said: "Clifford Irving says Howard Hughes looks like this—but did he ever see him?" The story inside the magazine was sharply cut, whole pages were dumped and new ones substituted, and everything was reshaped to make the magazine look as good as possible under absolutely terrible conditions. The frantic production exercise of fixing this issue to keep current with embarrassing events cost *Life* about $75,000, and readers of Graves's severely trimmed article, now called "The Hughes Affair, Starring Clifford Irving," would find no trace of the hopeful attitude toward the manuscript that had been in the original draft. Excised, too, was Graves's candid confession of early excitement about the project, and his *mea culpa* had even been beefed up a bit. "I was right to be skeptical," went his final draft, "and certainly wrong to be relaxed."

The hoax was collapsing now with soufflé speed, and perhaps fittingly for lovers of light farce, it came to a ludicrous end with the revelations of the Baroness Nina van Pallandt, a.k.a. the Danish Pastry. The word had somehow gotten abroad—quite possibly via Irving's irrepressible blabbing—that he hadn't exactly been traveling alone when he went to Mexico the first time to see Howard Hughes. Various investigators, reportorial as well as criminal, zeroed in at about the same time on the possibility that his companion was the beauteous van Pallandt, whom searchers found on an island in the Bahamas where she was taking a vacation from occasional television work in London. Under questioning by postal authorities and later by many others, she quickly made it clear that Clifford Irving had been much too preoccupied with her in Mexico to have spent any time at all interviewing Howard Hughes. The coup de grace was then administered by the honest outrage of reporter Jim Phelan, who had recognized much of the leaked Irving material as having come from Phelan's own manuscript. Side by side comparison of Phelan and Irving versions of many of the stories about Howard Hughes answered the lingering question about why Irving's work seemed so authoritative; much of it had been stolen from an authentic source.

While several jurisdictions (the United States, Switzerland, New York State) hassled over such grubby questions as how the Irvings and Suskind should eventually be punished, the inevitable recapitulations were taking place among the victims. Against the background of *Life*'s already disastrous financial situation, the hoax was a painful blow. Many onlookers, in and out of the publishing business, were delighted to see the often smug and arrogant operatives from Time Inc. made utter fools of by this obscure hustler. "There are a lot of people," wrote *Life* publisher Garry Valk in a memo to all department heads, "who take great delight in tossing darts at us and acting as Monday morning quarterbacks." But Valk was also ready with a sturdy, if vaguely absurd line of defense against the jokes. "Amidst the confusing cross-currents about the Hughes-Irving affair and our role," he went on, "let one fact shine through. It was Time Inc. management and investigative reporters on both *Time* and *Life* who uncovered virtually all the material that established the hoax."

That would be the company line in the snicker-filled days ahead. "Look, we got caught, but if it hadn't been for our detective work, the whole thing would have been a lot worse." Maybe so, but it is also

possible that the editors' determination to back their remarkable manuscript led them into a certain rigidity, a partial paralysis that prevented
them from dealing sooner and more bluntly with a worsening situation.
In a detailed and forthright report he wrote on what might have been
done differently, Ralph Graves concluded: "The major action that we
could have and should have taken was to press Irving harder on all
three fronts: the need for a current photograph [of Hughes], for a sample tape, for a witness to his meetings. We did press him for pictures
and, to a lesser degree, for tapes. He himself volunteered Richard
Suskind, his own researcher, as a witness. If I had leaned harder on
McGraw-Hill, asking them in turn to lean on Irving, Irving would of
course have explained that none of these corroborative adventures was
possible. I could have then proposed to McGraw-Hill that somebody
be sent undercover to observe Irving at his meetings with Hughes. If
this had been done, I think we could have learned that the manuscript
(or at least Irving's account of it) was a hoax. I don't know whether
McGraw-Hill would have agreed to such an action, but I wish I had
asked for it."

Editor-in-chief Hedley Donovan, in his own report on the matter
to Time Inc.'s board, said: "[Such tailing of Irving] might have precipitated a showdown in which McGraw-Hill might have said if you don't
have any faith in our author, why don't you withdraw from this project
and let us take the magazine rights elsewhere. If matters had come to
that point, I think Ralph and I would have backed down. The only other
possibility would have been that we do the tailing on our own without
telling McGraw-Hill, which would of course have been a violation of
our understanding with them."

Donovan went on to point out, as Valk had, that "Time Inc. had a
good deal to do with breaking the case," and that "both *Life* and *Time*
have gotten some very good stories out of the whole business. . . . I
think we have to assume that there is going to be some harm," he
continued, "at least temporarily, to our reputation. Or put it this way:
if we were to come along next month with some exciting manuscript of
mysterious origin, or even if we were presenting some sensational piece
of investigation by our own staff, like the Abe Fortas story of a few
years ago, I think we would have a certain credibility gap to overcome.
. . . Some nice people come up to me and say you have had millions
of dollars of free publicity, or what wonderful fun you've given all of
us, etc., etc. No doubt these are offsets to the embarrassment of being
fooled, but not quite total, I think . . .

"I'm afraid there was a certain kind of self-intoxication," Donovan
explained, "that developed as we went around repeating to each other

that nobody possibly could have invented some of these things in the manuscript, it just had to be Hughes himself talking. That was certainly my reaction."

Concluding, he said: "I do wish, however, that I had read Clifford Irving's previous book *Fake!* much sooner than I did. . . . It was Irving's story, you remember, that he made his original contact with Hughes by mailing him a copy of *Fake!*, got a fan letter back from Hughes saying what a sympathetic book it was, maybe we will meet some day, etc. After reading *Fake!*, I found it very difficult to believe Howard Hughes could have had the slightest interest in the book. It's a tiresome, repetitious book, and unless you happen to be very much interested in modern art and especially the world of art dealers, which there's no evidence Hughes ever has been, it would be a terrible bore. If I had read *Fake!* last April, perhaps I would have been moved to ask Graves some astute questions to ask McGraw-Hill to ask Irving. Perhaps not."

Some housecleaning details remained. Over the next months, *Life* pressed successfully for the return of the magazine's payments to McGraw-Hill and to get the book publishers to share some of the extraordinary expenses involved with clearing up the hoax. These included $60,000 in legal fees and about $70,000 in charges for various experts, among them the Osborns, who asked for $18,000 and whose final report (a bit late in the day) disclosed some evidence of forgery.

The guilty were eventually given their several punishments. Clifford Irving spent seventeen months in federal prison, Edith Irving spent two months in jail in America and then more than a year in Switzerland, and Richard Suskind served five months in prison in New York.

On February 14, 1972, all of *Life*'s copies of Irving's astonishing manuscript were shredded (by agreement with McGraw-Hill), while a photographer recorded the event. Two days later Howard Hughes, his privacy shattered beyond tolerance, slipped out of his hotel in the Bahamas and fled to a new hiding place.

20

The End

THOUGH NOBODY ON THE MAGAZINE COULD BEAR to face it directly—and in the highest corporate echelons, too, a sort of sentimental hope for the future obscured the hard facts of ruin—*Life* was utterly washed up by the start of 1972. Spasms of "rethinking" took place, various changes (of frequency, paper weight, page size) were considered, but all these were based on the wishful notion that stopgap relief measures could halt the steepening descent and somehow help set in motion a reversal, back to the good old days.

The truth was that everything was running against the survival of the magazine: production and mailing costs were much too high, important blocs of advertisers (foods, for one) were convinced that their money was better spent in television. And the readers themselves were just not finding the pleasure and punch they wanted in *Life*'s shrinking issues.

So it was really in a doomed cause that Graves and his reduced staff (another big, across-the-board cut had taken place in December 1971) looked somewhat groggily past the Irving fiasco and planned for the months ahead. Though the official line was that the Hughes hoax hadn't really hurt that much, virtually everyone on the staff felt the embarrassment of it and the sting of the grinning questions put by outsiders on all possible occasions. Then, as if some conspiring power wanted spirits kept low, a series of sad, premature deaths followed. In none of them was there the heroic quality of Larry Burrows's death-in-action. The deaths of John Thorne, Gene Farmer and Mary Leatherbee all bore the banal aspect of shocking and unexpected household accidents, yet in the light of *Life*'s predicament, they had a particularly strong symbolic impact. These three people represented what *Life* had been at its best—caring, smart, resourceful, adventurous, now and then inspired. And they had been completely devoted to the magazine. As it happened, all three had actually been pushed off the staff before they died, but this only gave the facts another sad spin, for each had wanted to stay.

John Thorne died in February, of a heart attack that hit him during a vacation in the Caribbean. He was fifty-six years old, and with the exception of a few wartime years as a bomber pilot, he had worked at *Life* since 1938. "I haven't been managing editor," he once said without much exaggeration, "but I've been just about everything else." His most recent job on *Life* had been as a sort of traffic manager for communications with the bureaus, and he didn't like it much. Shortly before he had gone on vacation, Thorne had been told that because of continuing staff reductions he would have to leave the magazine. Another job in the company, a good editing position at Time-Life Books, was offered to him, and he took it.

He did not make a big deal of leaving. It wasn't like Thorne to express his feelings heatedly, though he did complain at times, and he simply hated it when some scurrying co-worker passed him by in the hustle for extra credit. His responses to difficulty tended to be cool, mild, even jocular—he was a man of asides. Still, he was so especially knowledgeable about *Life*, so familiar with its techniques and inner workings, its failings and its strengths, its people, its history, that he must have been stunned—and hurt—to realize that "they" (for that is the vague and accusing way the corporate disinherited speak of an enemy they often know well) didn't value him enough to hang on to him in a tight situation.

Gene Farmer died suddenly in June at his home outside Boston. He was fifty-two, and he'd done his last major work for *Life* the previous fall and winter, when he carved three 10,000-word installments out of Clifford Irving's bogus Hughes transcripts. He'd also worked hard and skillfully at the shaping of the "Khrushchev Remembers" series, which ran with great success and wide public attention in 1970 and 1971.

In Farmer's best years at *Life* (the 1950s), the bright, dumpy, sometimes pompous young fellow from the little town of Huntsville, Arkansas, had been part of a group of perhaps six or eight who were marked for possible big things. He regarded Ed Thompson with affection and awe, as a power just short of deity, and Farmer worked like a dog—and loved it. Under Hunt, his star dropped. He wrote editorials and developed a special facility for condensing and editing articles drawn from books and big-name memoirs, Douglas MacArthur's *Rem-*

iniscences, for one. He worked on many stories involving the Apollo astronauts, and in 1969, in collaboration with Dora Jane Hamblin, one of the magazine's best reporters for years, he wrote a book on the historic flight of Apollo 11, *First on the Moon.*

In 1971, two years after Graves took over, Farmer left the staff and became an editor at Little, Brown, a Time Inc. subsidiary. It was clear to all who knew him that he'd been under pressure to move and would have much preferred to stay at *Life.* He was an absolute believer in the magic of the magazine, addicted to its fierce demands on his time and strength, and he craved more chances to show his loyalty. That loyalty was evident in a long memo he sent to Graves after he'd left. "If you get into a box," Farmer wrote amid a flurry of suggestions for *Life* stories, "and need someone to make a silk purse out of a sow's ear, I'm your man."

If anyone were to conduct a poll among the remaining survivors of *Life* asking who more than any other embodied the romantic spirit of the magazine at its peak, Mary Leatherbee would probably win it, hands down. She played her life headlong, with the wind machines blowing her hair. Her energy and vitality were palpable, and her death in a rafting accident in British Columbia in July left a very heavy silence at *Life,* a sort of black hole. She was sixty-one, and when she'd been told—by Graves in his sad role of bearer of awful tidings—that she would have to accept early retirement, she just had not been able to believe it.

Her most productive years had been spent in the entertainment department, where she and Tom Prideaux managed *Life*'s show business coverage for a couple of decades. In the mid-1960s, George Hunt moved her away from entertainment and made her the travel editor, with a franchise to look for good stories anywhere in the world. Later, with the need for improved newsstand sales assuming a crucial importance as the losses got bad, she was given the job of producing covers that would sell the magazine better.

She attacked both assignments with her usual full concentration. But it was not the same. The decline of the magazine depressed her, as it did virtually everyone, though it didn't cut the fierce concentration she gave. Once she got used to the idea that she was going to have to leave *Life,* she got around to figuring out how she was going to turn her strength to survival. A couple of weeks before her death, she had just about completed plans to attempt a modest lecture tour. She quite liked the idea; it would combine her need to be on stage with a chance to talk about experiences she'd loved.

Preliminarily, she'd worked out some subject titles for possible inclusion in her talks. Her list is a kind of joking digest of the joy she took in her job: "Irving Berlin Sings for Me," "Bicycling in Bali," "Picked Up on the Rome Express by Noël Coward," "Towed Down the Amazon by a Big Fish," "Marilyn Monroe Makes Up with Me." Mary Leatherbee's unashamed delight in her own journey revealed a personal investment in *Life* that many others over the years felt, too, but never dared express with such childlike candor.

"I never gave up completely until just a few weeks before we actually decided we had to," Hedley Donovan said over lunch one day in the Hemisphere Club, a suitably glass-windowed and carpeted executive restaurant on the top floor of the Time & Life Building. It was little more than four years after *Life* had folded, and Donovan's grindingly deliberate voice conveyed traces of the dismay he still felt as he considered what had happened and what might have been. "You can haunt yourself," he went on, "by trying to imagine what if anything we might or might not have done to save *Life*. But since I'm among those who couldn't think of anything different from the many things that we did, I'm not an impartial witness. But I've never heard of anything that sounded like a convincing explanation of how we could have kept it going. We could have changed to something very different, such as *People*, which was in fact discussed once or twice. But it's very difficult to take an existing magazine and its readers and advertisers and reputation and momentum and just kind of in front of everybody convert it into something quite different. The general argument against it, which I think was absolutely sound, was that the damage would be too great to people who had started either subscribing to it or advertising in it on the basis that it was one thing; to change that during the life of this contract, so to speak—you just can't do that.

"We cut back circulation," he continued, and his listing of the measures considered reflected the anxious tension of those last months. "It was not interpreted favorably. It was hard to put a positive construction on it. And what was terribly disillusioning and frightening internally was that with each of these cuts where you'd hoped we were getting rid of a million and a half of our worst circulation, we were also peeling off some really loyal and devoted *Life* subscribers. What had been a hopeful assumption on the part of several people, including me, that we'd be much closer to our real, natural, authentic circulation—well, we were closer, but not close enough. You know, some of the renewal figures we were up against were absolutely devastating, even when we got down to 5.5 million circulation. Sure, there were a lot of people who really liked *Life*—presumably the 2 million who leveled

all sorts of reproaches as to why did you ever stop this marvelous magazine. But there weren't enough who cared that much to support it.

"A thing that was very shortsighted for the whole magazine business (and one we've only now sort of barely corrected) was our selling
Life at those ridiculous prices for nine cents a copy and so forth for
years. We'd pretty much indoctrinated the public into thinking you can
have this magazine for almost nothing, and the advertisers or somebody,
they will pay for it and bring it to you. Part of the theory of cutting
back was that we hoped we'd hit layers of circulation that were more
seriously interested in the magazine and they'd be willing to pay something a little more resembling the cost. But that didn't work, and the
resistance to paying eleven cents or thirteen cents or fifteen cents a
copy was enormous."

There were other suggestions: to make it a women's magazine, to
make it a very inexpensive newsstand pictures-and-fun magazine with
very little wordage, like a 1930s rotogravure. "In all cases, the question
was whether or not you could graft such ideas on the existing body of
Life."

Granted the difficulty of keeping the magazine going, should it
have been closed down sooner and some part of the money and talent
devoted to inventing new projects? "Time Inc. is such a well-behaved
and civilized company that as far as I know no stockholder or director
has ever asked such a question," Donovan said. "I'm not uneasy in my
conscience about that question. I would rather be able to say that we'd
given the absolute maximum effort, including the maximum financial
support we could possibly justify to keep it going, than to say we were
so smart we stopped even two years before we had to. But it would
have been reckless to keep it going any longer than we did. The Time
Inc. board were quite wonderful about this. Nobody was jostling or
pressuring."

Donovan recalled that Luce had written somewhere that *Life* might
be like a long-running Broadway show, a tremendous hit but one that
wouldn't last forever. "One of the difficulties we had all during the last
dozen years," Donovan continued, "was getting *Life* to abandon any
area or claim of journalism. Harry at one time used to say—in dozens
of evenings of argumentation I had with him about this—that *Life* ought
to be absolutely universal. Of course, not everybody would take it, but
there shouldn't be any reason why you would say automatically that
[one kind of person] wouldn't. The Secretary of Defense should take it
and the taxi driver should take it. Some taxi drivers wouldn't, of course,
but you shouldn't be surprised if one did or a cabinet officer did. I used
to argue that you could no longer have such a tremendously broad

spectrum and that we ought to consider going after the top third of the audience, and we finally did sort of decree that. But we kept on trying to be practically everything."

Donovan's sense of regret about *Life*'s finish was palpable. "We were floundering at the end but in relation to the box office it was an understandable floundering. Things that had worked quite well in the sixties—not as well as they once worked in the fifties—were visibly not working. And just to say that what we're doing is right, and we believe in it, and goddamn it, you readers better shape up, that wouldn't quite work. I think that—second to coming up with the creations that were not forthcoming—the second most difficult thing was to decide among ourselves: Okay, we will stop trying to be this and this and this, and let somebody else do that better."

There were several others besides Donovan who were casting around in those last days for ways to keep *Life* afloat. Various ideas for survival were making the rounds, including one that would pitch it to a working-class audience. Another alternative was put forward by Tom Griffith, who'd been Donovan's deputy and a high-ranking editor of *Time*. In 1967 Griffith had come to *Life* in Thompson's place when the latter left to run *Smithsonian* and had stayed on with Graves. A shrewd, able man with a wry sense of humor, Griffith labored with great conscientiousness in the awkward editor–managing editor arrangement Luce had fashioned, and he worked with both Hunt and Graves without betraying any sense of impatience or pique that the managing editor ran things. Like Thompson, Griffith did not communicate fluently with his colleagues; spoken sentences trailed off and rattled into silence, and his handwriting was so pinched it needed magnification. For *Life* he managed the editorial page, sometimes doing the writing himself, and supervised many special projects. He suggested big stories (Norman Mailer on space flight) and reflected at considerable frequency and length on *Life* policy and direction. Griffith's memos about how *Life* could be improved began appearing on his colleagues' desks from the time he arrived. But they were always delivered with a kind of modesty, as if the author didn't want to seem too pushy, as if, in fact, he suspected that most people on the magazine regarded him more as an esteemed visiting lecturer than a regular staff person. In one of Griffith's last memos he asked: "Is it possible at this late date to think about a totally different *Life*? Common sense says that tradition, Time Inc. habits of thought and reader expectancy keep us from straying far . . . Of all ways to change *Life* dramatically I can think of only one which would be consonant with *Life*'s past and present, while giving us a chance to make a new start. It would be simply to declare that henceforth *Life* intends itself to be a magazine for those under 35. I don't mean it as a promotion stunt, but as a complete change of mind-set. This would soon give us a clearer audience profile, like *Redbook*'s 'young marrieds,' but we wouldn't go through any silly gimmickry about shutting off the subs of anyone over 35. We would merely assert that, after a time, many over 35 would not find *Life* speaking to them, but to any it does, glad to have you with us. We would instantly benefit from removing the worst albatross around our necks: those old-timers who are the grumbliest about our not being the old *Life,* as if we could wave a wand and return to a pre-television cocksureness in being first with the real pictures of anything and everything (or could afford the old lavishness in preparation and pages)."

Griffith acknowledged that his idea could create some delicate internal problems. "Oldies putting out a magazine for those under 35?" he asked, adding that he felt sure the present staff could manage it. "But present editors," he wrote, "would have to listen more to other voices, including those on their own staff . . . and would have to make way sooner than otherwise for the authentic under-35s.

"This is the one alternative I know," Griffith concluded, "that without doing violence to what we have stood for, gives most promise of giving us a lift, a renewed mission." Like so many others, his idea perished quickly.

It is at least interesting that the people most engaged in seeking new ways to provide that lift in *Life*'s last years were generally not those editors who had spent their careers on the picture magazine. Perhaps the *Life* people were too deeply involved to take objective views of the matter. More likely they believed, as a kind of faith, that the magazine was best when it was spontaneous, when it reflected the real enthusiasms of its editors, *their* surges of conscience and anger, *their* capacities for delight and caring. Tinkering—adding or dropping departments, moving people around in different jobs, changing emphasis here and there—was all right. But basically they deplored the idea that there was some perfect formula for this difficult moment, some new way to construct a winning editorial appeal. *Life,* when it was really good, they felt, represented them. Thus the magazine's painful and protracted failure was somehow a punishment for their own failures of imagination and nerve. They believed, largely because it had been the case, that when the magazine was "working," the readers would buy it in big numbers. The men on the business side, those others unencumbered with the sentimental baggage of close, personal memories of participation in a successful *Life,* were not as sanguine. But they kept telling themselves that *something* would make a difference and turn the whole thing around.

In a way *Life* was like an over-the-hill prizefighter who doesn't have the good sense to retire before his diminished gifts make him look foolish. Eyes swollen nearly shut, cuts leaking blood around the trainer's hasty patches, legs turning to water, he staggers around the ring under the battering of a much younger opponent. Watching the debacle, the crowd knows that nothing can be done to give him back his speed, his punch, his resilience. Even his will to win is gone, though he won't admit it. Such was really the case with *Life*, no matter how valiantly its managers tried to doctor the wounds, to alter its stance, to pump it up with some vital, new resolve. The great American magazine had outlived its own strength, was dead on its feet, and its fatal weakness was apparent in almost every issue. That weakness was clear in *Life*'s pitifully skimpy contents, in its obvious uncertainty about the temper and makeup of the audience it wanted to reach in an increasingly fragmented society, in the fact that the audience it did reach generally received it with a detachment far different from the impatient ardor with which subscribers in better days eagerly awaited the postman and buyers snatched it from the newsstands.

All that was left, really, was to kill *Life*. But Time Inc. had had unmatched success publishing magazines (even, in the cases of *Life* and *Sports Illustrated*, after big losses), and a massive, public failure was just not an acceptable corporate option. There were other reasons for reluctance: high-level fears about the bad effects that such a spectacular shutdown might have on the healthy image of the company, genuine compassion for the people whose lives would be badly disrupted in such a shocking change. The decision to bring it all to an end would not be reached until the figures (and the projections for the future) were so terrible that even the most tenderhearted of *Life*'s supporters in the corporate management (like board chairman Andrew Heiskell) bowed to the inevitable. The losses, tallied up at the end, were very stiff indeed: $40 million over the past four years, with commensurate losses predicted for the future, even with the circulation cut still more.

Long before the end, of course, the fourteen members of Time Inc.'s board had been deeply involved with the problems of *Life*'s downward spiral, and a number of the outside members seemed concerned that the management might prop up the corpse too long. They had already agreed to a progression of severe changes. In September 1970, they had, in fact, followed the advice of company bosses and actually empowered them, pending further analysis of the dismaying figures, to turn the picture magazine into a biweekly with a circulation of 8.5 million, effective in January 1971.

Two weeks later chairman Heiskell told the board that "after exhaustive reappraisal," the management was recommending that *Life* be continued as a weekly at 7 million circulation. One reason given for this switch was that the chopped-down circulation would make it possible to reduce page prices to advertisers (although the actual cost per thousand readers delivered at the new level would be somewhat greater), thereby—it was devoutly hoped—making the magazine more competitive with others, especially television. Plans were completed, too, to go ahead and stop publication of *Life*'s money-losing foreign editions (the first, the biweekly *Life International*, had been founded in 1946 and reached a circulation of almost 400,000). A year later, in November 1971, the board approved the next huge circulation reduction, to 5.5 million. A year before it actually happened, the members were getting accustomed to thinking the unthinkable.

On the editorial side of the magazine the man best qualified to deal with the worsening reality was the operational boss, Ralph Graves. Reflecting much later on the gifts of his predecessor, George Hunt, Graves had said: "One of his strengths as managing editor was that he didn't face the truth. He could convey his self-delusions to the staff and make them work." The Hughes caper notwithstanding, there was nothing self-delusional about Graves, nothing that would permit his own powerful wishes for success to interfere with his understanding of what was happening. Of course, the top managers didn't let him in on the final decision to fold the magazine until well after they made it. So there were some things he didn't know and others, naturally, that he wouldn't confide for fear of further damaging morale among his colleagues. But he had a solid sense of how precarious the *Life* position really was, and he was convinced that the best course under the circumstances was to drive himself hard, insist on good performance from his staff and try to keep the magazine as lively and interesting as possible. His communications tended to be matter-of-fact, as usual. "I hereby serve notice," he wrote a group of his editors in some annoyance, "that we have published our last 1972 entertainment textpiece in which the author explains and complains that the subject was a) reluctant, b) reticent, c) inarticulate, d) all three. If the subject won't talk, let us either drop the story or else find a way to do it without making an article out of the problem. The author's difficulties do not constitute subject matter." In midsummer he wrote Tom Griffith: "I hope you feel as good as I do about *Life*'s [Democratic] Convention issue, and as pissed off as I do about Hedley's niggardly praise. I can't remember when I've heard as many gratuitous compliments, both on and off the edit staff, since the Faces of the Dead in Vietnam . . . Men in England now abed will count their manhoods cheap, etc."

Graves's good working relationship with Donovan encouraged the straightforward exchanges between them. "I would like to make some points about your dictum this morning," Graves wrote the editor-in-chief, "that *Life* should plan to have an editorial page every week, and that absence of same should be the exception." Though editorials in *Life* had been appearing regularly since Luce instituted them in 1942, they had run less frequently in recent years, and Graves was anxious not to have them take up space that might otherwise be used for pictures in his small issues, issues that were already packed with writing. "One of our major problems," he went on, "is not only to keep the picture franchise, but to emphasize it . . . I must seriously question whether, in the present structure of the magazine, still another page of text—and current-form text at that—can be imposed as a weekly feature that does not enjoy and never has enjoyed wide readership. If a regular Time Inc. editorial statement has to be made, I again propose *Time* as a far more appropriate vehicle." Graves did not say so, but most members of the staff had always deplored the editorial page and rarely read it.

Donovan pushed his managing editor's objection aside. "I don't know whether a 'dictum' can get dicted in Time Inc.," he replied with a certain heartiness, adding bluntly that he did want the editorials to be a regular feature. "I think the magazine needs a visible spine of *Life* principle and viewpoint," he went on, "especially since so much varied opinion and emotion, in pictures as well as text, including outside writing, gets expressed in the magazine. An Editorial Page becomes a very effective reminder to us of that part of our responsibility, and a clarifier of *Life*'s character and personality."

Then his memo to Graves took on a tone that indicated how much *Life*'s trouble had a bearing on all plans for the future. "You—and others, me included—and Time Inc.," he continued, "have been devoting tremendous effort to keeping this magazine going. One reason for the company's commitment is the belief that *Life* is an important place to say important things to a particular audience (very little overlap with the *Time* audience), to express what Time Inc. 'stands for.' Not just for the sake of being 'on the record'—'somewhere'—with our views, in case somebody should ask, but actually in the hope of influencing people."

In June 1972, *The Gallagher Report*, a brash, rumor-packed and quite influential newsletter whose special audience included "marketing, sales, advertising and media executives," came out with an item that caught the pained attention of executives at Time Inc., where editor Bernard Gallagher's arrows often drew blood. "Death Struggle at *Life* Magazine," it was labeled, and it went on in typically staccato language to say: "Time Inc. chairman Bob Heiskell, president 'Brass Knuckles Jim' Shepley torn between loyalty to company's historic flagship, obligation to stockholders. This year perfect time to fold *Life* . . . Time Inc. president's insistence on ability to save *Life* could cost him his job . . . Jim insists *Life* on verge of breaking even . . . Ready to defy Federal Price Board in courts to boost one-year *Life* subscription from $10 to $17. Knowledgeable stockholders unimpressed. Downhill momentum too strong for *Life* to make full recovery . . . *Life* to lose estimated $15 million this year. Circulation cutbacks no solution without change in editorial . . . Heiskell, Shepley should bite bullet. Discontinue *Life* with year-end issue." Gallagher had been baying about the picture magazine's difficulties for some time, but this—which had the ring of insider talk—was a particularly chilling blast.

Life's own advertising people were putting a better face on the situation. "The agencies are responding well," said publisher Garry Valk to a columnist for *The New York Times*. Valk, formerly the publisher of *Sports Illustrated*, had been dragooned for the *Life* job when Jerry Hardy left in 1969 and was known as a brutally frank fellow and something of a wizard with figures. "The death rattle isn't there anymore every time you turn around," he confided comfortingly. A survey of ad agency attitudes by *Life* salesmen around the country brought good news from Los Angeles, where one Doyle, Dane, Bernbach executive said: "*Life* editorially has cut out the fat and is once again relevant and exciting." Not all the comments were so positive. "I personally know of major advertisers who won't spend a dime in *Life*," snarled one agency man. "Client top management not reading *Life*," reported another. "*Gallagher Report* comments causing them to discount *Life* as already dead."

In his own efforts to help improve the magazine's image with the agencies, Graves met on several occasions with their executives and explained what he considered *Life*'s focus and direction. At times in these meetings he had to submit to the agency men's lectures on how a mass-circulation magazine should be edited. One agency's art director suggested how issues could be done differently and better. The message to Graves, as one *Life* business executive told him, was: "You're letting aesthetics get in the way." But Graves bore this sometimes arrogant interference with grace and good humor and held his ground. In response to word he'd received that admen were considering selling space he thought would too closely resemble editorial matter, he warned the magazine's publisher and the general manager: "Just want you both to know that I am quite alarmed by the first reports I hear of the special spread advertising package called '*Life* Style.' I have a preliminary hunch that I am going to be very upset about it, and if that should prove to be the case, I hope we can look at it and discuss it while it is still in the larva stage. Later on, it might become a great big ugly pterodactyl, which would conflict with our well-known bluebird policy." The idea was dropped.

Meanwhile, of course, the magazine was churned out each week, and even for issues as small as eighty, even seventy-two pages (issues in the best days were almost three times that big), the demand for material was constant. Stories on President Nixon's trip to China, a selection from the newest novel by Alexander Solzhenitsyn, coverage of the final days of the Apollo program, accounts of terrible floods in West Virginia and Iowa, studies of rising crime in good neighborhoods, revelations of the shockingly lax conditions at a Washington state prison, examination of the changing attitudes of American women and the phenomenon of the "dropout wife," all these and more filled the pages. A new department in the front of the magazine called "The Beat of Life" opened the issues with a burst of from six to ten pages of pictures, often in color. A department the readers seemed particularly to like consisted of pictures drawn from back issues of the magazine—"16 Years Ago in *Life*," "31 Years Ago in *Life*"; the audience seemed grateful for the undemanding splashes of nostalgia. And amid it all, the staff changes kept taking place. Graves replaced Irwin Glusker, the amiable and skillful art director he'd hired to replace Bernie Quint, with Robert Clive, who'd been an assistant under Quint and who Graves hoped would bring more journalistic punch and excitement to the magazine's design. Among the old-timers who took early retirement were Dick Pollard, who managed the photographers and had been one of *Life*'s earliest and most aggressive bureau correspondents, and Marian MacPhail, the magazine's chief of research. MacPhail, a gravel-voiced and sensible manager whose air of patient understanding made her the recipient of everybody's troubles and all important in-house gossip for the twenty-four years she worked at *Life*, was the target of one of the magazine's last old-style farewell parties, where one verse of a song sung to her (to the tune—roughly—of "Red River Valley") went: "She hired everyone and his brother, including the Managing Ed, and kept track of her charges' affairs, desk to desk and sometimes bed to bed."

Fun was not in particular abundance during that last year, so it is even more understandable that Graves was annoyed at Donovan's lack of enthusiasm about the coverage of the Democratic convention. It was one of those occasions where a special esprit took over on the story and reminded the participants of how lively it used to be in the old days. Graves took only thirteen people to Miami (in the 1950s there would have been five times that many) and he was jubilantly scornful at hearing that *Newsweek*'s convention staff numbered thirty-five and *Time*'s was seventy, including eighteen photographers. Such excess tickled him a lot in his own pinched circumstances, and he was especially delighted that *Time* had to come and ask him for a picture they wanted from one of *Life*'s two photographers. The situation stimulated the staff's competitive juices, the more so because one team on the magazine had what appeared to be a solid exclusive. Photographer Stanley Tretick (who'd worked for *Look* until that magazine folded in 1971) and staff writer Dick Meryman (whose best articles included pieces on Lawrence Olivier, Elizabeth Taylor and Andrew Wyeth) seemed to have a lock on a story about the leading candidate, George McGovern. They had installed themselves in the McGovern family's hotel suite, where Tretick was merrily shooting pictures to the light of a number of 200-watt bulbs he had thoughtfully put in all the suite's lamps. When McGovern's staff, under pressure from *Newsweek*, agreed to let in one of *their* photographers, Tretick removed all the bright bulbs and put the dim ones back. While the *Newsweek* man, complaining about the poor light, shot his pictures, Meryman, who as a reporter more than twenty years earlier had been trained to anticipate the urgent needs of *Life* photographers, ambled unobtrusively around the suite, turning off as many lights as he could. The story Tretick, Meryman and *Life* got in part because of these imaginative techniques ran for seventeen pages and a cover and, regardless of how unenthusiastic Donovan had been about it, was one of the rare high points in the magazine's painful last months. It involved the kind of beat-the-opposition enterprise so valued in earlier days, and Graves, thoroughly fed up with trouble, was enormously proud.

Such heartening performances were not making any difference at the box office. When Time Inc.'s top managing group—Heiskell, Shepley, vice president for magazines Arthur Keylor, treasurer Richard McKeough, circulation director Kelso Sutton and Valk—met to go over *Life*'s situation in late summer, the outlook was very poor. Significantly, they met in secret out of the office at the nearby Hotel Dorset, where no one would note their gathering and use it to float more rumors.

All the important indicators—ad sales, circulation, renewals—were down, and the prospects for improvement were nonexistent. Even projections for the next two years that called for a further big reduction in circulation to 4.5 million showed losses of more than $10 million each year and much more with no cutback. Among the men at the meeting there was no real argument now over what had to be done, though at least one, Art Keylor, had been insisting for some time, in keeping with his emerging corporate image as a hard-nosed executive, that *Life* should be shut down.

"I guess if anybody was trying to keep it pumped up, I was the one," Heiskell recalled fourteen years later. "After all that time [he'd been hired at *Life* in 1937], you get emotionally involved in the thing. But when it came to the bitter, bitter end, I don't think there was any disagreement. There wasn't anybody who put forward a solution that had any promise to it. And at the same time we were looking at a real abyss. We hadn't been that badly hurt *yet*, but every set of figures you looked at was really disastrous." Shortly thereafter, the inevitable decision—with a precision in timing that would have filled forecaster Gallagher with glee—was made to close down *Life* at the end of 1972, subject to the final approval of the board of directors.

Plans moved forward with the tightest possible security. Donovan, of course, knew of and concurred in the decision to fold, but the top managers were determined to keep the insiders to a minimum. They were extremely concerned about working out the details of dealing with the company's big liability (more than $40 million) in subscriptions that would now be unfulfilled; the Federal Trade Commission would have to approve whatever Time Inc. offered customers in the way of cash returns or subscriptions to other publications. And the Securities and Exchange Commission had strict rules about the disclosure of information that might affect the price of Time Inc. stock. Graves was not told until two weeks before the very end, when the editor-in-chief confided it to him over a private lunch. In retrospect, a question about that is inevitable: would such an event have been kept so long from the managing editor of *Life* in Luce's time? It seems at least doubtful, particularly if it had happened during the years when Luce, who after all ran everything, remained so involved in the editing process. Later on, as the company got bigger and more diversified and was basically controlled by the businessmen at the top, the managing editors were regarded more as middle echelon, not all that important, really, when it came to the big picture. In any case, Graves, who was good at keeping secrets, didn't get in on that one until very late, and he was presumably thus able to participate more easily with his usual sturdy conviction in the charade of *Life*'s last few months of publication.

On the surface, not much out of the ordinary seemed to be happening as Graves and his staff, down to little more than half the size it was when he became managing editor in 1969, turned out the issues. "When I dream about *Life*," he said years later, "we suddenly don't have any stories," and the grinding hunt for new material—a principal preoccupation for all managing editors—went on. There were stories about the wives of returning prisoners of war, about great, young college football players, about an Ohio town's weariness with the war in Vietnam—in short, stories of the kind that had been staples of the magazine's output for more than thirty-five years. One that particularly interested Graves was on the special place in American life of the "middle-age" child (from six years old through twelve), and into the story he put a questionnaire addressed to the kids, inviting them to reveal their attitudes on topics that interested them—parents, friends, animals, dressing, the environment, sex. Other questionnaires—on people's attitudes toward crime, for example—had drawn a lot of mail and interest, and Graves hoped this would happen again with the children.

In mid-October an editorial, overseen by Donovan and his deputy Louis Banks, was written supporting Richard Nixon for a second term. (The burglary of Democratic headquarters at Washington's Watergate Hotel had taken place earlier, in June, but the full implications of the scandal were not yet apparent.) After seeing a draft, Graves sent a memo to Donovan and Banks pointing out that he thought more needed to be said bluntly about Nixon's failures in Vietnam. He suggested various wordings for inclusion; some of them were followed. A few days later Graves wrote Donovan again, this time about the receipt of a petition from edit staff members strongly supporting George McGovern for the presidency and protesting the Nixon endorsement. They wanted their position somehow to be noted in the issue carrying the editorial. Graves reported that the document had been signed by 100 out of a possible 145 people, that it had been given to him with "courtesy" but that "the feeling expressed was no less strong for the manner of its presentation." The fact that the edit staff disagreed with the management about an editorial stance was not unusual; the fact that they stated their position in a formal declaration decidedly was. Their request for space was denied, with Graves agreeing with Donovan that the management was entitled to state company positions on the editorial page and always had been, without rebuttal by disagreeing employees.

Three weeks later, only a month before the end, Graves was still getting lengthy, after-the-fact critiques about his issues (on story concepts, layouts, reproduction, quality of writing, headlines, the covers), these last now from editorial director Louis Banks, a former managing editor of *Fortune*, who wrote in one: "I'm sure the weekly nattering gets boring, and there really isn't much to be said for it if we don't have a sense of trying to get something done." Graves wrote back assuring him that it wasn't boring, and his patient, detailed reply to Banks's points entirely concealed the likelihood that he was getting dreadfully tired of this traditional Time Inc. form of second-guessing. To respond to it so calmly under these deteriorating conditions, to justify his positions or acknowledge his errors week after week, must have been exhausting.

Still, Graves kept plugging. On his own initiative, he went to see Roy Larsen, an old friend of *Life*'s and a man who'd been very much there when Luce started it. The magazine was starving for promotion, Graves told Larsen, then vice chairman of the board and not as active in company affairs as he had been. Larsen had long been considered an expert on promotion. Wasn't there some way, Graves wondered, to let people know how good the magazine really was? Shouldn't the company get behind *Life* and push a little extra hard at this time? Larsen, of course, knew that it was all over by then. He agreed with Graves that more people should know about the magazine. But he was gently noncommittal about whether or not anything could be done about the problem just then.

By the time Donovan finally told Graves what was happening, the end was virtually at hand. Graves, who couldn't have been utterly surprised by the news, was nevertheless stunned by the suddenness of it. His whole working career, twenty-four years, had been spent at *Life*. Now the structure he knew so well had collapsed. And for the edit staff, at least, he was the man in charge, the man in the big job so many had wanted. He would be the last man to hold it, and he must have wondered, in those final days, if he could have somehow done it better. Had he been a good enough boss? Had he spoken up at the right time for the right things? Had he encouraged and protected his people? Would someone else, some creative star bursting with great ideas, have made it work? Most people who knew the situation would have agreed that Graves, in fact, did better under rotten conditions than any other plausible candidate would have done. He had been courageous, honest, hardworking and very steady. The wreck had been inevitable before he took the wheel, possibly long before. But Graves was too much of a realist to dwell for long on such questions; with a few reservations about things he might have done differently, he felt he'd done his best.

As was his style, he began to think practically about the immediate future. Definite plans made him feel comfortable, and he began concentrating on the final issues, on how they should be shaped, on what he should say to the staff when he told them. Most importantly, he began to think about how he and a few others could set about to find jobs in and out of the company for as many as possible of the people who were going to lose theirs. He got busy, in short, with the details of shutting down the business. Because he was an orderly man and the ones most affected were his colleagues, he wanted it to be done properly. "Somebody," he said much later, "has got to show up in dress uniform at Appomattox and see that things are done right."

But for a little while he had to keep the secret. Bonnie Angelo, a *Time* correspondent in Washington, had been selected only days earlier to become *Life*'s next bureau head in that office, the first woman to be picked for such a position. Graves did not tell her that she would never start work in the job. The magazine's copy editor, Chuck Elliott, who worked very closely with all the writers and was every bit as tidy about details as Graves, kept reminding the managing editor about the need to decide in advance on a single page of color to close for a January issue. Graves ignored Elliott for a time, but the copy editor kept needling, and Graves selected for closing a story on the environment he knew Elliott liked. One photograph had already been engraved as a full page and was being held in Chicago for use at any time. The choice appealed to Graves's frugal nature; the engraving was already paid for, and he could choose it without additional cost for inclusion in an issue that would never be published.

For one that would be published, the weekly magazine's last, dated December 29, Graves had a special, private plan. The questionnaire that had accompanied the story on the middle-age child back in October was drawing a tremendous response. Thousands of letters from kids, from many classrooms full of kids, were pouring into the magazine. Their comments, many of them complete with drawings, were arriving faster than they could be sorted and answered; the total number of children replying, either as individuals or in groups, was later estimated to be 250,000. Graves was terribly moved by this response, touched by the eagerness of the children and amazed at the power of the magazine to elicit such a deluge of enthusiastic mail. A story on the children's answers was originally scheduled for a January issue. Now that was impossible, and Graves, determined not to lose it, decided to run it in the year-end *Life*, which would now, it turned out, be the magazine's last weekly issue. Traditionally this was a sort of yearbook in pictures, and the kids' story would normally have no place in it. So without telling anyone what he had in mind, he began pushing Tom Flaherty, the editor in charge of the story, to get it ready much sooner than planned.

On December 5 the Time Inc. board ratified the management's earlier decision to close down *Life*, with the final action taken by an executive committee two days later. That day, December 7, Donovan and Graves told a group of the top editors, and that night Graves and his colleagues divided up the names and telephoned everyone on the New York staff, advising them that there would be an important meeting the next day, December 8. Plans were also made to try to reach everyone else on the staff, wherever they were.

The meeting took place the next morning, in an auditorium on the eighth floor of the Time & Life Building. About 300 people—editors, reporters, photographers, admen, lab technicians, men and women from the business office—came and sat silently on imitation-leather folding chairs waiting for the bosses to take their turns at a raised lectern at the end of the room. The crowd looked numb and stricken; the sense of what had happened was in the air even though the actual announcement was still to come.

When Graves arrived at the auditorium a few minutes before 10:45, he saw Heiskell and Donovan standing together talking. He approached them and asked what the order of speaking would be. Donovan said that he would speak first and then Heiskell would say something. Graves, who had come with some prepared remarks of his own, waited to be included. But Donovan said nothing more. There was a long moment of silence. Then Graves said: "Well, I would like to say something and so would Garry Valk." His request was accepted without comment.

Although the whole process of telling the staff went off smoothly and without incident, as did a press conference later, there had been a certain amount of corporate apprehension about possible problems. A briefing report prepared for company executives and handed out before the meeting and the press conference included a list of possible questions that might be asked and the appropriate answers. The first question listed: "Will Mr. Donovan or Mr. Heiskell resign as a result of this?" The second: "Will Mr. Donovan or Mr. Heiskell or other top executives take a salary cut as a result of this?" The answer suggested for the first was no. For the second it was: "The salaries of top executives are set by a committee of outside directors. It is not for us to comment on this question." Nothing as rude as either of these questions was asked, although a number of staffers in the throes of a drinking party later that evening agreed that since hundreds of people were, in effect, getting fired, it would be only just that the biggest heads should roll as well.

"I'm Hedley Donovan," the editor-in-chief began as he stood at the lectern, "in case any of us haven't met." His face was gray, the weight of his announcement almost visible on his big shoulders. "I'm here with a very painful report, to tell you that the company must suspend publication of *Life* at the end of this month." In his heavy voice, his expression utterly serious, Donovan then laid it all out—the years of losses, the various alternatives considered, the impossible projections for the future, why *Life* was folding. The basic emphasis in his straightforward remarks was that the management had made enormous efforts to save *Life* over a long period of time. He praised the staffs, both editorial and publishing. He tried to reassure his listeners that efforts would be made to find jobs for as many as possible within the company (some on magazines, he confided, that would probably be started soon) and that a schedule of severance benefits would be given to those who left. "We make no apologies whatever for publishing *Life* as long as we did. We think it was the right thing to do in the interest of our readers and advertisers, our staff, our stockholders, our whole company—to give *Life* every possible chance to make it."

Heiskell, looking exhausted and close to tears, said less, confining himself largely to a list of *Life*'s accomplishments—everything from its coverage of war to the publication of Ernest Hemingway's *The Old Man and the Sea*. "I'm only sad," he closed, "that with such a record of achievement *Life* should have such a short life."

Graves spoke of the worst loss, of that sense of closeness known particularly to older members of the staff. "We have seen each other," he said, blinking behind his glasses, "two hundred days or so a year for many years, and I, for one, never got tired of it. . . . I think we know each other better than we know anyone outside our own families. Ed Thompson used to say that at *Life* it was all very well to be a first-class journalist, but to really enjoy it you had to be something of a slob. He always said this about himself and he meant that no matter how many things went wrong, how many packets got lost or delayed, he never lost his affection for the staff and for the magazine. That goes for me and I trust for you. It is a very rare thing in the American corporate world today and now we must end it.

"This is a sad ending, but I hope none of you will remember *Life*, or each other, in terms of this morning. We worked on a great and famous magazine; we've published many wonderful stories and we had a remarkable experience together. . . . I won't pretend that any place else is going to be like what we shared together at *Life*. And I thank you all for that gift we gave to each other."

That about wrapped it up. We got out the last issue, ninety-six pages, with pictures of Nixon eating with chopsticks in Hangchow, of George Wallace getting shot at a Maryland shopping center, of Liz Taylor and

Liza Minnelli, of a dejected George McGovern and a jubilant Olympic gold medalist, Mark Spitz. There was a brief story on the end of the Apollo program, on the terrorist-caused deaths of Israeli athletes in Munich, on the sudden emergence that year of something called "the bare look," which was mostly an excuse to run pictures of good-looking midriffs.

There were four pages on the letters of the middle-age children ("The sixth graders in our school know more about sex than the P.T.A. thinks," read one) and three pages on "the autobiography that wasn't," the Hughes hoax, consisting mostly of paintings of an imaginary Hughes, commissioned by *Life* and done on the basis of spurious descriptions by the hoaxer. "What does Howard Hughes really look like today?" the text began. "We don't know and neither does Clifford Irving." Donovan's statement of regret about *Life*'s end opened the issue and Graves's closed it. In the bottom right-hand corner of the cover, tucked under the dateline and the price, was the word "Goodbye." Like the first issue thirty-six years earlier, this one was something of a mixed bag, and like the first, it was a sellout.

A lot of people—both on and off the magazine—were sad about its passing. They had grown up with it, its weekly blend of news, sensation, education and trivia a weekly staple in millions of households, and now it was gone. It had lived beyond its best time, after struggling along for years on the basis of its past power and reputation. "I have no feeling now," Graves said later, "that *Life* should have survived its mythology." How great its contributions to American life, how significant its journalism (excepting, of course, the thousands of marvelous photographs), is open to argument. "*Life* likes people," Henry Luce had said more than once, and perhaps that was the most important thing to remember about it. And people liked it back.

Bibliography

ALEXANDER, SHANA. *Talking Woman*. New York: Delacorte Press, 1976.

BOURKE-WHITE, MARGARET. *Portraits of Myself*. New York: Simon & Schuster, 1963.

BRINKLEY, WILLIAM. *The Fun House*. New York: Random House, 1961.

BURNS, JOAN SIMPSON. *The Awkward Embrace*. New York: Alfred A. Knopf, 1975.

CORT, DAVID. *The Sin of Henry R. Luce*. Secaucus, New Jersey: Lyle Stuart, Inc., 1974.

EDEY, MAITLAND. *Great Photographic Essays from LIFE*. New York Graphic Society, 1978.

ELSON, ROBERT T. *Time Inc.: The Intimate History of a Publishing Enterprise, 1923–1941*. New York: Atheneum, 1968.

———. *Time Inc.: The Intimate History of a Publishing Enterprise, 1941–1960*. New York: Atheneum, 1973.

FAY, STEPHEN; CHESTER, LEWIS; AND LINKLATER, MAGNUS. *Hoax: The Inside Story of the Howard Hughes–Clifford Irving Affair*. New York: The Viking Press, 1972.

FRIEDRICH, OTTO. *Decline and Fall*. New York: Harper & Row, 1970.

GRIFFITH, THOMAS. *How True*. Boston: Atlantic-Little, Brown, 1974.

HALBERSTAM, DAVID. *The Powers That Be*. New York: Alfred A. Knopf, 1979.

HAMBLIN, DORA JANE. *That Was the Life*. New York: W. W. Norton & Company, 1977.

HARMAN, JEANNE PERKINS. *Such Is Life*. New York: Thomas Y. Crowell Company, 1956.

HICKS, WILSON. *Words and Pictures*. New York: Harper & Brothers, 1952.

HOOPES, ROY. *Ralph Ingersoll*. New York: Atheneum, 1985.

IRVING, CLIFFORD. *The Hoax.* Sagaponack, New York: The Permanent Press, 1981.

JESSUP, JOHN K., ed. *The Ideas of Henry Luce.* New York: Atheneum, 1969.

KNIGHTLEY, PHILLIP. *The First Casualty.* New York: Harcourt Brace Jovanovich, 1975.

KOBLER, JOHN. *Luce, His Time, Life and Fortune.* Garden City, New York: Doubleday & Company, 1968.

THE EDITORS OF *LIFE. Larry Burrows, Compassionate Photographer.* New York: Time Inc., 1972.

MADDOW, BEN. *Let Truth Be the Prejudice: W. Eugene Smith: His Life and Photographs.* New York: Aperture, 1986.

MYDANS, CARL. *More Than Meets the Eye.* New York: Harper & Brothers, 1959.

NEW YORK GRAPHIC SOCIETY. *Gjon Mili, Photographs and Recollections.* Boston, 1980.

PRENDERGAST, CURTIS, AND COLVIN, GEOFFREY. *The World of Time Inc.: The Intimate History of a Changing Enterprise, 1960–1980.* New York: Atheneum, 1986.

SWANBERG, W. A. *Luce and His Empire.* New York: Charles Scribner's Sons, 1974.

THOMPSON, THOMAS. *Celebrity.* Garden City, New York: Doubleday & Company, 1982.

THURBER, JAMES. *The Years with Ross.* New York: Grosset & Dunlap, Inc., 1959.

WHELAN, RICHARD. *Robert Capa.* New York: Alfred A. Knopf, Inc., 1985.

WHITE, THEODORE H. *In Search of History.* New York: Harper & Row, 1978.

Index

A NOTE ABOUT THE AUTHOR

Loudon Wainwright started at *Life* as an office boy in 1949, and except for short leaves of absence to undertake other writing projects, he worked there as reporter, bureau correspondent, writer, editor and columnist until the weekly magazine closed down in 1972. Until his retirement in 1985, he served as a top editor on the relaunched monthly *Life*, for which he continues to write a column. Wainwright lives in New York City with the writer Martha Fay and their four-year-old daughter, Anna.

A NOTE ON THE TYPE

This book was composed in a computer version of Caledonia designed by W. A. Dwiggins (1880–1956). It belongs to a family of printing types called "modern face" by printers—a term used to mark the change in style of type letters that occurred about 1800. It borders on the general design of Scotch Roman, but is more freely drawn than that letter.

Composed by Brevis Press, Bethany, Connecticut. Printed and bound by The Haddon Craftsmen, Inc., Scranton, Pennsylvania. Typography and binding design by Tasha Hall.